The Best of AAMR

Families and Mental Retardation: A Collection of Notable AAMR Journal Articles Across the 20th Century

Edited by

Jan Blacher, Ph.D.
University of California at Riverside
and
Bruce L. Baker, Ph.D.
University of California at Los Angeles

David L. Braddock, Ph.D.
AAMR Books and Research Monograph Editor

AAMR
American Association on Mental Retardation

Published by
American Association on Mental Retardation
444 North Capitol Street, NW, Suite 846
Washington, DC 20001-1512
www.aamr.org

The points of view herein are those of the authors and do not necessarily represent the official policy or opinion of the American Association on Mental Retardation. Publication does not imply endorsement by the editor, the association, or its individual members.

Printed in the United States of America.

Library of Congress Cataloging-in-Publication Data

The best of AAMR : families and mental retardation : a collection of notable AAMR journal articles across the 20th century / edited by Jan Blacher and Bruce L. Baker.
 p. cm.
 Includes bibliographical references and index.
 ISBN 0-940898-76-4 (pbk.)
 1. Mentally handicapped—United States—Family relationships. 2. Mentally handicapped—Home care—United States. 3. Parents of handicapped children—United States. 4. Mental retardation—United States. I. Title: Families and mental retardation. II. Blacher, Jan. III. Baker, Bruce L. IV. American Association on Mental Retardation.

HV3006.A4 B42 2002
362.3'4'0973—dc21

2001053616

Editors of AAMR Journals

Journal of Psycho-Asthenics

1896 – 1917	Vol. 1–21	A. C. Rogers, M.D.
1917 – 1920	Vol. 22–25	Fred Kuhlmann, Ph.D.
1921 – 1924	Vol. 26–29	Benjamin W. Baker, M.D.
1925 – 1930	Vol. 30–35	Howard W. Potter, M.D.
1931 – 1935	Vol. 36–40	Groves B. Smith, M.D.
1936 – 1938	Vol. 41–43	E. Arthur Whitney, M. D.
1939	Vol. 44	Edward J. Humphreys, M.D.

American Journal of Mental Deficiency

1940 – 1948	Vol. 45–52	Edward J. Humphreys, M.D.
1948 – 1959	Vol. 53–63	Richard H. Hungereford, M.A.
1959 – 1969	Vol. 64–73	William Sloan, Ph.D.
1969 – 1979	Vol. 74–83	H. Carl Haywood, Ph.D.
1979 – 1987	Vol. 84–92(1)	Nancy M. Robinson, Ph.D.
1987	Vol. 92(2)	Earl C. Butterfield, Ph.D.

American Journal on Mental Retardation

1987 – 1993	Vol. 92(3)–97	Earl C. Butterfield, Ph.D.
1993 – 1998	Vol. 98–102	Stephen R. Schroeder, Ph.D.
1998 – 2002	Vol. 103–107	Donald K. Routh, Ph.D.
2002 –	Vol. 107–	William E. MacLean, Jr., Ph.D.

Mental Retardation

1963 – 1964	Vol. 1–2(5)	Glenn E. Milligan, Ed.D.
1964 – 1970	Vol. 2(6)–8 (5)	Robert L. Erdman, Ed.D.
1970 – 1977	Vol. 8(6)–15(4)	Sue Allen Warren, Ph.D.
1977 – 1979	Vol. 15(5)–16	Jim F. Brody, Ph.D.
1979	Vol. 17(1–4)	John F. Miller, Ph.D.
1979 – 1983	Vol. 17(5)–21(3)	Reginald L. Jones, Ph.D.
1983 – 1994	Vol. 21(4)–31	Louis Rowitz, Ph.D.
1994 –	Vol. 32–	Steven J. Taylor, Ph.D.

Contributors

Bruce L. Baker
Joel Bakken
Paula J. Beckman
Arnold Birenbaum
Jan Blacher
Elizabeth M. Boggs
David L. Braddock
Bettye M. Caldwell
Herbert J. Cohen
Keith A. Crnic
Arthur H. Cross
Edgar A. Doll
Carl J. Dunst
Harold B. Dye
Alan Factor
Maurice A. Feldman
William N. Friedrich
Laraine Masters Glidden
Mark T. Greenberg
Samuel B. Guze
Louis J. Heifetz
Tamar Heller
Viki E. Johnson
Leo Kanner
Kathleen L. Kashima
Marty Wyngaarden Krauss
Sandra J. Landen

Gwynnyth Llewellyn
Allison B. Miller
Sandra M. Magana
Maureen O. Marcenko
C. Edward Meyers
Judith C. Meyers
Phyllis Mickelson
Raymond G. Miltenberger
Iris Tan Mink
Max A. Murray
Kazuo Nihira
Charles D. Nixon
Philip Roos
Scott Schauss
Marsha Malick Seltzer
George H. S. Singer
Harold M. Skeels
Mary A. Slater
Zolinda Stoneman
Carol M. Trivette
Ann P. Turnbull
H. Rutherford Turnbull, III
Jim L. Turner
Charles L. Vaux
Nicole Walton-Allen
Lynn M. Wikler
Andrea G. Zetlin

Contents

Introduction

This volume brings together 32 papers that we believe well represent the perspectives that American Association on Mental Retardation (AAMR) authors have taken on families and mental retardation during the 20th century. You will find here some "Golden Oldies," classic papers that spoke forcibly to issues of their times and often anticipated concerns of our time. You will also find some papers so recent that we cannot judge their impact, but we chose them for their timeliness. What all of these papers share, though, is that their authors had genuine concern for families and strong beliefs about what families experience and need. These differ, of course, and there is a natural tendency to see one's perspective as the best, outweighing the old, naïve, and misguided perspectives of the past.

One cannot set out to look back without remembering the philosopher Santayana's often quoted remark, that those who do not remember history are condemned to repeat it. As we will see, families were not studied—indeed, they were rarely mentioned—in AAMR's early years. The assumption was that retardation was inherited or caused by poor or irresponsible behavior of "intemperate parents" (Shuttleworth, 1878, p. 47). Thus the standard practice was to recommend that children and young adults be institutionalized, to get them away from their families and to prevent them from having families of their own. Ironically, AAMR was a leading advocate for institutionalization.

After reviewing AAMR's published record, however, we would say to Santayana: "Fine, ok, there is some history we do not want to repeat. But note also that those who do not remember history are missing a lot of good stuff—provocative and forward looking ideas that should not be lost, especially to a later generation with more resources to study or implement them."

The "Best of AAMR" Project

This volume was inspired by a conversation at an AAMR Publications Committee meeting about the gold mine of AAMR's published articles. If these could be drawn together carefully under selected topics, they would comprise a series of books that would be a valuable resource for professionals and for students. "Families" was suggested as an opening topic. This book is our effort to mine AAMR's publications and initiate a "Best of AAMR" series. To mix metaphors, the canary has lived and we think we have struck gold.

The publications. AAMR came into being in 1876, when six institution superintendents came together at the nation's centennial celebration in Philadelphia (Sloan & Stevens, 1976). The first 20 years of AAMR (1876–1895) are recorded in the annual *Proceedings of the Association of Medical Officers of American Institutions for Idiotic and Feebleminded Persons.* The Proceedings contained each Annual Meeting's addresses and discussions and, beginning in 1886, the Presidential Addresses. Beginning in 1896 (through 1939) the annual publication became the *Journal of Psycho-Asthenics.* The meaning of the newly coined title was less clear than the expanded aim of the journal, to publish selected articles and items of information from all sources, in addition to papers from the Annual Meeting. In 1940 the publication became the *American Journal of Mental Deficiency,* published quarterly. The name changed once again in 1988, after several decades of debate, to the *American Journal on Mental Retardation.* In 1963 a second journal, *Mental Retardation,* was launched to relieve space pressure in *AJMD,* which had grown to 1,000 pages a year and sometimes included a monograph length manuscript. At that time, *AJMD* was to be the scientific journal and *Mental Retardation* more a house organ for AAMR. Over time, however, both journals became premier research publications. Indeed, *Journal Citation Reports,* based on 1999 data, ranked *AJMR* and *MR*

1st and 2nd respectively among 21 special education journals and 1st and 3rd among 45 rehabilitation journals.

Our selections. The reader might be interested in how our "Best of AAMR" collection was assembled. We began by examining the Contents of every AAMR journal issue from 1876–2000, making copies of each paper concerned with families, parents, or siblings. We read and evaluated each paper, with the help of a small review team at UCLA. At the same time, we wrote to about 25 AAMR leaders and/or family researchers and sought their opinions about topics, authors, and specific papers to include. We have included a "Bibliography" in the Appendix. The reader will, no doubt, find errors of omission (hopefully not your paper!), and we apologize for these.

That was the easy part. We then had to choose from among hundreds of meritorious pieces the 32 that we have included here. We need to say at the outset that these choices are, of course, subjective and we are not even sure ourselves but that one or another article should have been substituted. These are certainly among the best, however, and they are those that had the best fit with our particular criteria. These criteria were to favor papers that: (1) Spoke well to a salient issue of its times; (2) Had an influence on the field; (3) Had methodological interest and contributed to diversity in the volume; (4) Were written by leaders in family studies; and (5) Were readable for a broad audience. All papers needed to meet the first criterion, as well as several other criteria. We also decided not to include more than one paper by the same first author.

We should add that some notable family researchers are not represented in this collection because they did not have the "wisdom" to publish in AAMR journals or because they published their best work elsewhere. We have made reference to some of them in our essays introducing each unit. Our selections also reflect an intentional recency bias, as just over two thirds of them were published in the last two decades of the 20th century. While we were captivated by the "Golden Oldies," and might have included more, we did not want this to be a primarily historical work. Rather, we wanted the volume to appeal to the concerns of today's families, professionals, and students, and to show how these concerns evolved over time.

A Few Methodological Points

Our selections represent myriad ways in which authors reached their conclusions and presented their findings. As researchers we struggled at first with whether this volume should be limited to research papers, only to be eventually guided by the literature to a different criterion—whether the paper represented the accepted, indeed the possible, methodology of its time. During AAMR's first 75 years or so, the accepted methodology was essentially experiential or, in some instances, rudimentary surveys. Despite advocacy for research within the organization almost from its inception, there was little financial support; moreover, measures, designs, and analytical techniques were still in their infancy. Most of the early papers we have cited or included contained no data or references and were usually presentations at an Annual Meeting (Vaux, 1935; Doll, 1937; Murray, 1959). Some relied totally on personal observation of individual cases (Kanner, 1953). Sometimes when the methodology of a study was spelled out, it was remarkably subjective. For example, Zuk (1959) utilized social workers' personal assessments of parents' intelligence and socioeconomic status in describing his sample. Despite these instances of what today causes methodological squeamishness, these authors identified themes and issues early on that inspired later researchers, who did indeed pay more methodological attention.

By contrast, in the past quarter century the literature has exploded with more sophisticated studies often using multiple measures, comparison groups, and elaborate methods of analysis. Among the influences that fueled this growth were (1) An increased national concern for persons with mental retardation and their families, with President Kennedy as the catalyst. This concern brought with it a host of researchable questions; (2) A concomitant and exponential increase in federal funding for research and training, for university-based centers and individual investigators; (3) The computer era, making sophisticated analyses possible to do—and to do on one's own PC.

We have tried, then, to represent diverse methods and designs, each aiming in a particular way to increase our understanding of families. The information presented in these papers was gathered through personal experiences, literature reviews, case studies, surveys, direct observation, testing, coding tape recorded interactions, interviews, questionnaires, and public records. Twelve papers do not have a research design in the traditional sense. Seven of these are thoughtful essays on critical issues (Boggs; Doll; Kanner; Murray; Roos; Turnbull & Turnbull; Vaux). Three papers make conceptual points and review relevant literature (Blacher & Meyers; Crnic, Friedrich, & Greenberg; Stoneman). Two papers represent qualitative research methodology, with numerous interviews over time (Llewellyn; Zetlin & Turner).

The remaining 20 papers broadly span quantitative research approaches. There are three descriptive survey studies, a methodology often relied upon in setting public policy (Braddock; Birenbaum & Cohen; Mickelson). There are six correlational studies that seek main effects and, in some cases, moderating relationships, within a single group of subjects (Beckman; Dunst, Trivette & Cross; Heller, Miller, & Factor; Magana; Mink, Nihira, & Meyers; Seltzer & Krauss). There are two studies involving comparison groups (Caldwell & Guez; Feldman & Walter-Allen). There is also a cross-sectional design (Wikler) and a longitudinal one (Glidden & Johnson). In studies evaluating services, one utilized a single subject design (Bakken, Miltenberger, & Schauss), two employed a single group pre-post design (Baker, Landen, & Kashima; Meyers & Marcenko), and four employed a multiple group comparison pre-post design (Heifetz; Nixon & Singer; Skeels & Dye; Slater). Surely one could teach a research methods course based upon the incredible variety of ways that AAMR professionals writing about families have approached their topic.

Our Organization

We have divided the papers into four units, and within each we have organized the papers chronologically. We begin with *Historical Views of Families* (3 papers); each of these papers is from the 1930s, reflecting the invisibility of families in AAMR's earlier years. Second is *Family Adjustment and Coping* (11 papers), which focuses on families of children and adolescents with mental retardation and contains the traditional core of family studies: family reactions to disability, stress, adaptation and coping, social support, and recent broader conceptions of family. Third is *Families of Adults with Mental Retardation* (8 papers), a generally more recent focus of family researchers examining transition to adulthood, older adults, and adults with mental retardation as parents themselves. Fourth is *Family Intervention, Support, and Social Policy* (10 papers), covering a range of approaches to supporting families, from individual counseling to social policy. We have introduced each of these units, trying to set the papers in a broader context and acknowledging other prominent work, especially from AAMR publications.

Acknowledgements

We appreciate foremost the efforts of all AAMR authors over the past 125 years, who have provided us with such a wealth of scholarship. We especially thank David Braddock, Editor of AAMR's books and monographs, for his encouragement, support, and wise advice. This work was supported in part by the Archives and Library on Disability, Coleman Institute for Cognitive Disabilities, University of Colorado System, Boulder, Colorado (D. Braddock, Director), and also by National

Institute of Child Health and Human Development Grants # 21324 (J. Blacher, PI) and #34879-1459 (K. Crnic, P.I., and B. L. Baker, J. Blacher, and C. Edelbrock, Co-PIs).

We are indebted to Steve Warren for initially suggesting a "Best of AAMR" series, and to Steve Schroeder, then Editor of AJMR, for his enthusiastic support. We appreciate Doreen Crosier's hospitality in the Washington office as we worked through the earlier volumes in the AAMR archives and her support throughout this project. At UCLA, many thanks to Lesley Keeler, Christopher Macauley, Sandra Minassian, and Michael Rothman for helping us track down and review the articles. We also appreciate the support from the staff of the UC Riverside Families Project. We appreciate the suggestions on content that we received from other colleagues: Don Bailey, Laraine Glidden, Tamar Heller, Claire Kopp, Marsha Seltzer, Gary Seltzer, Bob Schalock, Ann Turnbull, Patricia Noonan Walsh, and Steve Warren.

References

Doll, E. A. (1937). The institution as a foster parent. *Journal of Psycho-Asthenics, 42,* 143–148.

Kanner, L. (1953). Parents' feelings about retarded children. *American Journal of Mental Deficiency, 57,* 375–383.

Murray, M. A. (Mrs.) (1959). Needs of parents of mentally retarded children. *American Journal of Mental Deficiency, 63,* 1078–1088.

Shuttleworth, G. (1878). Intemperance as a cause of idiocy. *Proceedings of the Association of Medical Officers of American Institutions for Idiotic and Feebleminded Persons,* 46–51.

Sloan, W., & Stevens, H. A. (1976). *A century of concern: A history of the American Association on Mental Deficiency 1876–1976.* Washington, D.C.: American Association on Mental Deficiency.

Vaux, C. L. (1935). Family care of mental defectives. *Journal of Psycho-Asthenics, 40,* 168–189.

Zuk, G. H. (1959). The religious factor and the role of guilt in parental acceptance of the retarded child. *American Journal of Mental Deficiency, 64,* 139–147.

1-14-01

Authors

Jan Blacher, Ph.D., University of California, Riverside, and **Bruce L. Baker, Ph.D.,** University of California, Los Angeles.

PART ONE

Historical Views
The Invisible Family: AAMR from 1876 to 1939

As we enter the 21st century, *the family* has become one of America's most sacred, prominent, and studied institutions. When a family member has mental retardation, the family plays many highly visible roles from the time of diagnosis and evolving across the lifespan. This stands in sharp contrast to how the families of persons with mental retardation were viewed by professionals who comprised the earliest forms of the current American Association on Mental Retardation, The Association of Medical Officers of American Institutions for Idiotic and Feeble-Minded Persons, American Association for the Study of the Feeble-Minded, and the American Association on Mental Deficiency. From the first published paper in 1876 (in the *Proceedings of the Association of Medical Officers of American Institutions for Idiotic and Feeble-Minded Persons*) until 1939 (in *The Journal of Psycho-Asthenics*), the family was essentially invisible.

What do we mean by invisible? During the first 64 years of AAMR, the word "family" appears in only nine journal paper titles. The organization at first, as its cumbersome title implies, was dominated by medical officers of institutions; and a primary focus of addresses and writings was on institution issues, sometimes with quaint titles such as "Cases Which Succeed Outside the Institution Better Than Inside Under Extra-Institutional Supervision and a Little of That" (Bernstein, 1920). Indeed, AAMR promoted institutions in its own charter. There was a strong supposition that persons with mental retardation were best off in institutions—away from their families.

The first two articles that mentioned families in the title pertained more to the clinical description of specific conditions, such as microcephaly (Murdock, 1902) and Mongolism (Davenport, 1925), than to families *per se*. This was consistent with mental retardation scholarship of the time, which was also much focused on classification and description of mental defectives (Singer, 1910), with papers on topics such as dental irregularities (Tremaine, 1908/1909) and growth curves (Goddard, 1909/1910).

The last seven references to family in early publication titles pertain to out-of-home care; most of these use the term "family care," similar to the current term "foster care," where the child or young adult with retardation would live in someone else's family (Vaux, 1935, 1936; Doll, 1937; Doll & Longwell, 1938; Kuenzel, 1939; Pollock, 1938, 1939). Some reasons given for the need for alternative care, or foster care, included "bad environment," poor parentage, physical disorder, or malnutrition (Vaux, 1936). The biological family, widely held to be the cause of retardation, was essentially excluded from considerations of treatment.

The 1920s and 1930s were, we remember, the period in our nation's history when the eugenics movement was in full force, with immigration restrictions in the service of hereditary convictions and racist assumptions. A natural outgrowth of this movement was to prevent individuals with mental retardation from reproducing, through sterilization and institutional separation. Enthusiasm for sterilization was fueled by studies describing high rates of retardation within poor families (e.g., the Kallikaks), which, following the tenor of the times, was interpreted as evidence for heredity (Goddard, 1912). Virginia passed a law in 1924 permitting the state to sterilize individuals found to be incompetent because of feeblemindedness, insanity, alcoholism, epilepsy, or other factors (Smith & Polloway, 1993). Supreme Court Justice Oliver Wendell Holmes, writing for the majority and upholding the law, concluded that "three generations of imbeciles are enough!" (*Buck v. Bell*, 1927). By the late 1930s the majority of states had passed sterilization laws, and the practice continued to some extent into the 1970s (Smith and Polloway, 1993). Against this backdrop, we can understand better why AAMR authors paid scant attention to natural parents as viable caregivers.

We decided to include two of the articles on "other family care." The first, and the earliest to appear in AAMR journals, is a 1935 paper by Charles Vaux, superintendent of the Newark State School in New York, entitled *Family Care of Mental Defectives*. Vaux modeled his experimental program after the centuries-old program in Gheel, Belgium; he moved residents out of the institution into family homes in a nearby village, noting subsequently that they "can enjoy a happier, more normal kind of life with more liberty" (Vaux, 1936, p. 87). The second is a 1937 paper by Edgar Doll, Director of Research at the Training School at Vineland, New Jersey, entitled *The Institution as a Foster Parent*. Doll tempered the argument in favor of out-of-home care. Writing from a perspective sympathetic to both institutional care and to natural family care, Doll argued their relative benefits and in some ways foreshadowed the normalization philosophy. Doll wrote: "The success of family care both before commitment and after discharge suggests the very great importance of emulating family care as far as practicable within the institution" (p. 147).

Fortunately there were other early AAMR members who countered the trend of finding fault with the biological families of persons with retardation. Walter Fernald, longtime superintendent of the Massachusetts School for the Feeble-Minded (1887–1924), acknowledged in his 1924 Presidential Address to AAMR that "defectives" may come from "average American homes, from the homes of the poor and of the middle class, and of the well-to-do, with industrious, well behaved parents" (p. 213). These sentiments were elaborated upon by Stanley Davies (1925), Executive Secretary of the New York State Committee on Mental Hygiene:

It is a great hardship to the child and parents to send a child of tender years away from home to a distant institution to be cared for by strangers. In spite of the great advantages to be obtained in the institution, the child is deprived of the normal home life, the moral and social influence of the mother, and wholesome relations with the community. There is no substitute for good, average home care, and the love and individual attention which the child receives in the normal relationship between parent and child. In the past it may have been assumed that because the child was mentally defective, the parents were probably mentally defective also, and therefore unfit guardians for the child, but with the latest evidence as to the heredity of mental deficiency indicating that much mental deficiency is of the non-hereditary type, it is apparent that many mentally defective children may have entirely normal and intelligent parents (p. 213).

The perspective that a family environment can be healthy and even therapeutic gained further momentum from the classic 1939 paper by Harold Skeels (Psychologist, Board of Control of State Institutions, Iowa City, Iowa) and Harold Dye (Superintendent, Institution for Feebleminded children, Glenwood, Iowa), entitled *A Study of the Effects of Differential Stimulation on Mentally Retarded Children*. While this study did not involve natural families, we include it because it countered the biological determinism of the times and foreshadowed interest decades later in early intervention and parent training. The authors make a strong case for "bonding" between a child and one or two adults as a "dynamic factor of great importance" (p. 133). The finding that the children with retardation who had more intense personal contacts made greater gains in intelligence than those in more "limited" environments set the stage for much of our family intervention efforts today. Also, this was the first controlled study pertaining to family issues published by AAMR.

References

Bernstein, C. (1920). Cases which succeed outside the institution better than inside under extra-institutional supervision and a little of that. *Journal of Psycho-Asthenics, 25*, 90–93.

Buck v. Bell (1927). 274 U.S. 200, 47 S. Ct. 584.

Davenport, C. B. (1925). Family studies on Mongoloid dwarfs. *Journal of Psycho-Asthenics, 30*, 266–286.

Davies, S. P. (1925). The institution in relation to the school system. *Journal of Psycho-Asthenics, 30*, 210–226.

Doll, E. A. (1937). The institution as a foster parent. *Journal of Psycho-Asthenics, 42*, 143–148.

Doll, E. A., & Longwell, S. G. (1938). Social competence of feeble-minded in family care. *Journal of Psycho-Asthenics, 43*, 211–215.

Fernald, W. E. (1924). Thirty years' progress in the care of the feeble-minded. *Journal of Psycho-Asthenics, 29*, 206–219.

Goddard, H. H. (1909/10). A growth curve for feeble-minded children. Height and weight. *Journal of Psycho-Asthenics, 14*, 9–11.

Goddard, H. H. (1912). *The Kallikak family: A study in the heredity of feeblemindedness.* New York: Macmillan.

Kuenzel, M. W. (1939). Social status of foster families engaged in community care and training of mentally deficient children. *Journal of Psycho-Asthenics, 44*, 244–253.

Murdoch, J. M. (1902). Notes on the family history of five microcephalus children. *Journal of Psycho-Asthenics, 7*, 33.

Pollock, H. M. (1938). A visit to a French family-care colony. *Journal of Psycho-Asthenics, 43*, 40–46.

Pollock, H. M. (1939). The future of family care of mental patients. *Journal of Psycho-Asthenics, 44*, 234–237.

Singer, D. (1910/11). The classification of mental defectives. *Journal of Psycho-Asthenics, 15*, 3–16.

Skeels, H. M., & Dye, H. B. (1939). A study of the effects of differential stimulation on mentally retarded children. *Journal of Psycho-Asthenics, 44*, 114–136.

Tremaine, W. F. (1908/09). Dental irregularities associated with mental infirmities. *Journal of Psycho-Asthenics, 13*, 48–50.

Vaux, C. L. (1935). Family care of mental defectives. *Journal of Psycho-Asthenics, 40*, 168–189.

Vaux, C. L. (1936). Family care. *Journal of Psycho-Asthenics, 41*, 82–88.

Family Care of Mental Defectives

Charles L. Vaux, M.D.
1935

General Considerations

People see new institutions being built and new buildings added to old institutions and think of increased costs and taxes and wonder where it is all going to end. The boarding of some of the patients in the homes of private families has been suggested as an aid in solving the problem of further construction. In New York State a Committee was appointed in the Department of Mental Hygiene to investigate home and community care. As a member of this committee, I attended their deliberations, heard their analysis of the methods of conducting boarding homes in many of the countries of Europe, and was privileged to accompany the Chairman on a round of the hospitals having boarding homes in the State of Massachusetts. There was soon realized the difficulty in estimating exactly what could be expected from the use of boarding homes, in view of the wide variation in factors and conditions. This difficulty is more than hinted at in the Chairman's report. In one of his concluding paragraphs, Dr. Woodman says—"Notwithstanding all that has been said up to this point, going to show that Family Care in Europe is 65% for a different class than our insane given in communities organized for the purpose and not yet available here; and notwithstanding the failure of boarding from one to six patients in families to attain any large proportion in any place it has been tried; and notwithstanding that an example of the cost of following this latter method indicates only moderate economy which may perhaps be swallowed up in other unseen factors, such as loss of services of employable patients, or board for patients that might be able to maintain themselves, nevertheless, some patients are unquestionably better cared for and happier than when crowded in our large institutions, and they can live in this way at a cost below the average cost of institutional maintenance." This difficulty in exact definition explains why a brief physical description of our community has given way to a discussion and elaboration of considerable length. Quotations have been freely used from the 20th Annual Report of the General Board of Control for Scotland for 1933, to fortify our own opinions by citing the results of their greater experience. In Scotland, boarding homes have been used for 80 years and are now caring for nearly 3,000 patients about equally divided between the insane and the mental defectives. Many of the keen observations and pertinent comments in this report apply equally well to our own work, although the set-up is not the same.

Selection of Community

In Scotland, boarding homes are scattered throughout the country, while ours are confined to a small community, more like the method at Gheel, Belgium. For this small community we chose the Village of Walworth for many reasons which still hold good. A pleasant rural village of 300 people, it is located back in the country several miles from the railroad and the main highways, where the patients can walk the roads un-endangered by traffic. Situated within 17 miles of the Newark State School, it is accessible at all times in emergency and for frequent visits for supervision. Small farms and large gardens assure abundant food supply. Up to the year previous to beginning this experiment, orphan children from Rochester were boarded with many families, so that the idea of boarding homes was not totally unfamiliar. The fact that it was once an academy town is said to assure a superior class of residents. The absence of industries makes improbable any future change that would affect our settlement. The first patients were placed in January, 1933. By September, we had placed 32 in fourteen homes. No more have been placed in the past 18 months, solely because no more funds were available.

Selection of Homes and Guardians

Some patients live right in the village; others on near-by farms. Patients were placed only with going families; that is the family must not require the board money for their own support. The standard rate is $4.00 per week, which is not enough to provide for a patient in any place run as a regular boarding house. It is thought, however, that one or two extra mouths can easily be filled on a farm well stocked with food products of its own raising. The regular succession of dollars from this home-made market can be found very acceptable in a rural district where real money is usually so scarce. One or two to a family is thought most desirable. In most of the homes we placed two so they could be company for each other, and because their guardians felt that the second one would be no more trouble. We feel that in larger numbers they will not be absorbed into the family to the degree that we would wish. It is true that in two of our homes there are four patients, but here conditions are exceptional. One of these homes formerly boarded six boys and connected with it is a farm with cows, chickens and a truck garden so prolific that the patients live on the fat of the land.

Selection of the homes was made with the advice of two people from the village, the health officer and a practical nurse, both of whom were life residents there. Applications were numerous and many were rejected upon their advice. The Scotch report commends such local help in these words—"The knowledge and discrimination of the local Public Assistance Officer are great assets in the boarding-out system. In the choice of guardians for patients it is invaluable. In discussion with these officials one realized that they knew the people and all about them; the rough mannered type who were kindly folk, the smooth ones who needed watching, the people who applied for patients and whose characters were too well known for them ever to get them. One wishes to create the strongest link between central administration and the local knowledge and distribution."

Whenever a home was recommended, the written report of the home investigation was brought to the Clinical Director containing a description of the home. This report followed the pattern that has been in use for years in investigating homes for parole cases, shown in the following report of the first home contacted at Walworth:

Boarding Home Investigation

MRS MYRNA C.
Walworth, N.Y.   Jan. 6, 1933
Recommended by: Dr. E. E. Esley

Home: The house is located in the center of the village. The house is large and pleasant and the lawn is spacious. The rooms consist of a hall, living room, dining room, kitchen, bedrooms, billiard room and bathroom. The girls' room is located at the front of the house on the south side, is a very pleasant room and very comfortably furnished. All modern improvements. The town of Walworth is about 17 miles from the school and about 7¼ miles from the main road north of Palmyra. The road is a good country road. Walworth is a town of about 300 inhabitants, with two churches, a Baptist and a Methodist, three grocery stores, one of which is a grocery and dry goods combined, a high school and a grange hall.

Family: Mr. and Mrs. C. are in their late forties. They are very refined people and are highly recommended by Dr. Esley. There are two daughters, aged 15 and 16 years of age, and an aunt of Mrs. C.'s makes her home with them. She is 83 years of age, and pays $10.00 per week for her board.

Religion: Protestant.

January 9, 1933—Reba Dumbleton and Mary Norton were taken to Mrs. C.'s home this date. Board paid—$4.00 per week.

> S.T. BANCKERT,
> Assist. Social Worker

Selection of Patients

Selection of patients is made by the Clinical Director and takes into account what might be described as the accumulation of institutional dead wood. Patients who do nothing and for whom nothing special needs to be done are only in the way. If they can but sit they might just as well do their sitting elsewhere to make room for those who can benefit by the training or medical care that the institution provides. Our patients are selected for this reason regardless of the degree of intelligence, so that the intelligence quotient has the wide range of 19 to 84. The average I.Q. is 50, half the patients rating as morons; the other half, imbeciles. Those in the high range, as might be expected, have something else the matter with them. One is blind, two have paralysis-agitans; one is epileptic; one a cripple, and more than one partly psychotic.

Adaptation of Patients

The blind woman quickly learned to find her way about the small house, whereas the large institution building offered more difficulty. The epileptic had no convulsions until her new people had become acquainted with her. By that time, they had become attached to her and did not want to let her go, but gladly carried out directions for diet and medication. One woman, who had

Family Care of Mental Defectives

episodes of depression with a sulky period of several days' duration, has had no spells for the two years she has been out. The patients with the tremors do not feel so conspicuous in a small home as in a large institution. Of two patients from Binghamton State Hospital, one is still actively psychotic, but her disturbed spells no longer frighten her guardian and between times she helps with the house work. The chronological ages range from 33 to 65. The older patients were the first ones placed. Some of these patients had been in the institution for twenty years, and were considered to have settled into most rigid and routine habits. It was surprising that even such cases rapidly made the adaptation to their new life and quickly made themselves at home in their new surroundings. We may remark that with all living expenses provided for, life in a rural family is simple and natural and really makes few demands on the ability to adapt. In the Scotch report, Dr. Thomson extols this aspect of Family Care as follows:—"I have been profoundly impressed by the value and the possibilities of the boarding-out system, but consider it not only could, but should be developed further. It fosters a root principle of human life, namely life in a family, which is accepted as a normal healthy unit. I do not think any person would deny that he would willingly give up electric lights and other institutional conveniences with the abnormal life of the large group for a life with less material comfort in a small family unit. Surely a mode of life that runs along the normal course of natural feeling must tend to greater mental betterment. It is on this principle that the boarding-out system is working, and it is a sound and proper principle." Our patients have entered into the life of the family and almost invariably become a part of it. They fit into the picture and look no different than the middle aged aunt or sister found in so many homes. The guardian was always given to understand that the patient's board was paid, and that she was under no compulsion to work for it or to earn her own way, but that idleness was not a natural state and the patient should be taught to interest herself in little tasks about the house and grounds for her own welfare. We thus find patients peeling potatoes, setting the table and occupying themselves in small ways as though they had always been a part of the household. The co-operation of the guardian is, of course, necessary to this happy state. The Scotch believe you can depend on this co-operation. Their Dr. Fraser says—"I have much pleasure in testifying once more to the high standard of care bestowed upon the pauper lunatic and rate aided

mentally defective patients under guardianship in private dwellings. I should like to draw special attention to the attitude of guardians toward the whole welfare of the patients under their care. Very few, indeed, consider their duty to be accomplished when they have complied with the regulations by providing suitable accommodations, suitable occupation, suitable food, and adequate supervision. They go much further and by stimulation, by arousing interest, by arranging for recreation and occupation for leisure time and by giving them a real home life they add materially to their happiness and frequently develop latent capacities hitherto undiscovered. This applied more especially to the certified defective who responds readily to environmental influences and who, under such treatment, develops self-respect and comes to feel that, after all, he is of some use to the world and not a being apart as his previous treatment has so often led him to believe. The success in boarding-out can be attributed to many factors; for example, the selection of patients, the care and supervision exercised by the local authorities, the care and interest of the medical officers, and the careful selection of guardians. All of these factors are important, but the real success is due to the guardians. Were it not for their infinite patience, understanding, kindness and care, boarding-out would not have reached the high level at which it stands today."

One of the guardians, who had many misgivings and was a long time in deciding to take patients, soon found she could turn over the entire care of her three-year old daughter to one of the patients. The other one helped her around the house, but especially endeared herself by her banter with the woman's husband which kept him always in good humor. Now this woman would be most reluctant to part with her patients and treats them most kindly. In another home, without any suggestion being made, the guardian moved her patients downstairs when winter approached, as she thought they would be warmer in a room opening off the living room which was heated by the parlor stove. In still another home the patients run the house while the guardian is doing her farm chores. It is ludicrous to find an imbecile doing the honors when you enter; greeting you, ushering you to chairs and initiating the conversation. If you have other visitors with you, they verge on hysterics as other patients join in this entertainment. The hilarity is by no means abated when their guardian enters, as her manner and talk are apt to be as silly as that of her wards, but despite this, she is reputed as most competent and they live like five big sisters. At the same time, you are impressed with the freedom and independence which this guardian allows and in which they take such content. In the majority of the homes, patients sit down at the table to eat with the family. In all homes patients are regarded as human beings just like themselves. This is favored by their living in such close proximity where the personal element is accentuated. There is nothing to develop the attitude of a nurse to her case, and no one has taught them the attitude of an attendant or keeper to a group of inmates.

It has been unnecessary to rearrange patients in more than a few homes. The guardians develop such a personal liking to them, that they do not like to exchange, no matter what trouble they may cause. One patient was annoyed by a small child, but adjusted all right in another home. Another adjusted all right when moved away from her patient companion. Another did no better after a change and had to be returned. In all, seven were returned, three for illness, three for failure to adjust and one for both reasons. These were promptly replaced by others who did adjust, and I wish to emphasize that the return of these patients had no appreciable effect on our ultimate success. We have the same conditions in our colony houses; girls sent out for employment can fail by the dozen and no one gives it a thought as others are quickly sent to take their places and the colonies continue to flourish undisturbed. There has been no haste or hurry in securing homes. Placements were made one at a time fitting each individual to a home which was a surer way than by attempting to place large numbers in a short time.

Two other factors are suggested as reasons for the ready adjustment of the patients—the change and the individual attention given. The improvement or recovery of an insane patient has repeatedly been reported for no other apparent reason than transfer to a different ward. Every superintendent has observed this. The boarding home constitutes a much more radical change. We have no way of knowing how much the patient lets down when she is absorbed into the mass of an institution. A course of treatment given by either the occupational therapist, the physical therapist, the nurse or the physician, often results in a decided mental improvement. Credit for this is then claimed on behalf of the respective occupational therapy, physical therapy, nursing or medical care, whichever was used. Many psychiatrists who have repeatedly observed this phenomena believe it to be due to the one factor common to every case, that the patient has been

singled out of the mass and treated as an individual, and that it mattered not a bit as to the means employed. Our boarding home patient is singled out at once as the object of attention and concern of her family. That three patients should improve so much as to take positions where they were self-supporting exceeded the bounds of imagined possibilities.

Supervision of Patients

One of our social workers handles all of the work of the community, in addition to her regular duties. There is an advantage in her familiarity with the country and people, due to her having always lived in this district. Then, many of the problems met with were not new to her. The school has nearly 400 patients on parole at home, or for employment or in colony houses in various towns. Homes and places of employment are continually being investigated and hardly a day goes by that patients are not returned or sent out to new places. These patients in colonies or on parole for employment must be capable of earning the standard rate of $3.50 per week, and so are not of the same class as those selected for boarding homes, but the work of judging the calibre of employees, of helping in the adjustment of the patient, and of supervising the patients' living conditions and welfare are much the same, so that this experience is invaluable for family care. The social worker visits every home once a month, but may visit a home several days in succession after placing its first patient, and calls at the community three or four times a month.

There is no question but what the superintendent, who has boarding homes, should be alert to all the dangers that threaten. Yet, I may say that we cannot name them from our own experience. Most of the things we dreaded never happened. The social worker gave to each new guardian the instructions as to the proper care of her patients, customarily given to those taking girls on parole, and any matters not understood were corrected on her next visit. The necessity for proper supervision was always stressed. A very important addition to the supervision is afforded in such a small village by the fact that every one is known to every one else. As more and more families become guardians, it becomes the interest of more and more villagers to have their village recognized as a safe shelter for the patients.

Of accidents, there have been none. There have been no escapes as there could be little motive at attempt to escape. The patients feel they have been placed on parole, many of them after having long given up any hope of such good luck. They are anxious to show that trust in them has not been misplaced, but most of all they are more comfortable than they have ever been in their lives before.

Neglect has never been seen. Rather, the patients gain weight as they greedily devour home cooking after years of institution meals. There are no strict regulations as to food. What the family eats is good enough, but patients must receive that. By means of a small portable scales always carried in her car, the social worker can weigh anyone she suspects of getting too little to eat. During the severe weather, patients were always found comfortably seated about the kitchen stove with members of the family in normal farm-house style. Our own contribution, an issue of double blankets to every patient, no doubt, helped at bed time. All patients have appeared clean and well cared for whenever visited.

Exploitation is a bug bear to many. The Scotch report takes this up in these words—"The second criticism was the natural one of exploitation. Were these patients, persons of reduced mentality, not in danger of being made drudges? This was a natural and right criticism, but it is a danger of which the local Medical Officers and Public Assistance Officials are fully aware and against which they are very alert and on their guard; so much so that I do not consider that in practice there is a serious risk on this score. Indeed, my experience has been rather in the other direction, as the following instance will show:—A young patient and an elderly man had been recently transferred to an experienced guardian. I asked the guardian's wife first about the young patient and then asked about the old man, who had been under guardianship elsewhere for some years and was now transferred for an entirely satisfactory reason. He was a somewhat aged man and considerably demented. I asked what he could do about the house. "Not a great deal." "Could he bring the water in?" "Oh, we do not ask him to do that, it is rather heavy for him, he is an old man." Seemingly, however, he was able to chop sticks and do a number of minor light tasks. Then, after some further inquiries, the guardian said, "You see, he is an old man; I give him his breakfast in bed." While I admit that this episode was exceptional, it illustrates an attitude of mind and of care which, in a lesser degree was far from uncommon."

That is surely an encouraging statement. The only

instance in our community turned out to be not so bad as reported. Two patients were supposed to be putting in a full day in the cider mill. This was a surprise because, while I do not claim that these patients never did any work at all before, they were never good enough for any regular employment. Investigation disclosed that one of the patients had been working part of the day on an apple evaporator. Her employer's eagerness to comply with our demand to stop her was thwarted by the patient herself. As she begged to be allowed to continue, it was ruled that she might attend the evaporator mornings only. Our experience with paroled cases is, that employers are more apt to be too lenient, and that in a small community some other employer will be jealous enough to report most infringements of any kind. With adequate supervision and quick action against offenders, it does not seem that exploitation can be carried very far. The incident of the old man's breakfast could be matched by us many times over. Passing over the many little gifts and birthday parties to something of more moment I would cite the measures taken when any illness develops. Then especially cooked dishes are brought to their bed, homely measures like hot mustard foot baths are given or hot water bags are applied. Simple medications are purchased at the local drug store without thought of reimbursement. Their whole concern is to relieve the pain, break up the cold or alleviate the distress and nothing is too much trouble.

Social Life and the Community Center

The small community affords good opportunities for social life. All patients have the freedom of their own premises, they go unattended on errands to the village and to visit in each others' homes. Hospitality is not lacking and they often chat with each other over a cup of tea or a dish of fruit. Some of them come to the village from a considerable distance and it was thought that they should have some place to rest other than the post-office steps. This was afforded when we established the community center. Such a center is one of the features of Gheel and its value is recognized by the Scotch. They speak of a district where they established a club for the boys to meet and say it has been the means of giving the boys many pleasant social hours and making them more content. We contracted with our first guardian whose residence was centrally located to operate a community center in her home and in addition to its use as a social center, arranged that it should serve as a center for social service, nursing care, a depot for clothing and supplies and for occupational therapy materials. She agreed to the following regulations for it:

Rules for Community Center

1. A large warm room provided which has easy access outside so that all of the community cases may feel free to come and go for social intercourse and recreation. Adjoining this room or in it, there should be at least two beds which should at all times be in readiness to receive any emergency sick cases or patients left at the room over night.

2. The day room should be provided with books, magazines, pictures, games, a radio and piano. Everything except the piano will be furnished by the institution.

3. The one in charge should act in the capacity of nurse, looking after feet, hair, etc., of the neighborhood inmates and should keep weight charts (which will be furnished) on each case once monthly. Corns and calluses should receive attention every three weeks or more often, if necessary. Hair should be trimmed once monthly.

4. In the event that an inmate becomes ill she may be brought to the rooms where she can receive first aid and minor treatments, or she may require bed care for a few days and a record of temperature, pulse, and respirations kept.

5. A girl may be left at the rooms if her boarding mother is obliged to go away for the day. Girls should not be left alone in their boarding places throughout the day.

6. The one in charge should endeavor to make the girls feel welcome and assist them in entertaining themselves.

7. Our occupational therapy director will provide various forms of suitable occupation for those visiting the rooms.

8. The rooms to be used as general headquarters where articles for the different girls may be left and clothing fitted, etc.

9. One in charge to keep Mrs. Banckert informed at all times of the various happenings and follow her advice in regard to general care, etc.

A supply of cathartics and some simple remedies are at hand at the center, but when a physician's services are required the local health officer is called and paid his regular rate. The occupational therapist visits all homes and lays out the projects, but depends on the center to replenish supplies. There is greater need for this than was expected. It seems that patients once content to sit in idleness have been stimulated to the point where they complain if they have nothing to do. The occupational therapist arranges the monthly parties at which there is always a good attendance, besides which patients are accustomed to drop in any hour of day for the social facilities of the center. The nurse owning the house accepted $50.00 per month, the pay of an attendant to cover her services and the use of the rooms thus engaged.

Attitude of the Villagers

The attitude of the community toward us has been increasingly favorable. A reluctance to accepting patients first encountered was due to a fixed idea that they were insane. The psychiatric distinction we offered carried no conviction, as they were convinced that the fact that they were in an institution was conclusive evidence that they were there for a good and sufficient reason. So that the first guardians rather took their patients on trust. Therefore, these first patients were selected with great care and with the idea that on observation of their conduct would depend the attitude of the community toward us. What a good impression they made may be judged from the ease with which we later placed two patients from Binghamton State Hospital who were actually insane. Patients are welcomed at church and at entertainments, in fact the admission rate is cut to fit the 25 or 50c per month they are given for spending money. Those who have been refused patients blame the nurse for not recommending them but their being disgruntled seems to do us no harm. Just how many will ultimately apply for patients we cannot judge, since we are refusing all applications at present. The general feeling is good and any attitude of suspicion and distrust has changed since they have seen the patients going about the village unobtrusively and have observed for themselves that they are not crazy. The Scotch remark on this in positive terms as follows:—"The benefits of boarding-out, both lunatic and defective patients, do not apply exclusively to the patients. I have noticed, within recent years, that the presence of such patients in the community is having a definitely educative effect. In areas where such patients are placed, people are ceasing to regard mental illness or mental defect as something to be shunned or feared. Greater sympathy and greater understanding is being shown by the general public, and a new and enlightened attitude is gradually being developed." Our experience is probably too brief to record an observation so general, but there is no question that many of the immediate guardians have developed an altruistic attitude toward all the patients.

Plans for the Future with Various Methods

In planning for the future various lines are open. Unquestionably our present community can be considerably enlarged. The possibilities for developing a similar community for men in another village seem good. It is our further ambition to organize a similar community for insane patients in cooperation with one of the State hospitals. Our hopes are not based solely on our success with two patients from Binghamton State Hospital, but from an acquaintance with such inmates derived from 25 years experience in one of the larger New York State Hospitals. There we have seen many patients whose acute symptoms had long since subsided; who had deteriorated to a state in which they resembled a mental defective in appearance and conduct and in which they required only about the same degree of care and attention. Such cases seem eminently fitted for the purpose. Then there are the broken down workers, those who were employed in the laundry or kitchen until their heart or their feet gave out. We become sentimental about an old horse and put him out to pasture, why not make the patient's declining years happy with the comforts of a small home after a life-time devoted to faithful and laborious work for the State. Some difficulty may well be anticipated in securing suitable patients owing to the almost universal endeavor of hospital employees to palm off troublesome cases and to hide the good ones. Careful selection of patients is obligatory in the beginning of a project like this. We consider that the community has an outstanding advantage over any other type of placement in that the experience will be accumulative. As they become accustomed to having patients about we feel that it is reasonable to expect that not only will the individual guardians become more willing to accept worse patients, but as the number of guardians increases there will be less looking askance at a patient of any kind. This is said to account for the success at Gheel where Family Care has been carried on through succeeding generations; those now caring for them having been familiar with their presence throughout their childhood. While we cannot hope to approach this in degree for a long, long time, nevertheless, those who are familiar with the small compact community at Walworth feel that this factor is already beginning to operate to our great advantage.

Entirely aside from our community placements we would like to place a patient whenever we find a good home for her no matter where that home may be, because we believe that the most important thing is to get the right kind of guardian. Instead of a fixed rate a sliding scale will be used. The highest rate will be paid for an idle patient in a city or where high prices prevail; lower rates in rural sections or for a patient with a little earning capacity, until we come down to nothing for one who can earn his own keep. Patients of this latter class are all we could afford so far. Of these we have six widely scattered in separate homes. Such cases might be called "paroles," but as our paroles have to earn the standard wage, no such patients were placed heretofore. It has long been customary for some counties to allow almshouse residents to go out to work for some family who could give them board and keep. This does not seem different from what we have proposed, and being able to add a little board money ought to make it easier to do.

Then there is the matter of paying board to a relative for the patient's care. Objection has been made to this because it could be subjected to grave abuse. I can see how this might be were it made mandatory which is hardly likely. Otherwise the superintendent could refuse to allow the relatives to take the patient home to board exactly as he now refuses to allow his parole for the same reason. We do not parole a patient to his relatives no matter how insistent they are unless the social service returns a favorable report regarding home conditions, adequate supervision, the reputation and standing of the family and the possession of sufficient means to support themselves. Where the added burden of the patient's support is the only thing that prevents the family from taking him, I see no objection to paying them for his board. No real mother would let her child suffer want to spend the money on herself. This practice has been successful in Scotland on a large scale. Dr. Fraser states— "In Glasgow and Govan by far the greater number are living in their own homes with relatives. At the end of the year there were remaining 395 certified defectives. Some of these are low grade imbeciles who can be well looked after in their own home provided conditions are good. The majority, however, are high grade imbeciles or belong to the feebleminded group who have attended special schools and who on leaving school cannot obtain employment and whose parents apply for assistance. Such cases necessarily require very careful supervision, a matter of great difficulty in a city where the surroundings are bad and often there is little parental control and where the patients have nothing to do and very little outlet for their energies. Although city life is unsuitable for the majority of cases, it says much for the care and supervision exercised by the local authority that of the 395 certified defectives in Glasgow, it was only found necessary to remove seven to institutions on account of improper control and that only two of the seven were charged with offences." After such an account of success under the worst of conditions there seems no reason for hesitating to try it where all conditions can be controlled.

Nursing homes where a retired attendant or practical nurse can care for a number of patients is another means of relieving overcrowding in the institutions and is of advantage for some types of patients. It does not provide, however, the attractions peculiar to family and community life and the rate paid should probably double that for boarding homes. If the rate is not sufficient, it is unreasonable to count on the person in charge going without in order to supply the patient, and of course the obverse of this cannot be countenanced.

The colony house run by school employees can also accommodate a number of patients. Here, too, the desirable features of family life will be lacking. The costs of running a colony house are rather high and serious consideration should be given as to whether it affords the patient sufficient advantage. The superiority of our own colony house at Watkins Glen is open to question, because on account of its distance it is operated at considerable inconvenience and lacks the provision for entertainment and recreation which the institution affords. The nursing home and colony house are mentioned here because, if established in such a community as Walworth or used as a community center, such objections as have been made might be overcome and an increased number added to the total cared for.

Classification of Methods in Use

As all these plans are in operation somewhere none of them should be ruled out as impractical until proved so by experience with them. We are now using more than one of these methods so that in recording the number of

patients in family care we have found it convenient to separate them and to refer to them as—
1. Family Care—Community.
2. Family Care—Individual.
3. Family Care—School.

Family Care—community is the designation used in referring to those boarding homes I have described at length. Family care individual I have mentioned as placements made anywhere and family care school is yet to be described.

Family Care—School is in some ways different. Its object is therapeutic rather than economic, but the procedure itself is simple. A child of school age, despite her commitment, is placed in a foster home in a village with a special class school and given another chance to grow up outside instead of being kept locked up in the institution. Starting this three years ago, we are now carrying nine children. Three (3) girls in the village of Lyons attend special class; in Newark 4 girls are in the sixth grade (two of them starting in special class); 1 boy is in the second grade, and one in first. Their ages range from 5 to 15, I.Q. 58 to 85. All except the little boy are "Scouts" and one girl is leader of her troop. A long story of these children's activities may be condensed by saying that it is in no particular different from that of any other child in the village. For their board we pay $6.00 per week, as they live down town where city prices prevail, and we give them each 25c for church, pencils and sundries, but especially to teach thrift. We buy their clothing outside.

Already, we can report some favorable results. One of the first girls to be placed, with an I.Q. of 47, left school last summer when she became 18 years of age, and has steadily been employed at housework and in caring for children. Thus, she has become self-supporting.

Arrangements have been made for a little girl of 15 years, who is leader of her scout troop, to take a position as soon as the school term closes. She is to be employed in a very high-class private school for mental defectives. In return for her work in helping with the children, she will receive her board and clothing and 50c per week. Furthermore, her education will be continued there, with the idea of fitting her for a nursery governess.

The Society who sent us the two little brothers have been practically compelled to take them back under their care upon our representation that they have been able to attend regular classes in the public school and live successfully outside in a foster home for the past two years. It is thought that their success does not necessarily prove that they should not have been committed. No, rather it shows that when given a chance, under conditions as nearly ideal as could be devised, including the active support of a psychiatric social worker, they were able to manage; while their histories show that they were unable to combat handicaps of bad environment, poor parentage, physical disorder or malnutrition, and inadequate school facilities, from one or all of which they suffered. Dr. Greenacre, a psychiatrist, not only said that even the normal child brought up in an institution shows the effects of repressive discipline and tends to become standardized, but so directed that the Department of Welfare of Westchester County prefers to subsidize a child in its own home or to pay board for it in a substitute home, rather than commit it to the best of modern institutions. Yet the normal child can better overcome this handicap than the slowly adjusting mental defective, separated throughout his formative years from the very experiences of living most necessary to his survival. So this idea serves as our idea. What is done at this time affects the entire future of the child, and may determine whether he will be confined for life or otherwise. We have many promising candidates selected for trial, and keenly feel that we are depriving them of their one big chance in life while we await funds to enable us to augment the numbers placed.

Economic Results

Descending from this high plane of consideration of the patients' welfare and therapy there is something more to be considered than the high rate of board. From an economic standpoint, the gain from keeping a patient out of the institution altogether is enormous in comparison with the few years board paid. Further the fact that you have kept a child out in a boarding home if only for a year makes a convincing argument for the return of the child to the authorities committing him. While on the subject I will mention that the same argument has been effective in regard to older cases. A reluctance to take a patient has been overcome when the county commissioner was assured that the patient had already adapted to a boarding home outside. Seven or eight vacancies made this way in our community were promptly filled by younger patients. As the opportunities for boarding increase so will these numbers increase. It would seem then, while the highest board paid does not exceed institution costs, that such other factors as

mentioned will effect an ultimate economy on a much larger scale. The Department's budget for next year allows each institution to allocate $20,000.00 for boarding homes, and we anticipate no difficulty in employing every cent of this sum to good advantage, and are planning to do so.

Conclusions

I have tried to describe frankly our experience with Family Care. The numbers we quote may seem insufficient to be conclusive when it is the fashion to speak so lightly in terms of billions. We expect to begin increasing the numbers this year, but as that simply means a continuing repetition of the same things we have already done over and over again, we do not anticipate that it will add anything of value to the knowledge already gained. In the main, it comes down to this. We have six colony houses, we would run them in just the same way if we had one or a hundred. In short, we have convinced ourselves of the practicability of family care. As to its benefits, I can do no better than to refer to the arguments collected in the concluding paragraph of Dr. Pollock's paper on Family Care of Mental Patients before the American Psychiatric Society last year. What he says of hospitals and the insane, in my opinion, applies equally well to schools for mental defectives. His summation is this:

"The advantages to be derived from family care would be fourfold: The patients placed in suitable families would resume a measure of community life with a natural environment and with more freedom than could be possible in a State hospital. The families receiving patients would have an outlet for their altruistic sentiments and would acquire a secure economic status. The State hospital relieved of many of its custodial cases could devote more of its energies to the scientific treatment of acute and recoverable patients. The State conducting an extensive system of family care would be relieved of the necessity of building new hospitals and would have a better opportunity to treat its mental patients in accordance with their individual needs."

Discussion

Dr. Charles S. Bernstein (Rome, N.Y.):—

Dr. Vaux has established a practice which seems awfully human and interesting and worth-while. I am sure we want to support him and give him a chance to go further.

Dr. J. M. Murdock (Faribault, Minn.):—

I visited the community in Gheel some years ago and was much impressed with the work there, where mental defectives have been cared for in private homes for one hundred years or so. Of course, they have grown up to the work, and the fact that Scotland has adopted this plan appeals to me, too.

Dr. Vaux is doing a wonderful piece of work. In connection with it I don't wish to again bring up the question of sterilization, but I do feel that if boarding out is carried on to any extent, we will feel better satisfied if the individual who is sent out has first undergone sterilization. I do feel that a lot of our older people who, as the Doctor says, just sit around and do little or nothing, might be more contented and have a more natural life in a family unit. I hope to hear more of Dr. Vaux's work. It is something we would all think of very seriously, now that our institutions are crowded, and we have long waiting lists.

Dr. Charles L. Vaux (Newark, N.Y.)—

Dr. Bernstein was very kind to suggest the offer of money. So far it has been a very great handicap because we carried on this work without any funds, and anybody who has tried to do anything or buy anything without any money with which to buy it knows the difficulty. But we have shown a number of these homes to our commissioner. He had a private conversation with the budget commissioner, and the first of July every hospital in New York State will be able to spend $20,000 of its money in boarding homes or family care, if it cares to do so.

At the Newark State School I am sure we will use all of the money allotted to us. We have been waiting for a year and one-half to go ahead. We have had applications coming in every week from people who want to take patients, and we have had to turn them down because we have had no money. We don't know how many homes we could have offered us because we have to turn down the ones who do apply and that discourages the others.

I think it is not because we disregard sterilization, but I think it is because we regard it very much in selecting the place. One of the first considerations was to get a place that was secluded, where all the people knew each other, and where any stranger in town would be a marked person. Because we can't have sterilization, we depend for protection on supervision, and we emphasize very close supervision both with the patients in this group of family care and with the great many patients we have out on parole.

I am sorry that the time didn't allow me to discuss an even more interesting group that we have in boarding homes, the group of smaller children of school age who are living down in the village in private homes, where they attend public school and have severed all connections with the institution and have gone on like any child in the village, getting their school work in the public school and getting their training in the home where the woman is paid for their board.

We have been carrying this on for three years, and so successfully that as soon as we get this increase in funds we expect to push it just as far as we can, because these children are taken from the institution within the first year that they are admitted, and they are placed outside and we never expect to bring any of them back.

Two of them have already been placed in private homes as they have grown older, and we expect to have no difficulty in placing these children in the community and having them grow up outside, without ever having to return to the institution. We think it makes the greatest difference in the world in their lives and think it is the most important thing we can do for the children.

Author

Charles L. Vaux, M.D., is the Superintendent of the Newark State School, Newark, New York.

The Institution as a Foster Parent

Edgar A. Doll, Ph.D.
1937

This paper is concerned with general questions of policy of institutional administration and training as related to the social competence of the patients or wards. Before commitment each patient has grown up in the care of some family. Many of these families are of low-grade social and economic status. Others are of definitely superior status. Mental deficiency, insanity, epilepsy, deafness, blindness, and other handicaps to social sufficiency may occur in the best of homes with the changing fortunes of environmental circumstances. The great majority of handicapped and dependent persons are usually cared for up to the limit of the resources of the home or the relatives of the patient before an appeal is made for institutional care. The major or predisposing condition which brings the patient to the institution is therefore usually accompanied by precipitating influences, sometimes termed "the plus factor," which then makes further home care impracticable. Thus, the feeble-minded child may be cared for at home if he is not crippled, or while he is still small, or while the family integrity is unimpaired.

The institution which receives the mentally deficient ward thereby assumes in addition to the feeble-mindedness the further burden of crippling, dependency, misconduct, or other circumstances which are associated with the mental deficiency. The *commitable* feeble-minded, then, are those in whom some serious additional factor is present. This corresponds to the English system of identification vs. certification, meaning by the former the professional diagnosis of feeble-mindedness, and by the latter the social circumstances which make commitment desirable.

This suggests that insofar as the institution can mitigate the plus factor the patient or ward might be considered eligible for return to the home environment, providing the feeble-mindedness itself is not likely to lead to some other and possibly much graver plus factor. The logical conclusion is that not all the feeble-minded require institutional care, and those who are committed do not necessarily require permanent custodial care.

Assuming, however, that we must deal with the major handicap as well as with the plus factor associated with it, what should be the policy of the institution toward the primary condition itself? Confining the discussion for the sake of illustration to feeble-mindedness as one major condition, we may examine the peculiar advantages afforded by the institution over those of the home or the community.

The feeble-minded person is defined as one who because of incomplete mental development is incapable of managing his own affairs with ordinary prudence. In the home situation the parents, relatives, and community agencies provide the oversight and care made necessary by the individual's inability to conduct his own affairs successfully. As the normal child matures, he outgrows his dependence on the parent and ultimately "shifts for himself." The successive stages of this progressive independence have been systematically formulated in the Vineland Social Maturity Scale. Throughout this course of normal child development the parent assumes responsibility for the child for those details of behavior in which the child is not yet independently competent. Similarly, the parent adapts himself to the social limitations of the feeble-minded child or adult, and "looks after" him where he can not look after himself. When such a feeble-minded person is committed to institutional care, the institution acts *in loco parentis*, and continues to safeguard the patient and society from the unfavorable consequences of the patient's incompetence.

When the patient is admitted to the institution, his social competence is appraised at face value and he is surrounded with those safeguards to behavior which seem necessary in the light of his capabilities and deficiencies. But the institution may not assume all the risks that the family might be willing to hazard, and therefore controls the patient more solicitously in many respects than the family may have done by setting up a more rigorous system of environmental opportunity and restraints than that provided by the family. This regimentation, as it is sometimes called, may be both favorable and unfavorable.

The consequent first result of institutional commit-

The Institution as a Foster Parent

ment is to increase the patient's degree of dependence through increased supervision, because the institution dares not assume the same risks that the family has previously hazarded. On the other hand, the institution undertakes to develop the patient in those activities which can be pursued to *better* advantage in the institution than could be done at home. In this respect the institution affords stimulation in association with other patients of like degree of ability and disability in group activities, so that in this direction the institution can be more helpful to the patient than the family could be. There is always the prospect, therefore, that the limitations imposed by the institutional environment may be offset by the compensating advantages. The institution also tends to be more objective in its treatment of the patient than the family has been, and encourages him to fend for himself in many directions where the family previously acted for him, especially in self-help and occupational pursuits.

In what directions and to what extent do these differences obtain? Can we compare the competence of the child in the institutional environment with that previously and subsequently observed in the home environment? Such comparisons are possible by means of the social maturity scale. This scale is standardized in terms of normal genetic development in the ordinary home environment. When applied in the institutional environment, the differences in environmental opportunity and restraint readily become apparent.

Our data show that the institution restrains the patient in self-direction and locomotion, urges him in self-help and occupation, urges him in the lower degrees of communication and socialization and restrains him in the higher. Thus, the young or low-grade child may have had the use of the fork at home, but in the institutional environment this may be considered too hazardous, or *vice versa.* He may have been permitted to roam the streets at home, but in the institutional environment this may be considered too difficult to control. He may have had his own money at home, but in the institution this may prove impracticable. On the other hand, he may have been *put* to bed at home, whereas in the institution he may be encouraged to put himself to bed.

The use of this social scale rather clearly reveals the specific advantages and disadvantages of the institutional environment as compared with that of the home. We have conducted experimental studies of this kind in institutions for the feeble-minded, the insane, the deaf,

and the blind. These studies reveal that the nature of the restrictions to individual expression of independence varies appreciably from one institution to another, and within each institution from one patient to another.

What are these institutional restrictions and opportunities? How do they limit or foster the expression of personal independence? To what extent do they handicap, safeguard, or promote the patient's social competence? The prohibitions and the training opportunities of the institution have a direct relation to the responsibility of the institution for the welfare of the patient and to the incompetence which these individuals may have demonstrated in the pre-institutional surroundings. Obviously, the institution should provide for adjustment of its administrative restrictions and training program according to the actual competence of the individual patient. Here the welfare of the individual must be related to that of the group, for many difficulties are encountered in providing personal freedom which is yet consistent with the total responsibility of the institution.

This embarrassment is not limited to institutions for the handicapped, but is found also in institutions for the normal such as boarding schools and colleges, as well as at home. Thus, the family itself observes definite restrictions to behavior where the welfare of the individual must be subordinated to that of the family. Likewise the community observes certain conventions which protect the welfare of the community as a whole. There is no such thing as complete freedom in social life, since the freedom of each individual must be related to that of every other individual. This situation is only somewhat more obvious in the institutional community than in the home community.

The institution as a training center must also consider the patient in relation to his *ultimate* social competence. It must have some objective toward which it is leading the patient. It is therefore necessary to make some more or less immediate prognosis as to the presumptive ultimate attainment of the patient and to formulate a program for him which is reasonably related to his ultimate welfare. In the progressive institution this is done by means of scientific diagnosis and practical evaluation of the patient, and these estimates are revised in the light of continuing experience. From this point of view the patient is not a foundling on the doorstep for whom permanent custody is to be provided, but is a growing adapting person, who no matter how badly handicapped may be expected to show some progress toward improvement with training. This ultimate condition should be estimated as accurately and as early as possible and the program of training systematically related to these reasonable objectives.

We reach the conclusion, then, that the regimen of the institution should be designed to capitalize the patient's aptitudes and to minimize his weaknesses. If the patient is incapable of handling money wisely, he should not be completely restricted in the use of money, but should be *taught* to spend and to save money wisely, within the limits of his capacity to do so. If he is incapable of feeding himself, he should be trained in this activity within reasonable limits. If he has no occupational skills, he should be brought to the highest practicable level of occupational attainment. If he shows poor self-direction, he should be encouraged to become as self-directing as possible. In short, instead of being *held back* in the direction of his shortcomings, effort should be made to remove those limitations as far as may seem practicable. That is to say, his competence and independence should be increased in all directions that seem reasonable. This means somewhat paradoxically that we should consider these frontiers of incompetence as the points at which our efforts should begin rather than end, and the restrictions to behavior or the limitations of environmental opportunity should be kept, as far as possible, at the upper extreme of the patient's success as reflected through systematic training.

If this point of view is accepted, the progressive institution finds itself faced with the problem of examining all the conditions of institutional regimentation in relation to the capabilities of the individual patient. The successful institution will therefore have no iron-clad rules. On the contrary, the patient will be viewed as growing and developing, or as responding to treatment and training, and this progress will be revealed in the extent to which the individual patient can be relieved of the responsibility of observing particular rules. The practicability of this point of view is readily demonstrated by means of the social maturity scale which clearly portrays in each individual the present extent of his independence and responsibility and reflects at the same time those directions in which the patient might progress if institutional regimentation were relaxed in his case, or where he does perform in spite of official restrictions. Indeed, the progress of the patient toward recovery can be revealed rather definitely in this way. The patient will then have gone through a pre-parole period of opportunity to

exercise those privileges which become his obligations after leaving the institution or before being considered ready to do so. It is unfortunate that within the limits of this paper experimental justification of these conclusions cannot be presented.

This argument starts from the assumption that family life is, under ordinary circumstances, the most ideal environment for individual welfare. It is clear that all patients originate in the family and that most of them have a considerable background in family life before coming to the institution. This adjustment in family life has presumably been more or less successful up to or shortly before the time of commitment. It would seem reasonable, therefore, to expect the institution to bend its efforts toward restoring the individual to some form of family life. If, for various reasons, the patient cannot be restored to his own family, perhaps he can be restored to some community or to some foster family. The practicability of family care of the handicapped is amply demonstrated by the success of the Gheel plan in Belgium and by the success attained at Walworth, New York, and in other places. The advantages, social, personal, and economic, of family care are well summarized in a recent book by Dr. Horatio Pollock[1] and others. It should be clearly understood that family care is not limited to socially successful individuals, but may be extended under favorable conditions to the lowest grades and the most handicapped types of patients.

The success of family care both before commitment and after discharge suggests the very great importance of emulating family care as far as practicable within the institution. Most modern institutions are definitely ahead of the average family in material advantages of plant and equipment, but gravely behind the standards of family care in terms of personal solicitude and individual freedom. The ordinary institution is too large and too unwieldy to reproduce the more desirable features of family care. On the other hand, the family is too small and too unstandardized to provide some of the advantages afforded by institutional care. We agree with Professor Johnstone and others that the institution is or can be a "standard-setter" for the family in many directions. We recognize also his success and theirs in reproducing many desirable features of family life within the institution. We see, also, however, numerous advantages on the part of the family as compared with the institution.

It can never be possible to provide for all the feebleminded in institutions, nor is it desirable to do so. Permanent institutional care for all of the feeble-minded is therefore no longer a defensible policy. The modern institution should be thought of as a treatment center for temporarily assuming and ultimately overcoming the difficulties reflected in the failure of the handicapped person. To accomplish this, the welfare of the patient and of society must always be considered as paramount and the welfare of the institution as secondary. This requires the courage to "graduate" the most successful and the best adjusted patients, and to retain the most dependent and the least adjusted.

To many earnest institutional workers these ideas will seem radical, if not ingenuous. But these ideas are neither new nor untried. They are merely a restatement of the views of those great figures in this Association whose words carry weight because of the respect which they command. Out of many such, the words of our beloved R. George Wallace may be quoted as representative:

In the construction and arrangement of a school for the feeble-minded, it is most necessary that those concerned should be thoroughly acquainted with the lives and activities of the pu-

pils, and be able to interpret those activities to the extent of shaping inanimate objects such as brick, stone, concrete, and so forth, around their lives, with due regard to their hopes, desires, pleasures, recreations, as well as to their more material physical comforts and conveniences. . . .

It is wonderful how simple these institution problems become when we solve them by means of the common denominator; what is best for the children, not how much does it cost or how hard a job or how long will it take or how disagreeable the task. Strange as it may seem, that which is the best for the children will prove to be the most economical as well as the most pleasant task to perform.

And may we add it is also the most fruitful and the most encouraging task that lies before us.

Note

[1]Pollock, H. M. *Family Care of Mental Patients*. Utica, State Hospitals Press, 1936, p. 247.

Author

Edgar A. Doll, Ph.D., *Director of Research*, The Training School at Vineland, N.J.

A Study of the Effects of Differential Stimulation on Mentally Retarded Children

Harold M. Skeels, Ph.D. and Harold B. Dye, M.D.
1939

The study of the nature of intelligence challenges the interest of psychologists and educators not only because of the theoretical concepts involved, but also because of the implications relating to child care and education. If, on the one hand, intelligence is static, a fixed entity and relatively unmodifiable by changes in environmental impact, then changes in living conditions and amount and kind of education can be expected to have little influence on the mental level of individuals.

On the other hand, if intelligence shows change in relation to shifts in environmental influence, then our concept must include modifiability, and the implications for child welfare become more challenging.

This latter concept was postulated by Alfred Binet. In his significant book entitled *Les Idees Modernes Sur Les Enfants*, published in 1911, Binet devotes an enlightening chapter to the topic, *Intelligence: Its Measurement and Education*. He is surprised and concerned at the prejudice against the concept of modifiability of intelligence.

To quote: "Some recent philosophers appear to have given their moral support to the deplorable verdict that the intelligence of an individual is a fixed quantity, a quantity which cannot be augmented. We must protest and act against this brutal pessimism. We shall endeavor to show that it has no foundation whatsoever" (p. 141).

Binet goes on to cite observations and situations relating to the teaching of subnormal children, summarizing as follows: "A child's mind is like a field for which an expert farmer has advised a change in the method of cultivating, with the result that in place of desert land, we now have a harvest. It is in this particular sense, the only one which is significant, that we say that the intelligence of children may be increased. One increases that which constitutes the intelligence of a school child; namely, the capacity to learn, to improve with instruction."

Statement of the Problem

The purpose of this study was to determine the effects on mental growth of a radical shift in institutional environment to one providing superior stimulation, introduced into the lives of mentally retarded children of early preschool ages. These children were placed singly or in some cases by twos on wards of brighter girls in an institution for feebleminded children. Preliminary observation had given some indication that such an environment was mentally stimulating for children two to three years of age. As a corollary aim, it seemed pertinent to study a contrast group of dull-normal and normal children of somewhat similar ages residing over a period of time in a relatively nonstimulating orphanage environment.

Origin of the Study

This research project was the outgrowth of a clinical surprise. Two children under a year and a half, in residence at the state orphanage, gave unmistakable evidence of marked mental retardation. Kuhlmann-Binet intelligence tests were given both children. C.D.,[1] thirteen months of age at time of examination, obtained an I.Q. of 46, and B.D.,[2] at sixteen months, scored an I.Q. of 35. Qualitative observations of the examiner substantiated a classification of imbecile level of mental retardation. In the case of B.D., the examiner felt that the child's actual level was perhaps slightly higher, but not to exceed ten points or an I.Q. level of 45. As check tests for further corroboration, the Iowa Tests for Young Children[3] were used. Mental ages of approximately six and seven months respectively were obtained.

Obviously a classification of feeblemindedness would not be justified if based on results of intelligence tests alone, particularly at these young ages. However, behavioral reactions in conjunction with the examinations of the pediatrician, and observations by the superintendent

A Study of the Effects of Differential Stimulation on Mentally Retarded Children   Harold M. Skeels and Harold B. Dye

of nurses relative to activity or lack of activity of these children in the nursery in contrast with other children, gave ample substantiation for a classification of marked mental retardation. C.D., at thirteen months, was making no attempts to stand, even with assistance. She could not pull herself to an upright position with the aid of crib or chair, nor did she display much manipulative activity with blocks or play materials. Spontaneous vocalization also was lacking. B.D., at sixteen months, was not vocalizing, was unable to walk with help and made relatively no responses to play materials in the nursery.

There were no indications of physiological or organic defects. Birth histories were negative, both children being full term normal delivery with no indications of birth injury or glandular dysfunction. Social histories were not flattering. Both children were illegitimate. In the case of C.D., the mother had been adjudged feebleminded and a legal guardian was appointed. Although the mother claimed to have finished the eighth grade at sixteen years, the social workers felt that she was very retarded and probably had had a difficult time in school. A Stanford-Binet (1916 revision) intelligence test given at the University Hospital showed a mental age of nine years and an I.Q. of 56. She had always been healthy. Her father was a miner, had been unable to learn in school and had deserted his family. Little is known of the father of the child, although it was reported that he had gone to high school.

B.D.'s mother was an inmate in a state hospital, diagnosed as psychosis with mental deficiency. She was slow to sit up, walk and talk, and went only to the second grade in school. The maternal grandfather drank to excess and his brother died in a state hospital of general paralysis of the insane. One maternal great aunt died of epilepsy. B.D.'s father is unknown; the mother named an inebriate formerly released from the state hospital.

Accordingly, these two children were recommended for transfer to the school for feebleminded.[4] We quote from the recommendations for transfer as follows: C.D.: "Diagnosis of mental ability: Mental deficiency of imbecile level, which will probably continue with an increase in age. Prognosis: Poor. With this deficiency in mental development, C.D. will be unable to make her way outside the care and protection offered by an institution for feebleminded children. Her relatives are not in a position to give her the continuous care she will need." Diagnosis and prognosis on B.D. were similar to the one just quoted.

Following this recommendation, the children were committed to the school for feebleminded. They were placed on a ward of older girls, ranging in age from eighteen to fifty years and in mental age from five to nine years.

Six months after transfer, the psychologist visiting the wards of the institution was surprised to notice the apparently remarkable development of these children. Accordingly, they were re-examined on the Kuhlmann-Binet, C.D. obtaining an I.Q. of 77 and B.D. an I.Q. of 87. Twelve months later they were tested again with I.Q.s of 100 and 88, respectively. Tests were again given when the children were forty months and forty-three months of age, respectively, with I.Q.s of 95 and 93.

In the meantime, inquiries were made as to reasons for this unusual development. Their "home" or ward environment was studied. It was observed that the attendants on the ward had taken a great fancy to the "babies." They were essentially the only preschool children on the ward, other than a few hopeless bed patients with physiological defects. The attendants would take these two children with them on their days off, giving them car rides and taking them down town to the stores. Toys, picture books and play materials were purchased by these admiring adults. The older, brighter girls on the wards were also very much attached to the children and would play with them during most of the waking hours. Thus it can be seen that this environment turned out to be stimulating to these preschool children of low initial mental level.

Following these last examinations, it was felt that the stimulation value of this particular kind of an environment had been pretty well exhausted. If the resulting level of intelligence was to be maintained a shift to a more normal environment seemed essential. Furthermore, since the children were then well within the range of normal intelligence, there ceased to be any justification for keeping them in an institution for the feebleminded. Accordingly, they were transferred back to the orphanage, and from there placed in rather average adoptive homes, their ages then being three years six months and three years eight months. After approximately fifteen months in the foster home, the children were again examined, this time using the Stanford-Binet. I.Q.s of 94 and 93 were obtained. From the evidence obtained, there is every indication that they will continue to classify as normal individuals as they increase in age. Accordingly, legal adoption has been completed in both cases.

A Study of the Effects of Differential Stimulation on Mentally Retarded Children   Harold M. Skeels and Harold B. Dye

From these startling preliminary findings, several questions were presented. Observations of similarly retarded children comparable in ages, remaining in an orphanage nursery, showed continued lack of mental development. In such a situation, the retarded child with numbers of other children of higher intelligence but of the same age seemed to make no gain in rate of mental growth. Also, since there was a ratio of only one or two adults to twelve to eighteen children, adult contacts were at a minimum and limited largely to physical care. Obviously, the retarded child could not be placed directly in an adoptive home as there could be no marked assurance that later development would be normal. Boarding home care to permit further evaluation and observation of development would, of course, be a logical solution of such a problem. However, the code of Iowa provides only for institutional care or placement in free or adoptive homes. Consequently, there seemed to be only one alternative, and that a rather fantastic one; namely, to transfer mentally retarded children in the orphanage nursery, one to two years of age, to an institution for feebleminded in order to make them normal. In view of the earlier preliminary findings, it was hoped that possibly 50 per cent of the cases might show at least some improvement. With cases not showing improvement, the transfer would be proper, and they could remain in that environment permanently. The suggestion was presented to the Board of Control, and although received with doubts and misgivings, was approved. It was decided that children so transferred would not be technically committed to the institution for feebleminded, but would rather be guests in residence at the school for feebleminded and would continue to appear on the orphanage population list. In other words, they would simply be temporarily hospitalized for therapeutic treatment. In this way there would not be the stigma of commitment to the school for feebleminded appearing on the case histories. Each case was to be evaluated from time to time. If and when improvement failed to ensue, final commitment was to be consummated.

Subjects

Experimental Group

Accordingly, from time to time, retarded children from the Iowa Soldiers' Orphans' Home at Davenport were sent to the Iowa Institution for Feebleminded Children at Glenwood. The experimental group includes all children so transferred who were under three years of age at time of transfer, a total of thirteen. The following tabulation shows sex, chronological age at time of examination before transfer, Kuhlmann-Binet mental age and I.Q., and chronological age at time of transfer.

The mean chronological age at time of transfer was 19.4 months, median 17.1 months, with a range from

Examination Prior to Transfer

Case	Sex	Chronological Age, Months	Mental Age, Months	I.Q.	Chronological Age, Months, at Transfer
1	M	7.0	6.0	89	7.1
2	F	12.7	7.2	57	13.1
3	F	12.7	10.8	85	13.3
4	F	14.7	10.8	73	15.0
5	F	13.4	6.0	46	15.2
6	F	15.5	12.0	77	15.6
7	F	16.6	10.8	65	17.1
8	F	16.6	6.0	35	18.4
9	F	21.8	13.2	61	22.0
10	M	23.3	16.8	72	23.4
11	M	25.7	19.2	75	27.4
12	F	27.9	18.0	65	28.4
13	F	30.0	10.8	36	35.9

A Study of the Effects of Differential Stimulation on Mentally Retarded Children   Harold M. Skeels and Harold B. Dye

7.1 to 35.9 months. Range of I.Q.s was from 35 to 89 with a mean of 64.3 and a median of 65.0. In eleven of the thirteen cases, additional tests had been given shortly before or in conjunction with the tests reported above. These were either repeated Kuhlmann-Binet examinations or Iowa Tests for Young Children. Such tests gave further corroboration of classification of marked mental retardation.

That such retardation was real and observable was substantiated by the reports of the pediatrician and the nurse in charge, indicating lack of development.[5] The orphanage policy is to place children and infants in adoptive homes as soon as possible. All children in this group were considered unsuitable for adoption because of mental retardation. In Case 1, although the I.Q. was 89, it was felt that actual retardation was much greater. At seven months this child could scarcely hold his head up without support. There was little general bodily activity as compared with other infants the same age. In Case 3, at twelve months, there was very little activity and sitting up without support was very unsteady. She could not pull herself to a standing position and did not creep. Case 11 was not only retarded, but showed perseverative patterns of behavior, particularly rocking back and forth incessantly. Cases 5, 8 and 13 were classified at the imbecile level. Descriptions of Cases 5 and 8 have been given under the origin of the study. Case 13, the oldest child in the group, showed perhaps the greatest amount of retardation. She was committed to the orphanage at twenty-eight months of age and came from a home where extreme neglect was typical. At thirty months of age she was unable to stand alone, could not walk with help and required support when sitting in a chair.

Following the transfer to the school for feeble-minded, examinations by the superintendent and other members of the medical staff further corroborated the reports from the orphanage as to the marked degree of mental retardation.

Contrast Group

This group did not exist as a designated group until the close of the experimental period. These children were simply examined as individuals from time to time along with the other children in the orphanage as routine procedure. It was only after the data on the experimental group had been analyzed that the decision was made to study a group of children remaining in the orphanage for contrast purposes. Children were included who (a) had had initial intelligence tests under two years of age, (b) were still in residence in the orphanage at approximately four years of age, and (c) were in the control group of the orphanage preschool study,[6] or (d) had not attended preschool. The study of the orphanage preschool referred to included two groups of children matched in chronological age, mental age, I.Q. and length of residence in the institution. The one group had the advantages of the more stimulating environment of preschool attendance, while the control group experienced the less stimulating environment of cottage life. Since the purpose of the contrast group for the present study was to include children in a relatively nonstimulating environment, children who had attended preschool could not be included. Such limitations, however, did not constitute a selective factor as far as the make-up of the children was concerned. A total of twelve children met these requirements and have been designated as the contrast group in the present study.

The following tabulation shows sex, chronological age at time of first examination, Kuhlmann-Benet mental age and I.Q.:

Case	Sex	Chronological Age, Months	Mental Age, Months	I.Q.
14	F	11.9	11.0	91
15	F	13.0	12.0	92
16	F	13.6	9.6	71
17	M	13.8	13.2	96
18	M	14.5	14.4	99
19	M	15.2	13.2	87
20	M	17.3	14.0	81
21	M	17.5	18.0	103
22	M	18.3	18.0	98
23	F	20.2	18.0	89
24	M	21.5	10.6	50
25	M	21.8	18.0	83

The mean chronological age at time of first examination was 16.6 months with a median at 16.3 months. The range was from 11.9 months to 21.8 months. The mean I.Q. for the group was 86.7 (median 90.0). With the exception of two cases (16 and 24) the children had I.Q.s ranging from 81 to 103.

Reasons for earlier nonplacement in adoptive homes were in general for those other than mental retardation. In fact, nine were, or had, been considered normal as far

A Study of the Effects of Differential Stimulation on Mentally Retarded Children   Harold M. Skeels and Harold B. Dye

as mental development was concerned. Five children were withheld from placement simply because of a poor family history. Two were held because of improper commitment, two because of luetic condition and one because of mental retardation.

Birth Histories of the Groups

In the examination of the birth histories of the two groups, no marked discrepancies were observed. In the experimental group, eight children were full term with normal delivery. Prematurity occurred in three cases (4, 7 and 9). Case 7, two months premature, spent the first two months in an incubator. The other two cases did not require special care. One case, 11, was delivered by Cesarean section. The remaining case, 13, was not admitted to the orphanage until twenty-eight months of age. No birth history was available.

The children of the contrast group present similar birth histories. Eight of this group were full term babies with normal labor. One, Case 23, was premature and delivered by breach extraction. Case 17 was delivered by low forceps at full term. As a result of difficult labor, he presented early symptoms of intracranial hemorrhage. There were periods of cyanosis and clonic convulsions, and feedings were taken poorly. At the end of a week, however, the cyanosis had diminished and there were no longer convulsions. By the end of fifteen days, the child appeared normal. Case 24 was admitted at fourteen months with no birth history available.

These data have been presented in summary form in the following tabulation:

Information Concerning Births*	Experimental Group	Contrast Group
Birth injuries		1
Pathological labor	2	3
Prematurity	3	1
Normal delivery	8	8
Unknown	1	1

*A given case may appear in more than one category.

Medical Histories

In the evaluation of the medical histories of both the experimental and contrast groups, little of significance was found in the relationship between illnesses and rate of mental growth. In the experimental group,

one child, Case 9, had congenital syphilis, but immediate antiluetic treatment following birth was adequate and serology was negative during the experimental period. In the contrast group, two children, Cases 14 and 16, were luetic, but Case 16 responded to early antiluetic treatment and all serology has been negative during the period of the study. However, in Case 14, a question may be raised as to the contributing effects of persistent syphilis. Blood Wassermann and Kahn were negative at nine months of age, but examination at thirty months revealed four plus Wassermann and Kahn. Treatment was again instituted, and at forty-six months both blood and spinal fluid serology were negative. Case 14, on admission to the orphanage, had enlarged spleen and liver, a tentative diagnosis of Gaucher's disease being made. This did not seriously affect the activity of the child during the course of the study.

Considering all children of both groups, they have had various upper respiratory infections, occasional contagious diseases, mild eczemas, but nothing more severe than the ordinary child of preschool age would have in the average home.

Family Backgrounds

Social histories revealed that the children of both experimental and contrast groups came from homes of low social, economic, occupational, and intellectual levels. The family background is comparable to that reported by Skeels and Fillmore[4] in their study of the mental development of children from underprivileged homes and Skodak's study[6] of children in foster homes placed at ages two to five. The backgrounds of the children in the two groups were comparable.

Mothers. — Information relating to education was available for eleven of the thirteen mothers in the experimental group and ten of the twelve mothers in the contrast group. The mean grade completed by mothers of children in the experimental group was 7.8 with a median at grade eight. Only two had any high school work, one having completed the eleventh grade and one the tenth grade (Cases 3 and 6). In one case, it was doubtful if the second grade had been completed (Case 8). Two (Cases 1 and 5) had dropped out of the eighth grade at the age of sixteen.

In the contrast group, the mean grade completed was 7.3 with a median at 7.5. One mother (Case 19) had completed high school and one had an equivalent of ninth grade education.

Occupational history of mothers, available on seven of the mothers in the experimental group and nine of the contrast group, included mainly housework, either in the homes of parents or working out as domestics. In only one instance was there a higher level indicated (Case 24 of the contrast group) in which the mother had been a telephone operator and had done general office work.

Intelligence tests[5] had been obtained on five of the mothers in the experimental group and nine of the mothers in the contrast group. The mean I.Q. for mothers of the experimental group was 70.4, with a median at 66. One additional mother, although not tested, was considered feebleminded and had gone only as far as the second grade. Four mothers had I.Q.s below 70, and one classified as normal with an I.Q. of 100.

Of the nine mothers in the contrast group, only two had I.Q.s above 70, one being 79 and the other 84. The others ranged from 36 to 66. The mean I.Q. was 63, with a median at 62.

Fathers. — Little information was available on the fathers, in fact in many cases paternity was doubtful. Ten of the children in each group were illegitimate. In the experimental group information relating to education was available on only four fathers. Two had completed the eighth grade, one completed high school, and one had gone to high school but how far was not known. Occupational status was indicated on only three of the fathers; one was a traveling salesman, one a printer, and one a farm hand.

In the contrast group, educational information was available on four. One had completed high school and one was considered talented in music (Case 24). Two had completed eighth grade (Cases 15 and 18), and one the sixth grade (Case 21). Occupational information was known on eight of the fathers. Three were day laborers, two were farm hands, one worked on the railroad section, one was a farm renter, and one was in a C.C.C. camp.

A qualitative analysis of social histories seems to justify the conclusion that within these educational and occupational classifications of true parents, the individuals represent the lower levels in such groups. Most of these fathers and mothers dropped out of school because of having reached their limits of achievement, and in no sense of the word represent the averages of their grade placements. The same may be said with reference to occupational status.

Description of the Environments

Experimental Group

Children in this group were transferred from the orphanage nursery to the school for feebleminded, and placed on the wards with older, brighter girls. Wards in the girls' school division were used. This included a large cottage of eight wards with a matron and an assistant matron in charge and one attendant for each ward. There are approximately thirty patients on each ward, including girls ranging in ages from eighteen to fifty years. On two wards (wards 2 and 3) are girls of the higher levels, mental ages from nine to twelve years. On two other wards (wards 4 and 5) the mental levels are from seven to ten years, and on another ward (ward 7) the mental ages are from five to eight.

With the exception of ward 7, there were few if any younger children on the wards aside from the experimental children. In some cases, there were one or two other young children on the ward, usually a mongol or a spastic paralysis case. In general, one, or at the most two, children in the experimental group were placed on a given ward.

The attendants and the older girls became very fond of the child placed on the ward and took great pride in its achievement. In fact, there was considerable competition between wards to see which one would have their "baby" walking or talking first. The girls would spend a great deal of time with the children, teaching them to walk, talk, play with toys and play materials, and in the training of habits.

Most of the clothing for these children was made by the older girls. The girls were so fond of the children that they would actually spend their small earnings and allowances to buy them special foods, toys, picture books, and materials for clothing. Similarly attendants gave of their time, money, and affection, and during their free hours frequently took the children on excursions, car rides, and trips. In addition, it was the policy of the matron in charge of the girls' school division to single out certain of these children whom she felt were in need of special individualization, and permit these children to spend a portion of time each day visiting her office. This furnished new experiences including being singled out and given special attention and affection, new play materials, additional language stimulation, and contacts with other office callers.

A Study of the Effects of Differential Stimulation on Mentally Retarded Children   Harold M. Skeels and Harold B. Dye

An indication of the interest in these children was shown by the fact that a baby show was held for one of the Fourth of July celebrations. Each ward made a float upon which its "baby" rode, dressed in costume. Prizes were awarded for the winning baby, most attractive costume, and best float.

The spacious living rooms of the wards furnished ample room for indoor play and activity. Whenever weather permitted, the children spent some time each day on the playground, supervised by one or more of the older girls. In this situation, they had contacts with other children of similar ages. Outdoor play equipment included tricycles, swings, slides, sand box, etc.

In addition to the opportunities afforded on the wards, the children attended the school kindergarten. They were sent to school as soon as they could walk. Toddlers remained for only half of the morning, whereas those of four and five years of age were in kindergarten the entire morning. Activities carried on in the kindergarten were more in the nature of a preschool than the more formal type of kindergarten.

As a part of the school program, the children each morning attended fifteen minute chapel exercises, including group singing and music by the orchestra. The children also attended the dances, school programs, moving pictures, and Sunday chapel services.

In considering this enriched environment from a dynamic point of view, it must be pointed out that in the case of almost every child, some one adult (older girl or attendant) would become particularly attached to a given child and would figuratively "adopt" him. As a consequence there would develop a rather intense adult-child relationship with the other adult contacts being somewhat more marginal. This meant that such a child had some one person with whom he was identified and who was particularly interested in him and his achievement. It was felt that this constituted an important aspect of the environmental impact on the child.

Contrast Group

The environment of the children in the contrast group is considered to be rather representative of the average orphanage. The outstanding feature is the profound lack of mental stimulation or experiences usually associated with the life of a young child in the ordinary home.

Up to the age of two years, the children were in the nursery of the hospital. This was limited to a rather small play room with additional dormitory rooms of two to five beds each. The children were cared for by two nurses with some additional assistance by one or two girls of ten to fifteen years of age. The children had good physical and medical care, but little can be said beyond this. Contacts with adults were largely limited to feeding, bathing, dressing, and toilet details. It can readily be seen that with the large number of children per adult, little time was available for anything aside from the routines of physical care. The girls who assisted the nurses accepted the work as a necessary evil and, in general, took little personal interest in the children as individuals. Few play materials were available and little attention was given to the teaching of play techniques. The children were seldom out of the nursery room except for short walks or short periods of time out of doors for fresh air.

At two years of age these children were graduated to the cottages. A rather complete description of "cottage" life is reported in the study by Skeels, Updegraff, Wellman, and Williams[5] on *A Study of Environmental Stimulation: An Orphanage Preschool Project*, from which the following excerpts are taken:

"Overcrowding of living facilities was characteristic. Too many children had to be accommodated in the available space and there were too few adults to guide them. . . . Thirty to thirty-five children of the same sex under six years of age lived in a "cottage" in charge of one matron and three or four entirely untrained and often reluctant girls of thirteen to fifteen years of age. The waking and sleeping hours of these children were spent (except during meal times and a little time on a grass plot) in an average sized room (approximately fifteen feet square), a sun porch of similar size, a cloak room, . . . and a single dormitory. The latter was occupied only during sleeping hours. . . . The meals for all children in the orphanage were served in a central building in a single large dining room. . . .

"The duties falling to the lot of a matron were not only those involved in the care of the children but those related to clothing and cottage maintenance, in other words, cleaning, mending, and so forth. . . . With so much responsibility centered on one adult, the result was a necessary regimentation. The children sat down, stood up, and did many things in rows and in unison. They spent considerable time sitting on chairs, for in addition to the number of children and the matron's limited time, there was the misfortune of inadequate equipment. . . .

"No child had any property which belonged exclusively to him, except, perhaps, his tooth brush. Even his clothing, including shoes, was selected and put on him according to size. . . ." (p. 10–11.)

From this it may be seen what a remarkable contrast there was between the environment of the experimental transfer group and the contrast group. Such a

A Study of the Effects of Differential Stimulation on Mentally Retarded Children   Harold M. Skeels and Harold B. Dye

radical shift in environment as was experienced by each of the children in the experimental group would scarcely occur in an unselected sampling of children in their own homes more than two or three times in a thousand cases.

Following the completion of these research studies on preschool children, the orphanage has made radical changes in the program for the preschool child. Number of children per cottage has been reduced, thus alleviating to a great extent the overcrowded conditions. Each cottage now has two matrons with additional domestic service. The preschool has been made an integral part of the school system with all children of preschool age in attendance. With the assistance of the state emergency nursery school program a preschool program has been set up for the children in the nursery under two years of age. A trained teacher, in addition to the regular nursing staff, spends full time with the infants providing a more enriched play and educational program.

Mental Development of Children in Experimental and Contrast Groups

The mental development of individual children in the experimental group is presented in Table 1. As the standard measure of intelligence the 1922 Kuhlmann Revision of the Binet was used, excepting in the cases of two or three tests on children who were four years of age or more where the Stanford-Binet (1916) was used. All examinations were made by trained and experienced psychologists. Test one was the measure of intelligence just prior to transfer. Tests two, three, and last test, were given at subsequent intervals of time following transfer. "Last test" is the test at the end of the experimental period, and represents the second, third, or fourth test, depending on the number of tests available at representative time intervals on a given child.

Table 1 Mental Development of Individual Children in Experimental Group as Measured by Kuhlmann-Binet Intelligence Tests Before and After Transfer

	Before Transfer		Chronological Age, Months at Transfer	After Transfer						Length of Experimental Period, Months	Change in I.Q. First to Last Test
	Test 1			Test							
				2		3		Last			
Case Number*	Chronological Age, Months	I.Q.		Chronological Age, Months	I.Q.	Chronological Age, Months	I.Q.	Chronological Age, Months	I.Q.		
1	7.0	89	7.1	12.8	113			12.8	113	5.7	+24
2	12.7	57	13.3	20.5	94	29.4	83	36.8	77	23.7	+20
3	12.7	85	13.3	25.2	107			25.2	107	11.9	+22
4	14.7	73	15.0	23.1	100			23.1	100	8.1	+27
5	13.4	46	15.2	21.7	77	32.9	100	40.0	95**	24.8	+49
6	15.5	77	15.6	21.3	96	30.1	100	30.1	100	14.5	+23
7	16.6	65	17.1	27.5	104			27.5	104	10.4	+39
8	16.6	35	18.4	24.8	87	36.0	88	43.0	93	24.6	+58
9	21.8	61	22.0	34.3	80			34.3	80	12.3	+19
10	23.3	72	23.4	29.1	88	37.9	71	45.4	79	22.0	+7
11	25.7	75	27.4	42.5	78	51.0	82**	51.0	82**	23.6	+7
12	27.9	65	28.4	40.4	82			40.4	82	12.0	+17
13	30.0	36	35.9	51.7	70	81.0	74**	89.0	81**	52.1	+45

* Arranged according to age at time of transfer from youngest to oldest.

**   Stanford-Binet I.Q.

A Study of the Effects of Differential Stimulation on Mentally Retarded Children   Harold M. Skeels and Harold B. Dye

Similar data showing the mental growth of the individual children in the contrast group are presented in Table 2. In the column marked "last test" is given the test on each child at the end of the period of study. This was either the third or fourth test, depending upon the number of available tests at representative time intervals on each child.

Mean, median, and standard deviation comparisons of mental growth from "first" to "last test" for experimental and contrast groups are presented in Table 3. Mean I.Q. at time of transfer was 64.3 with a median at 65. The average gain in intelligence quotient for the experimental group during the course of the experiment was 27.5 points with a median of 23. The mean I.Q. on "last" test was 91.8 with a median at 93. The difference between "first" and "last tests" yielded a critical ratio (Fisher's t) of 6.3 or practical certainty of a true difference. Every child showed a gain, the range being from 7 points to 58 points. Three children made gains of 45 points or more, and all but two children gained more than 15 points (Table 1).

The average chronological age at time of transfer

was 19.4 months with a range from 7.1 months to 35.9 months, the median being 17.1 months. Length of the experimental period was from 5.7 months to 52.1 months with a mean of 18.9 months and a median of 14.5 months. The length of the experimental period was not a constant for all children, but depended upon the rate of development of the individual child. As soon as a child showed normal mental development as measured by intelligence tests and substantiated by qualitative observations, the experimental period was considered completed; the child's visit at the school for feebleminded was terminated; and he was placed in an adoptive home or returned to the orphanage.

The mental growth pattern for children of the contrast group is quite the opposite from that of the experimental group. The mean I.Q. on "first" examination was 86.7, whereas on the "last" test it was 60.5, showing an average loss of 26.2 points. The critical ratio (Fisher's t) was 6.1. The median I.Q. on "first" test was 90 and on "last" test 60, with a median of individual losses of 32.5 points (Table 3). With the exception of one child who gained two points in I.Q. from first to last test, all chil-

Table 2 Mental Development of Individual Children in Contrast Group as Measured by Repeated Kuhlmann-Binet Intelligence Tests Over a Period of Two and One-Half Years

Case Number*	Test								Length of Experimental Period, Months	Change in I.Q. First to Last Test
	1		2		3		Last			
	Chronological Age, Months	I.Q.	Chronological Age, Months	I.Q.	Chronological Age, Months	I.Q.	Chronological Age, Months	I.Q.		
14	11.9	91	24.8	73	37.5	65	55.0	62	43.1	−29
15	13.0	92	20.1	54	38.3	56	38.3	56	25.3	−36
16	13.6	71	20.6	76	40.9	56	40.9	56	27.3	−15
17	13.8	96	37.2	58	53.2	54	53.2	54	39.4	−42
18	14.5	99	21.6	67	41.9	54	41.9	54	27.4	−45
19	15.2	87	22.5	80	35.5	74	44.5	67	29.3	−20
20	17.3	81	43.0	77	52.9	83**	52.9	83**	35.6	+2
21	17.5	103	26.8	72	38.0	63	50.3	60	32.8	−43
22	18.3	98	24.8	93	30.7	80	39.7	61	21.4	−37
23	20.2	89	27.0	71	39.4	66	48.4	71	28.2	−18
24	21.5	50	34.9	57	51.6	42	51.6	42	30.1	−8
25	21.8	83	28.7	75	37.8	63	50.1	60	28.3	−23

* Arranged according to age at time of transfer from youngest to oldest.

** Stanford-Binet I.Q.

A Study of the Effects of Differential Stimulation on Mentally Retarded Children   Harold M. Skeels and Harold B. Dye

Table 3 Mean, Median, and Standard Deviation Comparisons of Mental Growth from First to Last Test for Experimental and Contrast Groups

Measure	Chrono-logical Age, Months	Mental Age, Months	I.Q.	Chrono-logical Age, Months	Chrono-logical Age, Months	Mental Age, Months	I.Q.	Length of Experi-mental Period, Months	Change in I.Q., First to Last Test
Experimental Group (13 Children)									
	Before Transfer			Transfer	After Transfer				
Mean	18.3	11.4	64.3	19.4	38.4	33.9	91.8	18.9	+27.5
Standard deviation	6.6	4.2	16.4	7.4	17.6	13	11.5	11.6	15
Median	16.6	10.8	65.0	17.1	36.8	30.0	93.0	14.5	+23
Contrast Group (13 Children)									
	First Test			Transfer	Last Test				
Mean	16.6	14.2	86.7		47.2	28.7	60.5	30.7	−26.2
Standard deviation	2.9	2.9	14.3		5.9	6.4	9.7	5.8	14.1
Median	16.3	13.6	90.0		49.3	29.3	60.0	28.8	−32.5

Figure 1 Mean Comparisons of Mental Growth from First to Last Test for Experimental and Contrast Groups

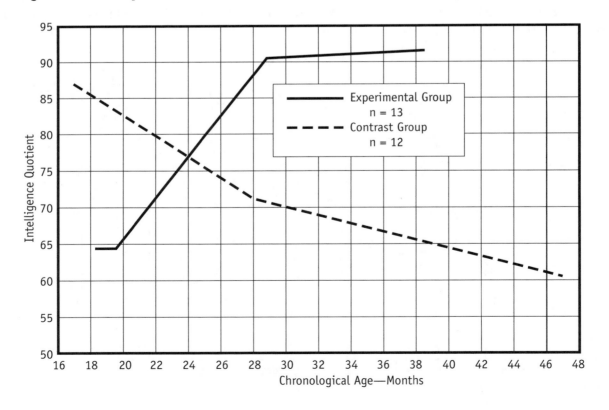

A Study of the Effects of Differential Stimulation on Mentally Retarded Children   Harold M. Skeels and Harold B. Dye

Figure 2 Mean Comparisons of Mental Growth from First to Last Test for Experimental and Contrast Groups, Showing Experimental Group Having Three Tests

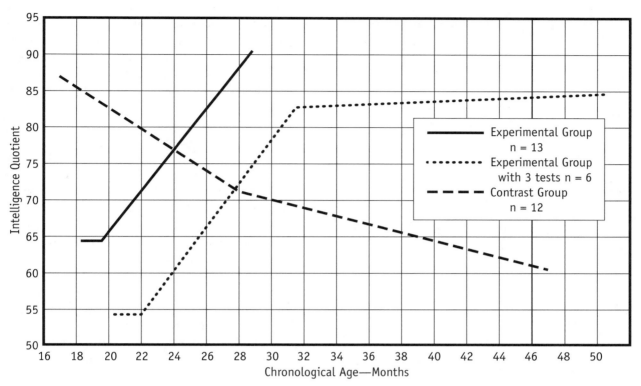

dren showed losses, the range being from –8 points to –45 points. Ten of the twelve children lost 15 or more points in I.Q. (Table 2).

Mean comparisons of mental growth from "first" to "last test" for experimental and contrast groups are shown graphically in Figures 1 and 2. Since the first examinations on children of the experimental group were made about one month before transfer, the unbroken line has been drawn horizontally from chronological age at time of first test to the time of transfer. In Figure 1, since some children in the experimental group had only two tests, the same I.Q. would appear in the second and "last" test landmarks on the graph. Accordingly, in Figure 2, these have been separated. The unbroken line represents the gain in intelligence from time of transfer to second test and includes all thirteen children. The broken line shows the rate of mental growth for six children having three tests reported and indicates the rate of growth from time of transfer to second test and from second test to third test. Since all children in the contrast group had at least three tests, such a division was unnecessary.

From Figures 1 and 2 and Table 1 it will be seen that as far as central tendencies are concerned, the greatest gain for children in the experimental group was made during the first ten months of the experimental period. Similarly, in Figures 1 and 2 and Table 2, the greatest loss for children in the contrast group was during the first year with a somewhat lower rate of loss during the second and third years.

In the following tabulation children in the experimental group have been arranged in the order of gains from the greatest to the least; children in the contrast group have been arranged in the order of losses from the greatest to the least.

There is a tendency for children in the experimental group initially at the lower levels to make the greater gains. The three children classifying at the imbecile level on first examination made gains of 58, 49, and 45 points I.Q. Also greatest losses in the contrast group were associated with the highest initial levels. Six children with original I.Q.s above 90 lost from 29 to 45 points in I.Q. While this shift may be partially due to regression, there

A Study of the Effects of Differential Stimulation on Mentally Retarded Children   Harold M. Skeels and Harold B. Dye

Case	Changes in First to Last Test	Chronological Age, Months First Test	I.Q. First Test
Experimental Group			
8	+58	16.6	35
5	+49	13.4	46
13	+45	30.0	36
7	+39	16.6	65
4	+27	14.7	73
1	+24	7.0	89
6	+23	15.5	77
3	+22	12.7	85
2	+20	12.7	57
9	+19	21.8	61
12	+17	27.9	65
10	+7	23.3	72
11	+7	25.7	75
Contrast Group			
18	−45	14.5	99
21	−43	17.5	103
17	−42	13.8	96
22	−37	18.3	98
15	−36	13.0	92
14	−29	11.9	91
25	−23	21.8	83
19	−20	15.2	87
23	−18	20.2	89
16	−15	13.6	71
24	−8	21.5	50
20	+2	17.3	81

are too small to permit statistical treatment of the data. Comparisons are therefore on a more general inspectional basis. In the experimental group, children whose mothers were classified as feebleminded showed as marked gains as children whose mothers were at a higher mental level. The greatest gain in intelligence (58 points I.Q.) was made by Case 8 whose mother was known to be feebleminded and had only gone as far as the second grade in school.

In the contrast group, the only child who failed to show loss in rate of mental growth (Case 20) from "first" to "last" test was the son of a mother with an I.Q. of 36. Case 24, the most retarded child in the group on first examination with an I.Q. of 50, had a rather flattering family history. His father had graduated from high school and was talented in music. His mother was an eighth grade graduate and had gone to evening business school. She had been a telephone operator and had done general office work.

That the gains in intelligence evidenced by the children of the experimental group were true gains and not due to an artifice in testing seems validated. Practice effects could not have been a contributing factor to these gains as the children in the contrast group, who showed continual losses in I.Q., actually had more tests than children in the experimental group. Improvement was noted independently by members of the medical staff, attendants and matrons, school teachers, and even the older girls on the wards. Teachers are required to submit written reports to the principal at the end of each semester on all children enrolled in classes. Repeated reference is made in these reports to the marked improvement of these children in the experimental group. The following excerpts are taken from such reports: Case 12 after one year preschool or kindergarten: "Well behaved, interested. Joins group for simple games and rhythms. From my observations she apparently possesses about average intelligence for a child her age." Later report: "Very great improvement. Has good vocabulary and muscular coordination. Takes directions readily and can be depended upon. A good leader in games. Does fair handwork." Case 3, after one year: "Very quiet. Has shown a very great improvement this year. Has a fair vocabulary and will take part in games when asked." (This child, two years of age, was one of the youngest in the group.) Case 9, after one year: "Has improved a good deal. Enjoys games and rhythms. Is speaking quite a little. Very attentive."

must be other factors operating to bring about such a large and consistent change.

These results, although more marked, are comparable to the findings reported in the orphanage preschool study of Skeels, Updegraff, Wellman, and Williams.[5] In that study, children of the preschool group initially at the lower levels made the greatest gains following a period of preschool attendance, and children in the control group originally at the higher levels showed the greatest losses.

There appears to be a marked lack of relationship between mental growth patterns and factors pertaining to the family histories of the children. Numbers of cases

A Study of the Effects of Differential Stimulation on Mentally Retarded Children   Harold M. Skeels and Harold B. Dye

A close bond of love and affection between a given child and one or two adults assuming a very personal parental role appears to be a dynamic factor of great importance. In evaluating these relationships, nine of the thirteen children in the experimental group were favored with such a relationship. The four other children tended to be less individualized and their adult relationships were more of a general nature involving more adults, the bonds of relationship being less intense with a given individual adult. It seems significant to note that the children favored with the more intense personal contacts made greater gains than those considered as being limited to the more general contacts. The nine children in the "personal" group made gains in I.Q. ranging from 17 to 58 points with an average of 33.8 points. gain. The four children in the more general contact group made average gains of 14 points. Two children made gains of only 7 points, one 19 points and one 20 points.

Two children (Cases 10 and 11) showed little progress on ward 7 over a period of a year and a half. This ward differed materially from the other wards in that there were from eight to twelve children of younger ages (three to eight years), and the older girls were of a lower mental level. The attendant on the ward was especially fine with young children, but, of course, was unable to give as much individual attention as was possible on other wards because of the large number of young children. At this time it was feared that these two children would continue to be hopelessly retarded. However, they were subsequently placed as singletons on wards with brighter girls, and after a period of six months with more individualization they showed marked gains in intelligence.

The possibility of "coaching" on test items may be ruled out as a factor. Adults and older girls working with the children were not in any way familiar with the tests used or when they would be administered. Results in terms of I.Q.s were never given out; the only reports made were qualitative ones indicating the general improvement of the child.

As has been indicated, all thirteen children in the experimental group were considered unsuitable for adoption because of mental deficiency. Following the experimental period, seven of these children have been placed in adoptive homes. Of the remaining six, five are considered well within the range of normality and were returned to the orphanage. Only one child (I.Q. 77) will continue in residence at the school for feebleminded for further observation as to subsequent mental development.

Of the children in adoptive homes, four have been examined following one year's residence in the foster home. These are Cases 1, 5, 7, and 8. Final I.Q.s are respectively as follows: 117, 94, 97, and 93. Three of the five children returned to the orphanage have been given an additional test following "last test" reported in Table 2. These are Cases 3, 10, and 11 with subsequent I.Q.s of 115, 84 and 85.

Accordingly, on a basis of last test reported, of the thirteen children two now classify as above average in intelligence with I.Q.s of 117 and 115; five have I.Q.s between 90 and 100; five at the 80 to 90 level and only one child with an I.Q. below 80. No child is now considered to be feebleminded.

In an evaluation of the contrasting mental growth patterns of children in the two groups, one is impressed by the marked relationship between rate of mental growth and the nature of the environmental impact. In the case of the contrast group, the psychological prescription was apparently inadequate as to kinds of ingredients, amounts, and relative proportions. Accordingly, the children became increasingly emaciated in mental growth as time went on.

Conversely, when the psychological prescription was radically changed, the children in the experimental group already retarded at the time of transfer showed marked improvement and either achieved or approached normal mental development after a period of time. The environment of the experimental group apparently included a more adequate prescription as relating to the kinds and proportions of ingredients needed by children of these young ages for normal mental development. It must not be inferred that the environment of the experimental group represented an optimum prescription. Perhaps even greater improvement would have resulted had there been greater facilities and more adequate knowledge of proportioning the ingredients operative in producing optimal mental growth. No instructions were given as to what should or should not be done with the children when they were placed on the wards. This was largely a matter of chance. The general prescription, however, did include certain unmeasured quantitative and qualitative ingredients such as love and affection by one or more interested adults; a wealth of play materials and ample space and opportunity for play with supervision and direction; varied experiences such as preschool or kinder-

A Study of the Effects of Differential Stimulation on Mentally Retarded Children   Harold M. Skeels and Harold B. Dye

garten attendance and opportunity to be in group gatherings; and a number of other diversified experiences associated with the opportunities afforded a child in a rather adequate home situation. This rather general prescription proved to be conducive to increase in rate of mental development.

With more adequate knowledge as to the correct proportioning of such ingredients in relation to the specific inadequacies or gaps in the developmental pattern of a given child, possibly even more marked mental improvement could have been brought about.

That such increase in rate of mental development may be brought about at older ages through provision of a more adequate psychological prescription is suggested in the studies of Kephart[3] at the Wayne County Training School. He found that boys of fifteen to eighteen years of age showed increase in rate of mental growth following environmental changes pointed toward alleviation of the developmental gaps or inadequacies.

It therefore appears that there is an added challenge in the education of the so-called "functional" feebleminded, that is those not evidencing physiological deficiencies or organic diseases. Not only should the educational program of a school for feebleminded include the teaching of skills at the individual's mental level, but it should be so individualized as to provide for the specific developmental needs of a given child with the strong possibility that the level of mental capacity can be materially augmented.

Summary

This study attempts to determine the effect on mental growth of a radical shift from one institutional environment to another which provided superior stimulation. The experimental group included thirteen mentally retarded orphanage children from one to two years of age, placed singly or by twos on wards with brighter older girls. This environment was stimulating and had many adult contacts. The mean I.Q. of the group at time of transfer was 64.3. As a contrast group twelve average and dull normal children (mean I.Q. 86.7) in an orphanage nursery were studied. Few adult contacts were afforded with limited opportunities for play and development.

Results and conclusions are as follows:

1. Over a period of two years the mean level of intelligence of the experimental group increased markedly while that of the contrast group showed an equivalent decrease. The experimental group made an average gain of 27.5 points while the contrast group showed a mean loss of 26.2 points.

2. Critical ratios (t's) based on differences between first and last tests for experimental and contrast groups were 6.3 and 6.1 respectively.

3. A change from mental retardation to normal intelligence in children of preschool age is possible in the absence of organic disease or physiological deficiency by providing a more adequate psychological prescription.

4. Conversely, children of normal intelligence may become mentally retarded to such a degree as to be classifiable as feebleminded under the continued adverse influence of a relatively non-stimulating environment.

5. An intimate and close relationship between the child and an interested adult seems to be a factor of importance in the mental development of young children.

6. In a child placing program if children are to be withheld from placement in adoptive homes pending further observation of mental development, it is imperative that careful consideration be given to the type of environment in which they are to be held.

7. The possibility of increasing the mental capacity of "functionally" feebleminded children should be considered as an essential objective in setting up an individualized treatment and educational program in a school for feebleminded.

Notes

[1] Designated as case 5 in Table 1.

[2] Designated as case 8 in Table 2.

[3] Ibid

[4] These two children were transferred to the state school at Woodward. All other children in the experimental group were sent to the state school at Glenwood.

[5] The writers are indebted to Dr. M. D. Ott, pediatrician, and Miss Sadie LeFevre, superintendent of nurses, Iowa Soldiers' Orphans' Home, for these observations and reports.

[6] Stanford-Binet (1916) intelligence tests. Most of these were given by psychologists either at the Psychopathic Hospital or the University Hospital of the University of Iowa. Maximum chronological age used was sixteen years.

A Study of the Effects of Differential Stimulation on Mentally Retarded Children   Harold M. Skeels and Harold B. Dye

References

Binet, Alfred: Les idees modernes sur les enfants. Paris: Ernest Flamarion, 1911. P. 346. Cited from Stoddard, George D.: The I.Q.: Its Ups and Downs. Educ. Rec., 1939, 20, 44–57. (Supplement for January.)

Fillmore, Eva A.: Iowa tests for young children. Univ. Iowa Stud., Stud. in Child Welfare, 1936, 11, No. 4, p. 58.

Kephart, Newell C.: The effect of a highly specialized institutional program upon the I.Q. in high grade mentally deficient boys. Unpublished study, Wayne Country Training School, Northville, Michigan.

Skeels, Harold M., and Fillmore, Eva A.: The mental development of children from underprivileged homes. Ped. Sem. and J. Genet. Psychol., 1937, 50, 427–439.

Skeels, Harold M., Updegraff, Ruth, Wellman, Beth L., and Williams, Harold M.: A study of environmental stimulation: An orphanage preschool project. Univ. Iowa Stud., Stud. in Child Welfare, 1938, 15, No. 4. p. 190.

Skodak, Marie: Children in foster homes: A study of mental development. Univ. Iowa Stud., Stud. in Child Welfare, 1939, 16, No. 1, p. 155.

This paper was presented at the annual convention of the American Association on Mental Deficiency, Chicago, Illinois, Section 2, Saturday afternoon, May 6, 1939.

The writers wish to express their appreciation to Senator Harry C. White, Senator F. M. Stevens, and Mr. E. H. Felton, members of the Iowa Board of Control of State Institutions, for approving this rather unusual venture; to Mr. Syl McCauley, Superintendent of the Iowa Soldiers' Orphans' Home, who has at all times co-operated in making possible research studies of wards in that institution; and to Mrs. Ethel Nichols, Secretary of the Children's Division of the Board of Control, for her co-operation and encouragement.

Authors

Harold M. Skeels, Ph.D., Psychologist, Department of Psychology, Board of Control of State Institutions, Iowa City, Iowa and **Harold B. Dye, M.D.,** Superintendent, Institution for Feebleminded Children Glenwood, Iowa.

PART TWO

Family Response to Disability:
The Evolution of Family Adjustment and Coping

American Journal of Mental Deficiency: The Early Years

In 1940, the *Journal of Psycho-Asthenics* became the *American Journal of Mental Deficiency*. About this time families became visible, with initial research interest in parental attitudes toward retardation, in AAMR journals (Stone, 1948; Thorne & Andrews, 1946) and others as well. Harriet Rheingold, who became one of the key figures in developmental psychology, published a paper in 1945 in the *Journal of Consulting Psychology*, "Interpreting Mental Retardation to Parents."

Thus, families—parents, primarily mother—catapulted to the forefront of research interest. This section of the book focuses on families of children and adolescents. Although much of what we refer to as the "family impact" literature has implications for intervention, papers on this topic are included in our final unit.

The "woe is me" years. For many people, the post-war late 1940s and 1950s connote a homogeneous media-fed image—the white, nuclear family, living in a house in the suburbs. Dad works. Mom is home when Dick and Jane arrive home from school. Absent is diversity in its many senses, and there is certainly no deformity or disability. The birth of a child with mental retardation shattered this picture, and thus was viewed as one of the worst things that could happen to a family. This sentiment is widely reflected in papers published in *AJMD* during the '50s, where the authors (rarely parents!) interpreted the situation in a "woe is me" fashion. These papers, fortified with the popular psychoanalytic perspective of the day, portrayed an overwhelmingly negative view of having a child with retardation, emphasizing hardship, stress, and disturbance. The assumption was that parents needed as much "fixing" (with the tools of counseling and therapy) as the children themselves. "Thus the problem becomes, not one of the individual subnormal child, but of the whole family unit" (Schonell & Watts, 1956, p. 219).

In the '50s, and well into the '60s, the discovery of families maintained this focus on parent attitudes, as exemplified in these *AJMD* titles: "Parental Attitudes Toward Mentally Retarded Children" (Grebler, 1952); "Selected Aspects in the Development of the Mothers' Understanding of Her Mentally Retarded Child" (Rosen, 1955); "Reactions of Parents to Problems of Mental Retardation in Children" (Gordon & Ullman, 1956); "Procedures for Evaluating Parental Attitudes Toward the Handicapped" (Thurston, 1959); and "Parental Attitudes Toward Mental Retardation" (Condell, 1966).

Psychological interpretations of family reactions abounded in this literature, often without regard to the behavior of the child with retardation. Wardell (1952) provides some illustrations of this:

> . . . it will help the counselor to understand the handicapped person better, for the retarded person almost always reflects the stability or emotional security of his family, especially in his ability to adjust to a new situation (p. 233).

> When families express some concern about the retarded member's ability to profit by his training, they are usually expressing their own anxieties for his success. They have a real need for him to succeed, yet have a reluctance to free him to the point of allowing him to try (p. 234).

The infrequent attempts to approach the subject through research had a similarly negative cast.

Worchel and Worchel (1961), studying parental acceptance, asked parents to rate the frequency of 40 traits in reference to " My child is. . . . " The procedure was then repeated in reference to " I wish my child were. . . " and "Most children are. . . . " The authors interpreted results to mean that "the more negatively the parent rated the child, the greater the rejection" (p. 784), ignoring alternative interpretations such as "the more disabled or low-functioning the child might be." Even Zuk (1959), who published an early and often cited paper on the role of religion in acceptance of a child with retardation, approached the issue as an "investigation of the 'parent problem'" (p. 139), assuming that *every* parent has guilt. The frequently noted conclusion of this paper was that Catholic mothers were judged to be more accepting of their child than Protestant and Jewish mothers. The interpretation of this finding was that Catholic mothers were given greater emotional support by their faith, which absolved them from a sense of personal guilt in the birth of the child with retardation.

On the positive side, some investigators did include caveats or notations that suggested a broader view of parental attitudes and adjustment. Condell (1966) investigated parental attitudes in 67 families using the Thurston Sentence Completion Form (Thurston, 1959) and concluded that parental attitudes could be quite varied. Furthermore, he noted that parental needs and professional goals may also vary, or contradict each other, a situation much later recognized in the professional literature (e.g., Turnbull & Turnbull, 1982, this volume). Schonell and Watts (1956) surveyed 50 families in Australia. While they concluded that the effects of the "subnormal child" on the family were "far reaching and intensely restrictive and destructive in nature" (p. 218), they did note that none of the children concerned attended any school or program, nor did their parents receive any help or guidance. They wondered about the possible positive effect on parents of having a child attend an educational program. A follow-up survey, after the children had six months or more of education, found 4 of 5 mothers reporting a better understanding of their problems; moreover 78 percent reported that their husbands were less embarrassed about the child and that there was less family tension (Schonell & Rorke, 1960).

Representative of this era, and yet looking beyond it, is a commentary by Leo Kanner, the noted psychiatrist. We have included his 1953 paper *Parents' Feelings About Retarded Children*, which contains four case studies with the caveat, "I know that it is difficult to speak in generalities about a subject which entails individual sentiments" (p. 375). We selected this paper not only because it represents the negative impact perspective, but also because it recognizes early on the kinds of information that parents needed to have. Kanner enumerates 24 questions frequently asked by parents that professionals should attempt to answer.

We have also included a 1959 address by Mrs. Max Murray, entitled *Needs of Parents of Mentally Retarded Children*. Mrs. Murray, who identified herself in this paper only with her husband's name, was the mother of a child with retardation and President of the Virginia Association for Retarded Children. She, too, emphasized that when addressing a broad topic like parental needs one must "think and speak in general terms rather than specific ones because of the variety of family situations" (p. 1078). She also noted how differences in the socioeconomic status of families and in specific child characteristics (e.g., whether the child also had a physical disability or whether he was "hyper-active") differentially affected the impact of the child with retardation. She lists six basic problems faced by families, which to varying degrees are still the subject of research and discussion today (e.g., acceptance of the child as retarded, anxiety over seeking lifetime care, and inept, inaccurate, and ill-timed professional advice). There is much wisdom in this paper.

Research on siblings. Some of the first studies that were more methodologically sound focused on the impact of a child with retardation on siblings; especially notable was the early work of Farber (1959, 1960) and Caldwell & Guze (1960). We included the 1960 paper by Bettye Caldwell and Samuel Guze, *A Study of the Adjustment of Parents and Siblings of Institutionalized Retarded Children*. This study represented a high level of methodological rigor for its time. For example, despite the relatively small sample size, the subjects were carefully described and groups were matched on relevant variables. Following the "devastating impact" theme of the '50s research, the authors conducted psychiatric interviews with mothers and clinical interviews with siblings. The comparison of two groups, one where the target child was institutionalized and one where he/she lived at home, was intended to address the question of whether or not institutionalization had a positive or deleterious effect on non-retarded siblings as well as on parents. Caldwell and Guze anticipated a perspective typically credited to much later work when they asked siblings about the positive impact of their brother or sister with retardation ("Tell me some good effects that (your sibling) has had on your family"). The findings were surprising, in that there were no appreciable differences between the groups for mothers or siblings. We were struck by the finding that "almost without exception the ideas of the brothers and sisters mirrored the family decision—i.e., siblings of the Institutional sample felt it better for retarded children to live away from home, while those of the Home sample expressed their conviction that it was better to have the children live at home" (p. 860). Despite the remarkable evolution in services, this identical finding was reported almost 40 years later by Eisenberg, Baker, and Blacher (1998).

The Response to Disability: Influence of Child and Family Characteristics

The study of parent adjustment and perceived family stress expanded during the 1970s and 1980s to include a father perspective as well (Bristol, Gallagher, & Schopler, 1988; Frey, Greenberg, & Fewell, 1989; Goldberg, Marcovitch, MacGregor, & Lojkasek, 1986; Gumz & Gubrium, 1972). By the 1980s a plethora of well-designed family studies appeared in AAMR journals; many of these focused on specific aspects of the child, parents, or home that might affect impact. Credibility was still given to the concept of "stages of adjustment" in parents of children with retardation (Allen & Affleck, 1985; Blacher, 1984), but the research focus expanded beyond mere description of parent reactions to more specific assessments of stress, adjustment, and well-being, all viable interests today.

Of the three papers selected for inclusion under this topic, one addresses child characteristics, one the parent-child relationship, and one the family environment. Paula Beckman's (1983) *Influence of Selected Child Characteristics on Stress in Families of Handicapped Infants* identified the contribution of child characteristics to parental reactions, a relationship suggested earlier by Mrs. Murray (1959) but empirically established by Beckman. In *A Review of Attachment Formation and Disorder in Handicapped Children*, Jan Blacher and Ed Meyers (1983) provided an analysis of attachment in children with handicaps, derived from the broader developmental psychology literature of the time. They established that mother-child attachment would be affected by a child's disability, especially a severe disability.

Inspired in part by Bronfenbrenner's (1977) ecological approach, family researchers began to study the influence of the broader home environment on parent-child-relationships. We have included an early paper by Iris Mink, Kaz Nihira, and Ed Meyers (1983), *Taxonomy of Family Life Styles: I. Homes with TMR Children*. This study, and subsequent related ones (Blacher, Nihira & Meyers, 1987; Mink, Blacher, & Nihira, 1988; Mink, Meyers, & Nihira, 1984) moved family research beyond its focus on child and parent characteristics to aspects of the home environment that may be facilitative (or detrimental) to family adjustment.

Broadening Perspectives on Families and Disability: Into the 21st Century

Having reviewed the last 65 years of family research published by AAMR, from its infancy in 1935, we believe that two specific publications marked its adulthood. One was the 1983 conceptual paper by Keith Crnic, William Friedrich, and Mark Greenberg, *Adaptation of Families with Mentally Retarded Children: A Model of Stress, Coping, and Family Ecology*, and the other was the publication in 1989 of an entire *American Journal on Mental Retardation* volume of research on families edited by Krauss, Simeonsson, and Ramey. We have included the paper by Crnic et al. (1983) here because of its strong influence on the subsequent development of the field (it is the most frequently cited AAMR family publication). This paper provided an integration of developmental, psychological, and ecological theory to produce a viable model for studying adaptation in families. It also had a more positive view of family outcome, to balance more negative perspectives inherent in the previous three decades of family research. With the exception of two articles, one of which appears in a subsequent unit, we opted not to reproduce the excellent 1989 volume of *AJMR* here, though we urge interested readers to review it, as it fairly represents the state-of-the-art of family research at that time. We did include in this section Zolinda Stoneman's (1989) methodological piece entitled *Comparison Groups in Research on Families with Mentally Retarded Members: A Methodological and Conceptual Review*; Stoneman makes many cogent points that should be considered in reading the papers in this volume and that are just as relevant today.

More methodologically sophisticated papers on coping with retardation followed the publication of Crnic et al., 1983. We included Carl Dunst, Carol Trivette, and Art Cross's (1986) *Mediating Influences of Social Support: Personal, Family, and Child Outcomes*, which identified social support as buffering parental reactions and underscored some of the more complex mechanisms that affect the impact of children on families.

At the juncture of the 20th and 21st centuries, family research has become more inclusive—focusing on broader family environments, on a wide range of coping strategies and outcomes, on fathers and siblings as well as mothers, on adults with retardation as well as children, and on ethnicities other than Euro-American or Caucasian. Regarding environment, Gallimore and colleagues introduced the term "ecocultural niche," expanding the concept of family environment and our understanding of parent-child interactions therein (Keogh, Garnier, Bernheimer, & Gallimore, 2000; Gallimore, Coots, Weisner, Garnier, & Guthrie, 1996; Gallimore, Weisner, Kaufman, & Bernheimer, 1989).

Research on broader outcomes is differentiating areas of specific impact. Dyson (1997), for example, found that in families with a disabled child, mothers and fathers experienced heightened child-related stress but did not differ in overall family functioning from families with normally developing children. Research on broader outcome following the paradigm shift from negative impact (family problem) to positive impact (family competence) is well represented in the work of Glidden and her colleagues (Flaherty & Glidden, 2000; Glidden, Valliere, & Herbert, 1988; Helff & Glidden, 1998). We have included Laraine Glidden and Viki Johnson's 1999 paper *Twelve Years Later: Adjustment in Families Who Adopted Children with Developmental Disabilities*, both for its unique perspective on adjustment in families who had adopted a child with retardation and for its longitudinal methodology. Glidden's studies of adoptive versus birth families have broadened our conceptualization of "family" and yet have retained measures and procedures used in other family research, making comparisons possible.

Papers focusing on cultural issues are now examining coping processes within and across ethnicities, often with the goal of determining what factors, within a culture, mediate or moderate stress or impact. As in the AAMR papers that were predecessors from four decades ago, these recent contributions seek to further understand the impact of a child with retardation on, for example, African-American families (Mary, 1990; Rogers-Dulan, 1998; Rogers-Dulan & Blacher, 1995), Chinese families (Chen & Tang, 1997; Cheng & Tang, 1995), and Latino Families (Blacher et al., 1997; Heller et al, 1994; Magaña, 1999). We selected Sandra Magaña's 1999 paper, *Puerto Rican Families Caring for an Adult with Mental Retardation: Role of Familism* for inclusion because of its emphasis on "familism" as a protective factor for maternal well-being in Puerto Rican mothers. Consistent with the other above-cited papers focusing on Latinos, Magaña's study pointed out the low socioeconomic conditions and poor health of many of these Latina mothers.

As we move into the 21st century, we hope that these now historical papers on family adjustment and coping continue to inspire studies that replicate, elaborate, and update the work of the past. The impact of the child with retardation on the family must change as the political climate in the United States changes, as the service delivery systems expands or contracts according to the winds of the economy, as genetics research leads to amelioration or even elimination of some disorders, and as definitions of retardation evolve. Families are now not only visible but key players.

References

Allen, D. A., & Affleck, G. (1985). Are we stereotyping parents? A postscript to Blacher. *Mental Retardation, 23*(4), 200–202.

Beckman, P. J. (1983). Influence of selected child characteristics on stress in families of handicapped infants. *American Journal of Mental Deficiency, 88*(2), 150–156.

Blacher, J. (1984). Sequential stages of parental adjustment to the birth of a child with handicaps: Fact or artifact. *Mental Retardation, 22*, 55–68.

Blacher, J., & Meyers, C. E. (1983). A review of attachment formation and disorder in handicapped children. *American Journal of Mental Deficiency, 87*, 359–371.

Blacher, J., Nihira, K., & Meyers, C. E. (1987). Characteristics of home environment of families with mentally retarded children: Comparison across levels of retardation. *American Journal of Mental Deficiency, 91*(4), 313–320.

Blacher, J., Shapiro, J., Lopez, S., Diaz, L., & Fusco, J. (1997). Depression in Latina mothers of children with mental retardation: A neglected concern. *American Journal on Mental Retardation, 101*(5), 483–496.

Bristol, M. M., Gallagher, J. J., & Schopler, E. (1988). Mothers and fathers of young developmentally disabled and nondisabled boys: Adaptation and spousal support. *Developmental Psychology, 24*, 441–451.

Bronfenbrenner, U. (1977). Toward an experimental ecology of human development. *American Psychologist, 32*, 513–531.

Caldwell, B. M., & Guze, S. B. (1960). A study of the adjustment of parents and siblings of institutionalized and non-institutionalized retarded children. *American Journal of Mental Deficiency, 64*, 845–861.

Chen, T. Y., & Tang, C. S. (1997). Stress appraisal and social support of Chinese mothers of adult children with mental retardation. *American Journal on Mental Retardation, 101*, 473–482.

Cheng, P., & Tang, C. S. (1995). Coping and psychological distress of Chinese parents of children with Down Syndrome. *Mental Retardation, 33*, 10–20.

Condell, J. F. (1966). Parental attitudes toward mental retardation. *American Journal of Mental Deficiency, 71*, 85–92.

Crnic, K. A., Friedrich, W. N., & Greenberg, M. T. (1983). Adaptation of families with mentally retarded children: A model of stress, coping, and family ecology. *American Journal of Mental Deficiency, 88*(2), 125–138.

Dunst, C. J., Trivette, C. M., & Cross, A. H. (1986). Mediating influences of social support: Personal, family, and child outcomes. *American Journal of Mental Deficiency, 90*, 403–417.

Dyson, L. (1997). Fathers and mothers of school-age children with developmental disabilities: Parental stress, family functioning, and social support. *American Journal on Mental Retardation, 102*, 267–279.

Eisenberg, L., Baker, B. L., & Blacher, J. (1998). Siblings of children with mental retardation living at home or in residential placement. *Journal of Child Psychology and Psychiatry, 39,* 355–364.

Farber, B. (1959). Effects of a severely mentally retarded child on family integration. *Monographs of the Society for Research in Child Development, 24* (Serial No. 71).

Farber, B. (1960). Family organization and crisis: Maintenance of integration in families with a severely mentally retarded child. *Monographs of the Society for Research in Child Development, 25* (Serial No. 75).

Flaherty, E. M., & Glidden, L. M. (2000). Positive adjustment in parents rearing children with Down Syndrome. *Early Education and Development, 11,* 407–422.

Frey, K. S., Greenberg, M. T., & Fewell, R. R. (1989). Stress and coping among parents of handicapped children: A multidimensional approach. *American Journal on Mental Retardation, 94*(3), 240–249.

Gallimore, R., Coots, J., Weisner, T., Garnier, H., & Guthrie, D. (1996). Family responses to children with early developmental delays II: Accommodation intensity and activity in early and middle childhood. *American Journal on Mental Retardation, 101*(3), 215–232.

Gallimore, R., Weisner, T. S., Kaufman, S. Z., & Bernheimer, L. P. (1989). The social construction of ecocultural niches: Family accommodation of developmentally delayed children. *American Journal on Mental Retardation, 94,* 216–230.

Glidden, L. M., & Johnson, V. E. (1999). Twelve years later: Adjustment in families who adopted children with developmental disabilities. *Mental Retardation, 37,* 16–24.

Glidden, L. M., Valliere, V. N., & Herbert, S. L. (1988). Adopted children with mental retardation: Positive family impact. *Mental Retardation, 26,* 119–125.

Goldberg, S., Marcovitch, S., MacGregor, D., & Lojkasek, M. (1986). Family responses to developmentally delayed preschoolers: Etiology and the father's role. *American Journal of Mental Deficiency, 90*(6), 610–617.

Gordon, E. W., & Ullman, M. (1956). Reactions of parents to problems of mental retardation in children. *American Journal of Mental Deficiency, 61,* 158–163.

Grebler, A. M. (1952). Parental attitudes toward mentally retarded children. *American Journal of Mental Deficiency, 56,* 475–483.

Gumz, E. J., & Gubrium, J. F. (1972). Comparative parental perceptions of a mentally retarded child. *American Journal of Mental Deficiency, 77*(2), 175–180.

Helff, C. M., & Glidden, L. M. (1988). More positive or less negative? Trends in research on adjustment of families rearing children with developmental disabilities. *Mental Retardation. 36,* 457–464.

Heller, T., Markwardt, R., Rowitz, L., & Farber, B. (1994). Adaptation of Hispanic families to a member with mental retardation. *American Journal on Mental Retardation, 99*(3), 289–300.

Kanner, L. (1953). Parents' feelings about retarded children. *American Journal of Mental Deficiency, 57,* 375–383.

Keogh, B. K., Garnier, H. E., Bernheimer, L. P., & Gallimore, R. (2000). Models of child-family interactions for children with developmental delays: Child-driven or transactional? *American Journal on Mental Retardation, 105,* 32–46.

Magaña, S. M. (1999). Puerto Rican families caring for an adult with mental retardation: Role of familism. *American Journal on Mental Retardation, 104,* 466–482.

Mary, N. L. (1990). Reactions of black, hispanic, and white mothers to having a child with handicaps. *Mental Retardation, 28*(1), 1–5.

Mink, I. T., Blacher, J., & Nihira, K. (1988). Taxonomy of family life styles: III. Replication with families with severely mentally retarded children. *American Journal on Mental Retardation, 93*(3), 250–264.

Mink, I. T., Meyers, C. E., & Nihira, K. (1984). Taxonomy of family life styles: II. Homes with slow-learning children. *American Journal of Mental Deficiency*, 89(2), 111–123.

Mink, I. T., Nihira, K., & Meyers, C. E. (1983). Taxonomy of family life styles: I. Homes with TMR children. *American Journal of Mental Deficiency*, 87(5), 484–497.

Murray, M. A. (Mrs.) (1959). Needs of parents of mentally retarded children. *American Journal of Mental Deficiency*, 63, 1078–1088.

Rheingold, H. L. (1945). Interpreting mental retardation to parents. *Journal of Consulting Psychology*, 9, 142–148.

Rogers-Dulan, J. (1998). Religious connectedness among urban African American families who have a child with disabilities. *Mental Retardation*, 36, 91–103.

Rogers-Dulan, J., & Blacher, J. (1995). African American families, religion, and disability: A conceptual framework. *Mental Retardation*, 33, 226–238.

Rosen, L. (1955). Selected aspects in the development of the mother's understanding of her mentally retarded child. *American Journal of Mental Deficiency*, 59, 522–528.

Schonell, F. J., & Watts, B. H. (1956). First survey of the effects of a subnormal child on the family unit. *American Journal of Mental Deficiency*, 61, 210–219.

Schonell, F. J., & Rorke, M. A. (1960). A second survey of the effects of a subnormal child on the family unit. *American Journal of Mental Deficiency*, 64, 862–868.

Stone, M. M. (1948). Parental attitudes toward retardation. *American Journal of Mental Deficiency*, 53, 363–372.

Stoneman, Z. (1989). Comparison groups in research on families with mentally retarded members: A methodological and conceptual review. *American Journal on Mental Retardation*, 94(3), 195–215.

Thorne, F. C., & Andrews, J. S. (1946). Unworthy parental attitudes toward mental defectives. *American Journal of Mental Deficiency*, 50(3), 411–418.

Thurston, J. R. (1959). A procedure for evaluating parental attitudes toward the handicapped. *American Journal of Mental Deficiency*, 64, 148–155.

Turnbull, A. P., & Turnbull, H. R. (1982). Parent involvement in the education of handicapped children: A critique. *Mental Retardation*, 20(3), 115–122.

Wardell, W. (1952). The mentally retarded in family and community. *American Journal of Mental Deficiency*, 57, 229–242.

Worchel, T. L., & Worchel, P. (1961). The parental concept of the mentally retarded child. *American Journal of Mental Deficiency*, 65, 782–788.

Zuk, G. H. (1959). The religious factor and the role of guilt in parental acceptance of the retarded child. *American Journal of Mental Deficiency*, 64, 139–147.

Parents' Feelings about Retarded Children

Leo Kanner, M.D.
1953

There was a time when, confronted with the task of dealing with retarded children, the educator's, psychologist's, or physician's main effort consisted of an examination of the child and advice to the family. No matter how expertly and conscientiously this was done, it somehow did not take in the whole magnitude of the problem. Parents were told of the child's low I.Q. in mournful numbers and were urged to think in terms of ungraded classes or residential school placement. The I.Q. figures may have been correct and the suggestions may have been adequate, and yet very often a major, highly important and, in fact, indispensable part of the job was somehow neglected.

It is recognized more and more that professional and at the same time humane attention should be given to the attitudes and feelings of people who are understandably puzzled by the lag in their child's development and progress. Whenever parents are given an opportunity to express themselves, they invariably air their emotional involvements in the form of questions, utterances of guilt, open and sometimes impatient rebellion against destiny, stories of frantic search for causes, pathetic accounts of matrimonial distensions about the child's condition, regret about the course that has been taken so far, anxious appraisals of the child's future, and tearful pleas for reassurance. It takes a considerable amount of cold, hard-boiled, pseudo-professorial detachment to turn a deaf ear on the anxieties, self-incriminations, and concerns about past, present, and future contained in such remarks. We have learned to take them into serious consideration and to treat them as the genuine, deep-seated, intrinsic perplexities that they are. We have learned to distinguish between abrupt, brutal frankness and a sympathetic statement of fact, between a dictatorial, take-it-or-leave-it kind of recommendation and the sort of presentation which would appeal to parents as the most constructive and helpful procedure, best suited under the existing circumstances.

I know that it is difficult to speak in generalities about a subject which entails individual sentiments. I know from experience that every couple who comes with a retarded child carries along a set of specific curiosities which must be understood and satisfied. For this reason, it may perhaps serve the purpose of this address if I were to introduce a few definite instances and, in so doing, to discuss the principal implications as they come along in the life of the retarded child and in the minds of his family.

Johnny Jones was brought to our clinic at the age of eight years. He was referred to us by his pediatrician with the request for a psychometric evaluation. Johnny was in his third year in school, had been demoted once, and after that had been given courtesy promotions, even though he did not master the required curriculum of his grade. The psychologist's examination showed that Johnny had a test age of six years and an I.Q. of 75. It was obvious that, with his endowment, he could not possibly be expected to do better than low first grade work. It would have seemed easy to say to the parents that Johnny should be in an ungraded class because of his low intelligence. It would have been very easy to give them the numerical result of the test and, if they balked, to offer them an authoritative explanation of the Binet-Simon or any other scale that had been employed. However, there was one big fly in the ointment. Mr. and Mrs. Jones were both college graduate people and moved in highly intellectual and sophisticated circles. Mr. Jones was a competent representative of a pharmaceutical firm and his wife had been a librarian prior to her marriage. They could see logically that their son had not been able to accomplish the scholastic functions expected of a child his age. But for years they had struggled against the very thought that something might be amiss with their Johnny's academic possibilities. As a result, they had kept looking for interpretations of his failures other than the one interpretation which they dreaded because they could not accept it emotionally. They had found fault with the "school system." There couldn't be anything wrong with the child: the problem must lie somewhere in the *method of instruction*: Johnny's teachers were either too young and inexperienced or too old and unfamiliar with modern education. They were alternately critical of what they chose to call either old-fashioned drilling or new-fangled frills. When, in the course of time, they had been convinced that the other children in Johnny's group got along all right under the same educational regime, they tried to seek the culprit in *Johnny's body*. After considerable search, they found one doctor who persuaded them that Johnny would do better if his tonsils and adenoids were taken out. They cherished this bit of wisdom because it fitted into their emotional pattern. They could say to themselves that, after all, their Johnny was all right and would learn better after the repair of a physical imperfection. This did not work. In order to satisfy their need for prestige, they began to pounce on *Johnny himself*. They decided that the child must be lazy. They scolded him, deprived him of privileges and sat with him for hours trying to hammer his homework into him. They pointed out to him how well his numerous cousins did without all the help such as he received from them. The child, smarting from the constant rebuff and rebuke, sat there, unable to grasp the parental instructions and, not knowing why he could not conform, came to think of himself as a wretched, miserable, ungrateful creature who let his parents down. He gave up completely. He lost all confidence in himself and, in order to find some compensation for his anguish, he took to daydreaming. Eventually, the parents thought that Johnny's salvation stared them in the face when they came upon an article in *The Reader's Digest* which told them that a certain drug, named glutamic acid, could brighten up children and make them learn better. They obtained the drug and got him to swallow tablet after tablet. For a time, they called off the dogs of daily tutoring and pushing, with the idea that glutamic acid would do the trick. Johnny, relieved of the pressures, perked up for a while and seemed brighter. He felt that being offered the tablets, however ill tasting they were, was better than being hovered over impatiently at the desk. The parents came to feel that the money they paid to the druggist was about the best investment they had ever made. But in the long run they realized that, as far as learning was concerned, there was no noticeable departure from the status quo. They felt disillusioned and finally decided to take the child to the clinic.

Betty Brown was a placid, likable little girl whose physical characteristics and marked developmental retardation had led the child's pediatrician to make the correct diagnosis of mongolism. He was able to help the parents to understand and accept Betty's limitations. The Browns were warm-hearted people and genuinely fond of their three children, of whom Betty was the youngest. Michael and Anne were healthy and bright and held out every promise of good academic achievement. They sensed their sister's handicaps, were helped by their parents to make the necessary allowances and, being secure in the warmth of a comfortable emotional climate, adjusted nicely to Betty's need for her mother's special attention. Anne, in fact, welcomed and invited opportunities to be mother's little helper in her ministrations to Betty.

This constellation of attitudes might have made for an ideal mode of family living. But a "bull in the china shop" charged into this peaceful home in the shape of Betty's paternal grandmother who lived a few doors away from the Browns. The elder Mrs. Brown stubbornly refused to acknowledge the doctor's diagnosis. She had always been a bit critical of her daughter-in-law but had found it difficult to hold on to a specific hat rack on which to hang her expressions of disapproval. Betty's failure to develop properly came to her as a godsend. She made up her mind that there was nothing wrong with Betty herself and that the whole trouble stemmed from the child's mother's inadequate methods of training. She offered no concrete suggestions. She did not substantiate her recriminations. But every morning, with clocklike regularity, she appeared at the home, looked at the child with a mien of profound commiseration, and uttered the same reproachful phrase: "When are you going to start making something of the child?"

Mrs. Brown took this as long as she could. She discarded as utterly futile her initial attempts to convey to her tormentor the reality of Betty's condition. She decided to remain silent. But eventually she could stand it no longer. It is not easy to be confronted daily with insult added to painful injury. She turned for help to her husband, imploring him to do something about his mother's stereotyped antics. All that he had to offer was the advice that she "pay no attention." After a few months, she brought Betty to our clinic. In reality, she brought herself and her misery rather than the child. She was obviously depressed and was seeking help for herself, which by that time she needed desperately.

Alan Smith was his parents' only child. He was severely retarded in his development. The Smiths, feeling that Alan would need all of their attention, had decided to deprive themselves of further offspring. There was also the dread of a possible repetition of the tragedy. But most pathetic of all was the boy's mother's constant self-searching for some shortcomings of her own which might be responsible for her son's intellectual defect. When she brought him to the clinic, she asked: "Doctor, did I have something to do with it? Did I do something wrong?" She eagerly gulped down the acquittal but went on: "Well—maybe before he was born—did I do something then?" When told that her child's retardation was not determined by anything that she had done, she was still puzzled. She wondered: "If it isn't what I have *done*, maybe it's what I *am* that brought it about." Again she seemed grateful for authoritative absolution. But still she went on. If she had not contributed to the fact of Alan's retardation, then she was surely guilty of not recognizing it in time, of pushing him beyond his capacity, of losing patience with him, of doing things for him which he might have learned to do for himself. Furthermore, she had been ashamed of his backwardness and tried to hide it from her friends and neighbors, and then she was ashamed of having felt shame. Of course, she could not gain peace through mere verbal reassurance, however thirstily she lapped it up. She needed many opportunities to talk herself out, more chances for this confessional type of expiation, and help in the suggested efforts to return to her previous social and communal life from which she had removed herself in sacrificial isolation because of her feelings of shame and guilt and remorse.

Larry White was brought to our clinic at the age of 7-1/2 years. His parents were distressed by his poor progress in school and by the suggestion that he be placed in an ungraded class. Larry was their only child who had come to them after eight years of married life. His birth, preceded by a miscarriage and much gynecological maneuvering, was greeted with jubilation. His mother, previously an efficient office manager, took Larry over as the biggest assignment of her career. Her feeding methods made and kept him nice and chubby. Speech development was somewhat delayed but this, she reasoned, is true of many children who later become regular chatterboxes. His faulty articulation was handled by sending him to a "teacher of expression and dramatics." He did well in nursery school and kindergarten. He was a happy, sociable, and well-mannered child.

Then the parents experienced their great shock. Larry could not do his first grade work, failed of promotion and finally was recommended for a special class. At first, the mother blamed his eyesight but three successive examinations convinced her that his vision was not

at fault. The mother tried to do his homework with him, and each attempt made her more impatient. She then employed a tutor for him. When his scholastic performance showed no improvement, the parents began to transfer the blame to Larry himself. The father found comfort in the formula that Larry was "mentally lazy." The mother began to nag and punish him and deprive him of privileges. Larry became rebellious under the many-sided pressures, was increasingly restless, at times even destructive, and developed behavior ostensibly intended to get even with his critics and oppressors.

His I.Q. was 77.

The mother reported that her nephews and nieces all had superior intelligence and remarked significantly: "I can't understand. Why does this happen to me?" The father, more genuinely fond of the child, said: "I think he is perfect apart from school," and added that his wife was disturbed because Larry obviously was not a genius. Thereupon she said categorically: "I want him to go to college. We can afford it."

It is clear that one could not use a sledge hammer in dealing with Larry's parents. Merely telling them that their son was not ready for first grade work did not solve the essential problem. They had known this for some time. But they needed help in learning to accept the child as he was without a sense of personal shame and failure. Larry's mother felt shamed and socially disgraced by having a child whom her society considers inferior. She felt guilty because the unpleasant thought must have kept obtruding itself that, after all her gynecological difficulties, she should perhaps have remained childless. She felt frustrated because her one great asset, her efficiency, and suffered defeat.

Examples such as these can be produced almost indefinitely. But even the small number of cited instances suffices to bring out a few highly important considerations. It is, of course, necessary for the expert to make the best possible use of the available test methods in order to obtain a scientifically valid assessment of a child's developmental potentialities. The application of these tests requires skill, experience, patience, and a setting in which the tested child would be at his ease and cooperate to his best ability. Many pitfalls must be avoided, such as testing a child during his regular naptime, failure to take into account an existing impairment of hearing or vision, psychometric examination immediately preceding or following a convulsion, or difficulty in allaying a child's acute anxiety which may manifest itself in speechless timidity or noisy defiance.

When a test has been completed satisfactorily and the child's intellectual endowment has been ascertained with reasonable accuracy, it is the expert's duty to report and explain his findings to the child's parents. It should hardly seem necessary to point out that such a report, if it involves the disclosure of a child's retardation, should be made tactfully, lucidly, and truthfully. But I have known parents who, without any concern for their emotional readiness, were thrown into a panic by the words feebleminded, imbecile, or moron hurled at them as if from an ambush. I have also known good-natured doctors who did not have the heart to confront the parents with the true state of affairs and mumbled something to the effect that Johnny or Janie may "outgrow" the developmental lag or "catch up" with other children of his or her age.

I once had a long-distance telephone call from a physician in a small town, who asked me to see a 6-year-old boy who was markedly retarded. For several years, he had "played along" with Billy's parents, who were his personal friends. He minimized, if not ridiculed, their apprehensions. When Billy did not begin to talk long past the expected time, he reminded the parents of a cousin of his who had not talked until the age of four years but then made up for lost time and eventually graduated from high school and college. He advised: "If Billy won't talk, just don't give him the things he wants unless he asks for them verbally." When this method did not work and the parents wondered whether they should have Billy tested, he said some unkind words about "all that psychology stuff." But when Billy was to be enrolled in the first grade, the school authorities refused to accept him. The heartbroken parents were enraged at the physician who, they felt, had either been inexcusably ignorant or had knowingly betrayed their trust in him. When I saw them, they asked again and again: "*Why* didn't he tell us?"

Adequate examination and the issuance of correct information are indeed indispensable. But they by no means constitute the whole of the expert's responsibility. The cited examples show that the mere procedure of Binetizing and Simonizing a child, the mere determination of an intelligence quotient, the mere pronouncement of the test result do not in themselves take care of the significant mater of family sentiments. It is true that each situation is unique and that different parents come with different problems. Yet it is possible to pick out from the large welter of cases several recurrent puzzlements which are voiced almost invariably. Allow me to enumerate some of the questions which are asked regularly with a great deal of feeling and to which the inquirers hope to get straightforward answers, without evasion and without hedging:

What is the cause of our child's retardation?
Have we personally contributed to his condition?
Why did this have to happen to us?
What about heredity?
Is it safe to have another child?
Is there any danger that our normal children's offspring might be similarly affected?
How is his (or her) presence in the home likely to affect our normal children?
How shall we explain him (or her) to our normal children?
How shall we explain him (or her) to our friends and neighbors?
Is there anything that we can do to brighten him (or her) up?
Is there an operation which might help?
Is there any drug which might help?
What about glutamic acid?
Will our child *ever* talk?
What will our child be like when he (or she) grows up?
Can we expect graduation from high school? From grammar school?
Would you advise a private tutor?
Should we keep our child at home or place him (or her) in a residential school?
What specific school do you recommend?
If a residential school, how long will our child have to remain there?
Will our child become alienated from us if placed in a residential school?
Will our child ever be mature enough to marry?
Do you think that our child should be sterilized and, if so, at what age?

These are some of the questions asked commonly by the parents of retarded children. These questions vary, of course, depending on the degree of the child's retardation, on the presence or absence of other children in the family, on the parents' financial resources, on their ideas about social prestige, on their degree of acceptance or rejection of the child.

It is not possible to answer every one of these questions unequivocally. Science has not advanced sufficiently—and probably never will—to make omniscient persons of the consulted physician or psychologist. Aside from the fact that causes of retardation are not always the same in all instances and that there may be multiple contributing factors in the same instance, the search for an ultimate cause often runs against the barrier of our incomplete knowledge. I have never encountered a parent who respected me less because, in answer to the question about the cause of his or her child's retardation, I made no secret of my inability to supply a definite answer. Intelligent parents usually realize fully that would-be erudite terms, such as innate, congenital, or constitutional, though literally correct, often beg rather than answer their question. What most of them hope to hear is indeed not so much a piece of etiological wisdom in words of Greek or Latin origin as an authoritative and sympathetic endorsement of themselves, of their human and parental competence, of their right not to blame themselves for what has happened.

Parents whose first child happens to be seriously retarded are almost invariably plagued by the question whether or not they should have another child. There is a conflict between the strong desire to enjoy the pleasure of having a healthy child and the simultaneous fear that things may go wrong again. The parents always wait for an opportunity to present this question to the person whom they consult about their handicapped offspring. They are disappointed if this opportunity is not forthcoming. It is not an easy thing to help in the solution of this conflict. For one thing, the question is not merely a desire for information. Behind it is sometimes a scheme, of which the parents themselves are not necessarily aware, to throw the whole burden of responsibility on the adviser. If the second child should also be afflicted, the parents are clear of any blame. They can point an accusing finger at the adviser who had told them what they wanted to hear. It has been my policy to remind parents that every childbirth entails a risk, that no one could possibly have predicted that their first child would be born handicapped. Though experience teaches that lightning does not usually strike twice in the same place, the risk, however small, must rest with the parents. But if they do decide in favor of having another child, they should do so only if they are capable of freeing themselves of any anticipation of disaster. Such constant dread before and after the arrival of the new baby would create

an attitude not conducive to a wholesome relationship even with the healthiest and sturdiest child.

There is no time to go into a discussion of all the questions which have been enumerated above. But the introductory examples show how profoundly the feelings of parents are involved in their types of curiosity, in the handling of their retarded children, and in their need for understanding and guidance. Like all human beings, the parents of retarded children react to their feelings. Their own life experiences, which have helped to shape their personalities, have contributed to the manner in which they adjust to pleasant and unpleasant realities in general, and to the presence of a handicapped child in particular.

In essence, one may distinguish three principal types of reaction:

1. Mature acknowledgement of actuality makes it possible to assign to the child a place in the family in keeping with his specific peculiarities. The child is accepted as he is. The mother neither makes herself a slave to him, nor does she take her inevitable frustrations out on him. She goes on functioning in her accustomed way. She continues her associations with her friends and acquaintances. The father shares her fondness for the child. Both parents manage to appraise the needs of their normal children as well and to distribute their parental contributions accordingly.

2. Disguises of reality create artificialities of living and planning which tend to disarrange the family relationships. The fact of the handicap is seen clearly but is ascribed to some circumstances, the correction of which would restore the child to normalcy. Some culprit is assumed in the child's character or body or in the educational inadequacy of the trainers. The child's poor scholastic progress in the regular grades is interpreted as a manifestation of laziness or stubbornness which must be exorcised with painfully punitive methods: the full burden is placed on the child himself. His low marks, his failure of promotion, the school's recommendation that he be placed in an ungraded class, are taken as a result of the blameworthy effrontery of a willfully unaccommodating child. Parental pressures to speed up his lagging speech development, to correct his indistinct articulation, and to improve his homework heap misery on the child, who finds it impossible to gain parental approval.

Instead of, or in addition to, the child himself, his body comes in for frantic attempts at correction. Tongues are clipped, prepuces are amputated, tonsils are evicted with the notion that somehow such measures will undo the reality of his handicap. Thyroid extract, caused to be swallowed by some physicians with hazy etiologic notions, and chiropractic adjustments of an allegedly misplaced vertebra are still much too frequently employed as a means of disguising reality.

3. Complete inability to face reality in any form leads to its uncompromising denial. The formula goes something like this: "There is absolutely nothing the matter with the child. Those who are anxious about his development are merely pessimistic spreaders of gloom. Some children walk or talk sooner than others, and some take their time." This is often the reaction especially of fathers who have no knowledge of children and do not wish to be bothered about them. They are away at work most of the day, have a glimpse of the child when he is asleep, hear the child's laughter on the rare occasion when they pick him up, and conclude with a shrug of the shoulder: "I can't see anything unusual."

A busy surgeon, the father of three children, could not see anything unusual about his youngest child, a severely withdrawn, autistic boy whom his mother brought to our clinic against her husband's wishes. The surgeon finally came, after several invitations. He had no idea of the child's developmental data; he left all this to his wife, he declared complacently. I tried to get an emotional rise at least by making him angry. I asked whether he would recognize any one of his three children if he met him unexpectedly in the street. He thought for a while, scratched his head, and then said calmly: "Well, I don't really know if I would." He felt that his wife's concern about the child was all nonsense but if she wanted to bring him to the clinic, that was all right, too; after all, this was her own business.

Any slightest acquaintance with the elementary principles of psychology is enough to indicate that all these different types of attitudes and resulting practices are deeply anchored in the emotional backgrounds of the individual parents and other relatives. Smothering overprotection, cold rejection, nagging coercion, or open neglect defended as proper tactics necessary to cope with the child's handicap, are in the main fundamental, dynamically evolved reactions which seize on the handicap as a readily accessible, superficial explanation.

All of this leads to the inescapable conclusion that the study and treatment of exceptional children would be sorely incomplete if the emotional factors of family relationships were left out of the consideration. In every instance, the place of the exceptional child in the family structure calls for a thorough overhauling, often with the urgent need for interviews with the parents. Frequently enough, the parents themselves beg for such an overhauling; they do so by asking seemingly specific or insignificant questions, and are most appreciative if such hints are understood and they are given an opportunity to talk themselves out before an experienced and sympathetic listener.

Presented at the Seventy-sixth Annual Meeting of the American Association on Mental Deficiency, held at Hotel Bellevue-Stratford, Philadelphia, Pennsylvania, May, 1952.

Author
Leo Kanner, M.D.

Needs of Parents of Mentally Retarded Children

Mrs. Max A. Murray
1959

In enumerating and studying the needs of parents of the mentally retarded the most logical beginning will be to look at some of the problems faced by those of us who are parents. Our needs are so closely related to our problems that to recognize and meet the needs we must first understand some of the most basic problems created by the birth of a retarded child into a family. It must be borne in mind while looking at family problems that we must think and speak in general terms rather than in specific ones because of the variety of family situations. We must recognize that the inherent disposition and nature of each parent, their educational and cultural backgrounds, their financial and social status in the community—these and other factors will all have some bearing on the kind of problems they will have. It is important that we keep in mind the over-all picture of the many types of families into which the mentally retarded are born. Obviously the problems will be somewhat different in a professional family to that of a day-laborer with an elementary school education who is scarcely known outside his immediate living and working circles. Situations which may present a very acute problem to one family may scarcely be noticed in another. This fact was brought to our attention several years ago by a college president who told me of his own small retarded boy of seven who was going through the agony of being considered a "dummy" by his little playmates who were sons of other educators. "Had he been born into a family with little education and no prominence in the community he would not suffer so much," his father said to me sadly, "but because he is *my* son, the son of a college president, he will always have an up-hill battle to fight because of his mental limitations."

In addition to the difference in family situations, we must also take into consideration the vast differences in the children themselves. Here again we see that the totally dependent bed or wheel-chair patient will present an altogether different set of problems from the trainable or educable child whose life will not only touch the family members but other persons in the community. The hyper-active, tense child who often responds in a de-structive manner will create problems never dreamed of by those who have dealt only with the dull, phlegmatic type of child who will sit quietly in one spot for hours. Keeping in mind that the specific problems will vary according to the individual family situation and the particular type child involved, let us look at some of the general problems. To touch on all of them would be impossible in a limited time but for constructive thinking we shall list six basic problems common to the families of the retarded. These are not necessarily listed in order of importance or degree—because here again the impact of the particular problem will depend upon the family setting as well as the child.

1. *The first severe problem which parents of retarded children face is the acceptance of the fact that the child is retarded.* Successfully coping with the total problem will center relentlessly about this foremost and basic problem. Dr. Leo Kanner, a leading psychiatrist in the field of mental retardation, describes parent reactions to mental retardation as variants of three specific types:

    a. "Mature acknowledgement of the actuality and acceptance of the child;

    b. disguises of reality with search for either scapegoats upon which to blame the retardation or the seeking of magic cures;

    c. complete denial of the existence of any retardation."

Dr. Kanner emphasizes that "since these basic attitudes will color all aspects of the care and management of the retarded child, it becomes the obligation of the physician to identify the attitudes present in the parents, and work for a 'thorough overhauling' in the direction of mature acceptance."

Various reasons can be supplied for parents who fall into any one of these three basic categories, but here again the nature and disposition of the individual parents, their educational and cultural, economic and social background, their fundamental philosophy for living—all of these aspects as well as many others will help to determine how parents meet this first and basic problem. It is true that a large percentage of parents *do* have difficulty in accepting the diagnosis of mental retardation in their child. The reasons given are many and varied, some superficial and some truly valid. However, one reason is often overlooked by the professional person— and it is probably overlooked because it is such a very simple one. It is the obvious fact that many parents come face to face with the diagnosis of mental retardation without ever having heard the term used or having seen such a child to their knowledge. Obviously it would be easier for any of us to accept a diagnosis of polio, or cerebral palsy, or rheumatic fever or any of the dozen other diseases or conditions because we at least *know* that they exist—but most of us know absolutely nothing concerning mental retardation until we are confronted with it first-hand. Another reason for our disbelief and great anxiety is our terrible fear of the word *mental* as against the word *physical* when used in connection with our child. Due to the present intensive educational program designed to remove the stigma from mental retardation as well as all other types of mental problems, we believe that the time will eventually come when parents can come face to face with the stern reality of a retarded child with far less emotional damage than has been true in past years. Once the true facts about the problem are known, not only by professional persons, but by the general public as well, we believe that a solution will be found to many, if not all, of our problems relating to non-acceptance of the fact of retardation.

2. *A second very real problem faced by the families of the retarded is a financial one.* Here again the problem varies in its severity according to the economic status of the family involved. In the low or even middle income group the amount of money required in seeking a diagnosis, providing proper medical care and possibly in later years a special training program for the defective child, can become a serious financial burden. Even in families of a higher income bracket, sacrifices are often made in some area in order to provide care for a child in a private residential setting. Parents who have difficulty in accepting the diagnosis of retardation will often spend sizeable sums (regardless of their economic status) going from one doctor to another, from one clinic to another, from one treatment center or training program to another until finally not only their financial situation has become critical but their health and general efficiency have been irreparably damaged. Perhaps the following true story will illustrate more clearly the point we are trying to make. Within recent years a middle-aged mother was left a widow with three children, a son and daughter in high school and a microcephalic child of about ten. Her husband had built up a modest estate of approximately $100,000 which with proper management would have enabled the two teenagers to acquire a college education and soon become financially independent in their own right. But because of the mother's overwhelming obsession that something *could* and *must* be done for the weaker and more helpless child, the entire estate soon dwindled away in the futile search for the cure which the mother blindly believed was always just around the next expensive corner. Both teenagers were forced by economic necessity to go to work immediately upon leaving high school instead of obtaining the college training which would have helped them to secure better positions as well as enabling them to make a more constructive contribution to the family and society in which they lived. Those of you who have worked in this field for a number of years could probably tell many similar stories—too many, in fact— in which the economic rights and privileges of an entire family have been sacrificed for the weaker child to such an extent that the lives of the normal children were permanently affected in adverse ways. Fortunate indeed are the parents who have been helped by some wise professional person to maintain an intelligent balance in the use of their income in relation to their retarded child. Many parents in their overwhelming anxiety for the welfare of the child will lose their sense of perspective and decide that money is of no consequence where the needs of the child are concerned. When this happens, the results are almost inevitably disastrous to the home situation because added to the terrific emotional strain through which they are passing is the additional burden of anxiety over the critical financial situation.

3. *A third very real problem faced by the parents of a retarded child is that of emotional tension built up by carrying a burden which they cannot find it possible to satisfactorily share with their fellowmen.* Those parents who refuse to admit their child *is* retarded must carry the double burden of grief and pretense—both of which tend to build within them great dams of emotional turmoil for which there seems to be no release. But even the parents who can and do admit their child's limitations often find it difficult if not almost impossible to share their sorrow because their friends, neighbors and relatives are hesitant to ask about the child's welfare. In the case of se-

vere physical illness or death we would think it inconceivable if our friends, relatives, or neighbors showed no concern for our need—yet in this case where the emotional shock is sometimes even more severe than in death, we are denied the privilege of sharing our grief with those closest to us because of a sense of embarrassment or shame. All of you know the real therapeutic value of being able to "talk out our troubles" with someone who understands. But often in the early stages of discovery of mental retardation within a family, the parents have difficulty in talking with one another—let alone with relatives or friends. Fortunately this is not the case too often, but it can and does happen. This inability to share our problem exists through no fault of the parents, or of the general public. It is simply the result of having looked upon mental abnormalities with superstition, with fear, with ignorance of the true facts, or, perhaps with the naive belief that if we just refuse to look at them or discuss them objectively they will somehow cease to exist. After talking with hundreds of parents it is my feeling that more real damage has been brought about by this inability to share their problem than by any other single factor. May we reiterate again and again that this is not the fault of the parents nor of society in general. It is simply a condition which exists—but one which is now crying out loud for correction.

4. *The fourth problem is one which is almost totally ignored by those professional persons whom parents are most likely to consult in regard to their child, and yet it is one of the most real and vital problems they face: we refer to the theological conflicts which arise in the minds of parents when faced with such a heart-rending situation within their own personal lives.* Death, they can accept—because death, at one stage or another, is a normal and natural part of life's history; physical illness they can accept because they have seen physical illness and deformity throughout their lives. Broken homes, loss of jobs and economical security, serious injury by accident—all these unfortunate circumstances are familiar to every adult couple and are within the realm of possibility in their thinking. But to suddenly face the fact that their child is a mental cripple and will remain so throughout life, well—this simply places them outside the providence of God's mercy and justice, or so they often feel—if they can indeed still believe that there *is* a God. If the parents have been reared in a somewhat puritanical concept they may possibly become so overwhelmed with a sense of guilt that it is totally impossible for them to see their problem from a rational viewpoint.

Any condition of life which destroys or permanently damages one's concept of a loving and merciful God presents a serious problem—a problem with which he must have help lest he finally sink into a state of despair from which there is no return. For this reason we believe that our Clergymen, our Priests and our Rabbis should have competent professional knowledge about the facts of mental retardation so as to be more able to advise and counsel wisely with the members of their parish who are faced with this problem.

5. *The fifth, and probably the most heart-rending of all the many problems we face is that of seeking a solution to the matter of satisfactory life-time care for our handicapped child, who, in many instances, will need adult guidance and care throughout his normal life span.* We believe that it can be safely said that very few professional persons can fully appreciate or understand the intense feelings of anxiety and concern on the part of parents over this acute problem of life-time care. The professional person, by the very nature of his training, is primarily concerned with finding a solution to the problem immediately at hand—and this is as it should be. The doctor endeavors to provide the small retardate with the healthiest, strongest physical body he can be given; the teacher works and thinks in terms of helping him learn to use and further develop his limited mental capacity; the social worker works in terms of helping the child and his family in making a satisfactory adjustment to his environment; the psychologist and psychiatrist endeavor to help both parent and child to an acceptance of his limitation and to a wiser understanding of their own feelings and motivations. Professional help is not only good, it is actually imperative in meeting the problems of the moment. But the professional person must always keep in mind that with the child's parent the problem is not for "just now" but for *always*. Such an attitude of understanding about the permanence of the problem from the standpoint of the parents will enable the professional person to work more constructively with us as parents in meeting the problems immediately at hand. In families where there are other children to be considered the problem of life-time care is intensified because we must take into consideration not only the handicapped child but the other children as well. Here again, there is no single, easy answer. Decisions must be made in the light of many, many factors—too numerous to go into at this time. But let it be said here that the decisions which must be made by parents on this one point alone are grave enough to

shake the emotional, spiritual and mental equilibrium of even the most stable personalities.

6. *A sixth and final problem with which most parents have to cope at one time or another during their experience is with inept, inaccurate and ill-timed professional advice.* Now I am well aware that such a statement as this coming from a parent contains potential dynamite! I must also confess that a sore temptation presents itself to cast all objectivity aside and give you some stories which parents have told me over the past few years—but I shall resist the temptation to do so. Instead, I would ask your permission to share with you material from several recognized leaders in the field of mental deficiency. All of their statements tend to lift up the point that we want to make here and it is this: parents can be spared much emotional damage and conflict if the professional persons they consult have two things,

A. A comprehensive knowledge of all factors concerning mental retardation so far as they are known.
B. The ability to counsel parents in a straightforward, honest but gracious manner.

To put it a bit more bluntly, the reaction of parents to their problem will depend to a great degree on the emotional and spiritual maturity of the professional person whom they consult as well as the professional person's knowledge or lack of knowledge concerning mental retardation. The first statement we would present for your consideration is lifted from an address by Dr. William M. Cruickshank, Director of Special Education, Syracuse University. This address was presented to the Virginia Public Health Conference, May 2, 1956 in Roanoke, Virginia.

I am concerned that in the first contact which parents have with a professional person they will be given an honest diagnosis and that they will also be given a realistic and honest prognosis. The diagnostic problem is the responsibility of the medical profession and the psychological profession. Both groups in the past have been remiss on many occasions and have frequently failed to bring to the child the best diagnostic procedure. Often times this has resulted from ignorance. This situation can be corrected and is now being the focus of attention of medical and psychological faculties. The problem of honest prognosis is more subtle because it is dependent on the emotional security of the professional person in his relation to the clients. Too often professional personnel simply do not have the ability to be able to tell parents the realities of a situation. Only recently a set of parents brought a ten-year-old child to our clinic. The child was markedly retarded. In the interpretive conference with the parent we asked why it was they had waited so long to seek assistance with their problem. "Surely you must have suspected long before this that your child was not developing properly." The mother replied: "We did suspect that something was wrong. He did not talk as soon as the other children had. He didn't walk as early as the others either. We took him to our pediatrician and he said: 'Don't worry Mrs. Jones, when Tommy is sixteen years old you'll never be able to tell him from other boys on the street.'" This is indeed inaccurate. It happens so frequently, however, that many of us are seriously disturbed. Educators likewise are to be criticized. I have a letter on my desk from a school principal to a mother. The school is recommending that her retarded child be placed in a special class. The mother objected. The principal's letter states: "I can understand your feeling about our recommendation for Stewart's placement in a special class. I wonder if we could suggest a compromise: Let us place Stewart in the special class for a year or two and then we will return him to the regular grades." This is more than inaccurate. It is an absolute mis-statement of the facts. It implies that while the child is in the special class, educators will wave a magic wand over the child's head, cure him of mental retardation, and thus put him back in the regular grades." In 1956, once mentally retarded, always mentally retarded in spite of the numerous articles to the contrary which appear in popular magazines. Educators, psychology, medicine cannot cure mental retardation. Can we not, however, be honest in our reporting to parents? Can we not be conservatively realistic? Parents may not like what we say, and their feelings we can appreciate. Nevertheless, basically they want an honest appraisal of the situation as distasteful as that may be. They need to be secure in the knowledge that the professions are shooting straight from the shoulder and that with such realism appropriate planning for the child can be undertaken.

The second statement is lifted from an article appearing in the *American Journal of Mental Deficiency* and comes from H. S. Storrs:

> Medicine is an art, and handling the relatives is one of the important functions of this art. In my opinion, every case is individual and should be investigated as such. I want to know all I can about the child, the family, and all situations connected with both the child and the family. . . . Doctors as a class do not seem to realize the enormity of the tragedy experienced by the parents when they find that their child is definitely defective. This should be appreciated by all doctors and they should size up the parents. I have always felt that it was a mistake not to tell the parents the whole truth. . . . Parents have in many instances been from doctor to doctor, spending their money; have been given evasive answers; have built up hopes over and over, only to have them dashed to the ground, finally. It always seemed to me that they should be told the truth as early as possible, with, as I have said, consideration for the individual family situation.

Other problems arise between the professional person and parents when the professional person tends to hide behind certain well-worn cliches such as the following: "These parents can't be helped because they just don't want to believe what we tell them"—or, "These parents believe that this just couldn't happen to them,"—or—more common still—"These parents have rejected their child so there is little that I can do to help them."

Some very well-qualified persons have come to feel that the over-use of these well-worn phrases usually arises from the fact that the professional person feels his own inadequacy in knowing how to successfully counsel with parents in a constructive manner. The professional person should ever bear in mind that the wrong kind of help or advice given to an emotionally disturbed parent is often worse than no help at all. And whether we like to admit it or not, most of us *are* disturbed to various degrees in the initial stages of our adjustment. We as parents need to have a wiser understanding of our own feelings during this period—but since many of us do not have, we must depend on you to sometimes go the second mile in trying to help us out of our emotional turmoil. However, let us hasten to add that just as we feel parents should not be harshly judged because they do not know how to handle their retarded children most

wisely, we should also recognize that professional persons should not be harshly judged because they often do not know how to handle parents wisely. We simply must take into account that the primary reason that both situations exist is due to ignorance and inexperience in most instances.

We have now considered six of the most basic problems faced by the parents of retarded children. What, then, is their greatest need?

After thirteen years experience as the mother of a retarded child and having talked and corresponded with literally hundreds of other parents, I have come to the conclusion that all of our many, many needs can be covered in one sentence and it is this:

> *The greatest single need of parents of mentally retarded children is constructive professional counselling at various stages in the child's life which will enable the parents to find the answers to their own individual problems to a reasonably satisfactory degree.*

In the early stages of our initial adjustment to life with a retarded child we need someone who can and will explain to us in lay language some of the numerous factors relating to mental retardation; we need someone to help us understand our own attitudes and feelings in relation to our handicapped child. We need someone to give us guidance in the simple, basic processes of home training. We need someone who can put us in touch with the various community and state agencies that can help with constructive management of the child. We need guidance from someone who can help us see that this thing which has happened to us, even though it may be a *life-shaking* experience does not of necessity have to be a *life-breaking* one.

Several years later we need guidance from those who can help us decide upon and provide a training program for the child. In later years we need guidance and help in making plans which will provide permanent care for our child when we are gone. Again, may we repeat that our greatest single need is for the kind of counsel which will enable us to find the answers to our individual problems. Please note that we are not suggesting that others should make our decisions for us, or that they should bear the burden of telling us what or what not to do,—only that we might be given the guidance that will enable us to make our own decisions in a way which will result in the greatest good for the child and the family of which he is a part.

If, then, constructive counseling seems to be our greatest need, what qualities do we as parents believe to be desirable in those who give guidance to us? Surely among the foremost qualities we want in those who attempt to help us in our need is absolute honesty. Perhaps some of you *think* we don't want honesty because of the parent's proneness for "shopping around" until he finds someone who will tell him what he wants to hear rather than the truth. But basically, we believe that parents *do* want honesty and in the final analysis will be deeply grateful to the professional person who has the courage to make a deep clean cut. All of you have heard this statement from your colleagues at one time or another: "But parents don't *want* to hear the truth"—of course we don't want to hear it. Not one of us present would *want* to hear that he had TB or cancer or heart trouble, but we would think a physician sadly remiss in his duty if he refused to give us an honest diagnosis of a physical ailment just because his patient didn't *want* to hear it. It would seem that this excuse is worn somewhat threadbare by those persons who just don't quite have the intestinal fortitude to face up to their own inadequacy in dealing with parents. On the other hand we hear from parents over and over: "If we had only found someone who would have given us an honest diagnosis from the beginning we may possibly have been able to begin constructive planning for the child years sooner." We do not believe that the word honesty implies that parents need to be informed of a child's condition in a blunt, cold or cruel manner. Surely the professional person in any area who is worthy of his calling should make every effort to develop the fine art of breaking such news in a manner which will leave at least some ray of hope and encouragement to which parents can cling during their blackest moments.

Another desirable attribute to be found in those who can most successfully counsel with parents of retarded children is that of an *understanding heart*. Please do not believe that we want sympathy, particularly the maudlin kind of sympathy which is damaging to the professional person as well as the parent. But we do need the kind of understanding personality which enables the professional person to put himself in the place of the parent.

An old Indian chief gave this saying which so aptly illustrates the kind of rapport which is necessary if parents and professional persons are to work together wisely for the good of the child—and I quote: "I cannot judge or advise any man rightfully and wisely until I have walked for ten moons in his moccasins." Surely if parents and professional persons could walk (figuratively speaking) in the moccasins of each other for ten moons, both would be more able to come to an understanding which would enable each to be mutually helpful in serving the needs of the child.

A third quality which we as parents greatly desire in those who attempt to give us help is the kind of integrity and stability of character which enables the professional person to work cooperatively with other professional disciplines for the good of the child—as well as with all those within his own particular profession. We are well aware that the question of professional jealousy is a very hot potato for one to try to juggle, and particularly so in front of an audience composed primarily of professional persons! But please forgive me if I play with this hot potato a bit to give you an idea as to what damage professional jealousy *can* and *does* do to the parents of a retarded child. In the initial stages of our problem, most of us are fairly young and very, very few have had any training or background of any type that would make us familiar with the complicated, many-sided angles of mental retardation. We come to the professional person (of any discipline) with the naive and innocent belief that he or she will surely have *all* the answers to our many questions because he or she has spent years of study about the problem. Rather soon we discover that many of the answers we hear and much of the advice we are given does not seem to be "compatible" shall we say. More often than you would like to believe we find capable, conscientious professional persons expressing to parents definitely contrary opinions to those expressed by another professional person concerning the child. Sometimes these contrary opinions are expressed within the same profession, sometimes in an allied one. Teachers will sometimes disagree strongly with an opinion rendered by a psychologist in regard to their child; psychologists will not always agree with the efforts of a conscientious social worker; physicians will express opinions which make it difficult for the parent to have proper respect and confidence in the field of psychiatry, and the members of the psychiatric profession will sometimes in turn take unprofessional little jabs at the ignorance of the general MD in matters of the mind. Worst of all, some few professional people are not above making derogatory remarks about those within their own profession. All of this tends to create a sense of tremendous confusion in the mind of an already disturbed parent and is in no way conducive to helping him think through his problem in an intelligent manner. We are in thorough accord with the idea that there is always room for an honest and sincere difference of opinion among professional persons in their study of the retarded child. Our deep concern is that such differences of opinion should be expressed to the parents in such a manner that will not cause them to lose respect for another professional person or discipline. Each of you have at times worked with parents who seemed very much on the "defensive" so to speak. Generally speaking, this is often blamed on a "guilt complex" (whatever that is!) but did it ever occur to you that this very defensiveness in parents may have been built up because of a former unfortunate contact with an emotionally immature and insecure professional person?

Please, please do not interpret what we have said as a reflection on professional people in general. We know that your ranks are composed of all kinds of persons— just like parents of retarded children in fact, strong ones and weak ones! We know too that sometimes an entire profession suffers because of the spiritual and emotional immaturity in a few of its members. Our only plea is that if you *do* have colleagues who suffer to a certain degree from the not so rare malady of professional jealousy, just urge them to be very cautious about exposing their symptoms before parents of retarded children. WE have enough decisions to make without trying to decide in our own bewildered minds who is right and who is wrong in a professional "tug-of-war!"

Even though we seem to have given a bit of a verbal spanking today to the few professional persons who cause real problems for the parents of retarded children, we certainly want to pay tribute to that vast army of professional persons who down through the years have worked so very hard to meet the needs of our children. It has disturbed me as a parent to hear some few overly-enthusiastic and uninformed parents make the statement that nothing had been done for our children until the recent formation of the parent associations. Those who have made the effort to find out the true facts recognize that for many years members of the International Council for Exceptional Children and of the American Association of Mental Deficiency have struggled long and hard to solve some of the problems posed by mental retardation. To these pioneer workers for our children we owe a deep debt of gratitude.

We are prone as human beings when seeking help in any field to search for those with the most training, the most knowledge, the most competent background. This is good—and as it should be—but it is not sufficient in itself when seeking answers to human problems so deeply involved as those produced by the love of a parent for a helpless child. Knowledge alone is not enough; experience alone is not enough; both together are not enough. Over and above all, the professional person who would be of the most help to parents of retarded children must have a dedicated desire to serve his fellowman and to help him in finding answers to the complex problems which he cannot solve alone.

To summarize: here are our major problems.
1. Acceptance of fact child is retarded. . . .
2. Intelligent use of income in relation to retarded child within total family needs.
3. Learning how to live successfully with emotional tension built up by carrying burden we find difficult to share with fellowman. . . .
4. Resolving the theological conflicts which may arise in our minds relative to the birth of our retarded child. . . .
5. Making decisions relative to life-time care for child. . . .
6. Learning to sift the wheat from the chaff in the professional advice given us over a long period of time. . . .

Our greatest need: Constructive professional counseling at various stages in the child's life which will enable us as parents to find the answers to our own individual problems to a reasonably satisfactory degree.

What do we want in those who help us from a professional standpoint?

1. Honesty—with a generous portion of graciousness poured on to relieve the sting. . . .
2. An understanding heart, the rare gift bestowed upon those who can look at a parent sitting across the desk and believe that "But for the grace of God, there sit I." . . .
3. Professional persons who have the wisdom to save all symptoms of professional jealousy to bestow on their colleagues rather than letting it leak out on the parents—it's most confusing to us!

In conclusion, may we leave you with the thought that even though we as parents of retarded children are faced with a multitude of problems, many unanswerable questions and a great deal of grief, yet we *do* have our compensations. During the past seven years as a volunteer member of the National Association for Retarded Children, Virginia Association for Retarded Children and my own local chapter it has been my privilege to have talked with hundreds of parents of retarded children. One of the favorite themes which permeates our conversation is how much our children have meant to us. This thought runs like a bright golden thread through the dark tapestry of our sorrow. We learn so much from our children, retarded children are wonderful teachers if we are not too proud to learn from them and the grief of parents leaves little room for pride. We learn so much in patience, in humility, in gratitude for other blessings we had accepted before as a matter of course; so much in tolerance; so much in faith—believing and trusting where we cannot see; so much in compassion for our fellowman; and yes, even so much in wisdom about the eternal values of life because deep agony of spirit is the one thing which can turn us from the superficialities of life to those things that really matter. We also gain much in developing a strange kind of courage which enables us to face life without cringing because in one sense we have borne the ultimate that life has to offer in sorrow and pain.

Where, in all of this wide, wide world could we go to learn such lessons as these—lessons dealing with the real meaning of life?

Where else could we ever learn so much from those who know so little?

Author

Mrs. Max A. Murray, President, Virginia Association for Retarded Children

A Study of the Adjustment of Parents and Siblings of Institutionalized and Non-Institutionalized Retarded Children

Bettye M. Caldwell and Samuel B. Guze
1960

The decision about whether to institutionalize a retarded child is never an easy one for families to make. It is a decision which may be made on the basis of presumed needs of the retarded child, or it may be made primarily on the basis of needs of the remainder of the family, often the other children. Professional advice regarding this problem is often strongly partisan and, if one can judge from the reports of parents, heavily weighted in favor of institutionalization. Parents often keenly resent this professional bias, not only because of the implied lack of concern for parental feelings in the matter, but also because it is often entirely unrealistic in terms of availability of institutional facilities in a given geographical area. At the same time, many parents clutch frantically at this recommendation, seeing in it an official permit to carry out their own internal desires in the matter.

Comparisons of institutionalized and non-institutionalized retarded children on one or another psychological variable (i.e., intelligence, personality traits, etc.) have been frequently made. However, one can find almost no literature relating to the effects of institutionalization for the retarded child upon other members of the family.

Despite the relative paucity of information about the effects on the total family situation of different kinds of living arrangements for retarded children, professional persons are often called upon to make recommendations which take this variable into account. For example, staff members of diagnostic and treatment centers for retarded children are confronted repeatedly with the anxious query of the parent of a retarded child, "What will be the effect of this child upon my other children?" Or, perhaps somewhat less frequently, one hears the comment from a worried husband, "The child seems to be doing all right, but I am concerned about my wife." In such situations there is a strong tendency to look to professional persons for authoritative answers based on facts; yet such facts are hard to obtain except in the form of clinical impressions gained from personal acquaintance with different family situations.

It is the purpose of this study to initiate a preliminary investigation into this important area of the adjustment of families of retarded children. Two main types of family structure were chosen for study—families in which the retarded child was present in the current living arrangement, and families in which the child no longer lived at home but resided in a state institution for retarded children. These are referred to as the "Home" group and the "Institutional" group, respectively. Two individuals within the family were singled out for especially close scrutiny—the mother, and one of the siblings, referred to throughout the paper as the key sibling. The main objective of this study was to ascertain whether the mothers and siblings in the group where institutionalization had been chosen differed in personal adjustment from the mothers and siblings of the group in which the retarded child lived at home. If such a difference could be found, it would have important implications for community and state programs of care for retarded children. If differences could not be detected, this finding would be equally important.

Procedure

Subjects

Subjects for the study were 32 mothers and 32 siblings of retarded children residing in the greater St. Louis area. Of the retarded children represented in the families, 16 lived in their own homes and 16 lived in the St. Louis State Training School, a state-maintained institution for the retarded. The non-institutional sample was obtained from a diagnostic and therapeutic clinic for retarded children and from a private school in St. Louis County for trainable retarded children.[1] All but one of the siblings lived in the parental home at the time of the study, the one exception being a girl who had married between the time the family was first contacted and the time the siblings were interviewed. Selection of subjects was predicated largely upon certain characteristics of the

A Study of the Adjustment of Parents and Siblings

Bettye M. Caldwell and Samuel B. Guze

retarded children, even though these children were not themselves directly studied in any way. It was decided that the retarded children in the two groups of families should be comparable in terms of age, sex, level of retardation, and ordinal position in the family with respect to the key sibling. This matching was done on the basis of records maintained by the institution, clinic, or school from which the subjects were secured.

Another factor which was controlled was one which might best be labeled *salience*. That is, certain retarded children are highly visible even to the untrained and uneducated eye, while others would not be recognized by the casual observer. It is conceivable that this salience factor might affect the total family adjustment to the child. Mongoloid children were chosen to represent high salience in the retarded children, and in each group approximately half of the retarded children were mongoloid. Low-salience children were those who, in the opinion of professional persons having close contact with them, would not be identified as abnormal on the basis of physical appearance.

In addition to matching on the basis of characteristics of the retarded children, an attempt was made to match the home and institutional samples on the basis of certain total family characteristics. These included number of children in the family, maternal and paternal age, socio-economic status, and age and intelligence level of key siblings. Socio-economic status was determined by use of an abridgment of Eells' modification of Warner's Index of Status Characteristics(2). In Table 1 can be seen a summary of the characteristics of the total sample. While the matching is obviously not perfect, it is surprisingly good when one considers the difficulties ordinarily encountered in eliciting cooperation from families for a project dealing with such a "delicate" subject. On those items where statistical tests of difference (X^2 or t test) were appropriate, no difference was significant at the .05 level of probability or better.

Table 1 Characteristics of the Sample

	Home (N = 16)		Institution (N = 16)			
	Mean	Range	Mean	Range	D	t
Socio-economic status	15.8	4–21	17.0	8–24	1.2	.71*
Number of children in family	3.4	2–7	4.6	2–8	1.2	1.52
Maternal age	39.8	30–48	40.8	25–55	1.0	.41
Paternal age	43.3	34–55	42.3	30–60	1.1	.44
Age, retarded child	8.6	2–16	10.8	2–17	2.2	1.41
Age, sibling studied	13.3	6–19	11.4	6–15	1.9	1.50
IQ, retarded child	41.6	10–65	32.3	16–57	9.3	2.00
IQ, sibling studied	104.1	90–139	105.6	81–138	1.5	1.09
Length of institutionalization			5.6 years			
Sex, retarded child						
Male	6	—	11	—	—	—
Female	10	—	5	—	$X^2 = 3.1$*	—
Sex, sibling studied						
Male	10	—	6	—	—	—
Female	6	—	10	—	$X^2 = 2.0$	—
Relative ordinal position						
Retarded child older	4	—	8	—	—	—
Retarded child younger	12	—	8	—	$X^2 = 2.1$	—
Salience of retarded child						
High (mongoloid)	8	—	10	—	—	—
Low (non-mongoloid)	8	—	6	—	$X^2 = 0.5$	—

*All P-values are greater than .05. Where distributions were continuous, the t test was employed; for dichotomous variables, X^2 was the statistic used.

Certain features of the two organizations which co-operated in providing subjects made for some slight, if not statistically reliable, differences between the two samples. Most of the children brought to the clinic from which subjects were obtained are in the preschool or early school age group. The State institution, on the other hand, does not as a rule accept children younger than five. Furthermore it has a long waiting list, which means that most children are in the middle years or older at the time of institutionalization. Thus it was difficult to match exactly for age, and the retarded children in the institution are on the average somewhat older. However, the difference is not statistically significant. Further sampling difficulties were encountered in attempting to control for the age of the key siblings. In order to be able to use the same assessment techniques with all cases and to be assured of some understanding of the meaning of mental retardation, only those siblings between 10 and 16 were initially considered eligible; however, in the attempt to secure a large enough sample, this restriction was relaxed and a few siblings beyond those age limits in either direction were included. The ordinal position of the siblings studied was of particular importance in the institution families. In some cases it might have been possible to secure siblings who fell within the desired age range but who were so young at the time the retarded child was institutionalized that they might have essentially no knowledge of the total situation and of their sibling's retardation. Therefore, an attempt was made with the institutional families to secure as the key sibling the child in the family hierarchy who was either immediately older or immediately younger than the retarded child.

One other difference of some magnitude in Table I warrants comment. This is the difference in IQ level, significant at the .10 level, between the retarded children of the two samples. It should be stated that the difference is probably not as large as it actually appears, as four of the IQ's of the institutionalized retarded children represent estimated rather than exact measures. These are children who had not been tested within the institution but for whom the medical diagnosis of "mental deficiency, severe" or "mental deficiency, idiot" was found in the child's record. As different diagnosticians have different subjective frames of reference for the application of the labels "severe" or "idiot," there might actually be considerable disparity between the estimate of 25 used in the calculations in all these instances and the actual functioning level of the child. Also the difference

might simply represent the frequently reported lowering of intellectual functioning within an institutional setting, and the two groups would probably be quite comparable (judging from such items as socio-economic status of parents in both groups) if this factor could be eliminated.

Experimental Procedures

Mothers

The mother and the key sibling were seen separately. Procedures used with the mother were as follows:

1. *Psychiatric Interview.* The psychiatric evaluation consisted of a partially structured interview of approximately 40–45 minutes duration. Each interview was begun in the same way. The subject was thanked for her willingness to cooperate and was given a very brief outline of the purpose of the study. The mother was then asked for certain identifying data about the family—the names and ages of her children with identification of the retarded child. At this time, the mother was asked to tell the interviewer about the index child—when she first "realized something was wrong," "what happened," etc. The interviewer noted the descriptive term the mother used for her child (e.g., mongoloid, retarded, etc.), and for the remainder of the interview this term was always used by the interviewer. The mother was encouraged to give her own version of the child's history with an attempt made by the interviewer to have her elaborate upon her own emotional responses and those of her husband to the various events.

At the conclusion of the interview, ratings were made on seven four-point scales: mother's guilt, love for child, rejection of child, over-all emotional disturbance, over-all acceptance of the situation, general attitude toward husband, and family morale. Each of the seven areas covered by the ratings was deliberately investigated during the course of the interview more or less in the same order and by the same gambits. For example, as the mother described the realization of the fact of her child's retardation, she was asked to characterize her husband's reactions to the situation and to tell more about the kind of man he is, how he handles the children, etc. This led to a statement from the interviewer that it was his experience that many parents in such a situation felt guilty about the child's condition, adding that he wondered what the mother and her husband had experienced about this. This furnished a satisfactory formula for getting the mother to talk about any guilt. Other areas were introduced by similar observations and questions.

2. *Cornell Medical Index.* This is a screening questionnaire requiring a "yes" or "no" answer to 195 questions about health. Approximately one-third of the questions deal with psychiatric symptoms

3. *Family Attitude Scale.* This is a 22-item questionnaire devised by one of the authors (BMC) to elicit reaction of different family members to the presence of a handicapped child in the family. The scale permits four categories of agreement (strong agreement, mild agreement, mild disagreement, and strong disagreement) to statements which attempt to assess love for the child, rejection of the child, shame and embarrassment about the child's condition, awareness of the child's handicap, and a desire to help and assist the child. The scale is subject to all the advantages and limitations inherent in such instruments and in techniques such as the interview described above. Crucial to their use is the ease with which true feelings and reactions can be disguised or denied. In the present instance it was hoped that the circumstances under which they were administered would decrease any such tendency on the part of the mothers.

4. *Parental Attitude Research Instrument (PARI).* This is an inventory of attitudes toward child rearing and family life assembled by Schaefer and Bell (3). The form used in this project consists of 23 sub-scales of five items each, all of which have been shown to have satisfactory psychometric reliability. For this project, the sub-scales were grouped into six major areas, based on factor analyses carried out by the authors of the inventory (4), with predictions made in advance as to direction of differences which would be obtained between the two groups. As it generally takes at least an hour to complete this scale, the mothers were permitted to take it home with them and return it by mail to the authors. Although this procedure involved the customary attrition rate, enough forms were returned so that it was still possible to analyze the data in terms of the initial hypotheses.

5. *Attitude Research Supplement.* The authors felt that there were certain broad areas of attitudes not sampled in PARI that might be related to the decision of whether or not to institutionalize a retarded child. Accordingly a scale similar in form to PARI but sampling a different universe of attitudes was developed for this study. It was designed to measure attitude areas labeled by the authors Acceptance of the Female Role, Positive Attitudes toward Family Life, Desire for Social Conformity, Attitudes toward Religion, and Acceptance of Appropriate Sex Roles. It was predicted that mothers of the non-institutionalized children would score higher in all these scales except Drive for Social Conformity, where it was felt that mothers who institutionalize their children would score higher. Preliminary standardization of this scale was done on 26 students taking college courses in the evening division of Washington University. The individual items elicit a consistent mode of response, as test-retest reliabilities after an interval of two weeks for the 5 sub-scales ranged from .67 to .82, with a median of .78.

Key Siblings

Procedures used with the key siblings were as follows:

1. *Stanford-Binet Vocabulary Test.* This was administered to all children as a brief check on intelligence level. The Binet Vocabulary was chosen because it is applicable to an extremely wide age range and also because it involves having the subject give his answers orally, thus providing an opportunity for the sibling and the interviewer to begin talking to one another. The answers were taken down verbatim and scored later according to the criteria established by Terman and Merrill (6).

2. *Children's Manifest Anxiety Scale.* This is a 53-item questionnaire developed by Castaneda, McCandless, and Palermo (1) which is intended as a downward extension of the Taylor Manifest Anxiety Scale (5). The scale attempts to determine the number and type of symptoms indicative of manifest anxiety possessed by a child. It can be most appropriately used with children between the ages of nine and twelve. As can be noted in the range of sibling age given in Table I, some of the key siblings in both groups extended beyond this age range. However, as stated earlier, the authors originally planned to study siblings who fell within a narrower age range, and the

Table 2 Means, Differences and t Ratios for Institutional and Home Samples on Cornell Medical Index

	Home Sample	Institutional Sample	D	t*
Total score	25.6	27.4	1.8	.76
Psychiatric symptoms	7.4	9.3	1.9	.28

*P-values greater than .05; therefore neither of the differences is considered statistically reliable.

extension was permitted only when it became increasingly difficult to obtain a sufficiently large sample. Those siblings who were either too old or too young to respond to this scale were omitted from the analysis of the data.

3. *Structured Clinical Interview.* This interview was similar to the one conducted with the mother except that, as the title implies, it was more structured and followed a more uniform course. It was designed to elicit the feelings, memories, ideas, suggestions, etc., of the key siblings about certain crucial questions pertaining to their retarded siblings. The exact content of the interview will be made clear in the discussion of results obtained by this method.

Results

Mothers

In Table 2 are presented the results of the analysis of the Cornell Medical Index. The average number of symptoms in the mothers with institutionalized children was 27.4 and in the mothers of the children living in their homes was 25.6. The average number of specific psychiatric symptoms in the first group was 9.3 and 7.4 in the latter. These data reveal no significant differences between the two groups with respect to prevalence of medical or psychiatric symptoms.

Table 3 represents the results of the analysis of the psychiatric interview with the mothers. In this phase of the study the evaluation of the mothers through a clinical interview was utilized, even though the limitations of the method are fully appreciated by the authors. The ratings made were based entirely upon interview material without recourse to other information and data obtained in the research. Objective information available about the families in the school and clinic records was not utilized—e.g., frequency of visiting, which might be an indicator of rejection, in the Institutional sample. However, in almost all cases the interviewer knew whether the retarded child in the family was institutionalized or lived at home, as this would inevitably come out in the discussion.

First it should be noted that it was the interviewer's general clinical impression that there were no appreciable differences between the two groups of mothers. This impression was borne out by the data. The ratings were based on a four-point scale, with four indicating the most desirable point in each scale, i.e., least guilt, least rejection, most love, highest morale, etc. The values shown in Table 3 indicate that in both groups most of the mothers appeared to be adjusting well to the situation, were accepting the retardation and coping with it as effectively as could be expected, had relatively little guilt, expressed strong love for the children, had little rejec-

Table 3 Means, Differences and t Ratios for Institutional and Home Samples on Psychiatric Interview

	Home Sample	Institutional Sample	D	t*
Guilt	3.9	3.7	.2	.92
Love for child	3.5	3.5	.0	.00
Rejection of child	3.8	3.8	.0	.00
Mother's emotional disturbance	3.4	3.4	.0	.00
Acceptance of child	3.5	3.6	.1	.50
Attitude toward spouse	3.1	3.8	.7	2.04
Family morale	3.1	3.7	.6	1.84

*P-values greater than .05; therefore none of the differences is considered statistically reliable.

tion of the child, had positive attitudes toward their husbands, and that family morale was high.

The differences between ratings of Attitude toward Spouse and Family Morale for the two groups were significant between the .10 and .05 levels. Although the authors had decided in advance that only P-values of .05 or less would be accepted as significant, these differences are certainly suggestive. It had been anticipated that any differences found on these scales would be in the opposite direction. The trends found in these data therefore warrant further investigation.

In terms of psychiatric diagnosis, one of the mothers of the Institutional group was clearly an hysteric. One of the fathers in this group was probably schizophrenic, judging both from the mother's story and from clinical records. One of the other mothers in this group had had a depression of the manic-depressive variety some time after the birth of her mongoloid child. (This mother had also given birth to a second mongoloid child who had died almost immediately after birth.) In the Home group, two of the mothers had also had a manic-depressive depression some time after the birth of the retarded child.

Considering the small numbers involved, no definite conclusions may be drawn from these observations, but it would seem that psychiatric illness was no more prevalent in one group than in the other.

The interviewer was impressed by the nearly universal courage, strength, and adaptability of these mothers. There was the general impression that as a result of their experiences nearly all of the women were more sensitive and sympathetic to people with all kinds of problems and handicaps.

In Table 4 can be seen an analysis of the Family Attitude Scale, the Parental Attitude Research Instrument (PARI), and the Attitude Research Supplement. The results of the analysis of all these scales can be summarized very briefly by the statement that there were no clear differences between the two groups on the attitudes sampled.

Of these three scales, PARI is the only one for which ample standardization data are available, and a more detailed analysis of the responses of these groups of mothers of retarded children is in process. It had been predicted that mothers who make the decision to institu-

Table 4 Means, Differences and t Ratios for Institutional and Home Samples on Three Attitude Scales—Family Attitude Scale, Parent Attitude Research instrument (PARI), and Attitude Research Supplement

	Home Sample	Institutional Sample	D	t*
Family attitude scale	77.7+†	76.0	1.7	0.22
Parent Attitude Research Instrument (PARI)				
Suppression and interpersonal distance	11.4	12.6+	1.2	.82
Hostile rejection of the homemaking role	26.6	27.7+	1.1	.38
Excessive demand for striving	17.8+	20.7	2.9	1.81
Over-possessiveness	22.4+	24.3	1.9	.78
Harsh punitive control	30.9	33.1+	2.2	.83
Approval of positive attitudes toward child rearing	14.6+	14.1	.5	.29
Definitiveness of attitudes	46.0	58.8+	12.8	1.03
Attitude research supplement				
Acceptance of female role	18.6+	18.1	.5	.58
Positive family attitudes	23.1+	22.5	.6	.08
Drive for social conformity	22.4	21.6+	.8	.62
Attitudes toward religion	20.9+	20.5	.4	.42
Acceptance of appropriate sex role	13.2+	13.3	.1	.89

*P-values greater than .05; differences not statistically reliable.
†Plus-marks indicate predicted higher scores for a given group on the sub-scales.

tionalize their retarded children, as contrasted to those who do not make this decision, would perhaps have discriminably different sets of attitudes toward child rearing that might led them toward this decision. Specifically it was predicted that the mothers of the institutionalized children would score higher on factors of Suppression and Interpersonal Distance, Hostile Rejection of the Homemaking Role, and Harsh Punitive Control. Also it was predicted that the mothers of the institutional sample would score higher in terms of decisiveness of attitudes—i.e., that they would have more strong agreements and disagreements than would the mothers of the non-institutionalized sample. Higher scores for mothers whose retarded children lived at home were predicted on the factors of Excessive Demand for Striving, Over-Possessiveness, and Approval of Positive Attitudes toward Child Rearing. These differences did not emerge in the analysis, and one would have to conclude that no drastic differences in attitudes toward child rearing exist in the two groups of mothers. The very fact that the one group is able to make the decision to institutionalize (while other parents vacillate about it for years) led to the prediction that the Institutional group would be more decisive in its attitudes toward child rearing (reflected by a greater number of "strong agreement" and "strong disagreement" responses to the scale). The difference was in the expected direction but was not statistically significant.

Key Siblings

Table 5 shows the results of the analysis of the Children's Manifest Anxiety Scale in the two groups of key siblings. This measure was chosen in an attempt to determine if the children who had retarded children living in the home would show a greater number of signs of anxiety than would children whose retarded siblings were "out of sight," as it were. Such a finding would tend to support the frequently espoused opinion that the presence of such a handicapped child in the home "harms" the other normal children in the home. As can be seen in Table 5, the slight difference found between the two groups is in the opposite direction—i.e., the children whose retarded sibs live in the institution show a slightly greater number of symptoms. However, the magnitude of the difference is not large enough to be statistically reliable.

In setting up an interview form to be used with the siblings, the authors were more concerned with adjust-

Table 5 Comparison of Scores on the Children's Manifest Anxiety Scale for the Siblings of the Home and the Institutional Sample

	Home Sample (N = 15)	Institutional Sample (N = 14)	D	t*
Score	11.2	15.1	3.9	1.44

*P-value greater than .05; difference not statistically reliable

ment *to* the situation than with adjustment *of* the siblings. Some of the most interesting material in the study emerged from the responses of the siblings to this structured interview. A skeleton form of the open-ended elicitors used by the interviewer is presented as Table VI. Wording of the questions as presented in the table was varied as required by the individual case. Also the questions were not necessarily presented in exactly the order as set up on the interview form.

Unfortunately the interview material cannot be condensed to a brief statistical table; nor can all the data be presented in detail. Accordingly the authors have chosen to summarize the qualitative material and to make quantitative comparisons whenever possible.

A few words should be said about the generalized reactions of the siblings. A few of the younger ones in each group evinced such limited comprehension of the total situation in casual preliminary conversation that the formal interview was not conducted for fear of upsetting the children. (This lack of comprehension or denial, as the case may be, was found in these children even though, in every instance, the mother had indicated that the key sibling understood about his brother's or sister's condition and would not mind talking about it.) Elimination of these younger children left 12 siblings in the Institutional sample and 13 siblings in the home sample.

Among these siblings, the over-all reactions ranged from a strictly casual, matter-of-fact approach ("There's nothing particularly special about having a retarded child in the family") to opposite poles of vehemence—i.e., to enthusiasm and appreciation for the opportunity to talk to someone about the problem or else to open hostility or sullenness. Several of the siblings, particularly those from the Institutional sample, appeared anxious at the beginning of the interview but in almost all instances

Table 6 Structured Interview used with Siblings of Retarded Children

1. When did you first become aware that there was anything "different" about X?
2. What did you notice?
3. How did you feel at the time?
4. What explanation did your parents give you?
5. Did the explanation satisfy you?
6. Did you talk to anyone else about it?
7. Do you think X understands anything about his condition?
8. Does X ask questions about why he can't do things other children do?
9. What do you think is the ideal way for parents to handle the explanation to brothers and sisters?
10. Have your friends asked questions about X?
11. What do you tell them?
12. Do you think you have fewer friends because of X?
13. Do all the brothers and sisters in the family react in pretty much the same way?
14. Do your mother and father feel about the same way about X?
15. There are probably some good and some bad effects on the family when there is a handicapped child in the home. Tell me some good effects that X has had on your family.
16. Now tell me some of the bad effects.
17. I want you to tell me honestly whether you think it is better for children like X to live at home or in some kind of training school or state institution.
18. What do you think would happen to X if something happened to your mother and father?
19. Tell me something that happened recently in connection with X that made you very unhappy or mad.
20. Now I want you to tell me something that happened recently in connection with X that made you very happy or pleased you a great deal.
21. Are there any other comments you would like to make?

relaxed as they realized that there was to be nothing really traumatic in the session. One or two of the siblings of the Institutional sample echoed their mothers' concern that selection for inclusion in the study might in some way be related to possible discharge of the retarded child from the Training School. In these cases there may have been too much protesting of the virtues of the institutional way of life lest negative comments encourage the Training School staff to send the child home. Extra effort was then taken to assure these children that there was no official connection between the research and the management of the institution.

One of the first topics covered in the interview was the age at which the sibling had become aware of his brother's or sister's retardation. It would seem that the siblings of retarded children living at home become aware of the nature of the problem earlier than do siblings of those children placed in an institution. For several of the brothers and sisters of the institutional children there

was an air of mystery about Training School placement which they did not understand for several years. As one child phrased it, "I didn't even know why she had to live out here until one of the sisters (nuns) at school told me." Or again, in one extreme case, "I didn't know I had this sister out here until last year." In general the siblings of the Home group who were able to respond to this question indicated that they just "always knew," and, since they had grown up with the problem in a more uninterrupted fashion, it was often more difficult for them to pinpoint just when they learned about their sibling's condition and understood the implications. In both groups, certain aspects of motor development, particularly speech, were most likely to be first noticed as the clue that something was wrong with their brother or sister. Many of the children had difficulty trying to describe their feelings *at the time* they learned of their sibling's retardation, a difficulty which was often related to their inability to remember just when they actually became aware of the condition. In other words, past and present feelings were so subtly blended that it was difficult to get meaningful answers to the question about how they felt at the time they learned about the retarded child's condition. The one emotion most frequently mentioned by the siblings in the Institutional sample was some variant of curiosity or wonderment, while an inability to denote any specific reaction was most characteristic of the Home sample. When they could specify an emotional reaction, it was most likely to be to the effect that they "loved the child anyway."

The two groups apparently had rather similar experiences with respect to parental explanation about etiology with a few minor but significant exceptions. Explanations in terms of trauma or illness were common in both groups. There appeared to be a greater tendency on the part of the parents of the Institutional sample to stress the hopelessness of the situation (e.g., that the child could never be normal or that nothing could be done) than was true in the Home group. There were a few children in both groups who either asserted that they were never given any kind of explanation, even though they had very much wanted one, or else that if one had been given they could not remember it. In view of the current semantic confusion rampant in this field regarding appropriate terminology, it is interesting to note that many of the youngsters spontaneously used the term "mentally retarded" either in describing the way the problem was explained to them or the way they had explained it to others. Apparently this is the most acceptable designation to this very important group of young people.

Approximately equal numbers in the two groups felt that the explanations they had received satisfied them, but a larger number of the siblings of the Institutional sample nevertheless found it necessary to talk to someone other than the parents for further explanations (8 as compared to 1 in the Home group). This may possibly indicate somewhat better rapport between parents and children in the Home sample, but it may also reflect the fact that when a decision is made to institutionalize a child, there is something sufficiently definite which warrants more "talking out" of the problem than is called for when the situation is handled as part of the daily living process without, in many instances, even being designated as a family problem.

Two questions which elicited different patterns of responses were those pertaining to whether the sibling felt that the retarded child understood anything about his own condition and, if so, how this awareness was revealed. Almost all the siblings of the Home group felt that their brothers and sisters were unaware of their condition, usually stressing that the family had taken pains to see to it that this was the case and to treat the child just like every other child in the family. On the other hand, about half of the siblings of the Institutional group indicated that their brothers or sisters seemed puzzled by their own conditions and often indicated their bewilderment by asking repetitive questions, such as why they could not live at home or why the siblings had certain things they could not have, etc. Apparently here is one area where there is a real difference between the groups, but the difference is in the retarded children and not in the key siblings.

There was very little basic difference between the responses of the two groups to the question pertaining to the ideal way in which parents should handle the explanation about a retarded child to his brothers and sisters. Only one child in either group felt that the siblings should not be told anything. ("Don't tell them anything; it might make them wonder too much.") Most of the children expressed—often quite vehemently—exactly the opposite point of view, namely, that they would be very resentful if the family had not told them.

Practically all the children in both groups indicated that their friends had asked questions about the retarded child in the family, with the main exceptions being three children in the Institutional sample who indicated quite candidly that their friends did not know about the retarded child living in the institution. One adolescent boy in the Home sample remarked that he was careful to see to it that his boy friends understood about his sister, bringing up the subject himself if they did not inquire. He then added that he had never brought a girl to his house for fear of what her reaction would be. None of the siblings in either group felt that they had fewer friends because of their retarded brother or sister.

Two of the questions pertained to the similarity of reaction in the total family group. Here there was greater solidarity among the Institutional sample. Eleven of the 12 felt that all the brothers and sisters felt the same way about the retarded child, and 10 of the 12 indicated that the parental reaction was harmonious. This undoubtedly reflects the low probability that a child will actually be placed in an institution unless both parents agree that this is the best solution. In the Home group there were many children who felt that they simply did not know if all the brothers and sisters reacted in the same way (in some instances the question was not appropriate, as there might be only the two children in the family). However, there was in this group also a perception of solidarity on the part of the parents. Thus perhaps it is not out of order to conclude that by and large the difficult decision about whether to institutionalize a retarded child will not be a unilateral one but one about which both parents must agree before a definite course of action is taken. Also it is worth commenting here on the rather amazing sophistication with which some of these young people could discuss the reactions of their parents.

The request for information on good and bad effects the retarded child might have had on the total family elicited some very interesting responses. In terms of good effects, several answers could be categorized as making the families more understanding of the problems of handicapped children. Many of the children commented that, as a result of their own personal experience with the problem, they were now more understanding of the problems of all retarded children and of people with other kinds of difficulties. Several in both groups expressed the conviction that family cohesiveness had been increased as a result of the presence of the retarded child in the family. In one case the sibling expressed the conviction that the family would have dissolved long ago had it not been for the presence of the retarded child who, because of her greater helplessness and needs for special care, had held the family together. Also frequently mentioned was an increased appreciation of religious values. In each group one child demonstrated the sine qua non of acceptance in response to this item—the retarded child was fun to be with and brought pleasure to the family. Bad effects most frequently mentioned were the extra expense of institution or school, medical bills, explanations to friends, and extra work for some member of the family, usually the mother. There were 5 children in the Home group and 8 in the Institutional sample who felt they could not specify any bad effects.

Probably the one question on which the two groups could be most clearly differentiated was the one asking for an opinion on whether it is better for retarded children to live at home or in a training school. In presenting this question, the interviewer requested their candid opinion, regardless of how the problem had been handled in their own families. Nevertheless, the answers seemed to parallel existing family policy. Eleven of the 12 siblings of the Institutional sample indicated without hesi-

tation or qualification that they felt it was better for retarded children to live in an institution. Only one of the siblings of the Home sample gave this response. Among the siblings of the Home sample there was more equivocation ("Sometimes I think one and sometimes I think the other") and perhaps a little more evasiveness. At the same time, there was also more vehemence in several instances about how wrong it is to deprive *any* child of the opportunity to live at home and receive the care, training, and love of his parents and brothers and sisters. The siblings of the Institutional sample often seemed quite defensive on this point, justifying their answer with the opinion that the retarded child could learn more in the institution or else that he would be happier among "other children like himself." Also, at the end of the interview when asked if there was anything else they might like to say, many of the Institutional sibs commented spontaneously on how wonderful they thought it was that such institutions were available. The question, "What do you think would happen to X if something happened to your mother and father," elicited some anxiety in several of the older children (who had obviously worried some about this very contingency) and in general was omitted in interviews with the younger ones. It was apparent that many of the siblings of the institutionalized children had given this no thought but had taken for granted the continued residence of their brother or sister in the Training School. ("I thought that once they accepted them here they kept them here as long as they lived.") Three of the siblings of the Institutional sample, after thinking about the question for a moment, indicated that one of the *other* siblings in the family would then assume responsibility; none said that he or she would do so. Relatively few of the siblings in the Home sample admitted having given any thought to this anxiety-producing contingency either. Two indicated that they guessed the retarded child would then have to go to a "school or home," usually offering some apologetic explanation for this action, such as "I would be in college and wouldn't be able to take care of her." Two of the siblings in the Home sample, however, indicated without hesitation that they felt it would be their responsibility to care for the retarded child. One 13-year-old girl, two years younger than her retarded sister, already had a very elaborate life plan worked out to cover such an emergency. In that particular family the parents were divorced, and the father had never been able to accept the older daughter's retardation. The sibling had selected nursing as her vocational goal in order to work in a residential school for the retarded so that her sister could live with her. The girl followed this rather elaborately described plan with the statement, "My sister and I have been together for 13 years, and there would be no reason for this to stop if something happened to my mother."

The last two questions requested the siblings to relate some recent experience (critical incident) associated with the retarded child that had made the siblings very unhappy or mad or very happy and pleased. The "unhappy or mad" incidents related by the two groups were very similar, with some kind of personal inconvenience caused by the retarded child leading the list in both groups. (E.g., "He scratched me the last time he was home," or "I had to stay home and watch him when all my friends were going to a movie.") While there was a modal incident for the Home sample on the "happy or pleased" incident, no such patterning could be found for the Institutional group. Ten of the siblings of the Home group related some incident that suggested progress or improvement for their brother or sister. For instance, one child reported, "He went to school for the first time and brought home a pot holder he had made, and that made me very happy." Again it was felt that this represented a real difference between the groups, as the siblings of the Institutional sample seemed to share the parental need not to be able to see improvement in the retarded children. Again, however, it should be stated that any generalizations must take into consideration the small sample and the possibly greater defensiveness of the siblings of the Institutional group.

One final bit of data pertaining to the sibling interview can be presented here. At the completion of each interview, the interviewer rated each child on a 4-point scale of *level of positive affect* shown for the retarded child (low numbers indicating minimal and high numbers indicating maximum positive affect). Such ratings are, of course, subject to the same limitations previously described for the ratings made following the psychiatric interviews with the mothers. The average rating assigned to siblings of the Home group was 3.0, while that in the Institutional group was 2.3. The difference between these two ratings is not statistically reliable (t = 1.63), again illustrating the espoused generalization that the two groups were, in most respects, more alike than different.

Discussion

The procedures used in this study failed to detect any impressive differences between the two groups studied. Mothers and siblings of retarded children living at home were not significantly better adjusted than were mothers and siblings of retarded children who have been removed from the home and placed in a state institution, or vice versa. At this point mention should again be made of the fact that the adjustment of the retarded children in these families was not investigated in this research; whether those living at home were significantly better adjusted themselves than those living in the institution is not known.

The results of this study should offer some reassurance to those groups trying to work out programs of care for the retarded which take into consideration the welfare of the entire family as well as that of the retarded child. They fail to buttress either of the partisan theories about *the* best living arrangement for retarded children when considered from the point of view of family members other than the retarded children themselves. However, the results should not be interpreted as indicating that in individual cases the choice of institution or home might not affect the adjustment of various family members. At least two mothers of the Institutional sample spoke to the investigators about improvements in the behavior of one or more siblings following the institutionalization of the retarded child. On the other hand, one mother spoke of the problems that had arisen with one of her children after institutionalization of the retarded child. No more than speculation is possible about the meaning of this experience to the normal children in the family, but it might be possible to arouse fears of rejection in any child whenever one child in the family is "sent away" from home.

One possible explanation of lack of significant differences in the siblings of the two groups is that certain selective factors operated to minimize whatever adjustmental differences actually existed. For example, in families where there is more than one unaffected sibling, one or another might react differently. Even though this may be true, every attempt was made to permit such selective factors to operate equally in both groups (e.g., by controlling for ordinal position with respect to the retarded child).

A Study of the Adjustment of Parents and Siblings   Bettye M. Caldwell and Samuel B. Guze

One finding of particular interest emerged from the psychiatric interview. This was the lack of difference between the ratings of "rejection" and "guilt" for the mothers in the two groups. If an objective criterion of rejection were to be sought, scarcely a better one could be found than actual expulsion of a child from the home. It would seem to follow logically that such an act would predispose the parents to stronger feelings of guilt than would be found where no such "rejection" had occurred. Yet the ratings made in these two areas were virtually identical in the two groups of mothers. One can find in this result some validity for the claims made by parents who institutionalize a retarded child that they do not love their child any the less but that they are merely seeking a realistic solution for what is at best a difficult family problem.

When interpreting between-group comparisons which might be expected to yield differences but which do not, one can either assume that no real differences exist or else that real differences exist but that they were not revealed by the methods employed. In the present study the findings of more similarities than differences might be challenged as spurious on methodological grounds. For one thing, no depth techniques were used. Perhaps it is unrealistic to hope to be able to obtain undisguised parental and sibling feelings about such an affect-laden situation as relationships with a retarded child when only straight-forward, objective, and possibly rather superficial techniques are employed. For example, the psychiatric ratings were based on only a single interview, and no projective techniques were used to probe deeper feelings for the siblings. While such a point of view has some merit, the so-called "depth" techniques are notoriously difficult to employ as research tools. However, in any repetition or extension of this study, it might be advisable to include more of such techniques in the research battery.

Also worthy of consideration in any repetition of the study would be the inclusion of more external criteria of adjustment. This was attempted briefly in the interview with the mothers by simply inquiring whether they had ever had treatment for any psychiatric disorder. However, as self-reports tend to minimize material that would reveal socially undesirable characteristics of the subject, this reporting may be biased. Also with the siblings the use of ratings by teachers and classmates would be helpful.

One final point which may be of relevance in accounting for the lack of difference between the two groups is the fact that one must always consider the possibility that the two groups are not really independent—i.e., that the Home sample is really an extension of the Institutional sample. While the subjects used in the Home group had not *at the time* of the study institutionalized their retarded child (and had disavowed any intention of doing so unless forced to by unforeseen circumstances), this does not necessarily guarantee that they would never do so. Thus they might be potential members of the Institutional sample, with no really distinct characteristics apart from those created by certain external factors (such as lack of success in arranging for institutionalization). Although this is a possibility to be considered, the fact remains that at the time of the study the retarded children in the one group resided in the institution and the retarded children in the other sample resided in their own homes. If a cross-sectional definition of the two groups be accepted—and this is really the only meaningful one—the two groups would have to be considered dichotomous and not overlapping. Also it should be noted that the potential crossing over of subjects from one group to the other would be of importance only for the observations made of the mothers; with the siblings the variable under consideration was whether the current presence, regardless of continuation for some prescribed period of time, of a retarded child in the home raised the manifest anxiety level of his siblings.

Summary

This study reports an attempt to investigate the reactions of mothers and siblings of two groups of retarded children: (1) a group residing in their own homes with their families at the time of the study and (2) a group living in a state institution for the retarded. The purpose of the study was to shed some light on the perennially raised question of whether, from the point of view of the rest of the family, it is "better" for retarded children to live at home or in a residential care program. Included in the research procedures used with the mothers were a psychiatric interview, a health questionnaire, and several attitude scales chosen to elicit maternal attitudes toward child rearing in general and to retarded children in particular. Techniques used with the siblings included a brief vocabulary test, a scale of manifest anxiety, and a lengthy structured interview designed to elicit feelings, memories, and cognitions related to the experience of having a retarded child for a brother or sister. Although the retarded children represented by the families were not directly studied themselves, matching of the two samples was done primarily in terms of characteristics of the retarded children.

Careful analysis of the data failed to reveal any striking differences between either the mothers or the siblings in the two groups. One notable exception to this generalization was found in the opinions of the siblings regarding the ideal living arrangement for retarded children. Almost without exception the ideas of the brothers and sisters mirrored the family decision—i.e., siblings of the Institutional sample felt it better for retarded children to live away from home, while those of the Home sample expressed their conviction that it was better to have the children live at home. This finding suggests that adolescents and pre-adolescents who have had the experience of a retarded child in the family are generally adaptable and that they can mold their value systems in this matter to conform to the family status quo. This would seem to be an important principle for parents to grasp.

On the basis of the findings of this study, the generalization is offered that the type of living arrangement made for a retarded child is not crucial for the adjustment of either the mother or the siblings. This study sheds no light on the equally important question of whether the experience of having a retarded child in the family, regardless of the type of living arrangement made for him, adversely affects the psychological adjustment of the parents or the siblings—i.e., whether parents or siblings of retarded children show a poorer adjustment than a comparable sample drawn from families in which there is no retarded child. In terms of the criteria used in the research, neither of the opposing points of view about whether it is best to keep a retarded child at home with the family or to institutionalize him finds support. If the decision about institutionalization is to be based largely upon the possible effects the retarded child will have on the other children in the family, then the reactions of the young people interviewed in this study should be of considerable interest. The suggestion is offered that par-

ents (and professional workers who may be called upon for counsel) can learn much from the attitudes and feelings of the group of siblings who cooperated in this study.

Note

[1]The authors wish to thank Dr. A. A. Hines, Medical Director of the St. Louis Training School, Mrs. Lucille Egen, Director of Egen-Tudor School, and Mrs. Nancy Holsen, Research Assistant in the Child Evaluation Clinic for their assistance in securing subjects for this study.

References

Castaneda, A., McCandless, B. R., and Palermo, D. S. "The Children's Form of the Manifest Anxiety Scale," *Child Development*, 1956. 27:3, 317–326.

Eells, K., Davis, A., Havighurst, R. J., Herrick, V. E., and Tyler, R. W. *Intelligence and Cultural Differences: A Study of Cultural Learning and Problem-solving.* Chicago, University of Chicago Press, 1951.

Schaefer, E. S., and Bell, R. Q. "Parental Attitude Research Instrument (PARI), Normative Data." Unpublished manuscript. Library, National Institutes of Health, Bethesda, Md., 1955.

Schaefer, E. S., and Bell, R. Q. "Structure of Attitudes toward Child-rearing and the Family," *Journal of Abnormal and Social Psychology*, 1957. 54, 391–395.

Taylor, Janet A. "The Relationship of Anxiety to the Conditioned Eyelid Response," *Journal of Experimental Psychology*, 1951. 41, 81–89.

Terman, L. M., and Merrill, Maud A. *Measuring Intelligence.* New York, Houghton Mifflin Company, 1937.

From the Child Evaluation Clinic and the Department of Psychiatry and Neurology of the Washington University School of Medicine, St. Louis, Missouri.

Authors

Bettye M. Caldwell and **Samuel B. Guze**

Influence of Selected Child Characteristics on Stress in Families of Handicapped Infants

Paula J. Beckman
1983

Abstract

Parents of 31 handicapped infants were interviewed to determine the extent to which specific kinds of behavior and characteristics of the child were related to the stress reported by mothers. Five characteristics were examined: rate of child progress, responsiveness, temperament, repetitive behavior patterns, and the presence of additional or unusual caregiving demands. All characteristics except rate of progress were significantly related to the amount of stress reported. The only demographic characteristic associated with the amount of stress reported was the number of parents in the home. Single mothers reported more stress than mothers in intact homes.

In recent years, researchers and interventionists have become increasingly interested in the parents and families of handicapped children. Although the focus of this interest has varied, one body of literature suggests that families of handicapped children often experience added stress (Beckman-Bell, 1981; Cummings, 1976; Cummings, Bayley, & Rie, 1966; Farber, 1959; Fotheringham & Creal, 1974; Friedrich & Friedrich, 1981; Gallagher, Beckman-Bell, & Cross, in press). Stress has been defined by Rabkin and Struening (1976) as an individual's response to events or changes that alter his or her social setting. This response may consist of one or more physiological or psychological reactions that can be both immediate and delayed. Thus, a number of responses, such as increased financial difficulties, marital problems, depression, and isolation, among others, have been considered indicators of high levels of stress (Farber, 1959; Farber & Ryckman, 1965; Gallagher et al., in press; Holroyd, 1974).

Despite evidence that stress may be a crucial factor in the lives of many families of handicapped children, little work has been carried out that systematically investigates factors associated with increased family stress. Findings from a limited number of studies suggest that certain characteristics of the child may be related to the amount of stress reported by parents. Variations in the amount of stress have been reported as a function of the child's diagnosis (Cummings, 1976; Cummings et al., 1966; Holroyd & McArthur, 1976). For example, Holroyd and McArthur (1976) found differences in the amount of stress reported by families of children who were autistic, had Down syndrome, and were outpatients in a psychiatric clinic. Other studies suggest that more family stress tends to occur in families of older handicapped children and that boys tend to be more stressful than girls (Bristol, 1979; Farber, 1959). Taken together, these studies provide valuable evidence suggesting that specific characteristics of handicapped children may influence the amount of stress the family experiences. For the most part, however, the characteristics that have been identified are relatively unalterable. It is unclear how other, more alterable characteristics are related to family stress. Such information could be valuable to educators and clinicians interested in assisting families of handicapped children.

Further, little information is available concerning stress in families of very young, handicapped children. Most studies have been focused on older children (Bristol, 1979; Farber, 1959). Since families of young children may only have known about the child's handicap for a short period of time, they may be experiencing a great deal of stress as a result of their initial attempts to cope with this information. Moreover, if characteristics and behavior of the child do contribute to parental stress, this early period may be critical to interventionists working with the family.

Thus, the present study was designed to determine whether specific characteristics of handicapped infants were associated with the amount of parent and family stress reported by mothers. I hypothesized that the amount of stress reported would be related to: (a) slower rate of development; (b) less social responsiveness; (c) more difficult temperament; (d) more repetitive, stereotypic behavior patterns; and (e) additional or unusual caregiving demands.

Method

Subjects

Subjects were 31 handicapped infants (9 females, 22 males) enrolled in a parent-based intervention program and their mothers. Infants ranged from 6.6 to 36.6 months of age (mean = 21.6, standard deviation [SD] = 8.04) and had been receiving intervention for a minimum of 3 months prior to their participation in the study. All had some identified, organic involvement that varied with respect to type (e.g., Down syndrome, cerebral palsy, spina bifida) and severity (mild to profound). Although an entire range of socioeconomic circumstances were represented, the bulk of the sample was white (n = 30) and middle class (Hollingshead Four Factor Index of Social Position, mean = 37.66, SD = 14.25). Approximately 26 percent of the families (n = 8) had only one parent present in the home. Mothers ranged from 19 to 39 years of age (mean = 28.4, SD = 4.81).

Procedure

Mothers were interviewed using several instruments. The Questionnaire on Resources and Stress (Holroyd, 1974) the primary measure used, is a 285-item questionnaire specifically designed to measure stress in families of handicapped children. Scores are obtained on 15 separate scales that can be summed to yield a total stress score. Three subscores can also be computed. The first, Parent Problems, deals specifically with problems of the individual parent as they relate to the handicapped child. The second, Family Problems, concerns problems experienced by the entire family. The last subscale, Child Problems, relates specifically to the problems of the child. For this study, the total number of parent and family problems was used as the index of stress.

Attempts to establish the validity of the Questionnaire on Resources and Stress have been limited, although successful. The questionnaire distinguishes among families of children with differing diagnoses (Holroyd & McArthur, 1976) and between families of institutionalized vs. noninstitutionalized children (Holroyd, 1974). Holroyd (1974) investigated the relationship between interviewer ratings of family stress and maternal responses on the Questionnaire. Families that were classified by interviewers as high stress scored higher on five Questionnaire on Resources and Stress scales than did those classified as low stress. Although no attempts to establish reliability have been reported, Bristol (1979)

conducted a study of stress in families of autistic children and reported mean scores on each of the 15 scales that were remarkably similar to those presented by Holroyd and McArthur (1976).

Mothers also completed a modified version of the Holmes and Rahe Schedule of Recent Experience, which is a checklist composed of 43 items pertaining to events that imply change in the respondent's life. It was chosen to provide a measure of stress that may exist in the family that is unrelated to the presence of a handicapped child. Holmes and Rahe (1967) found that diverse groups of judges were consistent when asked to judge the stressfulness of each item. The original scale requires subjects to indicate which of 43 life changes occurred in the last 6 months, year, 2 years, and 3 years. Weighted values are assigned and the scores are summed. In this study, an adaptation described by Bristol (1979) was utilized in which the respondents were asked to indicate which of the events occurred within the last 2 years. This technique yields a weighted, global measure of the life changes the family experienced.

Within 2 weeks of the interview, infants were observed during standard teaching sessions. Teaching sessions lasted about one hour and involved the infant, mother, and teacher. Teachers worked primarily on sensorimotor and language activities and assisted the mother in learning to carry out these activities. After the session, mothers and observers independently completed the Carolina Record of Infant Behavior (Simeonsson[1]), a rating scale designed to measure behavioral characteristics of young handicapped children. For purposes of this study, only observer ratings were used. This instrument has been adapted in part from the Infant Behavior Record of the Bayley Scales of Infant Development. Validity and reliability have been established and are presented in numerous reports (Blacher-Dixon & Simeonsson, 1981; Parse, 1982; Simeonsson, Huntington, Short, & Ware, 1982).

The Carolina Record of Infant Behavior was chosen because it provides an observational measure of three of the five child characteristics. Eight items were selected on an a priori basis to measure infant responsiveness. In the present study, responsiveness was viewed as the way infants responded to various forms of social stimulation. Items included responsiveness to persons, participation with examiner, expressive communication, receptive communication, responsiveness to caregiver, responsiveness to examiner, sound production, and affective behavior. Responsiveness scores were computed by orienting all items in the same direction and computing a mean across the eight items. The possible range of scores was from one to nine, with a nine indicating that the baby was very responsive. Temperament was viewed as the child's behavioral style and consisted of seven items from the Carolina Record of Infant Behavior: fearfulness, endurance, consolability, activity, reactivity, response to frustration, and attention span. Mean scores were also computed for temperament, with a possible range from one to nine. A score of nine indicated an "easy" temperament. Items in the repetitive behavior domain included 14 types of behavior, such as head banging, finger flicking, and other self-stimulatory behavioral patterns. Mean scores were also computed, with a possible range of one to five. A score of five indicated more repetitive behavior.

After initial training in use of the Carolina Record of Infant Behavior with several pilot subjects, two observers viewed 22 percent ($n = 7$) of the teaching sessions and independently completed the Carolina Record of Infant Behavior. Reliability estimates were determined using Pearson product-moment correlations and ranged from .823 to .981 (mean = .919). Thus, interrater reliability was judged sufficiently high to proceed with remaining analyses. In addition, since items were assigned to behavioral domains solely for the purposes of this study, an analysis of internal consistency was conducted for each of the three behavior domains. Coefficient alphas for the responsiveness, temperament, and repetitive behavior patterns were .86, .77, and .68, respectively.

Mothers and observers also independently completed an 11-item caregiving checklist, which I designed to tap the number of additional or unusual caregiving needs in the areas of feeding, handling, or medical considerations. For this study, only observer responses to the caregiving checklist were used as the measure of additional or unusual caregiving demands. Reliability estimates between two outside observers was obtained for 30 percent ($N = 10$) of the sample and ranged from .54 to 1.00 (mean = .81). (Copies of the checklist are available from the author upon request.)

Data from Bayley assessments collected as part of the child's ongoing program were used to measure the child's rate of development. To determine this rate, I subtracted the child's developmental age at the time of the first Bayley from the developmental age at the time of the most recent Bayley and divided by the number of months between assessments.

Results

The general approach to data analysis was correlational. Mean scores and SDs for each Questionnaire on Resources and Stress subscale are presented in Table 1. In these analyses, the total number of parent and family problems reported by mothers on the Questionnaire was used as the primary measure of stress. In addition, the weighted total obtained on the modified version of the Schedule of Recent Experience was also used as an index of stress.

Table 1 Means and SDs on Individual Subscores of the Questionnaire on Resources and Stress

Subscale	Mean	SD
Parent Problems		
Poor health/mood	3.61	2.44
Excess time demands	6.84	2.82
Negative attitude toward child	8.35	3.79
Overprotection	5.03	2.34
Lack of social support	3.58	1.65
Overcommitment	3.52	1.18
Pessimism	3.26	1.65
Family Problems		
Lack of family integration	3.71	3.25
Limits on family opportunities	1.81	2.07
Financial problems	5.29	3.29
Child Problems		
Physical incapacitation	6.45	1.96
Lack of activities for child	.84	1.07
Occupational limitations for child	4.19	2.05
Social obtrusiveness	2.13	1.06
Difficult personality characteristics	11.90	3.85

Correlations between the measures of stress and measures of the child characteristics are presented in Table 2. Four of the child characteristics (temperament, responsiveness, repetitive behavioral patterns, and caregiving demands) were significantly related to the amount of stress reported by mothers on the Questionnaire on Resources and Stress but not significantly related to the amount of stress reported on the Schedule of Recent Experience. Further, the amount of stress re-

Influence of Selected Child Characteristics on Stress in Families of Handicapped Infants   Paula J. Beckman

Table 2 Intercorrelations between Measures of Stress and Measures of Child Characteristics

Measure	1	2	3	4	5	6
Stress						
1. QRS[a]-Parent and Family Problems						
2. Schedule of Recent Experience	.27					
Child characteristics						
3. Extra caregiving demands	.81***	.12				
4. Social responsiveness	−.74***	−.21	−.68***			
5. Temperament	−.76***	−.15	−.75***	.83***		
6. Repetitive behavior	.52**	.08	.35*	.38*	−.43*	
7. Rate of progress[b]	−.22	.14	−.45*	.29	.23	−.39*

[a] Questionnaire on Resources and Stress.
[b] Correlations based on $n = 30$.
  * $p < .05$.
  ** $p < .01$.
  *** $p < .001$.

ported by mothers on each of the two scales was not significantly related.

One possible explanation for the high correlation between total caregiving demands and the number of parent and family problems was that the subscale (Excess Time Demands) from the Questionnaire on Resources and Stress contained information that overlapped that measured by the caregiving checklist. This possibility was tested by subtracting scores obtained on this subscale from the total Parent and Family problems score. The correlation coefficient between this adapted score and the total number of additional or unusual caregiving demands was .77, $p < .001$.

Intercorrelations among the five child characteristics are also presented in Table 2. With only two exceptions, all child characteristics were significantly associated with one another. Rate of progress was not associated with social responsiveness or temperament. Particularly strong associations were found between temperament and social responsiveness, temperament and caregiving demands, and caregiving demands and social responsiveness.

A series of post hoc analyses were conducted to determine the relationship between the amount of stress mothers reported and relevant demographic variables. Specifically, correlations were obtained between the two measures of stress and the family's score on the Hollingshead Four Factor Index of Social Position, maternal age, number of siblings, and number of parents. Results of these correlations indicated that the number

of parents in the home was associated with the amount of stress reported on the Questionnaire on Resources and Stress, $r = −.37$, and the Schedule of Recent Experiences, $r = −.43$, both significant at $p < .05$, but was not associated with the other demographic variables.

Finally, post hoc analyses were conducted to determine the relationship between two additional child characteristics reported in previous studies and the stress reported by mothers. First, a t test for unequal sample sizes was used to determine whether there was a significant difference between the amount of stress reported by mothers of boys and that reported by mothers of girls. A significant difference was not obtained. In addition, the results of a correlation between the child's age and the amount of stress reported also yielded no significant relationship.

Discussion

In general, results of the present study confirmed the hypothesis that there would be a significant relationship between specific characteristics of handicapped infants and the amount of stress reported by parents. Significant correlations were obtained between the Questionnaire on Resources and Stress and all child characteristics except rate of progress. Moreover, all correlations were in the expected direction. Specifically, mothers who reported more parent and family problems had infants who had a greater number of or unusual caregiving demands, were less socially responsive, had more diffi-

Influence of Selected Child Characteristics on Stress in Families of Handicapped Infants

Paula J. Beckman

cult temperaments, and displayed more repetitive behavioral patterns.

The relationship between stress and child characteristics was only obtained, however, when using the Questionnaire on Resources and Stress. There was no significant relationship between scores obtained on the Holmes and Rahe Schedule of Recent Experience and the Questionnaire on Resources and Stress nor to specific characteristics of the child. These findings have important implications for researchers interested in the area of stress. Both measures are commonly used indices of stress; however, the results of this study suggest that they tap very different kinds of family experience. Clearly, extensive generalization regarding the relationship between these measures is not possible since only a modified version of the Schedule of Recent Experience was used; however, these data suggest the need for further investigation of the relationship between the measures. Until such data are available, caution should be exercised when generalizing across various measures of stress.

The scores obtained on each of the individual Questionnaire on Resources and Stress subscales appear to be consistent with the findings of those in other studies (Friedrich & Friedrich, 1981; Holroyd & McArthur, 1976). Although the profile was slightly different, mean scores were similar to those reported by Friedrich and Friedrich (1981) for their handicapped group, as well as with those of the Down syndrome group reported by Holroyd and McArthur (1976). The most notable difference was that mothers in the present study scored substantially higher on two subscales than did mothers in any group in either of the above studies. Specifically, mothers in the present study had higher scores on Excess Time Demands and Physical Incapacitation. This may in part be due to the fact that children in the present study were infants. Studies comparing families of handicapped and nonhandicapped infants are needed to distinguish the added stress resulting from a handicap from that resulting simply from caring for an infant.

Another finding in the present study concerned the pattern of correlations obtained among the child characteristics themselves. The total number of extra caregiving demands was significantly associated with all other child characteristics. Rate of progress was significantly associated with repetitive behavioral patterns and total caregiving demands. A strong pattern of intercorrelations was obtained among temperament, responsiveness, and caregiving demands. This may suggest

that the three domains may tap a single dimension that reflects a general "difficulty of care." Rate of progress was not associated with responsiveness nor with temperament. Difficulty of care and rate of progress may reflect somewhat different characteristics. Further research is needed to investigate this issue since the two characteristics may require somewhat different intervention strategies.

In contrast with findings of previous research (Bristol, 1979; Farber, 1959), two child characteristics, age and sex, that have been associated with stress were not related to the amount of stress reported by mothers in the present sample. In part, these results may be a function of the restricted age range in the present study. Both Farber (1959) and Bristol (1979) studied children who ranged from 4 to 21 years of age. Children in the present sample were younger and represented a more restricted age range. Failure to find sex differences in the amount of stress reported by mothers of girls vs. the amount reported by mothers of boys may also be a function of the ages of the children in the sample. It may be that during the early period of adjustment to the child's handicap, sex is less important to parents than are other characteristics of the child.

The only demographic variable significantly related to stress was the number of parents in the family. Single mothers reported more stress than did mothers in two-parent families. This is consistent with the finding that the total number of caregiving demands is associated with higher levels of stress. Single parents are likely to have less help with caregiving activities, since relief in the form of another parent is unavailable.

These results have important implications for future research as well as for intervention with families. Of particular importance is recognition of the role played by the child in the stress experienced by all families. Over the past few years, researchers interested in interaction between nonhandicapped infants and adults have discovered that even very young infants may have a profound influence on the adults in their environment (Bell, 1968; Lewis & Rosenblum, 1974). Although this body of research may have important implications for parents of handicapped children, such a contribution has not been widely acknowledged. Understanding which characteristics of children contribute most significantly to problems experienced by the family may be extremely valuable to professionals interested in helping families solve these problems. For example, the variable most highly related to stress in this study was the number of additional caregiving demands made by the child. One way to reduce stress might be to expand the available respite care alternatives available to the family. Providing training in special caregiving techniques might be another way to reduce tress. Other characteristics associated with stress might also be the target of specific intervention strategies, either through direct intervention with the infant or by teaching mothers to use alternative responses.

Clearly, child characteristics are not the only potential sources of stress for families of handicapped infants. Beckman-Bell (1981) proposed that child characteristics may interact with family variables over time to produce differing amounts of stress for the family. Longitudinal studies are needed in which factors associated with stress over time are evaluated.

At the very least, results of the present study suggest that our view of parent involvement in intervention programs be expanded to incorporate knowledge about the potential impact of the child on the family. Such an expanded view is especially important at a time in which more parents are being encouraged to care for their children in their homes. Recognizing the stress that parents may be experiencing and developing ways to assist them as they cope with any added burdens could well be among the most useful ways of accommodating these goals.

Note

[1]Simeonsson, R. *Carolina Record of Infant Behavior* (CRIB). Chapel Hill: Carolina Institute for Research on Early Education of the Handicapped, University of North Carolina, 1979.

References

Beckman-Bell, P. Child-related stress in families of handicapped children. *Topics in Early Childhood Special Education*, 1981, *1*(3), 45–54.

Bell, R. Q. A reinterpretation of the direction of effects in studies of socialization. *Psychological Review*, 1968, *75*, 81–95.

Blacher-Dixon, J., & Simeonsson, R. J. Consistency and correspondence of mothers' and teachers' assessments of young handicapped children. *Journal of the Division of Early Childhood*, 1981, *3*, 64l–71.

Bristol, M. M. *Maternal coping with autistic children: Ad-*

equacy of interpersonal support and effects of child's characteristics. Unpublished doctoral dissertation, University of North Carolina, 1979.

Cummings, S. T. The impact of the child's deficiency on the father: A study of fathers of mentally retarded and or chronically ill children. *American Journal of Orthopsychiatry*, 1976, *46*, 246–255.

Cummings, S. T., Bayley, H., & Rie, H. Effects of the child's deficiency on the mother: A study of mothers of mentally retarded, chronically ill, and neurotic children. *American Journal of Orthopsychiatry*, 1966, *36*, 595–608.

Farber, B. Effects of a severely retarded child on family integration. *Monographs of the Society for Research in Child Development*, 1959, *24*(2, Serial No. 71).

Farber, B., & Ryckman, D. B. Effects of severely mentally retarded children on family relationships. *Mental Retardation Abstracts*, 1965, *2*, 1–17.

Fotheringham, J. B., & Creal, D. Handicapped children and handicapped families. *International Review of Education*, 1974, *20*, 355–373.

Friedrich, W. N., & Friedrich, W. L. Psychosocial assets of parents of handicapped and nonhandicapped children. *American Journal of Mental Deficiency*, 1981, *85*, 551–553.

Gallagher, J. J., Beckman-Bell, P., & Cross, A. Families of handicapped children: Sources of stress and its amelioration. *Exceptional Children*, in press.

Holmes, T. H., & Rahe, R. H. The social readjustment rating scale. *Journal of Psychosomatic Research*, 1967, *11*, 213–218.

Holroyd, J. The Questionnaire on Resources and Stress: An instrument to measure family response to a handicapped member. *Journal of Community Psychology*, 1974, *2*, 92–94.

Holroyd, J., & McArthur, D. Mental retardation and stress on the parents: A contrast between Down's syndrome and childhood autism. *American Journal of Mental Deficiency*, 1976, *80*, 431–436.

Lewis, M., & Rosenblum, L. A. *The effect of the infant on its caregiver.* New York: John Wiley & Sons, 1974.

Marcus, L. M. Patterns of coping in families of psychotic children. *American Journal of Orthopsychiatry*, 1977, *47*, 388–398.

Parse, S. W. *A comparative study of maternal and professional appraisals of handicapped preschool children.* Unpublished doctoral dissertation, University of North Carolina, 1982.

Rabkin, J. G., & Struening, E. L. Life events, stress, and illness. *Science*, 1976, *194*, 1013–1020.

Simeonsson, R. J., Huntington, G. S., Short, R. J., & Ware, W. B. The Carolina Record of Individual Behavior: Characteristics of handicapped infants and children. *Topics in Early Childhood Special Education*, 1982, *2*(2), 43–55.

Manuscript submitted 3/24/82.

This research was supported in part by the Carolina Institute for Research in Early Education of the Handicapped and the Research Training Program at the Frank Porter Graham Child Development Center. It was part of a doctoral dissertation submitted to the Department of Special Education at the University of North Carolina, in partial fulfillment of the requirements for the PhD degree. It was presented at the annual meeting of the Council for Exceptional Children, Philadelphia, 1980, and the annual meeting of the Association for the Severely Handicapped, New York, 1980. The author thanks Ronald Wiegerink, Craig Ramey, James Gallagher, Rune Simeonsson, and John Pelosi for their advice during the design and development of the study. Special thanks are given to Cordelia Robinson, director, and to the infants, families, and staff members of the Infant Development Program at Meyer Children's Rehabilitation Institute, Omaha, for their participation in the study. Reprint requests should be sent to P. J. B., Department of Special Education, 1308 Benjamin Building, University of Maryland, College Park, MD 20742.

Author

Paula J. Beckman, University of Maryland

A Review of Attachment Formation and Disorder of Handicapped Children

Jan Blacher and C. E. Meyers
1983

Abstract

Research pertaining to attachment formation of handicapped children against a backdrop overview of the general attachment literature was examined. Attachment development and disorder of handicapped populations was reviewed categorically by handicap and by the procedures used to study attachment and analogous behavior with populations of handicapped children. In general, evidence to date suggests that attachment between young handicapped children and their mothers or caretakers may be delayed, dulled, or even absent. Some critical methodological issues were discussed, and implications of the study of attachment for developing theory, providing services, and understanding child abuse were delineated.

A discussion of parent-child interaction would be incomplete today without reference to mother-infant attachment. The attachment of infants to their mother or caretaker is viewed as integral to their survival and development. The same may be presumed to be true for handicapped children. The presence and nature of attachment would seem to be pertinent to the crises and agonies confronting parents of disabled children. For example, the quality of attachment could well relate to the early burnout of parents as careproviders, to the inclination to place children out of the natural home, to abuse or neglect, to family accord or discord, and even to the quality of parent collaboration with service providers and school personnel.

In this paper we explored the application of the attachment concept to mentally retarded and other disabled groups. Space limitations dictate a cursory overview of the present status of general attachment theory and research; interested readers should consult Ainsworth (1973), Ainsworth, Blehar, Waters, and Wall (1978), Alloway, Pliner, and Krames (1977), Bowlby (1980), Parkes and Stevenson-Hinde (1982), and Waters and Deane (1982). We reviewed the few relevant investiga-

tions conducted with handicapped children, proposed areas open to research, and suggested adaptations of currently used procedures for use in studies of attachment with severely impaired populations.

Conceptual and Research Overview of Attachment

The word *attachment* was employed by Bowlby (1958) to avoid the one-way connotation of the word *dependency* in infant-mother interaction. Ainsworth and Bell (1970) have defined attachment as "an affectional tie that one person or animal forms between himself and another specific one—a tie that binds them together in space and endures over time" (p. 50). Discrete types of attachment behavior would be those that promote proximity or contact, e.g., smiling, looking, vocalizing, following, or clinging (Bowlby, 1969); however, any one of these types of behavior is not synonymous with attachment; rather, as Sroufe and Waters (1977) pointed out, attachment is inferred from such behavior. In distinguishing between attachment as a series of discrete types of behavior vs. an organizational construct, Sroufe and Waters (1977) emphasized the importance of looking at the context in which such behavior occurs, the meaning of each discrete behavior, and the age of the child.

Ainsworth (1973) described four phases of attachment development as originally proposed by Bowlby (1969). Initially, waking infants make suckling movements, smile, cry, and make other vocalizations toward environmental objects and seek and hold eye contact with people. At about 3 months of age, infants appear to differentiate people from inanimate features in their environment and become more selective in their responses.

A second phase occurs when infants differentiate the mother and perhaps one or two others for special contact and proximity seeking. This is noted after 6 months of age, when absence of the mother or presence of a stranger begins to lead to distress, best known by the popular expressions, "8-month anxiety," "stranger wariness," or "fear of strangers." Toward the end of the first year of life, the child has made good progress in the establishment of a mother-object constancy or person permanence, i.e., knowing the mother in her absence and recognizing her voice and other attributes at a distance.

This interdependency increases until about age 4 to 5 years, when a full trust may be established. This marks the fourth phase, one which is more cognitive–representational in nature. Delays in achieving this degree of attachment are evident in those 4- or 5-year-olds delivered at school who are distressed at the mother's departure; the secure child accepts her departure, demonstrating trust and an understanding of the mother's right and need to go now, for her own reasons. In Piagetian terms, the child has made the transition from egocentrism to reciprocity, being able to take the mother's perspective in the given situation. Attainment of this fourth phase of attachment marks a bond that presumably endures even when abuse has occurred.

Although attachment is conceptualized as a mutual development between mother and infant, most of the literature has reported on only the development of the child's attachment to the mother. Investigators have rarely provided information on how the mother performs. We propose that the nature of the mother's attachment is a critical variable in the development of family–severely impaired child dynamics.

Assessment of Attachment

The most commonly employed assessment procedure is a set of eight episodes described by Ainsworth and Wittig (1969; see also Ainsworth et al., 1978). These are employed with infants in the first 2 years of life; modifications are required for older children. The episodes provide for a strange situation: the mother leaving temporarily, the child alone, the child alone with a stranger, a reunion between child and mother, and so on. Observations are recorded of proximity seeking and maintenance, distress, resisting contact with the stranger, crying, and other behavior. Results are usually presented in terms of Ainsworth's three principal categories (qualities, not degrees): (a) Type A is avoidant or passive; (b) Type B is a secure bond, characterized by the child's tolerating reasonably well the mother's absence, being alone, and in a stranger's presence, (c) Type C is ambivalent or resistant. Not every child can be neatly fitted into one of these classifications. The standardized

procedures have been employed with mother–child dyads of "normal" families (e.g., Bell, 1970; Waters, Wippman, & Sroufe, 1979); at-risk or disadvantaged families (e.g., Vaughn, Egeland, Sroufe, & Waters, 1979), abusing parents (e.g., Egeland & Sroufe, 1981), dyads in which the newborn has been separated from the mother because of prematurity or illness (e.g., Rode, Chang, Fisch, & Sroufe, 1981; Barnard, Note 1), and secondary careproviders and day-care home operators (e.g., Anderson, 1980; Anderson, Nagle, Roberts, & Smith, 1981). The A-B-C-typology has also been related to nursery school adjustment, peer behavior, and the caretaking environment itself (Pastor, 1981; Vaughn et al., 1979; Waters et al., 1979).

The pediatric and child psychiatric literature recognizes attachment and attachment problems. The *Diagnostic and Statistical Manual-III* (American Psychiatric Association, 1980) includes "reactive attachment disorder of infancy" (pp. 15, 57). Call (1980) identified three varieties of this disorder, the first of which is called "primary attachment failure," defined as an absence of or a grave weakness of visual, vocal, and other forms of reciprocity occurring from neonatal days on. The cause may lie in sensory or motor defects of the child, early illness leading to hospitalization, or the mother's inability to respond to the child. The principal symptoms are apathy and failure to thrive. "Anaclitic" disorder is due to separation of mother and child after about 6 months of age, before which "normal" attachment has occurred. It is marked by behavior aberration followed by anxiety, depression, and generally poor psychological development and resembles Ainsworth's Type A or avoidant variety. Call referred to the third attachment disorder as "symbiotic," characterized by high insecurity, clinging behavior, and/or manipulation of mother's feelings; it resembles Ainsworth's Type C or resistant variety.

As one might expect, the secure Type B occurs more frequently with well-adjusted mothers and families, families without severe stress, with healthy infants, and so on. If an instance of the Type B occurs under conditions in which one would expect A or C, a secondary careprovider (e.g., a maternal grandmother) may have been supportive (Crockenberg, 1981). With abusing parents, Type B is less frequently found than Types A or C, but attachment does nevertheless develop.

Bowlby considers close emotional attachment an imperative for good adjustment throughout life. Furthermore, mother–infant attachment is an adaptive behav-

A Review of Attachment Formation and Disorder in Handicapped Children　　　　　　Jan Blacher and C. E. Meyers

ior system that serves both the infant and the species. Helpless infants receive physical protection; distress is minimized by comfort supplied by principal careproviders. Presumably, such bonding is dyadic and serves a role throughout life, as with friends, spouses, and members of one's social network. As Bowlby (1980) noted: "Intimate attachments of other human beings are the hub around which a person's life revolves. . . . From these intimate attachments a person draws his strength and enjoyment

of life, and, through what he contributes, he gives strength and enjoyment to others" (p. 442).

The proliferation of published studies of attachment, particularly the Ainsworth–Wittig procedures for infancy, has been accompanied by the expected complement of doubters and critics that attend any new emphasis. Conceptual and validity considerations have been raised by Ainsworth and Bell (1970), Cohen (1974), Masters and Wellman (1974), by selected authors in Parkes and

Table 1 Studies of Attachment and Analogous Behavior with Handicapped Populations

Subjects					
Type of handicap	Procedure	Focus	N	Age[a]	Investigator(s)
Down syndrome	Ainsworth–Wittig	Child	12	33.5 (median)	Serafica & Cicchetti, 1976
Down syndrome	Observations[b]	Child	14	18	Cicchetti & Sroufe, 1976
Down syndrome	Observations	Child	60	16	Cicchetti & Sroufe, 1978
Down syndrome	Ainsworth–Wittig	Child	18	24	Berry et al., 1980
Down syndrome	Ainsworth–Wittig	Child	42	30 to 42	Cicchetti & Serafica, 1981
Down syndrome	Structured procedures[c] and interviews[b]	Mother	6	4 to 12	Emde & Brown, 1978
Down syndrome	Observations	Child & mother	6	13 to 24	Jones, 1979
Mixed developmentally disabled[d]	Interviews	Mother	36	Not given	Rosen, 1955
Mixed developmentally disabled[d]	Structured procedures	Child	42	13.5	Greenberg, 1971
Mixed developmentally disabled	Observations	Child & mother	Not given	0 to 24	Bromwich, 1976
Various handicaps[e]	Structured procedures and interview	Mother	15	Infancy (specific ages not given)	Stone & Chesney, 1978
Various handicaps	Structured procedures	Mother	10	Postnatal	Nix, Note 2
Visually impaired	Structured procedures	Child & mother	9	Infancy (specific ages not given)	Fraiberg, 1971
Visually impaired	Structured procedures	Child & mother	10	23 days– 11 mos.	Fraiberg, 1974
Auditorially impaired/deaf	Structured procedures	Child & mother	28	51	Fraiberg, 1971

[a] Mean, in months, unless otherwise specified.
[b] Nature of attachment for (or analogous behavior) inferred from observations or clinical interviews.
[c] Structured procedures, but different from the Ainsworth–Wittig design.
[d] Most are mentally retarded, with various diagnoses.
[e] A combination of handicaps, e.g., epilepsy, Down syndrome, physical disability, etc.

A Review of Attachment Formation and Disorder in Handicapped Children

Jan Blacher and C. E. Meyers

Stevenson-Hinde (1982), Sroufe and Waters (1977), Vaughn et al. (1979), and Waters et al. (1979).

Attachment Study with Handicapped Children

Before we report on our substantive review of findings on attachment and cognate studies with handicapped children, some observations are necessary. First, standardized procedures such as those of Ainsworth and Wittig (1969) have only recently been employed, and because they are not appropriate for older children or cannot be employed at all with certain handicapped children, other procedures have been utilized. As listed in Table 1, these alternatives are other controlled procedures utilized to elicit discrete types of attachment behavior and inference of attachment status from observations of parent–child interactions or clinical interviews. Second, compared with the child-focused attachment literature with nonhandicapped children, the mother is a frequent focus when handicapped children are involved. This fact is noted in Table 1 and is the basis for certain recommended investigations discussed at the end of this paper. Finally, although in the general literature attachment is related to a variety of factors, the study of attachment with disabled individuals has not yet been connected to meaningful factors such as family integrity, marital harmony, and consideration of institutionalization.

Attachment Behavior of Down Syndrome Children

Attachment behavior of Down syndrome infants has received more attention than any other group of retarded individuals. Some of this research has been comparative in nature, and investigators have used the Ainsworth–Wittig procedures. Serafica and Cicchetti (1976), comparing Down syndrome and nonretarded children of approximately 33 months of age found that only one Down syndrome child cried during the observation period. The frequency of other vocalizations by the Down syndrome children was also much lower. On the other hand, there were no significant differences between the two groups of children in their smiling or locomotion to regain proximity to mothers. The authors considered the following explanations for their findings: (a) a lag in the development of attachment among Down syndrome children;

although they maintained comparable proximity to a visible mother, they did not utilize the signaling behavior at their disposal; (b) a difference in strength of attachment, untestable in the absence of appropriate procedures for assessing such strength (Ainsworth et al., 1972); and (c) a difference in the meaning the two groups attached to the situation, with the Down syndrome children less sensitive to cues denoting novelty, fear, or incongruity. Our own interpretation is that Serafica and Cicchetti's third proposal is simply a statement that the Down syndrome children's mental age (MA) was lower than that of the 33-month-old nonretarded children. Serafica and Cicchetti also speculated that the physical and personality characteristics of Down syndrome children tend to elicit such nurturant behavior from others that they may experience fewer opportunities or reasons to show fear. In related work Cicchetti and Sroufe (1976, 1978) studied affective and cognitive growth longitudinally in Down syndrome and nonretarded infants. They again found that the Down syndrome infants were comparatively delayed in both affective and cognitive growth, although the sequence was normal.

Berry, Gunn and Andrews (1980) showed that Down syndrome infants were qualitatively similar to nonhandicapped infants in their sensitivity to the strange situation in the episodes of separation from the mother and in the presence of a stranger. These investigators employed slightly modified Ainsworth–Wittig procedures. Cicchetti and Serafica's (1981) more recent report confirmed the Berry et al. findings. Although they again found quantitative differences in the degree of responsiveness of Down syndrome and nonretarded infants, the patterns of response were similar. Specifically, Down syndrome children showed the same range of behavior as did nonretarded children when they encountered a stranger.

Procedures other than the Ainsworth–Wittig have been employed to observe and describe discrete attachment behavior in Down syndrome groups. Emde and Brown (1978) used clinical interviews, developmental testing, and systematic observations of social interaction by employing "standardized approach and separation sequences by mother and by one or more strangers" (p. 303). Their observation of mother–child interactions revealed diminished eye contact, smiling, and overall social responsiveness of the Down syndrome infants. Emde, Katz, and Thorpe (1978) have also noted that the attachment of parents to their child may be affected by

A Review of Attachment Formation and Disorder in Handicapped Children

Jan Blacher and C. E. Meyers

the Down syndrome child's dulled emotional expression.

When examined in the broader context of mother–child interaction, Down syndrome children between approximately 1 and 2 years of age seem to be as active and to produce some appropriate types of potentially communicative behavior (Jones, 1979). Subtle communication difficulties, however, such as lack of eye contact or feedback, can lead to later problems in developing the mutuality so critical for attachment.

To summarize the Down syndrome literature in this area, the investigators employing the Ainsworth–Wittig procedures or its variations suggest that Down syndrome infants proceed through the same stages of attachment as do nonretarded infants, but at a slower pace and with less distress at separation. As pointed out by Cicchetti and Serafica (1981), such findings sustain Zigler's (1969) developmental or similar sequence position to include individuals with an organic impairment and suggest that lower intelligence per se need not result in a different developmental sequence. Although it is true that Down syndrome infants are biologically or organically impaired, they are behaviorally and physically different from other more severely impaired children. They are often cosmetically attractive and do not typically demonstrate bizarre, deviant behavior at early ages. Most who do not die young enjoy approximately normal perceptual and motor development in the first year and well into the second. Although they have a marked hypotonicity, they otherwise have physical capability for eye contact, recognition, remembrance, and selective responsiveness, all deemed critical for attachment development. Further, most Down syndrome children are most severely or profoundly retarded. The question of whether they can attain the highest level of attachment (Phase 4) seems not to have been investigated, except by Serafica and Cicchetti (1976).

Attachment in Other Retarded/Developmentally Delayed Children

The literature pertaining to attachment in other generic groups of retarded or developmentally delayed infants attests to the widespread acceptance of the attachment construct; however, in no study reviewed in this section was the Ainsworth–Wittig procedures employed, although several investigators used variations on the stranger or separation episodes or other forms of systematic observation (Bromwich, 1976; Greenberg, 1971; Stone & Chesney, 1978; Nix, Note 2).

Rosen (1955) provided an example of a mother-focus study. This and other reports differ from the child-focus in that the mother is observed, with the child perhaps also observed. Rosen conducted interviews with 36 mothers of retarded children. The data were interpreted in terms of his five stages of understanding that the mother of a retarded child is said to experience. The final stage is acceptance. One-half of the mothers indicated that their own feelings were obstacles to acceptance of their handicapped child, whereas the other half attributed their lack of acceptance (read "attachment") to symptoms in their child's behavior that they could not control or understand. This report and others indicate that impaired children are perceived to be different by mothers, who in turn seem incapable of the "normal" involvement-creating overtures and of responding to whatever overtures the infants might produce. Some might challenge whether Rosen's study concerns "attachment"; we suggest that it does as it represents a classic instance of a mother-focus study.

Greenberg (1971) observed a sequence of episodes with a stranger, separation from mother, and reunion in 42 "atypical" and 16 nonhandicapped infants. Responses of the atypical, or developmentally disabled, infants were less uniform than those of the nonhandicapped group and included the following: no response to separation, withdrawal, avoidance behavior, body rocking, and crying.

Stone and Chesney (1978) reported responses of mothers of a mixed collection of developmentally disabled children (including Down syndrome, blind, brain-injured, and multiply handicapped). Each of the 15 mothers selected from a list those types of attachment behavior that described her baby. Included were responses to being handled (e.g., tense, stiffening when handled, limp, unresponsive), smiling, crying, vocalizing. These data were then corroborated in subsequent interviews and observations of mother–child interaction. Disturbances were reported in one or more kinds of attachment behavior in all the infants. On the other hand, Nix (Notes 2) found no significant differences between ratings of attachment by mothers of handicapped and mothers of nonhandicapped infants. Nix employed a rating instrument called the Maternal Attachment Tool (Cropley, Lester, & Pennington, 1976) to record observations of discrete types of attachment behavior in the context of mother–infant interactions.

In contrast with the literature pertaining to Down

A **Review of Attachment Formation and Disorder in Handicapped Children**

Jan Blacher and C. E. Meyers

syndrome infants, results of investigations with developmentally delayed children suggest the presence of delays and disruptions in the development of attachment. Most severely retarded or delayed infants show sufficiently dulled perception or awareness to affect subsequent mother–child interactions. As aptly stated by Stone and Chesney (1978), "the failure of the handicapped infant to stimulate the mother leads to failure of the mother to interact with the infant" (p. 11).

Stone and Chesney's (1978) assessment pertains to the typical instance of the mother's relation with a severely impaired, non-Down syndrome child. All who work with families having such a child would accept the assessment as common but also know individual instances in which a strong attachment, in spite of the odds, has formed. It appears that when conditions such as medication, cerebral palsy, and hyperactivity preclude a normal cuddling relationship, there could be an attachment failure; however, individual cases indicate that if the child can form eye contact and give a smile of recognition, bonding can form even in the absence of ability to reach and embrace. Again, in common clinical instances without an objective data base, we adduce the classic description of the autistic baby who does not respond to parental overtures, leading to a failure of mutual relationships. Finally, we note that defective cosmetic aspects of many handicapped children tend to elicit less love and attention.

Attachment Behavior of Blind Children

Visual contact is believed by some to be the basis of human sociability (Rheingold, 1961). If this is the case, blind infants in particular may be especially vulnerable to impairment in social relationships because of visual inability to discriminate among people and to make eye contact with the mother. Specific disturbances in the development of discrete attachment behavior by blind infants have indeed been reported.

Fraiberg's (1971, 1974) observations and assessments of 10 blind infants showed that in most cases the following situation prevailed; (a) infants showed an absence of "eye language," creating problems for mothers trying to read their nonvisual sign language; (b) infant smiling in response to mother's (or father's) voice was not automatic or frequent; (c) the blind babies showed a meager repertoire of facial signs and expressions; (d) adaptive hand behavior (i.e., coordination of hand and sound) did not usually occur spontaneously; and (e) although blindness did not appear to be an impediment to language acquisition, there appeared to be differences in the quantity and quality of spontaneous vocalizations between blind and sighted infants. Using Decarie's scale (1965) to measure such behaviors as smiling, vocalizing, and tactile discrimination, Fraiberg demonstrated that blind infants made differential responses to mother and to strangers; such "attachment" responses were believed to be similar to those of sighted infants. In addition, Fraiberg (1974) used observational procedures and variations of stranger and separation sequences to obtain data on attachment between blind infants and their mothers. During their first year, blind infants seemed similar to sighted children in their discrimination, preference for, and valuation of mother. They demonstrated differential smiling, differential vocalization, manual tactile seeking, embracing, and other gestures of affection and comfort seeking. During their second year, the blind infants showed anxiety upon separation from mother and comfort upon reunion. With the onset of mobility (e.g., creeping and walking), these children showed some tracking of the mother as she moved from room to room, independent exploration, and return to mother as a "secure base." Fraiberg noted that these achievements pertaining to the development of human bonds compare favorably with those of sighted infants.

Although the subjects in Fraiberg's studies did have a severe visual impairment, they were not reported as having additional physical or cognitive handicaps. Furthermore, Fraiberg herself noted that she had an unusual sample of infants and mothers, and she provided intensive intervention efforts to develop adaptive substitutes for vision (particularly in speech and in the use of the hands, in locomotor functioning, and in body or self image). This intervention presumably led to sensorimotor organization and the establishment of a "dialogue" between mother and infant and the capacity for attachments to develop. Unfortunately, the relationship between communicative competence established in the mother–blind infant dyad and subsequent attachment formation has not been clearly addressed. Without any intervention, however, problems of disturbed attachment can develop. McGuire and Meyers (1971) studied 27 congenitally blind children. The vast majority exhibited hostility or passive aggression or compulsive solitary play or other behavior disturbance so severe that half the mothers sought to place the child out of the home because of inability to cope.

Attachment Behavior of Deaf Children

Greenberg and Marvin (1979) examined the development of attachment in 28 3- to 5-year-old profoundly deaf children and their hearing mothers. The investigators hypothesized that communicative competence in the mother–child dyad would reflect the attainment of Phase IV attachment. As in the Fraiberg (1971, 1974) studies, these investigators made systematic observations of mother–child interactions during various "attachment episodes," based on the measurement of discrete type of behavior coded prior to, during, and after separation sequences: the frequency of child-initiated approach and withdrawal; duration of mother–child proximity; and the frequency of smiling, touching, gaze aversion, and angry or aggressive behavior. Observations of communication were also obtained, enabling the investigators to show that communicative competence, not child age, was related to the pattern or level of attachment attained.

Greenberg and Marvin's (1979) study suggests that researchers should look more closely at both mothers' use of language and handicapped children's communication skills in the study of attachment. In considering other work that has demonstrated impaired communication and less than optimal interaction patterns between handicapped young children and their mothers (see, e.g., Greenberg's, 1980, or Wedell–Monnig and Lumley's, 1980, study with deaf children), Greenberg and Marvin's point is well taken. At the very least a hearing impairment may eliminate one important input from mother—the comforting effect of her voice. Ainsworth and her colleagues, for example, have asserted that the most important dimension associated with the infant's behavior toward his or her mother in the "strange situation" is the degree of maternal sensitivity in perceiving and interpreting the child's signals and in responding to them, i.e., in communicating with the child. Obviously, the more handicapped the infant or young child, and consequently the more impaired his or her communicative ability (due to single or multiple deficits in the cognitive, auditory, visual, or physical domains), the more dramatic the interruption in attachment formation is likely to be.

Conceptual Problems and Needed Research

The previously reviewed literature suggests that study of attachment within selected handicapped populations is proceeding, although collectively investigative efforts have been sporadic and somewhat uncoordinated. Indeed, there are a number of methodological, theoretical, and practical issues that merit further discussion.

Methodological Issues

The first issue is the adequacy of the procedures used for studying attachment in handicapped groups. The standard Ainsworth–Wittig procedure used extensively with Down syndrome infants and young nonhandicapped children has not been validated for use with more severely retarded and multiply handicapped children nor has the application of the A, B, and C classification for any handicapped group. Call's (1980) first type of attachment disorder, primary attachment failure, is not represented in the Ainsworth categorization. Other observational procedures have been utilized to assess attachment in selected retarded or developmentally disabled groups (e.g., Emde & Brown, 1978; Fraiberg, 1971, 1974; Greenberg, 1971; Nix, Note 2). The use of nonstandardized clinically oriented interview procedures with mothers of handicapped infants or young children have also yielded information on attachment development (Emde & Brown, 1978; Stone & Chesney, 1978).

There does seem to be a clear need, however, for systematic, workable procedures that can be used to study attachment behavior of handicapped young children who vary in level and type(s) of handicap. The most logical choice at this point is the Ainsworth–Wittig paradigm. As shown, there are ample data attesting to the validity of this procedure in the assessment of attachment behavior of nonhandicapped children through about 4 years of age and of Down syndrome children. This implies that the Ainsworth–Wittig design might be useful with severely handicapped children as old as 10 years, perhaps, but with MAs not exceeding 4 years. Slight modification or adaptation of the Ainsworth-Wittig procedure may indeed render it useful with more severely impaired populations. For example, throughout the sessions mothers may be allowed to use any alternative mode of communication that they normally use with their children; observations may take place in the natural home, where familiar furniture, surroundings, and adaptive equipment (such as mobility, positioning, or visual aids) are still available; and the timing of sessions may be adjusted to account for delays due to children who have more severe sensory or physical impairments. Such suggestions call for a great deal of pilot work incorporating these modifications.

A Review of Attachment Formation and Disorder in Handicapped Children Jan Blacher and C. E. Meyers

The Developmental Sequence of Attachment

The idea of stages or developmental levels of attachment is well documented in the literature and seems to be uncontested. One of the major theoretical issues of interest here is whether there is an "upper limit" in attachment stage attainment for handicapped populations. Although Serafica and Cicchetti (1976) have provided some evidence that Down syndrome children do not necessarily lag developmentally in the attainment of a full goal-corrected partnership, one can only speculate at this point as to the age at which full reciprocity would occur, if ever. Marvin (1977) found evidence of such reciprocity or "role-taking" in 4-year-old and a few 3-year-old nonhandicapped children. Given the acknowledged lag in the development of social–cognitive behavior by many retarded and other handicapped children (Simeonsson, Monson, & Blacher, in press), we can speculate that more severely handicapped children may never achieve the full reciprocity in social interactions that is necessary for attaining the highest level of attachment. It seems more likely that a plateau effect would occur somewhere around Phase 3, when, for example, the child knows his or her mother in her absence and recognizes her voice at a distance.

Delay or even absence of the development of attachment and responsiveness should not be surprising, given impairments in the sensory venues by which mother's signals can be detected (which may be further diminished by medication) and the retardation of cognitive growth that would impair discrimination among environmental events. Such impediments on the infant's side alone would be sufficient to account for delay. As to cognitive growth, Bell (1970) demonstrated the association of attachment development with the establishment of Piaget's object relations. As mentioned previously, Marvin (1977) showed how the advance of the child from the Bowlby–Ainsworth Phase III attachment to Phase IV required the ability to take the perspective of another person and to be less egocentric in the two-way social relationship. Furthermore, there is a related body of literature attesting to the fact that specific linguistic delays of young handicapped children affect subsequent mother–child and family–child interaction patterns (e.g., Cunningham, Reuler, Blackwell, & Deck, 1981; Gath, 1977; Jones, 1979). Thus, what the attachment literature is beginning to demonstrate with mentally retarded children comes as no surprise.

From the mother-focus point of view, additional reason for disturbance or delays in attachment can be adduced. The mother's overtures would fail to arouse the usual child responses and hence be subject to nonreinforcement. The child's lack of responding may constitute a threat to the mother's continued involvement or provide a limit on it.

A second issue of interest regards the similar sequence hypothesis. Will severely retarded children, known to have some organic brain damage, follow a developmental sequence of attachment level attainment that is similar to or different from that of nonretarded children of comparable MA? Cicchetti and Serafica's (1981) Down syndrome children did follow a similar but delayed developmental sequence, with no evident distortion. We would expect such a delay in mildly retarded, socioculturally retarded, or "at risk" populations. We question, however, whether Cicchetti and Serafica's findings really do extend Zigler's (1973) developmental position to include most individuals with organic impairments, specifically, other severely handicapped children; Down syndrome children have capabilities (motor, affective, and cognitive) and demonstrate many kinds of behavior similar to nonhandicapped children. Obviously, since this study is the only one to date that is specifically addressed to this issue, we need more of these data from other subgroups of severely handicapped young children.

Another theoretical notion that may have particular relevance for retarded populations is Bowlby's concept of "detachment." We propose that the detachment phenomenon, consisting of the sequences of attachment–loss–distress episodes of events, can be related to certain aspects of the careprovider–client relationships that occur so often in residences for mentally retarded people. In such living situations, it is not at all uncommon for even young children to develop a close relationship or "attachment" to staff members who, because of "burnout" or rotating staffing patterns, move on to another ward or job. Though some distress over the loss of a particular careprovider may occur, one might hypothesize that the entire sequence of events (attachment–loss–distress) will be repeated many times throughout the duration of retarded individuals' institutionalization.

Placement Issues

There are practical issues related to the study of attachment behavior of handicapped children, particularly the more severely impaired groups. An understanding of attachment or the family–handicapped child bond has implications for service providers involved in: (a) making recommendations about placing children out of the natural home; (b) making decisions about returning children to the natural home after periods of institutionalization or respite, and (c) soliciting parent or family involvement in the actual education of handicapped children.

Because of the overwhelming and often expensive burden of care they impose, severely handicapped children have historically been at great risk for institutionalization or other out-of-home placement (Meyers, Zetlin, & Blacher-Dixon, 1981). How well such children adapt to these placements may be related to their early attachment experiences (Marr & Kennedy, 1980). Some families, however, initially keep severely handicapped children at home and do form an attachment, and then later experience "burnout" due to the children's continuing daily care needs and helplessness, accompanied by larger physical bodies and/or maladaptive behavior. If such an initial attachment had formed, the burnout would be reflected in a fairly intense conflict for parents when actual placement becomes necessary. If attachment had been frail, or undeveloped, the conflict would presumably be less.

A related research focus would relate attachment to the concern parents demonstrate in securing services, utilizing social networks (both in the extended family and in the community), and participating in handicapped children's school programs. In general, attached parents would be expected to demonstrate more feeling, more intensity of relationship, and perhaps more competition and conflict with professionals or school personnel than would nonattached parents, who might acquiesce more readily to a routine program of care and educational services and accept the secondary care-provision of, perhaps, grandparents or day-care workers.

Child Abuse

A second practical issue concerns the dynamics of attachment as related to child abuse. Helfer (Note 3) proposed that parental abuse and neglect of young handicapped children may be due to interference during the normal bonding process between mother and infant. According to Ainsworth (1980), this interference or disruption in the formation of attachment can occur when infants are separated from caregivers at or immediately after birth, although recent attempts to demonstrate this have yielded contradictory findings (Grossmann, Thane,

& Grossmann, 1981; Rode et al., 1981). Clearly, severely impaired/handicapped infants, especially those who are premature, sickly, or have congenital malformations requiring immediate medical attention and prolonged hospitalizations, are more likely than nonhandicapped infants to undergo such separations.

Not surprisingly, handicapped children have been found to be overrepresented in abused populations (Friedrich & Boriskin, 1976). Frodi (1981) pointed out that infants born with mental, physical, or behavioral abnormalities may actually develop characteristics that invite abuse. For example, significantly maladaptive behavior (as is common among the severely impaired children) could blunt the development of mutual love and trust (i.e, attachment) between parents and handicapped children. Findings in this area are inconclusive, however, as a recent study by Starr, Dietrich, and Fischer (Note 4) failed to support the view that child characteristics play a major role in abuse. Furthermore, since parent–child relationships are interactional, parents may be the source of problems in attachment formation and abuse/neglect tendency (Meyers et al., 1981).

Proposed Investigations

Can a handicap defeat attachment formation between young children and their caretakers? The evidence to date suggests that it does not; however, we still do not know the extent to which it impairs or dulls attachment. There are at least three patterns of investigation that may be inspired by the attachment literature. The first concerns foster care, e.g., is adjustment a function of the degree of attachment formed with natural parents, or is it a function of attachment formed with foster parents? How is the adjustment of a handicapped child affected by frequent changes of foster families? A second area of investigation might focus on residential care, e.g., is adjustment in a residential environment related to preplacement attachment? How does attachment to careprovider personnel, especially as related to changes due to week-end or day-evening shifts in staffing, affect adjustment? To what extent can multiple attachments be formed with careproviding personnel? Finally, investigations might focus on the relationship between previously formed attachments, such as friendships between handicapped individuals or between handicapped residents and careproviders, and current adjustment.

These proposed investigations explore such broad issues as whether primary attachments can be developed

A Review of Attachment Formation and Disorder in Handicapped Children   Jan Blacher and C. E. Meyers

with handicapped children not living with their natural family; whether a primary attachment makes it easier to form new attachments, so important for severely impaired children who may undergo a series of foster care or residential placements; or whether previously formed attachments, as in the friendship patterns beautifully described by Berkson and Romer (Berkson & Romer, 1980; Romer & Berkson, 1980a, 1980b), should be carefully considered in the placement and relocation of handicapped people.

Reference Notes

1. Barnard, K. E. An ecological approach to parent-child relations. In C. C. Brown (Ed.), *Infants at risk: Assessment and intervention. An update for health-care professionals and parents.* Johnson & Johnson Baby Products Co., 1981.

2. Nix, K. S. *Maternal attachment behaviors with defective versus normal infants (Monograph: Mother-infant studies).* Denton: Texas Woman's University, College of Nursing, 1980.

3. Helfer, R. The relationship between lack of bonding and child abuse and neglect. In M. H. Klaus, T. Leger, & M. A. Trause (Eds.), *Maternal attachment and mothering disorders: A round table.* Johnson & Johnson Baby products Co., 1975.

4. Starr, R. H., Dietrich, K. N., & Fischoff, J. *The contribution of children to their own abuse.* Paper presented at the annual meeting of the Society for Research in Child Development, Boston, April 1981.

References

Ainsworth, M. D. S. The development of infant-mother attachment. In B. M. Caldwell & H. N. Ricciuti (Eds.), *Review of child development research* (Vol. 3). Chicago: The University of Chicago Press, 1973.

Ainsworth, M. D. S. Attachment and child abuse. In G. Gerbner, C. Ross, & E. Zigler (Eds.), *Child abuse: Agenda for action.* New York: Oxford University Press, 1980.

Ainsworth, M. D. S., & Bell, S. M. Attachment, exploration, and separation: Illustrated by the behavior of one-year-olds in a strange situation. *Child Development,* 1970, *41,* 49–67.

Ainsworth, M. D. S., Blehar, M. C., Waters, E., & Wall, S. *Patterns of attachment.* Hillsdale, NJ: Lawrence Erlbaum Assoc., 1978.

Ainsworth, M. D. S., & Wittig, B. A. Attachment and exploratory behavior of one-year-olds in a strange situation. In B. M. Foss (Ed.), *Determinants of infant behavior* (Vol. 4). London: Methuen, 1969.

Alloway, T., Pliner, P., & Krames, L. *Advances in the study of communication and affect* (Vol. 3). *Attachment behavior.* New York: Plenum Press, 1977.

American Psychiatric Association. *Diagnostic and statistical manual of mental disorders* (3rd ed.). Washington, DC: American Psychiatric Association, 1980.

Anderson, C. W. Attachment in daily separations: Reconceptualizing day care and maternal employment issues. *Child Development,* 1980, *51,* 242–245.

Anderson, C. W., Nagle, R. J., Roberts, W. A., & Smith, J. S. Attachment to substitute caregivers as a function of center quality and caregiver involvement. *Child Development,* 1981, *52,* 53–61.

Bell, S. M. The development of the concept of object as related to infant-mother attachment. *Child Development,* 1970, *41,* 291–341.

Berkson, G., & Romer, D. Social ecology of supervised communal facilities for mentally disabled adults: I. Introduction. *American Journal of Mental Deficiency,* 1980, *85,* 229–242.

Berry, P., Gunn, P., & Andrews, R. Behavior of Down syndrome infants in a strange situation. *American Journal of Mental Deficiency,* 1980, *85,* 213–218.

Bowlby, J. The nature of the child's tie to his mother. *International Journal of Psychoanalysis,* 1958, *39,* 350–353.

Bowlby, J. *Attachment and loss* (Vol. I). *Attachment.* London: Hogarth, 1969.

Bowlby, J. *Loss: Sadness and depression. Attachment and loss* (Vol. 3). New York: Basic Books, 1980.

Bromwich, R. M. Focus on maternal behavior in infant intervention. *American Journal of Orthopsychiatry,* 1976, *46,* 439–446.

Call, J. D. Attachment disorders of infancy. In H. I. Kaplan, A. M. Freedman, & B. J. Sadock (Eds.), *Comprehensive textbook of psychiatry* (Vol. III). Baltimore: Williams & Wilkins, 1980.

Cicchetti, D., & Serafica, F. C. Interplay among behavioral systems: Illustrations from the study of attachment, affiliation, and wariness in young children with Down's syndrome. *Developmental Psychology,* 1981, *17,* 36–49.

Cicchetti, D., & Sroufe, L. A. The relationship between affective and cognitive development in Down's syndrome infants. *Child Development*, 1976, *47*, 920–929.

Cicchetti, D., & Sroufe, L. A. An organizational view of affect: Illustration from the study of Down's syndrome infants. In M. Lewis & L. A. Rosenblum (Eds.), *The development of affect*. New York: Plenum Press, 1978.

Cohen, L. J. The operational definition of human attachment. *Psychological Bulletin*, 1974, *81*, 207–217.

Crockenberg, S. B. Infant irritability, mother responsiveness, and social support influences on the security of infant-mother attachment. *Child Development*, 1981, *52*, 857–865.

Cropley, C., Lester, P., & Pennington, S. Assessment tool for measuring maternal attachment behaviors. In L. McNall & J. T. Galeener (Eds.), *Current practice in obstetric and gynecologic nursing* (Vol. 1). St. Louis: C. V. Mosby, 1976.

Cunningham, C. E., Reuler, E., Blackwell, J., & Deck, J. Behavioral and linguistic developments in the interactions of normal and retarded children with their mothers. *Child Development*, 1981, *52*, 62–70.

Decarie, T. G. *Intelligence and affectivity in early childhood*. New York: International Universities Press, 1965.

Egeland, B., & Sroufe, L. A. Attachment and early maltreatment. *Child Development*, 1981, *52*, 44–52.

Emde, R. N., & Brown, C. Adaptation to the birth of a Down's syndrome infant. Grieving and maternal attachment. *Journal of the American Academy of Child Psychiatry*, 1978, *17*, 299–323.

Emde, R. N., Katz, E. L., & Thorpe, J. K. Emotional expression in infancy: II. Early deviations in Down's syndrome. In M. Lewis & L. A. Rosenblum (Eds.), *The development of affect*. New York: Plenum Press, 1978.

Fraiberg, S. Intervention in infancy: A program for blind infants. *Journal of the American Academy of Child Psychiatry*, 1971, *10*, 381–405.

Fraiberg, S. Blind infants and their mothers: An examination of the sign system. In M. Lewis & L. A. Rosenblum (Eds.), *The effect of the infant on its caregiver*. New York: John Wiley & Sons, 1974.

Friedrich, W. N., & Boriskin, J. A. The role of the child in abuse: A review of the literature. *American Journal of Orthopsychiatry*, 1976, *46*, 580–590.

Frodi, A. M. Contribution of infant characteristics to child abuse. *American Journal of Mental Deficiency*, 1981, *85*, 341–349.

Gath, A. The impact of an abnormal child upon the parents. *British Journal of Psychiatry*, 1977, *130*, 405–410.

Greenberg, H. A. A comparison of infant-mother interactional behavior in infants with atypical behavior and normal infants. In J. Hellmuth (Ed.), *The exceptional infant, Volume 2: Studies in abnormalities*. New York: Brunner/Mazel, 1971.

Greenberg, M. T. Social interaction between deaf preschoolers and their mothers: The effects of communication method and communication competence. *Developmental Psychology*, 1980, *16*, 465–474.

Greenberg, M. T., & Marvin, R. S. Attachment patterns in profoundly deaf preschool children. *Merrill-Palmer Quarterly*, 1979, *25*, 265–279.

Grossmann, K., Thane, K., & Grossmann, K. E. Maternal tactual contact of the newborn after various postpartum conditions of mother-infant contact. *Developmental psychology*, 1981, *17*, 158–169.

Jones, O. H. M. A comparative study of mother-child communication with Down's syndrome and normal infants. In D. Shaffer & J. Dunn (Eds.), *The first year of life*. New York: John Wiley & Sons, 1979.

Marr, P. C., & Kennedy, C. E. Parenting atypical families. In M. J. Fine (Ed.), *Handbook on parent education*. New York: Academic Press, 1980.

Marvin, R. S. An ethological-cognitive model for the attenuation of mother-child attachment behavior. In T. M. Alloway, P. Pliner, & L. Krames (Eds.), *Advances in the study of communication and affect* (Vol. 3). *The development of social attachments*. New York: Plenum Press, 1977.

Masters, J. C., & Wellman, H. M. The study of human infant attachment: A procedural critique. *Psychological Bulletin*, 1974, *81*, 218–237.

McGuire, L. L., & Meyers, C. E. Early personality in the congenitally blind child. *The New Outlook*, May 1971, 137–143.

Meyers, C. E., Zetlin, A., & Blacher-Dixon, J. The family as affected by schooling for severely retarded children: An invitation to research. *Journal of Community Psychology*, 1981, *9*, 306–315.

Parkes, C. M., & Stevenson-Hinde, J. *The place of attachment in human behavior*. New York: Basic Books, 1982.

Pastor, D. L. The quality of mother-infant attachment and its relationship to toddlers' initial sociability with peers. *Developmental Psychology*, 1981, *17*, 326–335.

Rheingold, H. L. The effect of environmental stimulation upon social and exploratory behavior in the human infant. In B. M. Foss (Ed.), *Determinants of infant behavior*. New York: John Wiley & Sons, 1961.

Rode, S. S., Chang, P., Fisch, R. Q., & Sroufe, L. A. Attachment patterns of infants separated from birth. *Developmental Psychology*, 1981, *17*, 188–191.

Romer, D., & Berkson, G. Social ecology of supervised communal facilities for mentally disabled adults: II. Predictors of affiliation. *American Journal of Mental Deficiency*, 1980, *85*, 219–228. (a)

Romer, D., & Berkson, G. Social ecology of supervised communal facilities for mentally disabled adults: III. Predictors of social choice. *American Journal of Mental Deficiency*, 1980, *85*, 243–252. (b)

Rosen, L. Selected aspects in the development of the mother's understanding of her mentally retarded child. *American Journal of Mental Deficiency*, 1955, *59*, 522–528.

Serafica, F. C., & Cicchetti, D. Down's syndrome children in a strange situation: Attachment and exploration behaviors. *Merrill-Palmer Quarterly*, 1976, *22*, 137–150.

Simeonsson, R. J., Monson, L. B., & Blacher, J. Social understanding and mental retardation. In P. Brooks, C. McCauley, & R. Sperber (Eds.), *Learning, cognition, and mental retardation*. Baltimore: University Park Press, in press.

Sroufe, L. A., & Waters, E. Attachment as an organizational construct. *Child Development*, 1977, *48*, 1184–1199.

Stone, N. W., & Chesney, B. H. Attachment behaviors in handicapped infants. *Mental Retardation*, 1978, *16*, 8–12.

Vaughn, B., Egeland, B., Sroufe, L. A., & Waters, E. Individual differences in infant-mother attachment at twelve and eighteen months: Stability and change in families under stress. *Child Development*, 1979, *50*, 971–975.

Waters, E., & Deane, K. E. Infant-mother attachment: Theories, models, recent data, and some tasks for comparative developmental analysis. In L. W. Hoffman, R. Gandelman, & H. R. Schiffman (Eds.), *Parenting, Its causes and consequences*. Hillsdale, NJ: Lawrence Erlbaum Assoc., 1982.

Waters, E., Wippman, J., & Sroufe, L. A. Attachment, positive affect, and competence in the peer group: Two studies in construct validation. *Child Development*, 1979, *50*, 821–829.

Wedell-Monnig, J., & Lumley, J. M. Child deafness and mother-child interaction. *Child Development*, 1980, *51*, 766–774.

Zigler, E. Developmental versus difference theories of mental retardation and the problem of motivation. *American Journal of Mental Deficiency*, 1969, *73*, 536–556.

Zigler, E. The retarded child as a whole person. In D. K. Routh (Ed.), *The experimental study of mental retardation*. Chicago: Aldine, 1973.

Manuscript submitted 2/8/82.

Authors

Jan Blacher, School of Education, University of California, Riverside and **C. E. Meyers,** University of California, Los Angeles.

Taxonomy of Family Life Styles: I. Homes with TMR Children

Iris Tan Mink, Kazuo Nihira, and C. Edward Meyers
1983

Abstract

A battery of instruments dealing with family social environment and family and child characteristics and behavior was administered to 115 families with children in trainable mentally retarded (TMR) classes. Cluster analysis was performed on the social environment variables. Five distinctive clusters of families, each with distinctive patterns of characteristics, were identified: cohesive, harmonious; control-oriented, somewhat unharmonious; low-disclosure, unharmonious; child-oriented, expressive; and disadvantaged, low morale. Comparisons among the clusters and ethnographic observations revealed significant differences in family characteristics and child adjustment at home and school.

In this paper we report on an exploration of homes of mentally retarded children designed to determine whether certain basic family life-style patterns could be identified, and if so, whether these could be meaningfully related to family and child characteristics. In previous research studies of these families, we employed multiple regression and canonical correlation analyses in the attempt to predict child adjustment from home variables (Nihira, Meyers, & Mink, 1980; Nihira, Mink, & Meyers, 1981). These studies revealed the importance of family environment in the child's development; however, we felt that certain combinations or interactions of home variables were related to the child's adjustment and that such patterns were not optimally ascertained by the analytical methods employed. Admittedly, each family may have a unique pattern of interactions, but it may be possible to identify subgroups of families who have similar patterns of interactions.

Attempts to specify family patterns have been made from data on deviant youth and problem families (Giovannoni & Billingsley, 1970; Minuchin, 1970; Minuchin, Montalvo, Guerney, Rosman, & Schumer, 1967; Pavenstedt, 1965). A search for patterns has also been made on a cross-section of problem and non-problem families (Kantor & Lehr, 1975; Moos & Moos,

1976; Westley & Epstein, 1970). In their determination of family types, Moos and Moos employed cluster analysis and identified six distinctive clusters of families: expression-oriented, structure-oriented, independence-oriented, achievement-oriented, moral/religious-oriented, and conflict-oriented.

Although the Moos and Moos (1976) typology provides a seemingly appropriate classification system for our families, a serious difficulty lies in their sample of families. The sample was composed of an ethnically mixed group of families from the community at large, from a psychiatric clinic, and from a probation department. Although the latter two groups have at least one family member with problems, it appears unwise to equate these families with those having severely retarded children (Begab, 1966; Farber, Jenne, & Toigo, 1960; Fowle, 1968; Grossman, 1972; Holt, 1958). Thus, a decision was made to develop a taxonomy of families with TMR children.

The statistic of choice in developing a taxonomy is cluster analysis. This is an objective method for deriving a classification system from multivariate data. Its use in the biological and social sciences dates from the publication of *Principles of Numerical Taxonomy* (Sokal & Sneath, 1963). Since that time clustering techniques have been employed with increasing frequency, especially in the attempt to classify persons with learning disabilities (Doehring, Hoshko, & Bryans, 1979; Fisk & Rourke, 1979; Hale, 1981; Kertesz & Phipps, 1977; Morris, Blashfield, & Satz, 1981; Petrauskas & Rourke, 1979).

There are many different cluster analytic techniques; all form groups by maximizing intra-group similarities while maximizing inter-group differences (Anderberg, 1973; Blashfield & Aldenderfer, 1978; Everitt, 1980). The two cluster analytic techniques in general use are the hierarchial agglomerative and the iterative partitioning.

In the iterative partitioning method, which was used in this study, the investigator chooses the number of clusters believed to be present in the data. This decision is based on knowledge of the general data field and familiarity with one's own data. Once the number of clusters is decided upon, estimates of the cluster centroids are found. Subjects are then assigned to their most similar clusters, and new centroids are computed. After all subjects are assigned to clusters, each cluster is rechecked for the goodness of fit of all its subjects. If a subject does not fit easily into a cluster, the subject is re-assigned to another cluster. This process is repeated until a stable solution is found. The investigator customarily performs several cluster solutions with different numbers of clusters and then selects the optimal solution.

Although cluster analysis is an objective method for determining classifications, certain precautions must be observed by users (Blashfield, 1980; Everitt, 1979). Chief among these is the external validation of the obtained cluster solution, which otherwise might be considered a statistical artifact. Therefore, once we determined that there were family types based on psychosocial variables that described the climate of the home, we proceeded to ask whether there were differences between the types in characteristics of the family and child and in the behavior of the child at home and at school.

Method

Subjects

Our sample consisted of 115 TMR children and their families. Children were selected from fifteen TMR schools in four Southern California counties and were studied for a 4-year period (1976 to 1980).

Father figures were present in 84 percent of these families, and over 47 percent of the mothers worked. Average family socioeconomic level was 48.0 on the Duncan scale (middle-class). Average number of children in the homes, under age 18, was 2.5.

Approximately 48 percent of the retarded children had Down syndrome; 57 percent were male. Ethnic composition was 79 percent white, 3 percent black, 16 percent Hispanic, and the remaining 2 percent other. Average age of the children was 12.7 years; their average IQ was 41.5, with a range of 12 to 70.

Instruments

All families answered a questionnaire and completed several instruments concerning family and child characteristics, attitudes, and behavior. Interviewers rated families on behavior at home, and teachers rated children on behavior at school. Instruments can be grouped into two categories: those providing variables to be used in the cluster analysis and those to be used in the criterion analysis.

Cluster analysis. Instruments were selected to provide a comprehensive picture of the home environment. Based on results of previous research, three areas of study were targeted: environmental-process variables, psychosocial climate and environmental press, and child-rearing attitudes and practices.

Environmental-process variables are those relating to reinforcement aspects of the environment. This approach is an extension of social-learning theory (Bandura, 1969; Mischel, 1968). A widely accepted instrument in this area is the preschool version of the Home Observation for Measurement of the Environment Inventory (HOME, Bradley & Caldwell, 1979). This instrument provides measures of parental reinforcement practices and educational stimuli/opportunities available to the child. The 55-item version of HOME yields eight subscales. Internal consistency coefficients range from .53 to .83 for the subscales and .93 for the total scale. Concurrent and predictive validity studies indicate that the subscales are significantly correlated with IQ.

The study of the psychosocial climate of the home derives, in large measure, from the work of Murray (1938, 1951). His theoretical formulations consider environmental press and individual needs. "Press" includes both the environmental forces and the individuals' own interpretation of the phenomena. The best known objective instrument that seeks to measure this is the Family Environment Scale. This instrument assesses general psychosocial climate of the home on 10 subscales. Reported internal consistencies range from .64 to .79, and test-retest reliability ranges from .68 to .86 (Moos, Insel, & Humphrey, 1974). Validation is provided by studies in which the scale relates to child-rearing attitudes (Schneewind & Lortz, 1978), differentiates between families with clinic and non-clinic children (Scoresvy & Christensen, 1976), and differentiates between families with academically successful and academically unsuccessful children (Tabackman, 1977). Family Environment Scale scores are also related to family adjustment and the development of educable mentally retarded children (Nihira et al., 1980).

Upon examining the intercorrelations between Family Environment Scale subscales for our sample, we felt it was feasible to decrease the number of subscales used without decreasing descriptive accuracy. Our factor analysis reduced the 10 subscales to six factors that describe: "(a) the interpersonal relations among family members, e.g., cohesion vs. conflict, expressiveness; (b) family values and orientation, e.g., achievement-orientation, intellectual-cultural orientation; and (c) rigidity of family rules and the degree of importance in structuring family relations" (Nihira et al., 1981).

The area of child-rearing attitudes and practices has been studied extensively over an extended period of time (Baumrind, 1971; Kagan & Moss, 1962; Schaefer & Bell, 1958; Sears, Maccoby, & Levin, 1957; Yarrow, Campbell, & Burton, 1968). These investigators, among others, have identified three basic parental attitudes and practices that appear across groups and across data-gathering techniques. These basic dimensions are variously termed but essentially similar and are: acceptance vs. rejection, restrictiveness vs. permissiveness, and concern for development vs. unconcern.

In order to measure these basic dimensions we developed the Home Quality Rating Scale (Meyers, Mink, & Nihira, Note 1). Factor analysis of the scale revealed five factors: harmony and quality of parenting, concordance in support of child care, openness and awareness of disability, quality of the residential environment, and quality of the residential area. Since these factors differ somewhat from the three basic child-rearing dimensions, we speculated that adjustment and coping strategies in families with retarded children are different from the norm. Internal consistency reliabilities of the factor scores were estimated using Cronbach's alpha. Reliability coefficients for factors one through five were, respectively, .83, .78, .76, .71, and .56.

The 19 factors from the three aforementioned instruments were used in the cluster analysis to establish family patterns or types.

Criterion analysis. Variables employed in this part of the study were chosen to describe family and child characteristics and behavior. Basic demographic data were obtained from interviewer questions, as were indices of adjustment for the family and child. The Schedule of Recent Experience, a measure of stressful life events (Holmes & Rahe, 1967), and a shortened form of the Adaptive Behavior Scale (ABS, Nihira, Foster, Shellhaas, & Leland, 1974) were employed. The retarded child completed the Primary Self-Concept Inventory, where the factors were: physical size, emotional state, peer acceptance, helpfulness, success, and student self (Muller & Leonetti, 1974). At school, the teacher rated

the student on the Self-Esteem Behaviors (Coopersmith, 1975), the Teacher Rating Scale (Agard & Kaufman, Note 2), and the ABS.

In addition to these instruments, yearly interviewer comments were collected and participant observers who were trained ethnographers were placed into homes that were selected prior to data analysis. We also secured in-depth interviews by independent home visitors after data analysis to augment the number of cases on which we had observation-based reports.

Procedures

The factors from the HOME, Family Environment Scale, and Home Quality Rating Scale that provided our psychosocial indicators of home environment, the variables on which the cluster anlaysis was based, were as follows.

Home Observation for Measurement of the Environment

Stimulation through toys, games, and reading materials (TOYSTIM)

Language stimulation (LNGSTIM)

Physical environment safe, clean, and conducive to development (PHYSENV)

Pride, affection, and warmth (PRIDE)

Stimulation of academic behavior (ACASTIM)

Modeling and encouraging of social maturity (SOCMAT)

Variety of stimulation (VARSTIM)

Physical punishment (PHYSPUN)

Family Environment Scale

Expressiveness (EXPRESS)

Achievement orientation (ACHIEVE)

Moral-religious emphasis (MORREL)

Control (CONTROL)

Cohesion, independence, and organization vs. conflict (COHCNF)

Intellectual-cultural and active-recreational orientation (INTREC)

Home Quality Rating Scale

Harmony of the home and quality of parenting (HARMONY)

Concordance in parenting and marriage (CONCORD)

Openness and awareness of disability (OPEN)

Quality of residential environment (RESENV)

Quality of residential area (RESAREA)

We chose the *K* means clustering procedure (Engleman, 1979). This is an iterative partitioning method that sorts a set of cases into clusters, based on the Euclidean distance measure between the cases and the centers of the clusters. We produced several solutions that had different numbers of clusters to determine the stability of the clusters and to decide which solution best described the data. Final determination of the optimal solution was based on examination of the distance matrix for each solution and inspection of cluster stability. This procedure for determining the optimal number of clusters is consistent with Everitt's (1980). He argued that formal tests of significance are unnecessary, that the investigator would do well to consider several alternative classifications, and that any rigid determination of the optimal number of groups may be counterproductive.

Once the cluster analysis was completed, we determined the differences among clusters on other family and child characteristics and behavior, using analysis of variance or chi-square, where appropriate.

Results

Cluster Analysis

Cluster analysis revealed five distinctive types of families. Mean standard score profiles of the clusters are graphed in Figures 1 through 5. The variables are from the instruments employed in establishing the clusters and have been coded with a shorthand designation to be found in the previous description of the variables. Thus, the first variable from the HOME, stimulation through toys, games and reading material, is coded as TOYSTIM.

In the following description of the clusters, the terms *high* or *low* are employed for relative status of the mean standard score of the cluster among all five clusters and will generally indicate the highest or lowest among the five or at least relatively high or low scores. Reference to the profiles in Figure 1 through 5 will help interpretation.

Figure 1 Cluster 1: cohesive, harmonious family (*N* = 35).

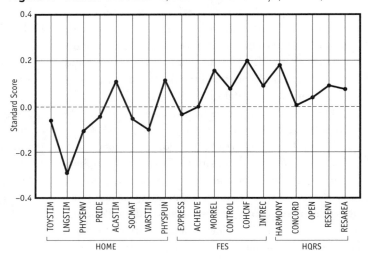

Figure 2 Cluster 2: control-oriented, somewhat unharmonious family (*N* = 34).

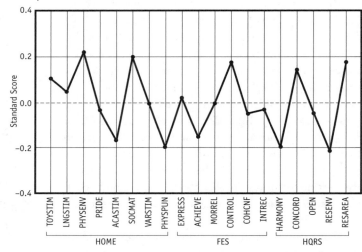

Figure 3 Cluster 3: low-disclosure, unharmonious family (*N* = 7).

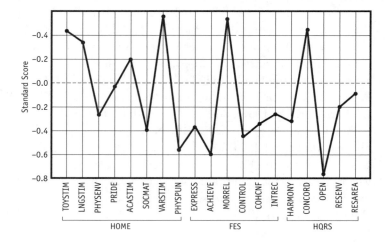

©American Association on Mental Retardation

Taxonomy of Family Life Styles: I. Homes With TMR Children Iris Tan Mink, Kazuo Nihira, and C. Edward Meyers

Figure 4 Cluster 4: child-oriented, expressive family (*N* = 27).

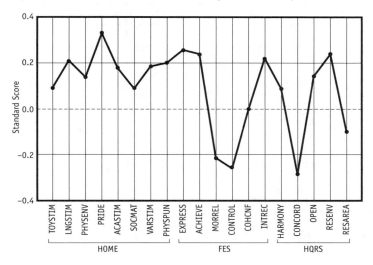

Figure 5 Cluster 5: disadvantaged family with low morale (*N* = 12).

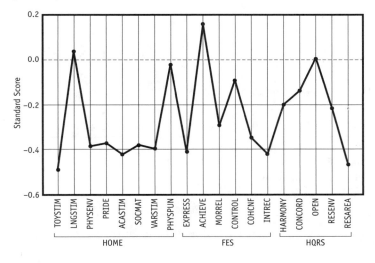

Cluster 1: cohesive, harmonious (35 families). These families scored high on cohesion vs. conflict and harmony. Moral-religious emphasis was somewhat elevated, but remaining scores hovered around the mid-points, except for language stimulation (see Figure 1).

Cluster 2: control-oriented, somewhat non-harmonious (34 families). Distinguishing features were high scores on physical environment, social maturity, and control. The low mean on physical punishment indicates use of physical punishment. Low scores also were found for harmony and residential environment; this differed from physical environment in that residential environment assessed the home as a place to rear children (see Figure 2).

Cluster 3: low disclosure, unharmonious (7 families). Figure 3 reveals a profile of extremes. The most distinguishing feature is the low score on openness and awareness. Families scored low also on physical environment, social maturity, and physical punishment; i.e., they used it. They were below average in expressiveness, achievement orientation, control, intellectual-recreational orientation, harmony, and residential environment.

These families also demonstrated high scores on stimulation through toys, language stimulation, academic stimulation, and variety of stimulation. Scores were high also on moral-religious and concordance in parenting. In fact, scores for this cluster were either very high or very low except for pride, affection, and warmth, and residential area.

Cluster 4: child-oriented, expressive (27 families). The outstanding feature of these families was high scores on factors concerned with the child's well being. Thus, scores on pride, affection, and warmth, language stimulation, and nonuse of physical punishment, may be noted in Figure 4. Also above median were expressiveness, achievement orientation, intellectual-recreation orientation, and residential environment. Low scores are on moral-religious emphasis, control, and concordance.

Cluster 5: disadvantaged, low morale (12 families). These families had low scores on almost all variables shown in Figure 5. Exceptionally low scores were on stimulation through toys, academic stimulation, expressiveness, intellectual-recreation orientation, and residential area. The only variables where means were above mid-line were language stimulation, and achievement orientation.

Criterion Analysis

As previously mentioned, we wanted to establish a better understanding of the child's home environment and home and school adjustment than could be derived from multiple regression approaches. We felt that constructing a taxonomy of family life styles would en-

Table 1 Description of the Parents and Family

| Variable | Cluster | | | | | | Test of significance[f] | |
	1	2	3	4	5	Total	Overall	Pairwise[g]
% father figures present	82.9	91.2	100.0	66.7	91.7	83.5	8.97*	
% father figures help with child care[a]	89.7	100.0	100.0	94.1	72.7	92.6	9.84**	2 ≠ 5**
% mothers who work	31.4	67.7	57.1	46.2	33.3	47.4	10.41**	1 ≠ 2***; 2 ≠ 4*, 5*
% father figures more than high school education[a]	65.5	71.0	42.9	55.6	45.5	61.5	3.86	
% mothers more than high school education[b]	40.0	47.1	71.4	53.9	41.7	47.4	2.98	
% of existing relationships where child has negative influence[a, c, d]	0	12.9	28.6	5.9	18.2	9.5	16.12**	1 ≠ 2**, 3***, 5**; 3 ≠ 4*
Mean family SES (Duncan)	48.5	52.3	49.4	47.9	34.8	48.0	1.25	
Mean N of children in home under age 18	2.9	2.4	2.1	2.2	2.3	2.5	1.08	
Mean occurrence of stressful life events (Holmes & Rahe)	56.4	62.5	122.3	84.0	86.3	71.8	3.22**	1 ≠ 3; 2 ≠ 3
Mean impact of child on home[e]	13.8	16.6	14.4	14.3	14.8	14.9	1.07	
Mean attitude to child's impact[d]	25.1	24.7	23.4	22.8	20.8	23.9	2.12*	1 ≠ 5; 2 ≠ 5

[a] Limited to 96 families with a father figure.
[b] Limited to 114 families where information was available.
[c] There were three levels of influence: negative, neutral, and positive.
[d] Interviewer rating.
[e] Parent report.
[f] Chi-squares are reported for the first 6 variables, Fs for the last 5.
[g] Level of significance: for chi-square as noted, for Duncan's multiple range test a = .05 on all comparisons.
 * $p < .10$.
 ** $p < .05$.
 *** $p < .01$.

able us to find meaningful patterns that would relate the nature of the home with the retarded child's adjustment. Accordingly, differences between clusters on manifold variables not used in the formation of clusters were examined.

The resulting percentages, means, and test of significance are presented in Table 1 for parent and family characteristics; Table 2, for child characteristics and behavior at home; and Table 3, for child behavior at school. When the overall test was significant, pairwise comparisons between clusters were made using Duncan's mul-

tiple range test or chi-square, whichever was appropriate.

Cluster 1: cohesive, harmonious. This family type had the lowest percentage of mothers who worked, an absence of negative child influence on the marriage, and the lowest occurrence of stressful life events among all groups. A high percentage of these children had Down syndrome. At home, the children had significantly high scores on Personal–Social Responsibility. At school, teachers rated them significantly high on self-esteem, and children reported themselves significantly high on physical size and peer acceptance, both self-concept dimensions.

Taxonomy of Family Life Styles: I. Homes With TMR Children   Iris Tan Mink, Kazuo Nihira, and C. Edward Meyers

Table 2 Description of the Child at Home

| Variable | Cluster | | | | | | Test of significance[b] | |
	1	2	3	4	5	Total	Overall	Pairwise[c]
% Down syndrome	65.7	38.2	42.9	44.4	33.3	47.8	6.95	1 ≠ 2***, 4*
% male	45.7	82.4	28.6	51.9	41.7	56.5	14.44***	1 ≠ 2***; 2 ≠ 3**, 4**, 5***
% white	65.7	88.2	85.7	96.3	50.0	79.1	16.69***	1 ≠ 2*, 4***; 2 ≠ 5**; 4 ≠ 5***
Mean age	12.7	12.6	12.8	12.7	12.9	12.7	.06	
Mean IQ	40.7	41.9	47.4	42.3	36.9	41.5	1.37	3 ≠ 5**
Mean Personal Self-Sufficiency	47.5	42.9	45.9	46.4	42.5	44.7	2.71**	2≠4, 4≠5
Mean Community Self-Sufficiency	30.3	24.9	39.4	32.8	24.7	29.3	4.44***	1 ≠ 2, 3, 5; 2 ≠ 3; 3 ≠ 5
Mean Personal-Social Responsibility	21.2	16.7	21.7	20.7	18.3	19.5	6.80****	1 ≠ 2; 2 ≠ 3
Mean Social Maladaptation	24.1	25.9	26.4	26.1	33.8	26.3	.48	
Mean Personal Maladaptation	7.1	7.7	9.9	6.9	12.6	8.0	1.05	
Mean general social adjustment[a]	41.0	37.8	43.1	40.7	37.1	39.7	2.85**	1 ≠ 2, 5; 2 ≠ 3, 4; 3 ≠ 5; 4 ≠ 5

[a] Parent report.
[b] Chi-squares are reported for the first 3 variables, Fs for the last 8.
[c] Level of significance: for chi-square as noted, for Duncan's multiple range test a = .05 on all comparisons.
   * $p < .10$.
  ** $p < .05$.
 *** $p < .01$.
**** $p < .001$.

Cluster 2: control-oriented, somewhat unharmonious. In this cluster, the majority of mothers were employed, and all father figures assisted with child care. These families had the highest socioeconomic level and a significantly low occurrence of stressful life events. Children were predominantly male and white. A relatively low percentage had Down syndrome. At home, they had significantly low scores on all dimensions of the ABS and general social adjustment. In school, Community Self-Sufficiency and self-esteem were significantly low.

Cluster 3: low-disclosure, unharmonious. All families reported that father figures were present and helped care for the child. Most of the mothers worked and were educated beyond high school level. Families also had the highest occurrence of stressful life events and negative impact of the child on the family. There were signifi-

cantly more girls in this cluster than in other clusters. A high percentage of the children were white, and IQ was the highest of all clusters. Children were significantly high on Community Self-Sufficiency, Personal-Social Responsibility, and general social adjustment at home. Teachers rated the children significantly high on Community Self-Sufficiency and self-esteem, whereas children rated themselves significantly high on peer acceptance.

Cluster 4: child-oriented, expressive. These families had the lowest percentage of father figures. When they were present, most assisted with child care. Very few of these children had a negative influence on the family. Almost all children were white. At home, they had significantly high scores on personal Self-Sufficiency. At school, they were average in most measures except for

Taxonomy of Family Life Styles: I. Homes With TMR Children   Iris Tan Mink, Kazuo Nihira, and C. Edward Meyers

Table 3 Description of the Child at School (Means)

Variable	Cluster						Test of significance	
	1	2	3	4	5	Total	Overall F	Pairwise[c]
Personal Self-Sufficiency[a]	36.1	33.8	34.8	34.7	33.2	34.7	1.59	$1 \neq 2, 5$
Community Self-Sufficiency[a]	27.7	24.3	37.4	26.8	20.9	26.2	4.29***	$1 \neq 3, 5; 2 \neq 3;$
								$3 \neq 4, 5; 4 \neq 5$
Personal–Social Responsibility[a]	21.7	18.9	25.8	21.0	20.2	20.8	2.40*	$1 \neq 2; 2 \neq 3$
Social Maladaptation[a]	23.1	24.7	8.8	12.0	22.8	20.2	1.67	
Personal Maladaptation[a]	3.9	6.2	6.2	3.1	8.0	4.9	1.49	
Self-esteem (teacher rating)	19.1	16.8	19.0	18.0	16.3	17.8	3.44***	$1 \neq 2, 5$
Self-concept (self-report):[b]								
Physical size	2.6	2.0	2.3	1.8	2.4	2.2	2.92**	$1 \neq 2, 4$
Emotional state	2.5	2.4	2.7	2.3	2.8	2.5	.63	
Peer acceptance	2.2	1.8	2.0	1.1	1.4	1.7	3.48***	$1 \neq 4$
Helpfulness	1.7	1.3	1.9	1.6	2.1	1.6	1.42	
Success	2.5	2.5	2.7	2.5	2.8	2.6	.36	
Student self	2.4	2.0	2.3	2.1	1.7	2.1	1.03	

[a] Limited to 109 children where information was available.
[b] Limited to 96 children where reliable report was available.
[c] Level of significance for Duncan's multiple range test a = .05 on all comparisons.
  * $p < .10$.
 ** $p < .05$.
*** $p < .01$.

maladaptation, where they were below average. The children rated themselves significantly low on physical size and peer acceptance.

Cluster 5: disadvantaged with low morale. Although the number of father figures present was above average, a significantly low percentage helped with child care, and most of the mothers were not employed. Education beyond high school level for mothers and fathers was relatively low. Frequency of occurrence of stressful life events was fairly high, parents' reported attitude to the child's impact on the family was poor, and interviewers rated an above-average number of the children as having a negative influence on the family. Children were equally divided into white and nonwhite groups, were below the total group average on percentage of males, and had the lowest percentage of Down syndrome. They also had the lowest IQ of all groups. At home, they were significantly low on Personal Self-Sufficiency, Community Self-Sufficiency, and general social adjustment. At school, they were rated significantly low on Community Self-Sufficiency and self-esteem.

Pairwise comparisons underscored the differences between clusters. In variables having to do with family stability (i.e., mother at home, good attitude, few life events), Cluster 1 was consistently better than were other clusters, particularly Cluster 3. In variables concerning self-esteem and acceptance at school, Cluster 1 children outperformed those from Clusters 2, 4, and 5. With regard to Community Self-Sufficiency and Personal–Social Responsibility at home and at school, Cluster 3 children scored consistently higher than those from other clusters, particularly Cluster 5 on Community Self-Sufficiency and Cluster 2 on Personal–Social Responsibility.

Comparisons between pairs of clusters were also computed on three variables not having a significant overall test: Down syndrome, IQ, and Personal Self-Sufficiency at school. Computation of the latter provided comparison with Personal Self-Sufficiency at home. Comparison of the number of Down syndrome children revealed a significant difference, .01 level, between

Clusters 1 and 2 and a nearly significant difference, .10 level, between Clusters 1 and 4. On IQ, children in Cluster 3 were significantly different, .05 level, from children in Cluster 5.

Ethnography and In-depth Interviews

Bogdan and Taylor (1975) stated that "when we reduce people to statistical aggregates, we lose sight of the subjective nature of human behavior" (p. 4). We are removed from their experience of life. Ethnography can provide investigators with information at this different level of discourse; therefore, to obtain a better understanding of the nature of our clusters and to confirm data secured in regular interviews, we employed ethnographic observers, trained in participant observation with families, to become very closely acquainted with a few families. We also had observers conduct in-depth interviews with other families. Assignment of the ethnographic observers was made prior to data analysis. After data analysis, several intense interviews were made to secure a few more family descriptions. In no case did these observers have any of the information secured by the regular interviewers. Hence, for these families we had extensive descriptive information regarding facts and dynamics of the families. We found that the regular interviewers were not deceived in what they obtained and, in general, got the right impressions. What they could not always obtain was the intensity of feeling, sometimes of despair, that only a close confident, as a participant observer, could obtain.

Cluster 1: cohesive, harmonious family. The participant observer described the Isaacs family, whose daughter Sara had Down syndrome. They lived in a tree-lined, pleasant, middle-class neighborhood. Mr. Isaacs managed a business and was in his 50s. He rejected a promotion that would have provided better retirement benefits because it involved moving to a new city, where he determined that the special education program was inferior to the one Sara locally enjoyed. Mrs. Isaacs, in her mid-40s, worked at home part-time as a bookkeeper. Sara was 10 and attractive, with long blonde hair. She was allowed considerable freedom in the neighborhood, walked her dog, played with children, or just "moseyed" around; but her parents required that she be home before dark.

She scored 36 on the Stanford-Binet Intelligence Scale; her major problem was expressive speech. The speech therapist believed that daily therapy would improve her articulation, and believed that Sara, of all the children in the TMR school, "has one of the better chances for being able to do something with her life" and should at least succeed in sheltered workshop.

Donald was 12.5-years-old, an adopted brother who used to tease Sara; the father counseled him about responsibilities of being a teenager, and the teasing stopped. The ethnographer noted the considerable amount of time spent by the parents with Sara and their warmth and affection. They were aware of her limitations, knew she would not be independent and would require a sheltered environment.

Sara did well at school and was in the highest achievement group for each activity. The teacher reported that her only problems were incomprehensible speech and occasional stubbornness; otherwise, she was a real pleasure, "the only child on the unit who is at peace with herself." The teacher reported her to be "free of the emotional problems that the other children have," attributing this to the attention and affection received at home.

Cluster 2: control-oriented, somewhat unharmonious family. The ethnographic report described the Jones family, who lived in a middle-class suburb of Los Angeles. Mr. Jones worked as a deliveryman and appeared to do well financially. The cars, house, and furnishings were of good quality. Charles was a retarded 10-year-old, good-looking, tanned rosy-cheeked, with dark brown hair, friendly, apparently bright; but he had unclear speech and difficulty recalling things. His IQ was 48.

Anthony was his non-retarded 13-year-old brother, not as good-looking, but bright and straightforward in manner, active in sports, with problems in controlling his temper. There was considerable sibling rivalry, which Mrs. Jones attributed to her husband, whom she described as "inflexible and non-empathetic." He was hard on Anthony, expecting him to be "the ideal son." Mrs. Jones regretted that Charles did not look retarded, for everyone expected him to act normally and had little patience or tolerance when he did not.

As an infant, Charles had scarlet fever; Mrs. Jones says she "didn't attend to it quickly despite, or because of her mother's urgings that this was something more than just a cold." Charles was finally hospitalized, and the doctors said that there might be damage from the high fever. He appeared normal for a while but showed slowness in the developmental stages for walking and talking. He was diagnosed as retarded at age 3.

The ethnographer described Mrs. Jones as "a pleasant and genuinely kind woman. She seems hard-working, but is disorganized and scatter-brained." She appeared to harbor some guilt for Charles' condition and felt confused because of his "appearance of normality" and frequent normal conversations. This contradiction led her to believe that "there may be something out there that can offer Charles a better chance for developing his potential to the fullest."

Mr. Jones was not sympathetic with his wife's search for treatment; "he wanted her to stop looking around so much," and felt that she developed false hopes and that each search ended in disappointment. Our ethnographer concluded that despite family participation in sports and an active social life, harmony was only on the surface; the father and Anthony had a strained relationship, whereas Anthony accused his mother of favoring Charles over him, "letting him get away with things because he's retarded." Mrs. Jones felt that her husband was hyper-critical, "stubborn, and spiteful in small ways." Mr. Jones was annoyed by his wife's unrealistic approach to Charles' condition.

Cluster 3: low disclosure, unharmonious family. Natalie Bolsky and her parents lived in a small city southeast of Los Angeles in an old, rundown section; mature trees provided a serene appearance. The house was a white clapboard that needed painting and landscaping attention. It appeared to be spacious but was actually small. It was uncluttered and sparsely furnished, but gave the appearance of disorganization. Family pictures appeared in the hall and included more of Natalie's two older brothers and their families than of her. She was a nice-looking 12-year-old with prominent Down syndrome features. Her IQ was 41.

Mrs. Bolsky ws an unattractive woman, short, fat, unkempt, with bowlegs and gray hair pulled back into a severe bun. Mr. Bolsky was never seen; he is a construction worker. Mrs. Bolsky reported "a happy marriage—for many years"; however, they rarely went anyplace, because the husband ws always working.

Our observer reported this to be the most difficult interview she ever conducted. After agreeing to the interview, Mrs. Bolsky responded with only a curt yes or no without elaboration. If a question touched on Natalie's disability, she would leave the room, ostensibly to do something, returning after a minute or so. She was described as "uncomfortable with questions and defensive in her answers." She once remarked to the interviewer that "these questions are ridiculous, they just don't ap-

ply to Natalie." Not once during the entire interview did Mrs. Bolsky mention that Natalie had Down syndrome or attended a special TMR class. In the four annual interviews, Mrs. Bolsky was reported to be upset that Natalie was not in regular class, never feeling she had a handicap. She agreed that Natalie might be "a little hyper" but was "just average." She gave the impression that she resented that Natalie was not "normal." She also gave the impression that "correct" responses were given to questions.

Cluster 4: child-oriented expressive family. The ethnographic visitor described Mrs. Thomas and her 14-year-old son, Evan. They lived in a "very working class" neighborhood, older but not deteriorating. The interior of the home was well decorated; "nothing clashes in any part of the house." There was no clutter; Mrs. Thomas was a fastidious housekeeper, and Evan kept his own room neat as well. She was an attractive woman in her early 30s, with short dark hair and awareness of what was fashionable. She was competent and hard-working as a sales representative of an import company. She was friendly, read, gardened, and was an active swimmer.

"She is good with Evan and genuinely likes him." She encouraged him to do his best; she was not overly protective and allowed him to take risks. He rode a two-wheeler without training wheels and a skateboard standing up. This competency enhanced his standing with the neighborhood children, who included him in their games.

The divorced father saw Evan about twice a month but was not otherwise conscientious about parental duties. The ethnographer described Evan as "tall and thin in a spidery manner. He has a smooth, almost expressionless face. It is obvious that he is not a normal child, but he is pleasant, neat, and engaging." He made friends with children and adults quite easily. He was not shy and was ready for conversation. His IQ was 38.

Evan was hyperactive and took medication. The ethnographer described an episode in which he became "hyper," jumping around, picking up things and tossing them, going from one thing to another, going inside and then outside, jumping up from his chair, exploring, looking, probing; but he was not loud, disruptive, or destructive.

The ethnographer believed that Evan hampered Mrs. Thomas's life. "She is not free to do things as she would do ordinarily, but it seems that she deals with this no differently than if she were any single parent." Mrs. Thomas would like to re-marry. She is philosophical

Taxonomy of Family Life Styles: I. Homes With TMR Children   Iris Tan Mink, Kazuo Nihira, and C. Edward Meyers

about her chances and good-natured even when Evan "ruins" her dates with his persistent questioning.

Cluster 5: disadvantaged, low-morale families. Andrew Larson, 14, lived with his parents in a Los Angeles suburb, in a run-down neighborhood with old, small houses needing attention both inside and outside. Mr. Larson managed a department in a store. The wife was a homemaker and hard-of-hearing. Both parents were in their late 50s. They appeared to be kind and warm but somewhat passive. Three older daughters lived away from home. "Andrew is their only son and he is special to them." He is tall, thin, and unattractive. With Down syndrome, he has poor coordination and very poor receptive and expressive speech. He and his parents were learning signing to effect better communication. Andrew's IQ was 27.

He was not hyperactive nor muscular, but his mother reported that he could be violent at times and could strike out. He had hit children who teased him and even his mother when she tried to punish him. He had no close friends; his play consisted of swinging in his backyard. He was not allowed out in the neighborhood because he had "no sense of direction." The family's lifestyle was limited; they kept to themselves, rarely socializing, and did not take Andrew out much because they were afraid that he would "act out."

Mr. Larson had some concern for Andrew's future and went "regularly to the library [to check] out books on mental retardation." He wanted to send Andrew to a "special training school so that he can learn some skills and become a bit more independent," but his financial situation precluded any such program. He was looking for something less expensive, but otherwise the Larsons had made no plans for Andrew's future.

Discussion

The five-cluster solution for families with TMR children made good conceptual and empirical sense. Two family clusters, Clusters 1 and 4, provided a good home environment for the developing child. Cluster 2 was not the best environment nor was it the worst; the worst was Cluster 5, where the attitudes and behavior of both the parents and the child were impoverished.

The remaining cluster, Cluster 3, the low disclosure, unharmonious family was a poor type from the standpoint of research. The parent informant was so lacking in openness and willingness to disclose information that

it is wise to question the validity of the interviews. The lack of cooperation most likely indicates the parent's unwillingness to confront the child's retardation, rather than a deliberate attempt to mislead the interviewer. Parental denial did not seem to affect the child adversely. In general, these children scored highest in measures of adaptive behavior and adjustment at home (parent report) and at school (teacher report).

Both the cohesive, harmonious family (Cluster 1) and the child-oriented, expressive family (Cluster 4) were characterized by ethnographers and interviewers as "caring" homes, ones where the child's abilities were realistically appraised and the parents encourged the children to develop their potential. Children in these families were often accepted by non-retarded neighborhood children as playmates and thus were not isolated. Statistical analysis of child variables bore out some of this appraisal. These children scored high, although not the highest, on measures of adaptive behavior at home. At school, Cluster 1, but not Cluster 4, children were high on self-esteem and self-concept.

The control-oriented, somewhat unharmonious family (Cluster 2) had a very high percentage of retarded sons and mothers who worked. Our findings may have been linked to this. Whatever the reason, these children had very low adaptive behavior and high maladaptive behavior both at home and at school.

In the disadvantaged family with low morale (Cluster 5), the parents appeared to be so demoralized that they restricted the children and exacerbated their isolation. These families were not only financially impoverished, they were also emotionally impoverished. Examination of the children's behavior at home and at school revealed very low adaptive behavior, high maladaptive behavior, and low self-esteem. Interviewers reported that these families were friendly but passive; an outreach program might effect positive changes.

In our other taxonomy, developed with families of slow-learning children (Mink, Meyers, & Nihira, Notes 3 and 4), there are three family types that resemble three of the types in this study. Examination of profiles (comparison is possible on the Family Environment Scale and the Home Quality Rating Scale) reveals that the cohesive, harmonious family (TMR) is quite similar to the child-oriented, concordant family (slow-learner) and that the disadvantaged family with low morale (TMR), with the exception of intellectual-cultural and active-recreational orientation on the Family Environment

Scale, is essentially the same as the disadvantaged family with little concern for the child (slow-learner). Low-disclosure, unharmonious families emerge in both taxonomies; however, the profiles were only identical on the Home Quality Rating Scale, not the Family Environment Scale factors; whether this is due to socioeconomic differences remains to be determined.

Although we have answered some of the critical questions associated with cluster analysis, there are several more questions that careful constructors of taxonomies should address, namely, (a) do the same types emerge when new variables are used and (b) do different groups respond differently to the same treatment (Everitt, 1979)? Unfortunately, the answers to both questions are beyond the scope of our present research.

With our current data we also were not in a position to address the question of why there were different family patterns. As suggested previously, however, some explanation may lie in the sex of the retarded child. Our data revealed significant differences in the percentage of boys in the clusters. Earlier research indicated that "sex of the retarded child produces differences in parental response and behavior" (Farber et al., 1960).

The differences between clusters on percentage of Down syndrome should also be considered. It varied by over 30 percentage points between the clusters. Two-thirds of the children in Cluster 1, a "good" psychosocial environment, had Down syndrome. Taking into consideration the effects of children on their caregivers, we may speculate that Down syndrome children will have a positive effect on the climate of the home.

We also speculate that the difference between clusters may be due to the availability of support systems, either financial, familial, or both and to the childhood upbringing of the parents. Neither of these possibilities was addressed in our present research. Further work is needed. As Blashfield (1980) said, "A cluster solution is the beginning of a research process, not the end."

Reference Notes

1. Meyers, C. E., Mink, I., & Nihira K. *Home Quality Rating Scale*. Pomona, California: Neuropsychiatric Institute-Pacific State Research Group, 1977.

2. Agard, J. A., & Kaufman, J. J. *Teacher Rating Scale, Project PRIME*. Austin: University of Texas Data Analysis Unit, 1973.

3. Mink, I. T., Meyers, C. E., & Nihira, K. Lifestyles in families with slow learning children: A taxonomy. *Working Paper of the Socio-Behavioral Group, No. 18*. Los Angeles: Mental Retardation Research Center, UCLA, 1981.

4. Mink, I. T., Meyers, C. E., & Nihira, K. A *taxonomy of family life styles: II. Homes with slow learning children*. Manuscript in preparation, 1983.

References

Anderberg, M. R. *Cluster analysis for applications*. New York: Academic Press, 1973.

Bandura, A. *Principles of behavior modification*. New York: Holt, Rinehart, & Winston, 1969.

Baumrind, D. Current patterns of parental authority. *Developmental Psychology Monograph*, 1971, 4, No. 1.

Begab, M. J. The mentally retarded and the family. In I. Phillips (Ed.), *Prevention and treatment of mental retardation*, New York: Basic Books, 1966.

Blashfield, R. K. Propositions regarding the use of cluster analysis in clinical research. *Journal of Consulting and Clinical Psychology*, 1980, 48, 456–459.

Blashfield, R. K., & Aldenderfer, M. S. The literature on cluster analysis. *Multivariate Behavioral Research*, 1978, 13, 271–295.

Bogdan, R., & Taylor, S. J. *Introduction to qualitative research methods*. New York: John Wiley & Sons, 1975.

Bradley, R. H. & Caldwell, B. M. Home Observation for Measurement of the Environment: A revision of the preschool scale. *American Journal of Mental Deficiency*, 1979, 84, 235–244.

Coopersmith, S. *Coopersmith self-esteem behaviors*. San Francisco: Self-Esteem Institute, 1975.

Doehring, D. G., Hoshko, I. M., & Bryans, A. Statistical classification of children with reading problems. *Journal of Clinical Neuropsychology*, 1979, 1, 5–16.

Engleman, L. K-means clustering. In W. J. Dixon & M. B. Brown (Eds.), *BMDP Biomedical Computer Program P-Series*. Berkeley: University of California Press, 1979.

Everitt, B. *Cluster analysis* (2nd ed.). New York: John Wiley & Sons, 1980.

Everitt, B. S. Unresolved problems in cluster analysis. *Biometrics*, 1979, 35, 169–181.

Farber, B., Jenne, W. C., & Toigo, R. Family crisis and the decision to institutionalize the retarded child. *Council for Exceptional Children NEA, Research Monograph Series*, 1960, No. A-1.

Fisk, J. S., & Rourke, B. P. Identification of subtypes of learning disabled children at three age levels: A neuropsychological, multivariable approach. *Journal of Clinical Neuropsychology*, 1979, *1*, 289–310.

Fowle, C. M. The effect of the severely mentally retarded child on his family. *American Journal of Mental Deficiency*, 1968, *73*, 468–473.

Giovannoni, J. M., & Billingsley, A. Child neglect among the poor: A study of parental adequacy in the families of three ethnic groups. *Child Welfare*, 1970, *49*, 196–204.

Grossman, F. K. *Brothers and sisters of retarded children: An exploratory study.* Syracuse, NY: Syracuse University Press, 1972.

Hale, R. L. Cluster analysis in school psychology: An example. *Journal of School Psychology*, 1981, *19*, 51–56.

Holmes, T. H., & Rahe, R. H. The social readjustment rating scale. *Journal of Psychosomatic Research*, 1967, *11*, 213–218.

Holt, K. S. The home care of severely retarded children. *Pediatrics*, 1958, *22*, 744–795.

Kagan, J., & Moss, H. A. *Birth to maturity: A study in psychological development.* New York: John Wiley & Sons, 1962.

Kantor, D., & Lehr, W. *Inside the family.* San Francisco: Jossey-Bass, 1975.

Kertesz, A., & Phipps, J. B. Numerical taxonomy of aphasia. *Brain and Language*, 1977, *4*, 1–10.

Minuchin, S. The plight of the poverty-stricken family in the United States. *Child Welfare*, 1970, *49*, 124–130.

Minuchin, S., Montalvo, B., Guerney, B. G., Rosman, B. L., & Schumer, F. *Families of the slums: An exploration of their structure and treatment.* New York: Basic Books, 1967.

Mischel, W. *Personality and assessment.* New York: John Wiley & Sons, 1968.

Moos, R. H., Insel, P. M., & Humphrey, B. *Family Environment Scale Manual.* Palo Alto: Consulting Psychologists Press, 1974.

Moos, R. H., & Moos, B. S. A typology of family social environments. *Family Process*, 1976, *15*, 357–371.

Morris, R., Blashfield, R., & Satz, P. Neuropsychology of cluster analysis: Potentials and problems. *Journal of Clinical Neuropsychology*, 1981, *3*, 79–99.

Muller, D. G., & Leonetti, R. *Primary Self-Concept Inventory.* Austin: Learning Concepts, 1974.

Murray, H. A. *Exploration in personality.* New York: Oxford University Press, 1938.

Murray, H. A. Some basic psychological assumptions and conceptions. *Dialectica*, 1951, *5*, 266–292.

Nihira, K., Foster, R., Shellhaas, M., & Leland, H. *AAMD Adaptive Behavioral Scale.* Washington, DC: American Association on Mental Deficiency, 1974.

Nihira, K., Meyers, C. E., & Mink, I. Home environment, family adjustment, and the development of mentally retarded children. *Applied Research in Mental Retardation*, 1980, *1*, 5–24.

Nahira, K., Mink, I. T., & Meyers, C. E. Relationships between home environment and school adjustment of TMR children. *American Journal of Mental Deficiency*, 1981, *86*, 8–15.

Pavenstedt, E. A comparison of the child-rearing environment of upper-lower and very low-lower class families. *American Journal of Orthopsychiatry*, 1965, *35*, 89–98.

Petrauskas, R., & Rourke, B. P. Identification of subgroups of retarded readers: A neuropsychological multivariate approach. *Journal of Clinical Neuropsychology*, 1979, *1*, 17–37.

Schaefer, E. S., & Bell, R. O. Development of a parental attitude research instrument. *Child Development*, 1958, *29*, 339–361.

Schneewind, K., & Lortz, E. Family climate and parental child-rearing attitudes. In K. Schneewind & H. Lukesch (Eds.), *Familiare Sozialisation: Probleme, Erghnisse, Perspektiven.* Stuttgart, Germany: Klett-Cotta, 1978.

Scoresvy, A. L., & Christensen, B. Differences in interaction and environmental conditions of clinic and non-clinic families: Implications for counselors. *Journal of Marriage and Family Counseling*, 1976, *2*, 63–71.

Sears, R. R., Maccoby, E. E., & Levin, H. *Patterns of child-rearing.* Evanston, IL: Row & Peterson, 1957.

Sokal, R. R., & Sneath, P. H. A. *Principles of numerical taxonomy.* San Francisco: W. H. Freeman, 1963.

Tabackman, M. A study of family psychosocial environment and its relationship to academic achievement in gifted adolescents (Doctoral dissertation, University of Illinois at Urbana-Champaign, 1976). *Dissertation Abstracts International*, 1977, *37* (10-A), 6381.

Westley, W. Q., & Epstein, N. B. *The silent majority: Families of emotionally healthy college students.* San Francisco: Jossey-Bass, 1970.

Yarrow, M., Campbell, J., & Burton, R. *Child-rearing.* San Francisco: Jossey-Bass, 1968.

Manuscript submitted 2/2/82

This study was supported by the National Institute of Child Health and Human Development Grants No. HD–04612 and HD–05540. A version of this paper was presented at the annual meeting of the American Academy of Mental Retardation, Detroit, May 1981. The authors thank Jill Korbin and Karen Ito for ethnographic material and Linda Brownlee Pearson for her assistance in data collection. All names used in the ethnographic and interviewer reports are pseudonyms.

Authors

Iris Tan Mink, Kazuo Nihira, and **C. Edward Meyers,** University of California, Los Angeles/Neuropsychiatric Institute.

Adaptation of Families with Mentally Retarded Children: A Model of Stress, Coping, and Family Ecology

Keith A. Crnic, William N. Friedrich, and Mark T. Greenberg
1983

Abstract

Research concerned with families of mentally retarded children has often yielded inconsistent, and at times, contradictory findings. This inconsistency is partly due to methodological inadequacies and a narrow focus on unidimensional variables with unimodal measurements. In addition, no succinct model has been presented to explain family adaptation and the range of possible outcomes. In this paper a critical review focused on parents, siblings, parent–child interactions, and family systems was presented. A comprehensive conceptual model was proposed that accounts for (a) the range of possible familial adaptations, both positive and negative, involving the impact of perceived stress associated with the presence of a retarded child; and (b) the family's coping resources and ecological environments as interactive systems that serve to mediate the family's response to stress.

The impact of mental retardation is never restricted to retarded individuals; members of the immediate and extended families are affected to varying degrees. The relationships and influences between retarded children and their families would also seem to be reciprocal and circular; i.e., although families are affected by the presence of retarded children, so too are the children affected by their families' responses. Indeed, satisfactory emotional development of retarded children may be dependent more upon the families' responses to them than to the extent of the handicap itself (Bentovim, 1972).

Yet, despite the acknowledged importance of the family, we know relatively little about the functioning of families of retarded children. Studies of cognition and behavior of retarded children far outnumber those focused upon specific variables related to family functioning. In addition, the existing studies of familial variables have a number of shortcomings. The research has had a narrow focus, proving generally to be unidimensional (focusing on a specific family member and/or a specific

variable) and unimodal (using only one type of measure: questionnaire, interview, rating scales, or, rarely, behavioral observations). The available descriptive studies generally present clinical case studies or group data without adequate control groups. Many report data from measures of undetermined or poor reliability and validity. Perhaps the most critical shortcoming is the lack of prospective longitudinal investigations detailing familial adaptation and functioning from the time at which retarded children are identified.

The unidimensional nature of the research is characterized best by the focus on individual family members, usually the parents (most frequently mothers) and occasionally siblings. The family as a system or functional unit has been studied infrequently. The unimodal characteristic of this research is clearest in the studies of parents of retarded children, which can be grouped according to the single measure of primary interest: attitudes toward child-rearing, personality or emotional problems, marital satisfaction, and psychosocial functioning. Even the few investigators of parent–child interaction who have attempted to expand the unidimensional focus by recognizing at least the presence of a dyad have measured only discrete behavioral interactions, without taking into account other, possibly contributory, variables.

No succinct model presently exists through which one can develop an empirical understanding of families of retarded children. Rather, investigators have seemed to rally around the concept of anticipated pathology in these families. Pathological adaptations are generally assumed to be a function of the stress associated with the presence of a retarded child (Cummings, 1976; Cummings, Bayley, & Rie, 1966; Farber, 1959), and have led to the development of a stress-reaction hypothesis to explain maladaptive family functioning (Erickson, 1969; Miller & Keirn, 1978; Pless & Pinkerton, 1975). Clinical experience with families of retarded children would suggest, however, that pathological reactions within these families are not uniform. A truly comprehensive model must encompass the range of possible positive and negative adaptations as well as the factors that serve as determinants of adaptation.

Although the stress associated with the presence of a retarded child is an important consideration, its impact on the family is likely to be related to the family members' cognitive appraisal of the stress situation (Lazarus, Kanner, & Folkman, 1980) and to the family's coping resources (Folkman, Schaefer, & Lazarus, 1979), which include the broad categories of health/energy/morale, problem-solving skills, social networks, utilitarian resources, and general and specific beliefs. In turn, the family's coping resources and functioning are likely to be mediated by the ecological systems (Bronfenbrenner, 1977, 1979) within which they must interact and be acted upon. Such ecological systems include not only the immediate environments of home, schools, agencies, neighborhoods, workplaces, and social networks, but also the interrelationships among these ecological systems as well as the institutionalized attitudinal patterns of the culture and subculture manifested in these systems. Thus, in the present paper we have attempted to integrate the concepts of stress, coping, and ecological systems into a single model to provide an impetus for investigating and understanding family adaptation and functioning.

In the following sections studies of the parents, siblings, parent–child interactions, and the entire family have been critically reviewed. This review is meant to be reasonably comprehensive, and studies were chosen for their specific relevance to the issues at hand as well as the adequacy of methodological information provided. Studies of other handicapping conditions that may involve retardation (e.g., cerebral palsy) were excluded. Following the review is a discussion of the proposed model, detailing the interrelationships among perceived stress, family coping resources, and the family's ecological environments as determinants of family adaptational response.

Research Review

Parental Attitudes

The attitudes of parents of retarded children have received a fair amount of research attention, but the lack of appropriate control groups, measurement inadequacies, and conflicting results limit the usefulness of much of this work. "Parental" attitudes may also be a misnomer, as mothers tend to be the exclusive subjects of much

of this research. In this regard, it is interesting to note that women have been found to be more accepting of handicapped children than are men (Fletcher, 1974).

Much of the attitudinal research has been focused on the dimensional structure of child-rearing philosophies: warmth–hostility, restrictiveness–permissiveness. The Parent Attitude Research Instrument (Schaeffer & Bell, 1958), which provides such a dimensional analysis of parental attitudes, has been used frequently with varying results. Generally, mothers of mildly and severely retarded children were found to be rejecting and punitive (Cook, 1963; Ricci, 1970), although mothers of more severely retarded children were also characterized as overprotective (Cook, 1963). In contrast, both Caldwell and Guze (1960) and Dingman, Eyman, and Windle (1963) found no differences between mothers with regard to the severity of the child's retardation. Rather, Dingman et al. (1963) found that differences on the Parent Attitude Research Instrument were related primarily to maternal education, a variable not measured in the Cook (1963) study. Indeed, this appears to be one of several deficiencies limiting the validity of this measure as a research instrument (Becker & Krug, 1965). Waisbren (1980), who did not use this instrument in her study of parent attitudes, also found that the parents of very young developmentally delayed children were angry and rejecting.

The overprotective attitudes of parents of retarded children appear to have significant implications for children's skill development. Landman (1979) found a significant negative relationship between overprotectiveness and developmental skill as measured by an applied performance test. Further, Strom, Rees, Slaughter, and Wurster (1981) divided parents of retarded children into groups with high or low expectations for their child and found that those with higher expectations complied more fully with home-based programming aimed at helping them teach their mildly to moderately retarded children.

Beyond specific child-rearing attitudes, general attitudes of parents toward mental retardation and related issues have been studied. Mothers of retarded children were found to have more positive attitudes about mental retardation than did a group of mothers of nonretarded children of similar socioeconomic status (SES) and education (Watson & Midlarsky, 1979), but resisted favoring normalization of their own child even though they supported the concept of normalization for the general population of retarded children (Ferrara, 1979). Watson and Midlarsky noted that the overprotectiveness seen with mothers of retarded children may arise less from maternal guilt feelings than from the factually based perception that other nonretarded individuals have relatively negative attitudes toward retarded people.

The suggestion of overprotective and less-positive parental attitudes toward their retarded children is compromised by the absence of control groups in all but the Ricci (1970) and Waisbren (1980) studies and by the measurement problems of the Parent Attitude Research Instrument. Further, such attitudes have apparent impact on child development (Landman, 1979; Strom et al., 1981), but it is unclear how such attitudes impact other family processes. The significance of various ecological factors (peer relationships, sociocultural attitudes, professional relationships) as mediators of parental attitudes requires attention. Certainly, both the Watson and Midlarsky (1979) and Ferrara (1979) studies suggest that prevailing sociocultural attitudes influence parental attitudes and behavior toward their retarded children.

Parental Personality and Emotional Difficulties

A moderate research effort has been directed at empirically examining the personality and emotional functioning of parents of retarded children, with the general assumption that the stress of having a retarded child has a deleterious effect on parental functioning. In general, this assumption has been validated.

Several studies have used the Minnesota Multiphasic Personality Inventory (MMPI) to compare parents of retarded children with parents of emotionally disturbed children and with MMPI normative groups. Parents of retarded children have significantly elevated profiles compared to the norm groups and more closely resemble parents of emotionally disturbed children, although total score elevations are somewhat less marked (Erickson, 1968, 1969; Miller & Keirn, 1978). The profile patterns suggest problems in impulse control accompanied by aggressive feelings. Using different personality inventories, other investigators have found that compared to parents of nonretarded children, mothers of retarded children show greater depressive and dysphoric affect, more preoccupation with the child, less sense of maternal competence, less enjoyment of the child, greater possessiveness (Cummings, Bayley, & Rie, 1966), and score higher on an unvalidated "malaise" inventory (Tew & Laurence, 1975). Fathers of retarded children have

also been found to be more depressed, to have lower self-esteem, to express a lack of interpersonal satisfaction, and to undergo long-term personality changes resembling a pattern of neurotic-like constriction (Cummings, 1976). Parental coping has also been found to be less successful for parents of retarded children, although coping was related to both the age and sex of the child and parent (Burke, 1973).

Unfortunately, no prospective studies exist that have been designed to examine parental characteristics prior to the birth or diagnosis of a retarded child. Nevertheless, each of the studies of parental personality has attributed the identified difficulties to a "stress-reaction hypothesis" (Erickson, 1969; Miller & Keirn, 1978). Only recently, however, have a number of investigators attempted to measure stress objectively in families with a retarded child. They used the Questionnaire on Resources and Stress (Holroyd, 1974), a 285-item inventory comprising 15 scales with three major scale clusters: parent problems, family problems, and child problems. This questionnaire has been found to relate to interview ratings of stress (Holroyd, Brown, Wikler, & Simmons, 1975), show a significant positive relationship to severity of a child's handicap (Beckman, 1983; Holroyd & Guthrie, 1979), and successfully differentiate families both within and between groups of handicapped and nonhandicapped children (Friedrich, in press; Friedrich & Friedrich, 1981; Holroyd & McArthur, 1976). The Questionnaire on Resources and Stress is, however, quite long, and a recent item and factor analysis has provided a more reliable and shorter (52 items) form (Friedrich, Greenberg, & Crnic, in press).

Stress does appear to be relevant to parental emotional functioning, as does coping ability. Indeed, the wealth of the research in this area suggests that parents of retarded children are at the least a group at high risk for emotional and personality difficulties. No investigators, however, have as yet attempted to integrate measures of stress and coping with family outcomes and, in general, the wealth of possibly influential ecological variables has been ignored. Studies of religiosity suggest the potentially powerful impact of one specific ecological context, as religious background and beliefs have been found to be significantly related to greater acceptance, more positive adaptation, less stress, and a greater orientation to caring for retarded children at home (Farber, 1959; Levinson, 1976; Zuk, 1959; Zuk, Miller, Bartram, & Kling, 1961).

Marital Satisfaction

Marital relationships in the families of retarded children have been a subject of much clinical concern, but relatively little direct research effort has been initiated. The research to date does not present a clear picture of marital functioning. Farber (1959) studied the effects of having a severely retarded child on marital integration in 240 families, finding that although marital integration declined with the presence of a severely retarded child, outcome was more strongly related to the marital integration of the parents prior to the presence of the child. Parents with high integration early in the marriage fared better than those whose integration had been initially lower. Sex of the child was also important to marital integration, as retarded male children had a more significant negative impact on the marriage. No control data were collected.

Several more recent studies have been designed specifically to assess marital relationships with the Locke-Wallace Marital Adjustment Inventory (Locke & Wallace, 1959), with conflicting results. Friedrich and Friedrich (1981), comparing matched groups of mothers of handicapped and nonhandicapped children, found a significant difference between groups on the Locke-Wallace, with the former group reporting lower satisfaction. Using multiple regression procedures to predict Questionnaire on Resources and Stress scores of 98 parents of handicapped children, Friedrich (1979) found that marital satisfaction was the most significant predictor, accounting alone for 33 percent of the total variance. In contrast, Waisbren (1980) found no differences in marital satisfaction between 60 well-matched couples, half of whom were parents of developmentally delayed infants. The conflicting findings of the two studies may be attributable to sample differences, as the children in the Friedrich study averaged 9.8 years of age as opposed to 13 months in the Waisbren report. Marital satisfaction may decrease over time in families with retarded children.

The variability in the findings on marital satisfaction suggests that marital response is not uniform and may be dependent upon factors aside from the presence of a retarded child. Such factors would include the severity of the handicap, the age and sex of the child, and the quality of the marital relationship prior to the presence of the child. The conflicting results noted may reflect the differences in subject samples on these charac-teristics. Again, however, it seems likely that the marital relationship will also be influenced by individual coping styles, community relations, support systems, and other ecological variables that have yet to be studied. Further, the prevailing focus on group differences may overshadow the importance of variables such as marital satisfaction as predictors of familial adaptation.

Psychosocial Problems

Although one would intuitively expect presence of a retarded child to have some impact on family's psychosocial status and SES, very little empirical work has been conducted in this area. In fact, research on these factors has been focused mostly on the converse process, i.e., the effect of family status on the child. The few studies available, however, are important, as they are among the most relevant to ecological considerations and suggest that the presence of a retarded child can be detrimental to familial psychosocial functioning. In a series of studies of approximately 400 families with severely retarded children, Farber (1960, 1968, 1970) found that social mobility was reduced. The earlier in the marriage that the retarded child was born, the greater the likelihood that mobility was reduced. Farber's work also indicated that parents who kept their child at home showed greater SES decline than those parents who institutionalized their child, although this difference may be somewhat misleading in that Gath (1972a) found that wealthier families were more apt to institutionalize their retarded child than were lower income families. Mothers of retarded children were also more likely to work only part-time rather than full-time (Watson & Midlarsky, 1979) and to have greater difficulty in arranging child care (Sells, West, & Reichert, 1974; Watson & Midlarsky, 1979).

Caution is necessary in interpreting these findings; Ward and Bower (1978) have noted that even in families who directly implicated the child's handicap in their difficulties, over half of the parents exhibited problems that rendered them especially vulnerable. Clearly, further research to clarify such issues is necessary and must be prospective and longitudinal. Descriptive studies of various ecological environments (e.g., work, neighborhood, agency contacts) and changes within such systems would provide a more meaningful context in which to understand parental psychosocial characteristics.

Adaptation of Families with Mentally Retarded Children   Keith A. Crnic, William N. Friedrich, and Mark T. Greenberg

Siblings

Siblings have received little research attention even within the literature on families of retarded children. The available research has been focused on the relationship between the siblings and the impact of the retarded sibling on the nonretarded sibling. Variation in methodological adequacy has produced conflicting results.

As one facet of his studies of family integrity, Farber (1960) interviewed the siblings of severely retarded children living at home. Two significant sibling relationship effects emerged: Siblings younger than the retarded child assumed a superordinate role, and female siblings were frequently encouraged to function as surrogate mothers for the retarded child. In a similar series of interviews, Miller (1974) found that the nonretarded siblings engaged primarily in instrumental activity with the retarded child and displayed more positive and less negative affect toward retarded siblings than toward nonretarded siblings. The children indicated, however, that their parents did not tolerate the expression of negative affect toward the retarded sibling, casting some doubt on the veracity of the siblings' self-report. Pfouts (1976), moreover, examined brother dyads with a projective Family Relations Test and found that the nonretarded brother was ambivalent toward the retarded brother, whereas the retarded brother was hostile toward the nonretarded brother. Indeed, Meuwisson (1971) has suggested that guilt may inhibit expression of negative feelings toward the retarded sibling.

Not only are sibling relationships affected by the presence of a retarded child, but there also appear to be detrimental effects on the nonretarded sibling's (primarily female) individual functioning, involving high degrees of anxiety and conflicts with parents, lower sociability or emphasis on interpersonal relationships, and the adoption of life goals involving dedication and sacrifice (Farber, 1960, 1963; Fowle, 1968). A retrospective study by Grossman (1972) found that older siblings and siblings from higher SES families were relatively protected from the adverse consequences of having a retarded sibling, whereas younger children and those from less advantaged families showed effects similar to those found in Farber's studies (1960, 1963). Grossman also noted that sibling reactions were related to parental reactions and ability to cope, the same finding noted in an earlier study of teenage sibling reactions to a retarded child (Graliker, Fishler, & Koch, 1962).

Two of the best designed studies in which the behavior of children with retarded siblings was examined merit closer attention. Gath (1972b) asked parents and teachers to complete behavioral surveys on two groups of school-age siblings, a group of 36 children who had a Down syndrome sibling and a group of 35 children who had a sibling with cleft palate. A well-matched control group was included. No significant survey differences among the three groups were found. In a subsequent study, however, when Gath (1973) compared similar behavioral ratings of 174 children with Down syndrome siblings with those of 143 age-matched controls, a significant group difference emerged. Twenty percent of the index group was rated as deviant by either the parents or teachers as compared to 10 percent in the control group, $p < .05$. When girls alone were considered, the significance level rose to .001, indicating that nearly the entire group difference could be accounted for by the increase in deviant behavior by the female siblings. Like Farber, Gath suggested that female siblings' behavior may reflect greater pressure to help with the retarded sibling at home. The conflicting findings in Gath's two studies may be a function of the smaller size of the earlier Down syndrome group as well as the relatively high incidence of behavioral problems found in the control group of the 1972 study. Certainly, the sample size in the 1973 study suggests that more confidence be placed in these results.

Research indicates that siblings of retarded children, particularly female siblings, are a population at-risk for behavioral problems. Little is known, however, about the emotional status of these children, their relationships outside their families, or those factors that mediate their response to a retarded sibling.

Parent–Child Interaction

Very few investigators have actually observed parent–child interactions in families of retarded children. This is especially surprising in view of the extensive discussion of the impact of a handicapped child on the family and the fact that parent–child interaction studies are a staple of the nonretarded child development literature. Available studies of parent–retarded child interaction can be categorized as: (a) analyses of mother–child linguistic patterns and (b) studies of responsiveness and communication styles in mother–child interaction. Studies of attachment behavior of Down syndrome infants have also been reported (e.g., Gunn & Andrews, 1980; Serafica & Cicchetti, 1976), but these will not be discussed as they have a specific focus on infant behavior and do not

Adaptation of Families with Mentally Retarded Children Keith A. Crnic, William N. Friedrich, and Mark T. Greenberg

report measures on the mothers (see Blacher & Meyers, 1983, for a review of these issues).

Mothers' speech to their retarded children has received the most attention, again with conflicting results. In the initial study in this area, Marshall, Hegrenes, and Goldstein (1973) measured the frequency of verbal operants during interactions between 20 mothers and their retarded children and 20 mothers and their nonretarded children matched for chronological age (CA). As expected, the nonretarded children used more and varied verbal operants, and mothers differed only in that mothers of retarded children used more commands. The use of CA controls was inappropriate, however, as overall developmental differences may account for the speech differences found. Further, the mothers of retarded children had fewer years of education and were of lower SES, confounding the results. Several subsequent investigators with more appropriate controls (matched for linguistic level) have reported either minimal group differences (Buckhalt, Rutherford, & Goldberg, 1978; Gutman & Rondal, 1979), or no differences at all (Rondal, 1978). In a recent mother–child interaction study comparing nonretarded and mild to moderately retarded children (Cunningham, Rueler, Blackwell, & Deck, 1981), group differences in mothers' mean length of utterance were not found. Within-group comparison, however, demonstrated that mothers' mean length of utterance with both nonretarded and retarded children with greater mental ages (MAs) were significantly longer than those with children of lesser MAs.

Several interaction studies measuring responsiveness and communication have produced meaningful differences between groups of mothers with retarded and nonretarded children. In a pioneering study, Kogan, Wimberger, and Bobbitt (1969) compared a group of 6 retarded children and their mothers with a control group of 10 mother–nonretarded child pairs on parameters of relative status, affection, and involvement. Mothers of retarded children displayed extreme degrees of warmth and friendliness less frequently. The retarded children generally displayed a more neutral status (neither dominant nor submissive). Several subsequent investigators measuring interactive behavior during free-play and structured situations (Breiner & Forehand, 1982; Eheart, 1982; Terdal, Jackson, & Garner, 1976; Thoman, Becker, & Freese, 1978; Vietze, Abernathy, Ashe, & Faulstich, 1978) have found a general asynchrony in the interactive behavior of mother–retarded child dyads. Mothers

of retarded children tend to be more active and directive with their children. Retarded children were found to be both less responsive and less compliant to their mothers than were nonretarded children.

The interactive patterns of mother–retarded child pairs suggest difficulties in reciprocity within the relationship. Vietze et al. (1978) found that developmentally delayed infants' vocalizations were not contingent on maternal speech as were the vocalizations of nondelayed infants. Similar findings were reported by Cunningham et al. (1981) and Terdal et al. (1976), with older retarded children responding less contingently to maternal social behavior than did nonretarded MA-matched children.

Of particular interest is the recent work reported by Stoneman and Brody (in press), which involves attempts to measure sibling interactions as well as triadic (mother–father–child) interactions within families of retarded children. Although the sample sizes were quite small (N = 5 to 7 sibling dyads, family triads) and no control data were collected, these studies are noteworthy in their attempt to broaden the perspective of interactive research with families of retarded children. Sibling interactions, although frequent, were found to involve distinct role asymmetries, with younger retarded siblings never assuming the role of teacher with their older nonretarded siblings, whereas older retarded siblings assumed the teacher role in only 4 percent of the interactive intervals. Also, retarded siblings complied with nonretarded sibling directives less frequently than with parental directives. For the triadic interactions, mothers were engaged more in interactions with the retarded child than were fathers and performed most of the caretaking; fathers interacted by playing and entertaining. Further, the retarded children complied more with paternal directives than maternal ones. It is unclear whether or how these interactive patterns differ from those of families with nonretarded children and whether within-group differences will emerge.

The paucity of interaction studies is distressing, especially given the suggestion of real differences in parent–retarded child involvement, affection, responsiveness, and reciprocity. Sample sizes have mostly been too small to permit generalization; and fathers, siblings, or triadic interactions have been generally ignored. Further, the settings and conditions under which interactions have been observed are few. Basic descriptive research on interactions among family members is needed before more than tentative conclusions can be reached.

The Family as a System

Assessment of the functioning of families of retarded children as a unit, or system, is the area that has received the least attention, although it may well prove to be the most informative. Only one study was found in which such a comprehensive approach was taken in delineating the impact of a retarded child on the family. Nihira, Meyers, and Mink (1980) studied 268 families of educable and trainable mentally retarded (EMR and TMR) children living at home, using numerous measures of the home environment, family adjustment, and child characteristics. Their results indicated that family adjustment and functioning were related not only to the severity of the child's retardation and degree of maladaptive behavior, but to family demographic characteristics, the psychosocial climate of the home (e.g., family cohesion, expressiveness, and harmony), and specific kinds of parental behavior toward their retarded children. In addition, the perceived impact was related to marital disharmony and family conflict other than that related to the retarded children.

The Nihira et al. (1980) study also demonstrated the interactional and reciprocal nature of the family–retarded child system, as the parents' feelings of impact were related to the retarded children's lack of adaptive competency, and the children's adaptive competence was related to the parents' successful coping with the problem of mental retardation. Although no control data were included, and some of the measures were of unknown reliability and validity, the Nihira et al. (1980) study suggests both the difficulties these families face as well as the variability of this impact within groups of families with retarded children. This is certainly a needed and promising direction for research, and represents an initial step in integrating measures of child and family to detail interactional outcomes within the family system.

Summary

In general, the available literature suggests that the parents and siblings of retarded children individually, as well as the family as a whole, are at-risk for numerous difficulties in comparison to families with nonretarded children. In spite of these suggestions, inconsistent and contradictory reports are common, due primarily to variations in methodological adequacy, inappropriate control groups, small and poorly defined samples, and the use of measures of greatly uneven quality.

A genuine bias has also existed toward expecting a deleterious or pathological outcome in these families. As more precise, appropriate, and controlled means of studying this population have emerged, however, the ubiquity of such impaired adjustment has certainly come into question. This uncertainty should lead to more appropriate considerations of the variables that are instrumental to the adaptation of these families (e.g., coping resources).

Further, there has been little consideration of more than a static perspective. No longitudinal data address how families of very young retarded children differ from those of older or adolescent retarded children. The few investigators who have followed samples over time suggest that such an approach could prove fruitful (e.g., lowered marital satisfaction across time [Tew, Payne, & Laurence, 1974]).

Finally, there has been a failure to study the individual in the larger context of the family, or to conduct broad-based, multivariate studies that address such basic issues as the child's age, type and severity of handicap, physical health, and appearance to parental, sibling and family outcome. These child-specific characteristics should serve as marker variables within individual studies of familial adaptation, as familial response is likely to vary as a function of such characteristics (e.g., Beckman, 1983; Nihira et al., 1980). Many of the studies to date, however, do not clearly specify these parameters of their samples. Indeed, research with retarded children reflects many of the prevailing misconceptions within the study of human development in general. Its approach has been low in ecological validity and generalizability because it has primarily been focused on the child or mother–child dyad, assumed a unidirectional causal sequence rather than a transactional model of development (Sameroff & Chandler, 1975), and has usually been focused on one setting (home, school, lab) without examining the interrelationships among such settings.

An Adaptational Model

Stress, Coping, and Ecological Systems

The variability found in the studies to date of families of retarded children not only reflects the variability in the quality of the work, but likely also reflects individual variations among families in their response to a retarded child. That familial response is likely to vary is substantiated by numerous studies of family outcome

Adaptation of Families with Mentally Retarded Children   Keith A. Crnic, William N. Friedrich, and Mark T. Greenberg

variables (Beckman, 1983; Burke, 1973; Farber, 1959, 1970; Friedrich, 1979; Nihira et al., 1980; Ward & Bower, 1978). Given such differential response, other factors must operate that mediate familial adaptation, and a comprehensive model must account both for such differences and the factors that influence them.

The model proposed here integrates concepts from three distinct bodies of research: stress, individual coping, and ecological influences on development and functioning. The presence of the retarded child represents a significant ongoing stressor within the family, precipitating numerous minor and major crises. Subsequent familial response to such stress will involve the various coping resources available both to the individual and the family as a whole. The coping resources available, as well as how and when they are used, are mediated by the various ecological domains in which the family members interact. In the present model, therefore, we have attempted to explain the range of familial adaptation as a response to stress moderated by the interaction of available coping resources and ecological contexts.

As is apparent from the preceding review, little research is presently available that tests the proposed model as a whole. Nevertheless, some of the previous research would certainly appear to support the application of the components separately. The stress associated with various crises in daily interactions with and about a retarded child, as well as the life transitions inherent in the developmental process, must certainly be considered a feature central to familial functioning. The concept of a stress-reaction hypothesis (Erickson, 1969; Miller & Keirn, 1978), therefore, has great utility. Although initially poorly defined and not measured objectively, subsequent studies of greater refinement have indeed demonstrated the increased stresses experienced by these families (Beckman, 1983; Friedrich & Friedrich, 1981; Holroyd & McArthur, 1976). Although this progress in the delineation of psychological stress is notable, the concept and measurement of stress needs to be expanded to include a life events model (Sarason, Johnson, & Siegel, 1978), because more numerous changes in the lives of family members are likely to occur in relation to the presence of a retarded child than a nonretarded child (e.g., major changes in social activities, recreation, or economic conditions). Such life stress, operationally defined as self-reported life changes, has shown significant relationships with numerous minor and major health changes, the seriousness of chronic illness, and various

psychiatric symptoms, including anxiety and depression (Rabkin & Streuning, 1976).

Although families respond differentially to various stressors, little attention has been given to those variables that appear to moderate or buffer the effects of stress. This lack is obvious from the focus of the existing literature on the differences between families of retarded and nonretarded children rather than relevant within-group differences. A more fruitful approach, however, would be to study also what it is that discriminates those families of retarded children that respond well to the evident stress from those who do not. Research on moderator variables suggests that several are powerful, particularly locus of control and social support (Sarason et al., 1978).

Considerations of the stress process involve not only the sources of stress, but also the mediators of stress (Pearlin, Lieberman, Menaghan, & Mullan, 1981). Although aptly delineating the sources, proponents of previous pathology-based concepts of adaptation have ignored the mediators. A competence or coping-based framework should be considered as an alternative to the pathology concept (Drotar, 1981), as it emphasizes the tasks and strategies involved in living with a retarded child. Coping is a process not readily operationalized, varying in mode (information-seeking or action), function (problem-solving or stress reduction), and outcome (more or less adaptive). Yet the strategies involved in coping with the stresses of having a retarded child should reveal the process as well as dictate the outcome of a family's adaptation.

The concept of coping resources presented by Folkman et al. (1979) provides a useful basis for understanding the coping process and subsequent familial outcome. Folkman et al. delineated five types of coping resources, each of which is assumed to moderate the adverse effects of stress as appraised within the individual's cognitive–phenomenological framework. Further, some of the research previously reviewed substantiates the relevance of these resources. First, parental health/energy/morale involves an individual's physical and emotional well being both prior to and during the course of a stressful event. The study of "chronic sorrow" in parents of retarded children (Wikler, Wasow, & Hatfield, 1981) bears specific relationship to such a factor. Second, problem-solving skills would involve both global and concrete abilities to search for and analyze information and generate various courses of action. Third, social networks involve potentially supportive relationships that may facilitate positive adaptations, as suggested by investigators to several studies of families with retarded children (Farber, 1959; Friedrich & Friedrich, 1981). Fourth, utilitarian resources including such factors as SES and income can have potentially powerful effects on adaptation, which can be seen in the studies of Farber (1970), Gath (1972a), and Nihira et al. (1980). The final resource area involves general and specific beliefs, which includes such person variables as an individual's feelings of self-efficacy, greater internal locus of control, and belief in some higher purpose (e.g., religious faith). Studies of religiosity among families of retarded children (Levinson, 1976; Zuk, 1959; Zuk et al., 1961), as well as the Strom et al. (1981) study of parents' belief in teaching their retarded child, offer some support to this notion.

Clearly the concept of coping resources has considerable utility in the study of familial adaptation to retarded children, as the families' differential response to stress is not solely related to the potential child marker variables of age, appearance, severity, and type of retardation. Future research with these families must present a more integrated perspective, assessing the relative impact and potential interaction of each of these five, and possibly additional, domains to the variations in family adaptational response.

Although perceived familial stress is moderated by coping resources, further consideration must also be given to the various ecological contexts of the individual, family, peer groups, and societal institutions, as well as the interactions within and between these contexts, as mediators of coping resources. Bronfenbrenner (1977) has proposed an ecological model of human development encompassing four levels of influence on individual development: interactions within immediate settings, e.g., home, school, workplace (Microsystem); the interrelations among major settings containing the individual (Mesosystem); the formal and informal social structures that impinge on the individual, e.g., neighborhood, media, government agencies (Exosystem); and the ideological institutional patterns of the culture and subcultures (Macrosystem). Each of these contexts is likely to exert some influence on the coping resources available to be employed and when and how they are used. Several previous investigators have suggested the importance of focusing on specific ecological factors (Farber, 1959; Rowitz, 1974), and Schoggen and Schoggen (1981) have recently noted the importance of various ecological factors in the prevention of psychosocial retardation. Yet

much of the previous research has focused exclusively on individual family members, ignoring ecological context as a mediator of behavioral response.

Presently, no systematic descriptive base exists detailing the environments in which families with retarded members function and by which they are influenced. It does appear intuitive that the ecology of these families will differ markedly from those of nonretarded children. Although families with retarded children operate under the same influences as families with nonretarded children (especially if there is a nonretarded sibling), they are also likely to have greater involvement with schools and teachers, social agencies, and service-delivery professionals as well as more limited social contacts (Farber, 1970; Watson & Midlarsky, 1979). Furthermore, they must cope with a set of cultural attitudes regarding the stigma of the handicap (Goffman, 1963). The behavior and attitudes of others in these various settings seem likely to influence such factors as an individual's beliefs, problem-solving, social contacts, morale, and other resources that in turn will affect the individual and familial response to the retarded child. These are relationships that must be assessed if familial patterns of adaptation are to be understood.

A few recent studies have begun to address these issues. In their study of the interrelationship of home environment and school adjustment (Mesosystem) of TMR children, Nihira et al. (1981) found that family harmony and quality of parenting, family cohesiveness, emotional support for learning, and cognitive stimulation available at home were significantly related to the child's school adjustment. These results suggest that familial coping within the specific home environment influences the retarded child's adaptation to a separate ecological context. Although Nihira et al. (1981) focused on a child outcome, several investigators have shown that social relationships and support available from several sources have a positive impact on parental functioning (Farber, 1959; Friedrich, 1979; Friedrich & Friedrich, 1981). A more descriptive study of use of support networks by parents of retarded children was recently conducted by Suelzle and Keenan (1981), who collected survey data cross-sectionally on 330 families of retarded children. Parents of younger retarded children utilized more support networks and were more supportive of mainstreaming whereas parents of older retarded children had less support, were more isolated, and had greater need for expanded services. The impact of such life cycle changes in support systems is in need of further study, as data are beginning to accrue suggesting that such relationships have significant effects on parents, the family, and child development (Cochran & Brassard, 1979; Crnic, Greenberg, Ragozin, Robinson, & Basham, 1983; Powell, 1979).

Although these few initial attempts at studying family coping and ecology are laudatory, they remain variable specific and, except for Suelzle and Keenan (1981), do not address the basic need for a major descriptive data base on such systems. Nihira et al. (1980) also certainly indicated that family coping and the ecological context of the family itself are related to family adjustment, although contexts outside the home are not considered. Nevertheless, these studies do suggest that coping and ecological context interact to influence adaptational response. Future researchers will, however, need to encompass the range of ecological systems relevant to the particular issue being addressed. For example, mainstreaming and normalization are concepts with ecological implications across each of the micro-, meso-, exo-, and macrosystems in which families operate. Ferrara's (1979) study of parents' attitudes toward mainstreaming has major ecological implications but offers no measures of variables that may influence a family's resistance to mainstreaming for their own child while favoring the concept in general. Such variables might include individual beliefs and social relationships as coping resources, as well as the specific ecological contexts of the school itself, the neighborhood, or general cultural belief systems.

The concepts of stress, coping resources, and family ecology provide a powerful explanatory model for the adaptation of families of retarded children. Differential family adaptation can be interpreted as a function of the coping resources available to the family, which moderate the impact of perceived stress associated with the presence of a retarded child. In turn, a family's coping resources are mediated by the various ecological systems in which the family interacts. Such an interactive model provides a more relevant context for the study of adaptation on both an individual and family system basis.

Conclusion

The research on families with retarded children has been hampered not only by methodological problems and a narrow focus, but also by the lack of a model that can account for individual variations in family adaptation. Family functioning cannot be considered simply as a response to a retarded child; rather, it is more meaningful to consider familial adaptation as a response to the child mediated by the coping resources available and influenced by the family's ecological environments. Future investigators, if they are to add to our understanding of families with retarded children, must not only attempt to measure differences in families with and without a retarded child, but must attempt to account for those variables that mediate these differences within a comprehensive conceptual framework such as the model proposed.

References

Ainsworth, M. D., & Wittig, B. A. Attachment and exploratory behavior of one-year-olds in a strange situation. In B. M. Foss (Ed.), *Determinants of infant behavior*. London: Methuen, 1969.

Becker, W. C., & Krug, R. S. The Parent Attitude Research Instrument: A research review. *Child Development*, 1965, 36, 329–365.

Beckman, P. J. The influence of selected child characteristics on stress in families of handicapped infants. *American Journal of Mental Deficiency*, 1983, 88, 150–156.

Bentovim, A. Emotional disturbances of handicapped pre-school children and their families: Attitudes to the child. *British Medical Journal*, 1972, 3, 579–581.

Blacher, J. B., & Meyers, C. E. A review of attachment formation and disorder in handicapped children. *American Journal of Mental Deficiency*, 1983, 87, 359–371.

Breiner, J., & Forehand, R. Mother–child interactions: A comparison of a clinic referred developmentally delayed group and two non-delayed groups. *Applied Research in Mental Retardation*, 1982, 3, 175–183.

Bronfenbrenner, U. Toward an experimental ecology of human development. *American Psychologist*, 1977, 32, 513–531.

Bronfenbrenner, U. *The ecology of human development: Experiments by nature and design*. Cambridge: Harvard University Press, 1979.

Buckhalt, J. A., Rutherford, R. B., & Goldberg, K. E. Verbal and nonverbal interaction of mothers with their retarded Down's syndrome and nonretarded infants. *American Journal of Mental Deficiency*, 1978, 82, 337–343.

Burke, L. B. Coping abilities of parents of moderately retarded children as they relate to the sex of the parent and the age and sex of the child. *Dissertation Abstracts International*, 1973, *34*, 1270–1271B. (University Microfilms No. 73–21, 623)

Caldwell, B. M., & Guze, S. B. A study of the adjustment of parents and siblings of institutionalized and non-institutionalized retarded children. *American Journal of Mental Deficiency*, 1960, *64*, 845–861.

Cochran, M. M., & Brassard, J. A. Child development and personal social networks. *Child Development*, 1979, *50*, 601–616.

Cook, J. J. Dimensional analysis of child-rearing attitudes of parents of handicapped children. *American Journal of Mental Deficiency*, 1963, *68*, 354–361.

Crnic, K. A., Greenberg, M. T., Ragozin, A. S., Robinson, N. M., & Basham, R. B. Effects of stress and social support on mothers and premature and full-term infants. *Child Development*, 1983, *54*, 209–217.

Cummings, S. T. The impact of the child's deficiency on the father: A study of fathers of mentally retarded and of chronically ill children. *American Journal of Orthopsychiatry*, 1976, *46*, 246–255.

Cummings, S., Bayley, H., & Rie, H. Effects of the child's deficiency on the mother: A study of mothers of mentally retarded, chronically ill and neurotic children. *American Journal of Orthopsychiatry*, 1966, *36*, 595–608.

Cunningham, C. E., Rueler, E., Blackwell, J., & Deck, J. Behavioral and linguistic developments in the interactions of normal and retarded children with their mothers. *Child Development*, 1981, *52*, 62–70.

Dingman, H. F., Eyman, R. D., & Windle, C. D. An investigation of some child-rearing attitudes of mothers with retarded children. *American Journal of Mental Deficiency*, 1963, *67*, 899–908.

Drotar, D. Psychological perspectives in chronic childhood illness. *Journal of Pediatric Psychology*, 1981, *6*, 211–228.

Eheart, B. K. Mother–child interactions with nonretarded and mentally retarded preschoolers. *American Journal of Mental Deficiency*, 1982, *87*, 20–25.

Erickson, M. T. MMPI comparisons between parents of young emotionally disturbed and organically retarded children. *Journal of Consulting and Clinical Psychology*, 1968, *32*, 701–706.

Erickson, M. T. MMPI profiles of parents of young retarded children. *American Journal of Mental Deficiency*, 1969, *73*, 728–732.

Farber, B. Effects of a severely mentally retarded child on family integration. *Monographs of the Society for Research in Child Development*, 1959, *24*, (Whole No. 71).

Farber, B. Family organization and crisis: Maintenance of integration in families with a severely retarded child. *Monographs of the Society for Research in Child Development*, 1960, *25*, 1–95.

Farber, B. Interaction with retarded siblings and life goals of children. *Marriage and Family Living*, 1963, *25*, 96–98.

Farber, B. *Mental retardation: Its social contest and social consequences.* Boston: Houghton-Mifflin, 1968.

Farber, B. Notes on sociological knowledge about families with mentally retarded children. In M. Schreiber (Ed.), *Social work and mental retardation.* New York: John Day, 1970.

Ferrara, D. M. Attitudes of parents of mentally retarded children toward normalization activities. *American Journal of Mental Deficiency*, 1979, *84*, 145–151.

Fletcher, J. Attitudes toward defective newborns. *Hastings Center Study*, 1974, *2*, 21–32.

Folkman, S., Schaefer, C., & Lazarus, R. S. Cognitive processes as mediators of stress and coping. In V. Hamilton & D. W. Warburton (Eds.), *Human stress and cognition.* New York: John Wiley, 1979.

Fowle, C. M. The effect of a severely mentally retarded child on his family. *American Journal of Mental Deficiency*, 1968, *73*, 468–473.

Friedrich, W. N. Predictors of the coping behavior of mothers of handicapped children. *Journal of Consulting and Clinical Psychology*, 1979, *47*, 1140–1141.

Friedrich, W. N., & Friedrich, W. L. Comparison of psychosocial assets of parents with a handicapped child and their normal controls. *American Journal of Mental Deficiency*, 1981, *85*, 551–553.

Friedrich, W. N. A validational study of the Questionnaire on Resources and Stress. *Children's Health Care*, in press.

Gath, A. The effect of mental subnormality on the family. *British Journal of Hospital Medicine*, 1972, *8*, 147–150. (a)

Gath, A. The mental health of siblings of congenitally abnormal children. *Journal of Child Psychology and Psychiatry*, 1972, *13*, 211–218. (b)

Adaptation of Families with Mentally Retarded Children   Keith A. Crnic, William N. Friedrich, and Mark T. Greenberg

Gath, A. The school-age siblings of mongol children. *British Journal of Psychiatry*, 1973, *123*, 161–167.

Goffman, E. *Stigma*. Englewood Cliffs, NJ: Prentice Hall, 1963.

Graliker, B. V., Fishler, K., & Koch, R. Teenage reactions to a mentally retarded sibling. *American Journal of Mental Deficiency*, 1962, 66, 838–843.

Grossman, F. K. *Brothers and sisters of retarded children: An exploratory study*. Syracuse, NY: Syracuse University Press, 1972.

Gunn, P. B. P., & Andrews, R. Behavior of Down's syndrome infants in a strange situation. *American Journal of Mental Deficiency*, 1980, 85, 213–218.

Gutman, A. J., & Rondal, J. A. Verbal operants in mothers' speech to nonretarded and Down's syndrome children matched for linguistic level. *American Journal of Mental Deficiency*, 1979, 83, 446–452.

Holroyd, J. The Questionnaire on Resources and Stress: An instrument to measure family response to a handicapped family member. *Journal of Community Psychology*, 1974, 2, 92–94.

Holroyd, J., Brown, N., Wikler, L., & Simmons, H. Stress in families of institutionalized and noninstitutionalized autistic children. *Journal of Community Psychology*, 1975, 3, 26–31.

Holroyd, J., & Guthrie, D. Stress in families with neuromuscular disease. *Journal of Clinical Psychology*, 1979, 35, 734–739.

Holroyd, J., & McArthur, D. Mental retardation and stress on the parents: A contrast between Down's syndrome and childhood autism. *American Journal of Mental Deficiency*, 1976, 80, 431–436.

Kogan, K. L., Wimberger, H. C., & Bobbitt, R. A. Analysis of mother-child interaction in young mental retardates. *Child Development*, 1969, *40*, 799–812.

Landman, S. H. A study of the relationship between parental overprotectiveness and the achievement of selected life skills among mildly retarded adolescents. *Dissertation Abstracts International*, 1979, 40, 5075-B. (University Microfilms No. 79–7476)

Lazarus, R. S., Kanner, A., & Folkman, S. Emotions: A cognitive-phenomenological analysis. In R. Plutchik & H. Kellerman (Eds.), *Theories of emotion*. New York: Academic Press, 1980.

Levinson, R. M. Family crisis and adaptation: Coping with a mentally retarded child. *Dissertation Abstracts International*, 1976, 36, 8336A–8337A. (University Microfilms No. 76–8221)

Locke, H. J., & Wallace, K. M. Short marital adjustment and prediction tests: Their reliability and validity. *Marriage and Family Living*, 1959, *21*, 251–255.

Marshall, N. R., Hegrenes, J. R., & Goldstein, S. Verbal interaction: Mothers and their retarded children vs. mothers and their nonretarded children. *American Journal of Mental Deficiency*, 1973, *77*, 415–419.

Meuwissen, H. J. Family adaptation to child with cystic fibrosis. *Journal of Pediatrics*, 1971, *78*, 543–549.

Miller, S. G. An exploratory study of sibling relationship in families with retarded children. *Dissertation Abstracts International*, 1974, 35, 2994B–2995B. (University Microfilms No. 74–26, 606)

Miller, W. H., & Keirn, W. C. Personality measurement in parents of retarded and emotionally disturbed children: A replication. *Journal of Clinical Psychology*, 1978, *34*, 686–690.

Nihira, K., Meyers, C. E., & Mink, I. T. Home environment, family adjustment, and the development of mentally retarded children. *Applied Research in Mental Retardation*, 1980, *1*, 5–24.

Nihira, K., Mink, I. T., & Meyers, C. E. Relationship between home environment and school adjustment of TMR children. *American Journal of Mental Deficiency*, 1981, 86, 8–15.

Pearlin, L. I., Lieberman, M. A., Menaghan, E. G., & Mullan, J. T. The stress process. *Journal of Health and Social Behavior*, 1981, *22*, 337–356.

Pfouts, J. H. The sibling relationship: A forgotten dimension. *Social Work*, 1976, *21*, 200–204.

Pless, I. B., & Pinkerton, P. *Chronic childhood disorder: Promoting patterns of adjustment*. London: Henry Kimpton Publishers, 1975.

Powell, D. R. Family-environment relations and early child-reading: The role of social networks and neighborhoods. *Journal of Research and Development in Education*, 1979, *13*, 1–11.

Rabkin, J. G., & Streuning, E. L. Life events, stress, and illness. *Science*, 1976, *194*, 1013–1020.

Ricci, C. S. Analysis of child-rearing attitudes of mothers of mentally retarded, emotionally disturbed, and normal children. *American Journal of Mental Deficiency*, 1970, *74*, 756–761.

Rondal, J. Maternal speech to normal and Down's syndrome matched for mean length of utterance. *Monograph of the American Association on Mental Deficiency*. Washington, D.C.: American Association on Mental Deficiency, 1978.

Rotwiz, L. Social factors in mental retardation. *Social Science and Medicine*, 1974, 8, 405–412.

Sameroff, A. J., & Chandler, M. J. Reproductive risk and the continuum of caretaking casualty. In F. D. Horowitz (Ed.), *Review of child development research* (Vol. 4). Chicago: The University of Chicago Press, 1975.

Sarason, J. G., Johnson, J. H., & Siegel, J. M. Assessing the impact of life changes: Development of the Life Experiences Survey. *Journal of Consulting and Clinical Psychology*, 1978, 45, 932–946.

Schaefer, E. S., & Bell, R. Q. Development of a parent attitude research instrument. *Child Development*, 1958, 29, 339–361.

Schoggen, P., & Schoggen, M. Ecological factors in the prevention of psychosocial mental retardation. In M. J. Begab, H. C. Haywood, & H. L. Garber (Eds.), *Psychosocial influences in retarded performance*. Baltimore: University Park Press, 1981.

Sells, C. J., West, M. A., & Reichert, A. Reducing the institutional waiting lists for the mentally retarded. *Clinical Pediatrics*, 1974, 13, 740–745.

Serafica, F. C., & Cicchitti, D. Down's syndrome children in a strange situation: Attachment and exploration behaviors. *Merrill-Palmar Quarterly*, 1976, 22, 137–150.

Stoneman, Z., & Brody, G. H. Observational research on retarded children, their parents, and their siblings. In S. Landesman-Dwyer & P. Vietze (Eds.), *The impact of residential environments on retarded persons and their care providers*. Baltimore: University Park Press, in press.

Strom, R., Rees, R., Slaughter, H., & Wurster, S. Childrearing expectations of families with atypical children. *American Journal of Orthopsychiatry*, 1981, 51, 285–296.

Suelzle, M., & Keenan, V. Changes in family support networks over the life cycle of mentally retarded persons. *American Journal of Mental Deficiency*, 1981, 86, 267–274..

Terdal, L. E., Jackson, R. H., & Garner, A. M. Mother–child interactions: A comparison between normal and developmentally delayed groups. In E. J. Mash, L. A. Hammerlynck, & L. C. Handy (Eds.), *Behavior modification and families*. New York: Brunner/Mazel, 1976.

Tew, B. J., Payne, H., & Laurence, K. M. Must a family with a handicapped child be a handicapped family? *Developmental Medicine and Child Neurology*, 1974, 16, Supplement No. 34, 95–98.

Tew, B. J., & Laurence, K. M. Some sources of stress found in mothers of spina bifida children. *British Journal of Preventive and Social Medicine*, 1975, 29, 27–30.

Thoman, E. B., Becker, P. T., & Freese, M. P. Individual patterns of mother–infant interaction. In G. P. Sackett (Ed.), *Observing behavior* (Vol. 1). Baltimore: University Park Press, 1978.

Vietze, P. M., Abernathy, S. R., Ashe, M. L., & Faulstich, G. Contingency interaction between mothers and their developmentally delayed infants. In G. P. Sackett (Ed.), *Observing Behavior* (Vol. 1). Baltimore: University Park Press, 1978.

Waisbren, S. E. Parents' reactions after the birth of a developmentally disabled child. *American Journal of Mental Deficiency*, 1980, 84, 345–351.

Ward, F., & Bower, B. D. A study of certain social aspects of epilepsy. *Developmental Medicine and Child Neurology*, 1978, Supplement No. 39, 1–63.

Watson, R. L., & Midlarsky, E. Reactions of mothers with mentally retarded children: A social perspective. *Psychological Reports*, 1979, 45, 309–310.

Wikler, L., Wasow, M., & Hatfield, E. Chronic sorrow revisited: Parent vs. professional depiction of the adjustment of parents of mentally retarded children. *American Journal of Orthopsychiatry*, 1981, 51, 63–70.

Zuk, G. H. Religious factor and the role of guilt in parental acceptance of the retarded child. *American Journal of Mental Deficiency*, 1959, 64, 139–147.

Zuk, G. H., Miller, R. L., Bartram, J. B., & Kling, F. Maternal acceptance of retarded children: A questionnaire study of attitudes and religious background. *Child Development*, 1961, 32, 525–540.

Manuscript submitted 8/12/82.

Appreciation is extended to Sharon Landesman-Dwyer for her helpful comments in the preparation of this manuscript. reprint requests should be sent to K. A. C., CDMRC, WJ-10, University of Washington, Seattle, WA 98195.

Authors

Keith A. Crnic, William N. Friedrich, and Mark T. Greenberg, University of Washington.

Mediating Influences of Social Support: Personal, Family, and Child Outcomes

Carl J. Dunst, Carol M. Trivette, and Arthur H. Cross
1986

Abstract

The mediating influences of social support were examined in a study of 137 parents of mentally retarded, physically impaired, and developmentally at-risk children. Social system theory was used as a conceptual framework for assessing the effects of social support on personal well-being, parental attitudes toward their child, family integrity, parental perceptions of child functioning, parent–child play opportunities, and child behavior and development. A series of hierarchical multiple regression analyses by sets, controlling for family socioeconomic status (SES) and income, child sex and age, and child developmental quotient and diagnosis showed that both satisfaction with support and number of sources of support had main and/or interactive effects in all sets of outcome measures. More supportive social networks were associated with better personal well-being, more positive attitudes, and more positive influences on parent–child play opportunities and child behavior and development. Findings were discussed in terms of both methodological and conceptual contributions to understanding the broad-based influences of social support.

The mediating influences of social support on families of mentally retarded, physically handicapped, and developmentally at-risk children were examined. The effects of support were investigated in relationship to a number of personal, family, and child outcomes, including parental and familial well-being, parent–child play opportunities, and child behavior characteristics. Both ecological and social network theories (Bronfenbrenner, 1977, 1979; Caplan, 1976; Cochran & Brassard, 1979; Hobbs, 1975; Holahan, 1977; Mitchell & Trickett, 1980) were used as a conceptual framework for generating predictions regarding the mediating influences of social support. Systems theory postulates that social networks and the support that members provide both directly and indirectly influence the behavior, attitudes, expectations,

and knowledge of parents and their offspring as well as other network members.

Social support networks are generally described in terms of linkages among individuals and groups (Bott, 1971; Mitchell, 1969; Mueller, 1980). Linkages are operationally defined in terms of network characteristics, including size, satisfaction, density, connectedness, and frequency of contacts (Mitchell & Trickett, 1980). Social support is a multidimensional construct that includes physical and instrumental assistance, attitude transmission, resource and information sharing, and emotional and psychological support. There is general consensus among social systems theorists that social support networks function to nurture and sustain linkages among persons that are supportive on both a day-to-day basis and in times of need and crises (e.g., Brim, 1974; Caplan, 1974; Cobb, 1976; Tolsdorf, 1976; Walker, MacBride, & Vachon, 1977; Weiss, 1974).

According to Bronfenbrenner (1979), ecological units, or social networks, may be conceived topologically as a nested arrangement of concentric structures, each embedded within one another. At the innermost level is the developing child and his or her family (mother, father, siblings). The family unit is embedded in broader ecological systems consisting of blood and marriage relatives, friends, neighbors, and other acquaintances. These formal and informal kinship units are embedded further in large social units, including neighborhoods, churches, social organizations, the parents' place of work, and school. A fundamental tenet of social systems theory is that ecological units do not operate in isolation but interact both within and between levels so that changes in one unit or subunit reverberate and impact upon other units.

A sizable body of literature indicates that social support has powerful mediational influences on personal and familial well-being (Bott, 1971; Dean & Lin 1977; McCubbin et al., 1980; Mitchell & Trickett, 1980). Recently, investigators have demonstrated both direct or indirect effects of social support on attitudes toward parenting (Crnic, Greenberg, Ragozin, Robinson, & Basham, 1983), styles of parent–child interaction (Crnic, Greenberg et al., 1983; Crockenberg, 1981; Embry, 1980; Giovanoni & Billingsley, 1970; Hetherington, Cox, & Cox, 1976, 1978), parental expectations and aspirations for their children (Lazar & Darlington, 1982), and child behavior and development (Crnic, Greenberg et al., 1983; Crockenberg, 1981).

In Bronfenbrenner's (1979) articulate formulation of an ecology of human development, he noted that if social support is to be implicated as either a mediational or causative factor, potentially confounding variables must be controlled and the mutual contributions of other explanatory variables examined. In addition, Bronfenbrenner noted the importance of determining the bidirectional influences of persons, settings, and their characteristics on outcome measures and cautioned that the influences of mediational factors should be determined for the child, parent, family, and other relevant network members. Unfortunately few social support studies have adhered to Bronfenbrenner's major tenets (see Crnic, Greenberg et al., 1983, for an exception). Consequently, the extent to which the outcomes reported in the studies cited previously were influenced primarily by social support and not confounded by uncontrolled factors is not directly discernible.

In the present study we employed a conceptual and methodological approach that permitted a determination of the unique mediational influences of social support on parental, family, and child functioning. Moreover, we simultaneously examined the influences of a series of family and child characteristics to determine the unique effects of these variables on the dependent measures. We hypothesized that, after controlling for these factors, provision of social support to parents of young children would both directly and indirectly influence parental well-being and attitudes, family integrity, parent–child play opportunities, and child behavior and development. Our major tenet was that social support would have major influences beyond those attributable to other explanatory variables and that social support would have both stress buffering and positive mediational influences.

We defined social support in terms of both satisfaction with various sources of support and the number of sources of support available to a family. Both Andrews and Withey (1976) and Barrera and Ainlay (1983) noted

that perceived satisfaction with support is a fundamental dimension of the social support construct, and the extent to which support is considered helpful should be related to well-being and other behavior outcomes. Evidence for this contention comes from Barrera (1981), who found that satisfaction with support was a better indicator of emotional well-being than was network size.

The study of the mediating influences of social support in families of young retarded, handicapped, and developmentally delayed children is instructive for several reasons. First, there is evidence that parenthood itself may be a crisis event (Hobbs, 1965; LeMasters, 1957; Miller & Sollie, 1980), but provision of support to parents is effective in buffering the stress associated with the birth of a child (Litwak, 1960). Second, the birth and rearing of a handicapped child can be devastating for parents (see Gabel, McDowell, & Cerreto, 1983), yet it is not known whether social support can buffer such reactions or mediate other parental, family, and child outcomes (Crnic, Friedrich, & Greenberg, 1983). Third, although there is evidence that child as well as family characteristics (Beckman, 1983; Nihira, Meyers, & Mink, 1980, 1983) influence behavior outcomes among retarded and handicapped children and other family members, it is not known what mutual contributions intrapersonal and intrafamily characteristics and support have on different parental, family, and child outcomes. Fourth, as Crnic, Friedrich, and Greenberg (1983) noted, an ecology of mental retardation is likely to become a reality only when a multidimensional approach is taken to the study of the influences of causal and mediational variables on child and family development and functioning. Based on this set of conditions, Crnic, Friedrich, and Greenberg (1983) stated the need "to conduct broad-based, multivariate studies that address such basic issues as the child's age, type and severity of handicaps, physical health, and appearance to (child), parental, sibling, and family outcomes" (p. 173).

Method

Subjects

Subjects were 137 parents (96 mothers, 41 fathers) of preschool children. All families were participants in an early intervention program for handicapped, retarded, and developmentally at-risk infants and toddlers. The program, which offered a wide range of support services to both children and parents (see Dunst, 1982, 1985), focused on provision or mediation of support services that allowed a child to be reared as normally as possible (within the home) through parental adaptation to and management of their child's developmental disability or delay. All families enrolled in the program at the time this study was conducted were asked to participate. The acceptance rates for mothers and fathers were 68% and 53%, respectively.

Seventy-four of the mothers were married. For over half of the married sample (55%), both mothers and fathers completed the questionnaires. To discern whether there were differences among the families for which fathers did or did not participate in the study, we performed preliminary analyses on a set of background variables (parents' educational levels and ages; SES and income; years of marriage; child chronological age (CA), mental age (MA), developmental quotient, birth order, and number of siblings; and three measures of social support

(see later discussion). Of the 17 separate analyses, there was a significant difference on only one measure: SES, t (72) = 3.14, $p < .01$.

The children fell into three separate groups: retarded ($N = 38$), physically impaired ($N = 29$), and developmentally at-risk ($N = 29$). The retarded group was comprised of children with known etiologies (e.g., Down syndrome) and those diagnosed as retarded (using American Association on Mental Deficiency criteria, Grossman, 1973) without physical impairments. The physically impaired group included children who had cerebral palsy, spina bifida, or other physical impairments. The at-risk group included children with slight developmental delays and children at risk for developmental problems due to social-environmental factors.

Selected characteristics of the parents and their children are shown in Table 1. The three family groups differed only in terms of SES. There were no significant

Table 1 Selected Characteristics of the Sample

| | Total sample | | Diagnostic group (children) | | | | | | |
| | | | Mentally retarded | | Physically impaired | | Developmentally at-risk | | |
Characteristic	Mean	SD	Mean	SD	Mean	SD	Mean	SD	F
Parents									
Mother's age (years)	28.98	8.52	30.71	8.71	27.72	6.09	27.96	10.12	1.31
Father's age (years)	33.17	8.09	33.85	7.64	31.90	6.42	33.14	7.08	0.62
Mother's education level[a]	11.50	2.57	11.36	1.97	11.62	2.53	10.58	2.86	2.26
Father's education level[a]	11.53	2.76	11.23	1.76	12.38	2.82	11.25	2.46	2.42
Social economic status[b]	26.96	12.88	25.96	10.29	32.26	13.20	23.28	13.46	4.17*
Gross monthly income (dollars)	1173.90	743.73	1148.14	645.85	1307.91	843.04	1087.13	714.06	0.71
Children									
CA (months	37.52	13.75	38.86	13.13	35.89	15.67	37.38	12.78	0.38
MA (months)	22.90	12.70	17.20	9.21	22.83	13.07	30.45	12.46	10.94**
Developmental quotient[c]	63.88	26.10	44.69	20.48	68.48	22.91	84.41	15.81	33.52**
Social-adaptive age (months)	24.75	13.00	20.68	11.22	20.92	10.42	33.39	13.38	11.09**
Social Quotient[d]	70.70	27.98	55.11	25.79	69.34	25.17	91.42	19.12	18.31**

[a] Highest grade completed.

[b] Hollingshead (1975) five-level model of social status.

[c] Bayley Scale Mental Development Index or Stanford-Binet IQ.

[d] Vineland Social Maturity Scale.

* $p < .05$.

** $p < .001$.

differences in the distribution of married parents in the three subsamples of subjects.

The three groups of children did not differ in CA but did differ on the four developmental indices (MA, developmental quotient, social age, and social quotient), reflecting their differential developmental delays. There were 52 male and 44 female children, equally distributed among the three subsamples of children.

Procedure

Parents completed a number of questionnaires: Family Support Scale (Dunst, Jenkins, & Trivette, 1984), Questionnaire on Resources and Stress (Holroyd, 1973, 1974), and Parent-Child Interaction Rating Scale (Dunst, 1984). All scales are self-report measures. Over 90% of the parents were able to read well enough to complete the scales independently. The remaining parents had the scales read to them by either a relative, friend, or staff member of the early intervention program. Order of completion of the scales was counterbalanced.

Current family demographic information (income, education, age, occupation, and SES) was obtained from both the respondents, and records were maintained on the families by program staff members. As part of the program involvement, regular assessments were conducted with the children at which time family information was updated, and a number of developmental tests were administered to the children. Two sets of child data were abstracted from client records: Bayley scale MAs and Mental Development Indices or Stanford-Binet Intelligence Scale MAs and IQs corresponding to the time at which the parents completed the questionnaires and the same set of data obtained at the previous year of data-collection. These child data were used to derive measures of child behavior and development (see *Dependent Variables* section). The average time between administration of the two measurement occasions was 11.69 months (*SD* = 2.85).

Independent Variables

The mediating influences of five sets of independent variables were examined: family characteristics, child characteristics, child diagnosis, satisfaction with social support, and number of sources of support. Family characteristics included both gross monthly income and SES scores, using the Hollingshead (1975) four-factor index of social status. Child characteristics were child sex and child CA (in months). Child diagnosis consisted of developmental quotient scores (either Bayley Mental Development Index scores or Stanford-Binet IQ) and diagnostic group (retarded, physically impaired, or at-risk). (Dummy variable coding [Cohen & Cohen, 1983] was used to render the information of group membership into g − 1 dichotomies. The comparisons were retarded vs. physically impaired and at-risk, and physically impaired vs. retarded and at-risk.) Satisfaction with social support was measured using the Family Support Scale, which determines how helpful (i.e., supportive) 18 sources of support have been to parents in caring for their preschool child. The sources of support include individuals (e.g., spouse, parents, friends, physician) and groups (e.g., church, school, day care) at the ecological levels posited by Bronfenbrenner (1979). On a 5-point scale ranging from not at all helpful (0) to extremely helpful (4), respondents indicate the helpfulness of each source. The sum of the 18 ratings was used as the measure of satisfaction with support. Coefficient alpha computed from the average correlation among the 18 scale items was .77. Test–retest reliability of the total Family Support Scale scores, taken one month apart, was .91. Number of sources of support was comprised of three variables: number of Family Support Scale sources of support available to the respondent and number of services provided by the early intervention program to (a) the child and (b) the family. Three categories of child services and five categories of family services were potentially available to the children and their parents.

Dependent Variables

The influences of the independent variables were examined in relationship to six sets of dependent measures: personal well-being, attitudes toward the child, family integrity, child functioning, parent–child play opportunities, and child behavior and development.

The Questionnaire on Resources and Stress was employed as the measure of both personal well-being and attitudes toward the child. (This instrument is also used to measure family integrity and selected aspects of child functioning.) The Questionnaire on Resources and Stress is a true–false instrument that measures various dimensions of parental, family, and child functioning. The discriminative validity of this questionnaire has been demonstrated in a number of studies in terms of the differential influences of handicapping conditions on parent, family, and child outcomes (e.g, Holroyd, 1974; Holroyd & Guthrie, 1979; Holroyd & McArthur, 1976). It includes two personal well-being scales (physical and emotional health and time demands placed upon the respondent by the handicapped child) and four scales that measure attitudes toward rearing a handicapped child (negative attitudes toward the child, dependency of the child on the respondent, overcommitment of the respondent to the care of the child, and the respondent's pessimism toward the child).

The measures of family integrity were the three Questionnaire on Resources and Stress family-level scales: (a) family integration, (b) limits placed on family opportunities due to the child's handicapping condition, and (c) financial problems and burdens on the family.

Selected aspects of child functioning were assessed using the five Questionnaire on Resources and Stress child characteristics scales: (a) physical problems and limitations placed on the child, (b) degree of behavior engagement of the child in his or her home, (c) use of specialized community resources for the child, (d) social acceptance of the child, and (e) the child's degree of behavior problems/social-adaptive competencies. These scales specifically measure the respondent's perceptions of the influence of the child's problem or disability.

The Parent-Child Interaction Rating Scale (Dunst, 1984) was used as a measure of opportunities to engage in parent–child play. This scale measures how often and how many different "games" parents play with their child. Ratings are made for 24 games that are typically played between parents and their preschool children (e.g., pat-a-cake, "this little pig," pretend phone conversations, repeating the alphabet). Parents are asked to indicate how frequently they play the games with their child. Ratings are made on a 4-point scale ranging from do not play at all (0) to play almost every day (3). The dependent measures of parent–child play opportunities were the number of different games played and the frequency at which the games were played. The latter was computed as the total of the ratings for the 24 individual scale items. Coefficient alpha computed from the average correlation among the items was .95. Test–retest reliability for the total scale score, taken one month apart, was .87.

The dependent measures of child behavior and development were developmental quotient difference scores and developmental gain scores. Developmental quotient difference was computed as the child's developmental quotient score at the time the parents completed the questionnaires for this study minus the child's developmental quotient one year before. Developmental gain was computed as the difference between MAs at the first measurement occasion minus those at the second measurement divided by the corresponding differences between CAs $[(MA_2 - MA_1) / (CA_2 - CA_1)]$. The latter was a measure of amount of child progress between the tests that corrected for differences in amount of time between the measurement occasions (mean = 11.69 months, $SD = 2.85$). (The measures of child progress were used for exploratory purposes only. Because they were obtained on a post hoc basis, the relationships found between support and child progress must be considered suggestive regarding the mediating influences of support.)

Method of Analysis

The data were analyzed by a series of hierarchical multiple regression analyses by sets (Cohen & Cohen, 1983), using the structurally related groups of measures, previously defined, as the independent variables. Each hierarchical analysis involved 11 F tests. Under an omnibus null hypothesis for the 18 separate dependent measures, the expectation is for .05 x 198 = 10 significant findings by chance; however, when only the F tests for the analyses testing the main effects of the social support measures are considered, the expectation is for only .05 x 36 = 2 significant chance findings. Likewise, when the F tests for the analyses involving the interactions of support with the covariates are considered, the expectation is for only .05 x 108 = 5 significant findings. Type I errors would therefore be expected to be minimized.

The order of entry of the sets into the analyses was as follows: family characteristics, child characteristics, child diagnosis, satisfaction with social support, and number of sources of support. The rationale for this hierarchical ordering derives from the ecological model upon which this research is based (Bronfenbrenner, 1979). Family characteristics were expected to have first-order effects; child characteristics and child diagnosis, second-order effects; and support, mediating effects on parent, family, and child functioning resulting from negative reactions to the birth and rearing of handicapped children.

In each analysis the increments (I) in R^2 were ascertained each step to determine whether the different sets of independent measures accounted for a significant proportion of variance in the dependent measures. The increments in R^2 for the interactions between the two sets of social support measures and the other three sets of independent variables were also tested. Interactions with satisfaction with support were entered first into the analyses followed by entry of the interactions involving number of sources of support. These particular second-order interactions were the only ones tested because they were most germane to the purpose of the study.

Results

Preliminary t tests comparing single vs. married mothers, male vs. female respondents, and mothers vs. fathers (pairs in which both completed the questionnaires) were performed on each of the dependent measures. Only five significant differences were found for the 54 separate comparisons. Single mothers reported more financial problems than did married mothers, t (94) = 3.33, p < .01. Females played more parent–child games with their children than did males, t (135) = 2.04, p < .05, and played the games more frequently, t (135) = 2.19, p < .05. Wives reported poorer emotional and physical health than did their husbands, t (84) = 2.20, p < .05, and greater time demands placed upon them by their child, t (84) = 3.25, p < .01. Although these differences were not unexpected, these few could have occurred entirely by chance; therefore, the regression analyses were not performed separately for subgroups of parents.

Personal Well-Being

Table 2 shows the results for the two Questionnaire on Resources and Stress personal well-being scales. Satisfaction with support was the only main effect independent measure significantly related to physical and emotional health. Respondents indicating more satisfaction with their support networks reported having fewer physical and emotional problems. The Child Characteristics x Number of Sources of Support interaction revealed that the largest proportion of variance, I = .08, F (3, 109) = 4.01, p < .01, was accounted for by the combination of child sex and number of sources of support. Support was more likely to influence well-being among parents with male offspring. Both the family characteristics and satisfaction with support sets were significantly related to amount of time demands placed upon the respondent. Families with higher incomes and respondents indicating more satisfaction with support reported fewer time demands with regard to the care of their child.

Attitudes Toward Child

Child diagnosis was the only independent variable significantly related to the negative attitudes toward the child and overcommitment scales (see Table 2). Developmental quotient but not diagnostic group accounted for the major proportion of the variance on both outcome measures. Respondents with children with lower developmental quotients had more negative attitudes and reported being overly committed to their child's care.

Both child diagnosis and satisfaction with support were significantly related to overprotection of the child. Respondents with physically impaired children reported being more protective of their offspring compared to parents of retarded or developmentally at-risk children; and respondents indicating more satisfaction with their support networks indicated being less protective of their children. The Child Characteristics x Support interaction showed that the largest proportion of variance, I = .03, F (1, 121) = 4.14, p < .05, was accounted for by support and age of the child. Overprotection increased with increasing age of child for respondents with low support but not for respondents with high support. The Child Characteristics x Number of Sources of Support interaction showed that the largest proportion of variance, I = .10, F (3, 106) = 5.64, p < .001, was accounted for by the combination of child sex and number of sources of support. Support was more likely to affect overprotection among parents with female offspring.

Pessimism toward the child's future status was significantly related to both child characteristics and child diagnosis. Respondents were more pessimistic about females than males and older than younger children; also, parents were more pessimistic toward retarded than physically impaired or developmentally at-risk children. The Child Characteristics x Support interaction showed that a significant amount of variance was accounted for by a combination of support and both age, I = .03, F (1, 122) = 5.32, p < .05, and sex, I = .04, F (1, 121) = 5.70, p < .05, of the child. Pessimism increased with increasing age of the child among respondents with larger degrees of support, and support was more likely to influence pessimism among parents with male offspring.

Family Integrity

The results of the analyses for the three Questionnaire on Resources and Stress family integrity scales are show in Table 3. The family characteristics set accounted for a significant amount of the variance on all three out-

Table 2 Multiple Regression Coefficients and Increments (I) in R^2 for the Questionnaire on Resources and Stress Personal Well-Being and Parental Attitude Scales

Independent Variable	df	Well-being						Attitudes toward child					
		Emotional and physical health		Time demands		Negative attitudes		Over-commitment		Over-protection		Pessimism	
		R^2	I	R^2	I	R^2	I	R^2	I	R^2	I	R^2	I
Family characteristics	2, 134	.034	.034	.058*	.058*	.008	.008	.017	.017	.014	.014	.021	.021
Child characteristics	2, 132	.060	.026	.072*	.014	.040	.032	.056	.039	.037	.023	.086*	.065**
Diagnosis of child	3, 129	.012*	.042	.112*	.040	.185****	.145***	.158***	.102***	.100	.063*	.184****	.098***
Satisfaction with support	1, 128	.137**	.035*	.148**	.035*	.185****	.000	.161***	.003	.129*	.029*	.187****	.003
N of sources of support	3, 125	.142*	.005	.163**	.015	.204***	.019	.193***	.032	.148*	.019	.188***	.001
Family x Support Satisfaction	2, 123	.143	.001	.169*	.006	.217***	.013	.195**	.002	.148	.000	.188**	.000
Child x Support Satisfaction	2, 121	.162	.019	.191*	.022	.236***	.019	.219**	.024	.191*	.043*	.257****	.069***
Diagnosis x Support Satisfaction	3, 118	.170	.008	.199	.008	.237*	.001	.225*	.006	.226*	.035	.279***	.022
Family x Support Sources	6, 112	.207	.037	.230	.031	.274**	.037	.258*	.033	.234	.008	.322***	.043
Child x Support Sources	6, 106	.295*	.088*	.294*	.064	.294*	.020	.310*	.052	.355***	.121**	.351***	.028
Diagnosis x Support Sources	9, 97	.337*	.042	.320*	.026	.359**	.065	.329	.019	.448****	.093	.387**	.036

* $p < .05$.
** $p < .01$.
*** $p < .005$.
**** $p < .001$.

Table 3 Multiple Regression Coefficients and Increments (I) in R^2 for the Questionnaire on Resources and Stress Family Integrity Scales

Independent variable	df	Family integration		Family opportunities		Financial problems	
		R^2	I	R^2	I	R^2	I
Family characteristics	2, 134	.064*	.064**	.071**	.071**	.447****	.447****
Child characteristics	2, 132	.109***	.045*	.076*	.005	.448****	.001
Diagnosis of child	3, 129	.207****	.098***	.107*	.031	.477****	.029
Satisfaction with support	1, 128	.219****	.012	.122*	.015	.480****	.003
N of sources of support	3, 125	.235****	.016	.134	.012	.489****	.009
Family x Support Satisfaction	2, 123	.236****	.001	.148	.014	.495****	.006
Child x Support Satisfaction	2, 121	.255***	.019	.193*	.045*	.496****	.001
Diagnosis x Support Satisfaction	3, 118	.263***	.008	.204*	.011	.498****	.002
Family x Sources of Support	6, 112	.283*	.020	.223*	.019	.560****	.062*
Child x Sources of Support	6, 106	.337***	.054	.338***	.115**	.600****	.040
Diagnosis x Sources of Support	9, 97	.357*	.020	.352****	.014	.661****	.061

    * $p < .05$.
   ** $p < .01$.
  *** $p < .005$.
 **** $p < .001$.

comes. Respondents from high SES families and families with larger incomes indicated that they had more integrated family units, more family opportunities, and fewer financial problems.

Both child characteristics and child diagnosis were also significantly related to family integration. Child sex and developmental quotient were the two variables that accounted for significant proportions of variance on the criterion measures. Families with male offspring and those with children with higher developmental quotients had more integrated family units.

Both social support sets interacted with child characteristics in affecting family opportunities. The Child Characteristics x Satisfaction With Support interaction showed that a significant amount of variance, I = .04, F (1, 122) = 5.38, $p < .01$, was accounted for by child age and support. Family opportunities decreased among families with older children if they had minimal support. The Child Characteristics x Number of Sources of Support interaction showed that a significant amount of variance, I = .07, F (3, 106) = 3.63, $p < .05$, was accounted for by child sex and support. Support was more likely to affect family opportunities among parents with female offspring.

The significant Family Characteristics x Number of Sources of Support interaction for the financial prob-

lems scale showed that a significant amount of variance, I = .05, F (3, 115) = 3.77, $p < .01$, was accounted for by income and support. Families with larger incomes and more sources of support reported having fewer financial problems.

Child Functioning

Table 4 presents the findings for the five Questionnaire on Resources and Stress child functioning scales. Both child diagnosis and number of sources of support were significantly related to physical problems and limitations. Respondents with children who had low developmental quotients and respondents with children who were physically impaired indicated that their offspring had more limitations in terms of both intra- and extra-family opportunities The significant main effect for number of sources of support showed that respondents with larger social support networks had children who had fewer limitations placed on them in terms of intra- and extra-family opportunities The Child Characteristics x Support interaction showed that a significant amount of variance, I = .04, F (1, 122) = 9.45, $p < .05$, was accounted for by age and support. Limitations increased with increasing child age among families with limited social support.

Mediating Influences of Social Support Carl J. Dunst, Carol M. Trivette, and Arthur H. Cross

Table 4 Multiple Regression Coefficients and Increments (I) in R^2 for the Questionnaire on Resources and Stress Child Functioning Scales

Independent variable	df	Physical limitations		In-home engagement		Use of community resources		Social acceptance		Behavior difficulty	
		R^2	I	R^2	I	R^2	I	R^2	I	R^2	I
Family characteristics	2, 134	.005	.005	.085***	.085***	.004	.004	.004	.004	.027	.027
Child characteristics	2, 132	.025	.020	.136****	.051*	.020	.016	.011	.007	.034	.007
Diagnosis of child	3, 129	.357****	.332****	.157****	.021	.143***	.123***	.107*	.096**	.244****	.210****
Satisfaction with support	1, 128	.368****	.011	.173****	.016	.169***	.026*	.131*	.024	.262****	.018
N of sources of support	3, 125	.415****	.047*	.180**	.007	.211****	.042	.181**	.050	.300****	.038
Family x Support Satisfaction	2, 123	.416****	.001	.198**	.018	.225***	.014	.197**	.016	.312****	.012
Child x Support Satisfaction	2, 121	.460****	.044**	.198*	.000	.254***	.029	.201*	.004	.346****	.034*
Diagnosis x Support Satisfaction	3, 118	.471****	.011	.207*	.009	.264***	.010	.211*	.010	.360****	.014
Family x Sources of Support	6, 112	.480****	.009	.237	.030	.278*	.014	.280*	.069	.383****	.023
Child x Sources of Support	6, 106	.499****	.019	.272	.035	.311*	.033	.317*	.037	.426****	.043
Diagnosis x Sources of Support	9, 97	.530****	.031	.326*	.054	.361*	.050	.369*	.052	.447****	.021

* $p < .05$.
** $p < .01$.
*** $p < .005$.
**** $p < .001$.

Family and child characteristics were significantly related to behavior engagement in the home. Respondents from higher income families and respondents with male offspring reported that their children had more opportunities to engage in entertaining activities.

The child's use of specialized community resources was significantly related to both child diagnosis and satisfaction with support. Respondents with children with low developmental quotients reported accessing fewer resources, and respondents with more supportive networks reported less use of community resources. At first glance this finding seems inconsistent with our social support hypothesis, but upon reflection indicates that if informal sources of support are effective mediators, then more formal support services may not be necessary. (This finding is consistent with predictions made by Gourash [1978] regarding help-seeking. Help-seeking from formal support networks is viewed as necessary only when informal sources of support cannot "buffer the experiences of stress which obviates the need for help" [p. 516]).

Child diagnosis was significantly related to social acceptance. Children with low developmental quotients were perceived as being less socially accepted by members of their community; however, both satisfaction and number of sources of support, when aggregated, accounted for a significant amount of variance, I = .07, F (4, 125) =

2.82, p < .05. Respondents with more supportive social networks indicated that their children were more accepted and integrated into the community.

The extent to which the respondents believed that their child's particular developmental problem or disability represented a behavior problem or difficulty was significantly related to child diagnosis, indicating that children with lower developmental quotients were perceived as having more difficult behavior characteristics. Again, however, when the two sets of support measures were aggregated, a significant amount of the variance, I = .06, F (4, 125) = 2.50, p < .05, was accounted for in the dependent measure, indicating that "how difficult a behavior is perceived" is in part mediated by the nature of support available to a parent. The more supportive the respondent's network, the less troublesome the child's behavior appears to be. The significant Child Characteristics x Support interaction showed that child age and support accounted for a significant amount of the variance, I = .03, F (1, 122) = 4.79, p < .01. Behavior problems increased with increasing age of child among parents with minimal support.

Parent–Child Play Opportunities

Table 5 shows the findings for the two parent–child play outcome measures. Number of sources of support

Table 5 Multiple Regression Coefficients and Increments (I) in R^2 for the Parent–Child Interaction and Child Behavior and Development Dependent Measures

| | | Parent–child games | | | | Developmental gains | | | |
| | | Number | | Frequency | | IQ difference | | Gain scores | |
Independent variable	df	R^2	I	R^2	I	R^2	I	R^2	I
Family characteristics	2, 134	.004	.004	.008	.008	.055*	.055*	.058*	.058*
Child characteristics	2, 132	.011	.007	.040	.032	.070*	.015	.060	.002
Diagnosis of child	3, 129	.067	.056	.068	.028	.379***	.309***	.622***	.562***
Satisfaction with support	1, 128	.083	.016	.082	.014	.380***	.001	.625***	.003
N of sources of support	3, 125	.144*	.061*	.096	.014	.380	.000	.658***	.033*
Family x Support Satisfaction	2, 123	.149	.005	.115	.019	.397***	.017	.680***	.022
Child x Support Satisfaction	2, 121	.150	.001	.115	.000	.448***	.051**	.682***	.002
Diagnosis x Support Satisfaction	3, 118	.156	.006	.122	.007	.487***	.039*	.698***	.016
Family x Sources of Support	6, 112	.224	.068	.198	.076	.516***	.029	.726***	.028
Child x Sources of Support	6, 106	.253	.029	.198	.000	.567***	.051	.737***	.011
Diagnosis x Sources of Support	9, 97	.333*	.080	.293	.113	.621***	.054	.763***	.026

* $p < .05$.
** $p < .005$.
*** $p < .001$.

was significantly related to the number of different types of games parents played with their children. Respondents with larger numbers of sources of support reported playing a wider variety of games with their children.

Child Behavior and Development

Developmental quotient difference scores were significantly related to both family characteristics and child diagnosis (see Table 5). Children from high-income families showed smaller developmental quotient losses between measurements. (For 46% of the cases, actual developmental quotient gains were observed. The distribution of gains for the mentally retarded, physically impaired, and at-risk groups were, respectively, 39%, 48%, and 55%. A chi-square analysis showed no significant difference in the relative percentage of cases who were likely to show developmental quotient gains among the three groups of children.)

Not unexpectedly, children whose developmental quotients were high to begin with were the same individuals whose developmental quotient gain scores were greater. Of theoretical and conceptual importance was the significant Child Diagnosis x Satisfaction With Support interaction. Children were more likely to show smaller developmental quotient losses if they were offspring of parents with supportive social networks. The Child Characteristics x Satisfaction With Support interaction showed that age and support accounted for the major proportion of the variance, $I = .04$, $F (1, 124) = 9.60$, $p < .01$. Larger developmental quotient losses were shown with increasing age among children of parents with minimal amounts of support.

The amount of progress (developmental gain) made by the children over the course of a year was significantly related to family characteristics, child diagnosis, and number of sources of support. Children from high SES and high-income families were found to make more developmental progress compared to children from low SES and low-income families. Again, not surprisingly, children whose developmental status was better to begin with made the greatest amount of progress; but number of sources of support available to the families was significantly related to amount of progress. Children from families with larger social support networks made significantly more developmental progress.

Discussion

In this study we examined the mediating influence of social support on personal, family, and child functioning. Our analytical strategy deserves comment to place the findings in proper perspective. The method of analysis used to assess both the main and interactive effects of social support discerned the unique and nonshared variance accounted for in the dependent measures by, respectively, satisfaction with support and number of sources of support. The hierarchical model partialled out (in an analysis of covariance sense) the shared variance between the seven covariates and the social support measures before the unique contributions of social support were determined. Thus, small but statistically significant amounts of variance accounted for by social support may be considered particularly robust. Taken together, our findings demonstrate rather complex relationships between social support and personal, family, and child outcomes, although the results were entirely as predicted by social systems theory.

Previous researchers have shown that support mediates both personal well-being (Bott, 1971; Dean & Lin, 1977; McCubbin et al., 1980; Mitchell & Trickett, 1980) and parental attitudes toward their children (Crnic, Friedrich, & Greenberg, 1983; Crnic, Greenberg et al., 1983). The positive effects of social support on personal well-being found here not only replicate results of previous research but also demonstrate the moderating influences of social support on even a potentially devastating event such as the birth and rearing of a handicapped child. Both the emotional and physical health and the time demands placed upon the respondents were related positively to social support. Our findings also replicate previous work in which investigators found that at least one dimension of parental attitudes—overprotection—is not related to degree of intellectual delay (see Crnic, Friedrich, & Greenberg, 1983), although our results showed that parents of physically impaired youngsters were more protective of their children than were parents of retarded or developmentally at-risk children. Our findings did show that overprotection is influenced by satisfaction with social support. Parents with more supportive social networks reported being less protective of their children, independent of their child's diagnosis or severity of developmental delay. This indicates that if parents had network members that were helpful with regard to the care of their child, such help mediated the

Table 6 Zero-Order Correlations Between the Family Support Scale (FSS) Items and the QRS Family Integrity Scales

FSS items	Family integration	Family opportunities	Financial problems
Respondent's parents	−.08	.10	.00
Spouse's parents	−.19*	−.14*	−.23*
Relatives/kin	−.25**	−.05	−.03
Spouse's relatives/kin	−.16*	.01	−.17*
Spouse	−.25**	−.23*	−.39**
Friends	−.09	.01	−.07
Spouse's friends	−.17*	−.05	−.21*
Respondent's children	−.06	−.05	.10
Other parents	−.21*	−.14*	−.09
Professional helpers	.06	−.11	−.02
Family/child's physician	.00	−.04	−.03
Coworkers	.01	.00	−.07
Parent groups	.02	.12	.05
School/day care	.04	−.15*	−.07
Professional agencies	.02	−.04	.27**
Early intervention progra	−.03	−.05	−.18*
Social groups/clubs	.00	.06	−.05
Church	−.12	−.17*	−.12

* $p < .05$.
** $p < .01$.

degree to which the parents felt it necessary to overcompensate by sheltering their child.

Contrary to expectation, social support had no main effects in terms of influencing family integrity. The findings for the family integrity outcome measures indicate that social support had some but less mediational influences on family functioning compared to either personal well-being or parental attitudes toward the child. Tentatively, the results suggest that social support has more powerful influences in intrapersonal behavior than it does on family functioning. This contention is based, in part, on findings from our other social support research. Satisfaction with intrafamily role sharing (Gallagher, Cross, & Scharfman, 1981) accounts for a significant proportion of the variance on the Family Integration Scale, whereas in the present study support was not significantly related to this particular outcome but was the only main effects variable significantly related to intrapersonal physical and emotional well-being. One might expect, then, that family integrity is related more to certain types of informal social support rather than to support in gen-

eral, and, in fact, the zero-order correlations between the three Questionnaire on Resources and Stress family-level scales and the individual Family Support Scale items show this to be the case (see Table 6). These findings indicate that different types of support have differential influences. The work of Crnic, Greenberg et al. (1983) has, in fact, demonstrated the differential effects of support. They found that intrafamily support had greater influences on maternal behavior and attitudes than did either friendship or community support. A potential line of inquiry as part of social support research would be the delineation of the differential effects of different types of support.

Bronfenbrenner (1979) and Cochran and Brassard (1979) posited both direct and indirect influences of social support on parental and child behavior and development, and the findings from the present study offer support for their contentions. For example, Cochran and Brassard hypothesized that the members of a parent's social network serve as models that may affect child-rearing practices and that parents are likely to adopt or modify their parenting styles if esteemed network members demonstrate effective and nurturing behavior. In the present study number of parent–child games played was significantly related to number of sources of support available to the respondents. It is reasonable to speculate that these different network members provided multiple exemplars that influenced the types and breadth of games parents played with their children.

Mediating influences of social support on child behavior and development were also found in this study, providing further support for the indirect effects of social support on child outcomes (Bronfenbrenner, 1979; Cochran & Brassard, 1979). Perhaps most impressive was the fact that the amount of progress the children made over the course of a year, despite being heavily influenced by developmental status, nonetheless was also affected by social support; i.e., children were more likely to make developmental progress if they were offspring of parents with supportive social networks. Changes in developmental quotients were also affected by social support. Children were more likely to show smaller losses if their parents reported having more supportive social networks.

Converging evidence for the indirect influences of social support on child behavior and development comes from the results for three of the Questionnaire on Resources and Stress child functioning analyses. Social support was related to parental perceptions of their childrens' physical limitations, social acceptance, and behavior problems. Parents who reported having more supportive networks indicated that their children had fewer physical limitations, were more socially accepted by others, and had fewer behavior problems and difficult personality characteristics. Taken together, our findings indicate that both real and perceived behavior characteristics of children are influenced by their parents' social support networks. Our data add to a growing body of evidence demonstrating the influences of social support on child outcomes (Crnic, Greenberg et al., 1983; Crockenberg, 1981).

A fundamental tenet of ecological–social support theory (Bronfenbrenner, 1979) is that social support is likely to have differential impacts at different developmental junctures and transitions; i.e., during the course of development, one would expect that the effects of support would differ depending upon the age of the child. This predicted Age x Support interaction was found on a number of the dependent measures. The same pattern emerged in the majority of cases. For the Questionnaire on Resources and Stress overprotection, family opportunities, pessimism, physical problems and limitations, and behavior problems scales, as well as for developmental quotient difference scores, negative effects were more likely to have been found with increasing age of the child among families with minimal support. In terms of the particular outcomes examined in this study, support would seem to be more important as a child becomes older if parent, family, and child functioning are not to be adversely affected.

Although this study was exploratory in nature, it nonetheless produced information that contributes to our understanding of an ecology of both human development (Bronfenbrenner, 1979; Cochran & Brassard, 1979) and mental retardation (Brooks & Baumeister, 1977; Crnic, Friedrich, & Greenberg, 1983; Schoggen & Schoggen, 1981). On one hand, the cumulative and interactive effects of social support that we found provide indications that qualitative as well as quantitative dimensions of support have both direct and indirect influences on pa-

rental, family, and child functioning (although the exact causal or mediational relationships are at this time not entirely clear). This evidence provides support for the contentions of both Bronfenbrenner (1979) and Cochran and Brassard (1979), who hypothesized that behavior is affected by events in settings in which developing persons are not even present. On the other hand, our data provide indications that social support can influence parent, parent–child, and child functioning in families with retarded and handicapped children. This evidence provides support for the adaptational model of Crnic, Greenberg et al. (1983), who noted that although the presence of a retarded child often has a detrimental effect on different family members, ecological influences, including social support, can have positive effects on the development and functioning of the target child and his or her family members.

One underlying theme emerged from this study, namely, social support has differential impacts and effects, and future investigators should consider these differential influences if the construct of social support is to contribute to an ecology of human development and mental retardation. Through identification of what types and dimensions of support have what particular impacts, we will begin to further our understanding of the differential influences of support on parents and the family, as well as the child.

References

Andrews, F., & Withey, S. (1976). *Social indicators of well-being.* New York: Plenum.

Barrera, M. (1981). Social support in the adjustment of pregnant adolescents. In B. Gottlieb (Ed.), *Social networks and social support* (pp. 69–96). Beverly Hills, CA: Sage.

Barrera, M., & Aimlay, S. (1983). The structure of social support: A conceptual and empirical analysis. *Journal of Community Psychology, 11,* 133–143.

Beckman, P. (1983). Influences of selected child characteristics on stress in families of handicapped infants. *American Journal of Mental Deficiency, 80,* 150–156.

Bott, E. (1971). *Family and social networks.* London: Tavistock.

Brim, J. (1974). Social network correlates of avowed happiness. *Journal of Nervous and Mental Diseases, 158,* 432–439.

Bronfenbrenner, U. (1977). Toward an experimental ecology of human development. *American Psychologist, 32*, 513–531.

Bronfenbrenner, U. (1979). *The ecology of human development: Experiments by nature and design.* Cambridge: Harvard University Press.

Brooks, P., & Baumeister, A. (1977). A plea for consideration of ecological validity in the experimental psychology of mental retardation. *American Journal of Mental Deficiency, 81*, 407–416.

Caplan, G. (1974). *Support systems and community mental health.* New York: Behavioral Publications.

Caplan, G. (1976). The family as a support system. In G. Caplan & M. Kililea (Eds.), *Support systems and mutual help* (pp. 19–36). New York: Grune and Stratton.

Cobb, S. (1976). Social support as a moderator of life stress. *Psychosomatic medicine, 38*, 300–314.

Cobb, S. (1976). Social support as a moderator of life stress. *Psychosomatic Medicine, 38*, 300–314.

Cochran, M., & Brassard, J. (1979). Child development and personal social networks. *Child Development, 50*, 601–616.

Cohen, J., & Cohen, P. (1983). *Applied multiple regression/correlation analysis for the behavioral sciences* (2nd ed.). Hillsdale, NJ: Erlbaum.

Crnic, K., Friedrich, W., & Greenberg, M. (1983). Adaptation of families with mentally retarded children: A model of stress, coping, and family ecology. *American Journal of Mental Deficiency, 88*, 125–138.

Crnic, K., Greenberg, M., Ragozin, A., Robinson, N., & Basham, R. (1983). Effects of stress and social support on mothers of premature and full-term infants. *Child Development, 54*, 209–217.

Crockenberg, S. (1981). Infant irritability, mother responsiveness and social influences on the security of infant-mother attachment. *Child Development, 52*, 857–865.

Dean, A., & Lin, N. (1977). Stress-buffering role of social support. *Journal of Nervous and Mental Disease, 165*, 403–417.

Dunst, C. J. (1982). *Social support, early intervention, and institutional avoidance.* Paper presented at the annual meeting of the Southeastern Association on Mental Deficiency, Louisville, KY.

Dunst, C. J. (1984). *Parent-Child Interaction Rating Scale: Reliability and validity.* Unpublished manuscript, Family, Infant and Preschool program, Western Carolina Center, Morganton, NC.

Dunst, C. J. (1985). Rethinking early intervention. *Analysis and Intervention in Developmental Disabilities, 5*, 165-201.

Dunst, C. J., Jenkins, V., & Trivette, C. M. (1984). Family Support Scale: Reliability and validity. *Journal of Individual, Family and Community Wellness, 1*(4), 45–52.

Embry, L. (1980). Family support for handicapped preschool children at risk for abuse. *New Directions for Exceptional Children, 4*, 29–58.

Gabel, H., McDowell, J., & Cerreto, M. (1983). Family adaptation to the handicapped infant. In S. G. Garwood & R. Fewell (Eds.), *Educating handicapped infants* (pp. 455–493). Rockville, MD: Aspen.

Gallagher, J. J., Cross, A. H., & Scharfman, W. (1981). *Parent Role Scale.* Unpublished instrument, Frank Porter Graham Child Development Center, University of North Carolina, Chapel Hill.

Giovanoni, J., & Billingsley, A. (1970). Child neglect among the poor: A study of parental adequacy in families of three ethnic groups. *Child Welfare, 49*, 196–204.

Gourash, N. (1978). Help seeking: A review of the literature. *American Journal of Community Psychology, 6*, 413–423.

Grossman, H. (Ed.) (1973). *Manual on terminology and classification in mental retardation.* Washington, DC: American Association on Mental Deficiency.

Hetherington, E., Cox, M., & Cox, R. (1976). Divorced fathers. *Family Coordinator, 25*, 427–428.

Hetherington, E., Cox, M., & Cox R. (1978). The aftermath of divorce. In J. Stevens & M. Mathews (Eds.), *Mother-child, father-child relations* (pp. 149–176). Washington, DC: National Association for the Education of Young Children.

Hobbs, D. (1965). Parenthood as crisis: A third study. *Journal of Marriage and the Family, 27*, 367–372.

Hobbs, N. (1975). *The futures of children.* San Francisco: Jossey-Bass.

Holahan, C. J. (1977). Social ecology. In I. Iscoe, B. Bloom, & C. Spielberger (Eds.), *Community psychology in transition* (pp. 123–126). New York: Wiley.

Hollingshead, A. B. (1975). *Four factor index of social status.* Unpublished manuscript, Yale University.

Holroyd, J. (1973). *Questionnaire on Resources and Stress.* Unpublished instrument, University of California, Los Angeles.

Holroyd, J. (1974). The Questionnaire on Resources and Stress: An instrument to measure family responses to a handicapped family member. *Journal of Community Psychology, 2,* 92–94.

Holroyd, J., & Guthrie, D. (1979). Stress in families of children with neuromuscular disease. *Journal of Clinical Psychology, 35,* 734–739.

Holroyd, J., & McArthur, D. (1976). Mental retardation and stress on parents: A contrast between Down's syndrome and childhood autism. *American Journal of Mental Deficiency, 80,* 431–436.

Lazar, I., & Darlington, R. (1982). Lasting effects of early education. *Monographs of the Society for Research in Child Development, 47* (2–3), Serial No. 195.

LeMasters, E. (1957). Parenthood as crisis. *Marriage and Family Living, 19,* 352–355.

Litwak, E. (1960). The use of extended family groups in the achievement of social goals. *Social Problems, 7,* 177–187.

McCubbin, H., Joy, C., Cauble, A. E., Comeau, J., Patterson, J., & Needle, R. (1980). Family stress and coping: A decade review. *Journal of Marriage and the Family,* 855–871.

Miller, B., & Sollie, D. (1980). Normal stress during the transition to parenthood. *Family Relations, 29,* 459–465.

Mitchell, J. (Ed.) (1969). *Social networks in urban situations.* Manchester, England: University of Manchester Press.

Mitchell, R. E., & Trickett, E. J. (1980). Task force report: Social networks as mediators of social support. *Community Mental Health Journal, 16,* 27–43.

Mueller, D. (1980). Social networks: A promising direction for research on the relationship of the social environment to psychiatric disorders. *Social Science and Medicine, 40,* 147–161.

Nihira, K., Meyers, C. E., & Mink, I. (1980). Home environment, family adjustment, and the development of mentally retarded children. *Applied Research in Mental Retardation, 1,* 5–24.

Nihira, K., Meyers, C. E., & Mink, I. (1983). Reciprocal relationships between home environment and development of TMR adolescents. *American Journal of Mental Deficiency, 88,* 139–149.

Schoggen, P., & Schoggen, M. (1981). Ecological factors in the prevention of psychosocial mental retardation. In M. Begab, H. C. Haywood, & H. Garber (Eds.), *Psychosocial influences in retarded performance (Vol. 1): Issues and theories in development* (pp. 47–64). Baltimore: University Park Press.

Tolsdorf, C. (1976). Social networks, support and coping: An exploratory study. *Family Process, 15,* 407–417.

Walker, K., MacBride, A., & Vachon, M. (1977). Social support networks and the crisis of bereavement. *Social Science and Medicine, 11,* 35–42.

Weiss, R. (1974). The provisions of social relationships. In Z. Rubin (Ed.), *Doing unto others* (pp. 17–26). Englewood Cliffs, NJ: Prentice-Hall.

This research was supported, in part, by Grants No. MH 38862 from the National Institute of Mental Health and No. 83527 from the Research Section, Division of Mental Health, Mental Retardation, and Substance Abuse Services, North Carolina Department of Human Resources. Appreciation is extended to Pat Condrey for her assistance in preparation of the manuscript. Requests for reprints should be sent to Carl J. Dunst, Western Carolina Center, Enola Rd., Morganton, NC 28655.

Authors

Carl J. Dunst and Carol M. Trivette, Western Carolina Center, Morganton, NC, and **Arthur H. Cross**, Appalachian State University.

Comparison Groups in Research on Families With Mentally Retarded Members: A Methodological and Conceptual Review

Zolinda Stoneman
1989

Abstract

A review and critique of the use of comparison groups in mental retardation family research was provided. Issues addressed include matching on age versus competency of the mentally retarded family member, description of comparison groups in published research, demographic equivalence of groups, matching strategies, populations from which samples were drawn, appropriateness of tasks/ instruments across groups, and the role of theory in comparison group selection. Unique concerns relating to sibling research and studies of mentally retarded parents were discussed. Caution was expressed concerning the translation of comparison research findings into intervention targets for families with mentally retarded members. Alternatives to comparison group designs were presented as well as recommendations for selecting and describing comparison samples.

Many studies on families with a mentally retarded member have been criticized because of the lack of nonretarded comparison groups (e.g., Byrne & Cunningham, 1985; Crnic, Friedrich, & Greenberg, 1983). Often investigators identified family problems (e.g., marital distress) and attributed these negative findings to the presence of a mentally retarded child in the family (e.g., Holt, 1958). In essence, families of mentally retarded children were being compared with a subjective ideal of what families should be. When families fell short, the mentally retarded family member was assumed to be either directly or indirectly responsible.

One solution to this problem, the use of nonretarded comparison groups, appears to be simple and straightforward. Rather than comparing families to a subjective ideal, comparisons are made with actual families drawn from the general population. By so doing, investigators can avoid pitfalls of previous research, and family characteristics that are specific to families with mentally retarded members can be identified. This simplicity, however, is deceptive. The dilemma becomes one of decid-ing exactly which families constitute an appropriate comparison. This dilemma is further intensified by recruitment difficulties, particularly when the sampling parameters are very specific.

A classic series of articles published in the late 1960s and early 1970s provides the clearest discussion of the use of comparison groups in mental retardation research. Some papers are directly focused on the selection of comparison groups (Baumeister, 1967; Heal, 1970), whereas others embed this information in arguments concerning the developmental/difference positions (Ellis, 1969; Milgram, 1969; Weir, 1967; Zigler, 1969). Those taking a developmental perspective (Zigler, 1969) argue for groups matched on mental age (MA), and those with a deficit orientation (Ellis, 1969) favor chronological age (CA) matches. These papers are focused on comparisons for individual children; family researchers must move beyond the individual and select comparisons for multiperson systems. Similar issues are applicable, but the systemic nature of families and family processes creates new demands for conceptualization of comparison groups. The purpose of this paper is to review and critique the use of comparison groups in mental retardation family research.

Reduction of Alternate Hypotheses

In classic experimental design, control groups are used to reduce the number of potential alternate explanations for a given effect. The aim is to hold all factors constant except the variable(s) under study so that clear causality attributions can be made. Although this control can never be achieved in family research, the notion of reducing alternate explanations remains sound. Zigler (1969) warned against attributing group differences in mental retardation research to subject factors (e.g., IQ) when groups also differ in other important ways. He concluded that "mischief and downright ambiguity" (p. 545) have accrued to mental retardation research from failure to address confounding variables.

Comparison Groups in Research on Families With Mentally Retarded Members   Zolinda Stoneman

Research on nonretarded families provides a wealth of insight into factors that impact on family functioning (and thus provide potential confounding variables in family research), including social class, parent age and education, race, family size, family form, child gender, and birth order (see Maccoby & Martin, 1983, for a review of this literature). It is not possible to equate groups for every factor that might covary with family dependent measures. As House (1977) suggested, variables are hopelessly confounded once one leaves the laboratory. Yet, each unaccounted-for variable yields potentially confounded findings, subject to multiple interpretations.

Table 1 provides an overview of how mental retardation family researchers have constituted comparison groups. Several points should be noted. *Family research* is defined broadly; an attempt was made to include a wide variety of studies that might fall under the general rubric of "family research." Not included, however, are studies of attachment or studies narrowly focused on children's language environments. All studies included families of mentally retarded persons and at least one nonretarded comparison group. In some studies cited in the table (e.g., Bailey & Slee, 1984; Dyson & Fewell, 1986), families with mentally retarded members were mixed together in a single group with families whose members had other disabling conditions.

Clusters of studies were divided by family subsystem and further subdivided by whether other disability groups, in addition to families with mentally retarded members, were included as separate sample groups (when multiple disability groups were included in a study, only information for the mental retardation group and its comparison were tabled). Entries for each matching variable indicate whether the investigator(s) matched for that variable (+), did not match for the variable (no), had groups that were similar on the variable, but not formally matched (S), or failed to report information concerning the variable in the description of comparison and/or mentally retarded subjects (NR). For studies containing more than one comparison sample, each was tabled on a separate line. When comparison group data were drawn from a previously published article, information provided in the original article was used in completing the tabled entry for that study. The time period covered was arbitrarily defined as 1965 to the present. Only journal articles were cited (books, book chapters, conference papers, dissertations, and in-press articles were excluded).

Matching on Age Versus Competency

Mentally retarded and comparison subjects are almost always matched on CA or MA or on another competency measure. Most family researchers have utilized matching strategies based on CA (see Table 1). The major methodological problem encountered in CA-match designs involves equating research tasks across groups when children differ in competency (e.g., Baumeister, 1967). This problem, which occurs most often when older or severely retarded children are studied, is addressed later in this paper. Conceptually, the CA-match design is limited in its ability to identify reasons for group differences. When CA-matched groups differ, one is left with the ambiguous attribution that "mental retardation" in one family member is responsible for the difference. Yet, "mental retardation" does not operate as an explanatory construct but, rather, as a global classifying variable. Thus, well-executed CA-match designs can identify facets about family life that differ in families with a mentally retarded member but cannot explain or identify the processes that underlie those differences.

Investigators use MA-match designs to attempt to equate mentally retarded and nonretarded individuals on general intellectual ability, thereby examining differences in family functioning when these competencies, central to a diagnosis of mental retardation, are similar. Matching on MA carries with it both conceptual and methodological problems, which have been discussed in detail elsewhere (e.g., Baumeister, 1967; Ellis, 1969; Heal, 1970). Mental age is a composite measure. When mentally retarded and nonretarded individuals are matched on MA, there is no assurance that their specific skills and competencies will be similar. In fact, it is probable that the skill patterns of two MA-matched individuals would be quite different.

Heal (1970) cautioned that in MA-match designs, IQ and CA are left confounded in subsequent sampling groups; to equate groups on MA, mentally retarded subjects must be older than comparison subjects. The older the mentally retarded subjects, and the more severe their mental retardation, the greater the discrepancy will be between the CA of these individuals and the CA of their MA matches. For example, a severely mentally retarded adolescent with an MA of 3 years would be matched with a nonretarded 3-year-old child. Few would argue that the situations confronted by the families of these two children would be similar or that comparisons of fam-

©American Association on Mental Retardation

ily functioning would be meaningful. The families of the two aforementioned children would be at different stages of the family life cycle. Parents of the mentally retarded adolescent would themselves be older and would differ in the support systems available to them. The educational programs experienced by the two children would differ dramatically, and the overall ecologies of the family's daily lives would be dissimilar. The confounding influence of large differences in child age on family functioning is so pervasive as to make most MA-match comparisons of families of older children conceptually meaningless. For this reason, MA-matching in family research is most frequent (and most valuable as a design strategy) when subjects are infants and the discrepancy between child MA and CA is minimal. Of 11 MA-match studies in Table 1, only 2 had subjects older than preschool age (Bailey & Slee, 1984; Cashdan & Jeffree, 1966). Investigators in both of these studies experienced major problems in their attempts to use an MA-match design with families of older mentally retarded children (the design problems they encountered are discussed later in this paper).

When MA-match designs are employed, ideally, MA data are obtained on the mentally retarded sample and then on a large pool of nonretarded subjects; MA matches are then drawn from this pool. The time and expense of this strategy can force researchers to employ shortcuts. Sometimes, no MA data are obtained on the comparison sample. The researcher assumes that for normally developing subjects, MA and CA are identical. This assumption is crude but allows completion of MA-match studies with limited resources. It is most common in infant studies (e.g., Maurer & Sherrod, 1987) where less distortion results than in studies of older children (the MAs of a group of infants would be expected to vary only by a few months; the MAs of a group of school-age children, on the other hand, could easily vary by several years).

Problems in using MA-match designs in studies of older children, as well as problems encountered when researchers use CA as a proxy for MA in defining a comparison sample, are pointed out in a study by Cashdan and Jeffree (1966), in which the *mean* MA of a group of mentally retarded children was matched to the CA of comparison children, with the assumption that the CAs of the nonretarded children could be used as an approximation of their MAs. The mentally retarded children ranged in age from 7 to 15 years and had a mean MA of

5.5 years. The comparison sample was recruited from a group of 5.5-year-old children attending a preschool. Because the range of MAs among the retarded children was not reported, it is impossible to know how widely the competency levels of these children varied around the mean of 5.5 years. Plausibly, a group of mentally retarded children between the ages of 7 and 15 could have a wide range of MA levels, making the mean of 5.5 only a very rough index of the range of MAs within the group. In addition, because the MAs of comparison children were not assessed, considerable variability would be expected to exist in the range of MA levels in the comparison group (few 5.5-year-old children would be expected to have an MA of exactly 5.5 years). When MA-matching strategies that include the error variance potentially involved here are used, interpretation of group differences becomes difficult, at best.

Difficulties in obtaining valid MA assessments can also compromise the use of MA-match designs, particularly with more severely retarded children. This dilemma arose for Bailey and Slee (1984) in a study of mothers of severely multiply handicapped children. Because of a lack of standardized instruments to adequately assess this population, they relied on professionals' clinical judgments to estimate MA. Although using this procedure is understandable, it unfortunately yields MA data of questionable reliability and validity.

Longitudinal studies point out another difficulty; as children develop, they outgrow scales such as the Bayley, necessitating use of two assessment instruments at different ages (e.g., Maurer & Sherrod, 1987). Across instruments, however, MA data are often not comparable. Other problems arise from inappropriate selection of MA assessments. Cunningham, Reuler, Blackwell, and Deck (1981) used the Peabody Picture Vocabulary Test to match children as young as 18 months on MA. This test assesses receptive vocabulary and is a questionable measure of MA, particularly for mentally retarded children. Further, it is normed on children older and more competent than those in the study (Dunn & Dunn, 1981). Mental age-match designs are only as strong as the measures used to assess MA. State-of-the-art of MA assessment is still imperfect, and these imperfections spill over into research using MA-matching strategies. In some cases, measurement problems are so pervasive as to hopelessly compromise study findings.

Using both CA and MA comparisons in studies of infants or young children can provide added interpre-

Comparison Groups in Research on Families With Mentally Retarded Members   Zolinda Stoneman

Table 1 Matching Variables in Studies With a Nonhandicapped Comparison Group(s)

Type of study/Author(s)	No. MR	No. C	CA	Sex	MA	Race	PEd	SES	# Par	B.O.	# Sib	PA
Mother												
Bailey & Slee, 1984	6	6	no	+	+	+	+	+	NR	NR	NR	NR
Barrera et al., 1987	19	24	S	S	S	NR	NR	S	S	S	NR	+
Berger & Cunningham, 1981, 1983, 1986	5	7	+	+	+	NR	NR	+	NR	S	+	S
Breiner & Forehand,	8	8	+	+	no	NR	NR	+	S	NR	NR	NR
1982		8	+	no	no	NR	NR	+	S	NR	NR	NR
Breiner & Young, 1985[b]	8	8	+	S	no	NR	NR	S	NR	NR	NR	NR
Buckhalt et al., 1978	10	10	+	+	no	NR	NR	S	NR	NR	NR	S
Cashdan & Jeffree, 1966	10	10	no	NR	+	NR	NR	S	NR	NR	NR	NR
Cook & Culp, 1981	8	8	no	+	+	NR	NR	NR	NR	NR	NR	NR
Cunningham et al., 1981	18	18	+	+	no	NR	+	+	NR	NR	NR	NR
Dyson & Fewell, 1986	15	15	+	+	+	+	S	+	+	NR	NR	S
Eheart, 1982	8	8	no	S	+	NR	NR	S	NR	NR	NR	S
Friedrich & Friedrich, 1981	34	34	S	NR	no	NR	NR	S	+	NR	S	S
Gunn et al., 1982	11	11	+	+	no	NR	NR	+	NR	+	NR	S
Herman & Shantz, 1983	12	19	+	no	no	NR	NR	S	NR	NR	NR	NR
Kogan et al., 1969	6	10	no	S	no	+	NR	no	NR	NR	NR	S
McAllister et al., 1973	281	784	NR	NR	no	+	NR	NR	NR	NR	NR	NR
Smith & Hagan, 1984	14	19	+	no	no	NR	S	S	NR	no	NR	no
Tannock, 1988	11	11	no	+	+	NR	+	+	NR	+	NR	+
Wilton & Renaut, 1986	42	42	+	+	+	NR	S	S	S	NR	NR	S
Wright et al., (1)	48	42	NR	NR	NR	NR	NR	NR	NR	NR	NR	NR
1985[c] (2)	62	1576	NR	NR	NR	NR	NR	NR	NR	NR	NR	NR
Mother (multiple disability groups)[d]												
Brooks-Gunn & Lewis, 1982[e]	57	156	+	NR	+	S	NR	NR	NR	NR	NR	NR
	20											
Cummings et al., 1966	60	60	S	S	no	NR	NR	S	+	NR	NR	NR
Hanzlik & Stevenson, 1986	10	10	+	NR	no	NR	NR	no	NR	NR	NR	NR
1986		10	no	NR	+	NR	NR	no	NR	NR	NR	NR
Kogan & Tyler, 1973[f]	6	15	no	NR	no	NR	NR	NR	NR	NR	NR	S
Ricci, 1970	20	20	+	+	+	NR	S	NR	NR	NR	S	S
Sigman et al., 1986	18	18	no	+	+	NR	+	NR	NR	NR	NR	NR
Wasserman et al.,	6	6	+	+	no	no	NR	+	NR	NR	NR	NR
1986[c]	6		+	+	no	no	NR	+	NR	NR	NR	NR
Mother-Father												
Abbott & Meridith, 1986	30	30	+	+	no	+	S	+	+	NR	S	S
Bristol et al., 1988	31	25	+	+	no	+	+	+	+	NR	S	+

Comparison Groups in Research on Families With Mentally Retarded Members

Zolinda Stoneman

Study	C	MR									
1988[h]	12	18	no	+	NR	NR	+	NR	NR	NR	NR
Levy-Shiff, 1986	20	20	+	NR	no	+	+	+	NR	no	S
Maurer & Sherrod, 1987	6	4	+	+	+	+	+	+	S	+	NR
O'Connor & Stachowiak, 1971[g]	8	8	+	S	S	S	S	+	+	+	NR
		8	+	+	S	S	S	+	+	+	NR
Routh, 1970	24	24	NR	NR	NR	NR	NR	NR	NR	NR	NR
Salisbury, 1987	31	33	S	S	S	S	S	S	NR	S	S
Stoneman et al., 1983	8	8	+	+	+	+	+	S	+	S	S
Waisbren, 1980	30	30	+	+	+	+	+	+	+	NR	NR
Williams & McHenry, 1981	30	30	NR	NR	NR	NR	NR	NR	NR	NR	NR
Mother–Father (multiple disability groups)[d]											
Kazak, 1987	36	33	NR	NR	+	+	+	+	NR	NR	NR
Miller & Keirn, 1978	50	50	S	no	S	no	no	S	NR	S	S
Father (multiple disability groups)[d]											
Cummings, 1976	60	60	NR	S	S	+	S	S	NR	NR	NR
Sibling											
Abramovitch et al., 1987[i]	14	71	NR	NR	NR	NR	no	NR	NR	NR	NR
1987[i]	12	48	NR	NR	NR	NR	no	S	NR	NR	NR
Gath, 1973	174	143	NR	NR	NR	NR	NR	+	NR	NR	NR
Gath & Gumley, 1987	95	95	NR	NR	NR	NR	NR	+	NR	NR	NR
1987	88	88	NR	NR	NR	NR	NR	+	NR	NR	NR
Lobato et al., 1987	24	22	+	+	S	S	+	+	+	+	S
Stoneman et al., 1987, 1988	16	16	+	+	+	+	+	+	+	+	S
Sibling (multiple disability groups)[d]											
Gath, 1972	36	36	NR	NR	S	S	S	+	+	+	NR
McHale et al., 1986	30	30	NR	NR	NR	no	NR	+	S	no	NR
Mentally retarded parents											
Feldman et al., 1986	8	8	NR	NR	NR	no	no	+	–	–	–
Peterson et al., 1983[j]	5	20	NR	NR	NR	no	no	+	–	–	–
1983[j]		20	NR	no	NR	no	no	+	–	–	–
Robinson, 1978	32	32	no	no	no	no	S	S	–	–	–
Mentally retarded parents (multiple disability groups)[d]											
Crittenden & Bonvillian, 1984	10	10	no	S	S	S	S	+	S	+	NR
1984	10	10	no	no	no	no	no	+	no	no	NR

Note. MR = mentally retarded, C = comparison, + = groups matched or identical as a result of a limited sampling frame, S = groups are similar—not formally matched, no = groups not matched or similar, NR = information not reported.

[a]MA = mental age or other child competence measure; PEd, parental education; # Par, one- or two-parent home; B.O., birth order; # Sib, number of children in the family; PA, parent age. [b]Data for the mentally retarded group taken from Breiner and Forehand, 1982; comparison group data taken from Griest et al., 1982. [c]The authors stated that groups were matched on race; however, the proportion of white families varied between the two groups. [d]Multiple disability group studies have at least one other disability group comparison. [e]Comparison group data taken from an unpublished manuscript (Lewis, 1978). [f]Data for the mentally retarded group and for 10 of the 15 comparison families taken from Kogan et al., 1969. [g]Sibling data also included. [h]Comparison group data on black families taken from Lewis and Looney, 1983. [i]Comparison group data taken from Abramovitch et al., 1986; ages of older but not younger siblings are matched in Sample 1 (younger dyads). [j]Comparison group data taken from Robinson and Eyberg, 1981.

tive power. Longitudinal studies afford researchers an opportunity to simultaneously employ CA and MA matching strategies by judicious selection of the longitudinal panel from which data are accessed for each child. Maurer and Sherrod (1987), for example, collected data on mother–child interactions of six infants with Down syndrome every 3 months and collected data on four comparison infants every 6 weeks. From this data set, both CA and rough MA matches were obtained. Similarly, Berger and Cunningham (1981) and Brooks-Gunn and Lewis (1982) were able to draw from longitudinal data to create groups equated on CA and MA. Using longitudinal data to select multiple comparison groups is a strong strategy that can provide close matches without the time-consuming, expensive search for comparison subjects required by cross-sectional studies. Longitudinal data offer maximum flexibility in comparison group selection, permitting case-to-case matches on multiple criteria that are difficult, if not impossible, in cross-sectional studies.

For those researchers without access to longitudinal data, simultaneously making MA and CA comparisons involves collection of two separate comparison samples. Of the studies cited in Table 1, only Hanzlik and Stevenson (1986) used this approach. Designs using multiple independent comparison groups are valuable options, but the time and effort required make them unattractive to most family researchers. Although designs using both CA- and MA-matched groups have sometimes been criticized (Ellis, 1969), they allow effects related to age and general ability to be disentangled. By so doing, investigators can gain important information concerning the processes underlying study findings. Use of these two comparisons can pit alternate hypotheses against each other within one study, thus illuminating causative mechanisms.

Baumeister (1967) and Heal (1970), among others, have decried the lack of attention to other individual difference factors that they believe deserve as much attention as MA in studies of mentally retarded persons. Only 3 of the studies in Table 1 utilized variables other than CA or MA to match groups. Tannock (1988) matched preschool children on expressive and receptive language, as well as MA. One of the most complex efforts was Eheart's (1982) study of mother–child interaction. She equated groups of young children based on their observed play complexity. In a competency matched study using multiple matching criteria, Cook and Culp

(1981) matched infants on object permanence and means–ends competencies as well as on the children's mean length of utterance, as reported by mothers. This strategy yielded groups that were similar on sensorimotor competency as well as on expressive language skill, providing a more precise and conceptually clearer group comparison than would result from using only a more global MA-match. It is unfortunate that family researchers have not made greater use of individual difference factors other than MA to match groups. Potentially important mediators of family processes (e.g., adaptive behavior, self-help skills, social skills, and language skills of the mentally retarded family member) would seem to be theoretically important to the quantity and quality of family interaction as well as to family coping. Similarly, the frequency and type of maladaptive behavior exhibited by a mentally retarded family member might override the intellectual competence of that person as a direct influence on family processes.

As is the case in the general mental retardation literature (Baumeister, 1967; Brooks & Baumeister, 1977), reasons for choosing one matching strategy over another often are not clearly articulated by family researchers. One is left with the impression that CA-match designs, which are by far the most popular, are frequently used by default. On the other hand, MA designs are often implemented without clear conceptualization of the MA construct, including its inherent measurement problems. Groups matched on competencies other than MA hold promise but have been underutilized in family research. Failure to employ more theoretically relevant matching variables is reflective of an overall lack of a clear conceptualization among family researchers about how mental retardation exerts an impact on families. As that conceptualization becomes more sophisticated, innovative matching strategies will be needed to test resulting hypotheses. The refinement of guiding conceptualizations and the linking of these conceptualizations to selection of matching strategies is one of the greatest needs in the area of family mental retardation research.

Description of Comparison Groups

One of the most striking aspects of Table 1 is the large number of "NR" entries, representing information about the comparison group (or the mentally retarded sample) not provided in the article. Table 1 may actually paint a more positive picture of the description of comparison samples than is warranted. A study is listed as providing information on a given demographic factor if the author(s) made a general statement that the groups were similar on that factor, even if no further supporting information (e.g., means, ranges) was provided. In other instances, group means were provided without information as to the ranges or standard deviations (SDs). Interpretation of such information is difficult. Descriptive data were sometimes available on only one group of families. Smith and Hagen (1984), for example, stated that all comparison families were two-parent but gave no similar information about their target group. Information provided in other studies is unacceptably vague.

Only Crittenden and Bonvillian (1984) provided information on all demographic factors; investigators in 5 papers described all but one (Abbott & Meredith, 1986; Bristol, Gallagher, & Schopler, 1988; Stoneman, Brody, Davis, & Crapps, 1987; Stoneman, Brody, Davis, & Crapps, 1988; Stoneman, Brody, Davis, & Crapps, 1989). The aforementioned studies did not necessarily match or equate groups on these demographic factors but did provide data on the sample that was sufficient for determination of whether the groups differed (or were similar) on these dimensions. Although it is usually not possible (and sometimes not desirable) to match groups on all the listed demographic factors, study families need to be described in sufficient detail to allow readers to make a judgment about the equivalence of groups. As can be seen in Table 1, this is seldom the case in the family mental retardation literature.

Demographic Equivalence of Groups

It is obvious from Table 1 that in many studies comparison groups differed from target families on dimensions in addition to the presence of a mentally retarded family member. Given the quantity of missing demographic information, one must assume that groups potentially differed on nonreported dimensions, as well as on variables for which groups were clearly not equated. Another important demographic factor, maternal employment status, was not included in the table because it was so seldom mentioned in the literature. This failure to adequately address demographic differences between groups weakens the conclusions that can be drawn from the existing research.

Even well-executed matching strategies sometimes break down at some point in a study. Cunningham et al. (1981) matched comparison children on gender, but when groups were divided into high- and low-MA subgroups, the gender distribution within subgroups became unequal. A similar problem occurred for Hampson, Hulgus, Beavers, and Beavers (1988). In their study, groups were originally similar on child sex and race. When they were divided into three age groupings for analysis, the younger group of mentally retarded children (6 to 8 years of age) had less healthy family functioning than did the two older groups (12 to 14 and 18 to 21 years). The younger group, however, had a higher proportion of male children and of white families. The confounding impact of gender and race on these findings is unknown.

In longitudinal studies differential attrition in the mentally retarded group versus the comparison group can create unbalanced groups over time (e.g., Berger & Cunningham, 1981). In addition, in studies using questionnaire methodologies, groups that are demographically similar when constituted can become distorted by different questionnaire return rates for the comparison and target groups (e.g., Friedrich & Friedrich, 1981; Salisbury, 1987).

Other factors, even less frequently addressed than family demographics, have been implicated as potentially important confounding variables in family research. Berger and Cunningham (1981), for example, found that differences between infant–mother gaze patterns of infants with and without Down syndrome disappeared when the gestational age of the babies was statistically equated. Differential health status (i.e., heart or respiratory problems, hearing loss) can be a confounding variable between groups. Barrerra, Watson, and Adelstein (1987) found that parents provide less stimulating home environments for infants with Down syndrome and heart defects as compared with more healthy infants with Down syndrome.

Another frequently overlooked factor is the participation of parents of retarded children in intervention programs that attempt to influence parent–child interaction patterns and strengthen family functioning. Group differences between these parents and a comparison group may be a direct result of what the parents of mentally retarded children have been taught in the intervention program. With the proliferation of family-focused intervention programs accompanying the passage of PL 99–457, this possibility becomes even greater. Obviously, one cannot match target and comparison families on the basis of intervention experiences, but it is imperative that researchers document the quantity and type of intervention experienced by the families to ensure that differences between target and comparison groups are not artifacts of services received by only one group.

In general, most comparison research on families with mentally retarded members has not been successful in addressing demographic and other differences between groups that constitute potential confounding variables and can distort research findings. In reading the family literature, one senses a confidence on the part of at least some researchers that mental retardation is such a powerful construct that its influences on family functioning swamp other potential sources of variance, such as those attributable to demographic differences between groups. Studies such as that by Salisbury (1987), however, suggest that this belief is unwarranted. In her study maternal reports of stress were related to single parenthood but unrelated to the presence of a mentally retarded child in the family. Researchers investigating the general family have vigorously argued for the necessity of addressing demographic variables in the study of family processes; mental retardation family researchers must do no less.

Strategies for Matching Comparison Samples

Three primary strategies have been used by mental retardation researchers to equate groups of families: case-by-case matching, group matching, and restricted sampling. Case-by-case matching is the most precise and difficult strategy to implement. Each family is individually matched to a comparison family on a set of predefined variables (e.g., Abbott & Meridith, 1986; Gunn, Berry, & Andrews, 1982; Hanzlik & Stevenson, 1986; Sigman, Mundy, Sherman, & Ungerer, 1986). In group matching, the means (and sometimes the ranges) of a set of variables in the target group are matched to the comparison group (e.g., Bristol et al., 1988), but individual cases are not matched. The final strategy, restricting the sampling frame, reduces differences between groups by limiting the population from which families are recruited; the resulting sample is homogeneous on specific variables. All families selected for study, for example, can be white (e.g., Bristol et al., 1988; Maurer & Sherrod, 1987; McAllister, Butler, & Lei, 1973; Smith & Hagen, 1984;

Waisbren, 1980), middle class (e.g., Buckhalt, Rutherford, & Goldberg, 1978; Herman & Shantz, 1983; Levy-Shiff, 1986), biological parents (e.g., Bristol et al., 1988; Routh, 1970) or have unemployed mothers (e.g., Eheart, 1982; Levy-Shiff, 1986). Children can all be male (e.g., Bristol et al., 1988; O'Connor & Stachowiak, 1971), for example, or all first-born (e.g., Smith & Hagen, 1984).

Each strategy has its strengths and weaknesses. Case-by-case matching provides a precise remedy to confounding demographic variables but is extremely tedious and expensive, particularly when families are recruited from the community and the number of matching variables is large. In some instances, even after exhaustive search, case matches cannot be identified for all families (e.g., Lobato, Barbour, Hall, & Miller, 1987). Detailed case-by-case matching can also unacceptably decrease variability between groups (Heal, 1970).

Group matching is less taxing to implement but carries an implicit assumption that group-matched demographic variables function as main effects rather than in interaction with other variables. Work such as that of Hetherington (1981), in which divorce was found to interact with child gender (to create increased risk for divorced mothers of sons), documents that this is not always the case. Consider a hypothetical study in which 5 families are divorced mothers with mentally retarded sons and 5 are two-parent families with retarded daughters. A group-matched comparison sample is recruited consisting of 5 divorced mothers with daughters; the remainder are intact families with sons. In this example, groups are equated for main effects resulting from child gender or divorce but not for interactive effects between gender and parent marital status (such as those identified by Hetherington). Negative outcomes for the families of mentally retarded boys would probably be attributed to the effects of mental retardation on families with sons but could quite plausibly be caused by the effects of divorce on sons instead. Another potential problem with the group-matching strategy occurs when the means but not the ranges or SDs of two groups are matched, potentially yielding groups that differ in the degree of variability of the matched variable.

The final strategy, limiting the sampling frame, avoids the complexities of matching groups on specified variables but sacrifices generalizability of findings to all but the specific subgroups studied. Finding families that fit the requirements of a limited sampling frame can also be difficult.

Because instituting case-by-case matching on all relevant variables is seldom practical (even if it were desirable), one compromise is to use a combination of strategies. One can match cases on those variables considered to be most important; use group matching on other, secondary variables; and limit the sampling frame to a specific subgroup of families. This strategy was used by Stoneman et al. (1987, 1988), who studied same-gender sibling pairs in which the younger sibling was mentally retarded (a limited sampling frame). Comparison siblings were matched case-by-case on sibling gender, age of each sibling, race, family income, parent marital status, and education. Group matching was executed on family size and birth order of the target sibling pair in relation to other children in the family.

When sampling and matching strategies fail to produce groups that are similar, or when matching strategies are not feasible, statistical remedies exist to artificially equate groups on important, uncontrolled variables. Covariance procedures and partial correlations, among others, can be used to examine the degree to which uncontrolled variables are influencing study results (Heal, 1970). Statistical controls are important tools that have been only sporadically used by mental retardation family researchers. These statistical procedures for exploring the influences of confounding variables improve the quality of mental retardation family research (e.g., Berger & Cunningham, 1981).

Populations From Which Target and Comparison Samples Are Drawn

Family recruitment can be difficult, and researchers vary widely in their strategies for identifying participant families. Concern arises when the comparison families and the families with mentally retarded members are drawn from very different populations. Ideally, each comparison family would be randomly drawn from a pool of families who are from the same population as the target families and all of whom match the target family on relevant demographic factors. Wilton and Renaut (1986) were able to use this strategy by having access to preschool rolls, waiting lists, and public health records in New Zealand. Friedrich and Friedrich (1981) asked each target family to nominate other families who were similar to them in socioeconomic status (SES) and had a nonhandicapped child the same age as their child. Comparison families were than randomly sampled from those nominated. McAllister, Butler, and Lei (1973) drew families from a random sampling of 1,065 households with children under 16.

Some investigators have used less than ideal sampling strategies. In their study of mentally retarded parents, Feldman et al. (1986) recruited comparison mothers from an exercise class; Gallagher, Scharfman, and Bristol (1984) recruited comparison families from a Catholic diocese (these families were dissimilar from target families in religion and demographic characteristics). Recruiting comparison families from college classes and personal acquaintances is a common practice (e.g., Abbott & Meridith, 1986). In all of these examples, comparison families were obtained from populations other than those from which the families of mentally retarded children were drawn, introducing possible bias.

Use of clinic families to constitute comparison groups is also common. Such studies frequently suffer from a lack of information about problems that brought families to the clinic and the possible ramifications of these problems for interpreting study findings. Routh (1970), for example, stated that, although his comparison sample of clinic families did not have a retarded child, they "evidently had some other reason to be concerned about the child's behavior" (p. 377). Without an understanding of the problems experienced by the clinic sample, study findings cannot be interpreted.

Rather than generate new comparison data, some researchers draw from data obtained for other purposes to constitute a comparison sample (e.g., Abramovitch, Stanhope, Pepler, & Corter, 1987; Briener & Young, 1985). Beavers, Hampson, Hulgus, and Beavers (1986) used a previously published study of black families to try to compensate for racial differences between families with mentally retarded children and comparison families. Peterson, Robinson, and Littman (1983) drew two comparison samples from an earlier study. Although the two samples were somewhat similar to each other, neither was similar to the mentally retarded parents being studied (see Table 1). In general, existing data sets are seldom well-suited to serve as comparison samples for mental retardation family research because they are almost never comparable in important demographic factors.

Ideally, comparison families should not just be similar to target families on important demographic characteristics but should be drawn from the same overall population. This reduces the chance of population biases entering into group comparisons and distorting findings in unforeseen and unknowable ways.

Sibling Studies

Unique considerations apply to research on sibling relationships. In addition to family factors discussed earlier, sibling gender combinations, birth order, and spacing (the number of months between the older and younger siblings' ages) also emerge as important factors. In research focusing on one child in the family, gender is a two-level factor. In sibling research, however, the possible gender combinations increase to four: two sisters, two brothers, older sister/younger brother, and older brother/younger sister. (The number expands geometrically when more than two siblings are considered.) Research suggests that the four sibling gender combinations are associated with different relationship patterns (e.g., Stoneman, Brody & MacKinnon, 1986).

In mental retardation research, the situation becomes even more complex because the retarded child can be the older or younger sibling. The four gender combination groups increase to eight when the birth order of the mentally retarded child (the older or younger sibling) is considered, as it must be. In addition, sibling spacing must be taken into account, as must the relative birth order of the sibling pair (compared to the birth orders of other children in the family). Case-by-case matching could become a search for the proverbial needle in a haystack if one should attempt to find, for example, two Caucasian siblings where the older child, age 9, is first-born and male and a second-born sister is 7. Their mother is a single parent, a high school graduate of lower-middle SES, who also has an infant daughter, age 9 months. The impossibility of this search necessitates use of multiple strategies, including a narrowed sampling frame, group matches on some variables, and statistical controls for others where sampling control is not feasible.

Sibling researchers have not always successfully dealt with these complexities. Gath (1972, 1973; Gath & Gumley, 1987), for example, recruited comparison families from the school classroom of the nonhandicapped sibling, selecting the next child on the class list. No further information was obtained on this child and his or her family, and no matching on any variables was attempted. Abramovitch et al. (1987) drew upon a previous study of siblings to constitute their comparison sample. They matched the ages of the nonhandicapped siblings of mentally retarded children to the ages of older siblings in their comparison data set. Unfortunately, this strategy confounded sibling birth order and the gender of both the older and younger siblings.

Authors of all of the sibling studies cited in Table 1 used CA-match designs. Numerous problems inherent in using competency matching strategies in sibling research probably account for its lack of popularity, the most serious of which are alterations in sibling age relations and birth orders that can occur. Consider, for example, a 10-year-old mentally retarded child with an 8-year-old sibling. If the mentally retarded child's MA were 6 years, comparison siblings would have approximate CAs of 6 and 8. The child matched to the retarded sibling (the 6-year-old), would be the younger, rather than the older child in the sibling pair. This would hopelessly entangle interpretation of study findings.

Assuming that the researcher is interested in the relationship between the mentally retarded child and one sibling (no mental retardation researchers have yet ventured into the uncharted domain of studying sibling groups of 3 or more) the nonretarded sibling to be studied must be selected in some way. This can be the child closest in age (e.g., Abramovitch et al., 1987) or a sibling of a particular gender and/or a particular birth order relation to the mentally retarded child (Stoneman et al., 1987, 1988, 1989). These selection criteria then translate directly into the definition of comparison sibling pairs, who must share these characteristics. Not all researchers, however, describe how target nonhandicapped siblings were selected in multichild families (Lobato et al., 1987; McHale, Sloan, & Simeonsson, 1986).

Sibling studies are made complex by the necessity to control for gender combinations of children, birth order, and spacing. Yet, these unique aspects are important in understanding sibling pairs including a mentally retarded child. Unless these factors are addressed in their interactive combinations, the processes impacting the sibling relationship cannot be clarified.

Studies of Mentally Retarded Parents

Special considerations also apply to comparison studies involving mentally retarded parents. Given the important social policy ramifications of comparing mentally retarded and nonretarded parents (which can result in judgments concerning the "fitness" of certain parents), extra caution seems prudent in selecting appropriate comparison groups. Only a few investigators have tackled these difficult questions, and comparison groups have often been less than exemplary. An examination of the final section of Table 1 reveals a lack of adequate description of comparison samples and nonequivalence of groups on important demographic factors. The low-income comparison group employed by Crittenden et al. (1984) provides the closest equating of mentally retarded and comparison parents. Comparisons made by Feldman et al. (1986), in which mentally retarded parents were compared to middle-class mothers recruited from an exercise class, and by Robinson (1978), whose comparison mothers had completed at least 2 years of college, fail to meet minimum requirements for equating groups. The Peterson et al. (1983) study, in which comparison data were drawn from a previous study, also failed to use workable strategies.

Further, before group differences between mentally retarded and nonretarded parents can be attributed to the limited intelligence of mentally retarded parents, potential child influences on parenting (e.g., Bell, 1968), such as age, gender, handicapping condition, and temperament, must be equated between groups, either statistically or through sampling/matching procedures. Child effects on parenting have been almost totally absent from the existing literature on parenting by mentally retarded individuals. Important differences in family context also have been largely ignored (mentally retarded parents are less likely to be married and more likely to have a benefactor who provides assistance) (Greenspan & Budd, 1986; Zetlin, Weisner, & Gallimore, 1985). Child sex, age, number of children, presence of a father or significant other, and living context (e.g., with extended family) as well as other child and contextual factors, must be similar between the mentally retarded parents and comparison parents before group differences in parenting (or other family factors) can be attributed to the mental retardation of one group of parents.

In research on mentally retarded parents, the global definition of groups based on parent IQ may prove less informative than groups matched on other competency factors (e.g., certain aspects of adaptive behavior or social competence). In addition, when public policy decisions are at stake, as they are here, it is important to conceptualize parenting as occurring within a family (including all persons taking important childrearing roles) rather than isolated to a dyadic relationship between one

parent and a child. Doing so takes into account the greater ecological family context experienced by the child, thereby providing more representative and important information about the child's well-being and childrearing environment as well as about the parenting behavior of mentally retarded persons.

This socially relevant area of research suffers from a lack of careful selection of comparison groups, which greatly compromises what can be learned about mentally retarded individuals as parents. Studies with inappropriate comparison groups can be potentially harmful. Poorly designed comparison studies provide policymakers with distorted findings, which may be translated into policy decisions. Careful studies are needed in which investigators conceptualize parenting as occurring in a larger family or social system and make well-articulated and well-executed comparisons between the parenting of matched groups of retarded and nonretarded persons.

Multiple Comparison Groups

The "if a little will do it, more will do it better" approach to comparison groups, criticized by Ellis (1969, p. 563), describes a frequent lack of theoretical rationale for the inclusion of multiple comparison groups. Although multiple comparison groups can add interpretive power to a research design, the comparison groups in some studies seem to have little conceptual relevance. A case in point is a study of childrearing attitudes of mothers of retarded children (Dingman, Eyman, & Windle, 1963), which includes a comparison group of social workers, another of psychiatric hospital technicians, and another of clerical and other hospital employees. No rationale is provided for inclusion of these groups. As is the case in explaining why one would climb tall mountains, some comparison groups seem to be included simply because "they are there." Unfortunately, the accessibility of comparison samples bears little relation to the theoretical importance of including them in research designs. (Some investigators engaged in family research might even suspect a perverse negative relation between the importance of a given comparison sample and the ease of finding that sample.)

Yet, researchers have effectively utilized multiple comparison groups to systematically examine important dimensions of their research questions. Wasserman, Shilansky, and Hahn (1986), for example, in their study of maternal interaction with infants with both mental retardation and physical disabilities, included two nonretarded comparison groups (with and without physical handicaps) in an attempt to tease apart the effects of physical disability from those of mental retardation. Maurer and Sherrod (1987) used both CA and MA comparisons to understand child contributions to maternal directiveness. Still others have been primarily interested in another disability, such as autism, and utilized mentally retarded samples to control for the functional deficits of autistic children. Ironically, some of these studies (e.g., Sigman et al., 1986), due to the tightness of the research designs used, contribute more to our knowledge about mental retardation than many family studies specifically designed for that purpose. Others (Dunst, Trivette, & Cross, 1986) have used multiple groups to demonstrate that the phenomena of interest (e.g., family social support) was relevant across disability groups.

The most difficult groups to equate on demographic characteristics tend to be those comparing different disabilities. Recruitment for each disability group is restricted by relatively low incidence in the population. Some frequent comparisons, such as Down syndrome versus other forms of mental retardation, often result in groups which are dissimilar on demographic factors, such as SES (e.g., Gath & Gumley, 1986) and maternal age. Multiple disability studies (with the exception of the autism studies previously discussed) tend to be less than explicit about the rationale for cross-disability comparisons. Strom, Wurster, and Rees (1983) perhaps speak for many researchers when they state that they focused on the only two disability groups that occurred with sufficient frequency in their sample to warrant statistical comparisons. One suspects the rationale for selecting disability groups to compare is equally pragmatic for many researchers.

Appropriateness of Tasks/Instruments Across Groups

An issue that frequently arises in mental retardation comparison group research concerns comparability of research tasks across groups (Baumeister, 1967; 1984; Ellis, 1969). When tasks are not equivalent measures of the same construct for both groups, or are differentially reliable, the integrity of the research is compromised.

In most of the self-report studies in Table 1, investigators used instruments developed for the general popu-

lation. It is not clear, however, whether these scales retain the same meaning when administered to families with mentally retarded members. Gath and Gumley (1984) suggested that the Behavior Problem Checklist used in their study failed to capture the behavior problems found troublesome by parents of children with Down syndrome. The Parent as Teacher Inventory (Strom, 1984), used with parents of young mentally retarded children, contains items such as "I like my child to make up stories" and "I feel unhappy when I don't know an answer to my child's questions." Such items may have little relevance to a parent of a child not capable of stories or questions. Numerous other self-report instruments contain items that may have dubious meaning when utilized in mental retardation research.

Using instruments developed to study families with mentally retarded members is even more problematic. Numerous investigators (e.g., Dyson & Fewell, 1986; Friedrich & Friedrich, 1981; Salisbury, 1987; Wilton & Renaut, 1986) have used the original or revised versions of the Questionnaire on Resources and Stress (Friedrich, Greenberg, & Crnic, 1983; Holroyd, 1974; Salisbury, 1985) to ascertain whether families with mentally retarded children experience more stress than do comparison families. Because this scale was designed for families coping with a disabled individual, numerous items have little or no probability of occurrence among comparison families (e.g., "I have accepted the fact that _____ might have to live out his/her life in some special setting such as an institution or group home"). Thus, the scale predisposes the emergence of group differences given its differential appropriateness for the two groups of families. Similar problems arise with other scales developed for families of disabled persons.

The appropriateness of the research task across groups is also an issue when observational methods are used. Three dimensions are relevant here: task difficulty, age appropriateness, and task novelty. When children differ greatly in competency, the same task can be easy for the more competent comparison children and quite difficult or totally beyond the skill level of mentally retarded children. This is a particular problem in CA-match designs. Differential task difficulty can be expected to create qualitatively different family interaction patterns across groups. When this occurs, study findings contribute more to our understanding of the effects of task difficulty than to our knowledge about families with retarded children.

Comparison Groups in Research on Families With Mentally Retarded Members   Zolinda Stoneman

Differences in task age-appropriateness can be a problem in designs where children are matched on competency and/or differ widely in age. Bailey and Slee (1984), for example, used Legos and doll-washing toys to study mother–child play with mentally retarded (ages 6 to 13 years) and comparison children (ages 2.5 to 10 years). These tasks were not age appropriate for the older children (two thirds of the sample were boys, for whom doll washing was also not gender-appropriate). Selecting tasks for a wide age span is challenging; reliance on preschool materials, however, potentially distorts interaction in older subjects, weakening the validity of study findings.

The final issue is one of differential task novelty. If the research task/materials are familiar to one group of families and novel to another, group differences can be detected that are direct effects of task familiarity. Stoneman et al. (1987) suggested that the ecologies of mentally retarded individuals are more restricted than those of nonretarded peers; activities that are common in the general population may occur less often (or not at all) in families with mentally retarded members.

Possible solutions include increased use of naturalistic observations (Breiner & Forehand, 1982; Levy-Shiff, 1986; Stoneman et al., 1987), materials that are structurally analogous but differentially complex across groups (Stoneman et al., 1983), observational contexts that occur in the daily lives of both groups (e.g., waiting rooms, Buckhalt et al., 1978), or pilot naturalistic observations to form the basis for task selection.

The Guiding Role of Theory

It might appear self-evident that selection of comparison groups should be driven by the theory or model guiding the research. Mental retardation research, in general, has been criticized for a lack of conceptual clarity in linking research goals to the selection of comparison strategies (Baumeister, 1967; Brooks & Baumeister, 1977). This criticism also applies to family research in mental retardation; the rationale for choice of a particular comparison group is rarely articulated in this research. Only a handful of studies cited in Table 1 can be considered to be theory-driven. The ABCX model of stress and coping has been adapted primarily by Bristol and her colleagues (e.g., Bristol et al., 1988), whereas role theory, which guided the early work of Farber (1959, 1960; Farber & Jenne, 1963), has been modified and used by

Stoneman and her colleagues (e.g., Stoneman, Brody, & Abbott, 1983; Stoneman et al., 1987, 1988, 1989). O'Connor and Stachowiak (1971) employed a systems model. Eheart (1982) based her work on symbolic interaction theory; researchers interested in parenting by mentally retarded persons have turned to behavioral models for guidance (e.g., Feldman et al., 1986; Peterson et al., 1983). In general, however, the family literature has its roots in previous research studies and clinical work rather than in theory or model-building.

Baumeister (1984) wrote of the "unsatisfying" nature of explaining differences between mentally retarded and nonretarded persons based on their relative position on "the normal distribution of IQs" (p. 25). The same can be said for attributing group differences in family functioning to the presence in some families of an individual who is mentally retarded. "Mental retardation" as a construct fails to explain why families differ and provides no information on the processes underlying such differences. Our understanding of families with mentally retarded members can only advance when causal relations are elucidated; such research must be guided by a theory/model of family functioning, as well as by a theory of mental retardation. Adding comparison groups to family studies is a step forward only when those groups are grounded in theoretical meaning.

Implications for Intervention

It is common for investigators comparing families with and without mentally retarded members to imply (or directly state) that findings are expected to have implications for intervention. This is not surprising given the press on researchers to demonstrate that their work has relevance for the lives of mentally retarded persons and those close to them. Yet, there is seldom a direct translation between the findings of comparison group research and intervention. In fact, this linkage can be fraught with value-laden dilemmas (Kazdin & Matson, 1981). Although one can speak with relative safety about normal language/cognitive development, "normal" loses meaning when applied to families. Using a language analogy, a diverse group of people probably would agree that having a larger vocabulary and using more complex grammar are worthy goals. Extrapolating to families, however, one would expect little consensus concerning the "best" type of family life. Cultural, religious, ethnic, and personal values all define what is desirable for a given family.

My purpose here is not to provide solutions to dilemmas inherent in selecting family intervention targets but, rather, to voice caution concerning the translation of differences found in comparisons with nonhandicapped families into intervention goals for families with mentally retarded members. There is sometimes a temptation to compare families with and without mentally retarded family members, identify differences, and then use this information to help the families with mentally retarded members become more similar to the comparison families. This approach is flawed and should be avoided. There is no single "ideal" mode of family functioning. It is incorrect to assume that because families with mentally retarded members differ in some way from other families that these differences are maladaptive. Satisfaction with intrafamily relationships and with the overall way in which the needs of each individual are met in the family context are more important considerations in planning interventions than whether a given family differs from comparison families.

Alternatives to Comparison Group Studies

Heal (1970) expressed puzzlement at the reliance of mental retardation researchers on what he termed "control-by-sampling" (p. 14), rather than studying the entire continuum of intelligence levels, using correlational strategies. Similarly, Baumeister (1967) questioned the rationale for the large number of comparison group studies in mental retardation research, and in a later paper, he described comparison studies as an "unnecessary excursion into a theoretical swamp inhabited by all sorts of conceptual and methodological monsters" (Baumeister, 1984, p. 26). Although comparison studies have much to contribute, comparison groups are not a necessity in family research. Many other strong design options exist.

Examples of family research without comparison groups include studies of stress and coping (e.g., Beckman, 1983; Chetwynd, 1985; Friedrich, 1979; Friedrich, Wilturner, & Cohen, 1985; McKinney & Peterson, 1987), predictors and consequences of different home environments (e.g., Affleck, Allen, McGrade, & McQueeney, 1982; Piper & Ramsay, 1980; Smith & Hagen, 1984), comparisons of mothers and fathers in the same family (e.g., McConachie & Mitchell, 1985), adaptation to diagnosis of retardation (Eden-Piercy, Blacher, & Eyman, 1986; Quine & Pahl, 1986), single-

subject designs (e.g., James & Egel, 1986; Lobato & Tlaker, 1985; Powell, Salzberg, Rule, Levy, & Itzkowitz, 1983), and studies examining families at different developmental periods (e.g., Suelzle & Keenan, 1981; Wikler, 1986).

Crawley and Spiker (1983) studied individual differences in interaction patterns between infants with Down syndrome and their mothers and, by so doing, shed light on the relation between maternal directiveness and sensitivity within this group of families. Mink, Nihira, Meyers, and colleagues (e.g., Blacher, Nihira, & Meyers, 1987; Meyers, Nihira, & Mink, 1984; Mink, Meyers, & Nihira, 1984; Mink & Nihira, 1986, 1987; Mink, Nihira, & Meyers, 1983; Nihira, Meyers, & Mink, 1983) have provided an intense examination of families of mentally retarded children without need for nonhandicapped comparison groups. Similarly, ethnographic studies (e.g., Winik, Zetlin, & Kaufman, 1985; Zetlin, 1986; Zetlin & Turner, 1985) provide rich data on small samples of families.

These studies underscore the multiplicity of design alternatives available to family researchers who prefer to avoid the conceptual and methodological complexities involved in comparing families with mentally retarded members to families without retarded members. "Conventional wisdom" sometimes suggests that mental retardation family studies without comparison groups are neither publishable nor fundable, but a review of the family literature suggests otherwise (many of the studies cited in the preceding paragraphs were funded through grants and awards from the National Institute of Health, the U.S. Department of Education, and other agencies).

Baumeister (1967, 1984) suggested that to gain an understanding of mental retardation, one should study mentally retarded persons. To paraphrase, researchers who hope to gain an in-depth understanding of families with mentally retarded members should study the processes that operate within those families. This is not to suggest that researchers should reject comparison designs. That would be a loss to the field. Yet, many research questions do not require comparison groups. Use of such groups when they are not needed is ill-considered given the wasted resources and the lack of interpretive power gained.

Conclusion and Recommendations

Comparison group designs are one of the most important tools available to mental retardation family researchers. Yet, comparison research can be misleading or uninterpretable if comparison strategies are not clearly conceptualized and well-executed. The overall quality of the existing body of family studies using comparison groups is disappointing. Table 1 lists 57 comparison family studies published in journals since 1965. With that quantity of work, one would expect a blossoming of understanding concerning families with mentally retarded members. Unfortunately, that is not the case. The existing comparison group literature is compromised by the selection of inappropriate comparison samples, lack of description of participant families, inattention to important demographic factors that constitute confounding variables, atheoretical rationale for comparison group selection, failure to equate research tasks across groups, and a lack of creativity and innovativeness in conceptualization and design.

Many of these problems are an outgrowth of family theories that defy operationalization and of the difficulty (and expense) involved in finding and recruiting families when sampling or matching parameters are narrowly defined. Family theory and mental retardation theory have yet to be blended into one perspective, leaving family mental retardation researchers with the difficult task of melding dissimilar theoretical traditions. Identifying participant families can be extremely tedious, often forcing researchers to choose between compromised sampling procedures or a never-to-be-completed research project.

Some deficiencies, however, are more easily remedied. The dramatic lack of information on study samples can be easily corrected. Participating families (both comparison families and those with mentally retarded members) need to be described in detail; means, ranges, and SDs for all demographic variables should be provided for each group. When groups are further subdivided for analysis (e.g., by gender, age), subject information for each subgroup is needed. The type of matching strategy (e.g., case-by-case matching) needs to be clearly stated. This is seldom done.

Other problems with the family comparison group literature yield less readily to easy solutions. However, a combination of careful conceptualization and design innovation hold promise of improving the state-of-the-art. The simplest and most straightforward solution is for researchers to employ rigorous matching procedures, including limited sampling frames, to ensure that groups are equated on important demographic variables. This takes time and expense but can be accomplished. Strat-

egies for equating groups must be built into the conceptualization of the research design rather than addressed after data are collected in hopes that groups will not differ. The common practice of using t tests or similar statistics to verify post hoc that groups are equated on important parameters is similar to trying to prove the null hypothesis. Researchers have a 95% or better chance of finding that groups are similar. Using such tests as sole support for claims of group equivalence is misleading and creates false confidence in the similarity of family groups.

The less common practice of using statistical remedies, such as covariance, to artificially equate groups on a few factors where matching has failed to yield group equivalence should be encouraged. These techniques broaden the tools available to researchers attempting to understand the role of confounding variables. However, even these techniques have limits and cannot be used to cure all ills resulting from poor research design. Using post hoc statistical controls as the primary strategy for dealing with demographic differences between groups can result in analyses with a very large number of covariates. Interpreting findings from such analyses requires what can best be described as a blind leap into the realm of mystical thought.

Creativity and design innovation are needed to provide new models for comparison group research. Researchers studying families of infants and young children (e.g., Berger & Cunningham, 1981, 1983, 1986; Maurer & Sherrod, 1987) have used combined cross-sectional and longitudinal designs to simultaneously match children on CA and on a competency-matching variable (usually MA). These designs are similar to those used over 2 decades ago by Schaie and Strother (1968) to study age changes in cognition. Such designs are flexible and innovative, allowing controlled examination of influences contributed by two or more individual difference dimensions. With further innovation, such designs could be expanded to explore more systemic family process variables across a wider age span. In these designs, as well as in more simple comparison designs, there is a need to use other individual difference dimensions, in addition to CA and MA, as group-matching variables.

Heal (1970) called for increased use of correlational designs to examine the whole individual-difference continuum. For family researchers, this could involve defining a sampling frame and then recruiting families with and without mentally retarded members from that restricted population. Data analyses could be used to examine the entire population simultaneously, with variables such as IQ or adaptive behavior as predictor variables, or the sample could be divided into subgroups (with and without mentally retarded members). In either case, demographic variables not controlled by the limited sampling frame would be utilized as predictor variables, either alone or in interaction with the individual difference variables under study. This design approach minimizes sampling distortion and sidesteps the question of whether families of retarded persons, as a group, differ from other families. This design option asks a more theoretically relevant question, namely, whether processes of influence are similar in the two family groups (or across the individual difference continuum).

Perhaps the most needed refinement is a strengthening of the link between the theoretical research question and the matching strategies used. The most popular research question in this literature seems to be, Are families of mentally retarded children different from families of nonretarded children? The major hypothesis is that differences will exist, usually with more negative outcomes expected for the mentally retarded group (e.g., more stress). These hypotheses rest on a poorly articulated conceptualization that mental retardation is "bad" and, thus, should be associated with "bad" things for families. Such a conceptual model fails to address definitional issues inherent in the construct "mental retardation" and provides no insight on the processes through which "mental retardation" impacts families.

Unfortunately, the more recent focus on family strengths offers little in the way of conceptual advancement. The focus has changed from mental retardation being "bad" to its being "not so bad," but both conceptualizations lack a process orientation that would begin to *explain* the impact that mental retardation has on families. The field needs fewer investigators simply trying to determine whether families with mentally retarded members are "different." Instead, theoretically driven research is needed that is focused on elucidating causative processes. New conceptualizations will push the field forward methodologically, requiring more sophisticated matching strategies than those currently in use.

Conceptual issues concerning appropriate comparisons still have not been resolved in other subdomains of mental retardation research, such as cognition (Baumeister, 1984), where the considerations are much simpler than those that face family researchers. Yet, family comparison group research has made great progress in the last decade. Although older classic studies still set the tone for the field, recent work has evinced striking advances in methodological rigor. For that progress to continue, conceptual and methodological advances related to the use of comparison groups are needed. It is hoped that this review will in some way contribute to those advances.

References

Abbott, D. A., & Meredith, W. H. (1986). Strengths of parents with retarded children. *Family Relations, 35,* 371–375.

Abramovitch, R., Stanhope, L., Pepler, D., & Corter, C. (1986). The influence of Down's syndrome on sibling interaction. *Journal of Child Psychology and Psychiatry and Allied Disciplines, 28,* 865–879.

Affleck, G., Allen, D., McGrade, B. J., & McQueeney, M. (1982). Home environments of developmentally disabled infants as a function of parent and infant characteristics. *American Journal of Mental Deficiency, 86,* 445–452.

Bailey, L., & Slee, P. T. (1984). A comparison of play interactions between non-disabled and disabled children and their mothers: A question of style. *Australia and New Zealand Journal of Developmental Disabilities, 10,* 5–10.

Barrera, M. E., Watson, L. J., & Adelstein, A. (1987). Development of Down's syndrome infants with and without heart defects and changes in their caretaking environment. *Child: Care, Health, and Development, 13,* 87–100.

Baumeister, A. A. (1967). Problems in comparative studies of mental retardates and normals. *American Journal of Mental Deficiency, 71,* 869–875.

Baumeister, A. A. (1984). Some methodological and conceptual issues in the study of cognitive processes with retarded people. In P. H. Brooks, R. Sperber, & C. McCauley (Eds.), *Learning and cognition in the mentally retarded* (pp. 1–38). Hillsdale, NJ: Erlbaum.

Beavers, J., Hampson, R. B., Hulgus, Y. F., & Beavers, W. R. (1986). Coping in families with a retarded child. *Family Process, 25,* 365–378.

Beckman, P. J. (1983). Influence of selected child characteristics on stress in families of handicapped infants. *American Journal of Mental Deficiency, 88,* 150–156.

Bell, R. Q. (1968). A reinterpretation of the direction of effects in studies of socialization. *Psychological Review, 75,* 81–95.

Berger, J., & Cunningham, C. C. (1981). The development of eye contact between mothers and normal vs. Down's syndrome infants. *Developmental Psychology, 17,* 678–689.

Berger, J., & Cunningham, C. C. (1983). Development of early vocal behaviors and interactions in Down's Syndrome and nonhandicapped infant-mother pairs. *Developmental Psychology, 19,* 322–331.

Berger, J., & Cunningham, C. C. (1986). Aspects of early social smiling by infants with Down's syndrome. *Child: Care, Health, and Development, 12,* 13–24.

Blacher, J., Nihira, K., & Meyers, C. E. (1987). Characteristics of home environment of families with mentally retarded children: Comparison across levels of retardation. *American Journal of Mental Deficiency, 91,* 313–320.

Breiner, J., & Forehand, R. (1982). Mother–child interactions: A comparison of a clinic referred developmentally delayed group and two nondelayed groups. *Applied Research in Mental Retardation, 3,* 175–183.

Breiner, J., & Young, D. L. (1985). Social interaction: A comparison of mothers with noncompliant, nondelayed, and developmentally delayed children. *Child and Family Behavior Therapy, 7,* 1–7.

Bristol, M. M., Gallagher, J. J., & Schopler, E. (1988). Mothers and fathers of young developmentally disabled and nondisabled boys: Adaptation and spousal support. *Developmental Psychology, 24,* 441–451.

Brooks, P. H., & Baumeister, A. A. (1977). A plea for consideration of ecological validity in the experimental psychology of mental retardation: A guest editorial. *American Journal of Mental Deficiency, 81,* 407–416.

Brooks-Gunn, J., & Lewis, M. (1982). Development of play behavior in handicapped and normal infants. *Topics in Early Childhood Special Education, 2*(3), 14–27.

Buckhalt, J. A., Rutherford, R. B., & Goldberg, K. E. (1978). Verbal and nonverbal interaction of mothers with their retarded Down's syndrome and nonretarded infants. *American Journal of Mental Deficiency, 82,* 337–343.

Byrne, E. A., & Cunningham, C. C. (1985). The effects of mentally handicapped children on families: A conceptual review. *Journal of Child Psychology and Psychiatry and Allied Disciplines, 26,* 847–864.

Cashdan, A., & Jeffree, D. M. (1966). Home background of severely subnormal children. *British Journal of Medical Psychology, 39,* 313–318.

Chetwynd, J. (1985). Factors contributing to stress on mothers caring for an intellectually handicapped child. *British Journal of Social Work, 15,* 295–304.

Cook, A. S., & Culp, R. E. (1981). Mutual play of mothers with their Down's syndrome and normal infants. *International Journal of Rehabilitation Research, 4,* 542–544.

Crawley, S. B., & Spiker, D. (1983). Mother-child interactions involving two-year-olds with Down syndrome: A look at individual differences. *Child Development, 54,* 1312–1323.

Crittenden, P. A., & Bonvillian, J. D. (1984). The relationship between maternal risk status and maternal sensitivity. *American Journal of Orthopsychiatry, 54,* 250–262.

Crnic, K. A., Friedrich, W. N., & Greenberg, M. T. (1983). Adaptation of families with mentally retarded children: A model of stress, coping, and family ecology. *American Journal of Mental Deficiency, 88,* 125–138.

Cummings, S. T. (1976). Impact of the child's deficiency on the father: A study of fathers of mentally retarded and chronically ill children. *American Journal of Orthopsychiatry, 46,* 246–255.

Cummings, S. T., Bayley, H. C., & Rie, H. E. (1966). Effects of the child's deficiency on the mother: A study of mothers of mentally retarded, chronically ill, and neurotic children. *American Journal of Orthopsychiatry, 36,* 595–608.

Cunningham, C. E., Reuler, E., Blackwell, J., & Deck, J. (1981). Behavioral and linguistic developments in the interactions of normal and retarded children with their mothers. *Child Development, 52,* 62–70.

Dingman, H. F., Eyman, R. D., & Windle, C. D. (1963). An investigation of some child-rearing attitudes of mothers with retarded children. *American Journal of Mental Deficiency, 67,* 899–908.

Dunn, L. M., & Dunn, L. M. (1981). *Peabody Picture Vocabulary Test-Revised.* Circle Pines, MN: American Guidance Service.

Dunst, C. J., Trivette, C., & Cross, A. (1986). Mediating influences of social support: Personal, family, and child outcomes. *American Journal of Mental Deficiency, 90,* 403–417.

Dyson, L., & Fewell, R. R. (1986). Stress and adaptation in parents of young handicapped and nonhandicapped children: A comparative study. *Journal of the Division for Early Childhood, 10,* 25–34.

Eden-Piercy, G. V., Blacher, J. B., & Eyman, R. K. (1986). Exploring parents' reactions to their young child with severe handicaps. *Mental Retardation, 24,* 285–291.

Eheart, B. K. (1982). Mother–child interactions with nonretarded and mentally retarded preschoolers. *American Journal of Mental Deficiency, 87,* 20–25.

Ellis, N. R. (1969). A behavioral research strategy in mental retardation: Defense and critique. *American Journal of Mental Deficiency, 73,* 557–566.

Farber, B. (1959). Effects of a severely mentally retarded child on family integration. *Monographs of the Society for Research in Child Development, 24*(2) (Serial No. 71).

Farber, B. (1960). Family organization and crisis: Maintenance of integration in families with a severely mentally retarded child. *Monographs of the Society for Research in Child Development, 25*(1) (Serial No. 75).

Farber, B., & Jenne, W. C. (1963). Family organization and parent-child communication: Parents and siblings of a retarded child. *Monographs of the Society for Research in Child Development, 28*(7) (Serial No. 91).

Feldman, M. A., Towns, F., Betal, J., Case, L., Rincover, A., & Rubino, C. (1986). Parent Education Project II: Increasing stimulating interactions of developmentally handicapped mothers. *Journal of Applied Behavior Analysis, 19,* 23–37.

Friedrich, W. N. (1979). Predictors of the coping behavior of mothers of handicapped children. *Journal of Consulting and Clinical Psychology, 47,* 1140–1141.

Friedrich, W. N., & Friedrich, N. (1981). Psychosocial assets of parents of handicapped and nonhandicapped children. *American Journal of Mental Deficiency, 85,* 551–553.

Friedrich, W. N., Greenberg, M. T., & Crnic, K. (1983). A short-form of the Questionnaire on Resources and Stress. *American Journal of Mental Deficiency, 88,* 41–48.

Friedrich, W. N., Wilturner, L. T., & Cohen, D. S. (1985). Coping resources and parenting mentally retarded children. *American Journal of Mental Deficiency, 90,* 130–139.

Gallagher, J. J., Scharfman, W., & Bristol, M. (1984). The division of responsibilities in families with preschool handicapped and nonhandicapped children. *Journal of the Division for Early Childhood, 8,* 3–12.

Gath, A. (1972). The mental health of siblings of a congenitally abnormal child. *Journal of Child Psychology and Psychiatry, 13,* 211–218.

Gath, A. (1973). The school-age siblings of mongol children. *British Journal of Psychiatry, 123,* 161–167.

Gath, A., & Gumley, D. (1984). Down's syndrome and the family: Follow-up of children first seen in infancy. *Developmental Medicine & Child Neurology, 26,* 500–508.

Gath, A., & Gumley, D. (1986). Family background of children with Down's syndrome and of children with a similar degree of mental retardation. *British Journal of Psychiatry, 149,* 161–171.

Gath, A., & Gumley, D. (1987). Retarded children and their siblings. *Journal of Child Psychology and Psychiatry and Allied Disciplines, 28,* 715–730.

Greenspan, S., & Budd, K. S. (1986). Research on mentally retarded parents. In J. J. Gallagher & P. M. Vietze (Eds.), *Families of handicapped persons* (pp. 115–127). Baltimore: Brookes.

Griest, D. L., Forehand, R., Rogers, T., Breiner, J., Furey, W., & Williams, C. A. (1982). Effects of parent enhancement therapy on the treatment outcome and generalization of a parent training program. *Behavior Research and Therapy, 20,* 429–436.

Gunn, P., Berry, P., & Andrews, R. J. (1982). Looking behavior of Down syndrome infants. *American Journal of Mental Deficiency, 87,* 344–347.

Hampson, R. B., Hulgus, Y. F., Beavers, W. R., & Beavers, J. S. (1988). The assessment of competence in families with a retarded child. *Journal of Family Psychology, 2*(1), 32–53.

Hanzlik, J., & Stevenson, M. (1986). Interaction of mothers with their infants who are mentally retarded, retarded with cerebral palsy or nonretarded. *American Journal of Mental Deficiency, 90,* 513–520.

Heal, L. W. (1970). Research strategies and research goals in the scientific study of the mentally subnormal. *American Journal of Mental Deficiency, 75,* 10–15.

Herman, M. S., & Shantz, C. V. (1983). Social problem solving and mother–child interactions of educable mentally retarded children. *Journal of Applied Developmental Psychology, 4,* 217–226.

Hetherington, M. A. (1981). Children and divorce. In R. Henderson (Ed.), *Parent-child interaction: Theory, research, and prospect* (pp. 33–58). New York: Academic Press.

Holroyd, J. (1974). The Questionnaire on Resources and Stress: An instrument to measure family response to a handicapped family member. *Journal of Community Psychology, 2,* 92–94.

Holt, K. S. (1958). The influence of the retarded child upon family limitations. *Journal of Mental Deficiency Research, 2,* 28–34.

House, B. J. (1977). Scientific explanation and ecological validity: A reply to Brooks and Baumeister. *American Journal of Mental Deficiency, 81,* 534–542.

James, S. D., & Egel, A. L. (1986). A direct prompting strategy for increasing reciprocal interactions between handicapped and nonhandicapped siblings. *Journal of Applied Behavior Analysis, 19,* 173–186.

Kazak, A. E. (1987). Families with disabled children: Stress and social networks in three samples. *Journal of Abnormal Child Psychology, 15,* 137–146.

Kazdin, A. E., & Matson, J. L. (1981). Social validation in mental retardation. *Applied Research in Mental Retardation, 2,* 39–53.

Kogan, K. L., & Tyler, N. (1973). Mother-child interaction in young physically handicapped children. *American Journal of Mental Deficiency, 77,* 492–497.

Kogan, K. L., Wimberger, H. C., & Bobbitt, R. A. (1969). Analysis of mother-child interaction in young mental retardates. *Child Development, 40,* 799–811.

Lewis, J. M., & Looney, J. G. (1983). *The long struggle: Well-functioning working-class Black families.* New York: Brunner/Mazel.

Lewis, M. (1978). *Effects of birth order on the mother-child relationship.* Unpublished manuscript, Educational Testing Service, Princeton, NJ.

Levy-Shiff, R. (1986). Mother–father–child interactions in families with a mentally retarded young child. *American Journal of Mental Deficiency, 91,* 141–149.

Lobato, D., Barbour, L., Hall, L. J., & Miller, C. (1987). Psychosocial characteristics of preschool siblings of handicapped and nonhandicapped children. *Journal of Abnormal Child Psychology, 15,* 329–338.

Lobato, D., & Tlaker, A. (1985). Sibling intervention with a retarded child. *Education and Treatment of Children, 8,* 221–228.

Maccoby, E. E., & Martin, J. A. (1983). Socialization in the context of the family: Parent-child interaction. In P. H. Mussen (Ed.), *Handbook of child psychology: Vol. IV* (pp. 1–101). New York: Wiley.

Maurer, H., & Sherrod, K. B. (1987). Context of directives given to young children with Down syndrome and nonretarded children: Development over two years. *American Journal of Mental Deficiency, 91,* 570–590.

McAllister, R., Butler, E., & Lei, T. J. (1973). Patterns of social interaction among families of behaviorally retarded children. *Journal of Marriage and the Family, 35,* 93–100.

McConachie, H., & Mitchell, D. R. (1985). Parents teaching their young mentally handicapped children. *Journal of Child Psychology and Psychiatry, 26,* 389–405.

McHale, S. M., Sloan, J., & Simeonsson, R. J. (1986). Sibling relationships of children with autistic, mentally retarded, and nonhandicapped brothers and sisters. *Journal of Autism and Developmental Disorders, 16,* 399–413.

McKinney, B., & Peterson, R. A. (1987). Predictors of stress in parents of developmentally disabled children. *Journal of Pediatric Psychology, 12,* 133–150.

Meyers, C. E., Nihira, K., & Mink, I. T. (1984). Predicting retarded students' short-term growth from home environment. *Applied Research in Mental Retardation, 5,* 137–146.

Milgram, N. A. (1969). The rationale and irrational in Zigler's motivational approach to mental retardation. *American Journal of Mental Deficiency, 73,* 527–532.

Miller, W. H., & Keirn, W. C. Personality measurement in parents of retarded and emotionally disturbed children: A replication. *Journal of Clinical Psychology, 1978, 34,* 686–690.

Mink, I. T., & Nihira, K. (1986). Family life-styles and child behaviors: A study of direction of effects. *Developmental Psychology, 22,* 610–616.

Mink, I. T., & Nihira, K. (1987). Direction of effects: Family life styles and behavior of TMR children. *American Journal of Mental Deficiency, 92,* 57–64.

Mink, I. T., Meyers, C. E., & Nihira, K. (1984). Taxonomy of family life styles: II Homes with slow-learning children. *American Journal of Mental Deficiency, 89,* 111–123.

Mink, I. T., Nihira, K. & Meyers, C. E. (1983). Taxonomy of family life styles: I Homes with TMR children. *American Journal of Mental Deficiency, 87,* 484–497.

Nihira, K., Meyers, C. E., & Mink, I. T. (1983). Reciprocal relationships between home environment and development of TMR adolescents. *American Journal of Mental Deficiency, 88,* 139–149.

O'Connor, W. A., & Stachowiak, J. (1971). Patterns of interaction in families with high adjusted, low adjusted, and mentally retarded members. *Family Process, 10,* 229–241.

Peterson, S. L., Robinson, E. A., & Littman, I. (1983). Parent-child interaction training for parents with a history of mental retardation. *Applied Research in Mental Retardation, 4,* 329–342.

Piper, M. C., & Ramsay, M. K. (1980). Effects of early home environment on the mental development of Down syndrome infants. *American Journal of Mental Deficiency, 85,* 39–44.

Powell, T. H., Salzberg, C. L., Rule, S., Levy, S., & Itzakowitz, J. S. (1983). Teaching mentally retarded children to play with their siblings using parents as trainers. *Education and Treatment of Children, 6,* 343–362.

Quine, L., & Pahl, J. (1986). First diagnosis of severe mental handicap: Characteristics of unsatisfactory encounters between doctors and parents. *Social Science and Medicine, 22,* 53–62.

Ricci, C. S. (1970). Analysis of child-rearing attitudes of mothers of retarded, emotionally disturbed, and normal children. *American Journal of Mental Deficiency, 74,* 756–761.

Robinson, E. A., & Eyberg, S. M. (1981). The Dyadic Parent-Child Interaction Coding System: Standardization and validation. *Journal of Consulting and Clinical Psychology, 49,* 245–250.

Robinson, L. H. (1978). Parental attitudes of retarded young mothers. *Child Psychiatry & Human Development, 8,* 131–144.

Routh, D. K. (1970). MMPI responses of parents as a function of mental retardation of the child. *American Journal of Mental Deficiency, 75,* 376–377.

Salisbury, C. L. (1985). Internal consistency of the short-form of the Questionnaire on Resources and Stress. *American Journal of Mental Deficiency, 89,* 610–616.

Salisbury, C. L. (1987). Stressors of parents with young handicapped and nonhandicapped children. *Journal of the Division for Early Childhood, 11,* 154–160.

Schaie, K. R., & Strother, C. R. (1968). A cross-sectional study of age changes in cognitive behavior. *Psychological Bulletin, 70,* 671–680.

Sigman, M., Mundy, P., Sherman, T., & Ungerer, J. (1986). Social interactions of autistic, mentally retarded, and normal children and their caregivers. *Journal of Child Psychology and Psychiatry & Allied Disciplines, 27,* 647–656.

Smith, L., & Hagen, V. (1984). Relationship between the home environment and sensorimotor development of Down syndrome and nonretarded infants. *American Journal of Mental Deficiency, 89,* 124–132.

Stoneman, Z., Brody, G. H., & Abbott, D. (1983). In-home observations of young Down syndrome children with their mothers and fathers. *American Journal of Mental Deficiency, 87,* 591–600

Stoneman, Z., Brody, G. H., Davis, C. H., & Crapps, J. M. (1987). Mentally retarded children and their older same-sex siblings: Naturalistic in-home observations. *American Journal on Mental Retardation, 92,* 290–298.

Stoneman, Z., Brody, G. H., Davis, C. H., & Crapps, J. M. (1988). Childcare responsibilities, peer relations, and sibling conflict: Older siblings of mentally retarded children. *American Journal on Mental Retardation, 93,* 174–183.

Stoneman, Z., Brody, G. H., Davis, C. H., & Crapps, J. M. (1989). Role relations between children who are mentally retarded and their older siblings: Observations in three in-home contexts. *Research in Developmental Disabilities, 10,* 61–76.

Stoneman, Z., Brody, G. H., & MacKinnon, C. E. (1986). Same-sex and cross-sex siblings: Activity choices, roles, behavior, and gender stereotypes. *Sex Roles, 15*(9/10), 495–511.

Strom, R. (1984). *Parent as Teacher Inventory.* Bensenville, IL: Scholastic Testing Services.

Strom, R. D., Wurster, S., & Rees, R. J. (1983). Parents as teachers of their exceptional children. *Journal of Instructional Psychology, 10,* 21–39.

Suelzle, M., & Keenan, V. (1981). Changes in family support networks over the life cycle of mentally retarded persons. *American Journal of Mental Deficiency, 86,* 267–274.

Tannock, R. (1988). Mothers' directiveness in their interactions with their children with and without Down syndrome. *American Journal on Mental Retardation, 93,* 154–165.

Waisbren, S. (1980). Parents' reactions after the birth of a developmentally disabled child. *American Journal of Mental Deficiency, 84*, 345–351.

Wasserman, G. A., Shilansky, M., & Hahn, H. (1986). A matter of degree: Maternal interaction with infants of varying levels of retardation. *Child Study Journal, 16*, 241–243.

Weir, M. (1967). Mental retardation. *Science, 157*, 576–578.

Wikler, L. M. (1986). Periodic stresses of families of older mentally retarded children: An exploratory study. *American Journal of Mental Deficiency, 90*, 703–706.

Williams, R. G., & McKenry, P. C. (1981). Marital adjustment among parents of mentally retarded children. *Family Perspective, 3*, 175–178.

Wilton, K., & Renaut, J. (1986). Stress levels in families with intellectually handicapped preschool children and families with nonhandicapped preschool children. *Journal of Mental Deficiency Research, 30*, 163–169.

Winik, L., Zetlin, A. G., & Kaufman, S. Z. (1985). Adult mildly retarded persons and their parents: The relationship between involvement and adjustment. *Applied Research in Mental Retardation, 6*, 409–419.

Wright, L. S., Matlock, K. S., & Matlock, D. T. (1985). Parents of handicapped children: Their self-ratings, life satisfaction, and parental adequacy. *Exceptional Child, 32*, 37–40.

Zetlin, A. G. (1986). Mentally retarded adults and their siblings. *American Journal of Mental Deficiency, 91*, 217–225.

Zetlin, A. G., & Turner, J. L. (1985). Transition from adolescence to adulthood: Perspectives of mentally retarded individuals and their families. *American Journal of Mental Deficiency, 89*, 570–579.

Zetlin, A. G., Weisner, T. S., & Gallimore, R. (1985). Diversity, shared functioning, and the role of benefactors: A study of parenting by retarded persons. In S. K. Thurman (Ed.), *Children of handicapped parents* (pp. 69–95). Orlando, FL: Academic Press.

Zigler, E. (1969). Developmental versus difference theories of mental retardation and the problem of motivation. *American Journal of Mental Deficiency, 73*, 536–555.

Partial support for the preparation of this manuscript was provided by Grant No. 04-DD-000-58 from the Administration on Developmental Disabilities, U.S. Department of Health and Human Services. Reprint requests should be sent to Zolinda Stoneman, Director, Georgia University Affiliated Program for Persons with Developmental Disabilities, Dept. of Child and Family Development, Dawson Hall, The University of Georgia, Athens, GA 30602.

Author

Zolinda Stoneman, The University of Georgia

Puerto Rican Families Caring for an Adult With Mental Retardation: Role of Familism

Sandra M. Magaña
1999

Abstract

The role of familism (a cultural value including interdependence among nuclear and extended family members for support, loyalty, and solidarity) in caregiving was explored for Puerto Rican mothers with children with mental retardation living at home. *Familism*—defined here as direct caregiving provided by family members to the person with mental retardation, mothers' social support networks, and mothers' obligations to other family members—was hypothesized to account for variation in maternal well-being. Better maternal well-being was predicted by larger social support networks, greater satisfaction with social support, and more minor children living in the household. A troubling but not unexpected finding is that these mothers faced many socioeconomic challenges and were in poor health in addition to the challenges of parenting a child with mental retardation.

In this paper I have explored the role of the family in providing care for adult Puerto Ricans with mental retardation. Caregiving experiences of Latino families with members who have mental retardation are important to study for several reasons. First, the role of the family in caregiving for persons with mental retardation has been increasingly recognized as important (Ramey, Krauss, & Simeonsson, 1989; Seltzer & Heller, 1997). Second, it is well-documented that families are a particularly important source of care for Latinos, as these families tend to utilize fewer services and place more importance on family caregivers than does the general population (M. Delagado & Tennstedt, 1997; Purdy & Arguello, 1992).

In order to conduct research about a specific Latino group, such as Puerto Rican families, it is important to understand current thinking about research in communities of color. Recent theorists emphasize the importance of measuring the *strengths* of ethnic and cultural values and of analyzing how variables such as racism, discrimination, and other sources of oppression may lead to negative outcomes. The importance of identifying specific cultural factors when accounting for differences between groups and when describing ethnic and cultural groups has been discussed as an important means of advancing the understanding of the role of culture (Betancourt & Lopez, 1993). In the past, however, deficit models have frequently been used in research about communities of color, resulting in a biased and negative image of those groups (García Coll et al., 1996).

Studies of people of color are beginning to be recognized as important by researchers in the field of mental retardation, as attested to by a recent increase in published articles about families from different cultural or racial groups (Blacher, Shapiro, Lopez, Diaz, & Fusco, 1997; Heller, Markwardt, Rowitz, & Farber, 1994; McCallion, Janicki, & Grant-Griffin, 1997; Pruchno, Hicks Patrick, & Burant, 1997; Rogers-Dulan, 1998; Chen & Tang, 1997). However, studies of specific ethnic groups in which researchers examine how cultural strengths and values impact the caregiving process remain sparse.

In most studies of Latino families who have a member with mental retardation, investigators have made comparisons to non-Latino groups, attributing group differences to ethnicity without identifying specific ethnic or cultural factors that account for the differences. Blacher et al. (1997) reported an important and serious concern about high rates of depression among 148 primarily Mexican American mothers of children with mental retardation. They found that mothers who had more family problems, worse health, fewer interactions with English-speaking persons, and more negative feelings about parenting had higher levels of depression than did those who did not. Blacher et al. did not, however, focus on specific cultural strengths of the mothers. A somewhat different conclusion was reached by Heller et al. (1994), who compared 51 Latino families with 195 Anglo families who had a child with mental retardation and found that Latino families were less burdened by the caregiving role than were the Anglo families. Although factors related to cultural practices such as religiosity and family support were examined, none were found to explain this difference. In a study comparing 60 Black, Latina, and White mothers who had a child with mental retardation, Mary (1990) examined the reactions of mothers and found no ethnic differences in ratings of maternal reactions. However, in a content analysis of an open-ended question, she found that Latina mothers reported more self-sacrifice with regard to the child, and Latino fathers were more likely to deny that their child had a disability than did Black or White fathers.

In contrast to previous researchers who have made between-group comparisons across different ethnic groups and have tended to focus on negative outcomes, I based the present study on a *cultural strengths* perspective and focused on the cultural value of familism among Puerto Rican families who care for an adult with mental retardation. *Familism* is a value that includes strong feelings of loyalty, reciprocity, and solidarity among members of the same nuclear and extended family (Marin & Marin, 1991). Sabogal et al. (1987) identified three types of value orientations within familism: reliance on family members for support, obligation towards family members, and use of relatives as referents. An underlying cultural element of these three value orientations is the concept of collectivism versus individualism. Collectivist cultures have high levels of interdependence, willingness to sacrifice for the good of group members, and trust of group members (Marin & Marin, 1991). Familism has been reported as one of the most preserved cultural characteristics of Puerto Ricans in the United States (Cortés, 1995) and has endured as a core value for Puerto Ricans, despite the influences of social and economic trends in the United States, frequent migration between the United States and Puerto Rico, and pressures of acculturation (Zayas & Palleja, 1988).

Studies of Latino families have been focused on either behavioral or attitudinal aspects of familism. *Behavioral familism* refers to the actual behaviors of the family in providing and receiving support and in demonstrating loyalty and solidarity. Studies that have investigated behavioral aspects of familism have examined the reliance on family members for support (largely through examining social support from the family) and have found that the extended and immediate family do provide substantial support for problem solving and protection of family members against stressors (Aranda & Knight, 1997; García-Preto, 1982; Keefe, 1978). Although large

family networks among Latino groups were found in early studies (Keefe, Padilla, & Carlos, 1979; Mindel, 1980), more recent researchers have found fewer differences between Latino and Anglo American families in the size of family support networks (M. Delgado, 1997; Heller et al., 1994). These changes may be the result of factors such as immigration, which results in separation from family members; acculturation of some family members; and economic demands put on family members in our society. In a study of 368 Puerto Rican older adults in Springfield, Massachusetts, M. Delgado (1997) found that family supports were not as prominent as expected and theorized that supports disappeared as these individuals migrated from Puerto Rico to the mainland and from one United States city to another before settling in Springfield, depleting the family network. Blacher, Lopez, Shapiro, and Fusco (1997) found that low family cohesion contributed to high depression rates in Latina mothers with a child who had mental retardation.

Attitudinal familism refers to beliefs and attitudes that family members have about their family. Researchers who have investigated attitudinal aspects of familism have examined this cultural value in relation to acculturation and found that Latinos retain some degree of attitudinal familism values despite differences in acculturation (Cortés, 1995; Rodríguez & Kosloski, 1998; Rogler et al., 1987).

Szapocznik and Kurtines (1993) have emphasized the importance of studying the individual in the context of the family and the family within the context of culture for Latinos. They emphasized, however, that culture cannot be seen as static or "culture as it occurred," but as changing and diverse or "culture as it occurs" (p. 404). "Culture as it occurs" refers to a changing multicultural context in which Latino Americans are a part. The multicultural context consists of American values, such as individualism, and Latino values, such as collectivism and familism. This dichotomy can cause conflict between family members, particularly between different generations. This is important from a caregiving perspective because Latino parents may have strong familistic values and expectations that their adult children who do not have a disability will participate in caregiving and provide support for the son or daughter with mental retardation, whereas the adult children may have more American values that promote their own independence and individual development.

In this paper I have focused on three different as-

©American Association on Mental Retardation

Puerto Rican Families Caring for an Adult With Mental Retardation   Sandra M. Magaña

pects of behavioral familism: (a) how family members participate in the caregiving process, (b) social support from the family, and (c) mothers' obligations to other family members. The relationship of these three aspects of familism to maternal well-being was examined. The model used in these analyses is an ecological multivariate model that consists of stressors, protective factors, and maternal well-being outcomes. Similar models have been used in research on family adaptation in the general population (Lazarus & Folkman, 1984; McCubbin & Patterson, 1983; Pearlin & Schooler, 1978), in family research in mental retardation (Crnic, Friedrich, & Greenberg, 1983; Flynt & Wood, 1989; Frey, Greenberg, & Fewell, 1989; Gowan, Johnson-Martin, Goldman, & Applebaum, 1989; Heller et al., 1994; Seltzer, Greenberg, & Krauss, 1995; Seltzer & Krauss, 1989) and have been recommended for use in research with Latino populations (Cervantes & Castro, 1985; García Coll et al., 1996).

Consistent with studies in the field of mental retardation (e.g., Seltzer & Krauss, 1989), I identified stressors as maternal and child risk factors. Maternal risk factors include low education and poor health, and child risk factors include maladaptive behavior, poor functional ability, and unmet service needs. Protective factors in this model are the familism aspects: the number of members in the mothers' social support network (I hypothesized that the majority of social support is provided by family members) and mothers' level of satisfaction with the support they receive. Familism is also measured by family participation in caregiving. Both social support and family participation in caregiving incorporate the familism value orientation of reliance on family members for support. To capture the value orientation of obligation to family members, I also examined additional family responsibilities, as characterized by the number of minor children living at home. The well-being variables for this model are maternal subjective burden and depressive symptoms.

Risk factors found to be associated with burden in studies of mothers who care for a child with mental retardation include poor physical health and younger age of the mother and more severe disability, maladaptive behaviors, and poor physical health of the child with mental retardation (Greenberg, Seltzer, & Greenley, 1993; Heller et al., 1994; Heller, Hsieh, & Rowitz, 1997; Seltzer & Krauss, 1989). Protective factors associated with lower burden in these studies include day program

participation by the son or daughter, more family cohesion, larger social support networks of the mother, and more maternal satisfaction with the social support networks (Greenberg et al., 1993; Heller et al., 1994; Seltzer & Krauss, 1989).

In studies of maternal depressive symptoms, researchers have found single marital status, poorer physical health, and lower education of the mother and child maladaptive behaviors to be risk factors associated with more depressive symptoms (Blacher, Lopez et al., 1997; Greenberg, Seltzer, Krauss, & Kim, 1997; Seltzer et al., 1995). Protective factors associated with lower depressive symptoms have included the size of the social support network, family cohesion, and active coping activities (Blacher, Lopez et al., 1997; Greenberg et al., 1997; Seltzer et al., 1995).

Although maternal burden and depression are related both conceptually and empirically, they have overlapping yet distinct predictors. In a longitudinal study examining both burden and depressive symptoms in mothers who care for adults with mental retardation, Seltzer, Greenberg, Krauss, and Hong (1997) found that residential placement of the son or daughter outside of the parental home was predictive of a decline in burden but was not associated with a change in depressive symptoms. More pessimism about the future was associated with increases in both burden and depressive symptoms. The size of the mothers' social support network was associated with decreases in depressive symptoms but not in burden (Seltzer et al., 1997). Burden, which is a role-specific measure, may be affected more by risk factors associated with the person being cared for, whereas depressive symptoms, which are more of a global well-being measure, may be related more to risk factors associated with the mother that are not necessarily related to the person being cared for. Of course, some overlap would be expected because risk factors associated with the mother may impact her ability to provide care and, consequently, affect her feelings of burden in the caregiving process.

On the basis of past caregiving research on families with a child who has mental retardation and to examine the role of familism in the caregiving process, I posed two research questions: Is familism a significant protective factor of emotional well-being for Puerto Rican mothers of adults with mental retardation? Are the protective and risk factors different for burden than for depressive symptoms in this population?

Method

Sample

Participants were 72 Puerto Rican families living in Massachusetts who met three criteria: the mother was the main caregiver for a son or daughter with mental retardation, the son or daughter lived at home, and the mother or son/daughter were of Puerto Rican descent. Both Spanish- and English-speaking families were eligible to participate. As shown in Table 1, the mothers in this sample represent a fairly homogeneous group with respect to place of birth and language preference. All but 3 mothers in the sample were born in Puerto Rico. One of the 3, whose father was Puerto Rican, was born in the Dominican Republic and raised in Puerto Rico. The other two were born in the Dominican Republic and Columbia, respectively, but the fathers of the children with mental retardation in these families were born in Puerto Rico. The level of acculturation was low for the majority of mothers, even though the average time sample members had lived in the United States was about 21 years. Mothers' ages ranged from 29 to 85 years old, with an average of 56.2 (standard deviation [SD] = 9.7). Level of education among this group was fairly low; 75% had less than a high school education. Income was also very low, with a median income in 1996–1997 of $12,500, which is well below the median for Massachusetts households of $35,714 (1990 census). Their mean income was $17,361 (SD = $10,104). Mothers' health was poor, with only 26% of the mothers reporting themselves to be in excellent or good health. About 40% of the mothers were married at the time of the study, with the remainder widowed, separated, or single. Very few of the mothers (9.7%) worked outside the home.

The mean age of the son or daughter with mental retardation was 28.6 years (SD = 9.4, range = 9 to 65). Slightly more than half were daughters and a quarter were born in the United States, with the remainder born in Puerto Rico. About two thirds of the mothers (63%) reported that their son or daughter with mental retardation was in good or excellent health, with the remainder in fair or poor health. Slightly more than half had severe or profound mental retardation (51.6%); only 27% had mild mental retardation.

Families were recruited with the help of personnel from 14 area offices of the Department of Mental Retardation and community organizations that serve Latino families who have a family member with mental retar-

Table 1 Characteristics of the Mother and Son/Daughter With Mental Retardation (N = 72)

Variable	%
Acculturation/migration characteristics of mother	
Where born	
United States (US)	0.0
Puerto Rico (PR)	95.8
Other Latin-American country	4.2
Language preference	
Spanish	77.8
English	1.4
English & Spanish equally	20.8
Acculturation	
Low	70.0
High	30.0
Average no. of years lived in PR	34.8[a]
Moved from United States to PR and	
back in past 5 years	11.1
Mothers have visited PR in past 5 years	68.1
Mothers who have had visitors from	
PR in past 5 years	54.4
Mother characteristics	
Marital status	
Married	40.3
Widowed	22.2
Separated/divorced	33.3
Single	4.2
Health status	
Excellent	6.9
Good	19.5
Fair	33.3
Poor	40.3
Education	
< than high school	75.0
High school	6.9
Trade/vocational or some college	11.1
Completed college	7.0
Work status	
Work full or part time outside	
the home	9.7
Son/daughter characteristics	
Gender, female	55.6
Where born	
US	25.0
Puerto Rico	75.0

Health status
Excellent	20.8
Good	41.7
Fair	26.4
Poor	11.1

Level of mental retardation
Mild	27.3
Moderate	21.2
Severe	36.4
Profound	15.2

Vocational status
Day activity program	62.5
Remains at home	37.5

Services
Average no. of services received	5.9[b]
Average no. of unmet service needs	3.6[c]

[a] $SD = 13.5$
[b] $SD = 2.5$
[c] $SD = 2.3$

dation. In addition, 8 families were identified by participating sample members. The service providers were asked to refer all families who met the three criteria mentioned previously. A key element of sample recruitment in this study was a reliance on personal contact of service providers with potential sample members. Because Latinos value personal interdependence and trust of other members of their group, as discussed earlier and because varying degrees of literacy were expected, I did not think a high response to a mailing of information would occur. Service providers presented information written in Spanish or English to the families and reviewed it with them. They then asked families if they would be interested in being contacted by the study staff. Although a sampling frame of Puerto Rican families that met the criteria of the study did not exist, only 2 families were reported by service coordinators or agencies as having refused to participate. All of the families referred by these agencies and those referred by other families agreed to participate. It is likely that the agency did not exhaust their caseloads of all of the families eligible for the study, but this was difficult to assess.

Measures

Characteristics of the mother considered were self-reported physical health status, years of education, and level of acculturation. Physical health was measured us-

ing a question taken from the Older Americans' Resources and Services Multidimensional Functional Assessment, on which mothers are asked to rate their own health from *excellent* (4) to *poor* (1). The criterion-related validity of this item with a physical examination has been reported to be .70 (Center for the Study of Aging and Human Development, 1978). Level of education was number of years of school completed. The Spanish Family Guidance Center Acculturation/Biculturalism Scale was used to measure acculturation (Szapocznik, Scopetta, & Kurtines, 1978; Szapocznik, Kurtines, & Fernandez, 1980). This scale consists of 24 items measuring behavioral acculturation along a 5-point Likert scale. The measures were developed and administered to Miami Cuban samples with reported high levels of reliability and criterion validity (Szapocznik et al., 1978) and have been used in hundreds of studies with Latino and immigrant populations (Buriel, Perez, De Ment, Chavez, & Moran, 1998; Dana, 1996). The higher the score on the acculturation scale, the more acculturated the person is. Sample items include the following: What language do you prefer to speak? What language do you speak at home (responses for these 2 items range from Spanish all of the time to English all of the time)? What sort of music do you listen to? What sort of places do you go out to (responses for these 2 items range from Latino all of the time to American all of the time)? Nineteen items were used in the data analysis of this sample; 5 items were eliminated due to missing data. In describing the scoring process of the scale, Szapocznik et al. (1978) indicated that up to 5 items can be eliminated without compromising the integrity of the scale. The cutoff for low acculturation was a score of 38, which indicates mean responses on acculturation items fell in the "Spanish/Latino all of the time" or "Spanish/Latino most of the time" categories. Alpha reliability for this sample was .93.

Migration variables were measured by a series of items about where the mother and son or daughter were born, the number of times the mother had ever moved back and forth between the United States and Puerto Rico, and whether she lived in Puerto Rico and for how long. In order to document recent migration patterns of these families between the United States mainland and Puerto Rico, I asked mothers whether they had moved back to Puerto Rico from the United States mainland in the preceding 5 years (to live for more than 3 months) and whether mothers had visited relatives in Puerto Rico or received visitors from Puerto Rico in the preceding 5 years.

Characteristics of the son or daughter included functional abilities, the number of maladaptive behaviors, and the number of unmet service needs. Functional abilities were measured using the revised Barthel Index (Mahoney & Barthel, 1965), a 31-point scale of instrumental and functional skills, with each item scored on a 4-point scale of independence. Higher scores denote more independence. Alpha reliability for this sample was .96. Maladaptive behaviors were measured using the Inventory for Clients in Agency Planning (Bruininks, Hill, Weatherman, & Woodcock, 1986). This measure contains eight questions that are grouped into three subscales: Internalizing Behaviors (e.g., hurtful to self), Externalizing Behaviors (e.g., destructive to property), and Asocial Behaviors (e.g., disruptive behavior). The alpha reliability for this sample was .75.

The number of unmet service needs was measured using a scale listing 15 services that are typically received by persons with mental retardation. Mothers were asked whether their son or daughter received the service, and if not, whether it was needed. The number of services needed but not received were totaled.

There were three measures of familism: caregiving support, mothers' social support network, and mothers' obligations to other family members. *Caregiving support* was the number of caregiving tasks (activities of daily living) for which relatives provide help to the son or daughter with mental retardation. This variable was constructed from the Barthel Index described earlier with a "who helps?" component. If the mother responded that her son or daughter was not able to perform a task independently, she enumerated all individuals and agencies who provided help. Items that were descriptions of caregiving tasks for which a relative helps were counted.

Measures of social support were based on Antonucci's (1986) Convoy Model, which indicates the number of people included in the mother's social support network (range = 0 to 10), the relationship of people in the social support network to the mother, and driving distance of these people from the mother. For those who were not relatives, the mother was asked whether she considered them to be part of the family (attempting to capture the concept of "fictive kin"). The mothers were also asked how satisfied they were with the overall social support network (rated on a 4-point scale ranging from 0, *completely dissatisfied*, to 3, *completely satisfied*).

The extent of mothers' obligations to other family members was measured by the amount of time spent caring for other family members with a disability, having minor children living at home, and having minor grandchildren living at home. The first of these was measured by an item that asked whether the mothers provided care to anyone with a disability other than the son or daughter who was the focus of the study and, if so, the number of people with a disability for whom the mother provided care. The latter two obligations were constructed from a series of questions about household composition.

Outcome variables were two measures: depressive symptoms and caregiver burden. Depressive symptoms were assessed using the Center for Epidemiologic Studies-Depression (CES-D) Scale (Radloff, 1977), a measure of the frequency of 20 depressive symptoms that had occurred over the last week, each rated on a 4-point scale. This scale has been shown to be valid and reliable with many populations and is often used in cross-cultural research (Blacher, Shapiro et al., 1997). However, researchers who have analyzed this scale with Latino populations caution investigators who use the measure for cross-cultural comparison that Latinos are more likely to report elevated symptoms than are members of other groups (Coelho, Strauss, & Jenkins, 1998; Guarnaccia, Angel, & Lowe Worebey, 1989; Kolody, Vega, Meinhardt, & Bensussen, 1986; Stroup-Benham, Lawrence, & Treviño, 1992). Researchers agree that this scale measures some form of mental distress among Latinos, and it is used in this study as a well-being measure within the Puerto Rican sample. The scale's alpha reliability was .88 for this sample.

Caregiver burden was assessed by the Zarit Burden Scale (Zarit, Reever, & Bach-Peterson, 1980), which consists of 29 items, each answered on a 3-point scale, ranging from 0 (*not at all true*) to 2 (*extremely true*). In this scale, Zarit et al. conceptualized burden as problems with the "caregiver's health, psychological well being, finances, social life and the relationships between the caregiver and the impaired person" (p. 651). The scale's alpha reliability for this sample was .88.

Data-Collection Procedures

Families who expressed interest in the study were contacted by telephone by bilingual, bicultural interviewers who explained the study in more detail and confirmed that recruitment criteria were met. Interviews conducted at the participants' homes were administered by bilingual, bicultural interviewers who received 2 days of train-ing in survey interview techniques. All but one of the interviews were conducted in Spanish. The majority of measures used in the study were already available in Span-ish (they were borrowed from a companion study in Mi-ami in which the back-translation method was used). Remaining items were translated into Spanish by a Puerto Rican interpreter and were checked for accuracy and piloted by a Puerto Rican interviewer. The measures al-ready translated into Spanish were also reviewed by the Puerto Rican interviewer to ensure they would have the same meaning for Puerto Rican Spanish speakers as they did for Cuban Americans. Although some measures are typically self-administered, all items were read aloud to the mothers because some of these mothers may not be able to read or may not be comfortable with a reading and writing component. They were paid $20 for the in-terview at the end of the visit as a gesture of respect for their time. Interviews lasted an average of 3 hours.

Results

The following is description of the extent to which the value of familism is manifested in this sample of Puerto Rican families caring for a son or daughter with mental retardation. One key aspect of familism is direct caregiving provided by family members. As reported ear-lier, mothers were asked whether the person with men-tal retardation needed help with 31 caregiving tasks and, if so, who helped him or her to perform these tasks. Mothers often reported more than one person who helped with each task. As shown in Table 2, mothers noted that these individuals provided help with more than three quarters of tasks in which the son or daughter needed help. Other relatives provided help with about one quar-ter of the tasks in which help was needed. These rela-tives were primarily fathers and siblings, with siblings playing a larger role in the day-to-day caregiving tasks than did fathers. Cousins, nieces, and nephews, an aunt, and a grandmother (to the person with mental retarda-tion) also provided help on some tasks.

Table 2 Familism Variables ($N = 72$)

Variable	Mean or %	SD
Family caregiving		
Mean no. of tasks with which mother helps[a]	13.7	6.7
Mean % of tasks with which mother helps[a]	77.3	14.6
Mean no. of tasks with which relatives help[a]	4.9	6.4
Mean % of tasks with which relatives help[a]	26.6	28.7
Mothers' social support network		
Mean size of social support network	6.3	4.2
Mean % of network who are relatives	87.7	25.2
Mothers who included relatives living in PR[b] as part of network	19.4	—
Satisfaction with social support network		
Somewhat satisfied	18.6	—
Completely satisfied	81.4	—
Mothers' other caregiving responsibilities (%)		
Have at least one minor child living at home	16.7	—
Have at least one grandchild living at home	15.3	—
Care for other family members with a disability	29.2	—
Have one or more other caregiving responsibilities	51.4	—

[a] Out of number of tasks in which help is needed
[b] Puerto Rico

Social support received from the family is another aspect of familism examined in this study. Social support includes emotional and instrumental support (e.g., having people in whom to confide, talk to when upset, and talk to about health). The average size of the social support network was about 6 people. On average, 88% of the persons defined by the mother as being part of her social support network were family members, and 19% of the mothers included family members living in Puerto Rico as part of their networks.

Another aspect of familism is obligations the mother has to other family members. Slightly more than half of the mothers had at least one other caregiving responsibility in addition to the person with mental retardation. Thirty percent of the mothers cared for at least one other relative with a disability (a child or children with mental retardation or another disability, a spouse, or a parent), 17% had at least one minor child still living at home, and 15% had at least one grandchild living with them.

Familism as a Protective Factor for Mothers' Well-Being

Intercorrelations among study variables and variable means are presented in Table 3. The only variable significantly correlated with higher depressive symptoms was poor maternal health; variables significantly correlated with lower depressive symptoms were larger maternal social support networks, greater maternal satisfaction with network, and more minor children living at home. Variables significantly correlated with higher burden were poor maternal health, more problematic behaviors, and more unmet service needs of the son or daughter; the only variable significantly correlated with lower burden was greater maternal satisfaction with the social support network.

Because the sample size limits the number of variables that can be used in regression analyses, some variables that have been reported as risk factors in previous research (e.g., low family income, older maternal age, single marital status, and caring for other family members with disabilities) were not included in the regression models (Blacher, Shapiro et al., 1997; Li, Seltzer, & Greenberg, 1999; Seltzer & Krauss, 1989). The decision to eliminate these variables was made based on lack of correlation of these variables with the dependent variables, high correlation of these variables with other independent variables in the model, and/or the priority of including other variables due to the theoretical framework of the model. For example, income was highly correlated with education and acculturation (see Table 3). Education was significantly correlated with burden, but income was not. Acculturation was important to maintain as a control variable because level of acculturation often varies in a Latino sample (Negy & Woods, 1992). In addition, all of the variables (including those excluded in the final models presented) were tested in regressions in which all variables were entered simultaneously and the patterns of findings did not differ.

The first research question was whether familism is a protective factor for mothers' well-being as measured by depressive symptoms and burden. Variables for both regression models were entered hierarchically by domain in the following order: maternal characteristics (Step 1), child characteristics (Step 2), and familism (Step 3) (see Table 4). Maternal characteristics, conceptualized as risk factors, were thought to have the most direct or proximal effect on the dependent variables, followed by child characteristics. Familism variables were entered last to determine how predictive this domain is of depressive symptoms or burden of caregiving after controlling for risk factors.

Of the maternal characteristics that might be risk factors for depressive symptoms, only maternal health status was a significant predictor (Step 1), and it remained significant regardless of the other variables included in Steps 2 and 3. No characteristics of the child were predictive of maternal depressive symptoms. Of the four measures of familism entered in the final step, three were significant predictors of maternal depressive symptoms: number of minor children living at home, size of the mother's social support network, and mother's satisfaction with social support. In total, these variables accounted for 42% of the variance in maternal depressive symptoms.

Poor maternal health was also a significant predictor for burden (Step 1). Maladaptive behaviors and the number of unmet service needs, entered in Step 2, were significantly related to increased burden. Once child characteristics were controlled, level of education became significantly predictive of higher burden. The only familism variable (Step 3) significantly related to lower burden was mothers' satisfaction with the social support networks. In total, these variables accounted for 52% of the variance in caregiver burden.

Table 3 Intercorrelations of Study Variables

Variable	1	2	3	4	5	6	7	8	9	10	11	12	13	14	15	16
1. CES–D[a]	1.00															
2. Burden	.54***	1.00														
3. Mother's age	.03	.05	1.00													
4. Age of S/D[b]	.16	.04	.66***	1.00												
5. Income	.07	.02	-.23*	-.12	1.00											
6. Years of education	-.18	-.22	-.24*	-.24*	.37**	1.00										
7. Mother's health	-.58***	-.42***	-.20	-.30*	.10	.21	1.00									
8. Married	.04	.10	-.40***	-.21	.56***	.25*	.00	1.00								
9. Behaviors of S/D	.22	.55***	-.24*	-.12	.17	.08	-.06	-.04	1.00							
10. Function level of S/D	.17	-.01	-.10	-.03	.26*	.03	-.11	.17	-.01	1.00						
11. Unmet service needs	.12	.30**	.01	.09	.11	.11	-.06	.31**	.19	.02	1.00					
12. Acculturation	-.06	-.13	-.24*	-.13	.39**	.39**	.29*	.11	.04	.18	-.09	1.00				
13. No. mother's network	-.27*	-.16	.28*	.05	-.10	-.01	.19	-.20	-.12	-.23	-.02	-.04	1.00			
14. Minor children	-.25*	-.08	-.53***	-.38***	.40***	.30**	.22	.43***	.03	.06	.01	.24*	-.12	1.00		
15. No. ADLS[c] relatives help with	-.11	-.03	.10	.01	-.13	.02	.03	.07	.00	-.50***	.11	-.31**	.31**	.01	1.00	
16. Network Satisfaction	-.25*	-.31**	.05	-.001	-.00	.02	.10	-.06	-.09	.10	-.12	.18	-.05	.05	-.01	1.00

[a] Center for Epidemiologic Studies–Depression.
[b] Son or daughter.
[c] Activities of daily living skills.
  * $p < .05$.
 ** $p < .01$.
*** $p < .0111$.

Table 4 Hierarchical Regression of Maternal Emotional Well-Being

Mother characteristics/Risk factors	Depressive symptoms			Caregiver burden		
	Step 1	Step 2	Step 3	Step 1	Step 2	Step 3
Health status	–.60***	–.56***	–.48***	–.40**	–.36***	–.34***
Year of education	–.11	–.13	–.11	–.15	–.23*	–.25*
Acculturation	.15	.13	.20	.04	.07	.09
Child characteristics/risk factors						
Functional skill level		.09	.11		.06	.07
No. of maladaptive behaviors		.18	.15		.50***	.48***
No. of unmet service needs		.07	.05		.22*	.21*
Familism variables						
No. of ADL[a] tasks with which relatives help			.08			–.03
No. of minor children at home			–.21*			.04
Size of social support network			–.21*			–.04
Satisfaction with social support network			–.23*			–.22*
Adjusted R^2	.33	.35	.42	.16	.50	.52

Note: Standardized beta coefficients are reported.

[a] Activities of daily living.

   * $p < .05$.
  ** $p < .01$.
 *** $p < .001$.

Differences in Predictors for Depressive Symptoms and Burden

The second research question concerned whether depressive symptoms and burden have similar or different predictors for this sample. Although depressive symptoms and burden were highly correlated with one another, $r (70) = .54$, $p < .001$, there were distinct differences in the predictors of these two indicators of maternal well-being. Table 4 (Step 3) shows that in the domain of maternal characteristics, poor maternal health was a strong predictor for both depressive symptoms and caregiving burden. Low education was a predictor for burden, but not for depressive symptoms. In the child characteristics domain, maladaptive behaviors of the son or daughter and unmet service needs were predictors of burden but not of depressive symptoms. In the familism domain, the size of the social support network and having minor children living at home were predictors of depressive symptoms but not of burden, whereas satisfaction with the social support network was predictive of both measures.

Table 5 presents the contribution of the subsets of variables to the overall models, which provides a more focused view of the distinctions between the models. In this analysis, specialized F tests were conducted in order to determine the contribution of each domain of variables (maternal characteristics, child characteristics, and familism) to each regression model. In this method, each model is estimated using the full set of variables. The subset of variables being tested is then dropped from the model and the model is re-estimated including only the remaining variables. The difference in R^2s between the two models is then tested with an F statistic. If the F is statistically significant, the null hypothesis that there are no differences between the model without subset and the original model is rejected. This shows that the subset of variables do make a statistically significant contribution to the original model (Crown, 1998).

In the present analysis, maternal characteristics as a domain contributed significantly to the dependent variables in both models. Child characteristics contributed significantly to the burden model, but not to the depressive symptoms model. The familism domain contributed significantly to the depressive symptoms model, but not to the burden model.

Discussion

Families were a very important part of the caregiving context for the Puerto Ricans with mental retardation in this sample. In the Puerto Rican family, many different relatives are involved in day-to-day caregiving tasks for the person with mental retardation, including fathers, siblings, cousins, nieces, and nephews. Family members are also an important part of the mothers' social support system, and some mothers receive social support from family members who live in Puerto Rico. When asked what message she would like to give to service providers, one mother said, "I would say they need to develop a little more understanding of our cultural background, and the unity of the family, the importance of taking care of our own and being respected."

Some aspects of familism were found to be protective factors for mothers' emotional well-being in this sample, particularly for depressive symptoms. The size of the mother's social support network and her satisfaction with social support were the aspects of familism most strongly associated with lower depressive symptoms. This is not unlike findings from studies of European American mothers who care for family members with mental disabilities. For example, Seltzer and Krauss (1989) found that social support was predictive of lower burden for mothers of a child with mental retardation, and Greenberg et al. (1997) showed that size of the social support network was predictive of lower depressive symptoms for both mothers of adults with mental retardation and mothers of adults with mental illness. One main difference between the present sample and the Seltzer and Krauss sample is in the composition of the social support network. In the present sample, 88% of the social support network members were relatives, whereas only 70% of the maternal social support network were relatives in Seltzer and Krauss' sample (Seltzer et al., 1995). An interesting comparison would be between a Latino sample and a European American sample on the familism variables measured in this study, including family social support.

Another aspect of familism—obligations to family members—might be an additional challenge for mothers, but for the mothers in the current study, this variable was associated with lower depressive symptoms. Two explanations may account for the positive influence of minor children. One involves motherhood as a central role for Puerto Rican women. The importance of motherhood in this population comes from the cultural notion of "Marianismo" and is based on the Catholic tradition in which the Virgin Mary is seen as a role model (Comas-Diaz, 1982; Sánchez-Ayéndez, 1989). Motherhood is thought to be a woman's main role, taking precedence over all others, and it is through motherhood that a woman receives her greatest satisfaction in life. In addition, because an underlying element of the familism value is collectivism, it would not be unusual for mothers to gain satisfaction from their obligations to the group. The other explanation is that perhaps other children living at home have strong relationships with the child with mental retardation that may increase the mothers' emotional well-being. One mother expressed the importance of siblings in the caregiving process by saying, "All of her sisters have loved her, have accepted her and have tried to help me as much as they can." In a study of the impact of siblings on the well-being of mothers with an adult child who has mental retardation, Seltzer, Begun, Seltzer, and Krauss (1991) found that having children who were more involved with the child who had mental retardation was predictive of more favorable well-being in mothers.

Surprisingly, direct caregiving by family members, another variable measuring familism, was not associated with better well-being. One explanation is that although performance of tasks by family members is important and probably expected in the caregiving process, emotional support is more meaningful to mothers. In an ethno-

Table 5 Multiple Regression: F Statistic Tests of the Contribution of Domains

Domain	Dependent Variables	
	Depressive symptoms R^2 change	Caregiver burden R^2 change
Mother characteristics	.21***(8.54)	.16*** (7.80)
Child characteristics	.03 (1.36)	.30***(14.74)
Familism variables	.10* (2.98)	.05 (1.78)

Note: F statistic in parentheses.
  * $p < .10$.
  ** $p < .05$.

graphic study of 16 Puerto Rican older women in Boston, Sánchez-Ayéndez (1989) reported similar findings with respect to the type of support provided by family members. Although the older mothers expected their children to help them in a variety of ways, what was most important to them was that their children call or visit frequently, not that they perform supportive tasks.

In the child characteristics domain, the finding that maladaptive behavior is significantly related to higher burden is consistent with other studies of mothers of a child who has mental retardation (Greenberg et al., 1993; Heller et al., 1994). In the current study, I did not find a relationship between low functional skills and high burden counter to past research (Heller et al., 1997; Seltzer & Krauss, 1989). The finding that level of functioning was not related to well-being in this sample can be explained in two ways. One possibility is that the lack of variability in this sample in the level of functioning may not have allowed for relationships to be detected. Another is that performing more caregiving tasks may not in itself pose a burden to Puerto Rican mothers because of the strong commitment to the role of motherhood. This commitment was expressed by a mother in the study who was explaining her response to doctors who were encouraging placement of her daughter:

> Many doctors have asked me about her situation and I have always said that I accept her as she was born into this world and as long as I live, I won't give her up to anyone, not even to a government that would demand me to; she would be better off with me.

In this study I found that unmet service needs of the person with mental retardation are predictive of high caregiving burden. This finding contradicts the explanation often given for low service utilization among Latinos, namely, that familism either replaces the need for services or becomes a barrier to service utilization (Purdy & Arguello, 1992; Rogler, Malgady, & Rodriguez, 1989). In this sample there was high involvement of family in the caregiving process, yet many mothers identified a number of services that they would like to receive for their son or daughter that are currently unavailable to them.

Among the most significant and troubling findings of this study are the poor health of the mothers and the strong relationship of poor health to poor emotional well-being. Poor health has been found to be related to low

socioeconomic status (SES), and Puerto Ricans as a group have lower incomes and higher poverty rates than any other Latino group (Zambrana, 1994). In a study comparing 773 Mexican American, 714 Cuban American, and 368 Puerto Rican older adults, Burnette and Mui (1995) noted that 65% of the Puerto Ricans reported themselves to be in fair or poor health as compared with 57% of the Mexican Americans and 46% of the Cuban Americans (Burnette & Mui, 1995). Tennstedt and Chang (1998) compared 683 African American, 591 Puerto Rican, and 702 White older adults in Massachusetts and found that the Puerto Rican sample was the youngest of the three groups, had the lowest SES, and had the most severe disabilities (Tennstedt & Chang, 1998). The demographic findings in the current study are consistent with results that show Puerto Ricans to be one of the most disadvantaged groups in the United States. Add to that the marginal status of women of color in our society, and the conditions are compounded for these mothers. Another factor that may contribute to poor health of the mothers in this study is the cultural expectation for mothers to be self-sacrificing (based on the concept of "Marianismo," and the underlying collectivist nature of familism as exemplified by the Spanish expression "la familia primero" or the family first). In this study, mothers' self-sacrificing commitment to providing care to their children with mental retardation may be at the expense of their own health and well-being.

The strong relationship between poor health and poor emotional well-being found in the current study is consistent with findings from other studies of Latina women in which investigators found either a very strong relationship between health ratings and depressive symptoms or a convergence of the affective and somatic factors in the Depressive Symptoms Scale (Blacher, Lopez et al., 1997; Guarnaccia, Good, & Kleinman, 1990; Kolody et al., 1986). One explanation for this relationship is that it may be a reflection of cultural factors, such as holistic belief systems among Latina women in which they do not conceptualize the mind and body as separate entities. This belief system is manifested in the cultural tendency to experience distress in mind, body, and spirit simultaneously (Angel & Guarnaccia, 1989; J. Delgado, 1997). In addition, it may be that because Puerto Rican women are taught to suppress their own needs for the good of their children, they the repress their emotional needs by somatizing their distress (Comas-Diaz, 1982).

Results of the present study show that although depressive symptoms and caregiving burden are highly correlated, there are differences in the predictors for each of the well-being measures. Child characteristics and formal supports for the person with mental retardation were not predictive of depressive symptoms but were for burden, whereas the familism domain was predictive for depressive symptoms but not for burden. Another interesting difference is that low education was predictive of high burden but not of high depressive symptoms. In addition, low education was not initially predictive of high burden, but when taking into account child characteristics, it became significant. One explanation is that having more unmet service needs and more difficult caregiving challenges (as a result of having a child with more problematic behaviors) force mothers to relate more to the service system, which can present additional stress for mothers with low education. Maternal characteristics may influence mothers' ability to provide care that also is associated with subjective burden. "Depressive symptoms" is a global well-being measure that is more related to characteristics of the mother and the support she receives in relation to her own needs. For this sample, the mother may perceive her obligations to the person with mental retardation as burdensome in a caregiving context but not as a major stress for her overall emotional well-being. In future longtudinal research, the relationship between burden and depression should be examined in order to understand better how they influence each other over time.

It is important to note that these findings are not representative of all Puerto Rican mothers with an adult child who has mental retardation because the sample was located through the service system. Puerto Ricans with mental retardation who are receiving some services appear to have disproportionately more severe disabilities than do the general population of persons with mental retardation. The high risk of poor health and elevated levels of burden and depressive symptoms in these mothers may be, in part, a reflection of more severe disability of the child in addition to the socioeconomic factors mentioned earlier. Lack of variability in many measures (e.g., acculturation, income, education, and functional skills level) may have reduced the chance of detecting relationships between many important variables in the study. Future research is needed that includes larger samples of Latino groups and that locates families not connected to the service system.

References

Angel, R., & Guarnaccia, P. (1989). Mind body and culture: Somatization among Hispanics. *Social Science and Medicine, 28,* 1229–1238.

Antonucci, T. C. (1986). Measuring social support networks: Hierarchical mapping technique. *Generations, 10,* 10–12.

Aranda, M., & Knight, B. (1997). The influence of ethnicity on the caregiver stress and coping process: A sociocultural review and analysis. *The Gerontologist, 37,* 342–354.

Betancourt, H., & Lopez, S. R. (1993, June). The study of culture, ethnicity, and race in American psychology. *American Psychologist,* 629–637.

Blacher, J., Lopez, S., Shapiro, J., & Fusco, J. (1997). Contributions to depression in Latina mothers with and without children with retardation: Implications for caregiving. *Family Relations, 46,* 325–334.

Blacher, J., Shapiro, J., Lopez, S., Diaz, L., & Fusco, J. (1997). Depression in Latina mothers of children with mental retardation: A neglected concern. *American Journal on Mental Retardation, 101,* 483–496.

Bruininks, R. H., Hill, B. K., Weatherman, R. F., & Woodcock, R. W. (1986). *Inventory for Client and Agency Planning* (ICAP). Allen, TX: DLM Teaching Resources.

Buriel, R., Perez, W., De Ment, T., Chavez, D., & Moran, V. (1998). The relationship of language brokering to academic performance, biculturalism, and self-efficacy among Latino adolescents. *Hispanic Journal of Behavioral Sciences, 20,* 283–297.

Burnette, D., & Mui, A. C. (1995). In-home and community-based service utilization by three groups of elderly Hispanics: A national perspective. *Social Work Research, 19,* 197–206.

Center for the Study of Aging and Human Development. (1978). *Multidimensional Functional Assessment: The OARS Methodology. A manual* (2nd ed.). Durham: Duke University.

Cervantes, R. C., & Castro, F. G. (1985). Stress, coping and Mexican American mental health: A systematic overview. *Hispanic Journal of Behavioral Sciences, 7,* 1–73.

Chen, T. Y., & Tang, C. S. (1997). Stress appraisal and social support of Chinese mothers of adult children with mental retardation. *American Journal on Mental Retardation, 101,* 473–482.

Coehlo, V. C., Strauss, M. E., & Jenkins, J. H. (1998). Expression of symptomatic distress by Puerto Rican and Euro-American patients with depression and schizophrenia. *Journal of Nervous and Mental Disease, 186,* 477–483.

Comas-Diaz, L. (1982). Mental health needs of Puerto Rican women in the United States. In R. Zambrana (Ed.), *Work, family and health: Latina women in transition* (Monograph No. 7). New York: Fordham University, Hispanic Research Center.

Cortés, D. (1995). Variations in familism in two generations of Puerto Ricans. *Hispanic Journal of Behavioral Sciences, 17,* 249–255.

Crnic, K., Friedrich, W. N., & Greenberg, M. T. (1983). Adaptation of families with mentally retarded children: A model of stress, coping and family ecology. *American Journal of Mental Deficiency, 88,* 345–351.

Crown, W. (1998). *Statistical models for the social and behavioral sciences.* Westport, CT: Praeger.

Dana, R. (1996). Assessment of acculturation in Hispanic populations. *Hispanic Journal of Behavioral Sciences, 18,* 317–328.

Delgado, J. (1997). *Salud: A Latina's guide to total health—Body, mind, and spirit.* New York: HarperCollins.

Delgado, M. (1997). Interpretation of Puerto Rican elder research findings: A community forum of research respondents. *Journal of Applied Gerontology, 16,* 317–332.

Delgado, M. & Tennstedt, S. (1997). Making the case for culturally appropriate community services: Puerto Rican elders and their caregivers. *Health and Social Work, 22,* 246–255.

Flynt, S. W., & Wood, T. A. (1989). Stress and coping of mothers of children with moderate mental retardation. *American Journal on Mental Retardation, 94,* 278–283.

Frey, K. S., Greenberg, M. T., & Fewell, R. R. (1989). Stress and coping among parents of handicapped children: A multidimensional approach. *American Journal on Mental Retardation, 94,* 240–249.

García Coll, C., Lamberty, G., Jenkins, R., Pipes McAdoo, H., Crnic, K., Hanna Wasik, B., & Vásquez García, H. (1996). An integrative model for the study of developmental competencies in minority children. *Child Development, 67,* 1891–1914.

García-Preto, N. (1982). *Puerto Rican families.* In M. McGoldrick, J. K. Pearce, & J. Giordano (Eds.), *Ethnicity and family therapy* (pp. 183–199). New York: Guilford Press.

Gowan, J. W., Johnson-Martin, N., Goldman, B. D., & Appelbaum, M. (1989). Feelings of depression and parenting competence of mothers of handicapped and nonhandicapped infants: A longitudinal study. *American Journal on Mental Retardation, 94,* 359–371.

Greenberg, J. S., Seltzer, M. M., & Greenley, J. (1993). Aging parents of adults with disabilities: The gratifications and frustrations of later-life caregiving. *The Gerontologist, 33,* 542–550.

Greenberg, J., Seltzer, M., Krauss, M., & Kim, H. (1997). The differential effects of social support on the psychological well-being of aging mothers of adults with mental illness or mental retardation. *Family Relations, 46,* 383–394.

Guarnaccia, P., Angel, R., & Lowe Worobey, J. (1989). The factor structure of the CES-D in the Hispanic health and nutrition examination survey: The influences of ethnicity, gender and language. *Social Science & Medicine, 29*(1), 85–94.

Guarnaccia, P., Good, B., & Kleinman, A. (1990). A critical review of epidemiological studies of Puerto Rican health. *American Journal of Psychiatry, 147,* 1449–1456.

Heller, T., Hsieh, K., & Rowitz, L. (1997). Maternal and paternal caregiving with mental retardation across the lifespan. *Family Relations, 46,* 407–415.

Heller, T., Markwardt, R., Rowitz, L., & Farber, B. (1994). Adaptation of Hispanic families to a member with mental retardation. *American Journal on Mental Retardation, 99,* 289–300.

Keefe, S. (1978). Why Mexican Americans underutilize mental health clinics: Fact and fallacy. In J. Casas & S. Keefe (Eds.), *Mental health in the Mexican American community* (Monograph 7). Los Angeles: Spanish Speaking Mental Health Research Center.

Keefe, S. E., Padilla, A. M., & Carlos, M. L. (1979). Mexican-American extended family as an emotional support system. *Human Organization, 38,* 144–152.

Kolody, B., Vega, W., Meinhardt, K., & Bensussen, G. (1986). The correspondence of health complaints and depressive symptoms among Anglos and Mexican-Americans. *Journal of Nervous and Mental Disease, 174,* 221–228.

Lazarus, R. S., & Folkman, S. (1984). *Stress, appraisal and coping.* New York: Springer.

Li, L. W., Seltzer, M. M., & Greenberg, J. S. (1999). Change in depressive symptoms among daughter caregivers: An 18-month longitudinal study. *Psychology and Aging, 14,* 206–219.

Mahoney, F. I., & Barthel, D. W. (1965). Functional evaluation: The Barthel index. *Maryland State Medical Journal, 14,* 61–65.

Marin, G., & Marin, B. (1991). *Research with Hispanic populations.* Newbury Park, CA: Sage Publications.

Mary, N. (1990). Reactions of Black, Hispanic, and White mothers to having a child with handicaps. *Mental Retardation, 28,* 1–5.

McCallion, P., Janicki, M., & Grant-Griffin, L. (1997). Exploring the impact of culture and acculturation on older families caregiving for persons with developmental disabilities. *Family Relations, 46,* 347–357.

McCubbin, H. I., & Patterson, J. M. (1983). The family stress process: The double ABCX model of adjustment and adaptation. In H. I. McCubbin, M. B. Sussman, & J. M. Patterson (Eds.), *Social stress and the family: Advances and developments in family stress theory and research.* New York: Haworth Press.

Mindel, C. H. (1980). Extended familism among urban Mexican-Americans, Anglos and Blacks. *Hispanic Journal of Behavioral Sciences, 2,* 21–34.

Negy, C., & Woods, D. (1992). The importance of acculturation in understanding research with Hispanic Americans. *Hispanic Journal of Behavioral Science, 14,* 224–247.

Pearlin, L. I., & Schooler, C. (1978). The structure of coping. *Journal of Health and Social Behavior, 19,* 2–21.

Pruchno, R., Hicks Patrick, J., & Burant, C. (1997). African American and white mothers of adults with chronic disabilities: Caregiving burden and satisfaction. *Family Relations, 46,* 335–346.

Purdy, J. K., & Arguello, D. (1992). Hispanic familism in caretaking of older adults: Is it functional? *Journal of Gerontological Social Work, 19*(2), 29–43.

Radloff, L. (1977). The CES-D scale: A self-report depression scale for research in the general population. *Applied Psychological Measurement, 1,* 385–401.

Ramey, S. L., Krauss, M. W., & Simeonsson, R. J. (1989). Research on families: Current assessments and future opportunities. *American Journal on Mental Retardation, 94*(3), ii–vi.

Rodríguez, J. M., & Kosloski, K. (1998). The impact of acculturation on attitudinal familism in a community of Puerto Rican Americans. *Hispanic Journal of Behavioral Sciences, 20,* 375–390.

Rogers-Dulan, J. (1998). Religious connectedness among urban African American families who have a child with disabilities. *Mental Retardation, 36,* 91–103.

Rogler, L., Malgady, R., & Rodríguez, O. (1989). *Hispanics and mental health.* Malabar, FL: Krieger.

Sabogal, F., Marin, G., Otero-Sabogal, R., Marin, B. V., & Perez-Stable, E. J. (1987). Hispanic familism and acculturation: What changes and what doesn't. *Hispanic Journal of Behavioral Science, 9,* 397–412.

Sánchez-Ayéndez, M. (1989). Puerto Rican elderly women: The cultural dimension of social support networks. *Women and health, 14,* 239–252.

Seltzer, G. B., Begun, A., Seltzer, M. S., & Krauss, M. W. (1991). Adults with mental retardation and their aging mothers: Impacts of siblings. *Family Relations, 40,* 310–317.

Seltzer, M. S., Greenberg, J. S., & Krauss, M. W. (1995). A comparison of coping strategies of aging others of adults with mental illness or mental retardation. *Psychology and Aging, 10,* 64–75.

Seltzer, M. S., Greenberg, J. S., Krauss, M. W., & Hong, J. (1997). Predictors and outcomes of the end of co-resident caregiving in aging families of adults with mental retardation or mental illness. *Family Relations, 46,* 13–22.

Seltzer, M., & Heller, T. (1997). Families and caregiving across the life course: Research advances on the influence of context. *Family Relations, 46,* 321–323.

Seltzer, M. S., & Krauss, M. W. (1989). Aging parents with adult mentally retarded children: Family risk factors and social support. *American Journal on Mental Retardation, 94,* 303–312.

Seltzer, M. S., Krauss, M. W., Walsh, P., Conliffe, C., Larson, B., Birkbeck, G., Hong, J., & Choi, S. C. (1995). Cross-national comparisons of aging mothers of adults with intellectual disabilities. *Journal of Intellectual Disability Research, 39,* 408–418.

Stroup-Benham, C., Lawrence, R., & Treviño, F. (1992). CES-D factor structure among Mexican American and Puerto Rican women from single- and couple-headed households. *Hispanic Journal of Behavioral Sciences, 14,* 310–326.

Szapocznik, J., & Kurtines, W. (1993). Family psychology and cultural diversity. *American Psychologist, 48,* 400–407.

Szapocznik, J., Kurtines, W., & Fernandez, T. (1980). Bicultural involvement and adjustment in Hispanic-American youths. *International Journal of Intercultural Relations, 4,* 353–365.

Szapocznik, J., Scopetta, M. A., & Kurtines, W. (1978). Theory and measurement of acculturation. *Interamerican Journal of Psychology, 12,* 113–130.

Tennstedt, S., & Chang, B. (1998). The relative contribution of ethnicity versus socioeconomic status in explaining differences in disability and receipt of informal care. *Journal of Gerontology, 53B,* S61–S70.

Zambrana, R. (1994). Puerto Rican families and social well-being. In M. Baca Zinn & B. Thornton Dill (Eds.), *Women of color in United States society.* Philadelphia: Temple University Press.

Zarit, S. H., Reever, K. E., & Bach-Peterson, J. (1980). Relatives of the impaired elderly: Correlates of feelings of burden. *The Gerontologist, 26,* 260–266.

Zayas, L. H., & Palleja, J. (1988). Puerto Rican familism: Family therapy. *Family Relations, 37,* 260–264.

Received 12/8/98, accepted 6/4/99

Support for the preparation of this manuscript was provided by grants from the National Institute on Aging (R01 AG08768), the National Institute of Child Health and Human Development (T32 HD 07194, T32 HD 07489), and the Merck Scholars II Program. Support was also provided by the Starr Center for Mental Retardation, Heller Graduate School, Brandeis University, and the Waisman Center at the University of Wisconsin-Madison. The author gratefully acknowledges the contributions of Marsha Mallick Seltzer and Marty Wyngaarden Krauss, who provided guidance in the research and feedback on drafts of the manuscript, and gives special thanks to Cynthia García Coll for providing suggestions about cultural issues and encouraging me as a Latina researcher. Requests for reprints should be sent to Sandra M. Magaña, Waisman Center, University of Wisconsin-Madison, 1500 Highland Ave., Madison, WI 53705-2280.

Author

Sandra M. Magaña, University of Wisconsin-Madison.

Twelve Years Later: Adjustment in Families Who Adopted Children With Developmental Disabilities

Laraine Masters Glidden, Ph.D. and Viki E. Johnson, B.A.
1999

Abstract

In most studies positive outcomes for families who have adopted children with developmental disabilities have been described. In this previous research, however, investigators have examined primarily short-term adjustment. In contrast, in the current longitudinal investigation 9 years after an initial interview, we assessed the adjustment and functioning of families who have adopted children with developmental disabilities. Results indicate that nearly 12 years after their adoptions, families remaining in the study reported generally positive outcomes and good adjustment to their adopted children. Whereas there were changes in these families, especially as the children approached adolescence and early adulthood, these changes were perceived as potential sources of reward as well as sources of stress.

It no longer surprises us to read that families adopt children with developmental disabilities nor that the outcomes of these adoptions are primarily positive. At least two reasons exist for this acceptance. First, the field of family research, in particular, and developmental disabilities, in general, has shifted from an almost exclusive focus on pathology to one of recognizing the prevalence of positive adaptation (Abbott & Meredith, 1986; Turnbull et al., 1993). Because we now believe that many birth families derive rewards from rearing their children with developmental disabilities, it is much easier to understand that some families choose this lifework. Second, a number of investigators have explored the adoptions of children with developmental disabilities, and their results are consistent with the interpretation of positive outcomes (Glidden, 1989, 1990, 1991; Lightburn & Pine, 1996; Marx, 1990; Todis & Singer, 1991). Indeed, on the basis of this research, Glidden (1994) was able to conclude that "these adoptions are, for the most part, resoundingly successful" (p. 200).

Nonetheless, some features of the research must qualify the generalizability of this conclusion. Of particular importance is the limited long-term follow-up data. Most studies involve only a single data-collection effort, often conducted fairly soon after the child's adoption. For example, Nelson (1985) reported very positive adjustment in a study of 257 special-needs adoptions, 78% of which involved a child with an impairment. However, she collected data only 2.6 years after the legal adoptions and 4.9 years after placement. Similarly, Rosenthal, Groze, and Aguilar (1991) reported many positive findings from a study of intact adoptions of children with disabilities. Data were collected at one point in time, on average 6.4 years after the child entered the home.

Groze (1996) did collect longitudinal data over a 2-year period and found that more than 95% of 133 parents who had adopted children with special needs indicated that they were getting along very well or fairly well with their adopted children. However, these children, like those in other studies, had been placed an average of only 4 years earlier and, on average, were only 11 years old. Furthermore, the data indicated that some deterioration of functioning had occurred since the previous year.

Simplistic or only partial conclusions result when data are from only one point in time and are collected soon after the adoption. Development of the child and the family system that must accommodate the child are dynamic processes that take place over time (Crnic, Friedrich, & Greenberg, 1983; McCubbin & Patterson, 1983). Adjustment to those processes may be different at different periods of time for all families, both birth and adoptive (Orr, Cameron, Dobson, & Day, 1993; Wikler, 1986). For example, there is ample evidence that birth families will be overpathologized when research explores only their early reactions to a child with a disability, when they are still recovering form the shock of diagnosis (Glidden, 1996; Schroll & Glidden, 1997). Investigators who have examined families at later points in time have frequently concluded that parents are better characterized by commitment rather than sorrow (Adams, Wilgosh, & Sobsey, 1990; Seltzer & Krauss, 1989). Lehman and Roberto (1996) found that parents of teenagers with disabilities actually view their children more positively than do parents of adolescents without disabilities.

Just as birth families have been overpathologized without a focus on the long term, adoptive parents might be glorified without adequate knowledge of the adoption's course during its entire history. It is possible that adoptive parents might adjust well initially because they were engaged in a task that they had freely chosen. This early adjustment might or might not predict success in later challenges, such as school program advocacy, dealing with emerging sexuality, and negotiating the maze of vocational training and placement.

The current study does not suffer from this flaw of early and one time only measurement. It is a report on the third data collection from families who had adopted at least one child with a developmental disability. We have previously described primarily positive outcomes from these families (Glidden, 1989; Glidden & Pursley, 1989; Glidden, Valliere, & Herbert, 1988). Glidden (1989) concluded that all but 5 of the 56 adoptions completed by these families were successful, as measured by a number of outcome items. However, the children had only been in the families an average of 25 months when those data were collected. In a follow-up, conducted approximately 3 years later, Glidden and Pursley (1989) reached the same conclusion.

The current study, then, has two primary purposes. First, it was designed to determine whether the early positive adjustments continue over time. This third data collection took place more than 9 years after the original study, a period of time allowing for a great deal of change and accommodation, potentially both successes and failures. Second, because the children and the families were older and in different stages of the life cycle than were samples in most previous work, in the current study we expanded the dimensions on which adjustment can be measured. At this time of assessment, issues dealing with puberty as well as independent living and job training and placement were part of the adjustment process for many of the families. A peek into the dynamic processes involving these domains of family life should provide insights into the nature of the adjustment process.

Table 1 Characteristics of Samples at Time 1

Follow-up

	Original (Time 1, n = 42)		1 (Time 2, n = 31)		2 (Time 3, n = 18)	
Variable[a]	Mean	SD	Mean	SD	Mean	SD
Parents educated beyond high school	60.00	—	60.00	—	60.00	—
Married	86.00	—	87.00	—	89.00	—
Down syndrome diagnosis	55.00	—	61.00	—	72.00	—
Socioeconomic status[b]	2.80	1.22	2.90	1.25	2.90	1.26
Age at Time 1 (years)						
Mother	37.60	7.57	37.70	7.85	36.50	7.52
Father	39.40	8.11	40.00	8.37	40.00	8.79
Child	8.40	9.47	8.00	10.53	6.00	4.62
Global Adjustment Scale	5.50	1.00	5.60	0.67	5.80	0.44

Note. Mother, father, and child mean ages are 9.6 years older at Time 3 (current) data collection than they were at Time 1.

[a] First three variables are percentages.

[b] Measured by the Registrar General's Index of occupations in Great Britain. 1 or 2 = RG1 or RG2, professional/intermediate; 3 = RG3, skilled manual or nonmanual; 4 = RG4, manual (semi-skilled); 5 = RG5, manual (unskilled) (Classification of Occupations, 1970).

Twelve Years Later: Adjustment in Families Who Adopted Children

Laraine Masters Glidden & Viki E. Johnson

Method

Participants

The participants in the original, or Time 1 sample, were 42 families who had adopted at least one child with a developmental disability. Eighty-eight percent of the families were referred to us by the adoption agencies that had placed the children, with the remainder referred by other families in the sample. Only one of these families refused to participate. Glidden (1986, 1989) reported detailed characteristics of that sample, some of which are summarized in Table 1. In addition to the family, parent, and child characteristics presented in this table, other relevant family information was collected. For example, although 57% of the original sample had no full biological children, 60% of the families had extensive child-rearing experience via step-parenting or previous adoptions in addition to biological children.

Extensive information was also available for many of the children. In addition to diagnostic information and level of functioning, histories prior to adoptive placement were collected. Forty-five percent of the children had been in institutional care for at least some time before the adoptive placement, and 40% had been adopted when they were older than 12 months.

Approximately 3 years after the original contact, we collected data from 31 of these original 42 families, a 74% return rate. Of the 11 other families, 4 could not be located and 7 did not return materials (Glidden & Pursley, 1989). The Time 2 sample of 31 families was representative of the Time 1 sample.

For the current follow-up, our initial mail inquiries to the 31 families in the Time 2 sample yielded data from 14 families within a 3-month period, with mail returned as not deliverable for 3 families. Four additional families responded after a mailed reminder. Subsequently, we attempted to contact the 10 families who had not returned materials after the second inquiry. This attempt was successful for an additional 3 families, and brief telephone interviews were conducted. The remaining 7 families could not be located. Thus, we had some follow-up information for exactly 50% of the Time 1 sample, and 68% of the Time 2 sample.

Sample representativeness. The Time 3 sample of 18 families who returned mail questionnaires was similar to both the Time 2 and Time 1 samples on demographic comparisons as well as comparisons of outcome measures taken at both Times 1 and 2. Characteristics for each of these groups are displayed in Table 1. As can be seen in this table, the majority of children in all three samples had a diagnosis of Down syndrome. Of the 5 children in the current sample who did not have Down syndrome, 2 had cerebral palsy, 1 had brain damage due to nonaccidental injury, 1 had autism along with mental retardation, and 1 had microcephaly. The range of mental retardation was severe/profound to mild. Moreover, some of the children had additional disabilities, including heart defects and physical and sensory impairments.

Although the children in the final sample were somewhat younger than those for whom follow-up information was not available, this difference was not statistically significant. Original mean scores on an outcome variable, the 2- to 6-point Global Adjustment Scale (see later description) also showed the three samples to be similar.

Another corroboration of the representativeness of the Time 3 sample was the similarity of the 3 families who were ultimately contacted by telephone after not responding to two mailings to the 18 families who had responded to one of the two mailings. The adoptees, two 17 years old and one 24 years, were still living at home. In addition, their mothers' responses to the Global Adjustment Scale (Table 2) and the Difficulty/Ease of Rearing (*Results* section) were similar to those of the 18 families who had responded to the mail inquiries. On the Global Adjustment Scale, 2 mothers gave their children

Table 2 Maternal (*n* = 18) Global Assessments (in %)

Score	Time 1	Time 2	Time 3
Outcome expectations			
3 Better	82	81	67
2 As well	8	19	28
1 Less well	—	—	5
Do it again?			
3 Yes	94	100	89
2 Not sure	6	—	5
1 No	—	—	5
Composite			
6 Excellent	76	81	67
5 Good	24	19	22
4 Average	—	—	5
3 Fair	—	—	—
2 Poor	—	—	5

the best possible rating of 6, and the third mother reported that she thought that the adoption had worked out as well as expected and that she would definitely do it again (score of 5). On the Difficulty/Ease of Rearing, a mean of 3.33 was actually a better outcome than the mean of the 18 "on-time" parents. These data lend further confirmation to the conclusion that the families who did not return their mail inquiries, and thus were lost to the sample, were not substantially different in outcomes from those who remained in the sample. Thus, we believe that the final, Time 3, sample of 18 families and their children is quite representative of the original sample.

Materials

Mothers were asked to complete a set of materials that included demographic information, current family structure, and a variety of items designed to assess adjustment outcomes. These adjustment items included (a) a 7-point scale measuring the ease or difficulty of rearing the target child; (b) the Global Adjustment Scale, which combines two 3-point scales, one comparing the adoption outcome to expectations and the other assessing whether the parent would adopt the child again; and (c) a set of 10 items, derived from Glidden and Pursley (1989), measuring the benefits and rewards as well as the problems and difficulties that may have resulted from the child being a part of the family. For this last section the mother was asked to rate individually five benefits and five problems, on a scale of importance from 1 to 5, with 5 indicating greater importance.

In addition, mothers and fathers completed a 102-item version of the Questionnaire on Resources and Stress—QRS (Clayton, Glidden, & Kiphart, 1994; Glidden, 1993). This version contains all the items necessary to re-create each of the three short forms currently in use (Friedrich, Greenberg, & Crnic, 1983; Holroyd, 1985; Salisbury, 1986). In the current paper we present results for the Friedrich short form, the most frequently used version. It contains two factors (Child Characteristics, Physical Limitations) that primarily tap the respondent's perceptions of the characteristics of the family member with disabilities and two factors (Parent and Family Problems, Pessimism) that tap parent and family functioning as well as the functioning level of the family member with disabilities (Clayton et al., 1994). The QRS is answered in a true/false format, and higher scores indicate greater demands, stresses, or strains.

Mothers of adoptees still living at home were asked, in open-ended questions, to descript the primary rewards and benefits as well as the difficulties and problems of the child's being a part of the family. These mothers were also asked to describe any benefits or problems they anticipated for the future in regard to the child being a part of the family. For adoptees no longer living at home, a separate set of questions covered current residence, reasons for the change in residence, frequency of family contact with the child, and whether the child was still considered to be a part of the family. Narrative descriptions of the transition and the current situation were also solicited.

Results

Global Assessments

Maternal global assessments, which combined both of the 3-point adjustment scales, indicated continued satisfaction with the adoptions (Table 2). At the current follow-up, 89% of the composite scores were either 5 or 6, with all but one mother responding in the top two categories with regard to outcome. A repeated measures analysis of variance of the mean global adjustment scores found no significant changes form the original interview to follow-up measurements.

Current Child Residence

Whether the adoptees remained part of their families an average of 11.5 years after their adoptions is an important measure of family adjustment. Nearly 10 years after the original interview, evidence of disruption was not found for the 21 families on whom follow-up information was available. Sixteen of the adoptees were still living at home. The remaining 5 had left home, having moved to residential schools or training centers or semi-independent group residences. Because the moves were made to age-appropriate settings, these cases were not considered to be adoption disruptions. Only one child had left home before age 17; the others left at an average of 20. Narrative responses and scores on adjustment variables indicated that these moves were positive transitions to adulthood for both child and family. For example, all but one of these five families received a 5 or 6 on the 2- to 6-point Global Adjustment Scale, as did 92% of the families with children still living at home.

All of the 5 children living away from home were still considered to be part of their families at the current

©American Association on Mental Retardation

follow-up. They all remained in regular contact with their adoptive parents and siblings. As an example, Chris (pseudonym) moved to a group home at age 21 but continued spending one night per week with his family. Tracy (pseudonym) moved to a group home when she was 19, allowing her to work at a nearby Adult Training Center. At the current follow-up, she had lived away from home for over a year, and her mother described the mixed emotions this transition had involved:

Hardly a day goes by without us missing her being here. We see her regularly—thank goodness! …It's taken over a year to shake off the feeling of guilt that we've "abandoned" her… Now we're able to see that it's the best thing that's happened. She has many people who love her, and although we're still legally responsible, not "isolated" anymore.

Even the "worst" outcome was not an adoption disruption. Sam (pseudonym), the youngest of the adoptees to leave home, was 16 when he began attending a residential "college" that his parents believed was the best placement for his special physical, mental, and behavioral needs. Serving a rural part of England, this school was more than 100 miles away from the adoptive home, so Sam came home usually only on longer holidays, spending a total of about 12 weeks a year with his adoptive family. There was evidence, however, that adjustment in this family had declined over time. Whereas at Times 1 and 2, the Global Adjustment scores had been 6 and 5, respectively, it was only 2 at Time 3. Also, Sam's

mother wrote that family life had improved since he had left and gave an average rating of only 1.8 to benefits and 3.2 to problems. Nonetheless, Sam was still considered to be part of the family. In his mother's words: "He will always be our son and a brother to his adopted brother and sister. We are in regular phone contact when he is away. We are planning for his future care."

Additional Adoptions

Another indicator of the success of the initial adoption is the adoption or fostering of additional children. Nine of the 18 families had adopted or long-term fostered at least one additional child in the intervening 10 years. A total of 17 additional children were eventually adopted or fostered, 14 of whom had a developmental disability. One family had adopted or fostered a total of 4 additional children.

Friedrich QRS

Maternal and paternal means for the four Friedrich QRS factors are displayed in Table 3. As expected, because the children were older, with more mature levels of physical and cognitive functioning, scores on both Child Characteristics and Physical Limitations had decreased between Time 1, the initial interview, and Time 3 (the current follow-up), indicating fewer demands and strains. However, both mothers and fathers showed some

Table 3 Friedrich Questionnaire on Resources and Stress Scores

Factor/Parent[a]	Time 1		Time 2		Time 3	
	Mean	SD	Mean	SD	Mean	SD
Family/Parent problems						
Mother	1.44	1.90	2.81	3.66	4.00	3.46
Father	2.42	3.45	2.50	3.50	3.33	2.42
Pessimism						
Mother	2.56	2.25	3.38	2.50	4.31	3.03
Father	4.08	2.78	4.08	2.71	4.92	1.88
Child Characteristics						
Mother	5.69	2.82	4.86	2.90	4.00	3.08
Father	6.42	3.66	5.25	2.86	5.75	3.08
Physical Limitations						
Mother	2.88	1.82	1.50	1.10	0.81	0.83
Father	2.67	1.61	1.33	.78	.92	.67

Note. Higher scores indicate greater demands and stress.

[a] *N*s = 16 mothers, 12 fathers.

increases in their scores on the Family/Parent Problems and Pessimism factors. In two separate multivariate analyses of variance for mothers and fathers, we assessed differences over time in the four Friedrich factors. The effect of time was significant for mothers, $F(8, 52) = 8.68$, $p < .01$, and fathers, $F(8, 36) = 3.49$, $p < .01$, using the averaged multivariate tests of significance or mixed-model approach as is recommended with small sample size (Norusis, 1994). Follow-up analyses with univariate F tests found the decreases in both Child Characteristics, $F(2, 30) = 4.63$, $p < .05$, and Physical Limitations, $F(2, 30) = 22.65$, $p < .01$, to be significant for mothers, but only the Physical Limitations decrease to be significant for fathers, $F(2, 22) = 14.44$, $p < .01$. In addition, the increase in the Family/Parent Problems scores was significant for mothers, $F(2, 30) = 4.42$, $p < .05$, but not for fathers. Neither mothers nor fathers showed significant changes over time in their scores on the Pessimism factor. In addition to tests of significance, we calculated effect sizes for both mothers and fathers for the change over time for each factor. Only the Physical Limitations factor showed substantial effect sizes, with n^2s = .57 and .60 for fathers and mothers, respectively. Effect sizes for the other three factors for both mothers and fathers ranged from n^2 = .05 to .24.

Difficulty/Ease of Rearing

At both the current follow-up, Time 3, and the previous contact, Time 2, mothers were asked to rate on a 7-point scale the difficulty or ease of rearing their child (1, *very easy*; 7, *very difficult*). At both times, the distribution of scores was normal, with 55% of the children receiving a 3, 4, or 5—neither very difficult nor very easy to raise. The mean at Time 3, 3.89 (standard deviation [*SD*] = 1.71) was slightly higher than the mean of 3.56 at Time 2, (*SD* = 1.46) but the difference was not statistically significant.

Ratings of Benefits and Problems

The mothers' ratings of individual benefits and problems, as displayed in Table 4, provide further evidence of a positive outcome for the majority of adoptions. Each of the five benefits was consistently rated as higher in importance than were the five problems by all but one mother. The average rating of all benefits items, 4.14 (*SD* = 0.78) on the 1- to 5-point scale, was nearly twice as high as the average rating for all problem items, 2.09 (*SD* = 1.07). Using a paired *t* test, we found this differ-

Table 4 Mean Ratings for Benefits and Problems

Category	Rating	
	Mean	SD
Benefits		
Giving and receiving love	4.6	0.9
Positive child characteristics	4.5	0.8
Pride in child's achievements	4.3	1.0
Happiness	4.2	1.0
Strengthen family	3.2	1.4
Problems		
Negative child characteristics	2.6	1.6
Worry, anxiety, or guilt	2.4	1.5
Developmental delay	2.1	1.3
Family disharmony	1.8	1.2
Lack of emotional bonding	1.7	1.3

Note. Items were rated on a scale of 1 to 5, with higher ratings indicating greater importance.

ence to be significant, $t(17) = 5.9$, $p < .01$. The benefit of giving and receiving love had the highest average, receiving a 4 or a 5 from 83% of mothers. The problem of negative child personality/temperament had the highest mean rating of all five problems and was rated a 4 or 5 by 33% of the mothers.

Correlations of the ratings of benefits and problems with both QRS and difficulty/ease of rearing scores were calculated. They were in expected directions, with the correlations for ratings of problems being large and significant both for the QRS total, $r = .73$, $p < .01$, and difficulty/ease of rearing, $r = .52$, $p < .05$. Moreover, each of the problem scores was significantly correlated with the Family and Parent Problems factor of the QRS, with negative characteristics = .54, worry = .67, developmental delay = .60, family disharmony = .63, and lack of emotional bonding = .58. The sum of benefits correlated −.38 and −.02, respectively, with the QRS total and the difficulty/ease of rearing. Neither was significant.

Narrative Reports

Narrative-response questions allowed mothers of the 13 children still living at home to describe the positive and negative outcomes of the adoption as well as the benefits and problems they anticipated for the future. Two independent raters divided the narrative responses into separate items, with 84% agreement on what constituted a specific benefit or problem. A third independent rater resolved the remaining 16% of items into the specific categories. Consistent with results at the Time 2 follow-up (Glidden & Pursley, 1989), the total number of benefits exceeded the total number of problems by nearly two to one, with 13 mothers describing 64 benefits and only 38 problems for the 13 children.

Benefits. Each mother described an average of 4.9 separate benefits (*SD* = 2.4), with all mothers naming at least one benefit in both current and anticipated categories. The benefits described were varied, but the largest category of current benefits (46% of the items) was related to positive child characteristics. These characteristics included intellectual achievements and progress towards independence as in the case of one mother who described her 11-year-old daughter's ability to read and enjoy books as rewarding to her, and a 20-year-old male's mother who wrote about the benefits of seeing him "thinking more for himself, making his own decisions... and growing into a reliable, sensible, caring young man." Personality features such as affection (e.g., "love and cuddles"), sense of humor, and good spirits were described. One mother wrote:

Family life is of prime importance to Drew (pseudonym) and I think we have all benefitted from having him around. Drew has a real zest for life and has shown us all that it is to be appreciated and enjoyed.

The majority of anticipated benefits (56% of the items) focused on pride in the child's future accomplishments. Securing employment, managing money, moving to a more independent setting, or other measures of independence and maturity were mentioned frequently.

Problems. The mothers each reported, on average, 2.9 specific problems (*SD* = 2.0). Again, the categories were varied, but 36% of the items listed as current problems were related to what mothers saw as troublesome behaviors or traits. For example, some mothers described problems stemming from the child's transition to adolescence. A few mothers expressed concern over their child's sexual development during puberty. These mothers described some worry about their adolescents' "budding sexuality"; for example, one mother was not sure how much and what kind of sex education was appropriate. Most of the problems anticipated for the future were categorized as general worry or anxiety over the child. Frequently, however, mothers mentioned concern for the child's ability to reach appropriate independence as an adult: Being able to live away from home, use public transportation, and handle money were cited.

Discussion

The results from this third time of measurement suggest continued good adjustment in almost all families who had adopted chidden with developmental disabilities. None of the adoptions had disrupted and when children did move out of their adoptive homes, it was generally to age-appropriate settings, usually for further education and training. Average maternal global assessments of the adoptions did not decline significantly over time, and although some demands and strains appeared to increase slightly as the children and families grew older, others declined. Indeed, as the children grew older, demands related to physical limitations and other child characteristics decreased as reported by both mothers and fathers, significantly so for the mothers. Mothers rated benefits as more important than problems and described more benefits than problems as being characteristic of their experience. Finally, 50% of the sample had adopted at least one additional child since the original interview almost 10 years earlier. That all these indices point toward positive adaptation is especially important in light of the long-term evaluation involved in the study. The families had a substantial amount of time—an average of 11.5 years—to fully evaluate the benefits and problems involved in raising a child with a disability.

Despite these positive indicators, these parents were not naive about, nor blind to, the difficulties. The significant increase over time in maternal scores on family/parent problems relating to the children indicates some additional demands and strains. Most of the mothers perceived their children's growth into adulthood as a significant source of both rewards and difficulties. Just as Tracy's mother had reported both relief and some guilt when her daughter left home, other mothers were looking forward to these milestones with a mix of anxiety and anticipation. This ambivalence is common to all parents, and parents of adolescents with developmental disabilities are no exception. The tendency to emphasize the positive over the negative, however, has been noted in other mothers rearing children with disabilities. In a recent study, Lehman and Roberto (1996) found that mothers of adolescents with severe disabilities emphasized their child's positive attributes more than did mothers of adolescents without disabilities. In both of these studies, mothers of children with disabilities expressed pride and happiness as a result of their children's personality and behavioral traits, especially their sociability, sense of humor, caring nature, and cooperativeness.

Our conclusions about the current research must be tempered with caution because we had follow-up information for only 50% of the original sample. Nonetheless, all analyses suggest that this sample is representative of the original. Furthermore, the data suggest continuity of functioning confirming the earlier positive prognosis for families who adopt a child with a developmental disability (Glidden, 1989; Glidden & Pursley, 1989; Glidden et al., 1988). What is especially valuable about the current results is that we have found positive family functioning as the child moves through adolescence and beyond. Narrative responses about anticipated benefits and problems indicate that this transition—to adolescence and to adulthood—is an important issue for all families raising a child with a disability. Our results show that this transition is a potential source of stress, but just as important, a source of substantial rewards.

References

Abbott, D. A., & Meredith, W. H. (1986). Strengths of parents with retarded children. *Family Relations, 35,* 371–375.

Adams, B., Wilgosh, L., & Sobsey, D. (1990). Sorrow or commitment: The experience of being a parent of a child with severe disabilities. *Developmental Disability Bulletin, 18,* 49–58.

Classification of occupations. (1970). Her Majesty's Stationery Office.

Clayton, J. M., Glidden, L. M., & Kiphart, M. J. (1994). The Questionnaires on Resources and Stress: What do they measure? *American Journal on Mental Retardation, 99,* 313–316.

Crnic, K. A., Friedrich, W. N., & Greenberg, M. T. (1983). Adaptation of families with mentally retarded children: A model of stress, coping, and family ecology. *American Journal of Mental Deficiency, 88,* 125–138.

Friedrich, W. N., Crnic, K. A., &, Greenberg, M. T. (1983). A short-form of the Questionnaire on Resources and Stress. *American Journal of Mental Deficiency, 88,* 41–48.

Glidden, L. M. (1986). Families who adopt mentally retarded children: Who, why, and what happens. In J. J. Gallagher & P. M. Vietze (Eds.), *Families of handicapped persons: Research, programs, and policy issues* (pp. 129–142). Baltimore: Brookes.

Glidden, L. M. (1989). *Parents for children, children for parents. The adoption alternative.* Washington, DC: American Association on Mental Retardation.

Glidden, L. M. (1990). The wanted ones: Families adopting children with mental retardation. *Journal of Children in Contemporary Society, 21,* 177–205.

Glidden, L. M. (1991). Adopted children with developmental disabilities: Post-placement family functioning. *Children and Youth Services Review, 13,* 363–377.

Glidden, L. M. (1993). What we do not know about families with children who have developmental disabilities: Questionnaire on Resources and Stress as a case study. *American Journal on Mental Retardation, 97,* 481–495.

Glidden, L. M. (1994). Not under my heart, but in it: Families by adoption. In J. Blacher (Ed.), *When there's no place like home: Options for children living apart from their natural families* (pp. 181–209). Baltimore: Brookes.

Glidden, L. M. (1996, July). *Longitudinal perspectives on the well-being of families rearing children with developmental disabilities.* Paper presented at the 10th World Congress of the International Association for the Scientific Study of Intellectual Disabilities, Helsinki, Finland.

Glidden, L. M, & Pursley, J. (1989). Longitudinal comparisons of families who have adopted children with mental retardation. *American Journal on Mental Retardation, 94,* 272–277.

Glidden, L. M., Valliere, V. N., & Herbert, S. L. (1988). Adopted children with mental retardation: Positive family impact. *Mental Retardation, 26,* 119–125.

Groze, V. (1996). A 1 and 2 year follow-up study of adoptive families and special needs children. *Children and Youth Services Review, 18,* 57–82.

Holroyd, J. (1985). *Questionnaire on Resources and Stress manual.* Unpublished manuscript, University of California, Los Angeles, Neuropsychiatric Institute.

Lehman, J. P., & Roberto, K. (1996). Comparison of factors influencing mothers' perceptions about the futures of their adolescent children with and without disabilities. *Mental Retardation, 34,* 27–28.

Lightburn, A., & Pine, B. A. (1996). Supporting and enhancing the adoption of children with developmental disabilities. *Children and Youth Services Review, 18,* 139–162.

Marx, J. (1990). Better me than somebody else: Families reflect on their adoption of children with developmental disabilities. *Journal of Children in Contemporary Society, 21,* 141–174.

McCubbin, H. I., & Patterson, J. M. (1983). The family stress process: The double ABCX model of family adjustment and adaptation. *Marriage and Family Review, 6,* 7–37.

Nelson, K. A. (1985). *On the frontier of adoption: A study of special-needs adoptive families.* New York: Child Welfare League of America.

Norušis, M. J. (1994). *SPSS advanced statistics 6.1.* Chicago: SPSS.

Orr, R. R., Cameron, S. J., Dobson, L. A., & Day, D. M. (1993). Age-related changes in stress experienced by families with a child who has developmental delays. *Mental Retardation, 31,* 171–176.

Rosenthal, J. A., Groze, V., & Aguilar, G. D. (1991). Adoption outcomes for children with handicaps. *Child Welfare, 70,* 623–636.

Salisbury, C. L. (1986). Adaptation of the Questionnaire on Resources and Stress-Short Form. *American Journal of Mental Deficiency, 90,* 456–459.

Schroll, K. M., & Glidden, L. M. (1997, April). *Parental adjustment to rearing children with and without disabilities.* Poster session presented at the biennial meeting of the Society for Research in Child Development, Washington, DC.

Seltzer, M. M., & Krauss, M. (1989). Aging parents with mentally retarded children: Family risk factors and sources of support. *American Journal on Mental Retardation, 94,* 303–312.

Todis, B., & Singer, G. (1991). Stress and stress management in families with adopted children who have severe disabilities. *The Journal of the Association for People with Severe Handicaps, 16,* 3–13.

Turnbull, A. P., Patterson, J. M., Behr, S. K., Murphy, D. L., Marquis, J. G., & Blue-Banning, M. J. (Eds.). (1993). *Cognitive coping, families and disability.* Baltimore: Brookes.

Wikler, L. (1986). Periodic stresses of families of older mentally retarded children: An exploratory study. *American Journal of Mental Deficiency, 90,* 703–706.

Received 7/22/97, first decision 9/22/97, accepted 2/6/98.
Editor-in-Charge: Steven J. Taylor

This manuscript was supported, in part, by Grant No. HD 21993 from the National Institute of Child Health and Human Development awarded to the first author.

Authors

Laraine Masters Glidden, Ph.D., Professor of Psychology, Department of Psychology, St. Mary's College of Maryland, St. Mary's City, MD 20686. **Viki E. Johnson, B.A.,** Graduate Student, Department of Psychology, University of Maryland, College Park, MD 20742. Requests for reprints should be sent to the first author.

PART THREE

Adults with Mental Retardation

The adult with mental retardation is a fairly recent concern of family researchers, for several reasons. The marked increase in life expectancy in general has been even greater for persons with mental retardation, insuring that many adults with disabilities in the 21st century will live with elderly and infirm parents or will outlive them (Braddock, 1999; this volume). Moreover, whereas a high proportion of persons with mental retardation have continued to live with their families all their lives, living apart in the community is becoming more normative; indeed, an increasing number are getting married and having children. This longevity and greater independence face families with new dilemmas and decisions and have led service providers and researchers to seek a better understanding of adult issues.

In the 1980s, family researchers began to embrace a lifespan perspective on the study of disabilities. Whereas research until then had focused primarily on families of children with handicaps, there was now heightened interest in families of adults—those families that are "off cycle" from normative parenting (Seltzer & Ryff, 1994; Turnbull, Summers, & Brotherson, 1986). The preponderance of adult research, however, was on older adults and was informed by the gerontology literature. Thus, with a few exceptions, we find family studies at the two extremes of the life cycle—children and older adults. One of us (Blacher, 2001) has written about the unique stresses on families during the launching stage (roughly ages 18-26), and has argued the need for greater study of this transition to adulthood.

> The transition to adulthood is a time of heightened opportunities but also of new risks. These challenges relate to the individual, the family, and the social service system. For example, the individual with retardation may seek increased independence. Indeed, vocational and adaptive programs for high school students with severe disabilities often reflect goals of autonomy and self-determination (Wehmeyer, 1996). Yet, this is also a time when the young adult is at heightened risk for behavioral and psychiatric disturbances. In the normative case the family system changes as well, as other children, without retardation, go off to college or jobs and usually move out of the family home (Bramston & Cummins, 1998). Perhaps most critically during this period, public school funding ceases and the quest for appropriate programs begins anew. Thus, this period is marked by growth and change, but also by increased uncertainties and challenges, and it is important to understand better the experience of persons and families going through this transitional period (Blacher, 2001).

We have included Andrea Zetlin and Jim Turner's 1985 paper, *Transition from Adolescence to Adulthood: Perspectives of Mentally Retarded Individuals and Their Families*, that used qualitative methodology in an intensive study of the transition period. The authors conducted repeated retrospective interviews with young adults and their parents, asking them detailed questions about the period of late adolescence. They then relate adolescent adjustment to the young adult's subsequent success in independent living.

We also have included Lynn Wikler's 1986 study, *Periodic Stresses of Families of Older Mentally Retarded Children: An Exploratory Study*, that is one of the earliest empirical papers examining family stress in young adulthood. Wikler demonstrated that family stress increased during transitions in developmental stage of the person with retardation. Her interpretation is that the onset of adulthood "may reactivate parental wistfulness over 'what is' in contrast to 'what might have been' " (p. 703-4). Yet the increased stress that was found also may have resulted from behavioral changes in the individual with mental retardation as well as new challenges in coping with the service delivery system (Blacher, 2001). In 1981, Suelzle and Keenan examined changes in available family support networks over the life cycle of persons with retardation; they found that parents of older children, ages 19-21, were less supported, more isolated, and more in need of expanded services than parents of younger ones. Although this may be less true today, parents do worry about what their sons or daughters will be doing when mandated public school services end at age 22 (Thorin, Yovanoff, & Irvin, 1996).

The majority of the AAMR literature, however, focuses on aging parents. There are three overlapping themes that have been of particular interest to family researchers at this stage of the life cycle. First is the overarching issue of "permanency planning," looking to the future and making specific plans, particularly regarding residential and financial security (Heller & Factor, 1991; Janicki & Wisniewski, 1985; Pruchno & Patrick, 1999; Seltzer & Seltzer, 1985). Arguably the primary concern for parents, and especially those who are elderly, is how their son or daughter with retardation will be provided for after their death. Oddly, however, despite the universality of the concern, studies in recent years have found that the majority of parents have taken few if any steps to formally plan ahead (Heller & Factor, 1988; Freedman, Krauss, & Seltzer, 1997). One drawback may be lack of information. Smith (1997) surveyed older mothers about their service needs and found that among the highest rated unmet needs were information about guardianship, financial planning, and residential programs.

Second is the cumulative effect of parenting over such a long period on maternal well-being, with emphasis not only on stress and burden but on caretaking satisfaction. There is evidence that caretaking burden and satisfaction are not two ends of the same continuum, but different domains that are affected by different factors. We have included Marsha Seltzer and Marty Krauss' paper from the 1989 AJMR special issue on family research, *Aging Parents with Adult Mentally Retarded Children: Family Risk Factors and Social Support*, that focuses on older mothers as caregivers of adult offspring with mental retardation. These authors found that maternal well-being was as high as or higher than in samples of mothers from the gerontology literature caring for aging elderly parents. It was particularly high when the mother perceived the family social climate positively.

Third is the related observation that co-residence brings positive benefits to both the individual with retardation and to the caregiver (Seltzer & Krauss, 1994). For many families the adult with mental retardation makes positive contributions to the parents, especially as parents age and are themselves in need of assistance (Greenberg & Becker, 1988). This includes performing actual household tasks as well as companionship more generally. Heller and Factor (1988) found that 61% of mothers in their sample said that caring for the family member with retardation "provided meaning to their lives." We have included a subsequent paper by Tamar Heller, Alison Miller, and Alan Factor (1997), *Adults With Mental Retardation as Supports to Their Parents: Effects on Parental Caregiving Appraisal*. Among the noteworthy findings of this study was this: "Parents who received support from their son or daughter with mental retardation experienced greater caregiving satisfaction and less caregiving burden." (p. 344).

Adults with Mental Retardation as Parents

Parenting challenges are multiplied when the adult son or daughter with mental retardation becomes a parent. This places their own children at particularly high risk for delays themselves, and adds a new dimension to the parenting responsibilities of the grandparents.

Historically, adults with mental retardation were strongly discouraged from having children. Misgivings about people with mental retardation as parents have been reflected directly in laws sanctioning sterilization, laws prohibiting marriage, and legal provisions for terminating parental rights (Scheerenberger, 1983). They also have been reflected indirectly by denied opportunities for social/sexual relationships, by community and family attitudes, by placement in institutions, and by gender separation within such settings. For families, perhaps the most difficult aspect of the modern principles of normalization and inclusion, is that romance and even marriage come with the territory. People with mental retardation increasingly are marrying and having children.

The key question is: Can people with mental retardation parent with at least the minimal competence that is a child's right (Whitman & Accardo, 1990)? Most of the literature focuses on mothers with mental retardation, excluding fathers. The ability of young women with mental retardation to adequately raise children has been discussed in AJMR journals throughout the century (Booth & Booth, 2000; Doll, 1929; Gamble, 1950; Mikelson, 1947, 1949), but with more intense attention in the past two decades. We have included Mikelson's 1947 study entitled *The Feeble-minded Parent: A Study of 90 Family Cases.* This is one of the earliest survey studies in the AAMR journals, examining the characteristics of families with at least one mentally retarded parent and at least one child. Mikelson divided parents according to the adequacy of child care (Satisfactory, Questionable, or Unsatisfactory) and contrasted them on child, parent, and family characteristics. One finding, that parents' serious mental health problems related strongly to the adequacy of child care, anticipates the considerable interest today in dual diagnosis (mental retardation and mental disorder). The reader may be intrigued by Mikelson's survey data and, at the same time, differ with her interpretations, which are framed in the pro-sterilization stance of the times.

A recent and provocative essay by sociologist Carol Ronai (1997), "On Loving and Hating My Mentally Retarded Mother," examines parenting from the child's point of view. Ronai focuses, in disturbingly graphic detail, on a childhood filled with sexual and physical abuse and acknowledges the deep ambivalence she feels. Although her abusive experience is extreme, the experience of having to be, in effect, parent to her parent, is more universal:

Though my mother loved me, I betrayed her by growing up. Year after year we grew further apart until I finally abandoned her to dolls, coloring, and make-believe. She was not growing with me, and as time went by, she became an embarrassment and a liability (430).

Whether I overtly knew about her retardation or not, the project, always, was to pass as a normal mother-daughter couple. Passing meant I wrote notes to school for my absences and had her recopy them in her own handwriting. Passing meant trying not to get into situations where my friends or their parents met her. . . . I became threatened by her when she violated this tacit contract of normalcy. When she took over my dolls, got my homework wrong, misread the book, slipped up in a speech performance, failed to protect me from my father, she was throwing it in my face, "I am not a normal mother" (p. 430).

In considering whether parenting is adequate, the legal system looks at provision of love and affection, performing housekeeping tasks, attending to the child's physical needs, and stimulating the child intellectually (Whitman & Accardo, 1990). There is evidence that parents with mental retardation are often deficient in meeting the medical, emotional, and cognitive needs of children, with a heightened incidence of child abuse and neglect (Schilling, Schinke, Blythe, & Barth, 1982).

Beyond the cognitive and adaptive behavior deficits that define mental retardation, these parents often face the multiple problems of poverty, discrimination, frequent isolation from formal and informal supports, and the absence of adequate parenting role models (Whitman, Graves, & Accardo, 1989). It has been important in studying parenting to distinguish between developmental risk to children associated with maternal intellectual limitations and risk associated primarily with poverty. In studies controlling for poverty, mothers with low IQ still have been found to be less sensitive, responsive, and reinforcing to their children when compared to mothers with normal IQ but low SES (Feldman, Case, Rincover, Towns, & Betel, 1989; Keltner, 1994; Tymchuk & Andron, 1992).

Feldman and his colleagues have conducted a series of studies focused on understanding the consequences to children of maternal mental retardation and the effectiveness of interventions to promote better parenting. We have included Maurice Feldman and Nicole Walton-Allen's 1997 paper, *Effects of Maternal Mental Retardation and Poverty on Intellectual, Academic, and Behavioral Status of School-Age Children*. This comparison group study teases out the separate effects on children of maternal mental retardation and poverty, and examines child development across a range of domains. Unfortunately, not a single child being raised by a mother with mental retardation escaped having significant deficits in at least one domain.

This raises the question, first asked by Mickelson in 1949, "Can mentally deficient parents be helped to give their children better care?" Budd and Greenspan (1985), reviewing the sparse intervention literature, concluded that parents' actual behavior toward their children is more important than intelligence in whether parents are adequate caregivers. There is some evidence that parents with mental retardation can benefit from intervention, especially when it is focused on specific skill areas (Slater, 1986 in this volume; Tymchuck, Andron, & Rahbar, 1988; Tymchuck, 1992). We have included a 1993 study by Joel Bakken, Raymond Miltenberger, and Scott Schauss, *Teaching Parents with Mental Retardation: Knowledge Versus Skills*; this is a methodologically strong demonstration of targeted intervention involving five mothers with mild mental retardation. These authors found that increasing knowledge about childrearing does not translate into practice unless actual skills are also taught.

Children's outcomes, however, are not a consequence of parenting inadequacies alone. In a qualitative interview study with adult children of parents who have "learning difficulties," Booth and Booth (2000) examined not only risk but also factors in the child's life context that contributed to resilience. For example, they introduce the notion of "distributed competence," pointing out that childrearing is a distributed enterprise including the influences of multiple persons who support parents in their parenting. Our final entry in this section looks to adults with retardation themselves to give voice to the parenting experience. We have included Gwynnyth Llewellyn's (1995) study of six couples in Australia entitled *Relationships and Social Support: Views of Parents with Mental Retardation/Intellectual Disability*. In interviews with the couples, the author explored "the shared experience of being a person with intellectual disability and a parent" (p. 350) and documented their views about "support they receive and the type of support they want, from whom, and in what way" (p. 360). The qualitative methodology, which involved numerous interviews and observations over two years, yielded personal perspectives that can inform the efforts of service providers.

References

Bakken, J., Miltenberger, R. G., & Schauss, S. (1993). Teaching parents with mental retardation: Knowledge versus skills. *American Journal on Mental Retardation, 97*, 405–417.

Blacher, J. (2001). The transition to adulthood: Mental retardation, families, and culture. *American Journal on Mental Retardation, 106*, 173–188.

Booth, T., & Booth. W. (2000). Against the odds: Growing up with parents who have learning difficulties. *Mental Retardation, 38*, 1–14.

Braddock, D. (1999). Aging and developmental disabilities: Demographic and policy issues affecting American families. *Mental Retardation, 37*, 155–161.

Bramston, P., & Cummins, R. A. (1998). Stress and the move into community accommodation. *Journal of Intellectual & Developmental Disabilities, 23*, 295–308.

Budd, K., & Greenspan, W. (1985). Parameters of successful and unsuccessful intervention for parents who are mentally retarded. *Mental Retardation, 23*, 269–273.

Doll, E. (1929). Community control of the feebleminded. *Journal of Psycho-Asthenics, 34*, 161–175.

Feldman, M. A., Case, L., Rincover, A., Towns, F., & Betel, J. (1989). Parent education project III. Increasing responsivity and affection in developmentally handicapped mothers: Component analysis, generalization, and effects on child language. *Journal of Applied Behavior Analysis, 22,* 211–222.

Feldman, M. A., & Walton-Allen, N. (1997). Effects of maternal mental retardation and poverty on intellectual, academic, and behavioral status of school-age children. *American Journal on Mental Retardation. 101,* 352-363.

Freedman, R. I., Krauss, M. W., & Seltzer, M. M. (1997). Aging parents' residential plans for adult children with mental retardation. *Mental Retardation, 35,* 114–123.

Gamble, C. (1951). The prevention of mental deficiency by sterilization, 1949–. *American Journal of Mental Deficiency, 56,* 192–197.

Greenberg, J., & Becker, M. (1988). Aging parents as family resources. *The Gerontologist, 28,* 786–791.

Heller, T., & Factor, A. (1988). Permanency planning among black and white family caregivers of older adults with mental retardation. *Mental Retardation, 26,* 203–208.

Heller, T., & Factor, A. (1991). Permanency planning for adults with mental retardation living with family caregivers. *American Journal on Mental Retardation, 96,* 163–176.

Heller, T., Miller, A. B., & Factor, A. (1997). Adults with mental retardation as supports to their parents: Effects on parental caregiving appraisal. *Mental Retardation, 35,* 338–346.

Janicki, M. P., & Wisniewski, H. M. (Eds.) (1985). *Aging and developmental disabilities.* Baltimore: Brookes.

Keltner, B. (1994). Home environments of mothers with mental retardation. *Mental Retardation, 32,* 123-127.

Llewellyn, G. (1995). Relationships and social support: Views of parents with mental retardation/intellectual disability. *Mental Retardation, 33,* 349-363.

Mickelson, P. (1947). The feebleminded parents: A study of 90 family cases. *American Journal of Mental Deficiency, 51,* 644–653.

Mikelson, P. (1949). Can mentally deficient parents be helped to give their children better care?: An analysis of the effects of community supervision, sterilization, and institutionalization upon 90 families. *American Journal of Mental Deficiency, 53,* 516–534.

Pruchno, R. A., & Patrick, J. H. (1999). Effects of formal and familial residential plans for adults with mental retardation on their aging mothers. *American Journal on Mental Retardation, 104,* 38–52.

Ronai, C. R. (1997). On loving and hating my mentally retarded mother. *Mental Retardation, 35,* 417–432.

Scheerenberger, R. C. (1983). *A history of mental retardation.* Baltimore: Brookes.

Schilling, R. F., Schinke, S. P., Blythe, B. J., & Barth, R. P. (1982). Child maltreatment and mentally retarded parents: Is there a relationship? *Mental Retardation, 20,* 201–209.

Seltzer, M. M., & Krauss, M. W. (1989). Aging parents with adult mentally retarded children: Family risk factors and sources of support. *American Journal on Mental Retardation, 94,* 303–312.

Seltzer, M. M., & Krauss, M. W. (1994). Aging parents with resident adult children. The impact of lifelong caregiving. In M. M. Seltzer, M. W. Krauss, & M. P. Janicki (Eds.), *Life course perspectives on adulthood and old age* (pp. 3–18). Washington, DC: The American Association on Mental Retardation.

Seltzer, M. M., & Ryff, C. (1994). Parenting across the lifespan: The normative and nonnormative cases. In D. L. Featherman, R. Lerner, & M. Perlmutter (Eds.), *Life-span development and behavior* (Vol. 12), Hillsdale, NJ: Erlbaum.

Seltzer, M. M., & Seltzer, G. B. (1985). The elderly mentally retarded: A group in need of service. In G. S. Getzel & M. J. Mellor (Eds.), *Gerontological social work practice in the community* (pp. 99–119). New York: Haworth Press.

Slater, M. A. (1986). Modification of mother-child interaction processes in families with children at risk for mental retardation. *American Journal of Mental Deficiency, 91*, 257–267.

Smith, G. C. (1997). Aging families of adults with mental retardation: Patterns and correlates of service use, need, and knowledge. *American Journal on Mental Retardation, 102*, 13–26.

Suelzle, M., & Keenan, V. (1981). Changes in family support networks over the life cycle of mentally retarded persons. *American Journal of Mental Deficiency, 86*, 267–274.

Thorin, E., Yovanoff, P., & Irvin, L. (1996). Dilemmas faced by families during their young adults' transitions to adulthood: A brief report. *Mental Retardation, 34*, 117–120.

Turnbull, A. P., Summers, J. A., & Brotherson, M. J. (1986). Family life cycle: Theoretical and empirical implications and future directions for families with mentally retarded members. In J. J. Gallagher and P. M. Vietze (Eds.), *Families of handicapped persons: Research, programs, and policy issues* (pp. 45–65). Baltimore: Brookes.

Tymchuck, A. J. (1992). Predicting adequacy of parenting by people with mental retardation. *Child Abuse and Neglect, 16*, 165–178.

Tymchuck, A. J., & Andron, L. (1992). Project parenting: Child interactional training with mothers who are mentally handicapped. *Mental Handicap Research, 5*, 4–32.

Tymchuck, A. J., Andron, L., & Rahbar, B. (1988). Effective decision-making/problem-solving training with mothers who have mental retardation. *American Journal on Mental Retardation, 92*, 510–516.

Wehmeyer, M. L. (1996). Self-determination as an educational outcome: Why is it important to children, youth and adults with disabilities? In D. J. Sands & M. L. Wehmeyer (Eds.), *Self-determination across the life span: Independence and choice for people with disabilities* (pp. 15–34). Baltimore: Paul H. Brookes.

Whitman, B. Y., & Accardo, P. J. (1990). *When a parent is mentally retarded.* Baltimore: Brookes.

Whitman, B. Y., Graves, B., & Accardo, P. J. (1989 - September). Training in parenting skills for adults with mental retardation. *Social Work*, 431–434.

Wikler, L. M. (1986). Periodic stresses of families of older mentally retarded children: An exploratory study. *American Journal of Mental Deficiency, 90*, 703–706.

Zetlin, A. G., & Turner, J. L. (1985). Transition from adolescence to adulthood: Perspectives of mentally retarded individuals and their families. *American Journal on Mental Retardation, 101*, 352-363.

Periodic Stresses of Families of Older Mentally Retarded Children: An Exploratory Study

Lynn McDonald Wikler
1986

Abstract

The relationship of transitions and stress in 60 families of older mentally retarded children were examined. Families whose offspring were entering adolescence (11 to 15 years old) and young adulthood (20 to 21 years old) were identified as being in transition. They were contrasted with families whose offspring were not those ages. Families were assessed once and then again 2 years later. Results at both points in time suggest support for a relationship between transition in developmental stage of the retarded person and increased levels of family stress.

Although the family crisis provoked by the initial diagnosis of mental retardation has been extensively examined (for a review of the literature, see Blacher, 1984), stresses of families of older retarded children have received less attention. Previous investigators have reported that families may find it increasingly complex to cope with their retarded children as the children get older (Birenbaum, 1971; Farber, 1968). In a study contrasting retrospective parent accounts of stress levels over time with perceptions of social services staff members about parental adjustment over time, human service workers underestimated the stresses of families in later periods of the life cycle (Wikler, Wasow, & Hatfield, 1981). Another study indicated that parents of older retarded children receive less support, are more isolated, and are in more need of expanded services than are those of younger retarded children (Suelzle & Keenan, 1981), but not all of their reported patterns could be explained by increased age alone, suggesting that certain life cycle stages require more service utilization than others.

That stress peaks periodically over time in families of retarded children has been suggested by various clinical observers (Adams, 1971; Berger & Foster, 1976; Humphrey & Jacobsen, 1979; Menolascino, 1977; Olshansky, 1962; Wikler, 1981), but periodic change in levels of family stress is just beginning to be examined systematically. The periodicity theory may be summarized as follows: Certain periods in the life cycle of a family with a retarded child may be associated with more manifest familial distress than are other periods. In this paper I have described a preliminary exploration of this proposal as it relates to older retarded children.

Two periods of transition of children with mental retardation were examined: the onset of adolescence and the onset of adulthood (the 21st birthday, ages 20 to 21). These are socially designated stages as well as developmental milestones and, therefore, normative transition periods for families. An assumption here is that later transitions in the life span of a retarded child may reactivate parental wistfulness over "what is" in contrast to "what might have been." Family stress levels were assessed once and then 2 years later, at which point many of the families had shifted into or out of a transition period.

Subjects were a nonrandom sample of 60 volunteer mothers of retarded children living at home. Letters inviting participation in a study of life changes were sent by the heads of two organizations: the Milwaukee, Wisconsin, Association of Retarded Citizens (37 out of 250 [15%] responded) and the Archdiocese of Milwaukee to families attending their special retreats (23 out of 98 [24%] responded). All of the families were white and from a large metropolitan area; all respondents but one were mothers; all were in intact marriages; 66% were upper-middle class; 31% were middle and lower-middle, and 3% were lower class (using Hollingshead & Redlich's, 1958, Four-Factor Index of Social Position).

A total of 60 families were assessed at Year 1 (Time 1); however, 3 children were younger than age 7 and were therefore not included in Time 1 data; 47 families were assessed at Year 3 (Time 2), with one younger than age 7, who was not included. Attrition at Time 2 was due to unreachable families or to not having time to participate; one child had died, and 2 families had placed their child outside the home.

The sample was divided by chronological age (CA) of the retarded child into five groups: latency (ages 7 to 10), onset of adolescence (11 to 15), middle adolescence

Table 1 Stresses of Families of Retarded Chidlren

Time	Life changes not related to retardation[a]		Family stress related to retardation[b]	
	Mean	SD	Mean	SD
Time 1				
Transition families (n = 28)	154.1	126.0	73.44	28.33
Nontransition families (n = 29)	161.0	131.9	53.90	26.36
Time 2				
Transition family (n = 14)	142.2	107.7	69.77	27.15
Nontransition family (n = 32)	149.2	81.6	55.68	24.62

[a] Schedule of Recent Events.

[b] Questionnaire on Resources and Stress.

(16 to 19), onset of adulthood (20 to 21), and early adulthood (22 to 25). Families with children at the onset of adolescence and onset of adulthood were combined as transition families: $n = 28$ in Time 1 and $n = 14$ in Time 2. The nontransition families were all others with children who were at least age 7: $n = 29$ in Time 1 and $n = 32$ in Time 2. Many of the families shifted categories between Times 1 and 2 measurements.

The subjects were sent an informed consent letter, a demographic questionnaire, the Questionnaire on Resources and Stress (Holroyd, 1974) and the Holmes and Rahe (1967) Schedule of Recent Events Checklist. Each

received a follow-up phone call from a research associate, with a second follow-up phone call for late responders. The same procedure was used at both time periods. A graduate student made all of the phone calls for each measurement period.

The dependent variable, level of family stress, was the total sum score of the Questionnaire on Resources and Stress (Holroyd, 1974). This measure is a 285-item true–false self-administered questionnaire designed to assess reported stresses of families caring for chronically disabled members. It is a frequently used instrument reported to differentiate types of stresses experienced by families raising children with varying handicapping conditions (Beckman, 1983; Friedrich, 1979; Holroyd, Brown, Wikler, & Simmons, 1975; Holroyd & McArthur, 1976) and to be an outcome measure indicating amount of stress mothers are experiencing. The questions were reviewed for content related to developmental transitions in order to rule out circularity between the independent and dependent variable. Scores on this instrument were used to determine whether the family showed increased stress levels during transition periods.

To assess additional life stressors during the 6 months preceding each assessment period that

Figure 1 Averages of Questionnaire on Resources and Stress sums for families.

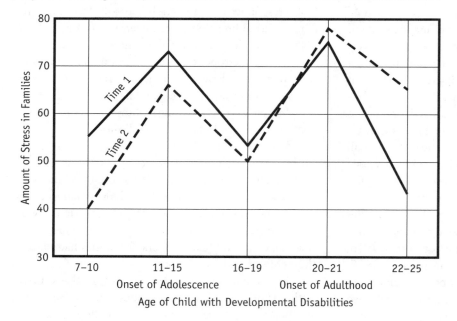

©American Association on Mental Retardation

might also vary with the transition vs. nontransition status of these families, I used a short, widely used instrument, the Holmes and Rahe Schedule of Recent Events (1967). Although there have been alternatives to this checklist proposed (Dohrenwend & Dohrenwend, 1974; Sarason, Johnson, & Siegel, 1978), there is support for its use in this kind of study (Tausig, 1982). Scores obtained with this second instrument provided an estimate of the number of recent life changes of the family that could produce stress but that were not specifically related to the child's handicap.

There were no significant differences between the transition and nontransition families on the Schedule of Recent Events scores for either time period. In contrast, the family stress scores on the Questionnaire on Resources and Stress were significantly higher at both times for transition families than for nontransition families.

In addition, total Questionnaire on Resources and Stress scores were plotted (Figure 1) for the five age groups so that the stress levels could be visualized for each age group. The resulting picture is an M-like figure emerging at Times 1 and 2, although many families shifted categories over the intervening 2 years. Consistent with my expectations, families had higher reported family stress related to the child's disability during these two period of transition. Because little is known about the self-selection process that took place in the sample, the generalizability of these exploratory results is limited. Furthermore, in the absence of a control group of families without handicapped members, it may be that the increased stress levels include stresses encountered by all families of children, including nondelayed children, but that possibility need not reduce the utility of these initial results for either practitioners or clinical researchers in the field of mental retardation. In addition, characteristics of the child and of the family and support network variables that might affect the impact of the transitions on stress levels of families should be assessed. For example, although increased stress may characterize different points in a family's history, different types of stress may occur over time, each of which might imply different service needs.

If periods of increased stress can be anticipated, clinical and policy strategies can be developed to aid families. Indeed, the family's awareness that an upcoming period may provoke family stress could be beneficial in coping with the impact of the stressor event (Golan, 1981). Information about periods of stress vulnerability could be used to plan for and to intervene with families of mentally retarded children proactively rather than in reaction to recurring crises. In this study two specific periods of transition of older retarded children that may be associated with increased disruption for families were identified.

References

Adams, M. (1971). *Mental retardation and its social dimensions.* New York: Columbia University Press.

Beckman, P. (1983). Influence of selected child characteristics on stress in families of handicapped infants. *American Journal of Mental Deficiency, 88,* 150–156.

Berger, M., & Foster, M. (1976). Family-level interventions for retarded children: A multivariate approach to issues and strategies. *Multivariate Experimental Clinical Research, 2,* 1–21.

Birenbaum, A. (1979). The mentally retarded child in the home and the family cycle. *Journal of Health and Social Behavior, 12,* 55–65.

Blacher, J. (1984). Sequential stages of parental adjustment to the birth of a child with handicaps: Fact or artifact. *Mental Retardation, 22,* 55–68.

Dohrenwend, B. S., & Dohrenwend, B. P. (Eds.). (1974). *Stressful life events: Their nature and effect.* New York: Wiley.

Farber, B. (1968). *Mental retardation: its social context and social consequences.* New York: Houghton-Mifflin.

Friedrich, W. N. (1979). Predictors of the coping behavior of mothers of handicapped children. *Journal of Consulting and Clinical Psychology, 47,* 1140–1141.

Golan, N. (1981). *Passing through transitions: A guide for practitioners.* New York: Free Press.

Hollingshead, A. B., & Redlich, M. (1958). *Social class and mental illness: A community study.* New York: Wiley.

Holmes, T., & Rahe, R. (1967). The social readjustment rating scale. *Journal of Psychosomatic Research, 11,* 213–218.

Holroyd, J. (1974). The questionnaire on resources and stress: An instrument to measure family response to a handicapped family member. *Journal of Community Psychology, 2,* 92–94.

Holroyd, J., Brown, N., Wikler, L., & Simmons, J. (1975). Stress in families of institutionalized vs. non-institutionalized autistic children. *Journal of Community Consulting Psychology, 3,* 26–31.

Holroyd, J., & McArthur, D. (1976). Mental retardation and stress of the parents: A contrast between Down's syndrome and childhood autism. *American Journal of Mental Deficiency, 80,* 431–436.

Humphrey, R., & Jacobsen, R. B. (1979). Families in crisis: Research and theory in child mental retardation. *Social Casework, 60,* 578–601.

Menolascino, F. (1977). *Challenges in mental retardation: Progressive ideologies and services.* New York: Human Sciences Press.

Olshansky, S. (1962). Chronic sorrow: A response to having a mentally defective child. *Social Casework, 43,* 190–192.

Sarason, T. G., Johnson, J. H., & Siegel, J. M. (1978). Assessing the impact of life changes: Development of the life experience survey. *Journal of Consulting and Clinical Psychology, 46,* 932–946.

Suelzle, M., & Keenan, V. (1981). Changes in family support networks over the life cycle of mentally retarded persons. *American Journal of Mental Deficiency, 86,* 267–274.

Tausig, M. (1982). Measuring life events. *Journal of Health and Social Behavior, 23,* 52–64.

Wikler, L. (1981). Chronic stresses in families of mentally retarded children. *Family Relations, 30,* 281–288.

Wikler, L., Wasow, M., & Hatfield, E. (1981). Chronic sorrow revisited: Attitudes of parents and professionals about adjustment to mental retardation. *American Journal of Orthopsychiatry, 51,* 63–70.

This research was supported in part by Grant No. 2-P30-HDO-3352. This paper is based on a report presented at the annual meeting of the American Association on Mental Deficiency, Dallas, May 1983. Sincere appreciation is extended to Dorothy Circo, Maggie Thompson, and Loretta Moir for data collection. Requests for reprints should be sent to Lynn McDonald Wikler, University of Wisconsin, School of Social Work, 425 Henry Mall, Madison, WI 53706.

Author

Lynn McDonald Wikler, University of Wisconsin-Madison.

Transition From Adolescence to Adulthood: Perspectives of Mentally Retarded Individuals and Their Families

Andrea G. Zetlin and Jim L. Turner
1985

Abstract

From ethnographic fieldnotes and life history interviews, basic descriptive data were presented that depict the adolescent life stage as it was recounted by 25 mildly retarded individuals and their parents. Patterns of adolescent adjustment are described in terms of the issues and concerns that preoccupied the retarded adolescents, the problem behavior exhibited by these young persons, and what parents did about their children's problems. Comparison of adolescent adjustment patterns and current adult status revealed that the central concerns of adolescence remain problems for only some mildly retarded adults. The majority regard normative achievements as most salient to their self-identity and well-being.

During adolescence, deep and lasting changes occur, including emancipation from parental attachment, development of attitudes and styles of behavior in social and sexual domains, emergence of a more complete concept of self, and formation of vocational plans and life aspirations (Bachman et al., 1969; Group for the Advancement of Psychiatry, 1968; Newman & Newman, 1979; White & Spiesman, 1968). It had traditionally been held that cognitive and emotional disorganization is pervasive as adolescents struggle through self-consciousness, impulsiveness, idealism, and intensity (Freud, 1969; Gaier, 1969; Jersild, 1963; Jessor & Jessor, 1977). As Erikson (1968) noted, "it is difficult to be tolerant if deep down you are not quite sure that you are a man or woman, that you will ever grow together again and be attractive, that you will be able to master your drives, that you really know who you are, that you know what you want to be, that you know what you look like to others, and that you will know how to make the right decision without committing yourself to the wrong friend, sexual partner, leader, or career" (p. 200). Recently, however, "sturm and drang" versions of the adolescent experience have been perceived as more myth than reality (Hill, 1980). Contemporary research supports the view that, for the majority of adolescents, change is of a gradual, emergent nature, not a time of upheaval and distress (Dusek & Flaherty, 1981; Offer, Marcus, & Offer, 1970).

Even in terms of movement away from the family context, recent studies reveal that although some families undergo a great deal of turbulence during this period, many others have a much more positive experience. The majority of parents respond to their maturing children with some degree of recognition and accommodation and with resulting transformations in family relations and styles of interaction. These parents provide increased support for individuation by gradually integrating into their children's daily lives the information and experience necessary for participation in adult life. As adolescents accumulate skills and knowledge, they begin to assume a more adult pattern of behavior.

For mentally retarded persons, it may well be that the adolescent developmental period is a unique stage of growth. Some investigators contend that although retarded individuals experience the same biological changes and drives as nonretarded youngsters, the issues associated with adolescence—emancipation, self-concept, sexuality—are exacerbated by the presence of their handicap (Abramson, Ash, & Nash, 1979; Irwin, 1977; Paulson & Stone, 1973; Sigman, in press). Retarded adolescents have to struggle with these highly charged issues with cognitive competencies similar to those of younger children. They also face conflicting role expectations from family, peers, and self due to the discrepancy between their chronological age (CA) and physical maturity and their functional capacity.

Because parents are uncertain or in conflict as to what retarded adolescents' adult roles will be, they are unsure how to prepare their teenagers for the transition to adulthood. They are more likely to encourage dependency, obedience, and child-like behavior rather than independence, self-direction, assumption of responsibility, and sexual awareness (Paulson & Stone, 1973; Winik, Zetlin, & Kaufman, in press; Zetlin, Turner, & Winik, in press). Even with limited cognitive ability, retarded adolescents are increasingly aware of their own limitations and exceptional status; theoretically, this awareness may lead to feelings of dissonance and be expressed in behavioral or emotional problems. Thus, for retarded young persons, adolescence may in fact be a time of increased turmoil and stress as they struggle to determine their relationship to society and the roles and lifestyles they will assume.

The life circumstances of the 25 individuals who comprised our sample serve to illustrate some of the major issues and concerns evident during this life stage. In what follows, we attempt to reconstruct patterns of adolescent adjustment from retrospective accounts by sample members and their parents. Through these depictions of the past, we can begin to understand how these retarded individuals conceptualize past life circumstances and what they regard as most salient to their self-perception as adolescents. Our observations of the current living status of our sample members also provide a base from which to explore whether issues perceived to be highly problematic during the second decade of life have become less salient for them as adults or whether they continue as central concerns.

Method

Sample

Between July 1980, and December 1981, 46 individuals living in the greater Los Angeles area were studied using intensive, naturalistic methods. One of the major goals of this research was to understand the personal and social adjustment of mildly retarded adults living independently in the community. More specifically, we sought to document the life experiences and coping responses of sample members as they adapt to everyday living.

Potential sample members were located through a variety of public agencies serving developmentally disabled persons, including California Regional Centers, residential facilities, sheltered workshops, social groups, and training programs. Some 60 individuals were nominated by agency staff personnel, and each person was then interviewed by a member of our research team to determine how well they met our criteria for inclusion: (a) Caucasian; (b) independent living status; (c) no significant physical handicap or mental illness; and (d) willingness to participate in the study. In all, 47 persons

Table 1 Basic Demographic Characteristics of Full Sample and Subsample

Characteristics	Full sample[a]	Subsample[b]
Males	25	13
Females	21	12
CA range[c]	23–60	23–33
Mean age[c]	35.4	28.11
Marital status		
Single	21	12
Married	23	11
Divorced	2	2
Residential arrangement		
With spouse	23	13
With roommate	11	9
Alone	12	3
Employment status		
Competitive job	20	14
Sheltered workshop	9	1
Unemployed	17	10
Delivery system involvement		
Supplementary security income	32	16
Regional center client	40	23
Independent living training program graduate	21	15

[a] N = 46.
[b] N = 25.
[c] In years.

were selected; their basic demographic characteristics are presented in Table 1. Of those not included, 5 chose not to participate, 4 were geographically distant, 1 had a history of emotional disturbance, and 3 had IQs above 80. Early in the course of the research, one sample member dropped out, yielding a final research cohort of 46 persons.

Although IQ data were not available for all of the sample members, they had all been classified as mildly retarded at some point in their development by a component of the service delivery system, and all except 2 had been placed in special-education classes during their school years. Of the 2 who were not enrolled in special education, 1 attended regular classes in a Catholic school until 7th grade and then remained at home, and 1 was ineligible for school because of an uncontrollable seizure condition. For the 28 sample members for whom IQs were available, most had scores within the 60 to 69 range; the mean IQ was 67.

Most sample members spent their childhood years living at home with family members; however, 7 spent some time in a state institution, 5 attended private special-education residential schools for various periods of time, and 3 resided in foster care or board-and-care homes from very young ages. The parents of all but 4 individuals were middle class; the remaining 4 sample members were from lower class families.

A subsample of 25 of the youngest sample members ranging in age from 23 to 33 years were selectively studied in an attempt to describe patterns of adolescent adjustment and to contrast features of adolescent adjustment and postschool adapation. (See Table 1 for demographic characteristics of the subsample.) Older sample members were excluded from this research effort to control for the effect of remoteness of the period being studied. The adolescent period covered in this report spans the junior and senior high school years.

Procedure

The principal means of data-collection was a form of participant observation developed by the Socio-Behavioral Group at UCLA to study general adaptation patterns of mentally retarded adults (Edgerton & Langness, 1978). This procedure allows a field researcher and sample member to engage in intensive interactions over a prolonged period of time. During that time discussions and observations occur as the sample member is involved in various typical activities Close relationships develop between researcher and sample member that result in intimate conversations on a range of topics.

Field researchers were assigned to sample members of the same sex and, with few exceptions, the same field researcher maintained contact with a sample member for the duration of the study. All field researchers had had previous experience working with mentally retarded individuals and had received extensive training in the technique of participant observation. Field researcher visits were scheduled at least once a month and lasted for a period of one to four hours. Regular telephone contact was also maintained. Over the course of 18 months, meetings took place in the homes of the sample members as well as in restaurants, bowling alleys, work locations, and relatives' homes to permit observation of the

individual in a variety of natural settings. The same kinds of information were collected on each member of the sample, including family relationships, self-maintenance in everyday activities, leisure, behavior in public places, communicative competence and involvement with the delivery system. Field researchers also questioned sample members about their adolescent experiences, including worries and concerns of the period, interpersonal conflicts, crucial incidents, and parent relations. A detailed narrative account of each contact was constructed, and the resulting fieldnotes permit examination of a number of features of the sample members' lives.

Structured life history interviews were also conducted with parents of the 25 sample members. These interviews covered the impact of the retarded child on family members' lives, the developmental history of the retarded child, as well as school, social, residential, and work histories. Both parents were respondents in 9 cases, mothers were the sole respondents in 15 cases, and in one instance, a father only was interviewed. Family contacts were initiated by field researchers and a total of 120 questions were asked, typically requiring two or three interview sessions and 6 to 9 hours for completion. A number of questions specifically focused on the adolescent period, and family members were asked to describe: (a) the behavioral characteristics of the retarded youth in terms of self-control, emotional adjustment, and feelings about self; (b) problem behavior, if any, and what parents did about it; and (c) in what ways the parent–child relationship changed during the teen years and what the characteristics of that relationship were.

Results

A major goal of the present study was to describe how mentally retarded adults and their parents view in retrospect the adolescent years and to compare that life stage with the retarded adults' current life circumstances. Field notes and life history interviews on each sample member were read independently by two researchers, and all references to the adolescent period were selected for more thorough examination. The majority of these materials, reflecting both parents and sample members' perspectives of the adolescent experience, fell into three broad categories: the issues and concerns preoccupying these retarded individuals as adolescents, the problem behavior exhibited by these young persons, and what parents did about their sons' or daughters' problems. More in-depth classification of each category was accomplished by further sorting the total group data into behavioral subcategories. As subcategories emerged, each sample member's data set was coded for occurrence; e.g., the two researchers reviewed individual data sets to determine whether the person had a history of throwing tantrums, if he or she engaged in homosexual activity, and so forth. Once all the data sets had been examined, percentage of occurrence across sample members was calculated for each subcategory. The retrospective nature of the data precludes reliable inference regarding frequency and magnitude of particular problems. There are, however, a number of reasons for believing that these data do accurately reflect what parents and sample members perceive the adolescent experience to have been. That (a) there was general agreement between parents and sample members with regard to problems and concerns; (b) sample members made repeated mention of the same issues, concerns, and problem behavior during informal conversations with field researchers; and (c) most parents felt the need to intervene, thus corroborating the magnitude of

Table 2 Distribution (in %) of Concerns and Behavior of Adolescents and Their Parents

Concerns and behavior	Distribution
Adolescent concerns	
Parent–child relations	56
Identity issues	84
Expectancy-performance	56
Acceptance-rejection	68
Problem behavior	84
Temper tantrums	32
Violent and destructive behavior	20
Antisocial behavior	24
Use of drugs/alcohol	8
Rebellious behavior	16
Withdrawal	16
Self-abusive behavior	12
Emotional lability	12
Parent management strategies	
Psychological evaluation	20
Counseling/therapy	20
Enrollment in school or training programs	44
Home confinement	4
Out-of-home placement	24

their child's problems, are indications of the internal consistency within these data and attest to the significance of the adolescent period for these mildly retarded individuals.

Issues and Concerns

From the combined reports of parents and sample members, two major foci of concern were identified as having affected the emotional adjustment of sample members during adolescence: parent–child relations and identity issues. Both are concerns that all adolescents must contend with; however, many of the specific complaints reported are somewhat unique to mentally retarded teenagers (see Table 2).

Parent–child relations. A key feature of adolescence is the gradual achievement of emotional and behavioral autonomy, which typically involves some amount of parent–child conflict. Therefore, that 56% of the sample featured the independence–dependence struggle as a major complaint was to be expected. In general, sample members objected to what they considered to be too much interference by parents in their daily lives. They felt that parental attitudes and practices were restrictive and conflicted with other pressures to achieve and become independent. They complained that parents imposed rules governing their conduct, such as curfews, restrictions on associates or telephone use, and demanded tidiness in appearanace or personal property. They resented parental protectiveness and reluctance to permit them to venture into new situations or experience normal activities. Most felt that parents treated them like children, making all decisions for them and dictating what they were to do.

Identity issues. The central task of adolescence is self-definition, the development of a person's ideas and attitudes about who and what he or she is. Erikson (1968) described it as a time of seeing yourself and your relation to others in a more differentiated and integrated way, comparing yourself to others, and perceiving the way others judge you. For 84% of our sample members, it was during the adolescent period that they became aware of their "differentness" and the effect of their social identity on their life. Two sets of experiences provided input into their developing sense of self: expectancy-performance and acceptance-rejection.

In terms of expectancy-performance, 56% of the sample reported that adolescence was a time in which they had to come to terms with the realities of their handicap. Their deficits were most likely to be perceived in terms of school performance. They were disturbed by their enrollment in special classes, their lack of achievement in math, reading, and other academic subjects, their slowness in grasping new material. They began to identify themselves for the first time as slow learners, and they felt inadequate, as though they were "nothing."

Many had normative expectations for themselves and became frustrated when they realized that their limitations were hindering the attainment of their goals. They wanted to do the same kinds of things they saw their siblings and nonretarded peers doing—graduating from high school, dating, getting a job, moving out on their own—but had difficulty trying to keep up. They became jealous as they saw their younger siblings surpass them and accomplish things that they had yet to achieve.

In terms of acceptance-rejection, 68% of the sample members reported having experienced some form of rejection either by family members or peers. Some sample members described having been aware that they were a disappointment to their parents. They perceived their parents "partiality to siblings," expressed in differential treatment, as evidence that their parents held their nonretarded sisters or brothers in higher regard. They interpreted being sent away to school while their siblings continued to live at home, the different standards of behavior that parents applied to them and their siblings, and the different manner by which parents spoke to each child as indications that they were not loved as much as their sisters or brothers.

Some sample members also reported rejection by siblings. In addition to reports of conflicts with their nonretarded sister or brother, they described how their siblings often criticized them for not doing more than they did. They complained that their siblings had not totally accepted them and would intentionally hurt their feelings by calling them retarded.

Some form of rejection by peers was described by over half of the sample; 85% reported being teased and taunted by schoolmates and neighborhood children. Some were occasionally beaten up as well. Twenty-three percent regretted having no friends with whom to share their free time. Another 23% were disappointed that they had no boyfriend or girlfriend as their peers had. The feelings of most of these sample members were summed up in the statement of one young man: "You were looked down upon as a person with not too much intelligence or smarts and what people were trying to tell you was 'too bad you couldn't live in our world and too bad you couldn't be

and act like us.' I felt very much left out of it."

Problem Behavior

A broad spectrum of problem behavior characterized our sample members during their adolescent years. At least 84% of these young persons had some type of emotional or behavioral reaction that became apparent during junior or senior high school (see Table 2). This problem behavior (e.g., temper tantrums and emotional lability) either had not been evident before that period or had noticeably intensified during the high school years.

The more serious problem behavior included temper tantrums, violent and destructive behavior, antisocial behavior, use of drugs or alcohol, rebellious behavior, withdrawal, and self-abusive behavior. Eight sample members reacted by throwing temper tantrums. Some had low frustration thresholds and blew up frequently; others seemed to let their frustrations build over time and exploded periodically. Most screamed and yelled and occasionally threatened; 5 were violent and destructive. Of those, 2 directed their hostility to parents or their property. For example, one young man threw his dad's transistor radio in the bathtub, tore up his mom's flower bed, and stuffed up the toilet bowl on numerous occasions. The other 3 threw or smashed things when frustrated. The increasing frustration of one young man eventually led to a breakdown that required brief hospitalization.

Six of the sample members committed delinquent or deviant acts. Two young men were picked up by the police, each for molesting a younger child. Four other sample members were petty thieves: one took trinkets from the local 7–11 store, one stole record albums, one "skipped out of restaurants without paying and lifted tips from tables," and the fourth charged $90 worth of calls to another telephone number. Other minor violations included the regular use of marijuana and occasional "uppers" and/or the daily consumption of a sizable quantity of beer by 2 sample members.

Four sample members were regarded as rebellious or defiant of parental attempts to control their activities or of school authorities. One young woman devised devious ways of sneaking out of the house to meet boys when her parents forbade dating, and one young man ignored parental objections to his choice of friends—local "hoods" involved in car thefts and other unlawful activities. One young woman refused to attend classes or complete assignments; the other's acting-out behavior caused her expulsion from a number of high schools.

Seven sample members, anxious or frustrated over pressures at home and at school, displayed symptoms indicating intrapersonal maladjustment. Four young persons became reclusive and withdrew from contact with peers or others. One, for example, sought solace in bed where she stayed for hours and sometimes days at a time; another showed signs of regression and sucked his thumb and publically masturbated. Two other sample members developed nervous habits and inflicted serious injury on themselves by biting their arms and nails, and one sample member would rip her clothing during crying episodes.

Three other sample members were described as emotionally labile teenagers. These young persons were depicted as impatient with themselves and depressed by their inability to attain friends and a dating relationship. They sulked or cried frequently and were overly sensitive to frustration.

Parent Management Strategies

Of the 25 families, 84% indicated awareness of the problems preoccupying the retarded teenager and most had tried to be understanding of their child's frustration and discontent. Parents attributed adjustment problems to loss of self-esteem due to inadequate educational programming, rejection by peers, lack of accomplishments, and bleak prospects for the future. To handle the acting-out or emotional problems that ensued, they intervened in ways that they believed were supportive. Some sought professional counsel and therapeutic intervention for their troubled child, some searched for more appropriate schools and training programs, and one kept the vulnerable teenager sheltered in the home. Most parents handled their sons' or daughters' problems within the family context, but six sample members were placed in boarding school, group, or foster home (see Table 2).

For those who remained in the home, parents mostly sought assistance from resources available in the community. Three sample members were taken for psychological evaluations to determine the seriousness of their problem and to find alternative ways to handle the inappropriate behavior. Five sample members were sent for individual counseling to help them learn more about themselves and to feel better about who and what they were. At least 11 parents maintained close contact with school personnel (counselors, psychologists, vice principals), some for advice on handling their child's misbehavior, others to monitor the appropriateness of their child's placement or programming. One parent, for instance, had her daughter transferred to another high school after she developed self-abusive habits, the result of daily harassment by schoolmates. In anticipation of high school graduation, a number of parents became alarmed at the possibility of their son or daughter vegetating at home and either searched for special programs in vocational training or independent living skills or investigated job oportunities to keep the young adult active. One parent, a widow, concerned with her son's increased nervousness, the result of peer teasing and school pressure, kept him in virtual isolation in the family home, where he mostly watched television.

Of the 6 parents who sought out-of-home placement, most believed that the new setting offered their son or daughter more than they could do for them at home. Alternative solutions had not succeeded in easing their child's adjustment problems. Some parents felt their child needed more structure and discipline than they could provide, some hoped their child would learn to be more independent and to develop social skills, some wanted to lessen the tension between siblings, and still others sought respite from the constant demands placed on them and other family members. For example, one young man had been so ostracized by neighborhood youths that he had to associate with children half his age, and his younger sister was taunted because she had a retarded brother who played with "babies." Finally, his parents sent him to a residential school so he could be with young men like himself and his sister could have some peace.

Sexuality Issues

Throughout the previous discussion, the retarded adolescent's increasing sexual drive and awareness of the excitement of a boy–girl relationship is evident. Most, however, received little formal sex education, and parents were generally uncomfortable discussing the topic with them. As one sample member complained, "My mother never talked about sex. She told me I'd have to find out when I get married. It was all Greek to me."

Parents, for their part, had to deal with their own anxieties about their child's emerging sexuality and possible pregnancy. Those with daughters were concerned that their maturing child lacked good judgment and was easy prey for higher functioning older men. Indeed, such was the case with 3 of these young women, one of whom subsequently became pregnant. Those with sons had to deal with other kinds of sexual problems. Two young men were having homosexual relations, and 2 had molested younger children. In many cases, parents imposed restrictions upon their retarded adolescent, which resulted either in inhibiting their child's sexual development or in adolescent defiance of the parental controls. For example, some parents tried to discourage or postpone dating, some carefully scrutinized their children's relationships and discouraged those they did not approve of, some parents "arranged" dates for their child and went along as chaperones. Some parents also took action to prevent pregnancies. Of 6 engaged couples, one member of each underwent sterilization when marriage was planned, and another sample member was sterilized after the delivery of her first child.

Adult Adaptation

One of the main criteria for sample selection was independent living status, which implies relatively effective personal and social adjustment. To delineate further the general adjustment patterns of sample members, we reviewed the field notes and parent interview data, and two researchers made independent judgments of each adolescent's degree of independence and self-maintenance in day-to-day living. Approximately one-third (10) of the sample had achieved near-normal lifestyles; another group (9) remained highly dependent on parents and were largely incompetent at managing their own affairs, whereas a final group (6) were interdependent and in conflict with parents. Interrater agreement averaged 83% across sample members.

Independent adults. Ten members of the sample handled most of the everyday affairs of their lives without assistance and only in times of crisis turned to parents for support. All were proud of their independence and self-sufficiency and readily identified themselves to others in terms of their normative accomplishments (e.g., managing their own apartment, being married, having a job). They also remained less involved and less dependent on delivery system support and agency counselors than did other sample members. Ninety percent of the group were employed, either competitively or in sheltered situations. Their employment histories were the most stable, and relationships with work supervisors were generally positive and nonproblematic. Six members were married, and the others were either engaged or involved in "steady" relationships. Almost all enjoyed large friendship networks, with relationships that appeared stable, enduring, and mutually satisfying. These individuals assigned little importance to their handicapped status and seldom dwelled on their limitations. They generally reported feeling satisfied with themselves and the quality of their lives at this time. As adolescents, members of this group displayed the lowest incidence of adjustment problems and when they did, it was most likely a form of emotional disturbance (e.g., withdrawal, emotional lability, self-abusive behavior).

Dependent adults. Nine persons looked to their parents for protection and guidance in virtually every dimension of their lives. Both parents and the retarded adults viewed this extensive parental involvement as necessary and desirable, and pressure for increased autonomy was minimal. These members were also heavily enmeshed in the service delivery system and dependent on agency counselors for routine as well as out-of-the-ordinary needs. They were more socially immature than were other sample members. Four were involved in unstable marriages, 2 had steady boyfriends their parents considered unsuitable, and the other 3 yearned for heterosexual relationships, but their lifestyles afforded little opportunity to meet members of the opposite sex. These individuals tended to have fewer and more shallow peer relationships and relied on their families for social interaction and recreation. They either denied experiencing a mental handicap or redefined their condition in terms of some less stigmatizing affliction. For the most part, they felt that they led a good life and had no plans or desire for change. They accepted their parents' protectiveness and their dependent status as best for them. As adolescents, these individuals were more likely to display problem behavior than were the independent adults, but like the independent adults, their adjustment reactions were most likely to be a form of emotional disturbance (e.g., withdrawal, emotional lability, self-abusive behavior).

Interdependent adults. The 6 members who made up this group were currently enmeshed in conflict-ridden relationships with parents. The retarded adults solicited extensive assistance but resented accompanying attempts by parents to exert control over their activities. Parents preferred less involvement but insisted on maintaining control over decisions affecting their child's life. These were the least well-adjusted members of the sample. Their employment records, independent living situations, and friendship patterns were marked by instability. Only 1 member was currently employed. The others worked on and off at part-time jobs or in sheltered workshops or spent periods of time enrolled in job-training program.

Most seemed indifferent to their unemployed status and appeared to prefer free time and a guaranteed income (SSI). They maintained very dependent relationships with counselors and agents of the delivery system who tended to regard them as manipulative and unchangeable. Most had not remained in one residence or the same living situation for any length of time. Three members were married, although 2 were in the process of filing for divorce. The other 3 expressed interest in finding a girlfriend, but had little success in attracting women. Their peer relationships, in general, were marked by shallowness, conflict, and instability. They had still not come to terms with their handicapped identity and viewed their dependent status as stigmatizing. Most reported dissatisfaction with the quality of their lives but avoided making significant changes in their day-to-day existence. During adolescence, these individuals were the most likely sample members to have acted out, and they tended to adopt antisocial forms of behavior (e.g., theft, rebelliousness).

Discussion

This study is a first attempt to learn about the adolescent life stage of mildly retarded individuals and to contrast adolescent adjustment patterns with current adult status. We relied upon the perspectives of the retarded adults and their parents for behavioral descriptions of the retarded young persons and on observations of current life circumstances for analysis of adult adjustment. From these accounts it appears that both parents and sample members viewed the adolescent experience as more problematic than either the childhood period or the adult years and generally agreed on the nature of the adolescent conflicts. For the most part, these retarded adolescents were concerned with the same issues that preoccupy nonretarded adolescents—personal identity and autonomy. They interpreted parental attitudes and practices as nonsupportive and issues of competence and self-definition as sources of frustration and self-conflict. Other concerns were more unique to a retarded population. The implications of their handicapped status as well as their limitations were salient concerns for the first time, and many of their experiences—parental restrictiveness, peer rejection, expectancy-performance discrepancies—contributed to their uneasiness and discontent.

Over three-fourths of the sample experienced somewhat serious adolescent disturbances that surfaced during the high school years and were either nonexistent or of less magnitude before that time. For most sample members, these disturbances continued well beyond their departure from high school until normative adult achievements, such as living on their own, steady employment, engagement, or marriage, had been achieved. During the adolescent years, a limited or unclear set of normative expectations by parents as well as the absence of a peer support network available to most nonretarded adolescents seem to have exacerbated adjustment disturbances in this sample.

As adults approaching the fourth decade of life, the issues perceived to be highly problematic during the teen years—concern with self-definition and autonomy—have, for the most part, become less salient. The independent adults were mostly self-sufficient. They maintained a balanced relationship with parents and were content with their life achievements. The dependent adults existed in an insulated reality, protected and regulated by parents. They felt good about themselves and were comfortable with their "perceived" independence. Only the interdependent adults continued their preoccuption with personal identity and parent–child relations as central concerns. They were the least well-adjusted members of the sample, discontent with their handicapped status and dependence on others but unwilling or unmotivated to make significant changes in their lifestyles. It therefore seems that for most of our sample members, achieving independent living status, acquiring material possessions, managing their own homes, holding down jobs, and maintaining heterosexual relationships contributed to their sense of self-worth and provided the security to regard concern with individuation and detachment as behind them.

References

Abramson, M., Ash, M. J., & Nash, W. R. (1979). Handicapped adolescents: A time for reflection. *Adolescence, XIV*, 557–566.

Bachman, J. G., Kahn, R. L., Mednick, M. T., Davidson, I. N., & Johnston, L. D. (1969). *Youth in transition* (Vol. 1). Ann Arbor, MI: Institute for Social Research.

Dusek, J. B., & Flaherty, J. F. (1981). The development of the self-concept during the adolescent years. *Monographs of the Society for Research in Child Development, 46*, 1–61.

Edgerton, R. B., & Langness, L. L. (1978). Observing mentally retarded persons in community settings: An anthropological perspective. In G. P. Sackett (Ed.), *Observing behavior: Theory and applications in mental retardation* (Vol. I, pp. 335–348).

Erikson, E. H. (1968). Identity and identity diffusion. In C. Gordon & K. J. Gergen (Eds.). *The self in social interaction* (Vol. I). New York: Wiley.

Freud, A. (1969). Adolescence as a developmental disturbance. In G. Kaplan & S. Lebovici (Eds.), *Adolescence: Psychosocial perspectives.* New York: Basic Books.

Gaier, E. L. (1969). Adolescence: The current imbroglio. *Adolescence, IV,* 89–110.

Group for the Advancement of Psychiatry. (1968). *Normal adolescence: Its dynamics and impact.* New York: Scribner's Sons.

Hill, J. P. (1980). The family. In *The Seventy-ninth Yearbook of the National Society for the Study of Education.* Chicago: University of Chicago Press.

Irwin, E. M. (1977). *Growing pains.* Plymouth, England: MacDonald & Evans.

Jersild, A. T. (1963). *The psychology of adolescence* (2nd ed.). New York: MacMillan.

Jessor, R., & Jessor, S. L. (1977). *Problem behavior and psychosocial development: A longitudinal study of youth.* New York: Academic.

Newman, B. M., & Newman, P. R. (1979). *An introduction to the psychology of adolescence.* Homewood, IL: Dorsey.

Offer, D., Marcus, D., & Offer, J. L. (1970). A longitudinal study of normal adolescent boys. *American Journal of Psychiatry, 126,* 917–924.

Paulson, M. J., & Stone, D. (1973). Specialist-professional intervention: An expanding role in the care and treatment of the retarded and their families. In G. Tarjan, R. K. Eyman, & C. E. Meyers (Eds.), *Sociobehavioral studies in mental retardation* (pp. 234–240). Washington, DC: American Association on Mental Deficiency.

Sigman, M. (in press). Psychotherapy with mentally retarded children and adolescents. In M. Sigman (Ed.), *Children with dual disabilities: Mental retardation and emotional disorder.* New York: Grune & Stratton.

White, K. M., & Speisman, J. C. (1968). *Adolescence.* Monterey, CA: Brooks/Cole.

Winik, L., Zetlin, A. G., & Kaufman, S. Z. (in press). Adult mildly retarded persons and their parents: The relationship between involvement and adjustment. *Applied Research in Mental Retardation.*

Zetlin, A. G., Turner, J. L., & Winik, L. (in press). Socialization effects on the adult adaptation of mildly retarded persons living in the community. In S. Landesman-Dwyer & P. Vietze (Eds.), *The impact of residential settings on behavior.* Baltimore: University Park Press.

This research was supported by National Institute of Child Health and Human Development Grant No. HD 11944 awarded to the Socio-Behavioral Research Group, Mental Retardation Research Center, UCLA. Requests for reprints should be sent to Andrea G. Zetlin, MRRC, 760 Westwood Plaza, Los Angeles, CA 90024.

Authors

Andrea G. Zetlin and Jim L. Turner, University of California, Los Angeles.

Aging Parents With Adult Mentally Retarded Children: Family Risk Factors and Sources of Support

Marsha Mailick Seltzer and Marty Wyngaarden Krauss
1989

Abstract

Predictors of four indices of well-being among 203 aging mothers of mentally retarded adults who live at home were examined. Maternal demographic variables (age, marital status, education, and income) correlated with maternal physical health and life satisfaction, whereas adult child risk factors (level of retardation, having Down syndrome, physical health, and functional skills) related more strongly to parenting stress and burden. Multiple regression analyses revealed that the family's social climate was a better predictor of maternal well-being than were formal or informal support, controlling for maternal and adult child risk factors. Results were considered in the context of previous findings in mental retardation and gerontology.

The phenomenon of life-long family care for a person with mental retardation has been studied only recently (Heller & Factor, 1988; Krauss, 1988; Seltzer, 1985). Although demographic research confirms that a substantial percentage of retarded persons live with their families throughout their adult years (Meyers, Borthwick, & Eyman, 1985), little is known about how their mothers, who provide direct care for decades, are affected.

The current interest in aging parents who provide long-term care stems from several sources. First, there is growing interest in the impacts on parents of the increased longevity of mentally retarded persons. It is now the rule rather than the exception for a retarded person to live well into old age (Janicki & Wisniewski, 1985). Second, there is growing interest in the heterogeneity of the aging process. Historically, aging was viewed as a pathological process, defined by declines in functional, cognitive, and social abilities (Rowe & Kahn, 1987). More recently, there is recognition that some persons maintain or even improve their adaptive capacities in selected functions during old age (Baltes & Baltes, 1980; Featherman, 1984; Featherman, Smith, & Peterson,

1988). In this context, the capacity of elderly persons to be family resources, rather than burdens (Horowitz, 1985), is being explored. The potential for reciprocity in intergenerational relationships is increasingly recognized (Greenberg & Becker, 1988).

Family caregiving is not an unusual role, especially for women. However, the experiences of aging mothers who continue to provide care is atypical for several reasons. First, direct caregiving by a parent for a child is not normative when the other is approaching or has reached old age and the son or daughter has reached adulthood. Farber (1959) first noted that families with mentally retarded children may experience an "arrest" in the family life cycle, because they are out of synchrony with their age peers whose children develop normally. Turnbull, Summers, and Brotherson (1986) proposed modifications within general stages of the family life cycle that may accompany parenting a child with a handicap. Families may be "off cycle" due to the prolonged and special nature of dependency of the retarded child, which in turn may affect the personal and social well-being of caregivers.

A second unique aspect of aging mothers of retarded adults is the duration of their caregiving responsibility. Care of an elderly relative tends to be relatively brief—about 5 years, on the average (Stone, Cafferata, & Sangl, 1987). In contrast, caregiving for an aging son or daughter with retardation can span 5 or 6 decades.

Third, parent caregivers are unique in that the rate of out-of-home placement of their sons and daughters is higher at this stage of life than at any earlier point (Meyers et al., 1985). Whether the factors associated with parents' placement decisions for older sons and daughters are similar to those for parents of young retarded children (Blacher, 1988; Cole & Meyer, 1989) is unknown.

The most prominent conceptual framework used in contemporary studies of stress in families is the Double ABCX Model of Adjustment and Adaptation (McCubbin & Patterson, 1983). This model emphasizes that the effects of unusual or difficult demands on a fam-

Aging Parents With Adult Mentally Retarded Children   Marsha Mailick Seltzer and Marty Wyngaarden Krauss

ily can be buffered by the availability of internal and external resources. The identification of specific resources or buffers, and the study of their meditating roles, have been investigated actively by family researchers (Wikler, 1986).

In the past investigators have focused almost exclusively on parents of young retarded children, seeking to identify *risk factors* for out-of-home placement and deleterious parent outcomes. These risk factors include greater severity of the child's retardation; poor functional skills, resulting in the need for extensive physical assistance from caretakers; the presence of maladaptive behaviors; and age (Blacher, 1984; Crnic, Friedrich, & Greenberg, 1983; Eyman, O'Connor, Tarjan, & Justice, 1972; Meyers et al., 1985; Seltzer & Krauss, 1984a, 1984b). Other researchers have identified *resources and supports* that families utilize to buffer the stress associated with caregiving, including strong and satisfying social support networks, particular characteristics of the family social climate, effective personal coping skills, and the receipt of formal services (Cole, 1986; Drotar, 1981; Mink, Blacher, & Nihira, 1988; Tausig, 1985; Wikler, 1986; Zimmerman, 1984).

Gerontological researchers also have examined the impacts of family caregiving. There is considerable evidence that caregivers for elderly family members are at risk for poor health, depression, and social isolation (Gallagher et al., 1985; Zarit, Todd, & Zarit, 1986). Furthermore, an adequate social support network can enhance the physical health, mental health, and longevity of elderly persons and buffer the effects of stress (Broadhead et al., 1983; House, Landis, & Umberson, 1988; Krause, 1986).

In the present cross-sectional analysis, drawn from a longitudinal study of aging mothers caring for adult children with mental retardation, we focused on two research questions. The first question was, To what extent is the well-being of aging caregiving mothers a function of adult child and maternal risk factors? We hypothesized that having a more severely impaired child, having a child whose retardation was due to causes other than Down syndrome, and having a child in poor physical health would be associated with poor maternal well-being. We further hypothesized that mothers who are older, less educated, widowed, and with less income would have poorer well-being than would younger, better educated, married, and more financially well-off mothers.

The second research question was, To what extent is the well-being of aging caregiving mothers a function of the supports provided to them? The sources of support we examined included characteristics of the family's social climate, the mother's social support network, and the amount of formal support services received by the family. Although we hypothesized that all three domains of support would relate to maternal well-being, we expected that social support would be the most important. Further, we recognized the need to adjust for maternal and adult child variables in the analysis of correlates of maternal well-being.

Method

Sample

The sample was 227 families with a mother 55 years of older who had a son or daughter with mental retardation who was living at home. All families volunteered to participate following recruitment by the Department of Mental Retardation, the Association for Retarded Citizens chapters, and the Executive Office of Elder Affairs in Massachusetts. Of the 262 mothers who met our eligibility criteria, 227 (87%) participated. The analyses presented in this report are based on 203 mothers for whom complete data were available.

Mothers averaged 66 years of age (standard deviation [SD] = 6.3). The majority (59.1%) were married; most of the others were widows. Almost a quarter (23.6%) had less than a high school education, 34.5% were high school graduates, 27.5% attended either trade school or some college, 9.4% were college graduates, and 5% attended graduate school. Median family income was between $15,000 and $20,000.

The retarded adults ranged in age from 19 to 51 years, with an average age of 34.7 (SD = 7.1), and 53.2% were male. Nearly half (49.3%) were mildly retarded; one third (35.0%), moderately retarded; and the remaining persons, either severely (10.8%) or profoundly (4.9%) retarded. One third (34%) had a diagnosis of Down syndrome. Their health status, as reported by mothers, was described as excellent (51.7%), good (36.9%), fair (9.9%), or poor (1.5%). Most (89.2%) attended an out-of-home day program. The retarded adults received an average of five formal services, most frequently transportation, vocational, recreational/social, financial, and social work.

Data-Collection Procedures

Data were collected by 10 interviewers who were advanced graduate students or recent graduates in special education, nursing, or social work. Interviews, averaging 67 minutes, were conducted with the mothers in their homes. The mothers then completed self-administered standardized measures. Information regarding the retarded adults' level of retardation was collected from the Massachusetts Department of Mental Retardation subsequent to the mother's interview.

Measures

Our measures were selected from the fields of mental retardation and gerontology, reflecting the cross-cutting nature of the problem and population studied. We used a multidimensional conceptualization of maternal well-being, involving four dependent variables. Maternal *physical health* was self-rated on a 4-point scale, with 0, *poor*; 1, *fair*; 2, *good*; and 3, *excellent* (mean for this sample = 2.0, SD = .7). The criterion-related validity of this item with a physical examination was reported to be .70 (Multidimensional Functional Assessment Manual, 1978). Maternal *life satisfaction* was assessed by the Philadelphia Geriatric Center Morale Scale (Lawton, 1972), which consists of 22 items answered *yes* (score of 1) or *no* (score of 0) (mean = 12.4, SD = 4.2). Alpha reliability for the present sample ranged from .64 to .74 for the scale's three subscales. This scale conceptualizes life satisfaction as "a basic sense of satisfaction with oneself, a feeling that there is a place in the environment for oneself, and an acceptance of what cannot be changed" (Lawton, 1972, p. 148).

The third indicator of well-being was the mother's generalized feeling of *burden*, assessed by the Zarit Burden Scale (Zarit, Reever, & Bach-Peterson, 1980). This scale consists of 29 items, each answered on a 3-point scale, ranging from 0 (*not at all true*) to 2 (*extremely true*) (mean = 29.1, SD = 7.4). Alpha reliability for the present sample was .91. In this scale, Zarit et al. conceptualized burden as problems with the "caregiver's health, psychological well-being, finances, social life, and the relationship between the caregiver and the impaired person" (p. 651). The fourth measure of maternal well-being, *parenting stress*, was assessed by the revised version of the Questionnaire on Resources and Stress (Friedrich, Greenberg, & Crnic, 1983). This scale consists of 52 items, answered *yes* (score of 1) or *no* (score of 0). The mean for the present sample was 17.6 (SD = 8.6); alpha

Table 1 Correlations Among the Dependent Variables (n = 203)

Dependent variable	1	2	3	4
1. Physical health	1.000			
2. Life satisfaction	.470*	1.000		
3. Burden	–.314*	–.622*	1.000	
4. Stress	–.253*	–.560*	.701*	1.000

$*p$ < .001.

Table 2 Means and SDs of Independent Measures (n = 203)

Independent measure	Mean	SD
Family social climate (FES)[a] subscale score		
Cohesion	7.7	1.6
Expressiveness	5.7	1.9
Conflict	1.7	1.6
Independence	7.1	1.6
Achievement	5.4	1.9
Intellectual/Cultural	5.9	2.2
Active/Recreational	4.9	2.3
Moral/Religious	6.4	1.9
Organization	6.8	1.8
Control	4.3	1.6
Mother's social support network		
Size	6.6	3.2
Satisfaction	2.7	.8
Support provided by network members to mother	.8	.2
Support provided by mother to network members	.8	.2
Formal supports to the family		
No. of services received by son or daughter	4.8	2.4
No. of services received by mother	.7	.9
Son or daughter attends day program	.9	.3

[a] Family Environment Scale.

reliability was .89. Stress was conceptualized by Friedrich et al. as consisting of three broad dimensions: parent problems, problems in family functioning, and problems the parent sees in or for the child.

The four measures of maternal well-being, although conceptually distinct, were highly intercorrelated. As shown in Table 1, the strongest relation was between burden and stress; the weakest, between physical health and stress.

Five domains of independent variables were examined. Two consisted of factors hypothesized to affect maternal well-being negatively: *maternal characteristics* of older age, single marital status, less education, and less income; and *the retarded adult's characteristics* of not having Down syndrome, having more severe retardation, poorer physical health, and poorer functional abilities. Functional abilities were measured by the revised Barthel Index (Mahoney & Barthel, 1965), a 31-item scale of personal and instrumental functional skills, with each item scored on a 4-point scale of independence. Higher scores denote more independence. The mean for the present sample was 65.4 (SD = 10.8). Alpha reliability for the revised Barthel Index was .93.

The other domains consisted of sources of support hypothesized to enhance maternal well-being (see Table 2 for means and SDs of these measures). *The family social climate* was assessed by the 10 subscales of the Family Environment Scale (Moos, 1974), each with a range of scores from 0 to 9. The alpha reliability across the 10 subscales was .76. *The mother's social support network* was assessed by Antonucci's (1986) Convoy Model, which indicates the number of people included in the mother's social support network (range from 0 to 10), the mother's level of satisfaction with her social support (rated on a 4-point scale ranging from 0, *completely dissatisfied*, to 3, *completely satisfied*), the amount of support provided to the mother by network members (calculated as the percentage of six support functions performed by each member of the mother's network and averaged across members), and the amount of support provided to network members by the mother (calculated as the percentage of six support functions performed by the mother for each member of her network and averaged across members). The *formal supports* received by the family were measured by the number of services received by the mother and the retarded adult and whether the retarded adult attended a day program (coded as 0, *no*; 1, *yes*).

In selecting the variables to study for the retarded adult, we did *not* use age, even though previous research has indicated age is a prominent risk factor for out-of-home placement and parental stress (Blacher, 1984). However, in the present sample, age of the retarded adult was highly correlated with age of the mother, r = .53, p < .001. To reduce redundancy in the independent variable set, we included only maternal age. Another prominent risk factor, maladaptive behavior, was not included in this analysis because the data set did not contain a measure of this domain. We note, however, that two thirds of the retarded sons and daughters did not receive and were reported not to need psychological services. Although not definitive, the low utilization rate of psychological services is consistent with a low estimated prevalence of severe behavior problems among samples of retarded persons in this age group and level of retardation.

Data Analysis

The SPSS-X (1988) was used to analyze the data. The principal analysis techniques were bivariate correlation and multiple regression, with a .01 level of significance.

Results

The mothers in the present sample compared favorably in their well-being with samples of age peers and samples of other caregivers. Regarding physical health, a higher percentage of the mothers in the present sample rated themselves as being in good or excellent health (78%) than did the members of either a national probability sample of caregivers for elderly persons—67% (Stone, Cafferata, & Sangl, 1987) or a national probability sample of older women—60% (Bumpass & Sweet, 1987). Regarding life satisfaction, the mothers in our sample had substantially better morale (mean = 12.4) than a comparison sample of caregivers for elderly persons (mean = 7.9) (Gallagher et al., 1985). Regarding perceived burden, our mothers reported slightly less burden than the standardization sample—means = 29.1 and 31.0, respectively (Zarit et al., 1980). Finally, regarding parenting stress, the mothers in the present sample had slightly lower stress scores (mean = 17.6) than did the standardization sample (mean = 18.6) used by Friedrich et al. (1983) in their revision of the Questionnaire on Resources and Stress. Thus, on an absolute level, our sample should be characterized as having above average health for their age, with a relatively favorable life satisfaction and about average levels of perceived burden and stress.

Table 3 Significant Relations Between Risk Factors and Dependent Variables (n = 203)

Risk factor	Physical health	Life satisfaction	Burden	Stress
Maternal[a]				
Age	−.158	−.078	−.155	−.084
Level of education	.247**	.226**	.046	.003
Marital status	−.092	.191*	.083	.010
Income	.305**	.313**	−.113	.096
Child[a]				
Level of retardation	−.092	−.136	.114	−.343**
Diagnosis	.139	.139	−.254**	−.213**
Functional level	.053	.068	.023	.405**
Physical health	.309**	.326**	−.272**	−.203*

[a] See text for coding conventions.
* $p < .01$.
** $p < .001$.

Table 3 summarizes significant correlations between maternal and adult child variables and measures of maternal well-being. Maternal characteristics tended to be more related to the mothers' physical health and life satisfaction, whereas the adult child variables correlated more with the mothers' generalized feelings of burden and stress associated with parenting. An exception was the retarded adults' physical health, which related significantly to all four measures of the mothers' well-being.

Specifically, risk factors for poor physical health in the mother were fewer years of education, having a lower income, and having a son or daughter who had poor physical health. Similarly, risk factors for low levels of life satisfaction included fewer years of education, not being married, having a lower income, and having a son or daughter who had poor physical health.

Risk factors for generalized feelings of burden included having a child with a diagnosis other than Down syndrome and having a son or daughter who had poor physical health. Risk factors for high levels of perceived parenting stress included having a child with severe retardation, having a child with a diagnosis other than Down syndrome, and having a son or daughter who had poor functional skills and poor physical health.

Maternal well-being was also analyzed in relation to family support, social support, and formal support. Only moderately significant correlations existed among the variables in each of these three domains, ranging from .14 to .62, suggesting that they represent empirically, as well as conceptually, distinct domains. (The full correlation matrix is available from the authors.)

Table 4 presents the bivariate correlations among the four measures of maternal well-being and the three domains of support. None of the support variables for maternal physical health was a significant correlate. Regarding maternal life satisfaction, mothers who were less satisfied perceived their families to be less cohesive, less expressive, more conflictual, less independent, less interested in intellectual and cultural activities, less likely to participate in active recreational activities, and less organized than did mothers who were more satisfied. In addition, mothers with lower levels of life satisfaction had smaller social support networks and perceived their level of social support to be less satisfactory than did mothers who were more satisfied with their lives. Finally, mothers who were less satisfied received a greater number of formal services.

Regarding perceived maternal burden, mothers who were more burdened perceived their families to be less cohesive, more conflictual, less independent, less likely to participate in active recreational activities, and less organized than mothers who reported less burden. In addition, mothers who reported more burden had smaller informal support networks and were less satisfied with their level of social support than were mothers not feeling as burdened.

Mothers who reported more parenting stress perceived their families to be less cohesive, more conflictual, less independent, less likely to participate in active recreational activities, and less organized than mothers who reported lower levels of stress. In addition, higher stress was associated with smaller social support networks and

Table 4 Significant Relations Between Support Domains and Dependent Variables ($n = 203$)

Supports	Physical health	Life satisfaction	Burden	Stress
Family				
Cohesion	.073	.448**	−.350**	−.338**
Expressiveness	.027	.289**	−.145	−.134
Conflict	−.107	−.284**	.444**	.259**
Independence	.081	.337**	−.310**	−.302*
Achievement	−.045	−.013	.089	.011
Intellectual/cultural	.061	.346**	−.104	−.095
Active/recreational	.053	.322**	−.267**	−.351**
Moral/religious	−.016	.030	−.033	.031
Organization	.022	.218*	−.222**	−.253**
Control	.048	−.088	.152	.004
Social				
Network size	.125	.340**	−.271**	−.260**
Level of satisfaction	.072	.290**	−.345**	−.193*
Supportiveness of network to mother	−.103	−.088	.154	.127
Supportiveness of mother to network	−.063	.014	.092	.125
Formal				
No. services received by son/daughter	.071	−.005	.012	.122
No. services received by mother	−.133	−.251**	.158	.262**
Son or daughter attends a day program	.149	.143	−.133	.064

* $p < .01$.

** $p < .001$.

lower levels of satisfaction with social support. Finally, as in the findings regarding life satisfaction, a higher level of parenting stress was associated with the mother's receipt of a greater number of formal services.

Finally, Table 5 presents the results of hierarchical multiple regression analyses for each dependent variable. The independent variables were entered in the following order: (a) maternal risk factors (age, level of education, marital status, and income), (b) adult child risk factors (level of retardation, diagnosis as Down syndrome or other, functional level, and physical health), (c) family social climate (the 10 subscales of the Family Environment Scale), (d) informal supports (the number of people in the mother's network, her level of satisfaction with the amount of support available to her, the supportiveness of the network to her, and the extent to which she is supportive of network members), and (e) formal supports (the number of services received by the retarded adult, the number of services received by the mother, and whether the retarded adult attended a day program).

The order of entry of the independent variables into the regression equations was a function of the research question, namely, whether sources of support would contribute to our understanding of maternal well-being, once maternal and adult child risk factors were controlled. The risk factors, therefore, were entered into the analyses first. The order of entry of the three domains of support—family, social, and formal—reflected our conceptualization of layers of support available to caregiving mothers. The family social climate variables were entered first because we thought that the mother's family environment would have the most immediate effects on her. Measures of her social support network, which potentially included friends as well as family members, were entered next because we believed that social support would be less intimate than the family environment but more intimate than formal supports, which was

Table 5 Multiple Regression Analysis of Maternal Well-being (n = 203)

Variable	r	R^2	R^2 change
Physical health			
Maternal risk factors	.33	.11	.11**
Child risk factors	.45	.20	.09*
Family social climate	.47	.22	.02
Social supports	.48	.23	.01
Formal supports	.49	.24	.01
Life satisfaction			
Maternal risk factors	.33	.11	.11**
Child risk factors	.47	.22	.11**
Family social climate	.63	.40	.18**
Social supports	.66	.44	.04*
Formal supports	.68	.46	.02
Burden			
Maternal risk factors	.28	.08	.08*
Child risk factors	.46	.22	.14**
Family social climate	.65	.42	.21**
Social supports	.70	.49	.07**
Formal supports	.71	.50	.01
Parenting stress			
Maternal risk factors	.18	.03	.03
Child risk factors	.53	.28	.25**
Family social climate	.67	.45	.17**
Social supports	.70	.49	.04*
Formal supports	.71	.50	.01

* $p < .01$.

** $p < .001$.

the domain entered last.

Although we entered the 25 variables separately, we present the data in Table 5 by domain for summary purposes. The full set of independent variables explained about one quarter of the variance in physical health, and about one half of the variance in life satisfaction, generalized feelings of burden, and parenting stress. However, the amount of unique variance associated with each of the domains differed for the four measures of maternal well-being. For physical health, only the maternal and adult child risk factors explained an appreciable amount of variance in the dependent variable. For the other three dependent measures, the family social climate and the mother's informal support network were predictive of

maternal well-being, even after controlling for the risk factors. However, the formal support domain was *not* predictive of any of the four measures of maternal well-being.

Specifically, regarding maternal life satisfaction, both maternal and child characteristics were associated with this measure of well-being. The family social climate also was highly predictive, accounting for an additional 18% of the variance. The mother's level of social support related only moderately to her life satisfaction, explaining 4% of the variance after the risk factors and family social climate were controlled. Regarding generalized feelings of burden, both maternal and adult child risk factors again were predictive; once these risk factors were controlled for, the family environment remained a very strong predictor, explaining fully 21% of the variance, whereas the mother's informal support network was only moderately related to this measure of well-being, explaining 7% of the variance.

The pattern of findings was somewhat different in the analysis of the mothers' parenting stress, with the child risk factors accounting for fully 25% of the variance and the maternal risk factors not being strongly associated with this measure. In addition, the family environment and, to a lesser degree, the mother's informal support network were predictive of stress, explaining 17% and 4% of the variance, respectively.

The order of entry of the support domains (family, social, and formal) was varied to determine whether the strong predictive power of family social climate, relative to social support and formal support, was a function of shared variance among these three sets of independent variables. We found that even when the formal support domain was entered before the other two support domains, it never explained more than a few percentage points of the variance in any of the dependent variables. However, the order of entry of the social support domain relative to the family social climate domain influenced the proportion of variance associated with each. When the social support variables were entered *before* the family social climate variables, they explained a larger proportion of the variance in three of the four dependent variables than when they were entered after the family social climate variables. The exception was physical health, where neither domain was predictive. Nevertheless, even when entered earlier, the social support variables, as a set, never explained more variance than did the family social climate variables.

Discussion

The study of aging mothers with adult mentally retarded children is derived from two research areas: studies of young families caring for a retarded child and studies of family caregivers for elderly persons Nevertheless, it is not known whether the confluence of the two factors of retardation and aging generates a different context for understanding the impacts of caregiving on older mothers. Our findings suggest both similarities and differences in this regard.

The mothers in this sample compared quite favorably with other samples of their age peers and samples of other caregivers. Despite the long duration of their caretaking roles, and despite the unique qualities of their children, many of the mothers appear to be resilient, optimistic, and able to function well in multiple roles. Specifically, the women in our sample were substantially healthier and had better morale than did other samples of caregivers for elderly persons and reported no more burden and stress than did other caregivers. The generalizability of these findings to families who are either not well integrated or more integrated into their state's service network is unknown. Further, the extent to which these findings *account* for the current residential placement of these retarded adults cannot be tested directly in this cross-sectional analysis. The longitudinal component of our study was designed, in part, to test this hypothesis.

One area of similarity with previous research on family caregiving for both a retarded and an elderly member is the salience of risk factors for the well-being of caregivers. Traditional sociodemographic risk factors of the mothers (age, level of education, marital status, and income) were strongly related to maternal well-being. These findings are generally consistent with past gerontological research on the characteristics associated with poor well-being among elderly individuals. Further, consistent with previous research on the impacts of caregiving on young families with a retarded child, the risk factor characteristics of the retarded adults were found to be associated with higher levels of parenting stress and feelings of burden in the mothers in the present sample. Lower levels of burden and parental stress were found for mothers whose adult children had Down syndrome than for mothers of those whose retardation was due to other factors, consistent with research on the effects of Down syndrome versus other diagnoses on par-

ents of young handicapped children (Holroyd & McArthur, 1976; Krauss, 1989). This difference may be due to a greater degree of knowledge available to families of retarded persons with Down syndrome about the etiology of the retardation and the expected development of their children.

A prominent finding for the well-being of caregiving mothers pertained to the importance of the *family social climate*, which emerged as the strongest of the three domains of support, irrespective of the order of entry of the support domains into the analyses. We expected that *social support* would be a stronger predictor of well-being for women at this stage of life than family social climate. This expectation was based on the fact that older women have diminished parenting and, in many cases, marital responsibilities and that friendships appear to increase in importance for women in their later years (Antonucci & Akiyama, 1987). However, our findings support the salience of the family social climate in predicting maternal well-being for women who continue to provide care to a dependent adult child. For these women, the parenting role remains a central part of their identity, even into old age. Thus, dimensions of the family social climate, including the relationships among family members, the value orientations of the family, and the organization of the family, may be more salient for the older women in our sample than for their age peers.

Further, although they reported that their social support networks were very satisfying, the mothers in our sample had substantially smaller networks than did their age peers who did not have a retarded child. Antonucci and Akiyama (1987) reported an average network size of 8.9 persons for a national probability sample of older persons, compared with 6.6 network members in the present study, which used the same measure. It is possible that smaller networks have less of an impact on well-being than do larger networks.

Finally, we were surprised to find that the formal support domain was not related to any of the measures of maternal well-being. Given the variability across states in community-based service structures, the generalizability of this finding is unknown. However, policy makers in both mental retardation and gerontology assume that formal services enable families to continue to care for a dependent member because services improve the well-being of caregiving families (Krauss, 1986). In fact, little research has actually been conducted to test this assumption. One recently reported study showed that the provision of respite to family caregivers of relatives with Alzheimer disease was unrelated to caregivers' feelings of burden and their mental health (Lawton, Brody, & Saperstein, 1989). Nevertheless, respite care recipients were able to maintain their impaired relative in the community significantly longer than were nonrecipients. The relation between formal support, the well-being of the caregiver, and the ability of the caregiver to continue to provide care appears to be more complex than initially assumed. The longitudinal component of our research, which involves two states (Wisconsin and Massachusetts), will provide a closer examination of these relations.

In conclusion, our data support the salience of both objective factors, namely, the family risk factors, and subjective factors, namely, perceptions of the family social climate, in shaping the well-being of long-term family caregivers to older adults with mental retardation. These two domains of variables appear to be enduring in their relation with maternal well-being in that they have been found to be predictive of the well-being of both younger caregiving families with a handicapped child and older family caregivers for elderly persons. These similarities suggest that although the families we studied had unique characteristics, there may be a relatively stable set of factors that affect the well-being of families in general, across the life cycle, and across the particular type of dependency of the family member receiving care.

References

Antonucci, T. C. (1986). Measuring social support networks: Hierarchical mapping technique. *Generations*, 10, 10–12.

Antonucci, T. C., & Akiyama, H. (1987). Social networks in adult life and a preliminary examination of the convoy model. *Journal of Gerontology*, 42, 519–527.

Baltes, P. B., & Baltes, M. M. (1980). Plasticity and variability in psychological aging: Methodological and theoretical issues. In G. E. Gurski (Ed.), *Determining the effects of aging on the central nervous system* (pp. 41–66). Berlin: Schering.

Blacher, J. (Ed.). (1984). *Severely handicapped children and their families: Research in review.* New York: Academic Press.

Blacher, J. (1988). *Families who place their severely handicapped child: Differentiating characteristics and influ-*
ences. Paper presented at the 21st annual Gatlinburg Conference on Research and Theory in Mental Retardation and Developmental Disabilities, Gatlinburg, TN.

Broadhead, W. E., Kaplan, B. H., James, S. A., Wagner, E. H., Schoenbach, V. J., Grimson, R., Heyden, S., Tibblin, G., & Gehlbach, S. H. (1983). The epidemiologic evidence for a relationship between social support and health. *American Journal of Epidemiology*, 117, 521–537.

Bumpass, L., & Sweet, J. (1987). *A national survey of families and households.* Madison: University of Wisconsin-Madison, Center for Demography and Ecology.

Cole, D. A. (1986). Out-of-home child placement and family adaptation: A theoretical framework. *American Journal of Mental Deficiency*, 91, 226–236.

Cole, D. A., & Meyer, L. H. (1989). Impact of needs and resources on family plans to seek out-of-home placement. *American Journal on Mental Retardation*, 93, 380–387.

Crnic, K., Friedrich, W. N., & Greenberg, M. T. (1983). Adaptation of families with mentally retarded children: A model of stress, coping, and family ecology. *American Journal of Mental Deficiency*, 88, 345–351.

Drotar, D. (1981). Psychological perspectives in chronic childhood illness. *Journal of Pediatric Psychology*, 6, 211–228.

Eyman, R. K., O'Connor, G., Tarjan, G., & Justice, R. S. (1972). Factors determining residential placement of mentally retarded children. *American Journal of Mental Deficiency*, 76, 692–698.

Farber, B. (1959). Effects of a severely retarded child on family integration. *Monographs of the Society for Research in Child Development* (Serial No. 71).

Featherman, D. L. (1984). *Plasticity: The challenge of aging.* Paper presented at the Joseph P. Kennedy Jr. Foundation Workshop, Bedford, MA.

Featherman, D. L., Smith, J., & Peterson, J. (1988). *Successful aging in a "post-retired" society.* Paper presented at the European Science Foundation Conference on Longitudinal Research and the Study of Successful Aging, Castle Ringberg, Germany.

Friedrich, W. N., Crnic, K., & Greenberg, M. T. (1983). A short-form of the Questionnaire on Resources and Stress. *American Journal of Mental Deficiency*, 88, 41–48.

Gallagher, D., Rappaport, M., Benedict, A., Lovett, S., Silven, D., & Kramer, H. (1985). *Reliability of se-*

lected interview and self-report measures with family caregivers. Paper presented at the 38th annual meeting of the Gerontological Society of America, New Orleans, LA.

Greenberg, J., & Becker, M. (1988). Aging parents as family resources. *The Gerontologist, 28*, 786–791.

Heller, T., & Factor, A. (1988). Permanency planning among black and white family caregivers of older adults with mental retardation. *Mental Retardation, 26*, 203–208.

Holroyd, J., & McArthur, D. (1976). Mental retardation and stress on the parents: A contrast between Down's syndrome and childhood autism. *American Journal of Mental Deficiency, 80*, 431–436.

Horowitz, A. (1985). Family caregiving to the frail elderly. *Annual Review of Gerontology and Geriatrics, 5*, 194–246.

House, J. S., Landis, K. R., & Umberson, D. (1988). Social relationships and health. *Science, 241*, 540–545.

Janicki, M. P., & Wisniewski, H. M. (Eds.). (1985). *Aging and developmental disabilities: Issues and approaches.* Baltimore: Brookes.

Krause, N. (1986). Social support, stress, and well-being among older adults. *Journal of Gerontology, 41*, 512–519.

Krauss, M. W. (1986). Patterns and trends in public services to families with a mentally retarded member. In J. J. Gallagher & P. M. Vietze (Eds.), *Families of handicapped persons: Research, programs, and policy issues* (pp. 237–248). Baltimore: Brookes.

Krauss, M. W. (1988). Long-term care issues in mental retardation. In J. Kavanagh (Ed.), *Understanding mental retardation: Research accomplishments and new frontiers* (pp. 331–339). Baltimore: Brookes.

Krauss, M. W. (1989). *Parenting a young child with disabilities: Differences between mothers and fathers.* Paper presented at the 22nd annual Gatlinburg Conference on Research and Theory in Mental Retardation and Developmental Disabilities, Gatlinburg, TN.

Lawton, M. P. (1972). The dimensions of morale. In D. Kent, R. Kastenbaum, & S. Sherwood (Eds.), *Research planning and action for the elderly.* New York: Behavioral Publications.

Lawton, M. P., Brody, E. M., & Saperstein, A. R. (1989). A controlled study of respite services for caregivers of Alzheimer's patients. *The Gerontologist, 29*, 8–16.

Mahoney, F. I., & Barthel, D. W. (1965). Functional evaluation: The Barthel Index. *Maryland State Medical Journal, 14*, 61–65.

McCubbin, H. I., & Patterson, J. M. (1983). The family stress process: The double ABCX model of adjustment and adaptation. In H. I. McCubbin, M. B. Sussman, & J. M. Patterson (Eds.), *Social stress and the family: Advances and developments in family stress theory and research.* New York: Haworth Press.

Meyers, C. E., Borthwick, S. A., & Eyman, R. K. (1985). Place of residence by age, ethnicity, and level of retardation of the mentally retarded/developmentally disabled population of California. *American Journal of Mental Deficiency, 90*, 266–270.

Mink, I. T., Blacher, J., & Nihira, K. (1988). Taxonomy of family life styles: III. Replication with families with severely mentally retarded children. *American Journal of Mental Retardation, 93*, 250–264.

Moos, R. H. (1974). *Family Environment Scale.* Palo Alto, CA: Consulting Psychologists Press.

Multidimensional Functional Assessment: The OARS Methodology. A Manual (2nd ed.). (1978). Durham: Duke University, Center for the Study of Aging and Human Development.

Rowe, J. W., & Kahn, R. L. (1987). Human aging: Usual and successful. *Science, 237*, 143–149.

Seltzer, M. M. (1985). Informal supports for aging mentally retarded persons. *American Journal of Mental Deficiency, 90*, 259–265.

Seltzer, M. M., & Krauss, M. W. (1984a). Placement alternatives for mentally retarded children and their families. In J. Blacher (Ed.), *Severely handicapped children and their families: Research in review* (pp. 143–175). New York: Academic Press.

Seltzer, M. M., & Krauss, M. W. (1984b). Family, community residence, and institutional placements of a sample of mentally retarded children. *American Journal of Mental Deficiency, 89*, 257–266.

SPSS. (1988). *SPSS-X user's guide* (3rd ed.). Chicago: SPSS Marketing Department.

Stone, R., Cafferata, G. L., & Sangl, J. (1987). Caregivers of frail elderly: A national profile. *The Gerontologist, 27*, 616–626.

Tausig, M. (1985). Factors in family decision-making about placement for developmentally disabled individuals. *American Journal of Mental Deficiency, 89*, 352–361.

Turnbull, A. P., Summers, J. A., & Brotherson, M. J. (1986). Family life cycle: Theoretical and empirical implications and future directions for families with mentally retarded members. In J. J. Gallagher & P. M. Vietze (Eds.), *Families of handicapped persons: Research, programs, and policy issues* (pp. 45–65). Baltimore: Brookes.

Wikler, L. M. (1986). Family stress theory and research on families of children with mental retardation. In J. J. Gallagher & P. M. Vietze (Eds.), *Families of handicapped persons: Research, programs, and policy issues* (pp. 167–196). Baltimore: Brookes.

Zarit, S. H., Reever, K. E., & Bach-Peterson, J. (1980). Relatives of the impaired aged: Correlates of feelings of burden. *The Gerontologist, 20,* 649–655.

Zarit, S. H., Todd, P. A., & Zarit, J. M. (1986). Subjective burden of husbands and wives as caregivers: A longitudinal study. *The Gerontologist, 26,* 260–266.

Zimmerman, S. L. (1984). The mental retardation family subsidy program: Its effects on families with a mentally handicapped child. *Family Relations, 33,* 105–118.

An earlier version of this paper was presented at the 22nd annual Gatlinburg Conference on Research and Theory in Mental Retardation and Developmental Disabilities, Gatlinburg, TN, March 1989. Preparation of this paper was supported, in part, by the Andrus Foundation and the March of Dimes Birth Defects Foundation. The authors gratefully acknowledge assistance of Leon C. Litchfield and Nao Tsunematsu, who conducted the data analysis. We also thank Laraine Masters Glidden and David L. Featherman for their helpful comments on this manuscript. Requests for reprints should be sent to Marsha Mailick Seltzer, University of Wisconsin, Waisman Center, 1500 Highland Ave., Madison, WI 53705.

Authors

Marsha Mailick Seltzer, University of Wisconsin and **Marty Wyngaarden Krauss,** Brandeis University.

Adults With Mental Retardation as Supports to Their Parents: Effects on Parental Caregiving Appraisal

Tamar Heller, Ph.D., Alison B. Miller, M.A., and Alan Factor, M.D.
1997

Abstract

This study was conducted to determine whether support provided to caregivers by their adult children with mental retardation would influence caregiving appraisals. We also examined how severity of disability of the adult child, personal and social resources of the caregiver, and amount of caregiver assistance to the adult with mental retardation influenced caregiving appraisals. Using surveys and interviews we collected information from 80 primary caregivers on caregiving burden and satisfaction and six predictors of burden and satisfaction. Findings indicate that greater support from the adult child to the caregiver resulted in greater satisfaction and less burden. Adaptive and maladaptive behaviors and caregiving assistance all predicted caregiving satisfaction but only maladaptive behaviors predicted caregiving burden.

Providing care to adults with mental retardation is likely to be experienced by caregivers as both rewarding and demanding (Heller & Factor, 1988, 1993). Many investigators have focused on how caregiving is appraised by caregivers of adults with mental retardation. These investigators have generally found that caregiving is perceived to be a burdensome activity, and they have not explored the more positive aspects of caregiving, such as caregiving satisfaction and the contribution adults with mental retardation make to their caregivers (Heller & Factor, 1991, 993; Seltzer & Krauss, 1989). Recently, researchers have begun to examine predictors of caregiving satisfaction instead of only caregiving burden (Pruchno, Patrick, & Burant, 1996; Smith, 1996). Although investigators are beginning to focus on caregiving satisfaction, they have ignored the influence that the supportive activities provided to the caregiver by the adult with mental retardation have on caregiving appraisals.

In the general population, Rossi and Rossi (1990) have documented that adult children provide considerable support and assistance to their aging relatives. Researchers, however, have often portrayed adults with mental retardation as sources of burden to their primary caregivers. In contrast, descriptive data from past research has demonstrated that adults with disabilities provide important support to their caregivers (Heller & Factor, 1988; Summers, Behr, & Turnbull, 1989). Yet, no research to date has been conducted to examine whether this support has any influence on caregiving burden or satisfaction. Thus, our primary goal in this investigation was to determine whether the amount of support provided by the adult with mental retardation to the caregiver influences the extent that caregivers appraise caregiving as burdensome or satisfying.

Caregiving appraisals are the cognitive and affective responses that caregivers have in reaction to the demands of caregiving (Lawton, Moss, Kelban, Glicksman, & Rovine, 1991). These appraisals generally fall into two categories: caregiving satisfaction and caregiving burden. In the present study, *caregiving burden* is defined as the perception of anxiety, depression, loss of freedom, or other form of psychological distress as a result of caregiving activities (Lawton et al., 1991). *Caregiving satisfaction* is defined as the realization that what one does or feels as a caregiver is a source of personal satisfaction (Lawton et al., 1991). Both appraisals of caregiving burden and caregiving satisfaction can occur simultaneously with separate antecedents.

Research on support provided by adults with other types of disabilities has been conducted. Investigators examining families of adults with mental illness have found that these adults provide social support to their families and that this support is related to lower levels of maternal subjective burden (Greenberg, 1995; Greenberg, Greenley, & Benedict, 1994; Horwitz, Reinhard, & Howell-White, 1996). Although such research in the area of mental retardation has yet to show a relation between support from the adult with a disability and caregiver well-being, several descriptive studies attest to the positive contributions that persons with mental retardation make to their families (Summers et al., 1989). Abbott and Meredith (1986) and Turnbull, Guess, and Turnbull (1988) noted that parents report receiving benefits from their children with mental retardation, such as stronger family ties, greater compassion, joy, and fulfillment. In Heller and Factor's (1988) research on future planning among aging parents, they found that many families report that their offspring with disabilities provide meaning to their lives, do chores for them, contribute financially through their Social Security Income, and keep them from feeling lonely. Persons with mental retardation are also likely to be living at home and lack competitive employment, which increases the possibility that they would be available to provide support to their parents. In addition, adults with mental retardation may become important sources of support to their parents as their parents age and possibly require greater assistance.

It seems possible that positive contributions increase the likelihood that caregivers will make positive appraisals about their role. It is also possible that a lack of contributions provided by persons with a disability would increase the subjective burden experienced by caregivers. Results of past research indicate that social support is associated with lower levels of burden (Seltzer & Krauss, 1989; Zarit, Reever, & Bach-Peterson, 1980). Therefore, we hypothesized that greater supportive activities by adults with mental retardation would be associated with greater caregiving satisfaction and that low levels of supportive activities would be related to greater caregiving burden. In addition, we examined other factors that have been reported in the literature to have an effect on perceived caregiving burden and satisfaction.

Results of past research on the experience of caregiving for relatives with disabilities suggest that there are other background factors that predict caregiving appraisals. We used Lawton et al.'s (1991) prominent gerontological model to explore what other antecedents may be related to caregiving burden and caregiving satisfaction among caregivers of adults with mental retardation. Lawton et al. designed the model to examine the relation of stressors and resources to positive and negative caregiving appraisals among spousal and adult child caregivers of aging relatives with Alzheimer disease. Furthermore, they examined the relation of these variables to the psychological well-being of the caregiver. In the current investigation we only focused on predic-

tors of appraisal and not on well-being. We used Lawton et al.'s model as a basis for choosing predictors of caregiving appraisals because it allowed us to examine both caregiving burden and satisfaction. Also, we expanded on this model by including support provided to the caregiver from the adult with mental retardation as a predictor.

In Lawton et al.'s (1991) model, the predictors of caregiving appraisals are (a) symptom severity of the relative with a disability, (b) personal resources (caregiver health), (c) social resources (informal assistance provided by friends and family), and (d) amount of help provided by the caregiver to the aging relative. Lawton et al. hypothesized that (a) greater symptom severity would increase caregiving burden and decrease caregiving satisfaction, (b) personal and social resources would decrease caregiving burden and increase caregiving satisfaction, and (c) a greater amount of caregiving assistance to the aging relative would simultaneously increase caregiving satisfaction and caregiving burden.

In the gerontological literature, there is some evidence that severity of disability (symptoms) is associated with greater caregiving burden (Lawton, Rajagopal, Brody, & Kleban, 1992; Pruchno, Peters, & Burant, 1995) and satisfaction (Lawton et al., 1991, 1992). The reasoning is that providing care for a person with a disability may simultaneously tax the caregiver's resources and affirm the caregiver's commitment to his or her relative. Thus, positive and negative appraisals are associated with providing care to persons with more severe disabilities. Among families of adults with mental retardation, however, researchers to date have only demonstrated that the severity of disability (lower adaptive functioning and higher maladaptive behaviors) are associated with greater caregiving burden (Heller & Factor, 1993; Pruchno et al., 1996). Pruchno et al. and Smith (1996) found no relation between severity of disability and caregiving satisfaction. We, therefore, hypothesized that for family caregivers of adults with mental retardation, severity of disability (adaptive functioning and maladaptive behaviors) will be associated with increased caregiving burden but not with caregiving satisfaction.

Among caregivers of aging relatives, researchers have demonstrated that the resources possessed by the caregiver aid in coping with life stressors such as caregiving activities (Lawton et al., 1991; Pruchno et al., 1996). Caregiver health (a personal resource) has been found to be associated with less burden but not with

Adults With Mental Retardation as Supports to Their Parents

Tamar Heller, Alison B. Miller, and Alan Factor

satisfaction (Lawton et al., 1991, 1992; Pruchno et al., 1995). Results of some research on caregivers of adults with mental retardation is consistent with these findings (Heller & Factor, 1993; Pruchno et al., 1996; Tausig, 1985), indicating that better caregiver health is associated with less caregiving burden. Smith (1996), however, found that caregiver health was not associated with either type of appraisal among maternal caregivers of offspring with mental retardation. Overall, results of past research seem to indicate that only negative appraisals are related to the caregiver's health. Therefore, we hypothesized that poor caregiver health will be associated with greater caregiving burden but not with caregiving satisfaction.

Researchers examining the influence of the social resource of informal assistance from friends and family (not including the relative with a disability) on caregiving appraisals have had inconsistent results. Contrary to their hypothesis, Lawton et al. (1991, 1992) did not find any relation between informal caregiving assistance and either type of caregiving appraisal among spouse and adult caregivers of aging relatives. Among families of adults with mental retardation, there is some evidence that informal supports are associated with lower caregiving burden (Heller & Factor, 1993; Seltzer & Krauss, 1989) but not with caregiving satisfaction (Smith, 1996). Therefore, on the basis of these results, we hypothesized that informal supports will decrease caregiving burden but have no influence on caregiving satisfaction.

Another important antecedent to caregiving appraisals hypothesized by Lawton et al. (1991) is the amount of assistance provided by the caregiver to the aging relative. As they predicted, Lawton et al. (1991, 1992) found that greater assistance was associated with increased burden and satisfaction among caregivers of aging relatives. They suggested that caregiving assistance increases both burden and satisfaction because it may simultaneously exceed the caregiver's resources and positively reaffirm his or her commitment to the person receiving care. In one of the few studies in which caregiver assistance among families of adults with mental retardation was examined, Smith (1996) found that greater caregiver assistance was not associated with burden or satisfaction. Pruchno et al. (1996), however, found greater assistance provided by maternal caregivers to their children with developmental disabilities or mental illness was associated with greater burden but not with satisfaction. Overall, it seems that the amount of help the caregiver provides increases negative appraisals but has

little or no effect on positive appraisals. Thus, we hypothesized that greater caregiving assistance would only be associated with greater caregiving burden.

To summarize, our hypotheses were as follows: (a) Greater supportive activities from adults with mental retardation would increase caregiving satisfaction and decrease caregiving burden. (b) Severity of disability, poor caregiver health, lower informal support, and greater caregiving assistance would be associated with greater caregiving burden but not with caregiving satisfaction.

Method

Sample

Study participants were 80 parents (primary caregivers) living with an adult son or daughter who had mental retardation. Primary caregivers were obtained from three states: Illinois (45%), Indiana (28%), and Ohio (28%). They were originally selected for a longitudinal study of residential transitions. Personnel from provider and case management agencies for persons with mental retardation were asked to identify parents who had an offspring with mental retardation who was 30 years of age or older. Of the 94 families designated by the agencies, 13 refused to participate and one could not be contacted, resulting in a response rate of 85%. The *primary caregiver* was defined as the parent primarily responsible for the care of their son or daughter.

The primary caregivers consisted of mothers (80%) and fathers (20%) whose mean age was 68.2 years. Eighty-eight percent of the sample was Caucasian and 12%, African American. Fifty-four percent of the caregivers were married, 43% were widowed, and 3% divorced. The health of 64% of the caregivers was reported to be good to excellent; another 28% reported that their health was fair, and 8%, that it was poor. The annual income of 55% of the families was under $20,000. Only 11% had incomes over $40,000.

The adult children (56% were males) of the primary caregivers had a mean age of 42 years. Forty-nine percent of them were classified as having mild mental retardation; 30%, moderate mental retardation; and 22%, severe to profound mental retardation. The Inventory for Client and Agency Planning (Bruininks, Hill, Weatherman, & Woodcock, 1986) was administered by agency staff. This instrument contains service levels for daily living. On the basis of these levels, 6% of the adult children were classified as needing total care; 14%, extensive care; 28%, regular personal care; 43%, limited personal care; and 9%, infrequent or no assistance.

Measures

Written surveys and follow-up phone interviews lasting about one hour were conducted solely with the primary caregiver. Information was obtained on the demographic characteristics of the child and the parents, the health of both parents and child, support provided between the caregiver and their son or daughter with mental retardation, other support resources, service use, and the parents' quality of life.

Level of disability. The Inventory for Client and Agency Planning was used to obtain information about the level of functioning of the persons with mental retardation. This measure includes a 72-item scale of adaptive behavior and an 8-item scale of maladaptive behavior. A low score indicates a lower level of functioning. The adaptive behavior scale includes items that assess motor skills, social and communication skills, personal living skills, and community living skills. The maladaptive behavior scale includes items such as the degree to which a person is hurtful to oneself or others and the degree to which a person engages in socially offensive or uncooperative behavior. The split-half reliability coefficients reported in the manual on samples of adolescents and adults with mental retardation were .96 for the adaptive behavior scale and .90 for the maladaptive behavior scale.

Personal resources. Two items from the Research and Service Oriented Multi-Level Assessment Instrument (Lawton, Moss, Fulcomer, & Kleban, 1982) were used to assess the health of caregivers. Caregivers rated their overall health on a scale of 1 (*excellent*) to 4 (*poor*). Also, they rated the extent to which any health problems they had interfered with their functioning on a scale of 1 (*not at all*) to 3 (*a great deal*). The two items had an alpha reliability of .69.

Social resources. This indicator was measured using a 21-item scale (Social Support Inventory Scale) designed to assess whether or not the caregiver received help from relatives, children (not including the child with mental retardation), and friends. The following seven areas of help were measured: helping them feel better when upset, helping with personal care, helping with chores, helping financially, keeping them from feeling lonely, sharing enjoyable activities, and giving useful advice and information. These items were adapted from the Parenting Social Support Index (Telleen, 1985). For this scale, caregivers reported whether or not their spouse, other children, other relatives, and friends provided support in the seven areas. The alpha reliability for the scale was .82.

Caregiver assistance. The amount of caregiver assistance provided to the adult with mental retardation was measured using the seven items just described. The Social Support Inventory Scale was used to assess the ex-

Table 1 Summary of Measures

Measure	Mean	SD	Range
ICAP[a]			
Adaptive functioning	473.8	32.0	399–487
Maladaptive functioning	−6.9	9.1	−49.0–0.0
Caregiver health[b]	3.9	1.3	2.0–7.0
Amount of informal support[c]	7.8	4.6	0.0–20.0
Caregiver assistance[c]	22.7	3.9	10.0–28.0
Support by adult child[c]	1.5	1.6	1.0–7.0
Caregiver burden[d]	2.4	0.7	1.1–4.4
Caregiver satisfaction[e]	7.9	2.0	1.0–10.0

[a] Inventory of Client and Agency Planning.

[b] Adapted from the Research and Service Oriented Multi-Level Assessment Instrument.

[c] Adapted from the Parenting Social Support Index.

[d] Adapted from the Zarit Burden Interview, using mean item score.

[e] Adapted from a caregiving scale developed by Lawton (1991).

Table 2 Correlations Between Study Variables

Variable	1	2	3	4	5	6	7	8
1. ICAP[a] adaptive	1.00							
2. ICAP maladaptive	0.39	1.00						
3. Caregiver health	0.05	0.09	1.00					
4. Informal support	0.08	0.05	0.06	1.00				
5. Caregiver assistance	−0.26	0.00	−0.07	0.04	1.00			
6. Support by adult child	0.12	0.09	0.06	0.56	0.04	1.00		
7. Caregiver satisfaction	−0.23	0.11	−0.20	−0.03	0.45	0.16	1.00	
8. Caregiver burden	−0.11	−0.24	0.09	−0.13	0.15	0.34	−0.32	1.00

Note. All correlations with absolute values greater than .2 are significant at the .05 level.

[a]Inventory of Client and Agency Planning.

tent to which the caregiver provided support to the adult with mental retardation in each of the seven areas. Items were rated on a scale of 1 (*not at all*) to 4 (*very much*). The alpha reliability of the scale was .68.

Support provided by the adult with mental retardation. Support to the parent referred to whether the adult with mental retardation helped the caregiver in the seven support functions listed previously. The Support to Caregiver scale was rated 1 (*no*) or 2 (*yes*) for each of the seven items. The alpha reliability was .75.

Caregiving appraisals. Caregiving appraisals included measures of caregiving burden and caregiving satisfaction. Caregiving burden was assessed with 22 of the 29 items of the Zarit Burden Interview (Zarit et al., 1980), which is a widely used instrument to measure subjective caregiving burden of elderly relatives. We omitted items that did not seem relevant to caring for an adult with mental retardation. On this scale, parents rate the extent to which they feel various aspects of burden ranging from 1 (*never*) to 5 (*nearly always*). The items measured the degree to which parents felt that caring for their child affected their health, psychological well-being, finances, social life, and relationships with others. The alpha reliability of this scale was .93.

Caregiving satisfaction was measured with the Caregiving Satisfaction Scale developed by Lawton et al. (1991). It includes 5 items ranging from 0 (*never*) to 2 (*very often*). For example, caregivers rate whether they enjoy being with their child and the degree to which being with their child increases their self-esteem. The alpha reliability was .69. A summary of the measures used in this study and information on their means, standard deviations [*SD*s], and ranges are provided in Table 1.

Results

Descriptive Data

Caregivers reported that their adult sons and daughters with mental retardation provided them with a wide variety of supports. The areas in which they were most likely to receive support from the adult with mental retardation were preventing the caregiver from feeling lonely (41%), helping with chores (39%), and sharing activities that they enjoyed (33%). Twenty-three percent reported receiving help in feeling better when upset, and 8% received advice and information from the adult sons and daughters. They were least likely to report receiving help with finances (3%) and personal care (4%).

Predicting caregiving appraisals. To determine the extent that the functioning level of the adult with mental retardation, caregiver health, other support resources, and caregiving assistance to and from the adult with mental retardation contribute to caregiving appraisals, we conducted hierarchical regressions, with adaptive and maladaptive behavior of adult with mental retardation and health of caregiver entered together first in a block. Informal support was entered second. Caregiver assistance (support from parent) was entered third and support from the adult with mental retardation entered fourth. The variables were entered in this order because we wanted to assess the impact of support to and from the adult with mental retardation with external supports and characteristics of the caregiver and their child already taken into account. The tolerance values of each independent variable indicated no multicollinearity. Correlations of the independent and dependent variables are provided in Table 2.

Caregiver burden. The results of this hierarchical regression are provided in Table 3. The first block of adult with mental retardation and caregiver characteristics did not account for a significant portion of the variance in caregiving burden. However, the individual variable of maladaptive behavior was significant, $p < .05$. Greater maladaptive behavior was associated with more caregiver burden. Neither the amount of informal support nor the amount of caregiver support to the adult with mental retardation was associated with caregiving burden. However, the amount of support provided by the adult with mental retardation to the caregiver significantly accounted for 10% of the variance in caregiving burden, $p < .01$. Caregivers who received more support from their son or daughter with a disability experienced less caregiving burden.

Caregiving satisfaction. The results of this hierarchical regression are also provided in Table 3. The first block

of adult with mental retardation and caregiver characteristics (adaptive and maladaptive behavior and caregiver health) accounted for 15% of the variance in caregiving satisfaction, $p < .01$. The specific significant variables in the first block were adaptive behavior and maladaptive behavior, $p < .01$ and .03, respectively. Caregiver health was marginally significant, $p < .06$. Greater caregiving satisfaction was reported by caregivers of children with lower levels of maladaptive functioning and lower adaptive functioning. Informal support did not explain a significant amount of variance. The amount of caregiver support provided to the adult with mental retardation accounted for 13% of the variance, $p < .001$, with greater satisfaction reported by caregivers who provided more support. Finally, the amount of support provided to the parent by the adult with mental retardation accounted for 5% of the variance, $p < .03$. Thus, increased levels of both parental support to the adult with mental

Table 3 Regressions of All Measures on Burden and Satisfaction

Variable	Beta	Beta	Beta	Beta
Burden				
Adult with mental retardation and caregiver characteristics				
ICAP[a] adaptive	−0.02	−0.01	0.05	0.07
ICAP maladaptive	−0.24*	−0.24*	−0.27*	−0.25*
Caregiver health	0.11	0.12	0.13	0.14
Informal support		−0.13	−0.14	0.06
Caregiver assistance			0.18	0.20
Support from adult child			0.07**	
r^2 change	0.07	0.02	0.03	0.10**
Total r^2 (unadjusted)	0.07	0.09	0.12	0.21**
Satisfaction				
Adult with mental retardation and caregiver characteristics				
ICAP[a] adaptive	−0.32**	−0.32**	−0.20	−0.21*
ICAP maladaptive	0.26*	0.26*	0.21	0.19
Caregiver health	−0.21	−0.21	−0.18	−0.19
Informal support		0.00	−0.03	−0.17
Caregiver assistance			0.38***	0.37***
Support from adult child				0.25*
r^2 change	0.15**	0.00	0.13***	0.05*
Total r^2 (unadjusted)	0.15**	0.15*	0.28***	0.33***

Note. All betas are standardized

[a] Inventory of Client and Agency Planning.

   * $p < .05$
  ** $p < .01$
 *** $p < .001$

retardation and adults support to their parents were associated with greater parental caregiving satisfaction.

Discussion

This study is unique in that it demonstrates how support from adults with mental retardation can play a significant role in reducing negative appraisals and increasing positive appraisals of caregiving. In addition, results of this study demonstrate that different patterns of caregiving burden and caregiving satisfaction are associated with various characteristics of the caregivers and their adult sons and daughters with mental retardation.

Support From the Adult Child With Mental Retardation

The support of adults with mental retardation to their parents was a key factor in predicting parents' degree of perceived caregiving satisfaction and caregiving burden. Parents who received support from their son or daughter with mental retardation experienced greater caregiving satisfaction and less caregiving burden. Specifically, adults with mental retardation provided considerable companionship support to their parents and help with household chores. According to our results, these forms of support have a positive influence on the experience of caregiving. Overall, these findings attest to the importance of understanding reciprocal caregiving roles and that persons with disabilities can play key supportive roles for their parents. This may be particularly important as parents experience frailty due to aging or become widowed.

Caregiver Assistance

The hypothesized association between caregiver assistance provided to the adult with mental retardation and caregiving appraisal was only partially supported by the data. Greater caregiving assistance was associated with caregiving satisfaction but not with caregiving burden. One explanation for this finding could be that providing care to a son or daughter with mental retardation helps give purpose to the caregiver's life. In Heller and Factor's (1988) report, 61% of families indicated that taking care of their relative with mental retardation at home provided meaning to their lives. Todd and Shearn (1996) noted that most caregivers of adults with mental retardation have provided life-long care to their child and are likely to be emotionally invested in the parental

role. The finding that providing care is more likely to be associated with caregiving satisfaction than caregiving burden is discrepant from the findings of Smith (1996) and Pruchno et al. (1996). They found significant relations between caregiving assistance and caregiving burden. One explanation for these differences is that their measures focused exclusively on instrumental support, whereas our measure also focused on socioemotional support.

Adults With Mental Retardation and Caregiver Characteristics

The results of this investigation indicate that the characteristics of adults with mental retardation influence both types of caregiving appraisals. Both adaptive and maladaptive functioning (severity of disability) were associated with caregiving satisfaction. Specifically, caregivers of adults with mental retardation who had lower adaptive functioning reported greater caregiving satisfaction, whereas parents of children with greater maladaptive functioning reported less caregiving satisfaction. Perhaps performing caregiving activities to compensate for a son or daughter's low adaptive functioning is affirming to the parent because such activities (e.g., bathing, feeding) are associated with the role of caregiver. On the other hand, coping with maladaptive behaviors may be stressful or demanding for the caregiver and, thus, reduce caregiving satisfaction. The demand of having to care for an adult child with maladaptive behaviors on caregivers is further demonstrated by the positive association between such behaviors and caregiving burden.

Although characteristics of the adult with mental retardation predicted caregiving appraisals, the health of the caregiver did not predict burden or satisfaction. This finding is similar to Smith's (1996) study, in which he found no significant relation between the caregiver's health and either type of appraisal. Although caregiver health does not appear to be a major determinant of caregiving appraisal, it should not be discounted as an important factor in the caregiving experience because it has been related to the well-being of caregivers (Pruchno et al., 1996; Smith, 1996).

Practical and Policy Implications

The results of the current investigation have some implications for practice and policy. Professionals should approach the family as the unit of focus by attending to the meaning and value of the relationships between parents and their children with mental retardation. Professionals who counsel families of persons with mental retardation, especially with regard to out-of-home placement, should be aware that some families may prefer to have their relative with mental retardation live at home. This preference may be due to the rewards of caregiving and the socioemotional and instrumental support the relative with mental retardation provides to the caregiver. However, as parents age or their health declines, they may need to consider alternatives to caring for their children in the home. These families may need support in conducting future planning for their children regarding living, legal, and financial arrangements. For those families who want to continue caregiving in the home, family support programs are needed to support both the aging parents and the adult with mental retardation. These programs should include services such as help with future planning, case management, and respite care (Heller & Factor, 1991).

Summary and Directions for Future Research

The disparate findings between the effects of parent caregiving efforts on caregiving burden and caregiving satisfaction are similar to those found by Lawton et al. (1991) regarding family care of elderly persons. Caregiving satisfaction and caregiving burden are different factors, not opposite sides of a continuum. Apparently, parents experience personal rewards for providing support to their child that they perceive as helpful. In fact, they are most satisfied when caring for a child who is more dependent in their adaptive behavior skills. This finding attests to the importance of focusing on the positive aspects of caregiving and not solely on the negative ones. In addition, we found that adult children with mental retardation provided important support to their parents, which played a significant role in reducing negative appraisals and increasing positive appraisals of caregiving.

There are several limitations to this study. First, because this study had a cross-sectional design, the relations of the predictors studied and caregiving appraisals are correlational. Therefore, inferences about causality based on the results of this investigation are questionable. For example, caregivers may provide more opportunities to their adult children to help if they are experiencing less burden (Greenberg, 1995). Second, the variables we examined in this study do not encompass all of the possible predictors of positive and negative caregiving appraisal. Other examples of possible predictors that should be examined are formal services, day program usage, cash benefits such as Supplemental Security Income, and the amount of support from other family members. Research with a longitudinal design is needed in order to better specify predictors of subjective appraisals and to explore possible causal relations between those predictors and appraisals.

Third, this investigation is based on a nonprobability sample of primary caregivers who volunteered to be in this study and who were known to the service system. Readers should, therefore, be cautious about generalizing the findings of this study. Finally, we focused on self-report data from the primary caregiver and obtained only the caregiver's perception of how much assistance the adult child with mental retardation provided. As this was not an objective measure, we may have obtained an over- or underestimate of the amount of support provided (Greenberg, 1995).

In the future researchers should expand on understanding the role persons with mental retardation play in the caregiving experience by including their perspectives on the support they provide to their caregivers. Persons with mental retardation may have a different perspective on the amount of reciprocal support that is provided between themselves and their caregiver and offer us insights into the experience of receiving care. Obtaining the perspective of the adult child with mental retardation may help illuminate how their quality of life is influenced by providing support to their parents. Providing support could have positive influences such as increased self-esteem or potentially negative effects such as increased levels of stress if demands for their support become too great. Finally, in the future researchers studying the reciprocal roles of caregiving should include families that are not currently included in the social service system and culturally diverse families.

References

Abbott, D. A., & Meredith, W. H. (1986). Strengths of parents with retarded children. *Family Relations, 35,* 371–375.

Bruininks, R. H., Hill, B. K., Weatherman, R., & Woodcock, R. W. (1986). *Inventory for Client and Agency Planning.* Allen, TX: DLM Teaching Resources.

Greenberg, J. A. (1995). The other side of caring: Adult children with mental illness as supports to their mothers in later life. *Social Work, 40*, 414–423.

Greenberg, J. A., Greenley, J. R., & Benedict, P. (1994). Contributions of persons with serious mental illness to their families. *Hospital and Community Psychiatry, 45*, 475–480.

Heller, T., & Factor, A. (1988). *Transition plan for developmentally disabled persons residing in the natural home with family caregivers* (Public Policy Monograph Series). Chicago: University of Illinois at Chicago.

Heller, T., & Factor, A. (1991). Permanency planning for adults with mental retardation living with family caregivers. *American Journal on Mental Retardation, 96*, 163–176.

Heller, T., & Factor, A. (1993). Aging family caregivers: Support resources and changes in burden and placement desire. *American Journal on Mental Retardation, 98*, 417–426.

Horwitz, A. V., Reinhard, S. C., & Howell-White, S. (1996). Caregiving as reciprocal exchange in families with seriously mentally ill members. *Journal of Health and Social Behavior, 37*, 149–162.

Lawton, P. M., Moss, M., Fulcomer, M., & Kleban, M. H. (1982). A research and service oriented multilevel assessment instrument. *Journal of Gerontology, 37*, 91–99.

Lawton, P. M., Moss, M., Kleban, M. H., Glickman, A., & Rovine, M. (1991). A two-factor model of caregiving appraisal and psychological well-being. *Journal of Gerontology: Psychological Sciences, 46*, 181–189.

Lawton, P. M., Rajagopal, D., Brody, E., & Kleban, M. H. (1992). The dynamics of caregiving for a demented elder among black and white families. *Journal of Gerontology: Social Sciences, 47*, 5156–5164.

Pruchno, R. A., Patrick, J. H., & Burant, C. J. (1996). Mental health of aging women with children who are chronically disabled: Examination of a two factor model. *Journal of Gerontology: Social Sciences, 51B*, S284–S296.

Pruchno, R. A., Peters, N. D., & Burant, C. J. (1995). Mental health of co-resident family caregivers: Examination of a two-factor model. *Journal of Gerontology: Psychological Sciences, 50B*, 247–256.

Rossi, A. S., & Rossi, P. H. (1990). *Of human bonding: Parent-child relations across the life course.* New York: Aldine de Gruyter.

Seltzer, M. M., & Krauss, M. (1989). Aging parents with mentally retarded children: Family risk factors and sources of support. *American Journal on Mental Retardation, 94*, 303–312.

Smith, G. C. (1996). Caregiving outcomes for older mothers of adults with mental retardation: A test of the two-factor model of psychological well-being. *Psychology and Aging, 11*, 1–9.

Summers, J. A., Behr, S. K., & Turnbull, A. P. (1989). Positive adaptation and coping strengths of families who have children with disabilities. In G. H. S. Singer & L. K. Irvin (Eds.), *Support for caregiving families: Enabling positive adaptation to disability* (pp. 27–40). Baltimore: Brookes.

Tausig, M. (1985). Factors in family decision-making about placement for developmentally disabled individuals. *American Journal of Mental Deficiency, 89*, 352–361.

Telleen, S. (1985). *Parenting social support reliability and validity.* Unpublished manuscript, University of Illinois at Chicago, School of Public Health.

Todd, S., & Shearn, J. (1996). Time and the person: The impact of support services on the lives of parents of adults with intellectual disabilities. *Journal of Applied Research in Intellectual Disabilities, 9*, 40–60.

Turnbull, H. R., Guess, D., & Turnbull, A. P. (1988). Vox populi and Baby Doe. *Mental Retardation, 26*, 127–132.

Zarit, S. H., Reever, K. E., & Bach-Peterson, J. (1980). Relatives of the impaired aged: Correlates of feelings of burden. *The Gerontologist, 20*, 649–655.

Received 9/4/96, first decision 11/12/96, accepted 12/30/96. Editor-in-Charge: Steven J. Taylor

Preparation of this article was supported, in part, by the Rehabilitation Research and Training Center on Aging with Mental Retardation, University of Illinois at Chicago, through Grant No. H133B30069 from the U.S. Department of Education, National Institute on Disability and Rehabilitation Research.

Authors

Tamar Heller, Ph.D., Associate Professor, **Alison B. Miller, M.A.,** PhD Candidate, and **Alan Factor, Ph.D.,** Senior Research Specialist, Institute on Disability and Human Development, University of Illinois at Chicago, 1640 W. Roosevelt Rd., Chicago, IL 60608.

The Feebleminded Parent: A Study of 90 Family Cases
An Attempt to Isolate Those Factors Associated With Their Successful or Unsuccessful Parenthood

Phyllis Mickelson
1947

"The better we understand the feebleminded and how to help them, the more faith we have in their capacity to respond to favorable conditions."

—A (relatively new) case-work saying.

Introduction

This is a study of 90 families in which one or both parent has been adjudged feebleminded. Its purpose was twofold: To attempt to identify those factors which appeared to have been associated with successful or unsuccessful parenthood, and to evaluate the effectiveness of institutionalization, sterilization and community supervision as measures of control. Special emphasis, however, was to be placed on the process of community supervision in the hope of developing principles, or hypotheses at least, for use with all such families. In these twenty minutes, however, only the results of the first part of the study can be presented.

Method and results will be better understood if it is explained first that in Minnesota the feebleminded are committed to the guardianship of the state—specifically the Director of Public Institutions—rather than to an institution, that guardianship is for life unless discharged by subsequent court action, and that it gives continuing authority to plan for the ward in whatever way seems best—in the institution or out. Under direction of the state office supervision in the community is given by the 87 county welfare boards which have by law the responsibility for administering all public welfare services. Entrances to and exits from the institutions are arranged through the state office with the cooperation of the institutions and the welfare boards. In conclusion Minnesota has a sterilization law which permits sterilization of the feebleminded, provided the written consent of the spouse or nearest relative is obtained.

Method

To secure comparable information on all family cases—those where either parent was under guardianship as feebleminded—the welfare boards were asked to send current information according to a special outline which contained the following items: (1) Living Conditions; (2) Income; (3) Health; (4) Family Relations; (5) Personality Traits; (6) Care and Adjustment of the Children; (7) Supervision Given; (8) Persistent Problems. In addition routine reports previously submitted by the welfare boards on these families and covering the period from commitment to inception of the study were reviewed.

Reports were received on 90 families: 79 or 88 percent from 41 rural counties and the remaining 11 or 22 percent from one urban county. With the exception of one parent who was committed in 1919, the year of commitment ranged from 1926 to 1946, the average number of years under state guardianship being 11. In 67 or 74 percent of the families the wife only was committed; in 8 or 9 percent the husband only; and in 15 or 17 percent both husband and wife were committed, a total of 105 parents who had been adjudged feebleminded. Distribution of their I.Q.'s was as follows:

Table 1 Distribution of IQs of the 105 Parents Adjudged Feebleminded

I.Q.	Approximate	
	No.	Percentage
30-39	1	1
40-49	13	12
50-59	44	42
60-69	33	31
70-75	12	12
Over 75	2	2 (now restored to capacity)
Total	105	

Their average I.Q. was 58.6.

The first step taken was to divide the 90 families into three groups based on the adequacy of care given to the children: Satisfactory, Questionable or Unsatisfactory. Thirty-eight or 42 percent of the families were rated as having given their children Satisfactory care; 29 or 32 percent were rated as having give Questionable care; and 23 or 26 percent were rated as having given Unsatisfactory care. Although necessarily subjective, this judgment was based in every instance on the absence or presence of social evidence which is customarily accepted as indicative of child neglect. For example, a rating of Satisfactory meant not only the absence of complaints from the community, but positive evidence that the children were kept clean, adequately fed, clothed and supervised, and regular in school attendance. A rating of Questionable indicated some inconsistency or inadequacy of care but not of sufficient degree to justify removal of the children as neglected. A rating of Unsatisfactory meant either that the children had been removed as neglected (there were ten such cases) or that their care was sufficiently poor to justify consideration of such action.

Various factors were then analyzed in an effort to determine their relationship to adequacy of child care.

Results

Number of pregnancies was considered first. (See Table 2.) For the total group there were 489 known pregnancies, an average of 5.4 per family. This average increased, however, from 4.0 for the Satisfactory group, to 6.2 for the Questionable group, to 6.7 for the Unsatisfactory group. It was found, furthermore, that the percentage of families with one to three total pregnancies decreased from 45 percent in the Satisfactory group to 21 percent in both the Questionable and the Unsatisfactory groups. All but one of the nine families with only one pregnancy were in the Satisfactory group. The percentage with 4 to 6 pregnancies decreased from 37 percent in the Satisfactory group, to 31 percent in the Questionable group, to 13 percent in the Unsatisfactory group. The percentage with 7 to 9 pregnancies increased, however, from 18 percent in the Satisfactory group to 34.5 percent in the Questionable group to 57 percent in the Unsatisfactory group. Finally the percentage with 10 to 12 pregnancies varied from 0 percent in the Satisfactory group, to 13.5 percent in the Questionable group, to 8 percent in the Unsatisfactory group. In other words, in

Table 2 Relationship of Number of Pregnancies to Adequacy of Child Care

No. of Children	Total Group No. Families	%		Satisfactory No.	%		Questionable No.	%		Unsatisfactory No.	%	
1	9	10		8	21		0	—		1	4	
2	7	8	31	4	11	45	2	7	21	1	4	21
3	12	13		5	13		4	14		3	13	
4	9	10		7	18		2	7		0	—	
5	8	9	29	4	11	37	3	10	31	1	4	13
6	9	10		3	8		4	14		2	9	
7	9	10		2	5		5	17		2	9	
8	15	17	34	2	5	18	4	14	34.5	9	39	57
9	6	7		3	8		1	3.5		2	9	
10	4	4		0	—		3	10		1	4	
11	1	1	6	0	—	0	1	3.5	13.5	0	—	8
12	1	1		0	—		0	—		1	4	
Total	90			38			29			23		

spite of certain exceptions, there was a tendency for child care to become less adequate as the number of pregnancies increased.

In this connection it should be noted that in 56 or 62 percent of the families one or both parent had been sterilized. The percentage varied from 73 percent of the families in the Satisfactory group to 55 percent of those in the Questionable group to 52 percent of those in the Unsatisfactory group. Thus, reducing the number of children in the home was one of the ways in which sterilization contributed to adequacy of child care.

A total of 300 children were currently living in the home, an average of 3.3 per family. (See Table 3.) This average increased, however, from 2.5 for the Satisfactory group, to 3.7 for the Questionable group, to 4.2 for the Unsatisfactory group. The percentage of families with one to three children in the home decreased from 71 percent in the Satisfactory group, to 52 percent in the Questionable group, to $47^2/_3$ percent in the Unsatisfactory group. The percentage with 4 to 6 children varied, however, from 26 percent in the Satisfactory group, to 41 percent in the Questionable group, to $34^1/_3$ in the Unsatisfactory group. The percentage with 7 to 10 children increased from 3 percent to 7 percent to $17^1/_3$ percent respectively. Again this would indicate a definite tendency for child care to become less adequate as the number of children in the home increased.

When age distribution of these 300 children was analyzed (see Table 4), it was found that for the group as a whole 19 percent were age 5 or under; 35 percent were between 6 and 10 years of age; 32 percent between 11 and 15 years of age; and the remaining 14 percent were 16 years of age or over. The only significant variation was that the percentage of children age 5 and under increased from 16 percent in the Satisfactory group to 19 percent in the Questionable group to 24 percent in the Unsatisfactory group.

Mental test results accompanied by a definite diagnosis were available for only 65 or 22 percent or these 300 children. (See Table 5.) Of these 18 or 6 percent had been diagnosed to be of average mentality or above; 3 or 1 percent as borderline or dull; and 44 or 15 percent as feebleminded. The distribution was approximately the same for the Satisfactory, Questionable and Unsatisfactory groups.

On the basis of their school achievements and social adjustment, effort was made to rate the mentality of the remaining children. Eighty-one or 27 percent of the children were judged to be of average intelligence and 70 or 23 percent as mentally retarded. No judgment was attempted for the remaining 84 or 24 percent of the children because of insufficient or conflicting information. The percent rated as average or above showed a definite increase and the percent rated as retarded a definite de-

Table 3 Relationship of Number of Children in Home to Adequacy of Child Care

No. of Children	Total Group			Satisfactory			Questionable			Unsatisfactory		
	No. Families	%		No.	%		No.	%		No.	%	
1	16	18		13	34		2	7		1	$4^1/_3$	
2	22	24	59	9	24	71	7	24	52	6	26	$47^2/_3$
3	15	17		5	13		6	21		4	$17^1/_3$	
4	14	16		7	18		4	14		3	13	
5	8	9	34	2	5	26	5	17	41	1	$4^1/_3$	$34^1/_3$
6	8	9		1	3		3	10		4	17	
7	6	6		1	3		2	7		3	13	
8	0	—	7	—	—	3	—	—	7	—	—	$17^1/_3$
9	1	1		—	—		—	—		1	$4^1/_3$	
Total	90			38			29			23		

Table 4 Relationship of Age Distribution of Children in the Home to Adequacy of Child Care

	Total Group		Satisfactory		Questionable		Unsatisfactory	
	No. Children	%	No.	%	No.	%	No.	%
0–5 years	58	19	15	16	20	19	23	24
6–10 years	104	35	32	33	42	39	30	31
11–15 years	97	32	36	37	29	27	32	33
16 or over	41	14	14	14	16	15	11	12
Total	300		97		107		96	

Table 5 Relationship of Mentality of Children Living in Home to Adequacy of Child Care

	Total Group		Satisfactory		Questionable		Unsatisfactory	
	No.	%	No.	%	No.	%	No.	%
1. Diagnosed as Average or Above	18	6 ⎤	7	7 ⎤	7	7 ⎤	4	4 ⎤
2. Reason to Believe Average	81	27 ⎦ 33	42	43 ⎦ 50	27	25 ⎦ 32	12	12 ⎦ 16
3. Diagnosed as Borderline or Dull	3	1 ⎤	2	2 ⎤	1	1 ⎤	—	— ⎤
4. Diagnosed as Feebleminded	44	15 ⎟ 29	15	15½ ⎟ 33	14	13 ⎟ 41	15	16 ⎟ 43
5. Reason to Believe Retarded	70	23 ⎦	15	15½ ⎦	29	27 ⎦	26	27 ⎦
6. Insufficient Information	84	28	16	17	29	27	39	41
Total	300		97		107		96	

crease as one went from the Satisfactory to the Questionable to the Unsatisfactory groups. However, since the accuracy of these ratings can be questioned, the specific distribution will not be given, although it is available in table form.

Turning to the parents, the *relationship of the mother's I.Q.*, in the 86 cases where it was known, was the first factor to be considered. (See Table 6.) Of the ten mothers with I.Q.'s between 30-49, 30 percent were rated as having given their children Satisfactory care, 50 percent as having given Questionable care, and 20 percent as Unsatisfactory care. Of the 35 mothers with I.Q.'s between 50-59 and the 26 mothers with I.Q.'s between 60-69—where distribution was almost identical—approximately 44 percent were rated as having given Satisfactory care; 33 percent as having given Questionable care and 23 per Unsatisfactory care. Of mothers with I.Q.'s of 70 and over 33 percent were rated as having given Satisfactory care; 27 percent Questionable care; and 40 percent Unsatisfactory care. In other words, while mothers with I.Q.'s between 30-49 were rated as having given less satisfactory child care than the group as a whole, the

difference lay in the relative distribution between Satisfactory and Questionable care. For mothers with I.Q.'s of 50-59 and 60-69 the distribution was almost identical with that for the total group, without regard to I.Q. And finally, mothers with I.Q.'s of 70 and over were rated as having given the most unsatisfactory care of all. One concludes that, with the exception of those with I.Q.'s between 30-49, the *degree* of the mother's mental retardation had no relationship to adequacy of child care.

Differences between the mentality of husband and wife were considered next. (See Table 7.) Mental test results for both spouses were available in only 29 or one-third of the families. Where the difference was less than 15 points, mentality was considered "approximately the same," and where it exceeded 15 points one spouse was considered "brighter." In 58 families the mentality of the spouse not tested was rated as "approximately the same" or "brighter" with no judgment being attempted in the remaining three cases because of insufficient information.

In only 11 or 12 percent of the families was one spouse diagnosed or judged to be considerably brighter than the other. Of these 27 percent were in the Satisfac

The Feebleminded Parent: A Study of 90 Family Cases

Table 6 Relationship of Adequacy of Child Care to Mother's I.Q. (In 86 Cases Where Known)

	Total Group		I.Q. 30–49		I.Q. 50–59		I.Q. 60–69		I.Q. 70 and over	
	No.	%	No.	%	No.	%	No.	%	No.	%
Satisfactory	35	41	3	30	16	46	11	42	5	33
Questionable	29	34 ⎤	5	50 ⎤	11	31 ⎤	9	35 ⎤	4	27 ⎤
Unsatisfactory	22	25 ⎦ 59	2	20 ⎦ 70	8	23 ⎦ 54	6	23 ⎦ 58	6	40 ⎦ 67
Total	86		10		35		26		15	

Table 7 Relationship of Differences Between Mentality of Husband and Wife and Adequacy of Child Care

	Total Group		Satisfactory		Questionable		Unsatisfactory	
	No.	%	No.	%	No.	%	No.	%
1. Diagnosed as approximately same (less than 15 points difference)	21	24 ⎤ 85	11	30 ⎤ 90	9	31 ⎤ 94	1	4 ⎤ 65
2. Reason to believe approximately same	55	61 ⎦	23	60 ⎦	18	63 ⎦	14	61 ⎦
3. Diagnosed as brighter (by 15 points or more)	8	9 ⎤ 12	1	2½ ⎤ 7½	1	3 ⎤ 3	6	27 ⎤ 31
4. Reason to believe brighter	3	3 ⎦	2	5 ⎦	0	0 ⎦	1	4 ⎦
5. Insufficient Information	3	3	1	2½	1	3	1	4
Total	90		38		29		23	

Table 8 Cases in which Differences in I.Q. Between Husband and Wife Exceeded 15 Points

	I.Q.		No. of Points "Brighter"	
	Man	Woman	Man	Woman
1. Satisfactory	45	70		25
2. Questionable	83	57	26	
3. Unsatisfactory	47	152 and		105 and
		135		88
	58	78		20
	76 (Est.)	52	24 (Est.)	
	129	59	70	
	96	68	28	
	52	70		18

tory group; 9 percent in the Questionable group; and 64 percent in the Unsatisfactory group. The two most extreme differences noted: a woman with an I.Q. of 59, married to a man with an I.Q. of 129, and a man with an I.Q. of 47 married to a woman who had earned I.Q.'s of 152 and 135. Both were in the Unsatisfactory group. (See Table 8.)

Assuming that valid judgments were made, a strong tendency was found for like to marry like. Where exceptions occurred, they tended to be associated with unsatisfactory child care.

Analysis of the *age difference between* husband and wife, for the 87 cases in which this information could be obtained revealed that in 77 or 88 percent of the families the husband was older than the wife—from 1 to 41 years older. (See Table 9.) In only 7 or 8 percent of the families was the husband younger than the wife (3 years being the average), and in only 3 or 4 percent were they the same age. For the group as a whole the husband av-

eraged 9 years older than the wife. This average varied, however, from 7 years older in the Satisfactory group, to 10 years 1 month in the Questionable group, to 9 years 9 months in the Unsatisfactory group. In other words, there was a strong tendency for the husband to be older than the wife, but where this difference exceeded 9 years, it was more often associated with Questionable and Unsatisfactory than with Satisfactory child care.

Marital relationship was rated on a five point scale: Excellent, Satisfactory, Fair, Serious Conflict, and Separated or Divorced. (See Table 10.) If points one through three were labeled Harmonious, and points four and five Inharmonious, one found that the percentage rated as having a harmonious marital relationship decreased from $92\frac{1}{3}$ percent in the Satisfactory group to 65 percent in the Questionable group to 56 percent in the Unsatisfactory group. Thus there seemed to be an extremely high correlation between harmonious marital relationships and adequate child care.

Table 9 Relationship of Differences Between Age of Husband and Wife and Adequacy of Child Care

	Total Group		Satisfactory		Questionable		Unsatisfactory	
	No.	%	No.	%	No.	%	No.	%
Husband younger—1 year and more	7	8	3	8	2	7	2	9
Same age	3	4	3	8	0	—	0	—
Husband older—								
1–9 years	42	48 ⎤ 78	19	53 ⎤ 78	13	$44\frac{1}{2}$ ⎤ 79	10	46 ⎤ $77\frac{1}{2}$
10–19 years	26	30 ⎦	9	25 ⎦	10	$34\frac{1}{2}$ ⎦	7	$31\frac{1}{2}$ ⎦
20–41 years	9	10	2	6	4	14	3	13
Total	87		36		29		22	

Table 10 Relationship Between Satisfactoriness of Marital Relationship and Adequacy of Child Care

		Total Group		Satisfactory		Questionable		Unsatisfactory	
		No.	%	No.	%	No.	%	No.	%
1. Excellent	⎤	5	6 ⎤	5	13 ⎤	—	— ⎤	—	— ⎤
2. Satisfactory	Harmonious	42	47 ⎟ 75	23	$60\frac{2}{3}$ ⎟ $92\frac{1}{3}$	14	48 ⎟ 65	5	22 ⎟ 56
3. Fair	⎦	20	22 ⎦	7	$18\frac{2}{3}$ ⎦	5	17 ⎦	8	34 ⎦
4. Serious Conflict	⎤	16	17 ⎤	2	5 ⎤	9	31 ⎤	5	22 ⎤
5. Separated	Inharmonious		⎟ 25		⎟ $7\frac{2}{3}$		⎟ 35		⎟ 44
or Divorced	⎦	7	8 ⎦	1	$2\frac{2}{3}$ ⎦	1	4 ⎦	5	22 ⎦
Total		90		38		29		23	

Table 11 Relationship of Serious Physical Problems of Either Spouse to Adequacy of Child Care

	Total Group		Satisfactory		Questionable		Unsatisfactory	
	No.	%	No.	%	No.	%	No.	%
1. Men only	18	56	4	45	8	73	6	55
2. Women only	9	31	4	45	2	18	3	27
3. Both	4	13	1	9	1	9	2	18
Total	31		9		11		11	

Table 12 Relationship of Serious Mental Health Problems of Either Spouse to Adequacy of Child Care

	Total Group		Satisfactory		Questionable		Unsatisfactory	
	No.	%	No.	%	No.	%	No.	%
1. Men only	24	65	8	100	10	77	6	37½
2. Women only	7	19	0	—	1	8	6	37½
3. Both	6	16	0	—	2	15	4	25
Total	37		8		13		16	

The relationship of serious physical and mental health problems of the parents to the adequacy of child care were considered next. (See Tables 11 and 12.)

In 31 or approximately 34 percent of the families one or both parent had a serious physical handicap or health problem, such as loss of one limb, blindness, deafness, heart disease, epilepsy, arthritis, etc. The proportion increased, however, from 29 percent in the Satisfactory group to 35 percent in the Questionable and Unsatisfactory groups. This would indicate only a slight correlation between physical health of the parents and adequacy of child care.

In 37 or approximately 41 percent of the families, one or both parents presented a serious mental health problem. (See Table 12.)

These problems fell into three main groups: excessive drinking and chronic alcoholism accounted for 70 percent of the total; a severe personality disturbance—extreme suspiciousness, depression, etc.—for 21 percent; and miscellaneous difficulties, such as gambling and extra marital attachments, for the remaining 9 percent. (See Table 13.) The distribution of these mental health problems increased, however, from 21 percent in the Satisfactory group to 35 percent in the Questionable group to 47 percent in the Unsatisfactory group. Another significant difference was that in the Satisfactory group *none* of the wives presented a serious mental health problem,

whereas in the Questionable group there were three families or 23 percent in which the wife only, or the wife as well as the husband, presented such a problem; and in the Unsatisfactory group there were 10 such families—an increase from 0 percent to 23 percent to 62½ percent respectively. Thus, where the wife was stable and the difficulties of the husband not too extreme, there was satisfactory child care in every instance. Where the wife was the one to be maladjusted, however, or where the difficulties of either parent were more extreme—in all cases, for example, where one or both parent could be considered a chronic alcoholic or suffered from an extreme personality disturbance—there was, in every instance, questionable or unsatisfactory child care. In conclusion it can be said that there appeared to be a definite correlation between mental health of the parents and adequacy of child care, but the greater correlation as might be expected, was with the mental health of the mother.

Adequacy of available income was the tenth and last factor to be analyzed. (See Table 14.)

During the depression years most of these families were on relief; today, however, only 17 or approximately 19 percent of the men remained unemployed—in every instance due to ill health or physical handicap.

Being employed and having an adequate income were not synonymous, however. For example, the amount earned did not always meet total needs when the family was large and the husband an unskilled laborer, nor was all of it available for use in homes where there was poor management or excessive drinking. When allowances were made for these factors it was estimated that 16 percent of the families in the Satisfactory group had an income in excess of needs; 21 percent an adequate income; 55 percent a marginal income; none an inadequate income; and 8 percent were on relief. Compare this with the ratings for families in the Questionable and Unsatisfactory groups where distribution was almost identical: none were rated as having a net income equal to or in excess of their needs; 75 percent were rated as having a marginal income; 10 percent an inadequate income; and 15 percent were on relief. This would indicate a definite correlation between adequacy of income and adequacy of child care.

Conclusion

We have now completed the first part of our study of 90 families in which one or both parent has been adjudged feebleminded. What have we learned? In the first place, that the care these parents gave their children varied all the way from Satisfactory to Questionable to Unsatisfactory, with somewhat less than half, it is true, having given satisfactory care, but with only one-fourth having given unsatisfactory care. Thus, the parents' mental status did not appear to be the sole determinant of adequacy of child care; otherwise all of the children would have been neglected. We therefore searched for other factors. Ten were considered. Of these five seemed most important; namely, the mental health of the parents but especially that of the mother; the degree of harmony between husband and wife; the number of pregnancies and the number of children in the home; and finally the adequacy of income. We had to analyze each of the factors separately; somewhat belatedly we call attention to one of their most important characteristics; their interrelatedness.

It is not the factors themselves, however, but their implications for treatment which interests us most. In the first place, the results would seem to tell us that sterilization did or could have helped these families in many ways—by reducing the number of pregnancies and number of children in the home it thereby contributed to the mental and physical health of both parents and to

Table 13 Relationship of Adequacy of Available Income to Adequacy of Childcare

	Total Group		Satisfactory		Questionable		Unsatisfactory	
	No.	%	No.	%	No.	%	No.	%
1. Drinks Excessively	14	33 ⎤	5	62 ⎤	5	33⅓ ⎤	4	20 ⎤
2. Chronic Alcoholic	16	37 ⎦ 70	—	— ⎦ 62	7	46⅔ ⎦ 80	9	45 ⎦ 65
3. Personality Disturbance	9	21	—	—	3	20	6	30
4. Other	4	9	3	38	—	—	1	5
Total	43		8		15		20	

Table 14 Relationship of Adequacy of Available Income to Adequacy of Childcare

	Total Group		Satisfactory		Questionable		Unsatisfactory	
	No.	%	No.	%	No.	%	No.	%
1. Exceeds needs	6	6 ⎤	6	16 ⎤	0	—	0	—
2. Adequate	8	10 ⎦ 16	8	21 ⎦ 37	0	—	0	—
3. Marginal	60	67	21	55	22	76	17	74
4. Inadequate	5	5 ⎤	0	— ⎤	3	10 ⎤	2	9 ⎤
5. On relief	11	12 ⎦ 17	3	8 ⎦ 8	4	14 ⎦ 24	4	17 ⎦ 26
Total	90		38		29		23	

the harmony between husband and wife, as well as to their economic well-being, by keeping the family's size in realistic relation to the husband's earning capacity.

In the second place the number of major health problems and the still larger proportion of such minor problems, of which no mention has been made, suggest that we may be underestimating the ability of the feebleminded to feel strain, to worry, and to be unhappy over problems in their personal life. By the same token we may be underestimating their capacity to respond to therapy or counseling. Perhaps, instead of arbitrarily excluding them from these services, we have the obligation to adapt our methods to their needs.

Yet to be discussed are the factors of institutionalization and community supervision. Their analysis, however, must be marked "To Be Continued" with this reminder only; that one of the prime purposes of the study was to make the use of all methods of control more sure, more knowing and more wise.

Author

Phyllis Mickelson, Social Worker, Bureau for Feebleminded and Epileptic, Division of Public Institutions St. Paul, Minnesota

Effects of Maternal Mental Retardation and Poverty on Intellectual, Academic, and Behavioral Status of School-Age Children

Maurice A. Feldman and Nicole Walton-Allen
1997

Abstract

The impact of low maternal IQ and poverty was examined through comparison of 27 school-age children of mothers with mild mental retardation to 25 similarly impoverished children of mothers without mental retardation. The children whose mothers had mental retardation had lower IQs and academic achievement and more behavior problems. Not one child with a mother who had mental retardation was problem-free. Boys were affected more severely than were girls. Quality of the home environment and maternal social supports were lower in the group with maternal mental retardation; both measures were negatively correlated with child behavior disorders. Results suggest that being raised by a mother with mental retardation can have detrimental effects on child development that cannot be attributed to poverty alone.

The relation between maternal and child IQ is well-established (Reed & Reed, 1965), and low parental IQ is related to child intellectual and language delays (Feldman, Case, Towns, & Betel, 1985; Feldman, Sparks, & Case, 1993; Gillberg & Geijer-Karlsson, 1983; Ramey & Ramey, 1992). Poverty is also implicated as a risk factor in child development and academic achievement (Campbell & Ramey, 1994; Parker, Greer, & Zuckerman, 1988; Zigler, 1967). Most parents with mild mental retardation also have low income (Fotheringham, 1971; Garber, 1988). Given the paucity of studies that directly compare development of children raised by low income parents with versus without mental retardation, it is not clear to what extent child problems are a function of variables related to low maternal IQ or to poverty.

In addition to the possible genetic transmission of low intelligence, parents with low IQ often exhibit deficits in basic child-care, nourishment, and positive interactions, which may jeopardize their children's well-being and development (Feldman, Case, & Sparks, 1992; Feldman et al., 1993; Keltner, 1992). In child maltreatment and custody studies, investigators have found that a disproportionate number of parents with mental retardation are incompetent or abusive (Schilling, Schinke, Blythe, & Barth, 1982; Seagull & Scheurer, 1986; Taylor et al., 1991). This overrepresentation in child custody cases may to some extent reflect society's bias against these parents, but their interactions with their children nonetheless resemble those of neglectful parents who do not have mental retardation (Crittenden & Bonvillian, 1984).

There is likely to be an increasing number of parents with low IQ. Courts are banning involuntary sterilization of persons with mental retardation and are upholding parenting as a basic right of all adult citizens (Hayman, 1990; Vogel, 1987). With virtually all persons with mild mental retardation now raised and socialized in the community, more of these individuals may exercise their parenting rights.

Despite concerns about the parenting abilities of persons with mental retardation and the demands that these families are placing on the social service system (Tymchuk & Feldman, 1991), relatively little is known about the development of their children. To complicate matters, investigators who have studied these parents have used varying definitions of mental retardation; some researchers included only those with IQs less than 70 (e.g., Reed & Reed, 1965), some used a cut-off of 75 (Garber, 1988; Keltner, 1994), and others have employed a social system perspective (Mercer, 1973) and accepted parents with IQs between 70 and 80 (Feldman et al., 1985; Tymchuk, Andron, & Tymchuk, 1990). Nevertheless, most investigators have reported that children of parents *labeled* as having mental retardation have lower mean IQs, and more of them have scores in the range of intellectual retardation than would be expected from a random, but not necessarily an economically disadvantaged, sample of the general population (Bass, 1963; Feldman et al., 1985; Garber, 1988; Gilberg & Geijer-Karlsson, 1983; Mickelson, 1947; Reed & Reed, 1965; Scally, 1973). Other researchers have reported significantly less vocalizations and speech for young children of mothers with mental retardation as compared to peers of low and middle SES whose parents did not have mental retardation (Feldman, Case, Rincover, Towns, & Betel, 1989; Feldman et al., 1986, 1993).

Most studies of children raised by parents with mental retardation have been focused on intellectual and language deficits (e.g., Feldman et al., 1985; Reed & Reed, 1965). In a study assessing behavioral adjustment, O'Neill (1985) used interviews and projective tests and found behavior problems (e.g., oppositional behaviors, pseudo-retardation) in approximately 50% of 19 "normal" or "bright" children of parents with mental retardation. Likewise, in a retrospective study of 41 offspring of 15 mothers with mental retardation in Sweden, Gillberg and Geijer-Karlsson (1983) found that 58% of the children had required psychiatric services.

Few investigators who have examined parents with mental retardation have focused on factors that may predict child development, such as the quality of the home environment and familial variables. Feldman et al. (1985) found a significant positive correlation between total Caldwell Home Observation for Measurement of the Environment—HOME Inventory (Caldwell & Bradley, 1984) scores and Mental Development Index scores on the Bayley Scales of Infant Development (Bayley, 1969) in twelve 2-year-old children of parents with mental retardation. Keltner (1994) reported that mothers with IQs less than 75 had significantly lower HOME scores than did a low income comparison group of parents with IQs of 85 or over. Considered in light of the results of Feldman et al., Keltner's findings suggest a greater risk of developmental delay for the infants of the parents with low IQs, but she did not provide developmental test data. Maternal social isolation/support is another predictor variable that has not been adequately studied in parents with mental retardation. Social support has been shown to be related to child outcomes in families from low SES backgrounds (Bee, Hammond, Eyres, Barnard, & Snyder, 1986) and in families of parents without mental retardation raising children with disabilities (Dunst, Trivette, & Cross, 1986).

We are aware of no study in which the intellectual, academic, and behavioral statuses of school-age children raised by parents with mental retardation have been simultaneously examined. Few investigators in this area have examined predictor variables and incorporated a low income comparison group of parents without mental retardation to control for the impact of poverty per

se on child development. To fill significant gaps in knowledge, we designed the present study to investigate the effects of low maternal intelligence and poverty on several crucial areas of child development by comparing the performance of children raised in poverty by mothers with and without mild mental retardation on a battery of standardized measures of intelligence, academic performance, and behavioral adjustment. We also explored the relation of child outcome to the quality of the home environment and maternal social isolation/support.

Method

Subject

Two groups of families with children between the ages of 6 and 12 years participated. Although there were no restrictions regarding ethnicity of the families, all 34 referred families were Caucasian. Referrals came from 10 community agencies providing advocacy and support services to adults with mental retardation in southern and eastern Ontario (where Caucasians are the substantial majority). We avoided referrals from child welfare agencies because we did not want to have an overrepresentation of parents with mental retardation who were known to maltreat their children (however, we did not exclude parents whom we subsequently found to be involved with a child protection agency). Agency workers initially contacted their clients who met our eligibility requirements (see later discussion) and referred interested parties to us. Although we do not know the exact number of parents who said they were not interested in participating, the workers told us that most of the eligible parents agreed to allow us to contact them; no parent we contacted subsequently refused to participate or dropped out.

To address the possibility that the parents with mild mental retardation may have had difficulty giving informed consent, their workers accompanied us on the first visit, witnessed our explanation to the parents, and had the opportunity to express any reservations about the parents' ability to give informed consent (this was never an issue with any of the participants).

Criteria for inclusion in the mental retardation group required a current maternal full-scale Wechsler Adult Intelligence Scale-Revised (WAIS-R) IQ less than 70 (the accepted *Diagnostic and Statistical Manual-III* [American Psychiatric Association, 1987] and AAMR cut-off at the time of the study [Grossman, 1983]) and previous independent diagnosis of mental retardation with no known biological conditions associated with cognitive deficits (e.g., Down syndrome, brain damage). Total family income had to be below the Statistics Canada urban poverty level (Ross & Shillington, 1989). Seven families were excluded because maternal IQ was greater than 70 (despite a diagnosis of mental retardation), leaving a total of 27 in the group with maternal mental retardation.

To recruit the comparison group, we placed flyers in community resource and drop-in centers located in low income neighborhoods in the same Ontario communities in which the target parents with mental retardation resided. Resource and drop-in centers are used quite frequently in these communities because they offer a variety of free recreational and educational programs, advice, and support for children, families, and adults. The

first 25 mothers who responded to the flyers and did not have mental retardation or a history of special education placement participated, and none dropped out.

Table 1 provides a comparison of group demographics. For the most part, mothers in both groups were between 30 and 35 years of age, more than 50% were married (or in a conjugal relationship), total family incomes were below the poverty level, a majority were receiving welfare, and few were employed. Eighteen comparison mothers agreed to take an intelligence test, and all had WAIS-R IQs over 80. The seven low income mothers who refused to take an intelligence test were included in the study as comparison subjects because their backgrounds suggested at least average intellectual development (high school and community college diplomas; previously or currently employed in the secretarial or

Table 1 Demographic Information by Group

Variable	Parents with mental retardation ($n = 27$)	Parents without mental retardation ($n = 25$)
Subject-selection variables		
Mean maternal IQ (WAIS-R)	63.6 (5.5)	93.8 (11.2)**
Mothers received special ed. services (%)	48.1	0**
Mean no. of social service agencies involved per family (SD)	2.27 (1.44)	0
Median range of annual family income[a]	7–10.5	7–10.5
Other variables		
Mean maternal age in years (SD)	35.1 (4.7)	33.7 (6.1)
Single mothers (%)	44.4	44.0
Mothers institutionalized (%)	3.7	0
Mothers receiving welfare (%)	88.9	68.0
Mothers employed (%)	11.1	24.0
Living in subsidized housing (%)	63.0	48.0
Mean crowding ratio (SD)[b]	1.62 (0.6)	1.49 (0.4)
Father reported to have MR or received special ed. services (%)	66.7	8**
Target child's sibling removed (%)	14.8	0
Child welfare supervision (%)	22.2	0*
Mean child age (SD)	9.7 (2.2)	10.2 (2.3)
Mean birth order of target child (SD)	1.1 (0.4)	1.3 (0.5)
Proportion of boys to girls	19/8	12/13

[a] In thousands of dollars. Exact incomes are not available because parents were asked to indicate income within (Canadian) $5,000 intervals from $0 to $5,000 to more than $25,000 (converted here to U.S. funds).

[b] Total number of persons living at home divided by the total number of rooms

 * $p < .05$.

 ** $p < .01$.

Effects of Maternal Mental Retardation and Poverty Maurice A. Feldman and Nicole Walton-Allen

Table 2 Means and *SD*s of Dependent Measures

| | Parents with mental retardation | | | | | | Parents without mental retardation | | | | | |
| | Total | | Boys | | Girls | | Total | | Boys | | Girls | |
Measure	Mean	SD	Mean	SD	Mean	SD	Mean	SD	Mean	SD	Mean	SD
Home[a]	36.52	8.07	34.11	7.71	41.33	6.80	44.64	6.34	46.18	6.14	34.09	6.43
Social isolation[b]	39.85	6.00	41.33	6.15	36.89	4.65	33.75	7.16	33.33	6.73	34.17	7.84
WISC-R	80.54	14.32	80.11	15.13	81.50	13.22	102.88	14.25	103.58	16.66	102.23	12.28
WRAT-R												
Reading	73.20	19.10	71.05	19.49	77.75	18.65	94.25	16.80	97.18	23.34	91.77	8.50
Spelling	71.56	21.38	66.88	21.42	81.50	18.77	89.54	17.50	93.09	20.34	86.54	14.86
Math	69.68	14.68	68.12	14.06	73.00	16.38	89.21	13.12	89.27	16.80	89.15	9.75
CBCL[c]												
Conduct	6.30	5.43	7.28	5.62	4.33	4.69	2.36	2.06	2.75	2.14	2.00	2.00
Hyperact.	5.44	2.71	6.17	2.71	4.00	2.18	2.76	2.50	3.17	2.33	2.38	2.69
Emotional	5.93	2.56	6.06	2.26	5.67	3.20	4.44	3.50	3.50	2.61	5.31	4.07

[a] Home Observation for Measurement of the Environment.

[b] Higher scores indicate more maternal social isolation and less social support

[c] Child Behavior Checklist.

accounting fields). There were no significant differences between the 7 mothers who refused to take an intelligence test and the remaining 18 comparison families on any of the measures reported in Tables 1 or 2.

None of the children in either group had known disabilities that could affect their development. Both sets of families were eligible for services for economically disadvantaged families, such as regular home visits by a public health nurse and access to community resource centers. Mothers with mental retardation were also eligible for advocacy services. When the children were younger, early intervention programs for children living in poverty (or for children of parents with mental retardation) were not as readily available as they are today. In fact, only one mother (who was in the group with maternal mental retardation) received specialized early intervention services for the target child in this study (another mother with low IQ received similar services for a subsequent child not included in this study).

Dependent Measures

Intelligence and Academic Achievement. The Wechsler Intelligence Scale for Children-Revised—WISC-R (Wechsler, 1974) was used. The WISC-III (Wechsler, 1991) was not available when this study was conducted. Reading, spelling, and arithmetic achievement were assessed using the Wide Range Achievement Test-Revised—WRAT-R (Jastak & Jastak, 1984). The educational placements of the children were also noted.

Behavior disorders. Behavioral adjustment was measured using the Ontario version of the Child Behavior Checklist (Statistics Canada, 1987), which was validated and normed on 3,294 children as part of a well-documented Ontario Child Health Study (Offord et al., 1987). It is an augmented version of the original Child Behavior Checklist (Achenbach & Edelbrook, 1981) and is divided into four behavior disorders: conduct, hyperactivity, emotional, and somatization (the latter scale was not used as there were no subjects over the required age of 12 years). Each mother was asked to judge her child's behavior over the last 6 months. To determine whether the mothers with mental retardation were consistent in reporting on their children's behavior problems, we also asked them to complete the Parent Attitude Test (Cowen, Huser, Beach, & Rappaport, 1970), which contains questions that are similar to those on the Child Behavior Checklist. Significant Spearman Rank correlation coefficients were found between the Parent Attitude Test total score and the three Child Behavior Checklist subscales: conduct, $r = .59$, $p < .001$; hyperactivity, $r = .40$, $p < .05$; and emotional, $r = .33$, $p = .05$.

Quality of the Home Environment and Maternal Social Isolation/Support. The elementary school-age version of the HOME Inventory (Caldwell & Bradley, 1984) was used to assess quality of the home environment. We devised a measure of the mother's social isolation/support by adding the raw scores on the Social Isolation and Marital Satisfaction subscales of the Parenting Stress Index (Abidin, 1990). Items in these scales measure the degree of the mother's social and spousal support (e.g., "I have a lot of people to whom I can talk, get help or advice." "My spouse has not given me as much help and support as I expected."). The mother's perception of support on the Parenting Stress Index subscales was partially corroborated by the listing of all services received by the family on the demographics form. As per the directions of the Parenting Stress Index, mothers who were not married were asked to base their responses on support by their closest friend.

Design and Procedure

A nonequivalent between-group design was used to compare the children of low income mothers with mental retardation to similar age children of low income mothers without mental retardation. The tests were given in the family home by one of two experienced testers, who were aware of the study purpose and design and group classification of the family. The child received the WISC-R and the WRAT-R in a quiet room free from distractions with only the tester present (the same conditions applied when the WAIS-R was administered to the mothers). Because many of the mothers with mental retardation had poor reading skills, the questionnaires (e.g., Child Behavior Checklist, Social Isolation/Support) were administered orally to all of them; none of these mothers had any problems understanding and responding to the verbal questions, and their responses were consistent with other similar measures (e.g., Parent Attitude Test, demographic questionnaire).

Results

The scores on all the primary dependent measures in the group with maternal mental retardation failed the test of normalcy even when subjected to several logarithmic transformations (i.e., base 10, 1/2 log, and arcsine). Thus, we felt it was more appropriate to use non-parametric statistical tests, such as the two-tailed Mann-

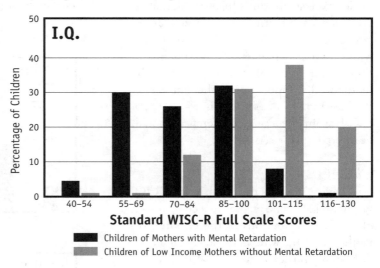

Figure 1 Distribution of WISC-R full scale IQ scores for children of parents with mental retardation and low income comparison children of parents without mental retardation.

Whitney U (z scores were used for $n > 20$, see Daniel, 1978), Wilcoxon signed-rank and chi-square tests for between-group comparisons and the Spearman sign-rank coefficient for correlational analyses. Table 2 presents means and standard deviations [SDs] of the nine dependent measures for both groups by gender and total group.

Demographics

As can be seen in Table 1, in addition to differences due to subject selection criteria (the first four variables), the two groups differed significantly on the percentage of families (a) who were involved with child protection agencies and (b) where the mother reported the father as having mental retardation or special education experience.

Home Environment

Table 2 shows the Caldwell HOME Inventory mean total scores. Scores of the group with maternal mental retardation were significantly lower than those of the comparison group, $z = 6.94$, $p < .001$. Note, however, that the mean total scores of both groups were within one SD of the school-age HOME Inventory normative group reported in Bradley, Rock, Caldwell, and Brisby (1989). As seen in Table 2, in the group with maternal mental retardation (but not in the comparison group), the boys' HOME total scores were significantly lower than those of the girls, $z = 2.74$, $p < .01$; this finding should be interpreted cautiously due to the disproportionate number of boys to girls in this group.

Social Isolation

The mean maternal social isolation score of the mothers with mental retardation (see Table 2) was significantly higher than that of the comparison mothers without mental retardation, $z = 10.4$, $p < .001$. In the group with maternal mental retardation (but not in the comparison group), there was significantly more social isolation among the mothers of the boys than those of the girls, $z = 10.63$, $p < .001$; again, these gender differences should be interpreted conservatively.

Child IQ

Table 2 presents the group WISC-R IQ means and *SD*s, and Figure 1 is a comparison of the IQ distributions of the children of mothers with and without mental retardation. A Mann-Whitney *U* test revealed that the children's IQs in the group with maternal mental retardation were significantly lower than those in the low income comparison group, $z = 4.27$, $p < .001$. The group difference upheld for both boys, $z = 3.33$, $p < .001$, and girls, $z = 2.78$, $p < .01$. Note that the mean IQs of the children in both groups were higher than those of their mothers (see Table 1), perhaps reflecting regression to the mean. A Wilcoxon signed-rank test revealed that these mother–child IQ differences were significant for both the group with maternal mental retardation, $z = -3.81$, $p < .001$, and the low income group, $z = -1.99$, $p < .05$.

Academic Achievement

Table 2 presents the group WRAT-R means and *SD*s and Figure 2 illustrates the distributions of scores of the children of mothers with and without mental retardation. As expected, the academic achievement of the comparison group children was lower than the norm, but to a lesser degree than that of the children whose mothers had mental retardation. Two-tailed Mann-Whitney *U* tests revealed that the children of mothers with mental retardation scored significantly lower than did the children of mothers without mental retardation on reading, $z = 3.58$, $p <$

Figure 2 Distribution of WRAT-R Reading, Spelling, and Arithmetic standard scores for children of parents with mental retardation and low income comparison children of parents without mental retardation.

ACADEMIC ACHIEVEMENT

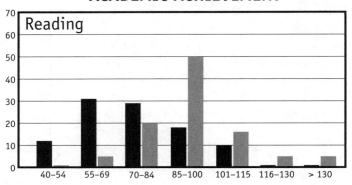

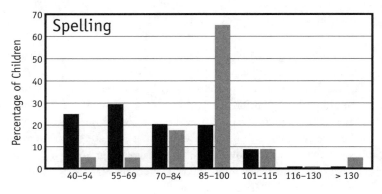

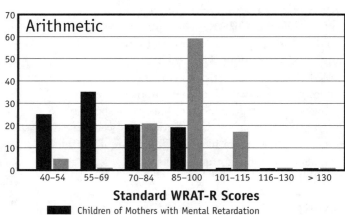

Figure 3 Percentage of children of parents with mental retardation, low income comparison children of parents without mental retardation, and Ontario norms for Child Behavior Checklist (CBCL) scores above the threshold for clinically significant behavior disorders.

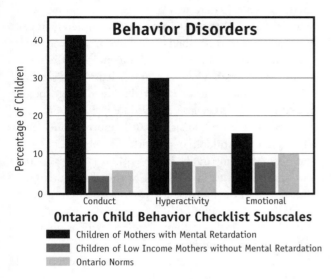

.001, spelling, $z = 3.04$, $p < .003$, and math, $z = 3.96$, $p < .001$. Between-group differences were significant for boys (reading: $z = 2.79$, $p < .006$; spelling: $z = 3.06$, $p < .003$; and math: $z = 2.95$, $p < .004$); the girls showed marginally significant differences in reading, $z = 1.78$, $p < .08$, and math, $z = 1.87$, $p < .07$, and no statistically significant difference in spelling, $z = .48$, $p > .6$ (because the relatively small number of girls increases the risk of Type II error, their marginally significant results are reported for the WRAT-R (see earlier discussion) and the Child Behavior Checklist (discussed later).

Using the local school board's diagnostic criteria for learning disabilities (i.e., average IQ with a 15-point split between performance and verbal WISC-R scores and at least one year behind in either reading, spelling, or math achievement test scores), we found that more of the children of mothers with mental retardation than the children of parents without mental retardation (36.4% and 4.5%, respectively) met the criteria, Chi Square = 5.8, $p < .02$. Also, 59.3% of the children of mothers with mental retardation were receiving various special education services for children identified as having "mental retardation," "learning disabilities," or "behavioral maladjustment" (e.g., full- or part-day self-contained classes, specialized curriculum and instruction, availability of an education aide in the regular classroom, tutoring) com-

pared to 12% of the children of parents without mental retardation; this difference was also statistically significant, Chi Square = 11.5, $p < .001$.

Behavior Disorders

Figure 3 shows that the group with maternal mental retardation had a higher percentage of children scoring above the Child Behavior Checklist clinical thresholds for behavioral disorders than did the low income comparison and the Ontario normative groups. Table 2 shows that the children of mothers with mental retardation had significantly higher scores than did the low income comparison children in conduct disorders, $z = 2.80$, $p < .005$, hyperactivity, $z = 3.30$, $p < .001$, and emotional disorders, $z = 2.20$, $p < .03$. Between-group Child Behavior Checklist differences for boys were significant on all three scales (conduct and emotional: both zs = 2.47, ps < .02; hyperactivity: $z = 2.70$, $p < .007$); the girls showed marginally significant differences in hyperactivity, $z = 1.76$, $p < .08$, but differences on the other two scales did not approach significance for the girls.

We tested the hypothesis that more competent children of slow parents would have more social maladjustment (O'Neill, 1985) by examining the percentage of children with clinically significant behavior problems (as determined by Child Behavior Checklist cut-off scores) with each group subdivided into child IQ below 85 or 85 or above. In the group with maternal mental retardation, a greater percentage of children with IQs 85 and over compared to those whose IQs were less than 85 ($n = 11$) had at least one behavior problem (63.6% vs. 43.8%, respectively). Although this numerical difference was not statistically significant, an examination of children with multiple behavior problems revealed that although no children with low IQ scored above the clinical threshold on all three scales of the Child Behavior Checklist, 27.3% of the children with IQs over 85 did; this difference was significant, $z = 2.22$, $p < .02$, but did not hold for the low income comparison children because none of these children had all three behavior problems. Thus, the children who met criteria for multiple behavior problems had IQs over 85 and mothers with mental retardation (IQs < 70).

Correlations

Because the results just discussed indicated that children of mothers with mental retardation apparently were not all affected in the same way, despite being raised by mothers with similar IQs, we ran a series of simple correlations using the Spearman sign-rank coefficient, appropriate for nonnormal distributions. We correlated the child outcome measures with maternal WAIS-R, Social Isolation/Support, and Caldwell HOME Inventory scores. These variables have been shown to be related to child development in low income families (Parker et al., 1988), and they were significantly different between the groups in this study. The coefficients are presented in Table 3.

In the group of children whose mothers had mental retardation, maternal IQ was not significantly correlated with any child measure. Maternal social isolation was significantly positively correlated, and HOME total scores were significantly negatively correlated with child conduct and hyperactivity disorders; HOME total score was also significantly correlated with WRAT-R math scores.

With respect to the low income mothers without mental retardation, maternal IQ was significantly correlated with WRAT-R math scores. Maternal social isolation was significantly related to child hyperactivity and emotional disorders; the HOME total score was significantly correlated with WISC-R and WRAT-R reading and math scores. Thus, both groups had in common significant correlations between maternal social isolation and child behavior problems as well as HOME scores and math achievement.

Discussion

Results of this study reveal the risk status of school-age children of mothers with mental retardation across intellectual, academic, behavioral, and family environment domains. There was no child in the group with maternal mental retardation who was completely free of problems. Close to 60% had IQs below 85, and even those children who were of average intelligence met the criteria for either a behavior disorder or a learning disability. These problems cannot be attributed solely to being raised in poverty because the children of mothers with mental retardation had significantly more deficits than did similar age children of parents without mental retardation from comparably impoverished families in the same communities. In addition to the child outcomes, we found that the mothers with mental retardation were providing less stimulating home environments and were more socially isolated than were comparison mothers without mental retardation.

Maternal mental retardation did not affect boys and girls in the same manner. Although both boys and girls of mothers with mental retardation had significantly lower IQs than did their low income counterparts raised by mothers without mental retardation, only the boys had significantly lower academic achievement and significantly higher behavior problem scores. These gender differences may be partly related to the boys' significantly lower quality of home environment and the sig-

Table 3 Correlation Coefficients of Parental IQ, Social Isolation, and Home Environment Scores With Child Outcomes

Measure	Parents with mental retardation			Parents without mental retardation		
	WAIS-R	Soc. isol.[b]	HOME[c]	WAIS-R	Soc. isol.	HOME
WISC-R	−.30	.20	.22	.10	.13	.51**
WRAT-Read	.17	.09	.25	−.04	.04	.47*
WRAT-Spell	−.20	−.09	.30	−.27	.09	.27
WRAT-Math	−.14	.08	.45*	.42*	.07	.60**
CBCL[a]-Conduct	−.30	.48*	−.43*	.04	.18	−.04
CBCL-Hyperactivity	−.08	.47*	−.39	.29	.45*	−.21
CBCL-Emotional	.10	.30	.14	.09	.37*	−.11

[a] Child Behavior Checklist

[b] Social isolation.

[c] Home Observation for Measurement of the Environment.

  * $p < .05$.

** $p < .01$.

nificantly greater social isolation of their mothers; no other variables (as listed in Table 1) were significantly different between the boys and girls. Further research is needed with a larger sample to explore possible gender differences in this population.

Given the finding that the boys in the group with maternal mental retardation were generally more negatively affected than the girls, it is conceivable that the between-group differences on the dependent measures may have been influenced by the group disparities in the proportion of boys to girls. To ascertain this potential confound, we reformed the two groups so that they had the same number of boys ($n = 12$) and girls ($n = 9$). This was accomplished by randomly selecting 12 boys from the original pool of 18 in the group with maternal mental retardation and adding them to the original 9 girls in this group. In the low income comparison group, we randomly chose 9 girls from the pool of 13 and added them to the original 12 boys in this group. Between-group Mann-Whitney U tests on all the dependent measures were still highly significant, $zs < .001$. Nevertheless, between-gender differences in this study should be viewed conservatively because of the relatively small number of girls in the group with maternal mental retardation.

The results of this study suggest that there may be two distinct types of school-age Caucasian children raised in poverty who can be differentiated by their mothers' intelligence. Although these findings await replication with more subjects and naive testers, the between-group differences found here suggest that researchers investigating the impact of poverty on child development should more closely examine parental IQ as a contributing factor in the variable and often adverse child outcomes seen in economically disadvantaged families (Garber, 1988; Garner, Carson Jones, & Miner, 1994; Ramey & Ramey, 1992).

The children's intellectual problems were also reflected in their poor academic achievement, especially for the boys. Besides having significantly lower WRAT-R scores than did the comparison children, the children of mothers with mental retardation were eight times more likely to meet the local school board's criterion for a diagnosis of learning disabilities and five times more likely to receive special education services. The special education placements provided some independent corroboration of our test scores.

The boys of mothers with mental retardation were also at considerable risk for behavior problems as mea-

sured using the Ontario Child Behavior Checklist. More data are needed with a larger sample to determine whether child behavior problems may be related to the inadequate knowledge and skills in basic child management strategies, such as positive reinforcement, supervision, limit-setting, and consistent discipline, that has been found for parents with mental retardation (Fantuzzo, Wray, Hall, Goins, & Azar, 1986; Tymchuk et al., 1990).

In the group with maternal mental retardation, the children with average intelligence were more likely to have multiple behavior problems than were the children whose IQs were below 85. There is currently no substantiated explanation of this result. One can speculate that conflicts may arise when the parents fail to set reasonable limits and do not comprehend their (average IQ) children's more abstract communications. These children may quickly learn to take advantage of, and rebel against, less competent parents. Early anti-social acts directed at their parents (e.g., disobedience, stealing) may subsequently generalize to other authority figures (O'Neill, 1985). Further research with more subjects is needed to determine why and how the combination of having average intelligence and parents with mental retardation places children at-risk for behavioral maladjustment.

Not all the children of mothers with mental retardation were adversely affected in the same way. On the WISC-R, 37% of the children had IQs less than 70 (i.e., mental retardation range), while 40.7% had IQs over 85. Moreover, 26% of the children of mothers with mental retardation were at or close to expected grade level in reading, spelling, and arithmetic, and about 36% did not exhibit clinically significant behavior problems.

Correlational analyses of key variables likely related to differential outcomes revealed that for the group with maternal mental retardation, maternal social isolation/support and the quality of the home environment were related to child behavioral, but not intellectual, outcomes. It may be the case that factors other than the ones we examined in this study may also be implicated in the development of school-age children of parents with mental retardation. For example, maternal depression has been shown to be related to negative child outcomes (Hammen, Burge, & Stansbury, 1990), and the prevalence of depression is relatively high in adults with mild mental retardation (Eaton & Menolascino, 1982). Perhaps a measure of depression in the mothers with mental retardation in this study would also have been significantly related to child developmental and behavioral outcomes.

A transactional approach (Sameroff & Chandler, 1975) that describes the interaction of organismic and environmental variables on child outcome could be utilized to help identify variables affecting the vulnerability and resiliency of these children (Crittenden, 1985). In the future researchers should try to differentiate children of parents with mental retardation who are at greater risk of subsequent problems. Following the transactional model, it is important to examine the accumulating impact of adverse preconceptual genetic influences (e.g., fragile X syndrome), prenatal (e.g., maternal nutrition, smoking, stress), and perinatal factors (e.g., low birthweight, congenital cytomegalovirus infection) in conjunction with subsequent environmental, nutritional, personality, and mother–child interactional variables (Bee et al., 1982; Breitmayer & Ramey, 1986; Parker et al., 1988).

Given the results of this study in the context of an increasing societal trend to both protect parenting rights and provide supports and services to try to keep the natural family intact, further attention should be paid to the development and evaluation of specialized services for these families (Feldman, 1994; Walton-Allen & Feldman, 1991). Several studies have shown that child language and cognitive delays can be reduced either by teaching mothers with mental retardation to interact in a more sensitive, reinforcing, and responsive manner with their children (Feldman et al., 1993; Slater, 1986) or enrolling the child in a specialized preschool (Garber, 1988; Ramey & Ramey, 1992). In the present study, the one child in the group with maternal mental retardation whose mother received interaction training when he was an infant had an IQ of 97. Future early intervention efforts should focus on the prevention of not only intellectual and academic deficits but also behavioral and psychiatric disorders in these children. Considerable work is still needed in first identifying, and then preventing, eliminating, or compensating for factors that promote the intergenerational recurrence of child developmental and other problems in families with parents who have mental retardation (Ramey, 1992; Zigler, 1967).

References

Abidin, R. R. (1990). *Parenting Stress Index—manual.* Charlottesville, VA: Pediatric Psychology Press.

Achenbach, T. M., & Edelbrook, C. S. (1981). Behavioral problems and competencies reported by parents of normal and disturbed children aged four through sixteen. *Monograph on Social Research in Child Development, 46*(1, Serial No. 188).

American Psychiatric Association (1987). *Diagnostic and statistical manual of mental disorders* (3rd ed., rev.). Washington, DC: Author.

Bass, M. S. (1963). Marriage, parenthood, and prevention of pregnancy. *American Journal of Mental Deficiency, 68,* 320–335.

Bayley, N. (1969). *Bayley Scales of Infant Development: Birth to two years.* New York: Psychological Corporation.

Bee, H. L., Barnard, K. E., Eyres, S. J., Gray, C. L., Hammond, M. A., Spietz, A. L., Snyder, C., & Clark, B. (1982). Predictions of IQ and language skill from perinatal status, child performance, family characteristics, and mother-infant interaction. *Child Development, 53,* 1134–1156.

Bee, H. L., Hammond, M. A., Eyres, S. J., Barnard, K. E., & Snyder, C. (1986). The impact of parental life change on the early development of children. *Research in Nursing and Health, 9,* 65–74.

Bradley, R. L., Rock, S. L., Caldwell, B. M., & Brisby, J. (1989). Uses for the HOME Inventory for families with handicapped children. *American Journal on Mental Retardation, 94,* 313–330.

Breitmayer, B. J., & Ramey, C. T. (1986). Biological nonoptimality and quality of postnatal environment as codeterminants of intellectual development. *Child Development, 57,* 1151–1165.

Caldwell, B., & Bradley, R. (1984). *Home Observation for Measurement of the Environment.* Unpublished manuscript, University of Arkansas, Little Rock.

Campbell, F. A., & Ramey, C. T. (1994). Effects of early intervention on intellectual and academic achievement: A follow-up study of children from low income families. *Child Development, 65,* 684–698.

Cowen, E. L., Huser, J., Beach, D. R., & Rappaport, J. (1970). Parent perceptions of young children and their relation to indexes of development. *Journal of Consulting and Clinical Psychology, 34,* 497–503.

Crittenden, P. M. (1985). Maltreated infants: Vulnerability and resilience. *Journal of Child Psychology and Psychiatry, 26,* 85–96.

Crittenden, P. M., & Bonvillian, J. D. (1984). The relationship between maternal risk status and maternal sensitivity. *American Journal of Orthopsychiatry, 54,* 250–262.

Daniel, W. W. (1978). *Applied nonparametric statistics.* Boston: Houghton-Mifflin.

Dunst, C. J., Trivette, C., & Cross, A. (1986). Mediating influences of social support: Personal, family, and child outcomes. *American Journal of Mental Deficiency, 90,* 403–417.

Eaton, L., & Menolascino, F. J. (1982). Psychiatric disorders in the mentally retarded: Types, problems, and challenges. *American Journal of Psychiatry, 139,* 1297–1303.

Fantuzzo, J. W., Wray, L., Hall, R., Goins, C., & Azar, S. (1986). Parent and social-skills training for mentally retarded mothers identified as child maltreaters. *American Journal of Mental Deficiency, 91,* 135–140.

Feldman, M. A. (1994). Parenting education for parents with intellectual disabilities: A review of outcome studies. *Research in Developmental Disabilities, 15,* 299–332.

Feldman, M. A., Case, L., Rincover, A., Towns, F., & Betel, J. (1989). Parent Education Project III: Increasing affection and responsivity in developmentally handicapped mothers: Component analysis, generalization, and effects on child language. *Journal of Applied Behavior Analysis, 22,* 211–222.

Feldman, M. A., Case, L., & Sparks, B. (1992). Effectiveness of a child-care training program for parents at-risk for child neglect. *Canadian Journal of Behavioral Science, 24,* 14–28.

Feldman, M. A., Case, L., Towns, F., & Betel, J. (1985). Parent Education Project I: The development and nurturance of children of mentally retarded parents. *American Journal of Mental Deficiency, 90,* 253–258.

Feldman, M. A., Sparks, B., & Case, L. (1993). Effectiveness of home-based early intervention on the language development of children of mothers with mental retardation. *Research in Developmental Disabilities, 14,* 387–408.

Feldman, M. A., Towns, F., Betel, J., Case, L., Rincover, A., & Rubino, C. (1986). Parent Education Project II: Increasing stimulating interactions of develop-

mentally handicapped mothers. *Journal of Applied Behavior Analysis, 19,* 23–37.

Fotheringham, J. B. (1971). The concept of social competence as applied to marriage and child care in those classified as mentally retarded. *Canadian Medical Association Journal, 104,* 813–816.

Garber, H. L. (1988). *The Milwaukee Project: Preventing mental retardation in children at risk.* Washington, DC: American Association on Mental Retardation.

Garner, P. W., Carlson Jones, D., & Miner, J. L. (1994). Social competence among low-income preschoolers: Emotion socialization practices and social cognitive correlates. *Child Development, 65,* 622–637.

Gillberg, C., & Geijer-Karlsson, M. (1983). Children born to mentally retarded women: A 1-21 year follow-up study of 41 cases. *Psychological Medicine, 13,* 891–894.

Grossman, H. J. (Ed.). (1983). *Classification in mental retardation.* Washington, DC: American Association on Mental Deficiency.

Hammen, C., Burge, D., & Stansbury, K. (1990). Relationship of mother and child variables to child outcomes in a high-risk sample. *Developmental Psychology, 26,* 24–30.

Hayman, R. L. (1990). Presumptions of justice: Law, politics, and the mentally retarded parent. *Harvard Law Review, 103,* 1201–1271.

Jastak, J., & Jastak, S. (1984). *Wide Range Achievement Test-Revised.* Wilmington, DE: Jastak Associates.

Keltner, B. R. (1992). Caregiving by mothers with mental retardation. *Family and Community Health, 15,* 10–18.

Keltner, B. R. (1994). Home environments of mothers with mental retardation. *Mental Retardation, 32,* 123–127.

Mercer, J. R. (1973). *Labelling the mentally retarded: Clinical and social system perspectives on mental retardation.* Berkeley, CA: University of California Press.

Mickelson, P. (1947). The feebleminded parent: A study of 90 family cases. *American Journal of Mental Deficiency, 51,* 644–653.

Offord, D. R., Boyle, M. H., Szatmari, P., Rae-Grant, N. I., Links, P. S., Cadman, D. T., Byles, J. A., Crawford, J. W., Blum, H. M., Byrne, C., Thomas, H., & Woodward, C. A. (1987). Ontario child health study: II. Six month prevalence of disorder and rates of service utilization. *Archives of General Psychiatry, 44,* 832–836.

O'Neill, A. M. (1985). Normal and bright children of mentally retarded parents: The Huck Finn syndrome. *Child Psychiatry and Human Development, 15*, 255–268.

Parker, S., Greer, S., & Zuckerman, B. (1988). Double jeopardy: The impact of poverty on early child development. *The Pediatric Clinics of North America, 35*, 1227–1239.

Ramey, C. T. (1992). High-risk children and IQ: Altering intergenerational patterns. *Intelligence, 16*, 239–256.

Ramey, C. T., & Ramey, S. L. (1992). Effective early intervention. *Mental Retardation, 30*, 337–345.

Reed, E. W., & Reed, S. C. (1965). *Mental retardation: A family study*. Philadelphia: Saunders.

Ross, D. P., & Shillington, E. R. (1989). *The Canadian fact book on poverty—1989*. Ottawa: Canadian Council on Social Development.

Sameroff, A. J., & Chandler, M. (1975). Reproductive risk and the continuum of caretaker causality. In F. Horowitz (Ed.), *Review of child development research* (Vol. 4, pp. 157–243). Chicago: University of Chicago Press.

Scally, B. G. (1973). Marriage and mental handicap: Some observations in Northern Ireland. In F. F. de la Cruz & G. D. La Veck (Eds.), *Human sexuality and the mentally retarded* (pp. 186–194). New York: Brunner/Mazel.

Schilling, R. F., Schinke, S. P., Blythe, B. J., & Barth, R. P. (1982). Child maltreatment and mentally retarded parents: Is there a relationship? *Mental Retardation, 20*, 201–209.

Seagull, E. A., & Scheurer, S. L. (1986). Neglected and abused children of mentally retarded parents. *Child Abuse and Neglect, 10*, 493–500.

Slater, M. A. (1986). Modification of mother-child interaction processes in families with children at-risk for mental retardation. *American Journal of Mental Deficiency, 91*, 257–267.

Statistics Canada. (1987). *Ontario Child Health Study Child Behaviour Checklist*. Ottawa: Author.

Taylor, C. G., Norman, D. K., Murphy, J. M., Jellinek, M., Quinn, D., Poitrast, F. G., & Goshko, M. (1991). Diagnosed intellectual and emotional impairment among parents who seriously mistreat their children: Prevalence, type, and outcome in a court sample. *Child Abuse and Neglect, 15*, 389–401.

Tymchuk, A. J., Andron, L., & Tymchuk, M. (1990). Training mothers with mental handicaps to understand developmental and behavioural principles. *Mental Handicap Research, 3*, 51–59.

Tymchuk, A. J., & Feldman, M. A. (1991). Parents with mental retardation and their children: A review of research relevant to professional practice. *Canadian Psychology/Psychologie Canadienne, 32*, 486–494.

Vogel, P. (1987). The right to parent. *Entourage, 2*, 33–39.

Walton-Allen, N., & Feldman, M. A. (1991). Perceptions of service needs by parents who are mentally retarded and their workers. *Comprehensive Mental Health Care, 1*, 57–67.

Wechsler, D. (1974). *Manual for the Wechsler Intelligence Scale for Children - Revised*. New York: Psychological Corp.

Wechsler, D. (1991). *Wechsler Intelligence Scale for Children* (3rd ed.). San Antonio: Psychological Corp.

Zigler, E. F. (1967). Familial mental retardation: A continuing dilemma. *Science, 155*, 292–298.

Received 8/26/94, first decision 11/28/94, second decision 2/24/96, accepted 7/10/96.

This research was sponsored by the Ontario Mental Health Foundation and the Ontario Ministry of Community and Social Services Research Grants Program (administered by the Research and Program Evaluation Unit). We thank J. Carnwell, L. Case, M. Garrick, W. MacIntyre-Grande, and R. Malik for their assistance in collecting the data; J. Berg and D. Yu for their feedback on earlier versions of the manuscript; and L. Atkinson for his statistical advice and insightful commentary. The first author is also affiliated with Ongwanada Hospital. Requests for reprints should be sent to Maurice Feldman, Department of Psychology, Queen's University, Kingston, Ontario Canada K7L 3N6.

Authors

Maurice A. Feldman, Queen's University, Kingston, Ontario, Canada and **Nicole Walton-Allen,** Chedoke-McMaster Hospitals, Hamilton, Ontario, Canada.

Teaching Parents With Mental Retardation: Knowledge Versus Skills

Joel Bakken, Raymond G. Miltenberger, and Scott Schauss
1993

Abstract

An educational program for parents ($N = 5$) with mild mental retardation was evaluated to assess whether knowledge gains results in corresponding skill acquisition. Generalization of parenting skills to the home environment following behavioral skills training procedures was also examined. Parenting knowledge was assessed as subjects responded to descriptions of parenting situations. Parenting skills were assessed in home observations. Following baseline, a knowledge training procedure was implemented in a small group format. A behavioral skills training procedure was then implemented in a small group training format. Finally, individual behavioral skills training was provided in the home setting. Although knowledge training produced sizable increases in the knowledge measure, neither it nor the behavioral group training produced increases in parenting skills. However, following training in the home, each of the parenting skills increased substantially. The results were discussed with regard to the problem of generalization, and future research was proposed.

Over the past decade, there has been an increased focus on the parenting skills of individuals with mental retardation (Budd & Greenspan, 1984; O'Neill, 1985; Schilling, Schinke, Blythe, & Barth, 1982). Parents who have mental retardation have been found to be less likely to display affection, praise, and appropriate discipline when compared to mothers without mental retardation of middle and low socioeconomic status (Feldman, Case, Towns, & Betel, 1985; Feldman et al., 1986; Peterson, Robinson, & Littman, 1983). Although recently investigators have begun to evaluate the effects of training procedures for parents with mental retardation (Feldman et al., 1986; Feldman, Case, Rincover, Towns, & Betel, 1989), very little research has been conducted in the area.

One of the first studies investigating procedures for training skills to parents with mental retardation was reported by Feldman et al. (1986). Using a number of behavioral techniques in a small group training format

in a home setting (the parents' home or an available group home), they successfully trained seven mothers with mental retardation who had 1- to 3-year-old children to exhibit important parenting skills (praising appropriate child behavior and imitating child vocalizations). Training involved group discussion, instructions, modeling, prompting, rehearsal, and praise. To facilitate generalization of the skills to the home setting, Feldman et al. used common stimuli and multiple exemplars (Stokes & Baer, 1977). Data were collected in the training setting and in the subjects' homes. The results showed that parenting skills increased in the home setting following training.

Feldman et al. (1989) extended their earlier findings by successfully training three women with mild mental retardation to praise, imitate, and show affection toward their children. The authors trained each subject in her home. Initially, they provided only verbal instruction for the subject to engage in the target skill. After finding minimal or no change in targeted measures in either the subjects or their children, they then used a training package similar to the one used in Feldman et al. (1986). Data were collected in the home and generalization measures were taken with the subjects interacting with their children doing different activities than originally targeted. When the full training package was used in the home, increases were noted in all of the targeted measures. These parenting skills continued to occur above baseline levels at a 6-month follow-up. Generalization measures showed that the parents increased their performance of the skills in the nontraining activities once they were told to use the skills during these activities.

In one other study investigating training for parents with mental retardation, Fantuzzo, Wray, Hall, Goins, and Azar (1986) evaluated the effectiveness of a parent and social skills training program. They found that using a modified version of the board game "Sorry" was effective in teaching verbal responses to common problematic parenting and social situations. They asked each subject to answer a parenting or social skill question correctly before he or she was allowed to move a game piece. Fantuzzo et al. demonstrated that these parents with mental retardation could learn the parenting and social skills information and retain the information in the generalized setting.

A limitation of the Fantuzzo et al. (1986) study was their question–answer format. Although answering questions correctly shows subjects' knowledge of a topic, it may not correspond with correct or consistent performance of the parenting skills in their home. Therefore, because the actual use of the parenting skills was not measured, it is not known whether the subjects actually exhibited the parenting skills with their children, even though they demonstrated knowledge gains following training. A strength of the study, however, is the nature of the training package. Fantuzzo et al. simplified the training strategy such that it could be readily used in a group training format by parents who had mental retardation. If found to be effective in actual parenting-skill acquisition, it would offer a more simplified and less expensive approach than the procedures used by Feldman et al. (1986, 1989).

The first part of the present study (knowledge training) was designed to replicate Fantuzzo et al.'s (1986) training procedure to determine whether parenting knowledge can be learned through a board game training format, and more importantly, to evaluate whether knowledge of parenting skills generalized to practical application of the skills in the home for five parents with mental retardation. Knowledge was assessed in group sessions in a clinic, and practical application of the parenting skills was assessed individually with each parent in his or her home. A multiple-baseline across-subjects design was used to evaluate the effects of the knowledge training.

The second part of the study (skills training) was designed to replicate and extend the work of Feldman and his colleagues (1986, 1989) by training parenting skills (praise and imitation) in the clinic and assessing generalization from the clinic to the home. Feldman et al. conducted their training in the subjects' own homes or a similar home environment. We sought to evaluate group training in a clinic setting and measure generalization to the home environment. We chose a clinic setting because it more closely approximates the training situation that is likely to be available in most human service centers or community mental health centers. Following evaluation of the clinic-based training, we evaluated home-based training similar to that used by Feldman et al. Acquisition of parenting skills was evaluated in a multiple baseline design across subjects and behaviors.

Method

Subjects

Subjects were 5 parents with mild mental retardation (IQs from 57 to 70) from an upper Midwest city with a population of 100,000. Subjects ranged in age from

Table 1 Demographic Characteristics of Subjects

Characteristic	Subjects[a]				
	1	2	3	4	5
Age	26	29	33	33	27
Gender	F	F	M	F	F
Married	Y	Y	Y	N	N
IQ	57	70	65	61	69
Previous child protection	Y	Y	Y	Y	Y
Employed	N	Y	Y	Y	N
No. of children	2	1	1	1	1
Age of first child	3	5	5	1	3
Child has DD[b]	Y	N	N	N	Y

[a] Subjects 2 and 3 were married to each other. Their 5-year-old child was involved in the training provided separately to each parent.
[b] Developmental disabilities.
Y = yes
N = no

26 to 33 years. All of them had at one time been involved with child protection agencies because of child neglect; however, no cases were active during the course of the study. The subjects were recruited from a parent training group that was being conducted by the local human service center. Participation was strictly voluntary, and all subjects expressed an interest in learning better parenting skills. The subjects had no previous professional contacts with the experimenters. All subjects lived in apartments in the community. Subject 1 was married to an individual without mental retardation. Subject 2 and Subject 3 were married to each other. Subject 4 had a boyfriend without mental retardation who was the father of her child, and Subject 5 had a boyfriend without mental retardation who was not the father of her child. Of these subjects' 5 children, 2 were diagnosed as having developmental disabilities. The subjects' characteristics are summarized in Table 1.

Settings and Materials

Group training sessions were conducted in several adjacent meeting rooms (5 m x 7 m) at a local human service center. Skills training in the latter phases was conducted in the subjects' apartments.

A commercially available table game ("Sorry," Parker Brothers, Salem, MA) was used in knowledge assessment and training. A special deck of 24 cards, used in conjunction with the regular game cards, included parenting situations designed to evoke a verbal description of appropriate parenting skills from the player before he or she was allowed to move the game piece. These cards were the same as those used by Fantuzzo et al. (1986). The cards were divided into three basic areas: positive reinforcement, discipline, and parent–child interaction. (The cards may be obtained from the first author.)

Data Collection and Dependent Measures

Parenting knowledge. Parenting knowledge was assessed during the board game by the experimenter, who read the situation to the subject and scored the subject's response as either incorrect, correct, or correct and elaborate (Fantuzzo et al., 1986). *Correct* and *incorrect responses* were defined by the inclusion or exclusion of certain responses stated in the answer guide (which may be obtained from the first author).

A *correct and elaborate response* was not only pertinent to the content of the interaction but also (a) expanded or extended the interaction or (b) identified the child's behavior that the parent was attempting to increase or decrease with positive reinforcement or discipline (Fantuzzo et al., 1986). Any response scored as correct and elaborate was also scored as correct. Reliability was assessed by a second experimenter who listened to a tape recording of the sessions.

Parenting skills and child behaviors. Parenting skills and child behaviors were assessed in 10- to 15-minute observation sessions in the home through the use of a 10-second partial interval recording procedure (Bailey & Bostow, 1977). These behaviors were assessed under two conditions: play and normal. In the play condition, subjects were told to play with their children while the observer was in their home. In the normal condition, subjects were told to do what they would normally do at that time of the day. These instructions were given just prior to data collection in the home. During the observations, observers stationed themselves such that they could view the living room and kitchen. Data were recorded for all intervals in which the subject and child were in view for the entire 10-second interval. Observers were told not to interact with the subjects or their children during the observation sessions. Two graduate and five undergraduate students in psychology performed the observations. They were all trained by the first author, who provided instructions and feedback as they practiced scoring videotape simulations of the target behaviors. Observers received approximately 2 hours of training, which was conducted until they achieved over 85% interobserver agreement with the experimenter. The dependent measures, adapted from Feldman et al. (1986), were defined as follows:

1. *Praise:* comments made contingent on child behavior that express approval or pleasure.
2. *Parental Attention:* (as) *Facing* (watching the child for at least 2 seconds), (b) *Touching* (physically touching the child in nonaggressive manner), and *Talking* (directing verbalizations to the child that are not demanding or requesting).
3. *Imitation of Child Vocalizations:* verbally repeating or approximating (within 5 seconds) words or sounds made by child or for the older children, verbally expanding on their vocalizations.
4. *Noncorporal Discipline:* using removal of some specified amount of a reinforcer, withdrawal of social approval, contingent observation (i.e., when a child engages in maladaptive behavior, the parent does

not verbally or physically interact with the child for approximately 2 minutes), or time-out within a room used immediately upon the exhibition of a negative behavior by the child.

5. *Child Maladaptive Behavior*: any aggressive, inappropriate social behavior or other negative behavior exhibited by the child that would typically require parental intervention. This would include hitting, slapping, pinching, playing with objects not intended to be played with (e.g., lamps, telephones), yelling, and ignoring a parental request to stop a behavior.

6. *Child Vocalizations*: any vocal sounds or words from the child, excluding crying, burping, whining, and screaming.

Interobserver Agreement

Interobserver agreement was assessed in 14% of the sessions for the knowledge-level responses and 26% of the sessions for parenting skills. Interobserver agreement for knowledge and skills was calculated by dividing the number of agreements by the number of agreements plus disagreements. When assessing knowledge-level responses, we defined *agreements* as both observers scoring the response as incorrect, correct, or correct and elaborate. For parenting skills, agreements were scored when both observers recorded the occurrence or nonoccurrence of a behavior in the same interval. The mean percentage of interobserver agreement for all subjects was 100% for the knowledge-level responses and 88% for the parenting skills (range = 62% to 100%). For the parenting skills, we also calculated interobserver agreement on occurrence of the behavior only (a more conservative measure for low-frequency behaviors). The mean percentage of interobserver agreement on occurrence for all subjects was 70%, with a range of 50% to 92%.

Experimental Design

A multiple baseline design across two groups of subjects was used to evaluate knowledge training and group skills training in the clinic. Subjects were initially assigned to one of two groups based upon the amount of contact they had with each other. For example, two participants were married and two others were close friends; therefore, members of each pair were assigned together. This was done in order to preserve the integrity of the multiple baseline design (i.e., so the partners or friends received training at the same time). Once group train-

ing was no longer used, skills training was provided on an individual basis within a multiple baseline design across subjects and behaviors (Bailey & Bostow, 1977).

Procedure

General procedure. At the initial meeting, subjects were told that the experiment concerned the evaluation of parent-training procedures. The experimenter then explained the consent form and interviewed each subject for reinforcer preference. He then told the subjects how much time would be involved in the study and described the benefits (i.e., that they would be able to interact better with their children).

After the original session, subjects were observed in their homes approximately twice per week. These sessions were scheduled in the morning or afternoon at the participants' convenience. Initially, weekly group sessions were also held and used to assess and train subjects in parental knowledge and skills. These weekly sessions took place for 12 weeks throughout the first three phases (baseline, knowledge training, and clinic training–praise). In the latter phases, all assessment and training sessions were completed in the subjects' homes.

Baseline. Parenting knowledge and skills were both assessed in weekly group sessions throughout this phase. During the knowledge assessment sessions, the experimenter read the parenting situations to the subjects and asked them how they would respond. After the subject's response, the experimenter instructed the subject to move his or her game piece the number of places indicated on the regular game card. Subjects were praised for complying with these requests, but not for the content of their answers. In the home observations, except for cueing the parents to the play and normal conditions, the observers did not interact with the subjects. No feedback or other consequences were provided to the subjects.

Knowledge training. During this phase, verbal responses to the three classes of parenting situations were trained in weekly group training sessions. The training procedures were the same as those described by Fantuzzo et al. (1986). Training included specific verbal feedback, modeling when necessary, reinforcement in the form of praise and the opportunity to move game pieces, and individual performance criteria for rewards for each subject. Home observations continued to be conducted during this phase.

Clinic training—praise. Because subjects in neither group substantially improved their parenting skills as measured in the home during the knowledge training phase, the first group of subjects (Subjects 1, 2, 3) was trained in a specific parenting skill in the clinic setting. Training was held once a week for approximately one hour per session. Subjects were trained to praise their child(ren) using behavioral skills training procedures consisting of instructions, discussion, modeling, prompting, praising, and simple generalization strategies as described by Feldman et al. (1986). Subjects were given a goal to independently praise their children 30 times each session. All subjects achieved this goal each session. Subjects were rewarded for attending and participating in the five training sessions. At the end of every session, subjects were instructed to praise their children in their homes when the children behaved appropriately. No other instructions were given at any time. Data were collected only in the home.

Home training—praise. This phase was added because the subjects in the first group did not increase their use of praise at home even though they had consistently demonstrated this skill in the clinic. The second group was not involved in the clinic training phase because clinic training failed to produce improvements during home observations in the first group. Training in this phase was similar to the training that occurred in the clinic, except the training occurred in the home prior to the observation sessions. After the initial training sessions in the home in this phase, the experimenter did not complete the entire behavioral skills training sequence in each session. Rather, prior to the observation session, the subjects were only reminded of the skill, asked if they had any questions, and told that their goal was to praise the child at least 10 times in the next 10-minute period. Participants were rewarded for achieving their goal five times.

Home training—imitation. In this phase, parental imitation of child vocalizations was trained in the subjects' homes. Strategies previously described for the home training—praise phase were used to teach this skill. The goal was for the subject to imitate or expand upon child vocalizations at least 10 times in the observation period. They were rewarded for achieving their goal in five observation sessions. Subjects were also reminded to praise their children often, although no goal was established for that skill in this phase. Following each training session, data were collected during the 10-minute observation period.

Home training—praise and imitation. For those sub-

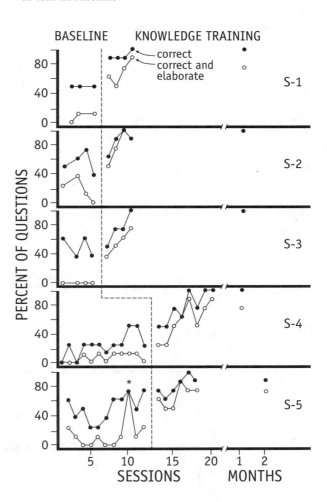

Figure 1 Percentage of subjects' responses to questions that were correct or correct and elaborate across baseline and knowledge training conditions. The asterisk for Subject 5 indicates a situation in which she inadvertently observed a training session for the first group while she was still in baseline.

jects who showed a substantial decrease in their frequency of praise during the imitation training phase, a combination training phase was added. This phase consisted of instructing subjects to not only praise their child 10 times but also to imitate or expand upon their child's vocalizations 10 times in the 10-minute period. No formal skills training procedures (e.g., modeling, rehearsal, feedback) were conducted in this phase. Rather, the two goals were established with the subjects prior to observation sessions. Subjects were rewarded for achieving their goal in three observation periods. Data collection occurred following each training session.

Follow-up. Six months following the end of the last treatment phase, a follow-up observation was conducted. This observation was identical to those conducted in the play condition described earlier.

Results

Figure 1 depicts the percentage of subjects' correct responses and correct and elaborate responses to orally presented descriptions of parenting situations. In baseline, subjects generally maintained a rather low level of correct responses and an even lower level of correct and elaborate responses. During the knowledge training phase, subjects progressively increased to 100% for correct responses and to or near 100% for correct and elabo-

rate responses. Follow-up measures of subjects' responses showed that all subjects maintained the improvements in this knowledge measure, although 2 of the subjects' percentages of correct and elaborate responses were slightly lower (Subjects 1 and 4) and 2 were slightly higher (Subjects 2 and 3).

The percentage of intervals that subjects praised their child(ren) in the play and normal conditions is presented in Figures 2 and 3, respectively. Throughout baseline, subjects praised their children very little, if at all. Praise continued to occur at a low rate throughout the knowledge training phase and the clinic training— praise phase. Praising child behavior did not increase substantially for Subjects 1 through 4 until it was trained in the home (home training—praise). Subject 5 withdrew from the project before this phase, stating that home

Figure 2 Percentage of intervals from home observations in the play condition in which the parents praised their child. The phases labeled "praise," "imitation," and "praise & imitation" were home training phases.

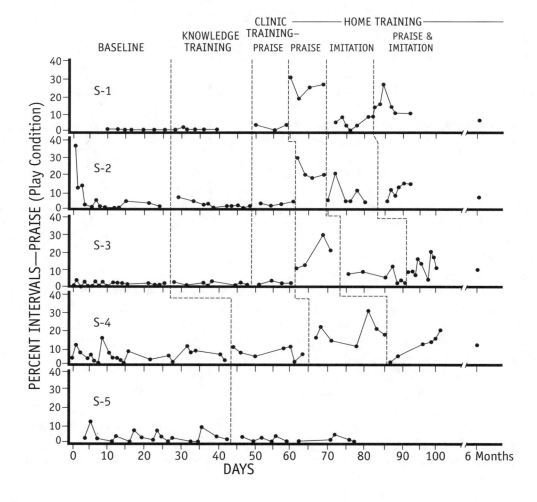

visits had become too "inconvenient." The frequency of Subject 4's praise maintained in the following phase when the focus of training was imitation (home training—imitation); however, for the other 3 subjects, the frequency of praise substantially decreased when imitation was trained. Only when the observers cued praise and imitation together in the final phase (home training—praise and imitation) did these 3 subjects' praise increase to or near the previously attained level. A 6-month follow-up showed a decrease in each subject's performance of this skill. However, the level of the behavior at follow-up was above the baseline mean for each subject.

Figures 4 and 5 show the percentage of intervals that subjects imitated child vocalizations in the play and normal conditions, respectively. Imitation rarely occurred for Subjects 1, 2, and 3 across baseline, knowledge training, clinic training—praise, and home training—praise phases. Subject 4's data were somewhat higher, but still stable across these four phases. All subjects substantially increased their imitation in

Figure 3 Percentage of intervals from home observations in the normal condition in which parents praised their child. The phases labeled "praise," "imitation," and "praise & imitation" were home training phases.

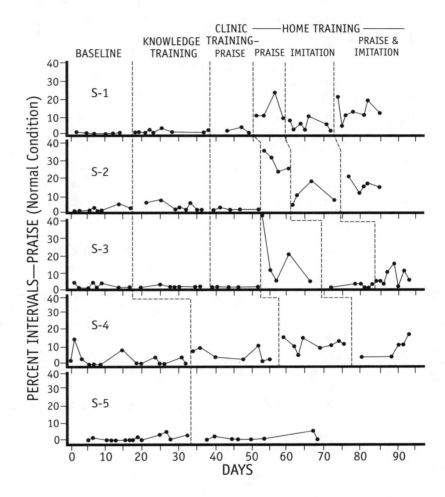

Table 2 Mean Intervals (in %) for Remaining Parent and Child Behaviors by Study Phase

Behavior	Phase[a]					
	B	KT	C—R	H—R	H—I	H—RI
Attention						
Facing	62	60	58	86	88	91
Touching	16	15	14	25	16	18
Talking	47	42	34	71	71	80
Child maladaptive behavior	2.9	2.0	3.4	0.5	0.9	1.2
Discipline	0.2	0.2	0.1	0.2	0.2	0.0
Child vocalizations	62	62	63	68	68	64

[a] B = baseline, KT = knowledge training, C—R = clinic training—reward, H—R = home training—reward, H—I = home training—imitation, H—RI = home training—reward & imitation.

both observation conditions only when imitation was the focus of training (home training—imitation). In the normal condition, however, there was less of an increase. In the final phase (home training—praise and imitation), imitation was maintained at or near the level of the previous imitation training phase. Follow-up revealed maintenance of the skill for all 4 subjects.

Table 2 shows the means of the other dependent measures (parental attention, parental discipline, child maladaptive behavior, and child vocalizations) in each of the different conditions. These behaviors were highly variable throughout the study. There were no definite trends in these data except for two of the three attention variables (i.e., facing and talking). Both behaviors substantially increased once training was initiated in the home and maintained at that higher level while train-

ing continued in this environment. Child maladaptive behavior was quite low throughout the study, making discipline virtually unnecessary by the parent. Child vocalizations were above 60% throughout the study, providing ample opportunity for imitation by the parents across all phases.

Discussion

The results of this study demonstrate that these parents with mental retardation could learn important parenting knowledge but that the acquisition of this knowledge did *not* lead to increases in the execution of parenting skills in the home setting. The subjects learned to describe the parenting skills that were required in a variety of parent–child situations but did not show a

Figure 4 Percentage of intervals from home observations in the play condition in which parents imitated child vocalizations. The phases labeled "praise," "imitation," and "praise & imitation" were home training phases.

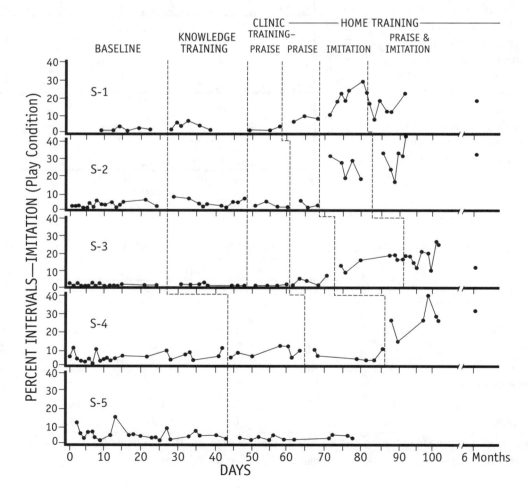

corresponding increase in the frequency of these same skills in home observations. These results suggest that the subjects' parenting knowledge and skills were independent. It would, therefore, seem that training that is focused on an increase in knowledge or "understanding" of the appropriate behavior (e.g., Fantuzzo et al., 1986) is inadequate to produce greater performance of the behavior in a criterion setting. These results question the utility of the earlier findings of Fantuzzo et al. (1986) and, in fact, question the utility of *any* training procedure involving only verbal responses without actual criterion skill measures.

Although these results suggest that knowledge training is ineffective for skill acquisition, one cannot rule out the possibility that knowledge training may have had an impact on subsequent skill training phases because of the sequencing of experimental conditions in this study. The present results should be interpreted somewhat cautiously due to the problem of sequence effects and the limited number of subjects participating in the training program.

The results of this study also demonstrate that there was little or no generalization from the clinic to the home setting, where observations were conducted without any prompts or cues for the subjects to engage in the targeted skill. Whereas Feldman et al. (1986, 1989) conducted training in the subjects' homes or another home environment and found an increase in parenting skills during observation sessions there, we conducted training in a clinic setting and found that there was no increase in the parenting skill in the home environment following training (which was nearly identical to training provided by Feldman et al., 1986, 1989). This suggests that training in the criterion setting (home) by Feldman et al. (1986, 1989) played a role in the generalization of the skills from training to observation sessions. With training in a setting that was quite different from the home in the present study, gen-

Figure 5 Percentage of intervals from home observations in the normal condition in which parents imitated child vocalizations. The phases labeled "praise," "imitation," and "praise & imitation" were home training phases.

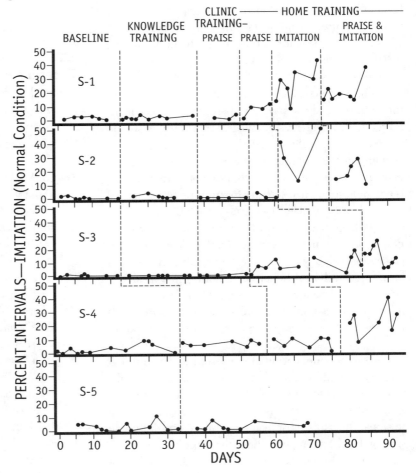

eralization did not occur in the home. We consider this to be an important finding because training conducted in a group format in a setting other than the home (e.g., a human service center or community mental health center) is more cost-effective and, therefore, more likely to occur in most nonresearch settings. Our results suggest that such training may have limited usefulness regarding skill performance in the home.

Following the failure of clinic-based training to produce an increase in parents' praising at home, this skill was taught in the home setting. With the implementation of this home-based training, praising increased for each subject. Imitation of child vocalizations also increased when this skill was trained in the home. However, when the focus of training shifted from praise to imitation, praising decreased from the previous training level. Only when praising and imitation were trained together in the final phase did both occur together in the home setting. It is disappointing that the increased level of praising was not maintained once the training focus was shifted to imitation. This finding suggests that when there is a need for training multiple skills, training should occur in a cumulative rather than a sequential fashion across skills.

These results have a number of implications for future training and research with parents who have mental retardation. The results suggest that training should not focus exclusively on verbal skills (knowledge or understanding), but rather on the acquisition and performance of actual parenting skills. From our experience, it is common in applied settings for training to occur on a knowledge or verbal level with groups of individuals (e.g., social skills groups, dating skills groups, parenting groups). Practitioners seem to take it on faith that "learning" takes place as a result of such training. Our results, on the other hand, suggest that, although such training may influence clients' verbal behavior, it does not by itself lead to the performance of important skills. Rather, specific skills training procedures are necessary for skills to be exhibited.

A second implication of our results is that training programs should ensure that criterion skills are occurring and being reinforced in criterion settings. It is not sufficient that clients exhibit the skills during training sessions; the skills must also be exhibited in the home setting. Furthermore, contingencies must be in place to maintain the skills there. Our results and the results of previous studies (Feldman et al., 1986, 1989) strongly suggest that some training activities must occur in the home setting in order for important parenting skills to be utilized there.

Although the present results suggest that the utility of knowledge training is limited, future research should evaluate whether initial knowledge training may enhance the value of subsequent skills training approaches. Another fruitful area of research may be the evaluation of self-instructional training for promoting parenting skills, as self-instructional training has been shown to influence other skills in individuals with mental retardation (Agran, Fodor-Davis, & Moore, 1986; Agran, Salzberg, & Stowitschek, 1987). Finally, researchers should investigate the value of other self-management strategies (see Browder & Shapiro, 1985, for a review of self-manage-

ment with individuals who have mental retardation). Because important parenting behaviors occur in the home and trainers can only be present in the home on a periodic basis at best, the investigation of strategies through which clients may manage their own behavior has great appeal.

References

Agran, M., Fodor-David, J., & Moore, S. (1986). The effects of self-instructional training on job-task sequencing: Suggesting a problem solving strategy. *Education and Training in Mental Retardation, 21,* 273–281.

Agran, M., Salzberg, C. L., & Stowitschek, J. J. (1987). An analysis of the effects of a social skills training program using self-instructions on the acquisition and generalization of two social behaviors in a work setting. *Journal of the Association for Persons with Severe Handicaps, 12,* 131–139.

Bailey, J., & Bostow, D. (1977). *Research methods in applied behavior analysis.* Tallahassee, FL: Copy Graffix.

Browder, D. M., & Shapiro, E. S. (1985). Applications of self-management to individuals with severe handicaps: A review. *Journal of the Association for Persons with Severe Handicaps, 10,* 200–208.

Budd, K. S., & Greenspan, S. (1984). Mentally retarded women as parents. In E. Blechman (Ed.), *Behavior modification with women* (pp. 477–506). New York: Guilford Press.

Fantuzzo, J. W., Wray, L., Hall, R., Goins, C., & Azar, S. (1986). Parent and social skills training for mentally retarded mothers identified as child maltreaters. *American Journal of Mental Deficiency, 91,* 135–140.

Feldman, M., Case, L., Rincover, A., Towns, F., & Betel, J. (1989). Parent education project III: Increasing affection and responsivity in developmentally handicapped mothers: Component analysis, generalization, and effects on child language. *Journal of Applied Behavior Analysis, 22,* 211–222.

Feldman, M. A., Case, L., Towns, F., & Betel, J. (1985). Parent education project I: Development and nurturance of children of mentally retarded parents. *American Journal of Mental Deficiency, 90*(3), 253–258.

Feldman, M. A., Towns, F., Betel, J., Case, L., Rincover, A., & Rubino, C. A. (1986). Parent education project II: Increasing stimulating interactions of developmentally handicapped mothers. *Journal of Applied Behavior Analysis, 19,* 23–37.

O'Neill, A. M. (1985). Normal and bright children of mentally retarded parents: The Huck Finn syndrome. *Child Psychiatry and Human Development, 15*(4), 255–268.

Peterson, S., Robinson, E., & Littman, I. (1983). Parent-child interaction training for parents with a history of mental retardation. *Applied Research in Mental Retardation, 4,* 329–342.

Schilling, R. F., Schinke, S. P., Blythe, B. J., & Barth, R. P. (1982). Child maltreatment and mentally retarded parents: Is there a relationship? *Mental Retardation, 20,* 201–209.

Stokes, T. F., & Baer, D. M. (1977). An implicit technology of generalization. *Journal of Applied Behavior Analysis, 10,* 349–367.

Manuscript submitted: 7/16/90; first revision requested: 10/29/90; accepted 3/26/91.

This study is based on a thesis conducted by the first author, who is now at Southeast Human Service Center (Fargo, ND). The third author is now at West Virginia University. We thank Rita Lall, Scott McGuire, and Denise Menzel for their assistance. Reprint requests should be sent to Raymond G. Miltenberger, Department of Psychology, North Dakota State University, Fargo, ND 58105.

Authors

Joel Bakken, Raymond G. Miltenberger, and Scott Schauss, North Dakota State University.

Relationships and Social Support: Views of Parents With Mental Retardation/Intellectual Disability

Gwynnyth Llewellyn, Ph.D.
1995

Abstract

From the professional perspective, parenting by people with mental retardation, or intellectual disability, is regarded with concern. Little attention has been paid to what constitutes social support for these parents. A qualitative design was used to explore views of parents with intellectual disability about their relationships and social support for their parenting. Most emphasis was placed on the support received from and given to their spouses or partners. Support was not always viewed as beneficial; rather, it was sometimes viewed as a restraint as well as a resource for parenting. Parents also exhibited a preferred sequence in seeking help, beginning with their partners, then family members, and, finally, professionals. Implications in light of policy and service provision were discussed.

Parents who have mental retardation (referred to hereafter as intellectual disability, consistent with Australian terminology) overwhelmingly receive a negative press (Whitman & Accardo, 1990). In most reports, with few notable exceptions (e.g., Booth & Booth, 1993; Taylor, in press), authors delineate parental deficiencies and express grave concern for the well-being of the children. There is an increasing literature on assessing parenting skills of parents with intellectual disability and developing intervention strategies (McGaw & Sturmey, 1993; Tymchuk & Andron, 1992). These parents, however, are rarely asked for their views about their parent education and training needs. The present study was designed to redress this oversight through exploration of the views of parents with intellectual disability on their experiences of parenting. Specifically, parents' views about their social relationships and the support they receive, and seek, with the tasks of parenting were examined.

Exactly what constitutes suitable social support for parents with intellectual disability is yet to be determined (Llewellyn, 1994c). In the research literature there are a number of suggestions, but little empirical data. For example, investigators have observed that the absence of social support may predict parenting breakdown (Espe-Sherwindt & Kerlin, 1990) or lead to child removal (Andron & Sturm, 1973; Seagull & Scheurer, 1986). However, social support for these parents has been investigated in only two studies (Tucker & Johnson, 1989; Zetlin, Weisner, & Gallimore, 1985). In both of these studies, results showed that social support comes primarily from close kin (grandparents or adult siblings) and seems to be proffered without regard for the parents' wishes. In neither study did the authors examine the role that spouses (or partners) might assume as "support providers" for each other, the possibility of support from outside the family, nor the role that parents might play in soliciting or rejecting social support. Most important, the views of the parents themselves were not considered.

In contrast, the present study was designed to investigate how parents with intellectual disability view their relationships and the support provided in relation to their parenting. For the purposes of this study, *social relationships* were defined as relationships with spouses (or partners), family members, friends, neighbors, and others (e.g., professionals) whom parents regarded as part of their personal social network. This definition follows the approach taken by McCallister and Fischer (1978) and Tracy (1990) in which the boundaries of one's personal social network are self-determined. The *nature* and *extent* of social support were defined to include assistance, advice, or intervention offered to parents as well as the role that parents play in seeking or receiving support. Together, these definitions permitted the exploration of a broad range of relationships and the ways in which these relationships supported or constrained everyday family life from the parents' point of view.

Method

Data collected as part of an ongoing study on the shared experience of being a person with intellectual disability and a parent were used (Llewellyn, 1994b). The study design chosen to explore this shared experience fits within the symbolic interactionist tradition (Blumer, 1969). Thus, following Blumer, I assumed that the way parents conduct their parenting is formed, in part, by socially constructed, community views. I also assumed that the way to identify the parent viewpoint is by listening to, observing, and talking with parents about what they think, feel, say, and do as they carry out parenting. Parents' perceptions, expressed by their words and observed in their actions, therefore, constituted the data for the study. In the following sections, I have described the parent sample and study procedures that were derived from those suggested by Strauss and Corbin (1990) to develop grounded theory. (This study was granted ethical approval by the Human Ethics Committee, University of Sydney, August 5, 1991.)

Parent Sample

A social systems perspective (Mercer, 1973) was used to determine criteria for inclusion of parents. Parents with *intellectual disability* were defined as those who received health or welfare services in which they had been identified as having intellectual disability. Suitable parents were those primarily responsible for parenting their young child or children. Those whose children had been permanently removed or who had little or no involvement in parenting their children were not included.

Parents were recruited indirectly from several agencies, including services for people with intellectual disability, generic community-based family support services, early intervention services, and advocacy organizations. Parents who met the criteria were approached by a contact person from the agency who explained the research

Table 1 Sample Characteristics

Family configuration	Occupation	Location/economic	Child attributes, age[a]
Couple 1			
Mark (husband)	Project officer (advocacy group)	Rented public housing	Samantha, 3 years old (developing typically)
Elizabeth (wife)	Home duties/parttime project officer (disability unit)	Working class area: outer suburbs	Anthony, 18 months old (developing typically)
Couple 2			
Sue (wife)	Home duties	Own home	Molly, 4 years old (developmental delay)
Morris (husband)	Factory job	Middle class area: suburbs	
Couple 3			
Jane (wife)	Home duties	Rented public housing	Tom, 5 years old (developmental delay)
David (husband)	Factory job	Working class area: suburbs	
Mary (Jane's mother)	Home duties/volunteer work		
Couple 4			
Margaret (divorced)	Home duties/parttime assistant to Robert	Rented public housing	Rebecca, 14 years old (developing typically)
Robert (de facto partner)	Fair equipment worker	Working class area: outer suburbs	Katrina, 12 years old (developing typically)
Couple 5			
Ruth (wife)	Home duties	Own home	James, 7 years old (developmental delay)
Allan (husband)	Parttime shift work, motel kitchen helper	Working class area: country town	Beth, 4 years old (developmental delay)
Couple 6			
Ros (wife)	Home duties	Own home	Bruce, 22 months old (developmental delay)
Gary (husband)	Painter and decorator	Middle class area: suburbs	

[a] At end of study.

project. If they expressed interest and willingly provided name and address, they were contacted.

My focus was the parental viewpoint on the everyday experience of parenting. The purpose, therefore, was not generalization but, rather, an in-depth exploration of parents' experiences. I set out to explore the common patterns in their lives in order to produce an account that reflects the everyday family lives of parents with intellectual disability. Six couples participated over the 2 years of the study. In all but 2 of these couples, both parents had intellectual disability. Summary information about all participating parents is contained in Table 1.

The following case studies are included to expand on this summary information. The couples described are those whose everyday family life experiences most clearly illuminate the topic of relationships and social support. These couples represent the range of characteristics across the parent sample on several dimensions: type of housing, socioeconomic class, age of child and presence of developmental delay, and, most pertinently, involvement with other people. The case studies permit a brief glimpse into the shared experience of being a person with intellectual disability and a parent.

Couple 1: Mark and Elizabeth. Elizabeth (28 years of age) moved out of her family home when she was in her early 20s. Mark (35) grew up in a state mental institution, which he left at the age of 18. Mark had little contact with his natural family; what contact he did have was generally not positive. Elizabeth, on the other hand, had frequent family contact despite the 300 km that separated them. She grew up in a country town and spoke warmly of her childhood with her mother, father, sister (since deceased), and younger brother. She did not maintain contact with her former classmates (she attended a special school for her primary schooling and a special class at senior level) but kept in touch intermittently with fellow workers from the sheltered workshop she attended after leaving school.

Mark and Elizabeth met through a self-advocacy group for people with intellectual disability. As their friendship developed, they talked about possibly sharing an apartment sometime in the future. When they discovered Elizabeth was expecting a child, they decided to marry (a commitment they had previously made, should Elizabeth get pregnant). Mark's parents totally disapproved; Elizabeth's parents were very worried about how they would manage but eventually decided to support them in their decision to proceed with the pregnancy

and get married. Subsequently, they moved together into a rented apartment in a large metropolitan city.

After the baby was born, Mark and Elizabeth went to a residential mother and baby unit with their infant daughter to learn how to care for her. They viewed the assistance they received there as positive; they frequently contacted the maternity ward for help in the first few months. They also received family assistance. Elizabeth's aunt provided assistance in the house, "time out" by baby sitting, and helpful ideas about child care and household management. They felt confident to ask others to aid them when necessary, although they found the advice given by others was often conflicting or confusing.

Mark and Elizabeth had a circle of friends, acquaintances, and support people through their work with a disability advocacy group. They regarded this as having benefits and disadvantages. The benefit was having people "to turn to"; the disadvantage, that everybody "knows their business." Mark was particularly ambivalent about intrusions in their family life. He felt strongly that he wanted to be involved in changing things for other people with intellectual disability, but this resulted in a busy and not very private family life.

Mark and Elizabeth spent a considerable amount of time clarifying their personal views with each other and negotiating child care and household management tasks. They had developed a workable family and parenting style with ongoing, but not intrusive, help from a diverse group of people. They both strongly desired to show others that even though they had intellectual disability, they too could bring up children. To this end, they endeavored to be as independent as possible.

Couple 2: Sue and Morris. Sue (37 years old) had a very restricted upbringing. When she was a young child, her father left home and her mother returned to work, so she moved to her grandmother's house where she still lived at the time of this study. From Sue's account her grandmother "surrounded herself" with her and did not encourage her to meet other people. She went to a local Catholic school for the first few years but did not mix with the other children in class or the playground. Sue described herself as very, very shy. She was sent to a special school—"for people like me who learn slowly." After leaving this school when she was 16 years of age, Sue remained at home nursing her grandfather until his death and then her grandmother until she was moved to a palliative care hospital. She also "minded" her younger stepbrother; her mother had married again and had left her young son with Sue and her grandmother. Sue acted as his "mother": feeding him, dressing him, and taking him to and from school. There was never any talk about Sue having her own life away from the family, getting a job, or leaving home.

Morris (39 years of age) came from a large family of eight children. He described his mother as "tired out" and his father as running the family with a firm hand. After he left school when he was 15, he got a job in a factory. He continued to work at the same job, although since Molly's arrival he had not always been punctual, which caused problems with his boss. Morris met Sue at a local friendship group that Sue was allowed to attend for the first time when she was 27 years of age when her grandmother felt that she needed some friends. Sue and Morris wanted to go out together, but Sue's grandmother was not at all enthusiastic about this. After several months she apparently relented, and Sue and Morris were able to develop their friendship.

At this time "all the family became involved." Finally, Sue's uncle agreed to support Sue and Morris getting married and provided the wedding. Sue and Morris moved in with her grandmother. By the time Sue became pregnant, her grandmother had died, and she felt very alone. Her uncle did not support her keeping the baby, but, on Morris' insistence, Sue went ahead with the pregnancy, received good antenatal care, and successfully delivered a baby daughter.

After Molly's birth, Sue's uncle paid for her to go to a residential mother and baby unit. She says she learned "some things" there, but by the time the baby was a few months old, Sue's uncle sought outside help for Sue. Getting Molly into a manageable routine was, and at the time of the study still was, a big challenge for Sue. Sue and Morris both felt that everybody else seemed to have an opinion on what they should do with Molly and that at various times, other people (such as Sue's uncle and his wife) tried to take over caring for Molly.

Sue and Morris received family and professional assistance, but neither was welcomed nor willingly sought and were often actively resisted. Despite this, Sue expressed a desire to be more involved with others. Although she attended playgroup with Molly, she rarely talked to the other mothers and acknowledged that she had no friends. Morris, on the other hand, was satisfied with the way things were; he liked his work and his work colleagues and enjoyed the time he spent with his family. Occasionally, he asked his sister for advice on what

to do with Molly, but generally he preferred to do it his "own way."

Morris firmly believed that parents should be in control of their children and that other people should not interfere. He resented Sue's uncle's intrusions into their family life. This uncle was also a financial benefactor, and the resentment between the two men resulted in family arguments. Sue strongly desired to bring up Molly as she was brought up ("nicely" as she sees it) and believed that Morris did not understand this because his upbringing was "rough." Sue did not feel welcome in Morris's family. At the time of this study, Morris had been spending more time with his family, adding to Sue's loneliness and feelings of frustration with just being with Molly.

Sue and Morris had not yet developed a mutually agreed or satisfying family or parenting style. Nonetheless, both spoke positively about being parents and recommended that other "slow learners" should experience parenting if they wanted to. Each new development with Molly brought a fresh challenge and much attendant anxiety for her parents, particularly for Sue. Sue and Morris continued to lead rather isolated lives as they faced the challenges of parenthood with little support for their efforts but a great deal of rarely welcomed advice.

Couple 3: Jane and David. When I first met Jane (28 years of age), David (age 32), and Tom (5 years old), they were all living in Jane's family home with Mary, Jane's mother, a widow in her early 50s. Tom was only a couple of months old and recently home from the hospital after being born 6 weeks prematurely. David had lived in institutions or group homes before moving into Jane's family home. David did not have any family, and his only friend was an assistant from the workshop where he and Jane met. He attended a special school before being placed in this sheltered workshop. David was deaf, had a speech defect, and had difficulty communicating. He admitted that he preferred to be alone or playing ten-pin bowling, for which he had won a number of trophies. Jane, on the other hand, had always lived at home with her mother and father (since deceased) and her younger brother (now in another state) and was well-known in the local community.

Jane attended her local school. When she was 8 years old, she was placed in a special class and continued in special classes for the remainder of her schooling. After leaving school she spent one year at a Work Preparation Centre; however, this situation was not successful, and she was placed in a sheltered workshop. She had one friend from school who lived close by. Jane rarely saw her, however, because she worked, as did most young mothers in her community. Jane really enjoyed company, although she said she was happy to be alone. With her mother, she attended several women's groups at their local church.

Jane and David did not plan their pregnancy, although they had been friends for some time and had planned to marry in "a year or so." Several people opposed their having the baby. The staff members at the workshop were particularly concerned that Jane, although she managed adequately in her supportive (and at that time, rather dependent) home environment, could not possibly cope with the demands of a baby. Nonetheless, Mary supported Jane's decision to go ahead with the pregnancy and suggested that they live with her. Tom was a sickly child who was small for his age and quite delayed in his development. Jane had regular contact with a community nurse and occupational therapist since Tom's birth and attended a parenting group for mothers with intellectual disability. Jane described her early days with Tom as "having Mum here to help me" and "Mum and I took it in turns." These comments underplay Jane's contribution to Tom's upbringing.

Mary stated that having a child was the best thing that could have happened to Jane because she matured and acquired many skills that she did not learn at school or in the postschool work training program. Mary had always hoped that one day Jane and David would be able to manage on their own and move out to live together as a family. Meanwhile, she continued to be the mainstay of the family, initially instructing Jane in how to care for Tom and then assisting her with managing Tom's behavior. Both Jane and Mary thought that David did not do enough with Tom and what he did do was not right. Consequently, David was very much on the outside of the mother, son, and grandmother "circle." Mary was the driving force in this family, assisting Jane to gradually assume her parenting role. Mary's philosophy was that the "slow learners" like Jane and David should be "given a chance" and that with family support and encouragement they would succeed. Jane and David both appeared happy to accept Mary's views on parenting and her ongoing support to their family.

Data-Collection

The desired outcome of this study was to gain a full and rich picture of the experience of parenting by individuals with intellectual disability. This experience was to be described, as far as possible, by the parents themselves and supplemented by observations of them in their daily family lives. Contact with the couples, which was extensive during the course of the study, was maintained through participation in many aspects of the parents' lives, including 25 family outings, and by brief "informal" visits (N = 210) and telephone calls (over 200). More "formal" in-depth interviews averaged one a month over the 2 years of direct involvement with the couples (N = 24). Involvement with some couples was more intensive than with others. For example, the minimum involvement with a parent was 2 in-depth interviews, 6 informal visits, and bi-weekly phone calls for the last 8 months of the study and the maximum was 6 in-depth interviews complemented by weekly discussions in person and numerous telephone calls during the 2-year period.

My early meetings with parents involved visiting, joining in a shopping outing, or chatting over coffee. In this initial period I was able to develop rapport and trust to help build an ongoing relationship. All parents were given every opportunity to ask questions about the study and to seek reassurance about confidentiality and anonymity. When they were satisfied about what their involvement entailed, I asked them to sign an informed consent sheet. An advocate or family member assisted, if necessary, with understanding the informed consent procedure.

In-depth interviews. The initial in-depth interviews were generally unstructured to maximize breadth and width of information generated. Interviews began with an open-ended question, "What is it like to be a parent?" The interviewing approach, advocated by Spradley (1979), was comprised of three different types of questions: descriptive, structural, and contrast. Descriptive questions were designed to elicit portrayals of daily life events in the parents' own words. Structural questions were asked to determine how parents organize their knowledge (e.g., "What types of support do you get? Can you give me examples?"). Contrast questions were used to investigate "the dimensions of meaning which informants employ to distinguish the objects and events in their world" (Spradley, 1979, p. 60), for example, "I would like to check with you something you mentioned in our earlier conversations about getting support from _____ (partner). Would you say that this support is the same as, or different to the support you get from _____ (mother)?".

The content of the interviews was initially based on what the parents wanted to talk about and often loosely followed surrounding events (e.g., the child playing on the floor) or events of the previous day. In later interviews, I asked structural and contrast questions to follow-up on topics initiated by the parents. I did not use this process with all parents because it depended, in part, on parental ability to communicate and comprehend. For example, one parent's answers were generally monosyllabic and/or perseverative. Another parent took time to explain his point of view as clearly as possible. The abilities of the other parents lay somewhere in between.

Interviews were tape recorded with parental permission. In many instances, however, tape recording was inappropriate due to concern for privacy or background noise in a public place. In these circumstances, I made extensive field notes during the observation period or immediately after the meeting.

Field notes. My note-taking followed the method suggested by Spradley (1979). A condensed account was written during observation or interview and an expanded account written or recorded as soon as possible after each encounter "to fill in details and recall things that were not recorded on the spot" (p. 75). I included verbatim phrases in the condensed account, where practical, to ensure that as little translation as possible occurred. Note-taking immediately after meeting with the parents facilitated reflection on the data and the exploration of potential relations with previously gathered data.

Participant observation. Observations that were not part of the interview situation occurred at the parents' invitation. I observed in several settings, which included situations in which other individuals who were significant to the parents were present, for example, playgroups, shopping expeditions, family visits at home and in family members' homes, and family meals and outings.

Observing parents' daily behaviors and activities provided a means by which I could clarify and expand on informal discussions and in-depth interviews. Overall, participant observation provided me with the opportunity to (a) "check out" parents' intentions, views, or problem-solving processes as events took place; (b) watch parents "demonstrate" ideas and beliefs that they had difficulty describing verbally; (c) verify previously gathered interview data; and (d) generate issues to be addressed and questions to be asked in later interviews.

Observation supplemented the interviews and with the field notes contributed to meeting the requirements of triangulation of multiple methods (Stainback & Stainback, 1984). A field work journal kept during the study included dated entries of observations on the research process and ideas about ongoing collection of data and data analysis and provided a record or audit trail of the study.

Data credibility. Several consistency checks were possible across the data sources. Consistency was evaluated within each individual's account across time, settings, and people. Second, by observing parents, I was able to evaluate the consistency of their individual verbal reports. Third, data from other sources (such as family members) helped me evaluate practical information supplied by the parents. Fourth, the interview transcripts were available for scrutiny by the parents. Finally, consistency was evaluated through identification of patterns drawn from the parents' accounts of their common experience of having intellectual disability and being parents.

Data Analysis

Interviews were transcribed and analyzed wherever possible prior to the next contact with the parent. In the beginning stages this was a valuable aid for remembering information such as names of family members and sequence of family events. Later, the interview material provided questions for succeeding interviews. Towards the end of the study, the interviews were specifically focused on the emerging key concepts and the conceptual relations that comprise the shared experience of intellectual disability and parenting.

After 2 months of data collection, I began open coding, which involved applying a code to each designated unit of meaning in the interview transcripts and field notes (Strauss & Corbin, 1990) to generate a coding list. A second list was generated by reviewing the findings of an exploratory study on parent and professional perspectives on parenting (Llewellyn, 1991) and reviewing the literature (Llewellyn, 1990). Together, these lists provided a framework for evaluating the empirical data.

At this stage the codes represented concepts in the data. Constant comparative analysis (Glaser & Strauss, 1967) was used to compare and contrast these concepts to achieve a level of internal consistency and mutual exclusivity. Subsequently, this process was again used to cluster the empirically generated concepts into conceptual categories. Following this, I applied the axial coding paradigm suggested by Strauss and Corbin (1990) to the data, which involved determining under what conditions an instance occurred, the context to which this instance was embedded, what actions or strategies were taken to handle the instance, and what the consequences of these actions or interactional strategies were (Strauss & Corbin, 1990). From this process, general relations within and between the categories emerged.

To elaborate the conceptual categories and their relationships, I again applied the axial coding paradigm, which required a constant interplay between proposing (at the category development level) and checking (at the level of all coded instances of data). Following this, I combined two categories and refined the hypothesized general relations within and between the categories. In total, eight conceptual categories were identified.

All parent participants in this study experienced parenting as represented by these categories. However, as noted by Glaser and Strauss (1967), conceptual categories do not perfectly represent nor substantially distort each participant's experience. Rather, conceptual categories reflect the common patterns experienced by parents and identified within the parameters of the study design.

Relationships and Social Support in the Family Lives of Parents With Intellectual Disability

In the literature, parents with intellectual disability are presented as requiring substantial family support (Johnson, 1950; Kaminer, Jedrysek, & Soles, 1981; Peck & Stephens, 1965). Without evidence to the contrary, one could assume that parents receive and accept extensive support from family members or benefactors.

The findings in this study suggest otherwise. Not all parents have support available to them. Not infrequently, parents respond ambivalently to proffered support. Thus, parents may welcome support from other people in their family lives or such support may be barely tolerated. Of note are parental actions in seeking out or rejecting support. In contrast to the one-dimensional perspective presented in the literature, the parents' views demonstrate that involvement of other people in their family lives is multifaceted: It comes not only from family members and benefactors but also from professionals, although rarely from friends. Of central importance to parents is reciprocal support between themselves and their partners.

Partnerships

Household management typically involves a number of physical tasks, particularly in homes with young children. A central theme in the parents' accounts was whether these tasks were shared and, if so, how and with whom. Reciprocal getting and giving of support occurred with a partner or family member (often acting as an adjunct parent). Reciprocity was demonstrated by provision of physical help, support for the other person's views or wishes, and moral support. Parents exerted a great deal of influence over each other beyond the child management role. Influence between partners ranged from a preparedness to negotiate and compromise to neither parent being willing to listen to the other's viewpoint. For example, Morris insisted that Sue stay at home and not seek volunteer work, despite her strong desire to do so.

Parents shared decision-making or, in other instances, left all decisions to their partners. For some, this was a willing abrogation of the parenting role; for others, they felt they had no choice but to do this. For some parents this worked out amicably, as it did for Ruth and Allan. For example, Ruth had managed to get Allan to take a little more interest in the children, particularly the younger one, a girl who was nearly 3 years old. However, Ruth commented that "really Allan just leaves it all up to me," to which he responded, "Yes, well I am never here so, if I tell her I want to do it this way she just does it her way anyhow." For other parents, such as Jane and David, there was little support for each other's views. In this family unit, Jane and Mary (Jane's mother) had jointly developed a pattern of parenting with Tom that, in a very real sense, excluded David. Jane and Mary regarded this pattern as better than the way David carried out parenting. They viewed the way he parented as deficient because he grew up in an institution and had "never known a family."

Reciprocity was viewed most positively when this involved moral support. Parents expressed such support in several ways. One way was when the parents encouraged each other to take time out, not to worry, or to seek help. Another was when one parent helped the other to have more realistic expectations. For example, Elizabeth found managing a young baby and doing the housework very difficult. She continued to find being on her own with the children quite difficult. Mark, however, was always quick to reassure her about managing the housework. He noted:

Also what I'm trying to do is to make Elizabeth realize that you can only do a bit at a time, because you've got to try . . . you can space your time out. She likes to have everything neat, she's one of those sort of people who are fussy. You might notice that I shut the door in our bedroom because I haven't had a chance to pack the clothes away so I closed the door.

The empirical data from this study demonstrate the central importance of parent partnerships in managing everyday parenting. The literature, however, presents conflicting reports on these partnerships. Wayne and Fine (1986) commented that none of the women in their group "spoke in warm, loving terms about their partners, but instead consistently talked about needing more affection, attention, and help from them" (p. 98). On the other hand, Mattinson (1970) described many of the marriages of the 32 couples she interviewed as "remarkably effective." She concluded that this was due in part to the majority of these marriages working on "a complementary basis, the skill of one partner supplementing the inability of the other . . . and, they were able to take help from each other" (pp. 181–182).

This complementary support also featured in the lives of two couples in the present study: for Mark and Elizabeth and, to a lesser extent, Ruth and Allan. For these couples, reciprocal moral support extended into areas of their lives outside home. This included supporting each other to make contact with people outside the family, to assert themselves with professionals, and to communicate their views to other people.

Family Support

People with intellectual disability are unduly subjected to negative opinions about becoming a parent. Family members may react to impending parenthood with disbelief and dismay and view competent parenting as unlikely. Parents perceive their disability (not only their parenthood) as a major factor influencing these judgments. For example, Allan had experienced "a bloke at work, I don't know he thinks I am stupid but he doesn't know that I'm not. I don't let it worry me. You don't want to let them think you should be understanding more." When others judge parents in this negative manner, parents feel talked "down to" and their adult status disregarded. This signals their lack of capability in any setting, not just with parenting.

Later, parents fall prey to family members' opinions about their parental practices. New parents are the ones most likely to accept, with little questioning, support from their family and others. The following comments from

Ros illustrate her ready acceptance of advice. She recalled:

My parents thought it would be a good idea to get him into a good routine cause we discussed it with my mum and dad and they said if you feed Bruce at a certain time, for his breakfast, for his lunch and for his dinner you will be all right.

Parents were not so willing to comply if the advice conflicted with their own views. As parents gained experience over time, they were also less willing to accept advice from others, including family members. Jane, for example, apparently agreed with her mother while actively disregarding her mother's rules as the following example illustrates:

But the thing is you still had to watch him, because even Mum said he could only go as far as the letter box, that he's not allowed out. But I let him out yesterday onto the footpath, because I said to bring the brush, and he started wandering down the footpath, I said "back here" and he came back.

Parents perceive other people as a highly valued resource when they offered help that was a "good fit" with their own perceptions of their needs. Assistance from other people was also perceived positively when their understanding of a parent's limitations resulted in information being presented in an appropriate manner. For example, Elizabeth and Mark recalled that when they first realized Elizabeth was pregnant

a friend (one of their unofficial support people) talked to us about abortion if we wanted to get rid of it. He wasn't talking to us trying to get us to get rid of it, he was telling us what happened if we decided.

On the other hand, parents described other people as intrusive or unhelpful when their assistance was based on judgments by "outsiders" about parental needs and they ignored parental wishes. What could be considered a potential resource then became a constraint. An example of this was when grandparents offered to babysit only when the parent was not managing rather than for parent-desired activities, such as pursuing volunteer work or a leisure activity.

Some parents viewed the intrusion of other people as lack of confidence in their abilities. Some were concerned that family members of others wanted to take over care of the child, perhaps even wanting to take the child away. (No parent in the study had been threatened with imminent child removal.) Sue and Morris viewed the involvement of Sue's uncle and his wife in this way. For example, in the early days they organized Sue's time, determined the family routine (often going against Sue and Morris's expressed preferences), and placed restrictions on whom Morris and Sue could turn to for advice. In circumstances such as these, parental decision-making is actively discouraged and information withheld. Withdrawal of support may be implied if the parent carries out a particular action. For example, Sue's uncle recently stated that he would withhold financial support if Sue and Morris had another child.

For the couples in this study, family members were considered central to providing support. They were asked for ideas about how to care for the baby and, later, how to manage the child. There was usually a strong commitment to asking "because they are family," even when their ideas were not considered helpful. This commitment appeared to come from a sense of trustworthiness. Being geographically close to family was perceived a "back up" moral support, even when this support was not utilized.

Family members were called on for personal support or when the child was distressed. Mark and Elizabeth received regular support from Elizabeth's aunt, whom they regarded as "one of *our* family." Parents who did not have this support appeared to be chronically disappointed. For example, Ruth and Allan reported:

R: I haven't got family, no family around here, that I can go around and see or they can come around and help me if I am tired with the kids. I have got no one like that to call on to come and get the kids for a couple of hours.

A: They never helped you in O. (where they used to live) when they were there so what are you on about?

R: Oh well they never did, did they, no. I'd like to have family. Other people have said to me, sister, aunty or mum came and got the kids for a while and do housework or have a rest or something. I'd like that.

For some parents then, family support was, in Tucker and Johnson's (1989) terminology, competence promoting. This is how Mark and Elizabeth regarded the family support they received. For other parents, such as Sue and Morris, family support was competence inhibiting and contributed to their feelings of perceived inadequacy. For yet others, family support was neither competence promoting or competence inhibiting. It was, quite simply, not available, as was the case for Ruth and Allan.

The central yet equivocal place of family members in the lives of parents who have intellectual disability demands attention from policy makers and service providers. With increasing emphasis on community care in

Australia and elsewhere (Cant, 1992), there is frequently an expectation, at policy and service levels, that close kin will meet the caring and support needs of vulnerable members of the community. As Finch (1989) has pointed out, however, "it is obvious that we are bound to find considerable variation in people's experience of support between kin" (p. 13). This variation was evident in the couples' lives and is further supported by the literature. For example, Rosenberg and McTate (1982) observed that few parents in their group had any social support. This was assumed to result from conflicts with their extended families and the parents' tendency to overtax supportive people. Andron and Tymchuk (1987) noted that whereas winning approval from family members was important to parents, little support came from their families. This caused problems if professional advice differed from that of family members. Budd and Greenspan (1985) also stressed the crucial role of the client's extended family but reported that family involvement could aid or undermine treatment success.

The nature of family support as a resource or constraint must alert policy makers and service providers to do much more than assume—or propose—that parents can call on kin networks to provide support with the tasks of parenting. Rather, it behooves service providers to individually assess the support available to parents, taking into account the parents' views of this support as promoting or inhibiting their competence as parents.

Friendship Ties

The couples in this study engaged in a process of "self-questioning" based on how they have experienced other people throughout their lives. This process serves two purposes: one is negative and undermining, the other is positive and productive. For Sue and Ruth, for example, the results were negative. Sue questioned having a child (as she did not believe she ever would), having another child (due to her age and difficulty managing her first child), and standing up to disapproval from her overpowering uncle. She retreated into overtiredness and inability to manage child care and household tasks. Ruth's self-questioning was demonstrated by the concerns she expressed for her children (e.g., that her children would not have friends, as she did not; would not be able to stand up for themselves, as she felt unable to do; and would always be slow, as she considered herself to be). Consequently, Ruth has difficulty establishing friendships for both herself and her children.

Relationships and Social Support: Views of Parents With Mental Retardation   Gwynnyth Llewellyn

For only one couple in this study—Mark and Elizabeth—self-reflection helped to build their confidence as they became aware of their attributes as parents. For example, Mark commented:

Like some men experience hell, going through hell, in coming up to it and what's happening to them. This second time we have been fighting a lot, and that's a problem . . . and that's why I don't like Elizabeth pregnant. . . . I like the idea that she is pregnant . . . but that means going through hard times.

Discussing these circumstances with Elizabeth and others had led Mark to decide

not to worry about it too much. I don't worry for the reason that it's the pregnancy that is doing it . . . and we can cope, we have got to cope . . . that's what I said to her, you are not leaving me because of that . . . we are going to cope.

Not surprisingly, given the "negative" self-questioning of most of the couples, the parents had no friendship ties. Some parents had acquaintances (e.g., at playgroups and adult group activities); however, these acquaintances were not regarded as people to be asked for support. There was no one else to turn to except family members and professionals from service agencies. For example, Sue commented that "My grandmother used to like me for herself all the time and that's why I met Morris late in life because my grandmother used to hide me away practically in life and everything." Because of this solitary childhood, Sue had no friends from the past. She continued to find it very difficult to talk to people. This remained a sadness in her life. When I asked whether she had friends at school, she answered, "well I had a few but not so close really, not as close as I would have liked really. I would have liked to, that's what I would have loved in my life really." Ruth's school experiences also mitigated against her making friends. She recalled:

When I was younger I started going to school and still through my adult life I know that people can be very cruel. I don't know how to stop it, I had a friend and I don't know if she intentionally did it to me but I saw her every day and then all of a sudden that was it and I am not going to be . . . I'm not going to chase her around. Allan said, oh you shouldn't worry about it but I have had it happen before to me in life.

Others have also commented on parents' social isolation (e.g., Mattinson, 1970). Andron and Tymchuk (1987) reported that parents in Project Parenting had a "sense of being different" and this, along with their poverty, led to severe social isolation. For example, difficulties with transportation and/or babysitting precluded them visiting people with whom they had been friends before having children; lack of social skills prohibited

their acceptance by other groups of mothers with young children. Social skill difficulties have been identified as a factor affecting service provision (Llewellyn & Brigden, 1995).

Atkinson (1986) noted similar friendship difficulties for adults with intellectual disability, although none of her sample were parents. Some were able to "engage 'competent others', ordinary members of the general public, to supplement, sometimes to supplant, the careers assigned to them by the formal system" (p. 83). Others relied entirely on their formal support worker (e.g., a social worker) for social network support. The majority (26 out of 42) had no ordinary friends.

The increasing social isolation of many parents with young children has been noted in Australia and elsewhere (Finch, 1989; New South Wales, 1994). The isolation of the parents in this study (8 out of 10 not having friends they could call on for assistance) is outstanding. The lack of friends for the parents in this study appears to result from their not knowing other parents in similar situations. Not one of the participating parents was able to identify friends with intellectual disability who were also parents. Yet, other parents of young children value relationships with parents in similar situations (Cant, 1993). In-depth investigation of the reasons underlying the lack of friendship networks for parents with intellectual disability is clearly warranted. Providing opportunities for these parents to acquire friends by initiating parent-to-parent support groups and by teaching parents skills in developing friendships appears to be an appropriate social support intervention.

Professional Support

The literature abounds with examples of professional support to parents with intellectual disability. Often this unsolicited support is mandated by the protective or court systems (Whitman, Graves, & Accardo, 1989). Researchers have not given attention to whether parents solicit support from professionals. When asked, parents report they do actively seek this support.

Of note is the parents' preferred sequence of help-seeking. This sequence begins with partners, including family members, and ends with seeking help from professionals. This sequence is influenced by the type of help required, the urgency of need for help, and confidence in those who might give help. For example, help is mainly sought from professionals in novel or emergency situations. Sue recalled an instance where she noticed bubbles coming out of Molly's mouth as she played beside her while she was cleaning the bath. She remembered the following instance:

I rushed her right up to the doctors and um, he said it (the cleaning liquid) is really mild, it won't harm her at all. . . . I was just worried, you've got to be so careful I think. I got a shock I didn't expect her to do it, didn't do it before but that day she did. In the car and rushed her to the doctors and he said, it's quite mild, but you've got to really, you don't know these things, first child.

Support from professionals was not always welcomed. This was particularly true when professionals ignored any difficulty the parent had in understanding and learning new concepts or gave conflicting advice. The following conversation I had with Elizabeth provides a typical example of the latter:

Interviewer: And when you were saying people tell you all different sorts of things. You mean different advice?

Elizabeth: Yes. Try this. Try that. Like Samantha is just starting to get teeth through, so people have been saying try . . . they've told us three things, one person has said try this cream that you can get from the chemist, another has said rub lemon over the gums, and the other one has said buy these teething rings—the ones you stick in the fridge and then they chew on it, which makes their gums go cold which stops the gums from hurting, so . . . at the moment I've got the cream and I've got the teething rings in the fridge, I haven't tried the lemon yet. . . . And it's hard to know which one to go to.

Whitman et al. (1989) observed that previous "bad" experience with services may lead parents to avoid professionals, thereby shutting themselves off from potential support or help in a crisis. Espe-Sherwindt and Crable (1993) reported that parents may socially withdraw or engage minimally in conversational turn-taking when attending services. These authors suggest that this is not necessarily due to lack of motivation but rather that parents "may choose to remain isolated because they are uncomfortable and unsure of their skills in even the most simple interactions" (p. 160).

Andron and Tymchuk (1987) and Espe-Sherwindt and Crable (1993) suggested that the most overwhelming influence is the number of professionals from multiple agencies, all of whom bring their own perspectives to parenting, including their definition of "good" parenting. In interviews with professionals, Espe-Sherwindt (1991) (cited in Espe-Sherwindt & Crable, 1993) found, for example, that all of them defined *parenting skills* using personally unique terminology. Their perspectives on parenting were relevant to their own life stage: "my childhood experiences" (for nonparents); "be-

ing a parent myself" (for those with young children); and "when I look back at what I've done as a parent" (for parents with grown-up children). Parents with intellectual disability are subject to these differing professional perspectives on what is "adequate" parenting.

Parenting is simultaneously an intensely personal and a commonly shared experience. Personal experience occurs within a socially constructed view of what is regarded as parenting. Views of parenting are part of the taken-for-granted personal and cultural heritage. These views guide judgments of those whose lives, and their parenting experience, may be different from our own. Becoming a parent is a welcomed family event for most adults, but not for people with intellectual disability. A common view is that these people do not become sexually mature (Wolfensburger, 1972); therefore, when they announce their impending parenthood, family members or service workers may want the pregnancy terminated or the forthcoming offspring adopted. If the pregnancy proceeds, their parenting will most likely be scrutinized by child care and protection authorities. Family and professional concern for child well-being results in many parents being sent to specialized parent training programs. Professional knowledge of parents who have intellectual disability is derived from these sources, most often based on parents who are doing poorly. Reports of parents doing satisfactorily are rare, and their voices are seldom heard.

Results of the present study add to the growing awareness of the need to understand the lives of people who have intellectual disability in their own context and from their own perspective (Ferguson, Ferguson, & Taylor, 1992; Kaufman, 1988). This perspective has its roots in classic studies such as Edgerton's *Cloak of Competence* (1967, 1993), in which he discussed the community living experience of previously institutionalized adults. More recently, interpretivist studies of disability have been published on such issues as ways of thinking about and developing concepts of intellectual disability and the subjective experience in diverse contexts, including classrooms, institutions, families, and life experiences such as parenting (Booth & Booth, 1994; Taylor, in press).

By neglecting the views of parents, investigators have represented parents with intellectual disability as having little influence on or control over their own lives. The parents in this study, by their own accounts, challenge this view. The present study serves as a reminder of the importance of seeking out the views of people with intellectual disability themselves (Taylor & Bogdan, 1994).

Conclusion

In the present study I have explored and documented the views of parents with intellectual disability about the support they receive and the type of support they want, from whom, and in what way. The findings highlight the previously simplistic nature of our views on relationships and social support for these parents. The parents' viewpoint offers a more sophisticated perspective. The participating couples were not simply receivers of support from their own parents. Rather, getting and giving support, particularly with their partner, was an integral part of their daily family life. Support from family members was desired but not automatically regarded as helpful. Support was also sought outside the family and from professionals. Relationships with friends and neighbors were notably absent.

The limited time span of the study (92 years with the couples) made it impossible to determine whether parents' perceptions of their relationships and support remain stable or change, as their needs, and the needs of their children, alter over time. Additional longitudinal work is needed to help determine the nature of social support for parents at various points in their family life cycle.

Four issues raised in this study are pertinent to policy and practice. The study findings challenge the notion of "adequate" parenting. In the absence of an agreed legal or practical definition of *parenting adequacy* (Hayman, 1990), parents with intellectual disability are pronounced guilty on many counts, including homelessness, child abuse and neglect, and unemployment and poverty, irrespective of the lack of empirical data to support these claims (Whitman & Accardo, 1990). The results of this study suggest that parents are not judged a priori but that their personal histories and their unique parenting and family experiences are taken into account.

Second, the traditional concept of parenting must be challenged and indeed, *is* challenged by the study findings. Parenting in Australian society is viewed as the prerogative of relatively autonomous and independent individuals. Yet the significant presence of other people in the lives of parents with intellectual disability suggests collective and communal aspects to parenting. Taylor (in press) has explored in depth the breadth of involvement of kin in one family with disabilities. Further in-depth studies of the nature and extent of the collective and communal aspects of parenting are needed if

services are to respond adequately to parents' circumstances. An admirable beginning has been made by Wenger (1994), who developed a typology of support networks for older people. A typology of support networks for parents with intellectual disability would be equally helpful.

Third, the usual concept of family should be questioned. Families can no longer be examined from an "ideal" family, single point of reference. Families have to be understood as they are, and as they perceive themselves to be. Rather than judging family life in relation to perceived ideals of families, investigators must ask questions about these parents' role and position, their community, and their society. The study findings of variation and diversity in the parenting experience affirms the need for policy developers to take into account family relationships and preferred family styles. This point has been eloquently elaborated both by Taylor (in press) and Booth and Booth (1994) in their parent profiles.

Fourth, particularly worthy of further investigation is the parental viewpoint on services and whether these services provide resource benefits or impose constraints on their family lives. Viewing professional support in this differentiated manner would allow the development of a user-centered framework to guide practice. Booth and Booth (1993) have suggested that such a framework would "give parents a sense of control over their own lives and their children's lives" (p. 468). As Taylor (in press) noted:

Parents with mental retardation should be approached with the same assumption underlying family-centered support programs: that is, offer assistance, but help the family in ways in which they want to be helped and on their own terms. (p. 42)

Does this happen now? Typically, first-hand knowledge of parents with intellectual disability is not sought for service development and evaluation (Llewellyn, 1991; Llewellyn, 1994a; Walton-Allen & Feldman, 1991). Programs for such parents are developed mainly from the input of service providers and focus on parent training (Tymchuk & Andron, 1992). Other needs of parents have been ignored (Llewellyn, 1994c). The results of the present study demonstrate that parents do have concerns about their relationships and the support provided with the tasks of parenting. The couples in this study displayed abundant willingness to share this aspect of their daily family lives. The challenge before us is to be just as willing to incorporate the views of parents with intellectual disability into policy and practice.

References

Andron, L., & Sturm, M. L. (1973). Is "I do" in the repertoire of the retarded? A study of the functioning of married retarded couples. *Mental Retardation, 11,* 31–34.

Andron, L., & Tymchuk, A. (1987). Parents who are mentally retarded. In A. Craft (Ed.), *Mental handicap and sexuality: Issues and perspectives* (pp. 238–262). Tunbridge Wells, UK: Costello.

Atkinson, D. (1986). Engaging competent others: A study of the support networks of people with mental handicap. *British Journal of Social Work, 16*(Suppl.), 83–101.

Blumer, H. (1969). *Symbolic interactionism. Perspective and method.* Englewood Cliffs, NJ: Prentice-Hall.

Booth, T., & Booth, W. (1993). Parenting with learning difficulties: Lessons for practitioners. *British Journal of Social Work, 23,* 459–480.

Booth, T., & Booth, W. (1994). *Parenting under pressure. Mothers and fathers with learning difficulties.* Buckingham, UK: Open University Press.

Budd, K. S., & Greenspan, S. (1985). Parameters of successful and unsuccessful interventions with parents who are mentally retarded. *Mental Retardation, 23,* 269–273.

Cant, R. (1992). Friendship, neighboring and the isolated family: The case of families with disabled children. *International Journal of Sociology of the Family, 22,* 31–50.

Cant, R. (1993). Constraints on social activities of caregivers: A sociological perspective. *Australian Occupational Therapy Journal, 40,* 113–121.

Edgerton, R. B. (1967). *Cloak of competence.* Berkeley: University of California Press.

Edgerton, R. B. (1993). *Cloak of competence* (Rev. ed.). Berkeley: University of California Press.

Espe-Sherwindt, M. (1991). *Infinite permutations and combinations: Perspectives on parents with mental retardation.* Unpublished manuscript, The Ohio State University.

Espe-Sherwindt, M., & Crable, S. (1993). Parents with mental retardation: Moving beyond the myths. *Topics in Early Childhood Special Education, 13,* 154–174.

Espe-Sherwindt, M., & Kerlin, S. (1990). Early intervention with parents with mental retardation: Do we empower or impair? *Infants and Young Children, 2,* 21–28.

Ferguson, P. M., Ferguson, D. L., & Taylor, S. J. (Eds.). (1992). *Interpreting disability. A qualitative reader.* New York: Teachers College Press.

Finch, J. (1989). *Family obligations and social change.* Cambridge, UK: Polity Press.

Glaser, B. G., & Strauss, A. L. (1967). *The discovery of grounded theory.* New York: Aldine.

Hayman, R. L. (1990). Presumptions of justice: Law, politics and the mentally retarded parent. *Harvard Law Review, 103,* 1205–1271.

Johnson, B. S. (1950). A study of sterilized persons from the Laconia State School. *American Journal of Mental Deficiency, 54,* 404–408.

Kaminer, R., Jedrysek, E., & Soles, B. (1981). Intellectually limited parents. *Developmental and Behavioral Pediatrics, 2,* 39–43.

Kaufman, S. Z. (1988). *Retarded isn't stupid, Mom!* Baltimore: Brookes.

Llewellyn, G. (1990). People with intellectual disability as parents: Perspectives from the professional literature. *Australia and New Zealand Journal of Developmental Disabilities, 16,* 369-380.

Llewellyn, G. (1991, March). *Parents with an intellectual disability: Parent and professional perspectives.* Paper presented at the International Conference on Mental Retardation (IASSMD and HKASSMH), Hong Kong.

Llewellyn, G. (1994a). Generic family support services: Are parents with learning disability catered for? *Mental Handicap Research, 7,* 64–76.

Llewellyn, G. (1994b). *Intellectual disability and parenting: A shared experience.* Unpublished doctoral dissertation, University of Sydney, Sydney, Australia.

Llewellyn, G. (1994c). *Support and services required by parents with intellectual disability* (Grant application). Sydney, Australia: University of Sydney, Department of Human Services and Health International Year of the Family Funding.

Llewellyn, G., & Brigden, D. (1995). Factors affecting service provision to parents with intellectual disability: An exploratory study. *Australia and New Zealand Journal of Developmental Disabilities, 20,* 97–112.

Mattinson, J. (1970). *Marriage and mental handicap.* London: Duckworth.

McCallister, L., & Fischer, C. S. (1978). A procedure for surveying personal networks. *Sociological Methods and Research, 7,* 131–148.

McGaw, S., & Sturmey, P. (1993). Identifying the needs of parents with learning disabilities: A review. *Child Abuse Review, 2,* 101–117.

Mercer, J. (1973). *Labeling the mentally retarded: Clinical and social system perspectives on mental retardation.* Berkeley: University of California Press.

New South Wales International Year of the Family Secretariat, Social Policy Directorate. (1994). *Focusing on families: A report on consultations conducted by the NSW International Year of the Family Advisory Committee.* Sydney, Australia: Author.

Peck, J. R., & Stephens, B. (1965). Marriage of young adult male retardates. *American Journal of Mental Deficiency, 6,* 818–827.

Rosenberg, S. A., & McTate, G. A. (1982, January–February). Intellectually handicapped mothers: problems and prospects. *Children Today,* 24–27 and back cover.

Seagull, E. A. W., & Scheurer, S. L. (1986). Neglected and abused children of mentally retarded parents. *Child Abuse and Neglect, 10,* 493–500.

Spradley, J. P. (1979). *The ethnographic interview.* Fort Worth, TX: Holt, Rinehart & Winston.

Stainback, S., & Stainback, W. (1984). Methodological considerations in qualitative research. *JASH, 9,* 296–303.

Strauss, A., & Corbin, J. (1990). *Basics of qualitative research. Grounded theory procedures and techniques.* Newbury Park, CA: Sage.

Taylor, S. J. (in press). Children's Division is coming to take pictures. Family life and parenting in a family with disabilities. In S. J. Taylor, R. Bogdan, & Z. M. Lutfiyya (Eds.), *The variety of community experience: Qualitative studies of family and community life.* Baltimore: Brookes.

Taylor, S. J., & Bogdan, R. (1994). Qualitative research methods and community living. In M. F. Hayden & B. H. Abery (Eds.), *Challenges for a service system in transition* (pp. 43–63). Baltimore: Brookes.

Tracy, E. M. (1990, May). Identifying social support resources of at-risk families. *Social Work,* 252–258.

Tucker, M. B., & Johnson, O. (1989). Competence promoting vs competence inhibiting social support for mentally retarded mothers. *Human Organization, 48,* 95–107.

Tymchuk, A. J., & Andron, L. (1992). Project Parenting: Child interactional training with mothers who are mentally handicapped. *Mental Handicap Research, 5,* 4–32.

Walton-Allen, N. G., & Feldman, M. A. (1991). Perception of service needs by parents with mental retardation and their workers. *Comprehensive Mental Health Care, 1,* 137–147.

Wayne, J., & Fine, S. B. (1986). Group work with retarded mothers. *Social casework: The Journal of Contemporary Casework, 67,* 195–202.

Wenger, G. C. (1994). *Support networks of older people: A guide for practitioners.* Bangor, Wales: Centre for Social Policy Research and Development.

Whitman, B. Y., Graves, B., & Accardo, P. J. (1989). Training in parenting skills for adults with mental retardation. *Social Work, 34,* 431–434.

Whitman, B. Y., & Accardo, P. J. (1990). *When a parent is mentally retarded.* Baltimore: Brookes.

Wolfensburger, W. (1972). *Normalization. The principle of normalization in human services.* Toronto: National Institute on Mental Retardation.

Zetlin, A. G., Weisner, T. S., & Gallimore, R. (1985). Diversity, shared functioning, and the role of benefactors: A study of parenting by retarded persons. In S. K. Thurman (Ed.), *Children of handicapped parents: Research and clinical perspectives* (pp. 69–95). Orlando, FL: Academic Press.

Received 1/19/95, first decision 4/3/95, accepted 5/16/95. Editor-in-Charge: Steven Taylor

I thank the parents who shared their family life experiences. Names used in this article are fictitious. The study was supported by a Cumberland College of Health Sciences Research Grant, University of Sydney, 1992.

Author

Gwynnyth Llewellyn, Ph.D., Senior Lecturer in Developmental Disabilities, Faculty of Health Sciences, University of Sydney, PO Box 170, Lidcombe NSW 2141 Australia.

PART FOUR

Family Intervention, Support, and Social Policy

Families with a child with retardation enter the new century with more support than ever before. For the child we find a myriad of educational, vocational, and social programs, many mandated by law. This greater assurance of a "free and appropriate education" is perhaps the most effective intervention for reducing the stress and caretaking burden experienced by these families. For family members we find specific interventions and supports, such as counseling, support groups, educational programs, teaching guides, home visitation, advocacy organizations, school involvement, and respite care. The future holds promise for even greater supports, such as increasingly sophisticated genetic counseling, more universally available tax benefits and cash subsidies, and more age specific assistance (e.g. permanency planning for families of adults). Indeed, perhaps more than ever before, parents are enjoying their caregiving responsibilities and appreciating the positive impact of their child on the family.

It has not been this way for long. The present view of families as citizens entitled to support that meets their individual needs has emerged in recent decades as an amalgam of roles that professionals have prescribed for families over the century. We have already noted that families were all but invisible up until the early 1940s. (Then, as now, "family" typically referred only to parents and, implicitly, only to mother). The earliest "intervention" literature, in the 1940's and early 1950's, was focused on "getting along" with parents, from the perspective of institutions (Mason, 1953; Scher, 1955; Wardell, 1947). This is reflected in titles like "Developing and Maintaining Good Relations with Parents of Mentally Deficient Children" (Sampson, 1947) and "Better Parent Education Means More Effective Public Relations" (Barber, 1956). Since then, services have been loosely organized around three roles for parents, as: patients, teachers, and advocates.

Parents as Patients

Interventions that view parents as patients were logical bedfellows of the view that parents experience much that is negative in delivering and raising a child with retardation. Beginning in the 1950s, there was a focus on providing counseling and therapy for distraught parents (Coleman, 1953; Morris, 1955). Some papers spoke to particular professional groups, like social workers (Begab, 1958) and school psychologists (Ruzicka, 1958). The prevailing psychodynamic model provided constructs for understanding family troubles. However, Carl Rogers's (1951) "client centered" approach, with its emphasis on active listening, empathy, and positive regard for the client, was a simpler and more readily understood alternative that is reflected in the early papers on counseling. We have included a 1963 paper by Philip Roos, *Psychological Counseling with Parents of Retarded Children*. Roos, at that time the director of psychological services for Texas's state facilities, began with the then popular view that "the psychologist working with parents of retarded children should remember he is probably dealing with highly distressed people" (p. 345). Although modern perspectives would temper and balance this statement some, his observations of parents' experiences and his suggestions that counselors should conduct therapeutic interviews as active listeners rather than advice givers still have much to offer today.

Yet while being attuned to parents' emotional struggles is commendable, there is a downside when this is held as a singular perspective. Roos, also a parent, wrote 15 years later about how the view of parents as patients led professionals to turn a deaf ear to parents' legitimate observations. He decried

". . . the attitude on the part of some professionals that parents are complete ignoramuses so that any conclusion they reach regarding their own child is categorically ignored. Later I found that suggestions I would make regarding my own child would be totally dismissed by some professionals, while these same suggestions made as a professional about other children would be cherished by my colleagues as professional pearls of wisdom" (Roos, 1978, p. 15).

The parent as patient view continued to dominate in the 1960s, with numerous reports of individual and group interventions, and not altogether successful attempts at evaluation (Ramsey, 1967). Although the "parent as patient" perspective began to be overshadowed in the 1970s by the teacher role we consider next, this viewpoint has continued to the present, modified to fit the themes and tone of the times. A recent emphasis is not so much on reducing parental psychopathology as on increasing positive coping, seen as what parents do (actions) and think (cognitions) that reduces burden and helps parents appreciate the positives in childrearing (Summers, Behr, & Turnbull, 1989). An illustration is Singer, Irvin, and Hawkins's (1988) well-evaluated group intervention to help parents manage stress. We have included a subsequent paper, Charles Nixon and George Singer's 1993 study entitled *Group Cognitive-Behavioral Treatment for Excessive Parental Self-Blame and Guilt*. This intervention focused on altering cognitive processes that may have in part led to the negative impact of a child with mental retardation on the family and thereby reduced distress. Although the earlier "patient" perspective was patronizing and had its ill effects, sensitivity to parents' thoughts and feelings, and therapeutic interventions to be utilized when appropriate, certainly constitute an essential backdrop to the provision of other family supports.

Parents as Teachers

In the 1950s and 60s there was a focus, too, on education and information, and some recognition that parents are always teachers and could be helped in that role. For example, Strazzulla (1954) and Leberfeld and Nertz (1955) wrote "how to" guides for parents on language training. Matheny and Vernick (1968) in the late sixties framed an alternative model with their paper entitled, "Parents of the mentally retarded child: Emotionally overwhelmed or informationally deprived?"

By the 1970s the "parents as teachers" model had come into clear focus (Baker & Heifetz, 1976; Fredericks, Baldwin, McDonnell, Hofmann, & Harter, 1971; Lindsley, 1967; Mash & Terdal, 1973). A growing cohort of professionals viewed parents as a resource for their child's development and promoted education and information as opposed to emotion-directed counseling. Among the many influences for this model shift, two stand out. First, the successes of the "new" behavior modification approach to teaching children were striking and engendered a renewed optimism about the child's potential for learning. Second, increasing legal rights to education, codified in the landmark Education for All Handicapped Children Act of 1975, fueled this optimism, especially as school doors opened for children with more severe retardation. Both of these developments logically argued for greater parent participation. Moreover, with increased funding available for research, it was now possible to examine program outcomes more rigorously.

We have included Louis Heifetz's (1977) study, *Behavioral Training for Parents of Retarded Children: Alternative Formats Based on Instructional Manuals*, which is notable for its methodology—a multiple group design, large sample size, multiple measures, and focus on increasing child skills as well as reducing behavior problems. Most importantly, there was a family empowerment theme. The demonstrated utility of written manuals to guide parents' teaching underscored what parents could do, without professional counseling, if provided with the right tools.

A different but related interest that began in the 1960s and '70s was early intervention for high-risk infants and young children. The impetus here was the same as that for the "great society" programs of the 1960s that fostered, among other programs, Head Start. Early intervention programs were grounded in developmental psychology and, while many embraced behavior modification methods, they were more multi-modal in the intervention design. Selecting children at risk for mental retardation, these programs focused on a stimulating experience for children but typically included components to enhance parenting skills and the home environment. Among the most notable programs were the Carolina Abecedarian Project (Ramey & Smith, 1976; Ramey et al., 1983), and the Milwaukee Project, which has been reported in an AAMR book (Garber, 1988). We have included Mary Slater's (1986) study, *Modification of Mother-Child Interaction Processes in Families with Children At-risk for Mental Retardation*, as an excellent illustration of a parent training component. Slater conducted a short-term laboratory-based intervention, teaching low-IQ mothers to talk with their children in ways that increased the children's cognitive and language functioning.

By the 1980s, behavioral parent training had become a component of many intervention programs (Baker, 1984; 1989). With demonstrated successes and with right to education legislation mandating increased parental involvement, many child programs began to anticipate, indeed expect, greater parent participation. Some professionals wondered: "Are we professionalizing parents?" (Allen & Hudd, 1987). Two cautions were raised: (1) That extensive expectations for parent involvement might increase already high levels of parent stress; and (2) That parents' intentional teaching efforts would alter the natural parent child interactions that occur in families, to the ultimate detriment of the child (Gallagher, Beckman, & Cross, 1983). We have included Ann Turnbull and Rud Turnbull's 1982 thoughtful essay, *Parent Involvement in the Education of Handicapped Children: A Critique*, that questioned the assumptions about parent involvement inherent in the Education for All Handicapped Children Act of 1975. They argue that parent needs, wants, and abilities vary and, thus, also must their involvement. We have also included Bruce Baker, Sandra Landen, and Kathleen Kashima's 1991 empirical study, *Effects of Parent Training on Families of Children with Mental Retardation: Increased Burden or Generalized Benefit?*, that examined parental adjustment before and after participation in a group parent training program. Although the limited changes these authors found were positive, we should note that the program was voluntary and made very limited demands on parents.

Parent training or education, following applied behavior analysis, continues to be the non-drug treatment of choice for reduction of problem behaviors (Rush and Frances, 2000) and is widely utilized in skill teaching (Kaiser, Hancock, & Nietfeld, 2000). In the past decade, however, there have been fewer reports of intervention with families in AAMR journals. This reflects, in part, the considerable decrease in federal funding for intervention research in the mental retardation field and also the choice of applied behavior analysts to publish elsewhere. At the same time, there has been a shift in the interests of AAMR authors away from intervention on the individual level to social policies providing broader supports for care giving.

Parents as Advocates

Parent organizations as long ago as the 1930s advocated for services and filled some voids by providing them. The first was the Cuyahoga County (Ohio) Council for the Retarded Child, which in 1933 operated a class for the "gravely retarded" (Scheerenberger, 1983). By 1950, there were 88 local programs and the inception of a national organization (now the Association for Retarded Citizens of the United States). By 1970, the membership was 250,000. Throughout its history, the ARC has been concerned with providing support to its members, information to the public, advocacy for services, and operation of programs—classrooms before the government assumed this responsibility, group homes and vocational training, recreation, and educational classes for parents.

We have included a 1952 paper by Elizabeth Boggs, one of the foremost advocates of the century. Her paper, *Relations of Parent Groups and Professional Persons in Community Settings*, written a half-century ago, is just as meaningful today in its plea for parents and professionals alike to be honest with themselves and each other. Boggs speaks eloquently about the aims and activities of parent organizations and is prescient in her observations about genetics and counseling. Despite Boggs's encouragement of parent-professional cooperation, Scheerenberger's (1983) history of mental retardation recounts the friction between parents and professionals in the early years of advocacy.

Today parents and professionals work together more comfortably, often to influence social policy. Beginning in the 1980s, many advocacy efforts have coalesced around the theme of "family support" (Bradley, 1992; Dunst, Trivette, & Deal, 1994). The emphasis is on moving away from provider-driven services to consumer-driven ones, where families are given greater control of resources so that services can respond to their self-identified needs. Bradley (1992) notes that "changes in the American family—increased numbers of working mothers, more single parent families, smaller family size, and lack of available extended family—suggest that contemporary families have diminished resources at their disposal to provide the care required by their family member with a disability" (p. 1). In addition, many children with complicated medical conditions are now surviving and living at home, and a shift in social policy toward family care has increasingly closed the doors to out-of-home placements. The major goal of state family support programs is to enhance caregiving capacity and improve the quality of life for the family; a related goal is to prevent or defer unnecessary out-of-home placement (Bradley, Knoll and Agosta, 1992; Agosta and Bradley, 1985).

The primary family supports are financial supports (e.g. discretionary cash subsidy) and respite and child care. Other family supports include case management, environmental adaptations (e.g. home and vehicle modifications; purchase of special equipment), parent training, in-home assistance (e.g. home health care), counseling, information, and meeting daily needs (e.g. home repairs, special diet) (Knoll et al., 1992). Almost all states now provide some form of family support, but the extent is underwhelming. The most recent available data, from 1996, show that family support allocations amounted to 2.3% of the total mental retardation/developmental disabilities funding in the U.S. (Braddock, Hemp, Parish, & Westrich, 1998). At this time, 36 states provided some form of respite care activity and 20 states had initiated cash subsidy payments for families whose child with disabilities lives at home. However, only 18,361 families were receiving cash subsidies, with Texas and Michigan accounting for more than half of these (Braddock et al., 1998).

The fledgling family support movement, primarily described in books, has thus far undergone limited evaluation of the type that is reported in journals. The Michigan program, a model of broad-based family support, has one of the first cash subsidy programs and has provided for outcome evaluation. We include Judith Meyers and Maureen Marcenko's (1989) paper, *Impact of a Cash Subsidy Program for Families of Children with Severe Developmental Disabilities*. These authors found out-of-home placement to be lower in supported families. Subsequently Herman and Marcenko (1997) reported that respite care and cash subsidies indirectly affected parental well being. Parents who perceived that babysitting and money resources were adequate also perceived that they had time to do things for themselves, family, and friends; this positive perception of time resources was related to lower depression.

Advocates for family support are aided in promoting social policies by national surveys on key service-related issues. We include two exemplary papers that provide a statistical basis for policy formulation. The first is David Braddock's (1999) paper, *Aging and Developmental Disabilities: Demographic and Policy Issues Affecting American Families*. Against the backdrop of an aging society, the author speaks to aging caregivers and individuals with developmental disabilities (DD) themselves, and the implications for service delivery. For example, a half million people with DD are living with family caregivers who are at least 60 years old; these people will likely need residential services in the not-so-distant future. Indeed, in 1997 there were almost as many persons on waiting lists for residential services as the total services system expansion during the previous 20 years. The pressure to create both more residential services and viable alternatives (such as cash supports) is heightened by increasing longevity of persons with DD, who will require more years of services.

The second paper is Arnold Birenbaum and Herbert Cohen's (1993) *On the Importance of Helping Families: Policy Implications from a National Study*. The authors present data on non-medical expenditures in providing care for persons with autism or severe mental retardation as well as policy recommendations on financial ways to support maintaining the individual at home.

Families as Citizens

Families of persons with mental retardation in the United States enter the new century with the complex roles and rights of any citizen. That is, the focus is on providing wide-ranging supports that family members can draw on as needed. Counseling and therapy, education and training in parenting, and opportunities to advocate no longer reflect conflicting parental roles but are part of a hoped-for integrated system of supports. For the person with retardation, there is heightened value on self-determination, individual choice, home ownership or control, maximum quality of life, independence, and self-advocacy. For his or her family, there is emphasis on how social institutions can provide help with supports that will ensure a better caregiving environment for the individual's growth.

References

Agosta, J., & Bradley, V. (1985). *Family care for persons with developmental disabilities: A growing commitment*. Boston: Human Services Research Institute.

Allen, D. A., & Hudd, S. S. (1987). Are we professionalizing parents? Weighing the benefits and pitfalls. *Mental Retardation, 25*, 133–139.

Baker, B. L. (1989). *Parent training and developmental disabilities*. Washington, D.C.: American Association on Mental Retardation.

Baker, B. L. (1984). Intervention with families with young, severely handicapped children. In J. Blacher (Ed.), *Severely handicapped young children and their families: Research in review* (pp. 319–375). Orlando: Academic Press.

Baker, B. L., & Heifetz, L. J. (1976). The Read Project: Teaching manuals for parents of retarded children. In T. D. Tjossem (Ed.), *Intervention strategies for high risk infants and young children*. Baltimore: University Park Press.

Baker, B. L., Landen, S. J., & Kashima, K. J. (1991). Effects of parent training on families of children with mental retardation: Increased burden or generalized benefit? *American Journal on Mental Retardation, 96*, 127–136.

Barber, T. M. (1956). Better parent education means more effective public relations. *American Journal of Mental Deficiency, 60*, 627–632.

Begab, M. J. (1958). A social work approach to the mentally retarded and their families. *American Journal of Mental Deficiency, 63*, 524–529.

Birenbaum, A. and Cohen, H. J. (1993). On the importance of helping families: Policy implications from a national study. *Mental Retardation, 31*, 67–74.

Boggs, E. (1952). Relations of parent groups and professional persons in community situations. *American Journal of Mental Deficiency*, 109–115.

Braddock, D. (1999). Aging and developmental disabilities: Demographic and policy issues affecting American families. *Mental Retardation, 37,* 155–161.

Braddock, D., Hemp, R., Parish, S., & Westrich, J. (1998). *The state of the states in developmental disabilities,* 5th ed. Washington, D. C.: American Association on Mental Retardation.

Bradley, V. J. (1992). Overview of the family support movement. In V. J. Bradley, J. Knoll, & J. M. Agosta (Eds.) *Emerging issues in family support,* pp. 1–8. Washington, D.C.: American Association on Mental Retardation.

Bradley, V. J., Knoll, J., & Agosta, J. M. (1992). *Emerging issues in family support.* Washington, D.C.: American Association on Mental Retardation.

Coleman, J. C. (1953). Group therapy with parents of mentally deficient children. *American Journal of Mental Deficiency, 57,* 700–726.

Dunst, C., Trivette, C., & Deal, A. (Eds.) (1994). *Supporting and strengthening families.* Cambridge, MA: Brookline Books.

Fredericks, H. D. B., Baldwin, V. L., McDonnell, J. J., Hofmann, R., & Harter, J. (1971). Parents educate their trainable children. *Mental Retardation, 9,* 24–26.

Gallagher, J. J., Beckman, P., & Cross, A. H. (1983). Families of handicapped children: Sources of stress and its amelioration. *Exceptional Children, 50,* 10–19.

Garber, H. L. (1988). *The Milwaukee Project.* Washington, DC: American Association on Mental Retardation.

Heifetz, L. J. (1977). Behavioral training for parents of retarded children: Alternative formats based on instructional manuals. *American Journal of Mental Deficiency, 82,* 194–203.

Herman, S. E., & Marcenko, M. O. (1997). Perceptions of services and resources as mediators of depression among parents of children with developmental disabilities. *Mental Retardation, 35,* 458–467.

Kaiser, A. P., Hancock, T. B., & Nietfeld, J. P. (2000). The effects of parent-implemented enhanced milieu teaching on the social communication of children who have autism. *Early Education and Development, 11,* 423–446.

Knoll, J., Covert, S., Osuch, R., O'Connor, S., Agosta, J., & Blaney, B. (1992). Supporting families: State family support efforts. In. V. J. Bradley, J. Knoll, & J. M. Agosta (Eds.), *Emerging issues in family support,* 57–98, Washington, D.C.: American Association on Mental Retardation.

Leberfeld, D. T., & Nertz, N. (1955). A home training program in language and speech for mentally retarded children. *American Journal of Mental Deficiency, 59,* 413–416.

Lindsley, O. R. (1967). An experiment with parents handling behavior at home. *Johnstone Bulletin, 9,* 27–36.

Mash, E., & Terdal, L. (1973). Modification of mother-child intervention. *Mental Retardation, 11,* 44–49.

Mason, L. F. (1953). Developing and maintaining good parental relationships. *American Journal of Mental Deficiency, 57,* 394–396.

Matheny, A. P., & Vernick, J. (1968). Parents of the mentally retarded child: Emotionally overwhelmed or informationally deprived? *Journal of Pediatrics, 74,* 953–959.

Meyers, J. C., & Marcenko, M. O. (1989). Impact of a cash subsidy program for families of children with severe developmental disabilities. *Mental Retardation, 27,* 383–387.

Morris, E. (1955). Casework training needs for counseling parents of the retarded. *American Journal of Mental Deficiency, 59,* 510–516.

Nixon, C. D., & Singer, G. H. S. (1993). Group cognitive-behavioral treatment for excessive parental self-blame and guilt. *American Journal on Mental Retardation, 97,* 665–672.

Ramey, C. T., & Smith, B. J. (1976). Assessing the intellectual consequences of early intervention with high-risk infants. *American Journal of Mental Deficiency, 81*, 318–324.

Ramey, C. T., Bryant, D., Sparling, J. J., & Wasik, B. H. (1983). Educational interventions to enhance intellectual development: Comprehensive daycare vs. family education. In S. Harel & N. J. Anastasiow (Eds.), *The at-risk infant: Psycho-social-medical aspects* (pp. 75–85). Baltimore: Brookes.

Ramsey, G. V. (1967). Review of group methods with parents of the mentally retarded. *American Journal of Mental Deficiency, 71*, 857–863.

Rogers, C. R. (1951). *Client-centered therapy*. Boston: Houghton Mifflin.

Roos, P. (1963). Psychological counseling with parents of retarded children. *Mental Retardation, 1*, 345–350.

Roos, P. (1978). Parents of mentally retarded children—misunderstood and mistreated. In A. Turnbull & H. R. Turnbull (Eds.), *Parents speak out* (pp. 12–27). Columbus, OH: Charles, E. Merrill.

Rush, A. J., & Frances, A. (2000). Expert concensus guideline series: Treatment of psychiatric and behavioral problems in mental retardation. *American Journal on Mental Retardation, 195*, 159–228.

Ruzicka, W. J. (1958). A proposed role for the school psychologist: Counseling parents of mentally retarded children. *American Journal of Mental Deficiency, 62*, 897–904.

Sampson, A. H. (1947). Developing and maintaining good relations with parents of mentally deficient children. *American Journal of Mental Deficiency, 52*, 187–194.

Scheerenberger, R. C. (1983). *A history of mental retardation*. Baltimore: Brookes.

Scher, B. (1955). Help to parents: an integral part of service to the retarded child. *American Journal of Mental Deficiency, 60*, 169–175.

Singer, G. H. S., Irvin, L. K., & Hawkins, N. J. (1988). Stress management training for parents of severely handicapped children. *Mental Retardation, 26*, 269–277.

Slater, M. A. (1986). Modification of mother-child interaction processes in families with children at-risk for mental retardation. *American Journal of Mental Deficiency, 91*, 257–267.

Strazzulla, M. (1954). A language guide for the parents of retarded children. *American Journal of Mental Deficiency, 59*, 48–58.

Summers, J. A., Behr, S. K., & Turnbull, A. P. (1989). Positive adaptation and coping strengths of families who have children with disabilities. In G. H. S. Singer & L. K. Irvin (Eds.)., *Support for caregiving families* (pp. 27–40). Baltimore: Brookes.

Turnbull, A. P., & Turnbull, H. R. (1982). Parent involvement in the education of handicapped children: A critique. *Mental Retardation, 20*, 115–122.

Wardell, W. (1947). Case work with parents of mentally deficient children. *American Journal of Mental Deficiency, 52*, 91–97.

Relations of Parent Groups and Professional Persons in Community Situations

Elizabeth M. Boggs, Ph.D.
1952

The relation between parent groups and all persons engaged professionally in fields which touch that of mental deficiency is one of the utmost importance for everyone involved; the parents, the professionals, and the retarded. The mere fact that the first two groups may be genuinely concerned with the welfare of the third does not suffice to ensure complete harmony between them, any more than the fact that father and mother are both honestly interested in the welfare of their children suffices to bring about complete agreement as to the components of that welfare or how it can best be served. This is a large subject which, for parent groups, merges with the still larger one of public relations generally.

This paper will concern itself with a limited but very immediate aspect of this relation, which is intimately bound up with the organizational problems of parent groups. Our success, as laymen, in our ultimate broader aims will be influenced not a little by our direct group contacts with those key professional people from whom we seek specific advice about the activities which we may wish to promote within our groups, and it is essential that we ponder carefully the part we expect our resource people to play, and the factors to be considered in choosing them.

The role of the professional advisers to a parent group must be considered in relation to the role of the parents. Since mental deficiency is no respecter of persons, it is to be expected—and experience bears out the prediction—that we will find within the parent groups a wide variety of competencies, including some in professional fields having direct bearing on the needs of the retarded; we have lawyers, educators, biochemists, statisticians, nurses, doctors, clergymen, public relations men, bankers, and a vast assortment of business men, among others. Generally speaking, we may expect that such necessary activities as setting up a committee structure, auditing books, raising money, writing publicity, speaking in public, contacting community groups and persuading legislators, can usually be carried through adequately by the parents themselves. Anything which can be done by parents should be done by them, both for efficiency and morale.

The professional person whose advice is sought should be expected to contribute it primarily in his particular field of professional competence, although his competence as a human being will have much to do with the acceptance of his ideas. He should understand, among other things, that the parents must retain freedom of action in determining the policies of their group, after listening to advice from different sources. There is more to this position than a mere reassertion of the well established American principle of the supremacy of the civilian or the right of the patient to choose his physician. It is in the long range interests of our professional friends that our effectiveness in speaking out for programs which we favor shall not be impaired by the inference that we are acting as a front for any particular agency, individual, or faction, particularly if the professional individual or faction is associated with any public service.

This is a pragmatic principle; having the disadvantages of being late starters as parent organizations go, we should at least profit by the history of others who went before.

Consider, for example, the experience of the parents of normal children. Like the P.-T.A.'s, our groups intend to promote parent education, and like them we promote the welfare of our children by obtaining equipment or offering extras which supplement the facilities provided by the authorities; our benevolent and rehabilitation work at institutions is quite analogous to many P.-T.A. projects. The effectiveness of P.-T.A.'s in advancing some of the larger causes in education, however, has been seriously impaired by the written and unwritten rules governing their action, and by the fact that their advocacy is often discounted by legislators and others because of the extraordinarily high correlation between their expressed opinions and those of the national, state or local education associations. The fact that the P.-T.A.'s alone could not adequately fill a felt need to channelize and vocalize the interest of parents and citizens in promoting a still higher standard of public education in this country was recognized by the formation of the National Citizens Commission for the Public Schools (NCCPS).

Relations of Parent Groups and Professional Persons in Community Situations

Elizabeth M. Boggs

The objects of this steering body are "To help Americans realize how important our public schools are to our expanding democracy" and "To arouse in each community the intelligence and will to improve our public schools." Here too, we, the organized parents of retarded children, can see objectives analogous to our own—to increase public understanding, and to arouse a sense of community responsibility. It is significant for us, therefore, that the NCCPS, while soliciting advice from an impressive array of persons outstanding in the field of education, has considered it desirable in the promotion of its objectives to state that "Its members are U.S. citizens not professionally identified with education, religion or politics." It is significant, too, that the formation of the NCCPS as a sort of focusing agent for democratic activity on behalf of our schools has been welcomed by far seeing educators. If we parents of retarded children are to make up for lost time and to coordinate expanding opportunities on behalf of our children, it will be well for us to take on such of the functions of both these groups as may apply to mentally handicapped children.

One of the most important functions of parent groups, as of P.T.A.'s, is parent education, both formal and informal. Here is a vast field in which the cooperation of professional persons is of the essence. But it does not suffice that parents be hearers of the word only; they must be doers also. This is a psychological as well as a practical necessity. They must be permitted, nay, encouraged to act on their own collective behalf. For example, according to a survey conducted in the summer of 1950 by Mr. Woodhull Hay, now Secretary of the National Association for Retarded Children, one of the most popular forms of activity in parent groups throughout the country is some sort of project to aid the trainable child living at home, who is generally excluded from school. In some groups this activity has been directed toward revision of legislation on behalf of these children; in others it has meant the establishment of pilot or demonstration schools or classes under parent group auspices. There are many other popular projects—clinics, play therapy groups, camps, occupational training groups, recreation clubs and so on. Parent group leaders are all too keenly aware of the need for professional advice of various kinds in the formulation and prosecution of such plans.

Some years ago, the American Association on Mental Deficiency gave formal recognition in its structure to the fact that mental deficiency has its educational, so-cial, and psychological, as well as its medical side. The parents groups' needs for advice, whether in the field of parent education or of activity on behalf of the children, are at least as many faceted, and groups will gain by seeking advice from many sources, rather than placing all their eggs in one professional basket. Counsel should be sought not only from those whose prime concern is with the mentally deficient, but from those community organizations which inevitably touch the lives of the retarded. Since much that is being done for the retarded child today is experimental, parent group leaders will also want to gather different professional points of view on the same aspect of the problem. To avoid paralysis, decisions may have to be made and action taken which lean toward one school of thought rather than another, but parent leaders are on firmer ground when they are apprised that differences of professional opinion exist before they commit their group to act.

The Board of Advisers is an extremely useful device for embodying the multidisciplinary approach to some specific project, especially when the discussions of such a group result in the evolution of a more rounded point of view and program. It is well, however, to distinguish between the "big name" and a working resource person. Sometimes they are the same, sometimes not. No one should underestimate, moreover, the value of informal advice. The man who is willing to confer by phone, as details come up, who will take time to jot down an outline or comments on a sketch, who puts himself out to spend an informal evening with a group which would like to "kick it around," is a friend indeed. To those who have served parents groups disinterestedly in this exceptional way, we parents can but render humble gratitude.

The selection of each professional person who may be asked to advise a parents group involves some pregnant decisions. We must be concerned both with professional competence and with the essential character of the individual as a human being. In many ways the problem confronting the group resembles that confronting the patient in choosing a physician. No matter how well one cases the situation in advance, the proof of the pudding remains in the eating. Only after the appendectomy will one have the answers to some of the questions.

As an individual does, so must the group seek as advisers men and women who will tell us the truth, rather than merely provide us with a placebo which we would like to hear. Much could be said—and more should be said in medical schools—about *how* to convey unpleasant truths to clients. It is possible that an awareness of their own ineptness in the field of communication has deterred many physicians from taking the bull by the horns. In any case the pooled experience of parents indicates that, whether through ignorance, timidity, or laissez-faire, many general practitioners and even pediatricians put off the day of reckoning, with ultimate disservice to their defective patients and the parents. These parents agree that as individuals they would have preferred to have had the facts—even if these could only be stated as probabilities—concerning their individual children, as early as their physicians may have seriously suspected any abnormality. Parents who affirm this need as applied to them individually may not be as ready to accept it applied to them collectively, but parent leaders have an obligation to champion those resource people who are prophets of the truth, rather than panderers to wishful thought. At the risk of an overemphatic digression, it may be well to consider this point in the light of an example:

The parents of cerebral palsied children give much voice to the thesis that "c.p.'s aren't feebleminded." Given a choice among many different expert opinions as to the percentage of palsies who are mentally retarded, they naturally incline to take the low figure. Of course, the battle to win training programs, properly designed to recognize and release the intellective functions of the palsied children must command respect and sympathy from all of us. But there still remains a strong emotive factor in their rejection of an association with mental deficiency as indicated by instances where, even though the child may be functioning on a practical level far below that of most retardates in the matter of personal care or economic and social contribution, some solace yet seems to be found in the assertion that the child is not feebleminded. Clearly there is a strong desire to dispose of what is considered a stigmatization. As we who are their final haven know, the campaign to minimize the incidence of mental limitations among the c.p.'s has worked serious damage to those children (and their parents) who are deficient as well as palsied. The diagnosis of cerebral palsy has, for these parents, raised false hopes, and for the children often meant placement in an unsuitable program from which they must be eventually rescued by transfer to a program for the retarded. Although the information disseminated about cerebral palsy from responsible sources never denies a significant fraction of mental retardates among them, the de-emphasis

produces an evasion of the truth which injures a segment of the group. The injury is two fold—first the attempt of the majority to remove a stigma by denying that mental deficiency is an important concomitant rather than by denying that the condition of mental deficiency is shameful does nothing to relieve the sense of shame of the substantial minority who are left with the double condition; second by under-emphasizing the concomitant deficiency for public relations purposes, the majority are led to leave it out of account in the programs, to the detriment of the minority. Perhaps the campaign to have the c.p.'s classed as "crippled children," "physically handicapped" and so on has merit, but not if it evades the truth in a damaging way.

We parents of retarded children are naturally extremely vulnerable to a campaign which reiterates that c.p.'s should be helped "because they are not feebleminded," with all that might be inferred from such a hypothesis. But perhaps we ourselves make the same sort of mistake.

For us the word "hereditary" has the same emotive connotations that "feeblemindedness" has for the parents of cerebral palsies. Scientifically we cannot deny that heredity has a bearing in a certain proportion of cases. We feel warmly toward those researchers who tell us the proportion is small. Why? Because in our anxiety to remove the stigma from the public concept of mental retardation, we have not stopped to think whether we have a right to stigmatize by implication the individual among us who happens to be the carrier of an undesirable gene, or whether by minimizing the hereditary factor we may be omitting from our program help for those normal human beings in our midst who have a stake in a fuller knowledge of genetics.

Unfortunately the subject of heredity has become so involved with the question of sterilization of the higher grade retarded individuals, with its many ramifications and implications outside the field of mental deficiency proper, that it is often hard to conduct a rational discussion of the subject. For the public generally and for most parents the concept of heredity is associated with the idea that mental deficients are bred by mentally deficient parents. In the excitement of refuting this notion, parent groups have omitted from parent education programs the well substantiated information concerning certain clinically definable serious types of deficiency which are due to single recessive genes, where the hereditary mechanism is well understood. The appearance

Relations of Parent Groups and Professional Persons in Community Situations   Elizabeth M. Boggs

of a child of this type indicates a strong possibility that a second child in the same family may be similarly afflicted even though both parents and all other near relatives are quite normal. Even though these cases are quite rare, these parents are entitled to full information, as well as an enlightened attitude toward their particular situation. Having endured so much, let us not stop short of the full logic of our position.

Toward this end, in every aspect of our work, parent groups should seek advisers whose devotion to truth is such that they will voice it if it is germane, and whose professional competence is such that their statements command respect.

Fortunately, in judging competence, parents collectively have one advantage not enjoyed by an individual choosing his physician. They may seek nominations from organized professional groups. The American Association on Mental Deficiency has set up a standing committee on liaison with parent groups, one of whose functions is the designation of resource persons from the Association's membership to assist parent groups. Officers of local or state chapters of other organizations, e.g., medical societies, the psychological associations, councils for exceptional children or other educational groups, mental health associations and so on, will often assist a group to select a person whose opinions are respected within the profession.

Even such a designation will not protect the parents from some of the cross fire of conflicting professional opinion. Even though Dr. X. heartily disapproves the treatments recommended by Dr. Y., he seldom blames the *patient* for taking the advice. When a group is substituted for the patient, however, some of this reticence is likely to be abandoned, and the parents group itself may be criticized for taking a certain course, even though this was done on professional advice. Such criticism is especially hard to take if it is broadcast in such a way as to prejudice public opinion or undermine the confidence of the rank and file parent member.

The competent and honest adviser can distinguish—and can lead parents to distinguish—between well substantiated evidence and hypotheses which are still in the realm of conjecture, even if some of the pet theories of the adviser himself fall in the latter class. It is neither necessary nor desirable to resort to censorship. Rather than deploring the "irresponsibility" of the press, he should take the initiative in informing parents on new developments and the nature of the scientific method.

Since we are living in an era of expanding activity on behalf of the retarded, a period of experiment and new and untried approaches, parents must expect, and indeed, welcome, honest differences of professional opinion as harbingers of progress.

As long as the differences are honest and the criticisms reasonably objective, the parents may be expected to dodge the chips. It is only when these controversies are overlaid with professional jealousies and personal ambitions that the parents are endangered. No parent group can afford to let itself be used as the rubber stamp, the blind, the cow catcher, the megaphone, or the panzer division for any professional faction or individual.

In the end it comes down to a matter of character. As their professional advisers parent groups must seek men and women of the highest personal integrity, of unselfish interest, of large mindedness and vision and imagination and true humanity, persons who are capable of being honest without being brutal, who have the common touch without sentimentality, who regard a waiting list, whether for a clinic, an institution or a class, as a human tragedy rather than as job insurance, who understand what it means to help others to help themselves, who are without thought of personal aggradizement from association with parent groups, who have the insight to glimpse a little of what it means to be deeply concerned with the problem of mental deficiency, not because it is a vocation which one chose and for which one prepared, but because it was handed to one. Such people are not common, but they exist. Some of us in the parent group movement have been fortunate to have had their help. To identify them, to seek them out and enlist their aid, to develop a working partnership with them, is one of the major tasks confronting any nascent parent organization.

Based on a paper presented at the 75th Annual Meeting of the American Association on Mental Deficiency, May 1951 as part of the Parents Panel on "Problems and Procedures in Local Organizations."

Author

Elizabeth M. Boggs, Ph.D., Chairman, Education Committee, State Council, New Jersey Parents Group for Retarded Children.

Psychological Counseling With Parents of Retarded Children

Philip Roos, Ph.D.
1963

Abstract

Counseling with parents of retarded children presents psychologists with difficult and unique problems. A therapeutic interview technique is recommended since recognition of retardation in one's child tends to precipitate severe emotional reactions. Typical parental reactions to retardation are described in this article, and specific suggestions for counseling with parents are considered. Special attention is given to the use of evaluative techniques as part of the counseling process.

In their painful search for answers to their dilemma, parents of retarded children frequently turn to the psychologist for counseling and guidance. Fruitful interaction between parents and psychologists requires special skill and sensitivity on the part of the psychologist. This presentation is an attempt to clarify important ingredients in the successful counseling situation.

The psychologist working with parents of retarded children should remember that he is probably dealing with highly distressed people. Reactions to the very real trauma of recognizing retardation in one's own child are, of course, infinitely varied, but certain general patterns recur with enough frequency to be considered more or less typical. Understanding of these patterns by the psychologist is helpful in dealing with the parents.

Parental Reactions to Retardation

Many parents suffer a severe loss of self-esteem when they recognize retardation in their child. In our culture children are often considered by parents as ego-extensions; that is, the parent closely identifies with his child, taking pride in his accomplishments and basking in his reflected glory. A serious defect in the child tends to be experienced by the parent as his own defect. Hence, the parent may feel responsible for disappointing his mate, his own parents, and other family members by "presenting" them with a defective child. The possibility of genetic etiology leads some parents to renounce plans for having other children. Self-esteem may be further lowered by threat to the fantasy of immortality through one's children—the individual is suddenly faced with the prospect that he will leave no descendents after him. Life goals and basic approaches to the world may be abruptly and radically altered.

Closely allied to loss of self-esteem is the feeling of shame experienced by many parents. They may anticipate social rejection, pity, or ridicule, and related loss of prestige. It is not uncommon to find parents withdrawing from social participation and altering plans which might expose them to social rebuff. They tend to view their child's school years with particular apprehension, since during this time his defect will become most apparent.

Parents' feelings toward their retarded child are typically extremely ambivalent. Not only are they constantly frustrated by the child's lack of achievement, but the child's inadequate control often leads to extremely irritating behavior. Resentment and hostility generated by repeated frustrations may be expressed in death wishes toward the child and feelings of rejection. Typically such feelings arouse considerable guilt in the parent, who then tries to atone for his hostility by developing overprotective and overindulgent attitudes toward the child. The inconsistent reactions by the parent of demandingness, hostility and rejection, alternating with overprotection and overindulgence, are likely to disturb the child and thereby further reduce his efficiency, in turn increasing parental frustration. Such a self-perpetuating "vicious cycle" may further reduce the child's intellectual efficiency.

Hostility generated by frustration experienced in their interaction with the retarded child is often displaced by the parent onto other relationships. Parents may present a "chip-on-the-shoulder" attitude. Their irritable, resentful demeanor tends to alienate others and leads to rejection and avoidance by friends and relatives, further frustrating the parents and thereby increasing their resentment. The counselor should be alerted to the possibility that his clients may be in the grips of such a vicious cycle. Inappropriate attacks against the counselor are more easily accepted if recognized as manifestations of displaced hostility stemming from serious frustrations.

Feelings of depression are to be expected. The absence of such feelings, particularly when realization of the child's retardation is recent, is unusual enough to raise suspicions regarding the possibility of atypical techniques of handling emotions (e.g., repression and isolation of affect). Some parents react to the retarded child as if he had died and manifest the typical grief reactions associated with the loss of a loved one. Such extreme reactions tend to be most prevalent in highly intelligent parents who tend to equate being human with the possession of intelligence. Disappointment in the child and concern for his future are appropriate reactions typically accompanied by some degree of unhappiness. Parents' ambivalence toward the child may contribute to depression, inasmuch as the hostility toward the child may be redirected toward the self.

Feelings of guilt and self-reproach may accompany depression and usually reflect internalization of hostility toward the child. It is not uncommon for parents to indicate that they feel responsible for the retardation, which may be described as a form of punishment for sins or as the outcome of transgressions. Cause of the retardation is sometimes erroneously attributed to guilt-ridden sexual activities.

Some parents adopt a masochistic position, almost welcoming the suffering they anticipate will accompany rearing the defective child. They may think of themselves as "martyrs" who will devote all their energies and sacrifice all pleasures for the child. The retardate may become the focus of a lifelong pattern of self-sacrifice and lamentation. It almost seems as if such parents "love to be miserable." They may dwell in detail on the tragic and sordid aspects of their situation and often share their unhappiness with all who will listen. Such parents are typically reluctant to institutionalize their child—no matter how severely incapacitated he might be—and may neglect siblings, relatives, careers, etc., for the "welfare" of the child. In counseling with such parents, it usually becomes apparent that the retardate plays a very significant role in the parents' adjustment patterns.

Realization that a child is retarded often has disruptive effects not only on the parents but on the entire family unit, and possibly on friends, acquaintances, and neighbors as well. Siblings and grandparents are very obviously involved, and increased tensions typically develop within the family. Marital conflicts may be aggravated, and the retarded child may become the focus of

mutual blame and criticism by the parents. It is as if the child were a catalyst activating long-dormant conflicts into overt explosion.

Ambivalence toward the child may lead to defensiveness as well as to overprotection. Parents may become acutely sensitive to implied criticisms of the child and may react with resentment and belligerence. It may be difficult in such cases to present factual information which may be interpreted as depreciating the child.

A more extreme position is found in those parents who have attempted to protect themselves against the pain of recognizing retardation in their child by failing to become aware of its existence. Human beings can become highly skilled at remaining unaware of a certain aspect of reality, even when it is thrust upon them with some force. Mechanisms of denial, repression, and selective inattention have been described in detail as techniques whereby people are able to exercise control over the extent of their awareness. It is not unusual, therefore, to find parents who claim that "there is really nothing wrong" with an obviously severely retarded child. They may attribute the child's complete failure in school to a vindictive teacher, for example, or to bouts of tonsillitis. Parents may be helped in this self-deception by relatives, friends, and at times even professionals, who have reassured them of the child's "normality." Reluctance to face a painful and irrevocable situation is not limited to parents, and it is not surprising to find, therefore, that others have likewise failed to recognize the situation.

The trauma of experiencing retardation in one's child may precipitate serious existential conflicts. Concern with religion, the meaning of life, the tragedy of death, the inescapability of aloneness, and the relative insignificance and helplessness of man may preoccupy the parents. Although these concerns are usually less obvious than the other reactions described above, their significance should not be underestimated.

The Therapeutic Interview

Since parents of retardates typically approach the psychologist with several of the reactions just described, it is important to furnish them with the opportunity for a therapeutic interview. In its simplest form, parents should be given the opportunity to express their feelings in a non-threatening interpersonal interaction. The basic ingredients of such an interview include the following:

(1) The counselee should be treated with acceptance and respect. By treating his client with dignity, the counselor helps decrease the feelings of worthlessness, self-blame and shame which plague many parents of retardates. Feelings of loss of self-confidence and helplessness are decreased when the parents feel accepted, understood and respected.

(2) The psychologist should resist the temptation to assume an authoritarian role. Although the assumption of a godlike role may enhance the counselor's feeling of self-esteem, it tends to have the reverse effect on his clients. Furthermore, the authoritarian role tends to discourage parents from expressing their views and feelings; they tend instead to await expectantly the words of wisdom which the psychologist will bestow upon them.

Few competent psychologists regard themselves as authorities in the area of mental retardation, for, if one is at all in contact with the field, one cannot but be impressed with the vastness of our current ignorance. Therefore, assuming an omniscient role is a bit of a fraud, and most parents soon grow painfully aware of the counselor's real limitations.

(3) Perhaps the essence of the therapeutic interview is that it is an interpersonal transaction wherein the interviewer allows the interviewee free emotional expression. In this respect, it differs rather markedly from the great majority of interpersonal interactions, since typically one is constantly reminded that many emotional reactions are rejected, condemned, censored, etc. As a result, of course, it becomes increasingly difficult to tolerate these "condemned" feelings within one's self, and one develops any number of ingenious mechanisms for disguising, disowning, and otherwise rejecting one's own feelings. The parent's statement that "sometimes this child makes me so mad!" may have repeatedly been countered with statements that he "shouldn't feel that way," that the child "can't help" how he acts, and so on. After these reactions, the parent has never even allowed himself the much more "reprehensible" thought: "I wish this child were dead!"

By encouraging emotional expression without passing value judgments on the expressed feelings, the counselor helps the parent to tolerate his feelings with less guilt and anxiety and, consequently, to deal with the feelings more effectively.

(4) Since the parents, and not the psychologist, will have to share life with the retarded child, decisions should be reached by the parents rather than the psychologist. By encouraging the parents to make their own decisions, the counselor enhances their feeling of self-confidence and helps them to assume responsibility for their actions. The counselor's goal should be to help the parents reach their decisions with as full an awareness as possible of their own feelings and of the reality of the situation.

(5) An important principle in conducting interviews with such parents is to let the parents determine the direction of the interview. That is, counseling seems most helpful when it is parent-centered rather than counselor-centered. The psychologist may have preconceived notions regarding the content and course which the interview should follow, and he may indeed experience feelings of accomplishment and satisfaction upon completing an interview successfully directed into these directions. The parents, on the other hand, may have quite different expectations regarding the interview and may, consequently, leave disappointed, frustrated, or confused. After all, the goal of the interview is generally assumed to be to help the parents—not the counselor—and a parent-centered interview seems most successful in reaching this goal.

(6) The last important ingredient of a therapeutic interview is perhaps the simplest and most difficult; namely, honesty. Although most psychologists do not plan to deceive their clients, their own needs and tensions may tempt them to distort, minimize, evade, ignore, and otherwise tamper with reality.

Not infrequently, the psychologist's need for approval and for maintaining the myth of his own omniscience leads him to deceive his clients by disguising his own ignorance and by bombarding them with assorted bits of impressive information. To a parent's question regarding the etiology of his child's defect, for example, the counselor may vaguely indicate that the etiology of many forms of retardation is not yet fully understood, and he may then embark upon a truly engrossing review of chromosome studies in Mongolism. Such a discourse may impress as well as confuse the parents, especially if their child is not a Mongol. In an attempt to "protect" parents against anxiety and depression, some counselors distort reality by minimizing the degree of retardation or by focusing upon unrealistic possibilities of eventual treatment of "cure."

Importance of Listening

Perhaps the most difficult skill for the psychologist to acquire is the ability to listen to his client. Listening not only implies attentiveness, interest, and sensitivity, but it also involves the capacity to remain silent. Many people find it difficult to refrain from speaking. Psychologists and other professionals often act as though their mission in life is to pass to the less informed the great wisdom which they possess.

Careful listening by the counselor has numerous beneficial results. The client's statements, for example, can be a valuable clue to the appropriateness of the counselor's comments. One does not respond in exactly the same way to an uneducated laborer as one does to a university professor. Detailed accounts of the latest studies of the reticular formation may be a bit inappropriate when directed to a truck driver, just as basic explanations of the meaning of electroencephalography are inappropriately condescending when directed to a physician.

By attentive listening, the counselor should succeed in reaching more or less valid conclusions as to the parents' current needs. If the counselor listens to the parents with the question, "Why are they seeing me here and now?" constantly in mind, he may frequently find that the initially stated reason for the interview is indeed far removed from the real reason which brings the parents to him. Having ascertained the parents' real needs, the counselor is better prepared to supply them with information which will be meaningful to them, and he can more intelligently make recommendations with regard to further evaluation and planning.

The psychologist who succeeds in controlling his need to speak is more likely to encourage his clients to express their own feelings, concerns and opinions. The parents' observations of the retarded child are frequently of considerable value, and their estimates of functioning level are often quite accurate. It is not unusual to discover that parents come to the psychologist having already made important decisions and searching for support or a chance for catharsis rather than for information or evaluation. On occasion, encouraging parents to voice their opinions reveals surprising distortions and erroneous beliefs, indicating areas in which information is most needed.

Use of Evaluative Findings

Since psychologists are frequently requested to determine the presence of mental retardation, psychological evaluation often becomes the subject of the interview with the parents. If the parents and the psychologist agree that formal evaluation of the child may be desirable, the parents should be informed of the nature and purpose of the evaluation. It is important to acquaint parents with the answers they may expect from the evaluation. If the results may prove to be relatively meaningless, the parents should be so advised. Parents' resentment at being told of uninterpretable results of complex and often expensive procedures is not entirely inappropriate, particularly if they were not forewarned of this possible outcome.

The psychologist should endeavor to expedite evaluative procedures. Allowing parents to linger in the agony of doubt is cruel and destructive. The period of evaluation is usually experienced as highly stressful and distressing by parents, and it should be kept as short as possible. As soon as the evaluation has been completed, the parents should be informed of the results.

Evaluative findings should be presented in terms that will be meaningful to the parents. Operational formulations and concrete examples are to be preferred to abstract and theoretical constructs. Presenting the child's level of functioning in mental age equivalents is usually considerably more meaningful than references to the intelligence quotients or social quotients. As a matter of fact, parents are often surprisingly accurate in estimating the child's level of functioning in terms of developmental level.

Description of probably accomplishments in terms of illustrative behavior is usually extremely helpful. Emphasis on those activities which the child may be able to perform is more helpful than dwelling on areas of limitations and expected failure. A statement such as, "Your child will probably be able to master fifth or sixth grade work," is much less likely to cause pain than saying, "Of course, your child will never complete junior high school," and it is equally factual.

Parents should be acquainted with the limitations of the evaluative findings. Parents usually have questions regarding etiology, diagnosis, and prognosis, and the counselor will, in many cases, of course, have to indicate that in one or more of these areas he is making an "educated guess." Although the majority of parents are blissfully ignorant of such concepts as validity and reliability, it is meaningful to indicate the relative probability that the present findings are accurate and, particularly, the likelihood that predictions will prove to be correct.

Although it is neither realistic nor appropriate to present exact probability figures, the counselor can indicate that his predictions regarding a severely retarded, ten-year-old microcephalic are made with considerable confidence, whereas his predictions regarding a two-year-old, mildly retarded child with no apparent neuropathology are made with less assurance. Comments regarding the possible value of future evaluations can be helpful, and they may include acquainting parents with suitable referral sources.

Concluding the Interview

Even if further referrals are not indicated, the psychologist should encourage parents to formulate tentative plans. Some parents are so overwhelmed with their tragedy that they seem to flounder in the present and to recoil from the future. With tactful encouragement and support the counselor can help such parents to think constructively about the future. In attempting to plan for the child, the parents can be helped by presentation of factual information regarding community resources, referral agencies, institutions, psychotherapists, and so forth.

In concluding the interview—or series of interviews, as the case might be—the psychologist can be supportive by informing parents that he will remain available for further contacts should the need arise. The parents then leave the counselor with the feeling that they have been understood and that they are not completely alone in their misery.

Author

Philip Roos, Ph.D., is the supervisor of psychological services of the Board for Texas State Hospitals and Special Schools. He has an extensive background in psychological services for hospitals and sanitariums as well as private practice and has contributed papers to various professional publications and at conferences throughout the country.

In his present position, Dr. Roos is responsible for the direction and supervision of psychological services in the state mental hospitals, special schools, the research institute, adult outpatient clinics, and tuberculosis hospitals.

Behavioral Training for Parents of Retarded Children: Alternative Formats Based on Instructional Manuals

Louis J. Heifetz
1977

Abstract

A series of instructional manuals in behavior modification with retarded children was tested as a self-contained resource and as part of three larger training programs involving different amounts of professional assistance to parents: telephone consultations, training groups, training groups plus home visits. One hundred and sixty families were randomly assigned to the four training conditions or to a delayed-treatment control group. The 20-week treatment period emphasized the programming of self-help skills, but also provided an introduction to programming language skills and managing behavior problems. The manuals-alone format was as effective as the more extensive training formats in producing gains in children's self-help skills and fostering knowledge of behavioral principles in mothers. The two group-training formats produced more efforts at behavior-problem management, greater gains in knowledge of principles by fathers, and higher self-confidence as teachers. Telephone consultation was generally the least effective training format; the manuals-alone condition was surprisingly effective. Some implications of the results for future strategies of family intervention were discussed.

Behavior-modification procedures have emerged in the last dozen years as a most powerful tool for training and educating retarded persons in areas as diverse as self-help, language, academic, social, and living skills and in reducing inappropriate, disruptive, and maladaptive behavior (Begab, 1975; Graziano, 1971, 1975). To date, however, behavior technology has not substantially improved the delivery of services to retarded individuals; because of limited dissemination, its potential has been largely unrealized (Heifetz & Baker, Note 1). A major limiting factor has been "professional preciousness," the tendency to define problems in ways that require the services of traditionally trained professionals (Sarason, 1972). Such parochial formulations render the problems insoluble, because of the vast personnel shortages in mental health generally (Albee, 1959) as well as in mental retardation specifically (Lindsley, 1966).

A challenge to professional preciousness has recently appeared in the form of "manpower engineering" (Hobbs, 1964), as the training of paraprofessionals has increasingly been acknowledged as a realistic and promising avenue for improving systems of service delivery (Guerney, 1969). In the past decade, under the dual impetus of the behavior modification and paraprofessional movements, behaviorally oriented training has begun to offer new, more collaborative roles for parents and professionals.

The recent but rapidly expanding literature on parent training in behavior modification reveals some important lines of evolution (Berkowitz & Graziano, 1972; O'Dell, 1974). Early reports usually involved one highly motivated parent, a specific child behavior, and considerable professional involvement in treatment, which was often restricted to clinic or hospital settings. Lately, there have been several trends toward higher cost effectiveness: complex behavior being targeted; parents are being prepared for greater responsibility in all aspects of programming; there has been greater attention to training in and for the natural environment; and group-training formats, offering added efficiency, are becoming more common (Benassi, & Benassi, 1973; Hirsch & Walder, 1969). Behavioral training for parents would appear to hold great promise for families with retarded children. But the current literature should be viewed somewhat skeptically on three counts.

First, the research methodology is highly variable and often inadequate (Berkowitz & Graziano, 1972; Hamerlynck, Handy, & Mash, 1973). Some investigators report no data at all, while others present uncorroborated parental reports of changes in children's behavior. Improvements are frequently reported for specific kinds of target behavior, with no parallel assessment of positive or negative generalization to unprogrammed behavior. Case studies predominate, despite their low scientific value. Designs using multiple baseline and reversal procedures, while increasingly popular, have furnished inadequate approximations to experimental rigor

(Hartmann & Atkinson, 1973); rigorous experimental designs (Campbell & Stanley, 1963) are woefully underused.

Second, the majority of parent-training studies are only indirectly or partially relevant to parents of retarded children. Most training programs have emphasized short-term management of maladaptive, surplus behavior (O'Dell, 1974); less attention has been paid to children's skill deficits, which may require years of persistent and carefully structured teaching (Bricker, 1970; Kazdin, 1973). Parents who do not have the luxury of dealing with a few isolated behavior problems in an otherwise well-functioning child may be better served by training in a more comprehensive programming framework; e.g., initial assessment and choice of target behavior, behavioral observation and record-keeping, long-run maintenance of behavioral gains accomplished initially by the professionals, and preparation for independent development of future teaching programs. Relatively few programs have adopted these broad goals (e.g., Pascal, 1973; Walder, Cohen, Breiter, Daston, Hirsch, & Leibowitz, 1969; Baker, Note 2).

Third, while the field progresses beyond the earlier, narrowly circumscribed forms of training, it must still confront the paucity of professionals (Lindsley, 1966) available to train parents. Group-training formats may be more efficient, but at best contribute only a few more drops to the bucket. And as the goals of training become more complex and ambitious, it becomes difficult for trainers to provide adequate instruction for each family's needs without reducing the efficiency that groups offer over one-to-one training formats.

It may, however, be possible to reduce the need for direct professional contact by providing parents with self-instructional materials for shaping and managing their children's behavior. Although only a few researchers actually report using written instructions (e.g., Pascal, 1973; Salzinger, Feldman, & Portnoy, 1970; Wagner, 1968), the preparation of written programs, guides, and summaries has been a fairly common adjunct to training programs. Also, some "how to" books and manuals on behavior modification have been written for parents (Becker, 1971; Patterson & Gullion, 1968; Vallet, 1969). However, there have been virtually no rigorous attempts to evaluate these instructional materials per se or to compare their effectiveness with other approaches to training that require substantial amounts of professional time.

In the present study, a series of instructional manuals (Baker, Brightman, Heifetz, & Murphy, 1973, 1976) was evaluated as a self-contained resource and as part of three other parent-training formats with different amounts of professional instruction and consultation. Before and after a 20-week training period, which dealt primarily with the teaching of self-help skills, broad-based measures of child functioning were taken to obtain data on skills specifically programmed as well as on possible generalized effects of training. Measures were taken of parental knowledge of behavior-modification principles, participation in training, and attitudes related to retardation. It was predicted that parents in the four training formats (128 families) would acquire greater knowledge of behavior modification than would parents in a delayed-treatment control group (32 families) and that their children would display greater gains in self-help skills than the control children. It was also expected that the effectiveness of the four training formats would increase with the amount of professional assistance specific to each format.

Method

Instructional Manuals

The series contains ten manuals in areas where parents express the greatest need for guidance: teaching self-help skills, developing language skills, managing behavior problems, and teaching play activities. Each manual is designed to be self-contained and includes sections on choosing a target skill, setting the stage for teaching sessions, behavioral principles, data-keeping procedures, and answers to questions frequently raised by parents. Each manual also contains fictionalized "mini-case studies" highlighting central points in setting up and carrying out a program, many explanatory illustrations, and a large number of step-by-step outlines for programs.

Subjects

Families with a retarded child who lived at home were recruited through agencies and media announcements that described the project briefly and invited interested parents to phone. Parents who called ($N = 310$) were given more detailed information and provided some basic background data; 88 children functioning outside the skill levels covered by the manuals were thereby screened out. The 222 remaining parents were invited to one of several introductory meetings (165 attended) where the service and research components of the project were described. Parents then took the Behavioral Vignettes Test, a questionnaire designed to assess knowledge of behavioral principles (Baker, 1973; Heifetz, Note 3; Schwenn, Note 4) and saw part of a film on behavior modification (Bensberg, 1967). Parents were told that they would be randomly assigned to one of four training conditions (varying on amount of input supplementary to the manuals) or to a control group that would later participate in a program incorporating improvements suggested by the experience of the other four groups. They were informed that the manuals themselves were sufficient for effective teaching and had been successfully used alone by parents in pilot studies. Of the parents attending the introductory meetings, 160 (97 percent) chose to participate in the study.

Families were widely distributed over the five Hollingshead (Note 5) social classes (15.7, 20.9, 21.6, 34.0, and 7.8 percent for classes I, II, III, IV, and V, respectively). Annual income ranged from under $5000 to over $50,000, with a mean of $13,800. The average age of mothers was 39.1 years, and their average education was 13.4 years; average age for fathers was 41.7 years and their average education was 14.3 years. Most of the children would be classified as organically retarded, with reported levels ranging from mildly to severely retarded; none met the usual criteria for cultural-familial retardation (Heber, 1961). About one third of them fell in the intervals of 2 to 5, 6 to 8, and 9 to 14 years of age. Ninety-six percent of the children were receiving some form of continuous, ongoing schooling, 91 percent in a publicly funded facility.

Procedure

Participants were arranged into 32 clusters of five families matched on chronological age (CA) of the child and parents' pretreatment score on the Behavioral Vignettes Test. The members of each cluster were then randomly distributed across the five experimental conditions. Parents in the control condition received no manuals or any other training during the study, thus providing an independent baseline against which to compare the training conditions. Parents in the manuals-only condition used the manuals but received no other form of training or professional assistance. Those in the manuals and phone condition used the manuals and received telephone consultations every 2 weeks from a staff member. For the manuals and groups condition, manuals were provided, and members participated in eight-family train-

Table 1 Per-Family Cost of Training Conditions

Condition	Cost (in dollars)	Cost relative to manuals only
Manuals only	38	—
Manuals & phone	77	2.0:1
Manuals & groups	118	3.1:1
Manuals, groups, & visits	211	5.6:1

ing groups that met every 2 weeks with two staff members. Parents in the manuals and groups and visits condition used the manuals, met in groups as did those in the manuals and groups condition, and received a 1-hour home visit from a staff member between group meetings. Table 1 shows the per-family cost of training.

Trainers had backgrounds in clinical psychology, special education, and nursing. All were familiar with the theory and practice of behavior modification and had previously worked with retarded children and their families. Half of the trainers were male and half female; each of the eight sets of families in the manuals and groups and manuals, groups, and visits conditions was led by a male-female pair. During the training period, other ongoing services to the children and parents in each condition proceeded as usual. Thus, each of the four training formats was actually being tested for its marginal effectiveness over and above the preexisting services.

Parents in the four training conditions began by carrying out a comprehensive, fine-grained assessment of their children's skills, using the Behavioral Assessment Scales, a set of observational checklists and guidelines for their use that were written to accompany the manuals. After completing these scales, parents received the self-help skills manual appropriate to their child's current functioning. During the first half of the training period, parents programmed self-help skills exclusively. Midway in training, they received the *Behavior Problems* manual and, where appropriate, *Toilet Training*. Four weeks before training ended, parents received one of the language manuals. Programming patterns varied during the second half of training: some parents continued to work solely on self-help skills, progressing in some cases to higher level manuals; others also began programs for behavior problems, toileting, and/or language. In general, the great majority of parental programming was directed toward self-help skills. At the end of the 20-week training period, parents provided posttest data on the Behavioral Assessment Scales and the Behavioral Vignettes Test, completed a questionnaire on attitudes related to having a retarded child, and filled out a structured evaluation of the training program.

Results

The effectiveness of training formats based on instructional manuals was quite evident, particularly in terms of mothers' acquisition of behavior-modification expertise and children's gains in self-help skills. Unexpectedly, the manuals-only condition was equal or marginally superior to the more expensive formats in these two areas. Parents in the manuals and groups and the manuals, groups, and visits conditions showed some scattered evidence of superiority, but not the consistent superiority predicted. The manuals and phone format was generally the least effective.

Reliability of Parents' Behavioral Assessment Scales Data

Trained observers independently assessed a randomly chosen sample of 33 children pretraining and 17 children posttraining. This reliability check was restricted to self-help and language, since these were the only areas that could be accurately assessed at a single point in time; the behavior problems and toileting scales were not checked for reliability. The mean pretreatment reliability coefficients were $r = .89$ for self-help skills and $r = .87$ for language. Given the high pretest reliability and the concentration of training on self-help, the postreliability check was used only to examine self-help skills, yielding a reliability coefficient of $r = .93$.

Participation Rates

Four of the 32 control families withdrew before the end of the treatment period. Of the 128 families assigned to training conditions, 6 never began and 11 more dropped out during training; 111 families (87 percent) maintained continued participation. An additional 11 families did not return Behavioral Assessment Scales postmeasures, bringing to 100 the number of trained families in most analyses. The number of families with complete Behavioral Assessment Scales data was not significantly different across conditions.

Attendance was a relevant measure only for the manuals and groups and the manuals, groups, and visits conditions. Both training conditions showed similarly very high attendance, with families represented at an average of 90 percent of meetings (manuals and groups: mothers = 85 percent, fathers = 67 percent; manuals, groups, and visits: mothers = 87 percent, fathers = 71 percent). The modal family was represented by at least one parent at all meetings. Parents in the four training conditions were encouraged to fill out one-page "teaching logs" for each day of formal teaching. There was significant variance among training conditions in percentage of days with entries in the teaching logs ($F = 3.19, 3/95$ df, $p = .035$. In the manuals-only and the manuals and phone conditions, where logs were mailed, rates were similar and combined to 45 percent; in the manuals and groups and the manuals, groups, and visits conditions, where the logs were handed in, the combined rate of 59 percent was significantly higher ($t = 2.43, 97$ df, $p < .02$).

Extent and Diversity of Parental Programming

A one-way analysis of variance on a number of self-help skills programmed did not differentiate significantly

Table 2 Number of Families Programming Additional Areas

Condition[a]	n	Toilet training	Language	Behavior problems	Mean number of programmed self-help skills	Mean additional areas programmed
MO	25	6	5	8	3.7	.76
MP	23	3	11	6	5.4	.87
MG	24	4	12	19	4.1	1.46
MGV	28	10	10	22	3.8	1.50

[a] MO = manuals only, MP = manuals and phone, MG = manuals and groups, MV = manuals, groups and visits.

Table 3 Mean Improvement on Behavioral Vignettes Test by Mothers and Fathers in Each Condition

Group[a]	n[b]		Improvement	Pre-post t	Second-order t[c]
Mothers					
Control	27	(28)	1.70	2.43*	
Trained	93	(100)	3.85	10.53***	2.76**
MO	20	(25)	4.70	5.55***	2.75**
MP	23	(23)	2.30	3.44**	.61
MG	23	(24)	3.74	5.77***	2.10*
MGV	27	(28)	4.63	6.57***	2.94**
Fathers					
Control	17	(28)	1.71	3.24**	
Trained	60	(100)	2.83	5.91***	1.19
MO	13	(25)	1.31	1.26	−.37
MP	11	(23)	2.46	2.40*	.72
MG	16	(24)	3.19	3.12**	1.31
MGV	20	(28)	3.75	4.80***	2.09*

[a] MO = manuals only, MP = manuals and phone, MG = manuals and groups, MGV = manuals, groups and visits.
[b] Parents who took both pre- and post-Behavioral Vignettes Test. Numbers in parentheses denote parents who completed pre- and post-Behavioral Assessment Scales.
[c] Comparisons were made against the mean improvements of the control parents.
   * $p < .05$.
   ** $p < .01$.
   *** $p < .001$.

among the four training conditions. As shown in Table 2, the manuals and groups and the manuals, groups, and visits parents extended their programming efforts to nearly twice as many additional areas as the manuals-only and the manuals and phone parents; this tendency was particularly strong for behavior problems (Chi Square = 24.89, 1 df, $p < .001$).

Gains in Knowledge of Behavior-Modification Principles

Table 3 shows the mean pre- and posttest change in Behavioral Vignettes Test scores by mothers and fathers in each condition. Overall, trained mothers acquired significantly more behavioral expertise than control mothers. A one-way analysis of variance showed a trend-level difference among the four training groups ($F = 2.41$, 3/ 89 df, $p = .072$). Compared to the control mothers, significantly more improvement was shown by mothers in the manuals-only, the manuals and groups, and the manuals, groups, and visits conditions; mothers in the manuals and phone condition did not differ significantly from control mothers. Trained fathers, overall, were not sig-

nificantly different from control fathers nor were there significant differences among the training conditions. Individually, only manuals, groups, and visits fathers gained significantly more behavioral knowledge than control fathers, although there was a trend-level difference for manuals and groups fathers.

Improvement in Self-Help Skills: Overall, Programmed, and Unprogrammed

Table 4 shows the total change in the 43 self-help skills measured by the Behavioral Assessment Scales. Overall, trained children gained, in bits and pieces, 1.78 more self-help skills than control children during the 20-week treatment period. This difference was highly significant ($t = 3.35$, 126 df, $p < .001$). The net gain in self-help skills was also significant for each of the separate training conditions (manuals only: 2.26 [$t = 3.14$, 51 df, $p = .002$]; manuals and phone: 1.44 [$t = 2.36$, 49 df, $p = .011$]; manuals and groups: 2.02 [$t = 3.34$, 50 df, $p = .001$]; and manuals, groups, and visits: 1.40 [$t = 2.71$, 54 df, $p = .004$]). Differences among the four training conditions were not significant.

Table 4 Mean Improvement in Self-Help Skills: Overall, Programmed, and Unprogrammed

Measure	Treatment[a]					
	Control	Trained pooled[b]	MO	MP	MG	MGV
Aggregate improvement, all self-help skills[c]	1.28	3.06	3.54	2.72	3.30	2.68
Aggregate improvement, programmed self-help skills[d]	—	1.43	1.28	1.57	1.59	1.29
Mean improvement, unprogrammed self-help skills[e]	.08	.11	.16	.09	.11	.09

[a] MO = manuals only, MP = manuals and phone, MG = manuals and groups, MGV = manuals, groups, and visits.
[b] Mean of children in trained conditions.
[c] Sum of improvements in the 43 self-help skills in the Behavioral Assessment Scales.
[d] Sum of improvements in self-help skills programmed by trained parents.
[e] Self-help skills not programmed and not already mastered at the time of the pretreatment Behavioral Assessment Scales and therefore had room for improvement. Since control children had no skills programmed, it was more apropriate to use mean improvement than aggregate improvement.

The average family in the four training conditions programmed 4.2 skills, or about 10 percent of the 43 skills measured by the Behavioral Assessment Scales. Table 4 shows the total change in programmed self-help skills. For the trained conditions pooled, and for each of the trained conditions separately, the mean aggregate gain in programmed self-help skills was significant at .001 or better and was equal to or greater than the total gain in all self-help skills for the control group. The evidence strongly supports the specific effects of parental-training efforts, with no significant differences across conditions.

Table 4 also shows the mean change in those skills that the parents did not program and that were not already mastered at the time the pre-Behavioral Assessment Scales were taken; thus, for control children, "unprogrammed skills" refers to all skills not mastered at the pre-Behavioral Assessment Scales. A comparison of the trained conditions pooled vs. the control condition showed a higher rate of improvement in unprogrammed skills on the part of trained children, a difference that approached significance ($t = 1.51$, 126 df, $p = .067$). Differences were not significant across the four training conditions. When compared separately to the control group, only children in the manuals-only condition showed significantly more gain ($t = 2.96$, 51 df, $p = .002$). None of the training conditions was inferior to the controls on this measure, thus indicating that the gains in programmed self-help skills were not achieved at the expense of other, unprogrammed skills.

Parent-Attitude Questionnaire

Parents rated their posttreatment feelings in relation to their retarded child on a 20-adjective scale, where positive attitudes (e.g., patient, friendly) and negative attitudes (e.g., frustrated, regretful) were rated "not at all," "a little," "a fair amount," or "very much." Summary scores were computed separately for positive and negative attitudes. Overall, there were no differences between trained and control parents, nor were there any differences among training conditions. The grand mean for negative attitudes was slightly below "a little"; the grand mean for positive attitudes was above "a fair amount," about one third of the way toward "very much." The training experience did not seem to have affected parents' already very positive feelings toward their retarded children.

On a series of items tapping attitudes toward services for retarded children, trained parents were very similar to control parents in expressing a great need for additional services, a great interest in further information on teaching, and a strong desire for additional and more productive communication between home and school. Trained parents did differ significantly from control parents on one item—feeling more able to evaluate the services being provided to their child ($t = 2.58$, 119 df, $p = .012$). Perhaps being trained as competent producers of services had given them a more discriminating stance as consumers of services.

A final set of items, regarding attitudes toward parents as teachers, revealed no overall differences between trained and control parents. When the four training conditions were compared individually to the control condition, however, it was found that manuals-only parents expressed significantly less confidence in teaching new skills ($t = 2.62$, 49 df, $p = .01$) and a trend toward less confidence in managing behavior problems ($t = 1.84$, 47

df, p = .07). Training seemed to have undermined the confidence of manuals-only parents in themselves as teachers, a finding that is striking in its inconsistency with the data on children's self-help gains and mothers' Behavioral Vignettes Test gains.

Discussion

The results clearly showed the utility of parent-training formats based on instructional materials. Trained mothers, as a group, acquired significantly more behavior-modification expertise than did control mothers. In self-help skills, the major focus of training inputs and of parental programming efforts, trained children on the whole showed significantly larger gains than did control children. Contrary to expectations, the successive increments in professional assistance provided by the manuals-only, the manuals and groups, and the manuals, groups, and visits conditions did not prove consistently more effective. In fact, the manuals and phone condition was in some areas less effective than manuals-only; the manuals and groups and the manuals, groups, and visits conditions showed only occasional evidence of superiority; and the manuals-only condition unexpectedly ranked first on some measures.

The four training conditions were statistically comparable on number of dropouts, overall improvement in self-help skills, improvement in programmed self-help skills, parents' posttraining feelings toward their children, and parents' perceived need for services. In comparison with manuals-only and manuals and phone parents, parents in the manuals and groups and the manuals, groups, and visits conditions made more extensive use of the teaching logs, were more likely to begin programs in areas other than self-help (especially behavior problems), showed more involvement by fathers as seen in greater Behavioral Vignettes Test gains, and expressed greater posttraining confidence as teachers (especially in contrast to manuals-only parents). Each of these advantages would seem to augur well for the quantity and quality of future teaching efforts.

On the other hand, parents in the manuals-only condition ranked first (although nonsignificantly) in overall self-help gain, showed the greatest generalized improvement in unprogrammed self-help skills (significantly better than the manuals and phone and the manuals, groups, and visits parents) and had the largest Behavioral Vignettes Test gain for mothers (significantly

larger than did the manuals and phone mothers). Yet despite this objective evidence of their ability, manuals-only parents felt less confident as teachers than did parents in either the other training conditions or the control parents.

These paradoxical results might be explained in terms of certain social-psychological features of the different training formats. The manuals and phone condition, unlike the manual and groups and the manual, groups, and visits conditions, could not readily be used for formal presentations of general principles; the natural tendency of phone calls was to focus on current problems. To many manuals and phone parents, it may have seemed more practical to seek solutions from the consultant than to deduce them from the manuals. Thus, from the outset, the manuals and phone format tended to foster dependence upon the consultant. In comparison, the manuals and groups and the manuals, groups, and visits parents—by being in groups with seven other families—participated in a range of ongoing programs and saw a variety of parental accomplishments, which might have raised their standards of achievement and boosted their confidence. But manuals and phone parents had no peer reference points to help raise their expectations. And the consultants, consistent with good clinical and didactic procedure, tended to reinforce whatever success had been achieved by the parents. Consequently, manuals and phone mothers felt rather confident in their teaching ability, even though they were the only mothers who did not significantly outperform the control mothers on the Behavioral Vignettes Test.

The manuals-only parents—by completing the pretreatment Behavioral Assessment Scales and then receiving a self-help skills manual that matched their child's functioning level—got an initial confirmation of their capacity for independent teaching and sufficient confidence to begin self-help programming. But with no consultants to give concrete suggestions, manuals-only parents had to learn general principles from the manuals and tailor them to their own situations. This generalized level of learning produced the greatest Behavioral Vignettes Test gains for manuals-only mothers and the greatest improvement on unprogrammed self-help skills for manuals-only children. Nevertheless, they were teaching without external feedback. And while this may have driven them to more conscientious teaching, it was not conducive to building confidence. This was shown by their low ratings of their teaching ability as well as by their comparative reluctance to venture beyond the familiar bounds of the self-help skills teaching area.

These results suggest that future training formats should combine the independence-fostering features of manuals only with the confidence-building elements of manuals and groups and manuals, groups, and visits. One such format could provide group meetings, but only at transitional points in the careers of parents as teachers, and would include feedback on previous stages and an orientation to the next stage. Future formats might also involve the coordination of school and home programming. During the present study, most children were in school placements costing $750 to $1500; the high marginal utility of parent training would be further enhanced by such coordination.

Parents less highly motivated than the present self-selected sample could profit from preparatory formats, whose initial emphasis would be more heavily clinical than didactic. Other investigators should address ways of getting fathers more actively involved in teaching. Also, various training methods should be studied not solely for their short-term impact but for their long-term effects as well; there is a real dearth of follow-up studies in the parent-training literature (the present sample is currently being followed-up). Finally, as a body of large-scale and methodologically rigorous studies accumulates, it should be possible to analyze family background variables in order to pinpoint correlates of success under different training formats, with a view toward more precisely custom-tailoring treatment programs.

The present findings carry a clear message of parents' ability to adopt realistic goals for their children's development and to assume an expert role in furthering it. This message runs counter to some durable and prevalent professional attitudes toward families of retarded persons. Until recently, the major focus was on the exploration and resolution of parents' emotional difficulties, often through dynamic forms of counseling and psychotherapy (Wolfensberger, 1967). But resolution of these emotional reactions should be seen as only a first step and in many cases need not be the primary focus of professional help (Menolascino, 1968). Many parents are not emotionally overwhelmed and are mainly in need of honest information about their children, implications for their future, and concrete strategies for coping with their special needs and doing so as "essentially mature and rational people" (Matheny & Vernick, 1968, p. 953).

Helplessness and loss of self-esteem are often cited as characteristic reactions of parents of retarded children. Training as active and effective contributors to their children's development offers a useful preventive measure and a more proactive strategy than simply relying on the palliative effects of psychotherapy. That an effective technology of teaching exists is clear; its potential for widespread dissemination is vast and has only begun to be explored.

Reference Notes

1. Heifetz, L. J., & Baker, B. L. Manpower and methodology in behavior modification: Instructional manuals for the paraprofessional parent. In L. J. Heifetz (Chair), *Manpower and methodology in behavior modification.* Symposium presented at the ninth Annual Convention of the Association for the Advancement of Behavior Therapy, San Francisco, 1975.

2. Baker, B. L. *Training in behavior modification for retarded children (Technical report).* Washington, DC: Social and Rehabilitation Service, 1972.

3. Heifetz, L. J. *Behavioral Vignettes Test: Instrument for measuring parental knowledge of behavior modification.* Unpublished manuscript, Yale University, 1972. (Available from author, Department of Psychology, Yale University, New Haven, CT 06520)

4. Schwenn, M. R. *The effects of parent training on generalization of therapeutic behavior change in retarded children from an educational camp to home.* Unpublished senior honors thesis, Harvard University, 1971.

5. Hollingshead, A. B. *Two-factor index of social position.* Unpublished manuscript, Yale University, 1957. (Available from author, Department of Sociology, Yale University, New Haven, CT 06520)

References

Albee, G. W. *Mental health manpower needs.* New York: Basic Books, 1959.

Baker, B. L. Camp Freedom: Behavior modification for retarded children in a therapeutic camp setting. *American Journal of Orthopsychiatry*, 1973, 43, 418–427.

Baker, B. L., Brightman, A. J., Heifetz, L. J., & Murphy, D. M. *The Read Project Series.* Cambridge: Behavioral Education Projects, 1973.

Baker, B. L., Brightman, A. J., Heifetz, L J., & Murphy, D. M. *Steps to independence: A skills training series for children with special needs.* Champaign, IL: Research Press, 1976.

Becker, W. C. *Parents are teachers.* Champaign, IL: Research Press, 1971.

Begab, M. J. The mentally retarded and society: Trends and issues. In M. J. Begab & S. A. Richardson (Eds.), *The mentally retarded and society: A social science perspective.* Baltimore: University Park Press, 1975.

Benassi V. A., & Benassi, B. An approach to teaching behavior modification principles to parents. *Rehabilitation Literature*, 1973, *34*, 134–137.

Bensberg, G. (Producer). *Teaching the mentally retarded: A positive approach.* Atlanta: National Medical Audio-Visual Center Annex, 1967. (Film)

Berkowitz, B. P., & Graziano, A. M. Training parents as behavior therapists: A review. *Behavior Research and Therapy*, 1972, *10*, 297–317.

Bricker, W. A. Identifying and modifying behavioral deficits. *American Journal of Mental Deficiency*, 1970, *75*, 16–21.

Campbell, D. T., & Stanley, J. C. *Experimental and quasi-experimental designs for research.* Chicago: Rand McNally, 1963.

Graziano, A. M. (Ed.). *Behavior therapy with children* (Vol. 1). Chicago: Aldine, 1971.

Graziano, A. M. (Ed.). *Behavior therapy with children* (Vol. 2). Chicago: Aldine, 1975.

Guerney, B. C. (Ed.). *Psychotherapeutic agents: New roles for nonprofessionals, parents, and teachers.* New York: Holt, Rinehart, & Winston, 1969.

Hamerlynck, L. A., Handy, L. C., & Mash, E. J. *Behavior change: Methodology, concepts, and practice.* Champaign, IL: Research Press, 1973.

Hartmann, D. P., & Atkinson, L. Having your cake and eating it too: A note on some apparent contradictions between therapeutic achievements and design requirements in N=1 studies. *Behavior Therapy*, 1973, *4*, 589–591.

Heber, R. A manual on terminology and classification in mental deficiency. *American Journal of Mental Deficiency*, Monograph Supplement, 1961 (2).

Hirsch, I., & Walder, L. Training mothers in groups as reinforcement therapists for their own children. *Proceedings of the 77th Annual Convention of the American Psychological Association*, 1969, *4*, 561–562. (Summary)

Hobbs, N. H. Mental health's third revolution. *American Journal of Orthopsychiatry*, 1964, *5*, 822–833.

Kazdin, A. E. Issues in behavior modification with mentally retarded persons. *American Journal of Mental Deficiency*, 1973, *78*, 134–140.

Lindsley, O. R. An experiment with parents handling behavior at home. *Johnstone Bulletin*, 1966, *9*, 27–36.

Matheny, A. P., & Vernick, J. Parents of the mentally retarded child: Emotionally overwhelmed or informationally deprived? *Journal of Pediatrics*, 1968, *74*, 953–959.

Menolascino, F. J. Parents of the mentally retarded: An operational approach to diagnosis and management. *Journal of the American Academy of Child Psychiatry*, 1968, *7*, 589–602.

O'Dell, S. Training parents in behavior modification: A review. *Psychological Bulletin*, 1974, *81*, 418–433.

Pascal, C. E. Application of behavior modification by parents for treatment of a brain-damaged child. In B. A. Ashem & E. G. Poser (Eds.), *Adaptive learning: Behavior modification with children.* New York: Pergamon Press, 1973.

Patterson, G. R., & Gullion, M. E. *Living with children: New methods for parents and teachers.* Champaign, IL: Research Press, 1968.

Salzinger, K., Feldman, R. S., & Portnoy, S. Training parents of brain-injured children in the use of operant conditioning procedures. *Behavior Therapy*, 1970, *1*, 4–32.

Sarason, S. B. *The creation of settings and the future societies.* San Francisco: Jossey-Bass, 1972.

Vallet, R. E. *Modifying children's behavior.* Palo Alto, CA: Fearon, 1969.

Wagner, M. K. Parent therapists: An operant conditioning method. *Mental Hygiene*, 1968, *52*, 452–455.

Walder, L., Cohen, S., Breiter, D., Daston, P. G., Hirsch, I. S., & Leibowitz, J. M. Teaching behavioral principles to parents of disturbed children. In B. G. Guerney (Ed.), *Psychotherapeutic agents: New roles for nonprofessionals, parents, and teachers.* New York: Holt, Rinehart, & Winston, 1969.

Wolfensberger, W. Counseling the parents of retarded children. In A. A. Baumeister (Ed.), *Mental retardation: Appraisal, education, and rehabilitation.* Chicago: Aldine, 1967.

Portions of this research were presented at the Fourth International Congress of the International Association for the Scientific Study of Mental Deficiency, Washington, DC, August 1976. This study was part of a 2-year research and development project supported by Contract NIH-NICHD-72-2016 (Project Officer, Michael J. Begab). The considerable advice and support of Project Director Bruce L. Baker is gratefully acknowledged.

Author

Louis J. Heifetz, Yale University.

Parent Involvement in the Education of Handicapped Children: A Critique

Ann P. Turnbull, Ed.D. and H. Rutherford Turnbull, III, LL.B., LL.M.
1982

Abstract

The policy and legislative (P.L. 94–142) assumptions underlying parent participation in the education of handicapped children are examined in the light of recent research on parent participation. It is argued that the assumptions are based more on what some advocates and policymakers think parents ought to be and do than on universally held parent preferences for participation. A model of parent participation—graduated according to degrees of participation based on an *individualized involvement* wherein parents determine the extent of their involvement—is advanced.

The concept of parent participation pervades the requirements of the Education for All Handicapped Children Act of 1975 (P.L. 94–142). This law extends the right and arguably the duty to parents of handicapped children to assume the role of educational decision maker. In this role, they are expected to receive and act upon information, consent, or withhold consent to proposed educational evaluations and placements, collaborate in making instructional and other service-provision decisions, and contest educators' decisions. The clarifications of Individualized Education Program (IEP) requirements issued by the U.S. Office of Special Education add weight to the parent's role by stating one of the major purposes of the IEP meeting as follows:

The IEP meeting serves as a communication vehicle between parents and school personnel, and enables them as equal participants to jointly decide what the child's needs are, what services will be provided to meet those needs, and what the anticipated outcomes will be (*Federal Register*, 1981, p. 5462).

Phrases such as equal participation and jointly decide convey the *active* role parents are expected to assume.

These requirements make it readily apparent that the roles played by parents of handicapped children have shifted dramatically during the past two decades. As suggested by Kirk and Gallagher (1979), parents have been scapegoats, program organizers, political activists, and program participants and partners. Whereas parents of handicapped children (usually considered a homogeneous group) not too long ago were viewed as part of the problem, they are now seen, in a rather sudden shift in philosophy (reflected in P.L. 94–142 requirements), as part of the solution. As Avis (1978) indicates, it is not surprising that many parents are experiencing *jet lag* because of the almost complete change in program philosophy and assumptions about them and their roles. The issue is what has caused this pendulum-like shift, and whether it is altogether warranted.

P.L. 94–142 Assumptions About Parent Participation

The Congressional debates concerning P.L. 94–142 reveal the assumptions upon which current parent involvement policy is based. As stated by Senator Williams, one of the bill's major proponents:

The individualized planning conference is also intended as a method of providing additional parent counseling and training so that the parent may bolster the educational process at home. This involvement is important to assure the educational services are meeting the child's needs and so both parents and child may be part of the process from which they're so often removed. . . .

One of the greatest benefits that can come to the handicapped child is to have the parents brought into the conferences, because the education of the child continues after the school doors close and the child is at home. This is one of the reasons the idea of the mandatory conference was developed, to make sure the parent is part of the education of the child. (126 Cong. Rec. S1950, daily ed., June 18, 1975) (Statement of Sen. Williams)

This testimony reveals the following beliefs about parent involvement:

1. the parents (and the child) should be part of the process from which they are so often removed—a belief in shared decision making;

2. parent participation should increase the appropriateness of the educational services—a belief in parent involvement as a means of insuring that schools satisfy their legal obligations to children; and

3. parents should receive counseling and training to prepare them to be part of the education of their child at home—a belief in the role of parent as teacher.

Thus, parent participation is expected to benefit the child. A different way of viewing parent involvement, however, is that it should have positive *parent* outcomes—reducing stress, increasing family coping, and improving relationships within the family (parent and sibling) and with the handicapped child. Nonetheless, the parent involvement policies of P.L. 94–142 are almost exclusively child-oriented and may even exacerbate family/parent-child relationships.

This article will synthesize data from a variety of sources, examine the three previously stated beliefs concerning parent involvement, and suggest an alternative model of parent involvement, based upon the following thesis:

A handicapping condition places not only the child but also the entire family at risk (Turnbull, 1976). A model of parent involvement is needed that responds to the needs and preferences of families a well as of handicapped children. Parents are a heterogeneous rather than a homogeneous group. They have different degrees of capability, time, energy, and interest in being education decision makers. The assumptions underlying parent involvement are based more on what some advocates and policy makers think parents ought to be and do rather than on universally held parent preferences for involvement. Expecting all parents to be *equal* participants in decision making is setting up many—if not most—parents to fail and many educators to be disillusioned by parents who do not fulfill this awesome and sometimes unwelcome responsibility.

Parents as Decision Makers

The belief that parents should share the rights and responsibilities of decision makers and be an integral part of the educational process is based on the following assumptions:

1. parents want to be involved in education decision making and, when given the opportunity, will take advantage of it; and

2. attending the meeting to plan their child's IEP will enable parents to be decision makers.

These assumptions are debatable, to say the least. Studies of parent involvement in IEP meetings have revealed consistently that, while parent attendance is fairly high, parent participation in actual decision making is very limited (Goldstein, Strickland, Turnbull & Curry, 1980; Marver & David, 1978; National Committee for Citizens in Education, Note 1). For example, the National Committee for Citizens in Education (Note 1) surveyed approximately 2,300 parents from 438 school districts representing 46 states. A slight majority (52%) of the respondents indicated that their children's IEPs had been completed *before* the IEP meetings. An observational analysis of IEP meetings conducted by Goldstein et al. (1980) corroborates these findings. That study revealed that the mean length of the IEP conference was 36 minutes; the teacher was observed talking more than twice as much as the parent; and the conferences typically consisted of a resource teacher describing an already developed IEP to the parents. In a follow-up study, Goldstein and Turnbull (1982) found that the majority of parent contributions in the IEP meetings were on the topic of personal/family issues, not on such educational issues as evaluation, curriculum, and placement.

To assess parents' perspectives concerning their own involvement in their child's educational program, Winton and Turnbull (1981) conducted a two-phase interview with 32 mothers of preschool handicapped children. When discussing factors important to them in their selection and evaluation of preschools, 65% of the respondents said they needed consistent professional involvement with their child so they could *take a break* from full-time educational responsibility. One upper middle-class mother, who previously had been extensively involved in an early intervention program, stated:

A lot of times I get tired of having a role-God. I don't want to solve that—I'm paying you to take him for three hours and, lady, make it work! Maybe that's a nasty attitude toward teachers but I kind of feel that way sometimes. It's not worth it to me if I have to figure it out—I might as well have him with me at those times. (p. 15)

This mother's need to *take a break* may be related to the documented stress felt by parents of handicapped children. Gath's (1977) two-year comparative study in

Parent Involvement in the Education of Handicapped Children   Ann P. Turnbull and H. Rutherford Turnbull, III

England of families with a handicapped child and families with a non-handicapped child found the major difference between groups to be *severe disharmony* in almost one-third of families with a handicapped child and in none of the control families. Moroney (1981) has indicated that families with handicapped children are more likely to have additional financial costs, stigma, considerable amounts of time given to personal care of the child, interruptions of family sleep, social isolation, limitations in recreational activities, difficulty in handling behavioral problems, difficulty in shopping and other normal household routines, and pessimistic feelings about the future. Farber & Ryckman (1965) have documented the extreme limitations posed by severely handicapped children in regard to taking vacations, finding babysitters, and having social opportunities in the community. Finally, a disproportionate number of abused children are handicapped, a result attributed to the increased stress within the family caused by the child's developmental delays (Embry, 1980).

Parents' needs to reduce stress and have time for themselves may be exacerbated by the current social emphasis on self-fulfillment. Yankelovich (1981) has indicated that the new emphasis on finding a ". . . rich life, ripe with leisure, new experience, and enjoyment . . ." (p. 36) is a sweeping, irreversible cultural revolution that is transforming the rules that once guided American life. In his recent survey, 66% of parents (drawn from general population of parents rather than being confined only to parents of handicapped children) indicated that ". . . parents should be free to live their own lives even if it means spending less time with their children" (p. 74). The implications of this trend for parent involvement are vast.

To be able to "live their own lives," parents of handicapped children surveyed by Winton and Turnbull (1981) repeatedly emphasized their need for competent teachers. Parents frequently expressed confidence in special educators' skills and a desire to defer to these *experts*. Their views of expert power and influence in education decision making are consistent with professionals' assessment of these same factors, as reported by Gilliam and Coleman (1981).

Another perspective on the role of parents as shared decision makers is available from Winton's study (Note 2) concerning the ideal preschool for a handicapped child. When asked to describe an ideal preschool, only a few parents, from a total of 32, mentioned parent in-

volvement *of any kind* as a component. When asked to rank the characteristics of an ideal preschool, the respondents identified parent involvement as the *least important* characteristic. They said, instead, that teacher competency is the most important characteristic.

In summary, parent participation in the education decision making process may be a benefit to some parents and a detriment to others. Further, parent *attendance* at an IEP conference does not necessarily equate with parent *decision making*. Finally, many parents apparently prefer a role of receiving and confirming information at the IEP meeting, not one of active and assertive contribution.

Parent Participation to Insure Handicapped Child's Rights

The second belief inherent in the parent participation policies is that parent involvement insures the child's rights to an appropriate education will be satisfied. The assumptions undergirding this belief are:

1. parents can improve the quality of decisions made by teachers;

2. parents are the best advocates for insuring the accountability of the school system; and

3. parents will represent only the interests of their child and there is no conflict of interests between parents and children.

Many parents are unconvinced that their contributions can improve the quality of decisions made by teachers. As stated by one parent, who is a nurse by training (Winton & Turnbull, 1981):

You've got to have a staff that is smarter than you . . . I'm no genius, I mean, my background is giving enemas . . . but you've got to know that the people who are teaching your child know their stuff. Now I leave him off in the morning and I feel like— phew—people more competent than me are taking him and that's a great feeling. (p. 15)

The topics that parents discuss in IEP conferences (Goldstein et al., 1980; Goldstein & Turnbull, 1982) and the emphasis that they place on having competent teachers (Winton & Turnbull, 1981) reflect this viewpoint. Many parents do not believe that their child needs to be protected from the special education system. They consider the special education system their greatest ally. It follows that some will be reluctant to attack a system that helps them and their child.

It also is not surprising that parents express a lack of self-confidence and skills in improving their child's education. If it requires a master's degree in special education to qualify a person in assessment, curriculum planning, methods and materials, and behavior management, it is questionable how parents without specialized training ever could be *equal* participants in developing an IEP, much less advocates for more appropriate IEPs, programs, related services, placements, or teachers.

Consider the hypothetical example of a person who has developed a rare form of cancer. In choosing a physician to treat the cancer, what criteria become most important? Are they criteria related to the doctor transferring the position of expertise to the patient; this would require the patient's expression of personal viewpoints on the method and extent of treatment most appropriate. Contrasting criteria include the doctor's providing extensive information to the patient on treatment options, the pros and cons of each, statistics on treatment success, and advice on the option best suited to the patient's condition. Then the patient would have an opportunity to ask questions, seek additional information, and decide whether to accept the advice of the doctor. In the IEP conference, many parents prefer to be involved according to the latter set of criteria.

Many parents are highly interested and successful in being advocates for their handicapped child (Goldberg & Goldberg, 1979). But the assumption cannot be made that all parents are suited to be advocates and will function as such, thereby insuring their children's rights and schools' accountability. More research is needed on the impact on parents of the continuing need to justify and be advocates for their child's rights. Parents' refusal to support systems that still reflect the belief that the child is expendable (if their child is, in a sense so are they) may have implications for the attachment between parent and child and the mental health of the parent. It clearly has implications about perceived stigma (Goffman, 1963). And, as Lavelle and Keogh (1980) point out, a mother's perception of society's view of her child can influence her feelings about her capacity to love and to care for the child.

Advocacy can exclude parents of handicapped children from the opportunity of having mainstreamed experiences with parents of non-handicapped children. A parent (Michaelis, 1981) of five children, one of whom is handicapped, has written:

Since funding for Special Education was tenuous, it also meant that to keep (my son) Jim in the class, I had to be involved. I lobbied at the school board and in the legislature. Keeping Jim in school also meant leaving housework and babies to attend parent conferences across town. No wonder I didn't have time to even try to mainstream myself into the coffee-cup conversation in the neighborhood kitchens. . . . Although sophisticated services are being implemented in many places, the Individualized Education Program conferences, the school visits, and the parent groups take more time for already busy parents. Early intervention means all of this starts sooner and it is possible that the parent and the child are labelled and 'out of the mainstream' even sooner. (p. 15)

If they function as advocates, parents of handicapped children frequently must choose between the conflicting demands of spending time with their child or going to one meeting after another to act as advocate for the child's needs (Turnbull, 1978). One mother explained why she stopped being an advocate as follows (Winton & Turnbull, 1981):

When (our son) was first born we really got involved, and it was tremendously beneficial. But now I just want to draw back and make sure that this little guy gets it at home. When you're putting in so much time that your family is no longer benefiting from it, then it's time to quit and let somebody else do it . . . that's where we got. (p. 17)

Finally, there may be a conflict of interest between the child and parent, a conflict that may be weighted against the child because of his or her minority and handicap and because the parent is the legal and natural guardian as well as the party to whom P.L. 94–142 extends so many rights. It is naively assumed that parents always will represent the child's interests, but it is only human nature for parents to represent their own interests as well (Turnbull, 1977). Some potential conflicts of interest are:

1. parents need the child *not* to be in a special education program (need for self-esteem) but the child needs specially designed instruction;

2. parents need to reduce stress by institutionalizing the child but the child needs the least restrictive alternative placement (Teitelbaum & Ellis, 1978);

3. parents need to protect their handicapped child (and themselves) from rejection and failure, but the child needs to take risks in the regular classroom.

Many questions must be answered associated with conflicts of interest. A few relevant ones are: Is it legitimate sometimes to give priority to parents' needs? Is meeting the parents' needs a strategy that also can help the child? Is it too narrow to think about handicapped children as being at risk? Are families of handicapped children also at risk?

Parent as Teacher of a Child

The third belief inherent in the parent involvement policies is that all parents should be both counseled and trained to be the child's teacher. This belief is based on the following assumptions:

1. all parents need and want counseling;

2. all parents can and should be teachers of their children;

3. all parents are interested and willing to receive counseling and training to fulfill this role; and

4. all handicapped children will benefit from receiving instruction at home.

But parents are not homogeneous; predictably, they have different reactions to being counseled. Two highly educated, middle-class mothers with similar backgrounds and experiences illustrate this variability toward structured parent counseling (Winton & Turnbull, 1981). Both mothers were moving from programs with parent support groups to programs without them. One mother responded:

I cried for two months last spring—I knew what was going to happen. I didn't know it would be as drastic. I was hoping that there would be some type of parental support but it just didn't happen. (p. 12).

In contrast, another mother answered the question, what is it like not having a parent group, by saying: "It is definitely refreshing." She added:

You really feel bad for the professionals who want to help you but don't know how. You know, the psychologists and the social workers have this concept that every parent with a handicapped child wants to talk about it all the time. That's garbage! (p. 12)

What is beneficial for one parent is not necessarily beneficial for another. Just as children have individual styles of learning, so parents have individual preferences for counseling, support, and other involvement.

Many parents of handicapped children have achieved impressive success as teachers of their own children (Boyd, 1980; Bricker & Bricker, 1976; Karnes & Teska, 1980). But being an effective teacher of one's own child is a formidable undertaking. For example, Karnes

& Teska (1980) list, at great length, those competencies desirable for parents to be teachers of their children. No less is required of every master's-level special education teacher. Below is an excerpt that includes *less than half* of the skills they identify as important for parents:

The parental competencies required for direct teaching of the handicapped child at home involve interacting with the child in ways that promote positive behavior; reinforcing desired behavior; establishing an environment that is conducive to learning; setting up and maintaining a routine for direct teaching; using procedures appropriate for teaching concepts and skills; adapting lesson plans to the child's interests and needs; determining whether the child has mastered knowledge and skills; keeping meaningful records, including notes on child progress; participating in a staffing of the child; communicating effectively with others; and assessing the child's stage of development. (p. 99)

The implication is clear: to be a good parent, one must have skills comparable to a master's level special educator, and still have time for IEP participation, self-fulfillment, individual and system advocacy, employment, and other family responsibilities.

A further case in point is the standard component of preschool programs funded through the Handicapped Children's Early Education Program Network (U.S. Office of Special Education in the Department of Education) for parent training. This component and the philosophy behind it (parents are teachers) are so widely accepted in preschool programs that Shearer and Shearer (1977) have made the following statement:

It thus becomes mandatory that projects develop training programs for parents with the objective of teaching parents to be effective in working with and teaching their own child. (p. 213)

If it is mandatory for the program to offer parent training, it is also probably mandatory that the parents attend the training—and appreciate the opportunity! Consider, however, the paradox observed by a handicapped child's mother who is an elementary teacher (Turnbull & Winton, in press):

I think you have to be removed as a parent from the situation. . . . Living with a child like this and trying to train him is just about an impossibility. It's just the constant supervision of a child like this that really gets to you after a while . . . it's frightening enough without having to teach him too.

Calvert (1971) has suggested that the success of a parent training program be partially defined by comparing the number of family members involved in carrying out a handicapped child's program with the total number of members in a child's family. It is as though the responsibility to assist the handicapped child to get better becomes the family project.

But what is the impact of such training on the parent-child relationship? Although the question has not yet been addressed in the literature, Sondra Diamond, a physically handicapped psychologist, has written (1981) insightfully:

Something happens in a parent when relating to his disabled child; he forgets that they're a kid first. I used to think about that a lot when I was a kid. I would be off in a euphoric state, drawing or coloring or cutting out paper dolls, and as often as not the activity would be turned into an occupational therapy session. 'You're not holding the scissors right,' 'Sit up straight so your curvature doesn't get worse.' That era was ended when I finally let loose a long and exhaustive tirade. 'I'm just a kid! You can't therapize me all the time! I get enough therapy in school every day! I don't think about my handicap all the time like you do!' (p. 30)

The consequences of parents being teachers of their handicapped children command far greater attention. The assumptions may be right for some, wrong for others. What are the consequences for the parent-child relationship? For the child's self-image? For the possible implicit message to the child: "You need to get well—you are unacceptable as you are." The recent Carnegie report on handicapped children (Gliedman & Roth, 1980) states that society's fundamental misconception is its view of handicapped people as perpetual patients. The need for parents to be teachers of their children day-in day-out, year-in year-out, may contribute to perpetuating this misconception.

Summary and Recommendations

The assumptions underlying the parent involvement policies of P.L. 94–142 are valid for some parents and invalid for others. Moreover, a dichotomy exists between P.L. 94–142 policies for children and those for parents. For children, a fundamental concept is individualization. And the law allows competing interests to be balanced against each other in selecting the child's placement: his or her needs for specially designed instruction and social interaction with nonhandicapped peers are balanced against the demands and expectations of the settings. It is time—indeed, beyond the time—to consider the needs, abilities, and preferences of parents in regard to the demands of their children and expectations of the school. Rather than mandating that all parents be equal participants with the school personnel to make decisions jointly

(*Federal Register*, 1981), public policy should tolerate a range of parent involvement choices and options, matched to the needs and interests of the parents.

First, a policy analysis should explicate the valuative criteria for determining effective parent participation practices. Heretofore, the major criterion seems to be obtaining a parent's signature on an IEP. More relevant criteria include improved adaptation of the family to the needs of the child, reduction of family stress, improved parent-child relationship, improved self-esteem for the family and child, reduction in the degree and frequency of parent burnout, and improved social competence for the child.

Second, a comprehensive evaluation of parent involvement activities should consider the viewpoint of parents, rather than that wholly of professionals or other policy makers. The study should investigate the relationships of child, family, and program variables to successful practices. Family variables might include parents' educational values, expectations for their child, expectations for service, level of stress, extent of accessible support systems, locus of control, assertiveness, educational background, and long-term goals for their child. The analysis should answer the question: What types of parents, with what types of children, benefit from particular types of parent involvement activities? A desirable result of the study would be a parent involvement model that takes into account the diverse needs and perspectives of parents. Such a model might provide, at the minimum, the following graduated (less-to-more) involvement options:

1. Allow some parents not to be involved with a school program if they so choose. If patients have a right to refuse medical treatment, parents of handicapped children should have the right to decline to be education decision makers. Perhaps taking on the responsibility of education decision making will be the greatest service the program can provide in helping some parents establish equilibrium between the stresses posed by adapting to the handicapping condition and their optimum coping skills.

2. Provide still other parents an opportunity to be informed of goals and objectives according to the decisions made by professionals.

3. Provide full and equal decision-making opportunities for parents who choose to participate at this level.

Such a model should recognize the evolving needs of parents and allow for flexibility in meeting these needs. Various strategies should be available to help family members address their priority concerns in learning to integrate their handicapped child successfully into the family. In essence, educational policy first should recognize and next create a range of options and choices for parents. It is an overly rigid policy—one that parents of handicapped children do not support uniformly—that lacks respect for their individuality and diverse capabilities.

Reference Notes

1. National Committee for Citizens in Education. Unpublished manuscript serving as basis for congressional testimony, 1979.
2. Winton, P. J. *Descriptive study of parents' perspectives on preschool services: Mainstreamed and specialized.* Doctoral dissertation, University of North Carolina at Chapel Hill, 1980.

References

Avis, D. W. Deinstitutionalization jet lag. In A. P. Turnbull & H. R. Turnbull (Eds.), *Parents speak out: Views from the other side of the two-way mirror.* Columbus, Oh.: Charles E. Merrill Publ. Co., 1978.

Boyd, R. D. Systematic parent training through a home based model. *Exceptional Children*, 1980, *45*(8), 647–650.

Bricker, W. A., & Bricker, D. D. The infant, toddler, and preschool research and intervention project. In T. D. Tjassem (Ed.), *Intervention strategies for high risk infants and young children.* Baltimore, Md.: University Park Press, 1976.

Calvert, D. Dimensions of family involvement. *Exceptional Children*, 1971, *37*, 655–658.

Diamond, S. Growing up with parents of a handicapped child: A handicapped person's perspective. In J. L. Paul (Ed.), *Understanding and working with parents of children with special needs.* New York: Holt, Rinehart, and Winston, 1981.

Embry, L. H. Family support for handicapped preschool children at risk for abuse. In J. J. Gallagher (Ed.), *New directions for exceptional children: Parents and families of handicapped children* (#4). San Francisco: Jossey-Bass, Inc., 1980.

Farber, B., & Ryckman, D. B. Effects of severely mentally retarded children on family relationships. *Mental Retardation Abstracts*, 1965, *2*, 1–17.

Federal Register. Washington, D.C.: U.S. Government Printing Office, January 19, 1981.

Gath, A. The impact of an abnormal child upon the parents. *British Journal of Psychiatry*, 1977, *130*, 405–410.

Gilliam, J. E., & Coleman, M. C. Who influences IEP committee decisions? *Exceptional Children*, 1981, *47*(8), 642–644.

Gliedman, J., & Roth, W. *The unexpected minority: Handicapped children in America.* New York: Harcourt, Brace, Jovanovich, 1980.

Goffman, E. *Stigma.* Englewood Cliffs, N.J.: Prentice-Hall, 1963.

Goldberg, P., & Goldberg, M. PACER Center: Parents learn about special education laws. *Education Unlimited*, 1979, *1*(4), 34–37.

Goldstein, S., Strickland, B., Turnbull, A. P., & Curry, L. An observational analysis of the IEP conference. *Exceptional Children*, 1980, *46*(4), 278–286.

Goldstein, S., & Turnbull, A. P. The use of two strategies to increase parent participation in the IEP conference. *Exceptional Children*, 1982, *48*(4), 360–361.

Karnes, M. B., & Teska, J. A. Toward successful parent involvement in programs for handicapped children. In J. J. Gallagher (Ed.), *New directions for exceptional children: Parents and families of handicapped children* (#4). San Francisco: Jossey-Bass, Inc., 1980.

Kirk, S. A., & Gallagher, J. J. *Educating exceptional children* (3rd ed.). Boston: Houghton Mifflin Co., 1979.

Lavelle, N., & Keogh, B. K. Expectations and attributions of parents of handicapped children. In J. J. Gallagher (Ed.), *New directions for exceptional children: Parents and families of handicapped children* (#4). San Francisco: Jossey-Bass, Inc., 1980.

Marver, J. D., & David, J. L. The implementation of individualized education program requirements of P.L. 94–142. Trends Park, Ca.: SRI International, 1978.

Michaelis, C. T. Mainstreaming: A mother's perspective. *Topics in Early Childhood Special Education*, 1981, *1*(1), 11–16.

Moroney, R. M. Public social policy: Impact on families with handicapped children. In J. L. Paul (Ed.), *Understanding and working with parents of children with special needs.* New York: Holt, Rinehart, and Winston, 1981.

Shearer, M. S., & Shearer, D. E. Parent involvement. In J. B. Jordan and others (Eds.), *Early childhood education for exceptional children.* Reston, Va.: CEC, 1977.

Teitelbaum, L., & Ellis, J. The liberty interest of children: Due process rights and their application. *Family Law Quarterly,* 1978, *12,* 153–202.

Turnbull, H. R. Families in crisis, families at risk. In T. D. Tjossem (Ed.), *Intervention strategies for high risk.* Baltimore, Md.: University Park Press, 1976.

Turnbull, H. R. Mainstreaming emotionally disturbed children: Legal implications. In A. J. Pappanikou (Ed.), *Mainstreaming emotionally disturbed children.* Syracuse, N.Y.: Syracuse University Press, 1977.

Turnbull, A. P. Moving from being a professional to being a parent: A startling experience. In A. P. Turnbull & H. R. Turnbull (Eds.), *Parents speak out: Views from the other side of the two-way mirror.* Columbus, Oh.: Charles E. Merrill Publishing Co., 1978.

Turnbull, A. P., & Winton, P. J. A comparison of specialized and mainstreamed preschools from the perspectives of mothers of handicapped children. *Journal of Pediatric Psychology,* in press.

U.S. 94th Congress, 6th Session. 104 et seq., *P.L.: 94–142, Education for All Handicapped Children Act of 1975.*

Winton, P., & Turnbull, A. P. Parent involvement as viewed by parents of preschool handicapped children. *Topics in Early Childhood Special Education,* 1981, *1*(3), 11–19.

Yankelovich, D. New rules in American life: Searching for self-fulfillment in a world turned upside down. *Psychology Today,* 1981, *14*(11), 35–91.

An expanded version of this paper was originally presented by the senior author at the Minnesota Round Table in Early Childhood Education VIII, June 1981. It will appear in the conference proceedings to be published by the Bush Program in Child Development and Social Policy, University of Michigan, a co-sponsor of the conference.

Authors

Ann P. Turnbull, Ed.D., Associate Professor, Department of Special Education, and Acting Associate Director, Bureau of Child Research, and **H. Rutherford Turnbull, III, LL.B., LL.M.,** Professor and Chairman, Department of Special Education, and Courtesy Professor of Law, The University of Kansas, Lawrence, KS 66045.

Effects of Parent Training on Families of Children With Mental Retardation: Increased Burden or Generalized Benefit?

Bruce L. Baker, Sandra J. Landen, and Kathleen J. Kashima
1991

Abstract

Parents of children with mental retardation have become increasingly involved in special education, including training programs to facilitate teaching at home. Although some writers have argued that families accrue generalized psychological benefits of such participation, others have cautioned that the result may be increasing the burden of child-rearing. Forty-nine families of children with mental retardation were assessed before and after a parent training program, on a variety of parent, marital, and family measures. Parents reported high satisfaction with the program and showed small but statistically significant decreases in reports of symptoms of depression, parent and family problems, overall family stress, and dissatisfaction with the family's adaptability. Family characteristics were also predictive of teaching at home one year following training. The families that reported doing the least productive teaching had entered training reporting a greater child-related stress and lower satisfaction with the marriage and the family.

Families with a child who has mental retardation are at risk for greater stress and adjustment difficulties than are families with a child who is developing normally (Blacher, 1984; Crnic, Friedrich, & Greenberg, 1983; Waisbren, 1980). This subject has received much study, and for many years the findings justified treatment for parents that was focused, sometimes exclusively, on their psychological needs (Wolfensberger, 1970). Behavioral parent training came on the scene, however, with a different perspective, namely, that intervention should address parents' needs for useful information. It seemed possible, though, that if parents learned to cope better on a daily basis with the child who had mental retardation, not only the child but also the parents would benefit (Baker, 1980). Parent training programs are now widely accepted as one effective component in the array of services for families with a child who has mental retardation. Numerous studies have demonstrated that these programs meet their specific goals: Parents teach their children better and their children show positive behavioral changes (Baker, 1984; Breiner & Beck, 1984; McConachie, 1986). The notion that such programs might affect parent and family adjustment, however, remains essentially unstudied.

The present study was designed to examine psychological characteristics of parents and families and to address two questions: First, what, if any, is the broader impact of parent training on participating parents and families? Second, are parent and family characteristics predictive of successful outcome?

Proponents of parent training assume benefits to participants beyond the specific skill gains assessed, and there is some evidence for what Griest and Forehand (1982) called "family generalization": positive changes on measures of personal, marital, or family adjustment (Forehand, Wells, & Griest, 1980; Forrest, Holland, Daly, & Fellbaum, 1984; Karoly & Rosenthal, 1977; Omizo, Williams, & Omizo, 1986; Webster-Stratton, 1985). However, these studies have involved only children without mental retardation who have behavior problems.

The issues may be different for families with a child who has mental retardation, and voices of caution are being raised. Parent training programs and other parent involvements, some writers have argued, sometimes make excessive or inappropriate demands, in some cases disturbing the parent–child relationship or increasing the perceived burden of raising a child with handicaps (Benson & Turnbull, 1986; Buckley, 1981; Featherstone, 1981; Foster, Berger, & McLean, 1981; Lyon & Preis, 1983; McConachie, 1986). Turnbull and Turnbull (1982) argued that parents' rights to involvement are being distorted into excessive program demands and noted that parents often express a desire not to be involved in their child's schooling (Winton & Turnbull, 1981). Allen and Hudd (1987) conjectured that when training programs place parents in the role of teacher and expect them to carry out a prescribed curriculum, parents often feel uncomfortable and may become frustrated if the child does not show progress. The question is summed up by

Gallagher, Beckman, and Cross (1983), who advised that professionals should consider whether asking parents to participate actively in the child's treatment by carrying out specific program activities may not, in fact, impose additional stress on the family. Nonetheless, although the literature presents personal opinions about family generalization, the issue has received little empirical study.

The second, and related, question recognizes that parent training will not be of benefit to all families. In prediction studies investigators have typically examined only a few variables, foremost among them demographic characteristics, and have primarily looked at immediate posttraining outcome. For example, socioeconomic disadvantage, including single parent status, consistently has been predictive of poorer outcome (Baker & Clark, 1987; Dumas, 1986; Dumas & Wahler, 1983; Webster-Stratton, 1985). Dumas, citing Zussman's (1978) argument that socioeconomic measures are "basket" variables that stand for parental dysfunctions and lack of parental skills, suggested that researchers should attempt to study these variables directly. Only a few investigators in studies with parents of children with conduct disorders have examined personal or marital adjustment as predictors of training outcome (Griest & Forehand, 1982). We do not know of studies in which psychological variables as predictors of long-term parent training outcome in families with children who have mental retardation have been assessed.

We chose to study adjustment problems for which parents and families with a child who has mental retardation have been found to be at heightened risk: depression (Cummings, 1976; Cummings, Bayley, & Rie, 1966), stress (Blacher, 1984; Crnic et al., 1983), and marital distress (Friedrich & Friedrich, 1981; Waisbren, 1980). We also examined family processes that might be affected by parent training and included measures of family cohesion and adaptability, satisfaction, and coping.

Method

Overview of Procedures

Forty-nine families of children with mental retardation completed an 11-session parent-training program focused on self-help skill teaching and behavior problem management. In addition to our standard measures of training outcome, we obtained measures of family functioning, which we examined for changes from pre- to posttraining and for prediction of parents' continued implementation of programs at home one year later.

Subjects

Staff members of four Regional Centers for the Developmentally Disabled in Los Angeles county recruited families with a child who had moderate or severe mental retardation to participate in behavioral parent-training programs that would meet at their sites. Seventy-two families completed a battery of pretraining measures and began training. Forty-nine of these (68%) met the completion criteria of attending at least five of the eight group meetings and three individual assessment sessions.

Table 1 Demographics for Families (N = 49) Who Completed Parent Training

Characteristics	
Primary parent	
Age (mean years)	36.2
Education (mean years)	14.0
Marital status: Single (%)	12.2
Prior behavior mod. experience (%)	50.7
Ethnicity (%)	
Caucasian	49.0
Black	16.3
Hispanic	20.4
Asian	10.2
Other	4.1
Family income (%)	
$16,000	10.4
17,000–34,999	33.3
35,000–49.999	25.0
> 50,000	31.3
Children	
Age (mean years)	6.1
Sex (% boys)	77.6
Diagnosis (%)	
MR, cause unknown	24.5
Down syndrome	24.5
Autism	16.3
Cerebral palsy	14.3
Other	20.4
Age at diagnosis (mean years)	1.3
Siblings (mean no.)	1.6

Table 1 shows demographic characteristics for the 49 completers. In each family, we designated a "primary parent" for data coding purposes. When both parents were equally involved, the mother was designated as the primary parent. There were four primary parent fathers; 3 of them were so designated because the mother did not read and/or speak English. The average primary parent was in her mid 30s, with 2 years of college education.

The target children were primarily boys between 2 and 11 years of age. Their most frequent diagnoses were mental retardation of unknown origin, Down syndrome, and autism. All target children were designated as mentally retarded, but standard intelligence scores were not obtained.

Training

The training program consisted of three individual and eight group meetings distributed over a 16-week period as follows: an individual pretraining assessment, four weekly group meetings on self-help skill teaching, 4 weeks of teaching at home with no meetings, an individual assessment and feedback session, four weekly group meetings on behavior problem management, 2 weeks for implementing behavior management programs at home, and an individual assessment and feedback session. Meetings were conducted in the evening, in groups of 4 to 7 families, and lasted about 2 hours. Homework involved reading a manual and teaching for about 10 minutes for 4 or 5 days each week. We used the UCLA Parents as Teachers training curriculum, which has been described elsewhere (Baker, 1989; Kashima, Baker, & Landen, 1988). We note that 41 of these families participated in a study contrasting video-directed and live-directed parent training for the four session self-help skills component of training (Kashima et al., 1988). Because these training conditions produced comparable posttraining and follow-through outcomes, we combined them for the present analyses.

Outcome Measures

Three outcome measures were administered pre- and posttraining. The Behavioral Vignettes Test (Baker & Heifetz, 1976) is a 20-item questionnaire that assesses knowledge of behavioral principles by posing teaching and behavior management situations and asking parents to select one of four responses that they believe would be the most effective. The Teaching Proficiency Test

(Brightman, Baker, Clark, & Ambrose, 1982), a videotaped 15-minute teaching session involving parent and child, is coded for components of good behavioral teaching (e.g., arranging antecedents, contingent reinforcement). The Teaching Interview (Baker, Heifetz, & Murphy, 1980; Brightman et al., 1982) is a structured interview, lasting about 30 minutes, that asks parents about teaching and behavior problem management during the previous 3 months. Pre- and postinterviews were audiotaped and scored by raters blind to condition and administration time for the extent and quality of teaching and behavior problem management being implemented in the home. Follow-up interviews were collected by telephone and coded during the interview.

The 23 item self-report Parent Evaluation Questionnaire, adapted from Forehand and McMahon (1981), was administered at the final assessment. This measure assesses parents' opinions about the appropriateness of the approach, helpfulness of the program, effectiveness of program components, and their own involvement in the program. Parents rate each statement on a 4- or 7-point scale.

Demographic and Psychological Measures

Two measures were administered at pretraining only. The Demographic Questionnaire obtained information about the parents (e.g., age, education, income, marital status, previous parent training experience) and their child (e.g., age, diagnosis, school placement). The Marital Adjustment Test (Locke & Wallace, 1959), a 15-item self-report questionnaire about aspects of married life, yields a total marital adjustment score.

Four other measures were administered pre- and posttraining. The Beck Depression Inventory (Beck, Ward, Mendelson, & Erbaugh, 1961), a 21-item self-report questionnaire in a multiple choice format, assesses cognitive, affective, and physiological symptoms of depression and yields a total score. The Questionnaire on Resources and Stress-Short Form (QRS-F) (Friedrich, Greenberg, & Crnic, 1983), a 53-item short form of Holroyd's (1974) QRS, assesses stress and attitudes related to a child with delays. The QRS-F yields a total score and four subscales derived from factor analysis: Parent and Family Problems, Pessimism, Child Characteristics, and Physical Incapacitation.

The Family Adaptive and Cohesive Environment Scale—FACES (Olson, McCubbin, Barnes, Larsen, Muxen, & Wilson, 1982) is a 30-item questionnaire assessing family adaptability and cohesion. Respondents complete it twice, first to describe how they perceive their family and then how they would ideally like their family to be. The discrepancy scores give measures of family satisfaction on these dimensions. The Family Coping Strategies—F-COPES (Olson et al., 1982) is a 30-item questionnaire assessing the strategies a family has available for coping with problems.

Follow-Up

Families were recontacted one year following training, and an appointment was made for a 30-minute Teaching Interview conducted by telephone. Thirty-nine of the 49 families were followed-up. Of the remaining 10, 1 refused the interview, 4 had moved away and were not reachable, 3 could not be scheduled, and 2 had placed their child out of the home.

Results

Interrater Reliabilities

For Teaching Interviews, 29 (36%) randomly selected audiotapes were coded by a second rater, with a resulting interrater reliability of .91 At follow-up, 8 (21%) randomly selected phone interviews were simultaneously coded by a second rater; the interrater reliability was .84.

Changes on Standard Outcome Measures

Pre- and posttraining scores on three outcome measures were compared by two-tailed t tests for the primary parents. Behavioral Vignettes Test scores increased from 10.1 to 14.3, reflecting significant gains in knowledge of teaching principles, $t(46) = 10.2, p < .001$. We have previously used a Behavioral Vignettes Test score of 15 (75% correct) as a proficiency criterion. Considered this way, 15% of parents met criterion before and 55% after training. Teaching Proficiency Test scores increased from 20.1 to 26.5, reflecting increased skill in implementing behavioral teaching, $t(42) = 5.75, p < .001$, and Teaching Interview scores increased from 12.2 to 21.6, indicating more and better teaching at home in the 3 months during training than in the 3 months before training, $t(45) = 8.24, p < .001$.

Table 2 Consumer Satisfaction Measure: Parents With High Positive Endorsement After Training ($N = 48$)

Measure	%
General[a]	
Appropriateness of the approach	100
Helpfulness of the group meetings	96
Helpfulness of the group leader	100
Competence of the group leader	96
Confidence in teaching self-help skills	81
Recommend the program to friend	
or relative	100
Program components, usefulness of[a]	
Lectures by leader	98
Videotapes	70
Group discussions	89
Group exercises (e.g., role plays)	73
Reading the manuals	80
Home observations and teaching	93
Self-Evaluation[b]	
Attending meetings	100
Completing readings	76
Teaching self-help skill at home	91
Keeping records of skill teaching	39
Programming behavior problem at home	85
Keeping records of behavior problem	52
Understanding material[c]	81

[a] Percentage of parents who reported *very much* (7) or *much* (6) on a 7-point scale.
[b] Percentage of parents who reported they did *all* (4) or most (3) of what was recommended.
[c] 5 or 6 on a 6-point-scale.

Consumer Evaluation

Parent Evaluation Questionnaire responses are summarized in Table 2. Every parent rated the approach as appropriate or very appropriate for his or her family and would recommend the program much or very much to other families. Parents were very positive about the helpfulness of the group meeting and the helpfulness and the competence of group leaders. Most parents left training confident in their ability to teach their child. In their self-assessment of participation, however, parents were not as consistently positive; most responded that they had met most or all of the requirements for attendance, skill teaching, and behavior problem programming, but a smaller proportion responded that they had met the requirements for record keeping during skill teaching or behavior problem programming.

Changes on Psychological Measures

The psychological measures were analyzed with two-tailed t tests. Table 3 shows prescores, postscores, correlations between pre- and postscores, and difference scores. The correlations indicated high stability, while the difference scores showed small changes, all in the positive direction. Beck Depression Inventory scores were reasonably stable, but decreased significantly, $t(40) = 2.58$, $p < .05$. A score of 16 or higher, the cutoff commonly used to designate moderate depression, was found for 4 parents pre- and only 1 parent posttraining. Questionnaire on Resources and Stress scores (QRS-F) were stable but decreased slightly on all scales except Pessimism, which remained the same. The decrease was significant for the Parent and Family Problems subscale, $t(42) = 2.75$,

$p < .01$, and for the total QRS-F score, $t(40) = 2.44$, $p < .05$. The mean F-COPES and FACES scores were almost identical from pre- to posttest. On the Family Adaptive and Cohesive Environment Scale, however, the satisfaction index (discrepancy between actual family and ideal family) improved significantly for adaptability, $t(39) = 2.54$, $p < .05$.

Spouse Completion

We were interested in whether any of the training benefits previously discussed were greater in families where both parents completed the training program. For the 43 intact families, we contrasted primary parent scores for the 19 families where both parents completed training with the 24 families where only one parent completed it. These two groups did not differ on posttraining or change scores for any of the standard outcome, consumer evaluation, or psychological measures that we previously considered nor did they differ on follow-through implementation.

Table 3 Parent and Family Measures

Measure	Prescore	Postscore	r^a	Diff.	r^b
Beck Depression Inv.	7.0	5.0	.65	−2.0*	−.05
Marital Adj. Test	108.0	NA	NA	NA	.29
QRS-F Total	24.7	22.6	.85	−2.1*	−.27
Parent/Family	7.3	6.2	.86	−1.1**	−.07
Pessimism	6.3	6.3	.74	0	−.10
Child Characteristics	8.0	7.3	.73	−0.7	−.41*
Physical	2.7	2.5	.81	−0.2	−.31
FACES					
Adaptability	45.8	46.5	.76	+0.8	.35*
Cohesion	61.9	62.6	.86	+0.7	.24
Satisfaction					
Adaptability	8.1	6.0	.66	−2.1*	−.62***
Cohesion	7.2	6.1	.55	−1.1	−.40*
F-COPES Total	94.9	95.3	.57	+0.4	.10

Note. QRS-F = Questionnaire on Resources and Stress-Short Form, FACES = Family Adaptive and Cohesive Environment Scale, F-COPES = Family Coping Strategies.
[a] Prescore–postscore correlations.
[b] Correlations of parent and family measure prescores with the Teaching Interview scores at follow-through.
   * $p < .05$.
   ** $p < .01$.
   *** $p < .001$.

Follow-Up Outcome

Teaching Interviews obtained one year after training covered the previous 3-month period. There was further increase from a mean of 21.6 posttraining to a mean of 25.8 at follow-up, $t(36) = 2.04$, $p < .05$, although this was confounded by the different data-collection methods (in person vs. phone). There was a good range of follow-up scores, from 5 to 44.

Prediction of Follow-Up Outcome

Teaching interview scores at follow-up were not significantly correlated with pre- or postscores on any of the three outcome measures or the consumer evaluation measure. With demographic indices, teaching at follow-up was significantly related only to primary parent employed, $r(37) = .41$, $p < .01$, with higher scores for employed parents. Teaching was not related significantly to parent age, education, income, ethnicity, marital status, family size, or prior behavior modification experience or to child age, sex, or diagnosis.

Table 3 also shows correlations between pretraining scores on the psychological variables and Teaching Interview scores at follow-up. The significant correlations were all in the direction of better adjusted families scoring higher on follow-through teaching. Parents with higher teaching scores at follow-up had reported significantly less stress (QRS-F) related to the child's behavior and marginally less related to the child's physical problems. On the FACES, parents who became more involved teachers had viewed their family higher on adaptability, and they were more satisfied with their families for both adaptability and cohesion. Moreover, they reported marginally higher Marital Adjustment Test scores.

Our primary interest was to predict the low follow-through families, so that alternative interventions might be attempted. We divided the sample into the lowest third of scorers on the Teaching Interview (low follow-through group: scores 5 to 22, $n = 13$) and the top two thirds (middle–high group: scores 23 to 44, $n = 26$), and compared these groups using t tests. Consistent with the correlational analysis, the low follow-through group had reported greater child-related stress on the QRS-F, $t(34) = 2.46$, $p < .05$. They also reported lower satisfaction on the FACES adaptability, $t(33) = 4.43$, $p < .01$, and cohesion, $t(33) = 2.03$, $p < .05$, scales, and on the Marital Adjustment Test, $t(31) = 2.18$, $p < .05$.

Discussion

Our first question concerned family generalization, or the psychological effects of participating in parent training. We found no evidence for the adverse outcomes hypothesized by some writers. The program had good social validity; parents evaluated the behavioral approach as very appropriate for their families and evaluated the program highly. Parents gained on the outcome measures of teaching knowledge and skills, and they increased programming at home during training and continued even one year afterwards. Posttraining psychological measures either remained at pretraining levels or changed positively. There were small but statistically significant decreases in reports of symptoms of depression, parent and family problems, overall family stress, and dissatisfaction with the family's adaptability.

Several factors limit the generalizability of these findings. First, there was no untrained group to control for effects of repeated testing. Although we know from other studies that the outcome measures are stable in untrained families (Baker & Brightman, 1984; Brightman et al., 1982), we do not know if the psychological measures might have decreased upon retesting without treatment. We can at last conclude that these families did not become worse on any psychological measure. Second, we only examined families who completed training. This program had an unusually high dropout rate (23%), perhaps in part because it was conducted in two separate modules; some families completed the first module but did not begin the second one. There may be merit to the argument that some families indeed found the program burdensome and that they simply dropped out. We note, however, that almost all dropouts in voluntary parent-training programs leave early, after one or several sessions (Dangel & Polster, 1984). Although some of these families may not feel comfortable with the training program, it is unlikely that they have suffered any significant burden from such brief involvement.

Third, our conclusions must be limited to the Parents as Teachers program. One might actually expect greater difficulties with this "packaged" program that affords limited opportunities to meet individual family needs. Yet, this is a voluntary and time-limited program that makes rather circumscribed demands on families. The evening meetings and the provision of child care reduced the difficulties of attendance. It is not surprising that a program of this limited intensity did not change the participants much, for better or worse. In a much more demanding and individualized parent-training program, and especially one that is not voluntary, it is logical to hypothesize more variance in outcome, with some families finding stronger benefits and others perhaps experiencing increased distress.

Our second question concerned the relation of family characteristics to the key outcome index of continued implementation at home. Although some authors include dropouts when considering treatment failures, we did not do so because the predictors of dropping out and completing but not implementing have been found to be different (Baker & Clark, 1987). The significant predictors of dropouts in this sample were single parent marital status, low marital adjustment, low income, low pretraining Behavioral Vignettes Test scores, and high F-COPES scores (Baker, 1989). As a consequence, the remaining range on these measures available for prediction to follow-up among program completers was restricted.

Mothers in families that were doing less productive teaching at follow-up were unemployed and perceived the family as low in adaptability before training. This is consistent with Dumas and Wahler's (1983) finding that unemployed mothers are more insular, less open to suggestions about changes in child-rearing methods, and therefore, less likely to implement programs at home. Our low follow-through families also entered training reporting more stress related to the child's disabilities. We cannot say from the present data whether this may in part reflect realistic handicaps that make the child more difficult to teach.

Perhaps most important, low follow-through families had entered training less positive about family life; they reported poorer marital adjustment and more dissatisfaction with their family's adaptability and cohesion. Other investigators have also found that marital status (single or intact) and/or the perceived quality of the marriage are critical variables in predicting family coping (Friedrich, 1979) and benefits of parent training (Webster-Stratton, 1985). Dadds, Schwartz, and Sanders (1987) reported that although standard parent training was sufficient for families with good marriages, it was only successful in families with poor marriages if accompanied by a separate behavioral communication skills training program directed toward enhanced marital adjustment. The present findings also suggest that the eventual success of parent training might be enhanced if programs also intervened to enhance marital satisfaction, or increase family adaptability, or decrease stress—areas that are predictive of poorer long-term outcome.

References

Allen, D. A., & Hudd, S. S. (1987). Are we professionalizing parents? Weighing the benefits and pitfalls. *Mental Retardation, 25,* 133–139.

Baker, B. L. (1980). Training parents as teachers of their developmentally disabled children. In S. Salzinger, J. Antrobus, & J. Glick (Eds.), *The ecosystem of the "sick" child* (pp. 201–216). New York: Academic Press.

Baker, B. L. (1984). Intervention in families with young severely handicapped children. In J. B. Blacher (Ed.), *Severely handicapped young children and their families: Research in review* (pp. 319–375). New York: Academic Press.

Baker, B. L. (1989). *Parent training and developmental disabilities.* Washington, DC: American Association on Mental Retardation.

Baker, B. L., & Brightman, R. P. (1984). Training parents of retarded children: Program specific outcomes. *Journal of Behavior Therapy and Experimental Psychiatry, 15,* 255–260.

Baker, B. L., & Clark, D. B. (1987). Intervention with parents of developmentally disabled children. In S. Landesman & P. M. Vietze (Eds.), *Living environments and mental retardation.* Washington, DC: American Association on Mental Deficiency.

Baker, B. L., & Heifetz, L. J. (1976). The Read Project: Teaching manuals for parents of retarded children. In T. D. Tjossem (Ed.), *Intervention strategies for high risk infants and young children.* Baltimore: University Park Press.

Baker, B. L., Heifetz, L. J., & Murphy, D. (1980). Behavioral training for parents of retarded children: One-year follow-up. *American Journal of Mental Deficiency, 85,* 31–38.

Beck, A. T., Ward, C., Mendelson, M. J., & Erbaugh, J. (1961). An inventory for measuring depression. *Archives of General Psychiatry, 4,* 53–63.

Benson, H. A, & Turnbull, A. P. (1986). Approaching families from an individualized perspective. In R. H. Horner, L. H. Meyer, & H. D. Fredericks (Eds.), *Education of learners with severe handicaps: Exemplary service strategies* (pp. 127–157). Baltimore: Brookes.

Blacher, J. (Ed.). (1984). *Severely handicapped children and their families: Research in review.* New York: Academic Press.

Breiner, J., & Beck, S. (1984). Parents as change agents in the management of their developmentally delayed children's noncompliant behaviors: A critical review. *Applied Research in Mental Retardation, 5,* 259–278.

Brightman, R. P., Baker, B. L., Clark, D. B., & Ambrose, S. A. (1982). Effectiveness of alternative parent training formats. *Journal of Behavior Therapy and Experimental Psychiatry, 13,* 113–117.

Buckley, S. (1981). Parents as partners—are we sometimes asking too much? *Early Childhood, 2,* 15–16.

Crnic, K. A., Friedrich, W. N., & Greenberg, M. T. (1983). Adaptation of families with mentally retarded children: A model of stress, coping, and family ecology. *American Journal of Mental Deficiency, 88,* 125–138.

Cummings, S. T. (1976). The impact of the child's deficiency on the father: A study of fathers of mentally retarded and of chronically ill children. *American Journal of Orthopsychiatry, 46,* 246–255.

Cummings, S. T., Bayley, H. C., & Rie, H. E. (1966). Effects of the child's deficiency on the mother: A study of mothers of mentally retarded, chronically ill, and neurotic children. *American Journal of Orthopsychiatry, 36,* 595–608.

Dadds, M. R., Schwartz, S., & Sanders, M. R. (1987). Marital discord and treatment outcome in behavioral treatment of child conduct disorders. *Journal of Consulting and Clinical Psychology,* Vol. 55, 396–403.

Dangel, R. A., & Polster, R. F. (1984). Winning: A systematic, empirical approach to parent training. In R. A. Dangel & R. F. Polster (Eds.), *Parent training: Foundations of research and practice* (pp. 162–201). New York: Guilford Press.

Dumas, J. E. (1986). Parental perception and treatment outcome in families of aggressive children: A causal model. *Behavior Therapy, 17,* 420–432.

Dumas, J. E., & Wahler, R. G. (1983). Predictors of treatment outcome in parent training: Mother insularity and socioeconomic disadvantage. *Behavioral Assessment, 5,* 301–313.

Featherstone, H. (1981). *A difference in the family.* New York: Basic Books.

Forehand, R., & McMahon, B. (1981). *Helping the noncompliant child: A clinician's guide to parent training.* New York: Guilford Press.

Forehand, R., Wells, K. C., & Griest, D. L. (1980). An examination of the social validity of a parent training program. *Behavior Therapy, 11,* 488–502.

Forrest, P., Holland, C., Daly, R., & Fellbaum, G. A. (1984). When parents become therapists: Their attitudes toward parenting three years later. *Canadian Journal of Community Mental health, 3,* 49–54.

Foster, M., Berger, M., & McLean, M. (1981). Rethinking a good idea: A reassessment of parent involvement. *Topics in Early Childhood Special Education, 1,* 55–56.

Friedrich, W. N. (1979). Predictors of the coping behavior of mothers of handicapped children. *Journal of Consulting and Clinical Psychology, 47,* 1140–1141.

Friedrich, W. N., Greenberg, M. T., & Crnic, K. (1983). A short-form of the Questionnaire on Resources and Stress. *American Journal of Mental Deficiency, 88,* 41–48.

Gallagher, J. J., Beckman, P., & Cross, A. H. (1983). Families of handicapped children: Sources of stress and its amelioration. *Exceptional Children, 50,* 10–19.

Griest, D. L., & Forehand, R. (1982). How can I get any parent training done with all these other problems going on?: The role of family variables in child behavior therapy. *Child and Family Behavior Therapy, 4,* 73–80.

Holroyd, J. (1974). The Questionnaire on Resources and Stress: An instrument to measure family response to a handicapped family member. *Journal of Community Psychology, 2,* 92–94.

Karoly, P., & Rosenthal, M. (1977). Training parents in behavior modification: Effects on perceptions of family interaction and deviant child behavior. *Behavior Therapy, 8,* 406–410.

Kashima, K. J., Baker, B. L., & Landen, S. J. (1988). Media-assisted versus professional led training for parents of mentally retarded children. *American Journal on Mental Retardation, 93,* 209–217.

Locke, H. J., & Wallace, K. M. (1959). Short marital-adjustment and prediction tests: Their reliability and validity. *Journal of Marriage and Family Living, 21,* 251–255.

Lyon, S., & Preis, A. (1983). Working with families of severely handicapped persons. In M. Seligman (Ed.), *The family with a handicapped child: Understanding and treatment* (pp. 203–232). New York: Grune & Stratton.

McConachie, H. (1986). *Parents and young mentally handicapped children: A review of research issues.* London: Croom Helm.

Olson, D. H., McCubbin, H. I., Barnes, H., Larsen, A., Muxen, M., & Wilson, M. (1982). *Family inventories: Inventories used in a national survey of families across the family life cycle.* St. Paul: University of Minnesota.

Omizo, M. M., Williams, R. E., & Omizo, S. A. (1986). The effects of participation in parent group sessions on child-rearing attitudes among parents of learning disabled children. *The Exceptional Child, 20,* 134–139.

Turnbull, A. P., & Turnbull, H. R. (1982). Parent involvement in the education of handicapped children: A critique. *Mental Retardation, 20,* 115–122.

Waisbren, S. E. (1980). Parents' reactions after the birth of a developmentally disabled child. *American Journal of Mental Deficiency, 84,* 345–351.

Webster-Stratton, C. (1985). Predictors of treatment outcome in parent training for conduct disordered children. *Behavior Therapy, 16,* 223–243.

Winton, P., & Turnbull, A. P. (1981). Parent involvement as viewed by parents of preschool handicapped children. *Topics in Early Childhood Special Education, 1,* 11–19.

Wolfensberger, W. (1970). Counseling the parents of the retarded. In A. A. Baumeister (Ed.), *Mental retardation: Appraisal, education, and rehabilitation* (pp. 329–400). Chicago: Aldine.

Zussman, J. U. (1978). Relationship of demographic factors to parental discipline techniques. *Developmental Psychology, 14,* 685–686.

This research was supported by Grant No. G008635232 from the National Institute of Disability and Rehabilitation Research to the senior author. This paper was completed while the senior author was a visiting Scholar at the May Institute (Chatham, MA). We gratefully acknowledge the contributions of our co-workers in the UCLA Project for Developmental Disabilities, especially Moi Wong. Requests for reprints should be sent to Bruce L. Baker, Department of Psychology, UCLA, Los Angeles, CA 90024–1563.

Authors

Bruce L. Baker, Sandra J. Landen, and **Kathleen J. Kashima,** University of California, Los Angeles.

Modification of Mother-Child Interaction Processes in Families With Children At-Risk for Mental Retardation

Mary A. Slater

1986

Abstract

An intervention study designed to investigate the effects of maternal behavior on children's cognitive and language functioning was conducted with 40 disadvantaged preschool children at risk for mental retardation and 20 control children. Intervention was based in part upon Sigel's distancing theory, with 20 mothers encouraged to increase inductive, responsive, and complex behavior and the other 20, only inductive and responsive behavior. Results indicated that both procedures were effective in increasing targeted maternal and child behavior; control measures remained stable over sessions. Posttest results suggested that training procedures significantly increased treated children's cognitive skills compared to the control children; the treated children who were encouraged to increase the complexity of behavior outperformed the others. Training generalized to the home environment. Implications of the results for early intervention were discussed.

Children from economically deprived environments with low-IQ mothers are at-risk for mental retardation (Heber, Dever, & Conry, 1968; Ramey & Smith, 1977), and as they become older, tend to show a progressive decline in IQ (Jensen, 1977; Ramey & Haskins, 1981). A number of static variables (e.g., mother's education, occupation of the head of household, and family income levels) are predictive of school success (Shipman, 1976), but what is unclear is why these static, molar variables are so predictive (Ramey, Sparling, & Wasik, 1981). This study was designed to determine whether specific aspects of maternal behavior may be related to cognitive development of children. Data were gathered to answer two basic questions. Can a low-IQ mother's behavior with her preschool child be modified? If so, do modifications varying in cognitive-distancing levels result in differential cognitive and language skills in the children?

Previous theoretical work and correlational and longitudinal studies have implicated maternal behavior as important to children's cognitive and language develop-

ment. Bruner (1973), for example, posited that children will only develop symbolic, as opposed to concrete, representation skills (skills allowing the child to go beyond the immediate situation to deal with concepts remote in time and space) through meaningful interactions with a significant other. He noted that children growing up in native villages of Senegal remain at a level of manipulation that is concrete and lacking in symbolic structures.

There is abundant correlational research suggesting that maternal behavior influences young children's cognitive development (e.g., Bee, Van Egeren, Streissguth, Nyman, & Leckie, 1969; Feshbach, 1973; Hess & Shipman, 1965; Schachter, 1979; White & Watts, 1973). These studies suggest that an optimum maternal behavior is characterized by asking the child questions, employing abstract language, emphasizing conceptual relationships in a categorical fashion, and encouraging the child to solve problems through responsiveness and positive feedback. In contrast, mothers of children functioning at a lower intellectual level display a process of interaction marked by: giving the child numerous commands; employing concrete language patterns; emphasizing conceptual relationships dependent on physical characteristics; discouraging, through negative feedback, the child's attempts to solve problems; and spending limited periods of verbal interaction with the child (e.g., Falendar & Heber, 1975; Snow et al., 1974; Wilton & Barbour, 1978; Wulbert, Inglis, Kriegsman, & Mills, 1975).

Sigel's (1970, 1971, 1972) distancing theory specifies more clearly the role that parents play. He delineated three levels of distancing strategies: Level I, low-distancing demands, requiring simple labeling; Level II, intermediate-distancing demands, requiring classification, identification of similarities/differences, sequencing, and enumeration; and Level III, High-distancing demands, requiring evaluation, inference of causal relations, and generalization. Telling and inquiry were denoted as two forms of distancing strategies, with inquiry encouraging more active responses. Sigel and his associates (e.g., McGillicuddy-DeLisi, Sigel, & Johnson, 1979) found that mothers who incorporated higher level distancing strategies into storytelling sessions had children who performed better overall on cognitive tasks.

Ramey and associates (e.g., Ramey, Bryant, Sparling, & Wasik, 1983) have attempted to modify mother–child behavior through an in-home parent-training program. Significant experimental–control differences were reported at 6 months of age (Ramey et al. 1981), but had disappeared by 3 years of age (Ramey et al., 1983). Slaughter (1983), focusing upon poverty mothers with children aged 18 to 44 months, found that in-home toy demonstration facilitated cognitive development, but a discussion intervention was more effective in enhancing the mother's interactive style with her child, as well as providing informal support.

The present study was designed as a short-term laboratory investigation focused upon identifying the effects of differential levels of maternal distancing behavior on young children's cognitive functioning. Age 4 was chosen because expanded language and abstract reasoning skills tend to emerge at this time (Bruner, 1973). The study was based upon the premise that low-IQ mothers employ a concrete, directive, nonresponsive form of interaction that serves to limit their children's cognitive functioning. More specifically, I hypothesized that mothers trained within a low-distancing mode of interaction would have children who showed increased language usage, but concrete usage primarily focused upon labeling presently occurring events. In contrast, those mothers trained within a high-distancing format would have children who employed increased language patterns marked as well by increased higher level concepts. On overall cognitive measures, the experimental children were expected to outperform those in the control group.

Method

Subjects

The subjects were 60, 4-year-old children and their mothers. All families were white, low-income, and lived in rural areas. They were selected on the basis of the following characteristics: (a) their earnings were $11,000 or less per year; (b) they had a history of educational problems and/or social service dependency; (c) they had a child between the ages of 36 and 72 months with no known physiological defects; and (d) the mother had limited verbal-intellectual ability, as measured by a scaled score of 6 or less on the vocabulary test of the Wechsler Adult Intelligence Scale (WAIS, Wechsler, 1955). There

were no significant differences between groups on pretest measures. All families attained a score of 11 or more on the High-Risk Index, a measure designed to identify families at-risk for mental retardation (Ramey & Smith, 1977). Sixty percent were referred after the child had failed to attain the local school district kindergarten-screening criterion score.

Sixty-two families were identified as meeting the basic project requirements. Two left the project during the pretesting phase: one mother moved from the project area; the other stated that she had too many family concerns. After pretesting interviews, triads of children and mothers were matched by maternal IQ, child's IQ (Stanford-Binet Intelligence Scale, Terman & Merrill, 1972) and child's age and sex and then randomly assigned to a control group or one of the two experimental groups. (There were no significant IQ or age differences among the children.) Twenty mothers and children were assigned to each group. Table 1 presents a summary listing of familial, maternal, and child characteristics for each group.

Treating matched triads as a random effect, a Model 3 analysis of variance (Neter, Wasserman, & Kutner, 1985) was conducted on the nonmatched family–child variables to test for similarity among groups. Nonsignificant differences existed on all measures.

Intervention Program Content

All families participated in a six-part intervention program: family-support social work services, field trips, storytelling, question, review training, and a toy-lending library service. Control families participated in all six components. In the review-training session, the control families were simply provided general positive feedback. The intervention program has been previously described (Slater, 1985). In brief, the program was designed to provide families with basic humanitarian services and a parent enhancement program varying in level of structure (semi-structured storytelling to structured question sessions) as well as new types of setting (real-life field-trip settings to more abstract settings such as the storytelling) in order to enhance generalization and transfer of learning. Although mothers were the primary focus of intervention, they were encouraged to share the training ideas with other family members. In fact, in a few families (n = 3), the maternal grandmothers were heavily involved because they assisted their daughters with child care.

Table 1 Characteristics of Families and Children

| Characteristic | Group | | | | | |
| | Low-distancing | | High-distancing | | Control | |
	Mean	SD	Mean	SD	Mean	SD
Family						
Mean maternal IQ	76.2	6.2	75.1	6.1	74.5	7.5
Mean maternal education[a]	10.8	1.5	9.9	1.6	10.1	1.7
Maternal special-education[b] involvement(%)	35.0		35.0		25.0	
Mean N children	2.6	1.2	2.8	1.5	2.6	1.6
Mean maternal age	29.4	5.6	27.4	5.4	30.4	6.3
Mean income (per year)	7,600.0	3,251.0	6,400.0	3,789.0	6,300.0	3,326.0
Mean High-Risk Index	18.4	8.4	21.9	7.3	22.7	8.9
Fathers present (%)	55.0		85.0		80.0	
Target child						
Mean IQ	86.3	15.6	82.5	10.8	82.9	11.8
Mean age (in months)	48.8	6.2	49.5	5.7	47.2	6.0

[a] Only grade level for those involved in regular-education classes were included.
[b] Involvement in some special-education programming (e.g., self-contained, resource room).

Procedure

Experimental situation. All storytelling, question, and training sessions were conducted in a mobile research laboratory (a Dodge motor home) furnished with video-tape equipment. All field trips were conducted in real-life settings.

Pretest

All mothers and children were pretested with the WAIS, the Stanford-Binet, the Verbal, Quantitative, and Memory subscales of the McCarthy Scales of Children's Abilities (McCarthy, 1972), and the Home Observation for Measurement of the Environment-Revised-Preschool Version (HOME, Bradley & Caldwell, 1979). The HOME was completed in the standardized fashion through a home-based interview.

Baseline

To provide a comparison for training, each dyad went on an initial field trip to a pet store and returned to the mobile lab. The mother was instructed to tell her child a story based on a picture with pets and to ask the list of written questions given to her. The list consisted of seven questions, one representing each of the following types: selective attention, categories of exclusion, imagery of future events, categorization, sustained sequential thinking, remembering, and critical evaluation (based in part on Blank, 1973; Blank & Solomon, 1968). Training followed the story-telling–question session.

Low-Level Distancing

The training encouraged this group of mothers to increase three behaviors: (a) asking questions, forming statements directed at asking, interrogating, or inquiring; (b) talking more, verbally informing, giving, offering information; and (c) talking with, expanding on what the child had previously said and/or expressing approval about what the child had done. Mothers were provided these rules verbally and pictorially. A self-analysis training procedure was employed in which the trainer and mother reviewed the previously video-taped session, with the trainer identifying maternal utterances that matched the rules. The trainer reinforced the mother for using these rules and assisted her in modifying remaining utterances to match the provided rules. Examples employed by the trainer were concrete, focusing on labeling specific items.

At the completion of the review session, the mother was asked to list the three rules (ask questions, talk more, and talk with), to use these rules at home and to attempt to encourage her child to talk as much as possible throughout the week. The trainer explained that the child was to be the director of these stories. The child should do most of the talking, and the mother was encouraged to think of questions that elicited "the longest sentences" from the child. The trainer suggested that other family members (father, siblings, grandparents) be asked to use a similar language pattern. Each mother was asked to report sample home dialogues at the next session.

Mothers in this group were given additional training for the question phase. They were encouraged to use a one-level prompt system: repetition, repeat (rephrase the question and wait for the child to respond). Training followed the same self-analysis procedure as the storytelling procedure.

High-Level Distancing

The trainer encouraged these mothers to increase the level of distancing strategies as well as the frequency of questions and responsiveness. They were encouraged to: (a) ask what and why questions that focused the child's attention on a major part of the picture; (b) talk more—label, describe (e.g., size, color, number, shape, taste), and identify functions and classes of items; (c) talk with (same as the low-distancing group); and (d) talk about "things in general" by noting the general function and classification of items (i.e., cars and trucks are used for traveling; apples and oranges are fruits). The same training procedure as summarized previously for the low-level distancing group was used.

High-distancing mothers were provided training in the question phase that encouraged a three-level prompt system: (a) repetition (same as low-distancing group); (b) orienting comments—highlight relevant parts of the picture (e.g., written question, "Who is the farmer?" orienting comment, "Which man do you think is the farmer?"); (c) focusing comments—suggestions about specific cues to the solution (e.g., written question, "What happened in the story?" focusing comment, "Weren't they building something?"). Mothers were informed that the use of orienting and focusing strategies would give children clues to the correct answer while at the same time modeling a problem-solving strategy. This prompt system was based in part on Bee et al.'s (1969) specificity scale and Blank's (1973) simplification procedures.

Control. As each control mother viewed her videotape the trainer commented that the mother and child were doing fine and that the mother should continue with the same type of story–question session during the next week.

Intervention–Retention

Mothers and children from all three groups accompanied the staff on five weekly field trips (farm market, hospital, farm, circus, and toy store) and then completed a story about a corresponding picture, a question session, and a training session.

At the completion of the sixth training session, three staff members readministered the Verbal, Quantitative, and Memory subscales of the McCarthy and the HOME. These staff members had not been trainers and were unaware of group assignment. One month after the last teaching session, each dyad was taken on the seventh trip (zoo). Following the trip, the mother was asked to tell her child a story about a corresponding picture.

Data Collected, Maintained, and Coded

All visits were tape-recorded and all story and question sessions video-taped. All story–visit sessions were transcribed in standard orthography from audio tapes dubbed from the video tapes. Utterances were segmented primarily by apparent terminal intonation context. A second observer evaluated all transcripts for accuracy. Discrepancies were noted and resolved. Maternal and child measures were collected[1] from the story and question session.

The rating scale, modeled after Caldwell's (1969) computer compatible APPROACH coding system, translated each story–visit utterance into a numerical code consisting of subject/predicate units. The scale consisted of six subject/predicate behavior units: declaratives, interrogatives, descriptive concepts, categorical concepts, abstractions, and positive/negative reinforcement.[1] Two measures of language complexity were calculated: mean length of utterance (Brown, 1973) and number of unique vocabulary items.

Responses during the question phase were scored separately for mother and child. Maternal comments were coded on a 4-point specificity scale: Level 1, repetition; Level 2, orienting; Level 3, focusing; and Level 4, details (providing the answer/solution). Children's responses were coded as a frequency of correct responses, with pointing and simple identification receiving a one-point designation and delineation of a reason/rationale for the choice as a two-point response.

Table 2 Summary of Planned Comparisons Between Groups During Story Sessions

| Variable | Training (Session 6) | | | | | | |
| | Low-distancing | | High-distancing | | Control[a] | | |
	Mean	SD	Mean	SD	Mean	SD	F
Mother–child							
Total Verbal Utterances	190.8	76.0	285.4	89.5	68.7	60.3	8.14***
Mother							
Form (frequency)							
Declaratives	49.1	20.7	62.4	32.1	22.8	18.8	4.62***
Interrogatives	58.7	26.8	108.4	56.1	19.9	8.6	5.88***
Higher order concepts (rate)							
Descriptive	2.2	1.5	3.1	1.2	2.7	2.8	.65[b]
Categorical	1.5	1.9	4.6	1.8	1.5	1.6	6.03***
Abstract	1.3	1.5	4.4	1.8	.8	1.6	6.16***
Total	5.0	7.3	12.1	3.8	4.9	4.5	2.82**
Feedback (rate)							
Positive	5.7	2.8	5.8	3.8	2.3	2.9	2.83**
Child							
Form (Frequency)							
Declaratives	67.6	25.9	100.7	28.6	23.7	24.6	7.28***
Interrogatives	11.9	6.0	10.6	4.7	1.5	1.0	2.09*
Higher order concepts (rate)							
Descriptive	1.2	.9	1.8	1.2	.4	.2	.75[c]
Categorical	1.5	1.2	2.3	1.1	.3	.5	1.95*
Abstract	1.3	1.3	2.3	1.2	.1	.3	9.27***
Total	3.1	3.1	6.3	2.7	.8	.8	3.00***
Feedback (rate)							
Positive	8.2	4.3	7.5	5.3	2.6	2.6	8.02***
Complexity							
Mean length of utterance	3.5	1.1	3.6	.6	2.5	.9	2.71*
Vocabulary	53.9	19.6	79.3	19.1	16.4	17.1	10.43***

Note. F values were derived by analyzing data from all seven sessions.
[a]Wilks' Lambda F statistic is reported (based upon discussion in Stevens, 1979).
[b]Wilks' Lambda for time effect was significant, $F (6, 48) = 4.17$, $p < .0001$.
[c]Wilks' Lambda for time effect was significant, $F (6, 48) = 6.01$, $p < .0001$.
* $p < .05$.
** $p < .01$.
*** $p < .001$.

Coding was conducted by 10 trained observers, with interrater reliability averaging 97% for all raters across all measures. Reliability checks were conducted every tenth session. Rate measures were calculated for higher order concepts and feedback measures to decrease the effects of time.

Analysis

To determine treatment effects, I conducted multivariate repeated-measures analyses on one dependent variable across time in a 3 (groups) x 7 (sessions) design for mother and child data separately. Because a matching method was employed to place subjects within groups, I used the REPEATED option of PROC GLM (SAS,

Figure 1 Maternal mean rate of higher level concept-oriented utterances

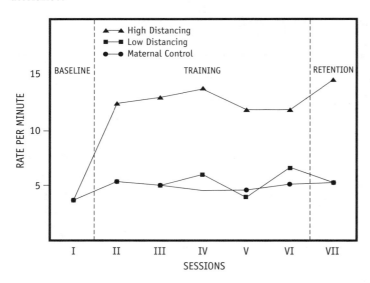

Figure 2 Child mean rate of higher level concept-oriented utterances

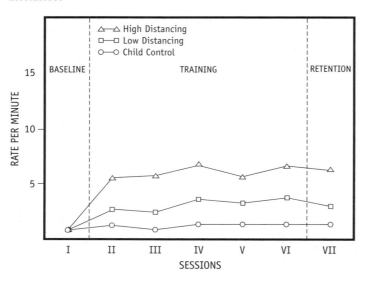

1985). This regression program performs multivariate general linear modeling that tests for subjects' measures to increase over time. Formally, this is called a "test for treatment time interaction yielding an *F* approximation." The Treatment x Time *F* approximations are reported in the *Results*, unless otherwise noted. Posttest data were analyzed with an analysis of covariance, with treatment group as the independent variable and pretest score as the covariate (SAS, 1985).

Results

Story Phase

A summary of the results for form, higher order concepts, feedback, and complexity measures is presented in Table 2. Although data from all seven sessions were analyzed in the multivariate repeated-measures analysis, descriptive statistics are presented for only the final training session.

Dyads in both experimental groups began emitting longer stories during the training sessions, as indicated by a significantly greater frequency of maternal and child declaratives and interrogatives, than did the control dyads. Differences between experimental groups were also found. Mothers in the high-level distancing group emitted a significantly greater frequency of interrogatives, $F(6, 30) = 2.89$, $p < .05$, and the children emitted a significantly greater frequency of declaratives, $F(6, 30) = 2.71$, $p < .05$, than did those in the low-distancing group. Higher level concepts (descriptive, categorical, and abstract) were noted by the high-distancing dyads significantly more often than by dyads in the other groups. Differences between the two experimental groups also were significant (mothers: $F(6, 30) = 4.42$, $p < .01$; children: $F(6, 30) = 2.26$, $p < .05$). Figures 1 and 2 graphically illustrate the differences in the rate of higher order concept usage for mothers and children separately across time.

During training and retention sessions, experimental dyads emitted approximately four times the rate of positive, responsive comments as did the control dyads. Across treatment sessions children in both experimental groups emitted more complex utterances than did those in the control group. Nonsignificant differences were noted on negative feedback measures. Children in the high-level program significantly outperformed those in the low-level group on vocabulary measures, $F(6, 33) = 2.91$, $p < .05$, but not MLU.

Retention. The majority of the measures remained at the same level as in the training period, with a number of the measures slightly increasing. Only the rate of higher order concepts and positive feedback measures decreased slightly for both experimental groups of children.

Table 3 Summary of Planned Comparisons in Question Phase Between Mothers on Specificity Scale Measures and Children on Correct Responses

| Variable | Training (Session 6) | | | | | | |
| | Low-distancing | | High-distancing | | Control[a] | | |
	Mean	SD	Mean	SD	Mean	SD	F
Mothers: Specificity scale							
Repetition	36.8	17.4	13.9	9.7	11.7	4.9	4.66***
Orienting	1.3	1.7	13.9	10.3	.8	.9	6.87***
Focusing	8.7	5.8	13.8	8.9	2.4	2.9	3.52**
Details	6.5	5.6	3.7	3.7	2.9	2.4	2.32*
Children: Correct responses							
Selective attention	1.9	.1	2.7	1.6	1.0	1.4	8.44***
Categories of exclusion	2.2	2.1	5.2	4.0	.5	.8	10.27***
Imagery of future events	1.9	1.1	2.1	.9	.9	.9	11.32***
Categorization	2.4	2.6	12.1	6.2	.3	.6	14.19***
Sequencing	1.6	1.1	1.9	.8	.9	1.0	8.94***
Memory	5.6	3.8	7.7	5.1	2.1	2.0	3.67*
Evaluating critically	.7	.9	2.8	3.2	.2	.4	9.68***
Total	16.1	6.9	34.4	15.5	5.8	4.3	8.01***

* $p < .05.$
** $p < .01.$
*** $p < .001.$

Question Phase

The question phase immediately followed the story phase of each session. Separate measures were derived for mother and child. Specificity scale measures on maternal behavior during the last training session are summarized in Table 3. Nonsignificant differences were noted on the four measures of specificity between groups during Session 1, baseline. Mothers in all groups emitted comparable responses. They repeated most of the questions once, then usually moved to the next question, infrequently giving the child the answer.

Across training sessions significant differences were noted. Low-level distancing mothers emitted a significantly greater frequency of repetitive and detail-related comments than did mothers in either of the other groups. In contrast, mothers in the high-level distancing group emitted significantly greater frequencies of orienting and focusing comments.

Significant differences were obtained between the two experimental groups of mothers. On orienting and focusing comments, differences favored those in the high-level distancing group (orienting: $F(6, 30) = 12.27, p < .001$; focusing: $F(6, 30) = 12.01, p < .0001$). Low-distancing mothers, however, outperformed the high-distancing group on frequency of repetitive and detail-related comments (repetition: $F(6, 30) = 5.20, p < .0001$; detail: $F(6, 30) = 4.90, p < .001$).

Descriptive statistics and F values of children's correct responses on each of the seven separate questions as well as total correct responses emitted during the last training session are also presented in Table 3. Nonsignificant differences were obtained among the children's responses by group during Session 1, baseline. A comparison by group during training and retention phases indicated significant treatment effects favoring experimental children on total number of correct responses as well as number of correct responses on individual questions.

Differential treatment analyses comparing training and retention performance of the two experimental groups indicated that those participating in the high-distancing group made significantly more total correct responses, $F(6, 30) = 7.12, p < .0001$, than did the low-distancing children. An inspection of the analyses by individual question revealed that these differences were most pronounced on items concerning categorization

Modification of Mother-Child Interaction Processes in Families

skills (categories of exclusion and categorization) and critical evaluation.

Retention. During retention no significant differences were noted on any measure compared to the sixth and last training session.

Visit Phase: A Generalization Measure

Data obtained during the visit sessions complemented the story data (See Table 4). Dyads in both experimental groups began emitting significantly more verbal utterances that did the control dyads during training and retention sessions. Experimental dyads outperformed

controls on number of declarative statements emitted. Interrogative data indicated, however, that only experimental mothers significantly outperformed control mothers. Experimental children emitted approximately twice the number of interrogatives as compared to control children, but these differences did not reach significance. No significant differences were noted between experimental dyads on declarative or interrogative measures.

Dyads in the high-distancing group significantly outperformed those in the other groups on all measures of higher order concepts. Positive, responsive feedback measures indicated that there was a significant differ-

Table 4 Summary of Planned Comparisons Between Groups During Visit Sessions

| | Training (Session 6) | | | | | | |
| | Low-distancing | | High-distancing | | Control[a] | | |
Variable	Mean	SD	Mean	SD	Mean	SD	F
Mother–Child							
Total verbal utterances	252.9	101.2	279.6	120.6	130.0	79.7	11.59**
Mother							
Form (frequency)							
Declaratives	88.0	38.0	72.4	50.4	42.4	18.2	9.53**
Interrogatives	63.0	39.0	77.3	40.3	30.3	20.5	5.58**
Higher order concepts (rate)							
Descriptive	2.0	2.6	4.9	3.1	2.2	.9	10.10**
Categorical	1.0	1.6	3.4	1.7	.7	.3	12.99**
Abstract	.8	1.8	3.3	1.9	.5	.4	11.45**
Total	3.7	4.3	11.5	6.0	3.2	2.2	13.70**
Feedback (rate)							
Positive	6.0	3.9	5.0	4.2	2.3	1.9	4.43**
Child							
Form (frequency)							
Declaratives	98.4	33.1	94.6	48.1	47.8	25.3	9.51**
Interrogatives	20.2	22.3	16.2	15.3	9.5	6.3	1.52
Higher order concepts (rate)							
Descriptive	1.7	1.2	2.2	2.3	1.2	.9	4.16*
Categorical	.9	.6	.9	1.4	.3	.3	5.40**
Abstract	.9	.9	1.9	1.2	.3	.4	4.84*
Total	3.7	2.4	6.6	3.7	1.8	1.4	5.60**
Feedback (rate)							
Positive	5.6	3.6	5.7	2.9	2.2	1.7	4.94**

[a] F values were derived by analyzing data from Sessions 1, 6, and 7. Wilks' Lambda F statistic is reported (based upon discussion in Stevens, 1979).
  * $p < .01$.
  ** $p < .001$.

ence between the experimental and control groups. No significant differences were found between the two experimental groups of mothers on the positive, responsiveness measure.

Retention. The majority of the measures remained at the same level as during treatment. Higher order concept rate measures for the high-distancing mothers increased slightly from Sessions 6 to 7.

Pre–Post Data

The analyses of the pretest responses on the HOME and the McCarthy scales indicated no significant differences among groups. Experimental groups showed significant differences on posttest measures as compared to the control group. Environments of both experimental groups differed significantly on total HOME scores as compared to the control group, $F(2, 57) = 120.81$, $p < .0001$. Significant treatment effects were obtained between the two experimental groups on total HOME scores, $F(1, 38) = 2.23$, $p < .001$, and on four subscales (Subscale I, "Stimulation Through Toys, Games and Materials; Subscale II, Language Stimulation; Subscale V, Stimulation of Academic Behavior; Subscale VI, Physical Punishment). These differences favored families in the high-distancing group.

Children in both experimental groups obtained significantly higher scores on the three subscales of the McCarthy than did the control children. Table 5 contains the descriptive statistics and analyses of covariate F ratios for differences on the three scale indices. Non-

significant differences between experimental groups were obtained at the subscale level. To identify more precisely the pattern of differences between the three groups, I analyzed scores from 10 or 11 tests derivable from the McCarthy using an analysis of covariance (Numerical Memory 2 was omitted because no child in this sample earned any credit on it). Covariate F comparisons (dfs = 2, 54) indicated significant group differences on Pictorial Memory I, $F = 6.51$, $p < .01$, Verbal Fluency, $F = 9.81$, $p < .01$, and Opposite Analogies, $F = 11.56$, $p < .001$. Covariate F comparisons (dfs = 1, 38) between the two experimental groups indicated that the higher level children significantly outperformed those in the low-level group on Number Questions, $F = 8.5$, $p < .01$, and Opposite Analogies, $F = 7.0$, p < .01.

Discussion

The data support the basic premise of this study: The style of interaction of low-IQ mothers significantly affects their children's language and cognitive functioning. High-level distancing training led to significant increases in the amount and cognitive level of maternal and child functioning within semi-structured storytelling sessions, structured question sessions, and generalized to real-life experiences. In contrast, training procedures that encouraged a low-level distancing style led to significant increases only in the amount of maternal and child language/cognitive patterns, not the level of concept usage. The HOME data indicated that both training procedures

Table 5 Means and SDs and Univariate F Ratios for Group Differences on Scale Indices of the McCarthy

Variable	Low-distancing		High-distancing		Control[a]		F[a]
	Mean	SD	Mean	SD	Mean	SD	
Pretest							
Verbal	40.8	6.8	39.7	5.5	39.1	7.2	.69
Quantitative	37.9	7.9	36.9	6.7	35.6	6.9	.55
Memory	37.3	5.5	38.6	5.3	36.3	5.9	.28
Posttest							
Verbal	46.1	7.7	48.6	4.9	39.1	4.5	10.37**
Quantitative	37.5	8.8	40.9	5.8	34.2	5.6	3.03*
Memory	43.6	6.2	43.6	4.1	37.2	5.6	10.00***

[a] $dfs = 2, 54$.
 * $p < .05$.
 ** $p < .01$.
 *** $p < .001$.

enhanced the low-IQ mothers' responsiveness language styles but that only the higher level training program encouraged the mothers to stimulate their preschool children's academic behavior.

Similarly, scaled scores on the McCarthy tasks suggested that the high-level program was more successful than was the lower level program in enhancing a child's complex cognitive skills. These data provide support for Sigel's (1970, 1971, 1972) distancing theory, suggesting that maternal interactional styles characterized by demands for classification, enumeration, and similarities/ differences may assist the child in developing higher order cognitive skills. It appears that mothers with limited intelligence may profit from short-term intensive training experiences. Furthermore, these data suggest that the amount as well as level of distancing strategies employed with young children may significantly impact on cognitive functioning. Training mothers to employ a responsive style with their young children may only be an initial step, with level of demand characteristics being a significant defining characteristics for cognitive functioning.

The training procedure itself—guided self-analysis coupled with the provision of simple rules—also appears to be effective in training low-IQ mothers. The rules provided structured directives to mothers regarding how they should interact with their children. Through the video-taped feedback sessions, the mothers became critical observers of their own behavior, seeing the effect that different types of questions, statements, and feedback had on their children's behavior. In addition, the guided self-analysis procedure led to rapid increases in targeted maternal behaviors, suggesting that the program focused upon enhancement, not initial development of skills. All the mothers in this study emitted examples of one or more of the rules spontaneously during the baseline session (e.g., labeled an item, expanded one of the child's comments, asked one question). Thus, the task of the trainer took on two major emphases: encouraging use of previously emitted behaviors and encouraging increased distancing level of previously emitted comments. No behaviors foreign to the mothers' behavioral repertoires were introduced or expected.

Employment of this simplified maternal training program resulted in an additional benefit. As the mothers became proficient in developing a high rate of responses that matched the rules and as they observed the concomitant positive effects on child behavior, their self-

confidence increased. During baseline many mothers noted that they should not be telling the stories to their children; rather, they requested that it be done by the trainer. By the third training session, however, not one experimental mother made this request. On the contrary, mothers made comments such as, "I asked Amy what she saw in the picture, and she talked for 3 minutes." Raven (1980) previously mentioned this same concern by noting that low-income mothers who were visited by a "toy demonstrator" similar to Levenstein's parent trainees became dependent on this individual and appeared to develop reduced self-confidence as mothers.

This study was only a beginning effort to identify some of the elements within the mother–child interaction process that may influence young children's cognitive functioning. Although no longitudinal conclusions can be drawn as to the effects of these interventions without follow-up data, the data do suggest that low-IQ mothers and their preschool children may benefit from parent enhancement programs, particularly programs that increase the concept level as well as the inductive and responsive elements of the interaction. Future longitudinal research is required to determine whether low-IQ mothers involved in a long-term intervention (e.g., 1 to 2 years) will develop styles of interaction that enhance their young children's cognitive and academic abilities during the preschool and elementary school years.

Note

[1]Coding schemes are available from the author upon request.

References

Bee, H. L., Van Egeren, L. F., Streissguth, A. P., Nyman, B. A., & Leckie, M. J. (1969). Social class differences in maternal teaching strategies and speech patterns. *Developmental Psychology, 1,* 726–734.

Blank, M. (1973). Teaching learning in the preschool: A dialogue approach. Columbus, OH: Merrill.

Bradley, R. H., & Caldwell, B. M. (1979). Home Observation for Measurement of the Environment: A revision of the preschool scale. *American Journal of Mental Deficiency, 84,* 235–244.

Brown, R. (1973). *A first language, the early stages.* Cambridge: Harvard University Press.

Bruner, J. S. (1973). *On knowing: Essay for the left hand.* New York: Atheneum.

Caldwell, B. M. (1969). A new APPROACH to behavioral ecology. In J. P. Hill (Ed.), *Minnesota symposia on child psychology* (Vol. 2, pp. 74–109). Minneapolis: University of Minnesota Press.

Falendar, C., & Heber, R. (1975). Mother-child interaction and participation in a longitudinal intervention program. *Developmental Psychology, 11,* 830–836.

Feshbach, N. D. (1973). Cross-cultural studies of teaching styles in four-year-olds and their mothers. In A. D. Pick (Ed.), *Minnesota symposia on child psychology* (Vol. 7, pp. 87–116). Minneapolis: University of Minnesota Press.

Heber, F. R., Dever, R. B., & Conry, J. (1968). The influence of environmental and genetic variables on intellectual development. In H. J. Prehm, L. A. Hamerlynck, & J. R. Crosson (Eds.), *Behavioral research in mental retardation* (pp. 1–22). Eugene: University of Oregon.

Hess, R. D., & Shipman, V. C. (1965). Early education and the socialization of cognitive modes on children. *Child Development, 36,* 869–886.

Jensen, A. R. (1977). Cumulative deficit in IQ of blacks in the rural school. *Developmental Psychology, 13,* 184–197.

McCarthy, D. (1972). *McCarthy Scales of Children's Abilities.* New York: Psychological Corp.

McGillicuddy–DeLisi, A. V., Sigel, I. E., & Johnson, J. E. (1979). The family as a system of mutual influences: Parental beliefs, distancing behaviors and children's representational thinking. In M. Lewis & L. A. Rosenblum (Eds.), *The child and its family* (pp. 91–106). New York: Plenum.

Neter, J., Wasserman, W., & Kutner, M. H. (1985). *Applied linear statistical models* (2nd ed.). Homewood, IL: Irwin.

Ramey, C. T., Bryant, D., Sparling, J. J., & Wasik, B. H. (1983). Educational interventions to enhance intellectual development: Comprehensive daycare vs. family education. In S. Harel & N. J. Anastasiow (Eds.), *The at-risk infant: Psycho-social-medical aspects* (pp. 75–85). Baltimore: Brookes.

Ramey, C. T., & Haskins, R. (1981). The causes and treatment of school failure: Insights from the Carolina Abecedarian Project. In M. Begab (Ed.), *Psychological influences and retarded performance: Strategies for improving social competence* (Vol. 2, pp. 89–112). Baltimore: University Park Press.

Ramey, C. T., & Smith, B. J. (1977). Assessing the intellectual consequences of early intervention with high-risk infants. *American Journal of Mental Deficiency, 81,* 318–423.

Ramey, C. T., Sparling, J. J., & Wasik, B. (1981). Creating social environments to facilitate language development: An early education approach. In R. Schiefelbusch & D. Bricker (Eds.), *Early language intervention* (pp. 447–476). Baltimore: University Park Press.

Raven, J. (1980). *Parents, teachers and children.* Edinburgh: The Scottish Council for Research in Education.

SAS user's guide: Statistics (Version 5 ed.). (1985). Gary, NC: SAS Institute.

Schachter, F. F. (1979). *Everyday mother talk to toddlers: Early intervention.* New York: Academic.

Shipman, V. C. (1976). *Disadvantaged children and their first school experiences.* Princeton, NJ: Educational Testing Service.

Sigel, I. E. (1970). The distancing hypothesis: A causal hypothesis for the acquisition of representational thought. In M. R. Jones (Ed.), *Miami symposium on the prediction of behavior: Effects of early experience* (pp. 99–108). Coral Gables, FL: University of Miami Press.

Sigel, I. E. (1971). Language of the disadvantaged: The distancing hypothesis. In C. S. Lavatelli (Ed.), *Language training in early childhood education* (pp. 60–76). Urbana: University of Illinois Press.

Sigel, I. E. (1972). The distancing hypotheses revisited: An elaboration of a neo-Piagetian view of the development of representational thought. In M. E. Meyer (Ed.), *Cognitive learning* (pp. 33–46). Bellingham: Western Washington State College Press.

Snow, C. E., Arlman-Rupp, A., Hassing, Y., Jobse, J., Joosten, J., & Vorster, J. (1974). *Mothers' speech in three social classes.* Unpublished manuscript, University of Amsterdam Institute for General Linguistics.

Stevens, J. (1979). Comment on Olson: Choosing a test statistic in multivariate analysis of variance. *Psychology Bulletin, 86,* 355–360.

Terman, L. M., & Merrill, M. A. (1972). *Stanford-Binet Intelligence Scale.* Boston: Houghton-Mifflin.

Wechsler, D. (1955). *Wechsler Adult Intelligence Scale.* New York: Psychological Corp.

White, B. L., & Watts, J. C. (1973). *Experience and environment* (Vol. 1). Englewood Cliffs, NJ: Prentice-Hall.

Wilton, K., & Barbour, A. (1978). Mother-child interaction in high-risk and contrast preschoolers of low socioeconomic status. *Child Development, 49*, 1136–1145.

Wulbert, M., Inglis, S., Kriegsman, E., & Mills, B. (1975). Language delay and associated mother-child interactions. *Developmental Psychology, 11*, 61–70.

This research was supported in part by Grant No. 16-P-56811-5-15, Rt-11, from the National Institute of Handicapped Research, Department of Education, and Grant No. G00-7800012 from the Office of Special Education and Rehabilitative Services. The author expresses her sincere appreciation to a number of individuals who gave most freely of their time and expertise: F. Rick Heber, William I. Gardner, Howard L. Garber, Jon F. Miller, and James McCarthy. Special thanks go to John Sawyer for his assistance in statistical analysis. In addition, the author extends appreciation to all the families who gave most generously of their time and effort. The author is now affiliated with Texas Tech University. Requests for reprints should be sent to Mary A. Slater, Department of Pediatrics, Texas Tech University Health Sciences Center, 1400 Wallace Blvd., Amarillo, TX 79106.

Author

Mary A. Slater, University of Wisconsin-Madison.

Group Cognitive–Behavioral Treatment for Excessive Parental Self-Blame and Guilt

Charles D. Nixon and George H. S. Singer
1993

Abstract

The effect of a short-term group intervention to reduce self-blame and guilt in parents of children with severe disabilities was examined. Thirty-four mothers were randomly assigned to treatment and waiting list control groups. They participated in classes led by a counselor on topics relating to cognitive processes associated with guilt and self-blame. Results showed significant reductions in measures of guilt, negative automatic thoughts, internal negative attributions, and depression. Theoretical and treatment literature concerning self-blame and guilt was briefly reviewed and the derivative treatment was described.

Parenting a child with severe developmental disabilities poses a number of extraordinary challenges and opportunities. Many parents and siblings are able to maintain normal or better morale and to eventually view their family member with developmental disabilities as a positive contributor to the family's quality of life. Summers, Behr, and Turnbull (1989) have suggested that many parents attain a sense of mastery, meaning, and enhanced self-esteem from their experiences.

However, an important number of parents experience excessive self-blame and guilt (Blacher, 1984; DeLuca & Salerno, 1984; LaBorde & Seligman, 1983). Parents feel guilty and responsible for the child's handicap even when they are clearly not at fault (Featherstone, 1980; LaBorde & Seligman, 1983). Singer, Irvin, Hawkins, and Cooley (1987) found a prevalence of self-blaming responses in the diaries of parents of children with disabilities. Bristol and Schopler (1984) found that one third of parents attributed their child's disability to inadequate parenting or punishment for past behaviors. Breslau and Davis (1986) reported that depressed mothers of children with a disability experienced significantly more guilt than did depressed mothers of children without disabilities.

As with the general population, guilt and self-blame in parents of children with disabilities are associated with depression, helplessness, and hopelessness (Meyerson, 1983) and low self-esteem (Featherstone, 1980). Guilt and self-blame experienced by parents of children with handicaps are also believed to interfere with parental attachment to their child (Kaiser & Hayden, 1984), effective parenting (Crocker & Crocker, 1970; LaBorde & Seligman, 1983), a healthy family system (Meyerson, 1983), a healthy sexual relationship between the parents (Kivowitz, 1977), and the ability of the parents to take care of their own needs (Meyerson, 1983). The prevalent recommendation in the literature is that parents of children with handicaps work through and reduce their self-blame and guilt (Blacher, 1984; LaBorde & Seligman, 1983; Meyerson, 1983). The present study was designed to develop and evaluate the effectiveness of an intervention to reduce excessive self-blaming attributions and guilt feelings experienced by parents of children with severe disabilities.

In the last decade, most of the research on self-blame has been related to attribution theory. Since the reformulation of Seligman's (1975) learned helplessness theory of human depression into an attributional framework by Abramson, Seligman, and Teasdale (1978), attribution theory has associated self-blame with internal attributions of causality for negative events. Only two outcome studies were found using self-blame as a dependent measure, and both of these attributional treatments were not successful in changing self-blaming attributions (Sober-Ain & Kidd, 1984; Ickes & Layden, 1978). However, there were two important components missing from these approaches. First, these unsuccessful interventions were instructional only and did not attempt to change the cognitive distortions that reinforce the self-blaming attributions. Second, in both studies the investigators employed individual treatments and could not use a group treatment effect such as social comparison, which is thought to be effective in externalizing and reducing self-blame (Lerner & Miller, 1978). Cognitive restructuring and social comparison were the central components of the intervention used in the present study.

The method of cognitive restructuring we used was cognitive therapy, which conceptualizes automatic thoughts, cognitive distortions, and negative schemas as the sources of self-blaming attributions (Beck, Rush, Shaw, & Emery, 1979). Automatic thoughts or images are out of awareness and are appraisals of specific situations, which are negative, reflexive, involuntary, and irrational. For example, when a negative event occurs related to their child with a disability, the automatic thought of a parent could be "I'm a bad parent." Cognitive distortions involve the thinking process by which a person comes to that particular appraisal. Holon and Beck (1979) have identified six cognitive distortions: personalization, polarized thinking, arbitrary inference, overgeneralization, selective abstraction, and magnification. Burns (1980) identified 10 cognitive distortions and called *personalization* the originator of self-blame and guilt. The belief of many parents that they are 100% responsible for their child's development is a form of personalization, for the parent must take responsibility and blame themselves for any lack of development. Finally, schemas consist of stable patterns of cognitions that can affect a broad range of cognitive judgments. Parenthood schemas often contain impossible goals that can set parents up for failure and self-blame. For example, the schema of "parenthood" can consist of an array of cognitive distortions such as parents should *always* be patient, kind, loving, nurturing, and perfect.

Cognitive therapy describes specific cognitive strategies and techniques that are used in cognitive restructuring (Beck et al., 1979; Burns, 1980). Cognitive distortions and automatic thoughts are first brought into awareness by daily monitoring, and then they are challenged using a variety of strategies. Reality testing challenges distorted cognitions by asking the question: What evidence does the client have to support their belief that they are to blame? Automatic thoughts and cognitive distortions are also challenged by demonstrating that they lead to feelings of self-blame, guilt, and depression. Burns noted that *should* statements are particularly guilt producing and need to be challenged using *should* removal techniques. Reattribution consists of helping clients accept part but not all of the responsibility for negative events. Schemas are changed by challenging the underlying cognitive distortions that make up the schemas. Another way to change schemas is to use a technique

called "alternative conceptualizations" (Beck et al., 1979), which involves helping the client reinterpret and restructure a schema such as parenthood so that the goals of parenthood are more realistic and not perfectionistic and unattainable.

Proponents of cognitive therapy (Beck et al., 1979) and attribution theory (Abramson et al., 1978) understand self-blame as related to internal attributions of negative events. Wortman (1976) reviewed the research in which investigators found that causal ambiguity is so aversive that people are willing to self-blame in order to avoid it. For parents the cause of their child's disability is often ambiguous, and the desire to know the cause leads parents to make extensive causal searches that can lead to self-blaming attributions (LaBorde & Seligman, 1983; Tennen, Affleck, & Gershman, 1986). According to attribution theory, ambiguity is so aversive because people need to explain and understand the changing events of their lives in order to perceive their world as predictable and controllable (Heider, 1958). Wortman (1976) has suggested that self-blame is an "explanation" that gives people some perceived control over the future occurrence of a negative event ("I did it, but I won't let it happen again in the future"). Self-blame may be more tolerable than concluding that no one knows who is to blame (ambiguity) and that the world is a chaotic place where negative events occur at random.

When parents are first faced with the reality of their child's disability, they do not feel in control of their world. Blaming themselves in order to maintain a sense of perceived control may explain why parents of children with disabilities irrationally blame themselves. However, there are more adaptive ways of increasing perceived control. Rothbaum, Weisz, and Snyder (1982) distinguished primary control over the environment from secondary control, which involves changing our thoughts and feelings about a nonmodifiable environment. Interpretive control is one kind of secondary control, and it is very similar to cognitive restructuring. Cognitive restructuring provides parents of children with disabilities with a more adaptive way of maintaining their sense of perceived control and eliminates the need to blame themselves in order to maintain a sense that the world is controllable and predictable.

In the most successful attempts at changing attributions, researchers have used social comparison. Attribution therapy was used to successfully help a woman alleviate her fears (Kopel & Arkowitz, 1975) and college freshmen perform better (Wilson & Linville, 1982) by having them compare themselves to "normal" people in similar situations. According to Lerner and Miller (1978), social comparison is effective at reducing self-blame: "The most effective way of externalizing blame is not to say you didn't intend to do it (you still caused it) but to compare yourself with others and conclude that is what any reasonable person would have done" (pp. 1039). Thoits (1986) proposed that social comparison and social support from people who have gone through a similar experience can validate feelings as "normal," thereby reducing self-blame. Coates and Winston (1983) proposed that one of the major therapeutic components of peer support groups is the validation and normalization of feelings.

Our hypothesis in the present study was that a group treatment emphasizing cognitive restructuring and social comparison would reduce self-blaming attributions and guilt feelings in parents of children with severe disabilities.

Method

One of our purposes in this study was to extend the research of Singer, Irvin, and Hawkins (1988) at the Oregon Research Institute. This research team has used behavioral and cognitive techniques to help parents of children with severe disabilities reduce their self-reported stress. The present study was an expansion of the "cognitive" component of their research into the area of self-blame and guilt in parents of children with disabilities.

Subjects and Procedure

The subjects were parents of children with severe developmental disabilities. The mean age of the children was 9.3 years. They attended public school programs for students with severe disabilities, and they all experienced intellectual deficits ranging from moderate to profound mental retardation. Most children had other disabling conditions, including autism, cerebral palsy, epilepsy, and sensory deficits.

The parents were recruited through the schools in three counties in a large metropolitan area. The administrators of special education programs in most of the school districts agreed to send flyers inviting parents of children with severe disabilities to a "stress management" class. Parents expressed their interest in participating by telephoning the researchers, and the parents' eligibility for the treatment was evaluated over the phone. At the time of the initial phone call, parents were randomly assigned to treatment and control groups and were informed of their assignment. Members of the control groups were informed that they would have to wait 5 weeks for their classes to begin. During the phone call, the class was described, and parents were invited to an orientation meeting. Parents were told that the purpose of the class was to reduce stress by changing the way people think. At the orientation meeting, the class was again described, and pretests were administered. Posttests were given to the parents at the last class meeting, and they were asked to complete the tests and mail them to the researchers within one week. Posttests were considered valid if they were returned within 2 weeks. Some parents were called and reminded of the importance of completing the posttests. Parents in the treatment group were paid $10.00 for participating, and the control group received $20.00.

In order to keep the treatment groups small (10 to 12 members) so as to maximize group participation and social support, we formed two treatment and two control groups. Fifty-eight subjects were randomly assigned to treatment and control groups, and 40 subjects completed pretests and posttests in this study (21 in the treatment group and 19 in the control group). There were six married couples who participated, but the independence of husband's and wife's scores could not be demonstrated; therefore, the scores of the 6 husbands were not used in this study. The study now consisted of 34 mothers, 18 (9 and 9) in the treatment groups and 16 (9 and 7) in the control groups. Demographic information was collected on all the subjects. Using analysis of variance and multivariate analysis of variance to statistically analyze all the research variables, we found no significant differences, $\alpha = .05$, between the four groups (2 control, 2 treatment) at pretest.

Treatment Program

The treatment consisted of five 2-hour sessions. Content was presented in lecture format, but the desire of the parents to talk with one another was so great that most of the time was spent in group discussions and small-group exercises. Homework, which consisted mainly of monitoring automatic thoughts, cognitive distortions, negative feelings, and attempts at cognitive restructuring, was assigned.

Each of the five treatment sessions focused on cognitive distortions that contribute to self-blame and guilt and techniques to deal with these cognitive distortions. In Session 1 we introduced a cognitive model of emotions (Beck et al., 1979; Burns, 1980) that is based on the proposition that people can change their feelings by changing their thinking. In Session 2 we presented strategies to change cognitive distortions and automatic thoughts. Session 3 dealt with cognitive distortions around the issue of control and Session 4, with the misattributions around the explanation of events such as the birth of a child with a disability. In Session 5 cognitive distortions and misattributions related to parental schemas were covered.

Instruments

According to the cognitive therapy of Beck (1967), self-blame and guilt are related to negative automatic thoughts, to internal negative attributions, and to depression. Measures of automatic thoughts, internal negative attributions, and depression were used to determine whether cognitions had been restructured. Each test instrument had standardized instructions that were used in the administration of the tests.

Situational Guilt Scale. The outcome measure of the dependent variable of self-blame and guilt was the Situational Guilt Scale (Klass, 1983, 1987), a 22-item self-report test in which subjects are asked to respond to brief descriptions of situations (e.g., breaking a promise) in four different ways: according to whether they are *regretful, disappointed in themselves, guilty,* or *ashamed.* The Total Guilt scale of the Situational Guilt Scale was used in this study. Klass (1987) has provided the only reliability and validity data on this measurement. Internal consistency (.74 to .92) and reliability (.84 to .90) have been demonstrated. Significant correlations with the Forced-Choice Guilt Inventory (Mosher, 1966) and the Depressive Experience Questionnaire (Blatt, D'Afflitti, & Quinlan, 1976) is evidence of its validity.

Attributional Style Questionnaire. This questionnaire (Peterson et al., 1982), which was used to measure changes in internal negative attributions, is a 12-item, self-report measure of patterns of explanatory style. *Explanatory style* is the tendency to select certain causal explanations for positive and negative events along the internal/external, stable/unstable, and global/specific dimensions. Only the measurement of internal, negative attributions (Attributional Style Questionnaire-Internal) was used in this study. Test–retest reliability (5-week) for this questionnaire was .64 (Peterson et al., 1982). Peterson and Seligman (1984) and Tennen and Herzberger (1985) provided reviews of the validity studies of the Attributional Style Questionnaire and found broad support for its ability to predict depression.

Automatic Thoughts Questionnaire. This questionnaire (Holon & Kendall, 1980) is a 30-item, self-report instrument designed to measure the frequency of automatic negative thoughts that people have experienced during the preceding week. Parents were asked to respond according to the frequency of automatic thoughts ([I'm no good") on a 5-point Likert scale. The split-half reliability coefficient was measured at .97, and coefficient alpha had a correlation of .96. Holon and Kendall (1980) reported that the convergent validity of the Automatic Thoughts Questionnaire was confirmed by its significant correlations with the Beck Depression Inventory (Beck, 1967).

Beck Depression Inventory. This inventory (Beck, 1967) is a 21-item test that measures categories judged to be characteristic of depression. Each item consists of four statements that are ranked from 0 to 3 to indicate the degree of severity. Beck reported an odd–even split-half reliability coefficient of .86 (with Spearman-Brown correction, .93). The Beck Depression Inventory is consistently and significantly related to clinical ratings of depression, with correlations ranging from .60 to .90 for a variety of samples (see Steer, Beck, & Garrison, 1986, for a review).

Research Design

We employed a pretest–posttest control group design, a 2 (groups) by 2 (waves) by 2 (times) mixed analysis of variance (Kirk, 1982). The group factor consisted of the treatment group and the control group, which were independent between-subjects factors. The waves consisted of the two treatment–control experiments, and the times factor was the within-subjects factor of the pretests and posttests. No effect was found for wave, so the wave factor was eliminated, creating a 2 x 2 analysis of variance design. Because of the pretest–posttest design, analysis of covariance was used to analyze the differences between treatment and control groups.

Results

Significant differences, a = .05, between treatment and control groups were found in self-blame and guilt

Table 1 Group Comparison Statistics by Measure

Measure[a]	Treatment posttests		Control posttests		
	Adj. mean	SD	Adj. mean	SD	F
SGS	257.1	41.3	286.0	64.4	8.8**
ATQ	51.4	13.3	60.4	16.2	7.6*
ASQ-IN	23.1	6.1	29.0	5.6	10.9**
BDI	10.6	7.1	13.6	8.7	6.5*

[a] SGS = Situational Guilt Scale, ATQ = Automatic Thoughts Questionnaire, ASQ-IN = Attributional Style Questionnaire-Internal Negative, BDI = Beck Depression Inventory.
* $p < .05$.
** $p < .01$.

(Situational Guilt Scale), internal negative attributions (Attributional Style Questionnaire-Internal), automatic thoughts (Automatic Thoughts Questionnaire), and depression (Beck Depression Inventory). These results are summarized in Table 1. Means were adjusted for differences in treatment and control group scores at pretest.

Effect size is an important tool in evaluating the effectiveness of treatment because it allows the effects of treatments to be compared (Smith & Glass, 1977). The effect sizes of the treatment were as follows: on the variables of self-blame/guilt, .39; internal negative attributions, 1.11; automatic thoughts, .34; and depression, .34. In one meta-analysis study, the average effect size for all therapies was .85 (Glass & Kliegl, 1983). For another comparison, Smith, Glass, and Miller (1980) reported that the average effect size was .83 for group therapy and .51 for family therapy.

Discussion

The purpose of the present study was to evaluate the effect of a group cognitive restructuring treatment program on the self-blame and guilt of parents of children with severe disabilities. Self-blame and guilt as measured by the total score on the Situational Guilt Scales was significantly reduced in the treatment groups. The effect size of the treatment on self-blame and guilt was only .39, but this effect size might have been modest because of the brevity of a 5-session treatment. The large effect size in the reduction of internal negative attributions (1.11) indicates that the treatment was more effective in externalizing negative attributions. The significant reductions in automatic thoughts, internal nega-

tive attributions, and depression indicate that cognitive restructuring was effective. Because of the controlled experimental design, cognitive restructuring must be seen as a significant contributor to the reduction in parental self-blame and guilt.

We were not able to find an instrument that would measure social comparison, but clinical observations provide some evidence that social comparison contributed to the reduction of self-blame. The group cohesion and the desire to talk and share with other parents was very strong. Social comparison with other parents could have led to the normalization of feelings and the reduction of self-blame (Lerner & Miller, 1978). For example, one mother shared the fact that the stress became so great at home once that she ran away for 3 days without telling her family where she was. A majority of the group then validated her experience by sharing that they had either run away or thought about it. It may be that this kind of support and validation can only come from other parents of children with severe disabilities. Validation and normalization of feelings is an *externalizing process* that counteracts the internalization of negative attributions and blame. Our clinical speculation that social comparison was effective at externalizing parental self-blame is consistent with the fact that the greatest effect size of this treatment by far was in the reduction of internal negative attributions.

In clinical observations social comparison sometimes seemed to be more effective in reducing self-blame and guilt than was cognitive restructuring. One mother described how her 10-year-old son with Down syndrome was a "genius" at unlocking locks and getting out of the house. She had installed the most sophisticated locks available, but her son sometimes still got out of the house and wandered the streets alone. The techniques of reality checking ("What more could you do?") and reattribution ("Are you 100% responsible for your child every moment of every day?") did not seem to help. Yet, having other parents describe how their child had run out into the street, got lost at the mall, or climbed onto the roof *did* seem to help. By comparing herself to parents in similar situations, this mother seemed to conclude that she was not a bad parent but was in fact like all the other parents in the group who were doing their best.

The opposite of positive social comparison that normalizes feelings is negative social stigma, which blames parents for having a child that has disabilities and is different. Parents shared many examples of how they felt blamed by others. They expressed their feelings that family, friends, and professionals placed excessive "shoulds" on them, which led to feelings of guilt. Even seemingly supportive expressions such as "As a parent, you are as patient as a saint" were experienced as stigmatizing and blaming by parents because (a) the standard of parenting being used to judge them was "sainthood"; (b) these expressions discounted their feelings, which were not saintly and patient; and (c) the message of such statements was that parents did not need help and support. Social comparison that normalizes people's feeling and experiences is an important component in the destigmatization of people (Coleman, 1986). Social comparison could have been effective in reducing self-blame in parents by helping them resist the stigma and blame from others.

In conclusion, this treatment was effective in reducing self-blame and guilt in parents of children with severe disabilities. Because there were significant reductions in automatic thoughts, internal negative attributions, and depression, there is evidence that cognitive distortions were effectively restructured. Therefore, there is evidence that cognitive restructuring was an important contributor to the reduction in parental self-blame and guilt. Clinical observations indicated that social comparison normalized and restructured parents' experiences and feelings and contributed to the reduction in self-blame and guilt. The major weakness of this study is that no valid, reliable measure of social comparison could be found to test the hypothesis that social comparison contributed to the reduction in self-blame and guilt. The possibility that social comparison is a powerful treatment tool in reducing self-blame and guilt needs further research.

References

Abramson, L. Y., Seligman, M. E. P., & Teasdale, J. D. (1978). Learned helplessness in humans: Critique and reformulation. *Journal of Abnormal Psychology*, 87(1), 49–74.

Beck, A. T. (1967). *Depression: Clinical, experimental, and theoretical aspects.* New York: Hoeber.

Beck, A. T., Rush, A. J., Shaw, B. F., & Emery, G. (1979). *Cognitive therapy of depression.* New York: Guilford.

Blacher, J. (1984). A dynamic perspective on the impact of a severely handicapped child on the family. In J. Blacher (Ed.), *Severely handicapped young children and their families: Research in review* (pp. 3–50). New York: Academic Press.

Blatt, S. J., D'Afflitti, J. P., & Quinlan, D. M. (1976). Experiences of depression in normal young adults. *Journal of Abnormal Psychology*, 85, 383–389.

Breslau, N., & Davis, G. C. (1986). Chronic stress and major depression. *Archives of General Psychiatry*, 43, 309–314.

Bristol, M. N., & Schopler, E. (1984). A developmental perspective on stress and coping in families of autistic children. In J. Blacher (Ed.), *Severely handicapped young children and their families: Research in review* (pp. 91–141). New York: Academic Press.

Burns, D. D. (1980). *Feeling good: The new mood therapy.* New York: New American Library.

Coleman, L. M. (1986). Stigma: An enigma demystified. In S. C. Ainlay, G. Becker, & L. M. Coleman, (Eds.), *The dilemma of difference: A multidisciplinary view of stigma* (pp. 211–232). New York: Plenum Press.

Coates, D., & Winston, T. (1983). Counteracting the deviance of depression: Peer support groups for victims. *Journal of Social Issues*, 39, 171–196.

Crocker, E. C., & Crocker, C. (1970). Some implications of superstitions and folk beliefs for counseling parents of children with cleft lip palate. *The Cleft Palate Journal*, 7, 124–128.

DeLuca, K. D., & Salerno, S. C. (1984). *Helping professionals connect with families with handicapped children.* Springfield, IL: Thomas.

Featherstone, H. (1980). *A difference in the family: Life with a disabled child.* New York: Basic Books.

Glass, G. V., & Kliegl, M. (1983). An apology for research integration in the study of psychotherapy. *Journal of Consulting and Clinical Psychology*, 51(1), 28–41.

Heider, F. (1958). *The psychology of interpersonal relations.* New York: Wiley.

Holon, S. D., & Beck, A. T. (1979). Cognitive therapy of depression. In P. C. Kendall & S. D. Hollon (Eds.), *Cognitive-behavioral interventions: Theory, research and procedures* (pp. 153–203). New York: Academic Press.

Holon, S. D., & Kendall, P. C. (1980). Cognitive self-statements in depression: Development of an automatic thoughts questionnaire. *Cognitive Therapy and Research, 4,* 383–395.

Ickes, W. J., & Layden, M. A. (1978). Attribution styles. In J. Harvey, W. Ickes, & R. Kidd (Eds.), *New directions in attribution research* (Vol. 2, pp. 119–152). Hillsdale, NJ: Erlbaum.

Kaiser, C. E., & Hayden, A. H. (1984). Clinical research and policy issues in parenting severely handicapped infants. In J. Blacher (Ed.), *Severely handicapped young children and their families: Research in review* (pp. 275–317). New York: Academic Press.

Kirk, R. E. (1982). *Experimental design: Procedures for the behavioral sciences.* Belmont, CA: Brooks/Cole.

Kivowitz, J. (1977). Counseling parents whose sexual relationship has been affected by a handicapped child. *Medical Aspects of Human Sexuality, 11,* 79–80.

Klass, E. T. (1983). *Guide to the use of a situational self-report measure of guilt.* Unpublished manuscript, Hunter College, City University of New York.

Klass, E. T. (1987). Situational approach to assessment of guilt: Development and validation of a self-report measure. *Journal of Psychopathology and Behavioral Assessment, 9*(1), 35–48.

Kopel, S. A., & Arkowitz, H. (1975). The role of attribution and self perceptions in behavior change. *Genetic Psychology Monographs, 92,* 175–212.

LaBorde, P. R., & Seligman, M. (1983). Individual counseling with parents of handicapped children: Rationale and strategies. In M. Seligman (Ed.), *The family with a handicapped child: Understanding and treatment* (pp. 261–284). San Francisco: Harcourt Brace Jovanovich.

Lerner, M. J., & Miller, D. T. (1978). Just world research and attribution process: Looking back and ahead. *Psychological Bulletin, 85,* 1030–1051.

Meyerson, R. C. (1983). Family and parent group therapy. In M. Seligman (Ed.), *The family with a handicapped child: Understanding and treatment* (pp. 285–308). San Francisco: Harcourt Brace Jovanovich.

Mosher, D. L. (1966). The development and multitrait-method matrix analysis of three measures of three aspects of guilt. *Journal of Consulting Psychology, 30,* 25–29.

Peterson, C., & Seligman, M. E. P. (1984). Causal expectations as a risk factor for depression: Theory and evidence. *Psychological Review, 91,* 347–374.

Peterson, C., Semmel, A., von Baeyer, C., Abramson, L. Y., Metalsky, G. I., & Seligman, M. E. P. (1982). The Attributional Style Questionnaire. *Cognitive Therapy and Research, 6,* 287–299.

Rothbaum, F., Weisz, J. R., & Snyder, S. S. (1982). Changing the world and changing the self: A two-process model of perceived control. *Journal of Personality and Social Psychology, 42,* 5–37.

Seligman, M. E. P. (1975). *Helplessness: On depression, development, and death.* San Francisco: Freeman.

Singer, G. H. S., Irvin, L. K., & Hawkins, N. J. (1988). Stress management training for parents of severely handicapped children. *Mental Retardation, 26,* 269–277.

Singer, G. H. S., Irvin, L., Hawkins, N., & Cooley, E. (1987). *Cognitive behavior modification for parents of developmentally disabled children: A content analysis.* Unpublished manuscript, Oregon Research Institute, Eugene, OR.

Smith, M. E., & Glass, G. V. (1977). Meta-analysis of psychotherapy outcome studies. *American Psychologist, 32,* 752–760.

Smith, M. E., Glass, G. V., & Miller, T. I. (1980). *The benefits of psychotherapy.* Baltimore: Johns Hopkins University Press.

Sober-Ain, L., & Kidd, R. F. (1984). Fostering changes in self-blamers' beliefs about causality. *Cognitive Therapy and Research, 8*(2), 121–138.

Steer, R. A., Beck, A. T., & Garrison, B. (1986). Applications of the Beck Depression Inventory. In N. Sartorius & T. A. Ban (Eds.), *Assessment of depression* (pp. 123–142). Berlin: Springer-Verlag.

Summers, J. A., Behr, S. K., & Turnbull, A. P. (1989). Positive adaptation coping strengths of families who have children with disabilities. In G. H. S. Singer & L. K. Irvin (Eds.), *Support for caregiving families* (pp. 27–40). Baltimore: Brookes.

Tennen, H., Affleck, G., & Gershman, K. (1986). Self-blame among parents of infants with perinatal complications: The role of self-protective motives. *Journal of Personality and Social Psychology, 50,* 690–696.

Tennen, H., & Herzberger, S. (1985). Attributional style questionnaire. In D. J. Keyser & R. C. Sweetland (Eds.), *Test critiques* (Vol. 4, pp. 20–32). Kansas City: Test Corporation of America.

Thoits, P. A. (1986). Social support as coping assistance. *Journal of Consulting and Clinical Psychology, 54,* 416–423.

Wilson, T. D., & Linville, P. W. (1982). Improving the academic performance of college freshmen: Attribution theory revisited. *Journal of Personality and Social Psychology, 42,* 367–376.

Wortman, C. B. (1976). Causal attributions and personal control. In J. Harvey, W. Ickes, & R. F. Kidd (Eds.), *New directions in attribution research* (Vol. 1, pp. 23–52). Hillsdale, NJ: Erlbaum.

Received: 11/5/90; first decision: 3/9/91; accepted 9/9/91.

This research was funded in part by Grant No. H023T80013-90 between the U.S. Department of Education and the Oregon Research Institute. Opinions expressed herein do not necessarily reflect those of the funders. The authors acknowledge Christine Lorenz for her assistance in preparing the manuscript. Requests for reprints should be sent to Charles D. Nixon, Oregon Research Institute, 1899 Willamette, Eugene, OR 97401.

Authors

Charles D. Nixon, Oregon Research Institute and **George H. S. Singer,** Dartmouth Medical School.

Impact of a Cash Subsidy Program for Families of Children With Severe Developmental Disabilities

Judith C. Meyers, Ph.D. and Maureen O. Marcenko, Ph.D.
1989

Abstract

The impact of a cash subsidy program on 81 families raising children with severe handicaps was examined. Families were interviewed prior to receiving the $225 monthly subsidy and one year later. Mothers reported significantly less family stress, particularly related to financial stress, and enhanced life satisfaction. Furthermore, they were less likely to anticipate out-of-home placement for their child after receiving the subsidy. In general, lower income and black mothers were less likely to plan placement. However, the number of families stating that they planned placement was too small to allow us to fully explore the interrelations between out-of-home placement and various social, cultural, and economic factors.

A survey conducted by Agosta and Bradley (1985) revealed that 49 states are providing some kind of support service to families raising children with developmental disabilities at home, with 33 states administering supportive service programs, 9 states providing cash assistance without supportive services, and 7 states administering a combination of the two. Two thirds of these programs have been established since 1980.

Program objectives include linking families with appropriate community services, reducing stress in the family, training families to better care for their children with disabilities, and increasing the family's quality of life. The broader goals are to maintain the integrity of the family and reduce, prevent, or forestall institutionalization or other out-of-home placement, which is potentially of great cost-saving benefit to the public.

Although there has been a proliferation of family support programs throughout the country, few have been carefully and systematically evaluated. The one notable exception is Zimmerman's (1984) study on the impact of a program in Minnesota, the first state to introduce such a cash-assistance program. Her results are based on a retrospective telephone survey with 36 families, 95% of whom were headed by two parents in their first marriages. Families had received the subsidy for varying lengths of time when interviewed. The subsidy was reported to be instrumental in assisting families to cope better in caring for their child at home. The subsidy was said to be most beneficial for families of lower socioeconomic status (SES). The small sample and retrospective design make it difficult to generalize from these findings.

In the present study we report the findings of an evaluation of a cash subsidy program implemented in Michigan in 1984. At the time of the study, Michigan's program provided $225 monthly to families who were caring for their children with a severe mental impairment at home. (The amount of the subsidy was patterned after the Social Security Disability rate. Therefore, as of September 1988, families were receiving $256.74 a month.) A family was eligible for a subsidy if there was a child younger than age 18 living at home who, according to special education guidelines, was severely mentally impaired, with cognitive development four or more standard deviations (SDs) below the mean; severely multiply impaired, with multiple handicaps including cognitive deficits similar to those associated with severe mental impairment along with physical impairments; or autistic impaired. These were children with the most extreme dependent care needs. Many were incontinent, nonambulatory, required assistance in personal care functions, and had severe behavioral problems. In addition, to quality for the subsidy, a family's taxable income for the prior year had to be $60,000 or less. The subsidy supplemented but did not supplant other public assistance benefits.

The money could be used at the discretion of the parents for the special needs of their child. Eligible families applied through their local Community Mental Health Boards and were required to report yearly the purposes for which the subsidy was used. As of August 1988, approximately 3,200 families were enrolled in the program at a cost of almost $10 million to the state.

As part of the state's evaluation, we used a longitudinal design and personal interview to examine the effects of the subsidy on a subsample of 81 recipients. In this paper we report on the impact of the subsidy on maternal stress, life satisfaction, and plans for out-of-home placement of the child.

Method

Subjects

Four Michigan counties were selected to participate. Based on a Michigan Department of Mental Health survey of services for persons with developmental disabilities (Herman, 1984), these counties represent three types of service areas: an urban county with many family support services available, an urban county with few available support services, and two rural counties with low levels of local services.

Letters inviting participation were sent by the school district in each of the four counties to all families known to have a child in one of the three eligible diagnostic groups. Of these 625 families, 50% ($N = 315$) agreed to participate. We excluded from the sample frame those families with the following characteristics: the child with handicaps was younger than age 3 or older than 16, there was more than one severely handicapped child, or the father was primary caretaker of the child. A stratified random sample of 100 families was then selected from among all eligible families who agreed to participate. Stratification was based on the age of the child with handicaps and estimates of SES.

Of the 100 mothers originally interviewed, 81 were included in the follow-up study. The 19 respondents who were not available for follow-up interviews were disproportionately black (58%) and from the lower income group (68%). They did not differ from the sample as a whole with regard to age, sex, diagnosis of child, or county of residence. Reasons for noninclusion in the follow-up study included late or nonenrollment in the subsidy program ($n = 10$), moved out of area ($n = 3$), critical illness or death of child ($n = 2$), or refusal ($n = 4$). Subject characteristics are presented in Table 1.

The sample selected in each county was compared to the population of families in that county who were enrolled in the Family Support Subsidy Program by diagnosis, sex, age, and race of the child with handicaps and by family income. The total sample was then compared to the families statewide who were enrolled in the program. Analysis by county showed that with the ex-

Table 1 Demographic Characteristics of Sample

Characteristic	%
Race of mothers	
White	52
Black	44
Hispanic	4
Education of mothers	
< High school	20
High school	49
College	31
Marital status	
Married	57
Single	43
County of residence	
Urban	84
Rural	16
Family income[a]	
< $8,000	22
8 to 24,999	44
25 to 60,000	33
Sex of children with handicaps	
Male	51
Female	49
Diagnosis	
Severely mentally impaired	44
Severely multiply impaired	35
Autistic impaired	21
Age of children[b]	
3 to 5	26
6 to 8	24
9 to 11	24
12 to 16	27

[a] Median income = $15,000.
[b] In years; median age = 10.

ception of special education category in one urban county, there were no significant differences between the sample and those families receiving the subsidy. A comparison of the four counties to the entire state of enrollees showed that the sample had more black families than the enrolled state population, but there were no other differences on the selected demographic variables.

Procedure and Measures

In-home interviews were conducted with the mothers, or in some cases grandmother, as primary caregivers in each family. A semi-structured questionnaire consisting of both closed and open-ended questions was utilized. Initial interviews (Time 1) were conducted 1 and 2 months before the start of the subsidy program. Follow-up interviews (Time 2) were conducted 1 year later. At Time 2, 72 of the families (89%) had been receiving the subsidy for 10 months. The remaining 9 families had been in the program 8 or 9 months. The interviews consisted of standard sociodemographic data, measures of stress, and questions about the child's condition and decisions to place the child out-of-home.

We modified Stein and Riessman's (1980) Impact on Family Scale to measure stress. Although the scale was designed for use with families having a chronically ill child, we felt that there were enough similarities between the two populations to warrant use of the instrument with families of children with developmental disabilities. The 25-item scale consists of statements about the impact of a child with handicaps on various components of family life, including financial problems, social interaction, subjective distress felt by the mother, and a positive sense of mastery that may emerge from coping with the stress. Responses to each item were given a score along a 4-point scale from *strongly agree* to *strongly disagree*. A mean item score was calculated; a higher mean score was associated with lower stress. Cronbach's alpha was computed for the scale, revealing an alpha reliability coefficient of .89. Regarding out-of-home placement, mothers were asked whether they presently or in the near future planned to place their child out-of-home and, if so, to what extent such reasons as stress, money, or the child's condition contributed to the decision.

Results

Stress

The amount of family stress (mean = 2.36) reported at the follow-up interview was significantly less than the amount reported at the time of the first interview (mean = 2.44), $t(80) = -2.61$, $p = .02$. An item-by-item analysis showed a significant reduction in stress on 6 of the 25 items. As seen in Table 2, significant change was most apparent in items relating directly to areas of financial stress, such as: "The cost of my child's care is causing financial problems for the family" or "I am unable to save much money because of my child's handicaps." Further analyses revealed no significant group differences by mother's marital status, employment status, or education or by child's age, diagnosis, or level of functioning nor

Table 2 Impact on Family Scale Items That Changed Significantly From Time 1 to Time 2

| Item | Time 1 | | Time 2 | | | |
	Mean	SD	Mean	SD	t	df
The cost of my child's care is causing financial problems for the family.	2.31	.79	2.62	.75	−3.34**	80
Additional income is needed in order to cover our expenses.	1.78	.65	2.05	.74	−3.22**	80
I am unable to save much money because of the expense of my child's care.	1.98	.72	2.23	.80	−2.80**	80
We have to borrow money to help pay for our child's care.	2.71	.74	2.92	.50	−2.51**	77
I think about not having any more children because of my child's handicap.	2.20	1.05	2.44	.98	−2.03*	79
Our family gives up things because of my child's handicap.	2.22	.85	2.38	.82	−1.97*	80

Note: Higher scores indicate lower stress. Range of possible scores, 1 to 4.
   * $p < .05$.
   ** $p < .01$.

were differences found by family income or county of residence.

Scores on the measure of life satisfaction showed a significant increase from the first interview (mean = 6.3) to the second interview (mean = 6.7), $t(80) = -1.97$, $p = .05$. Again, change in life satisfaction was not related to any of the sociodemographic variables tested in the analysis of the stress scale.

Out-of-Home Placement

There was a significant reduction in the proportion of mothers who said they anticipated placing their child away from home at some future point. During the first wave of interviews, 26 mothers (32%) had plans to place their child, whereas at follow-up, there was a decrease to 15 mothers (19%). Although there was a net decrease of 11, we note that in total 16 mothers (20%) changed from saying they planned to place their child at the first interview to saying they had no plants to place their child at the second interview, and 5 mothers (6%) changed in the reverse direction.

Comparisons were made between two groups: those who changed from saying that they planned placement at Time 1 to not planning placement at Time 2 and those who either said they planned placement at both Times 1 and 2 or changed from saying no to placement at Time 1 and yes at Time 2. Analyses revealed that there were no significant differences between the two groups on marital status; mother's employment; child's level of functioning, sex, or race; number of children in the family; or income.

Based on an analysis of Time 1 data, the families with higher incomes (> $15,000) were significantly more likely to anticipate placing their children than were lower income families, Chi Square $(1, N = 79) = 4.86$, $p < .05$, and white families were more likely to plan on placement than were black families, Chi Square $(1, N = 77) = 7.14$, $p < .01$. Results of the second interview also indicated a similar significant relation between income, race, and decision to place. The lower income group contained significantly more black than white families, so it is unclear whether SES or cultural factors contributed to the group differences. The sample was too small to adequately determine the contribution of each. Plans for placement were not significantly related to mother's age, marital status, or employment status nor influenced by the child's age or diagnostic group, number of children in the family, or county of residence.

Table 3 Extent to Which Factors Contribute to Decision to Place

Reason	Time 1	Time 2
Normal transition to adulthood	3.2	3.4
Child's lack of independent living skills	3.1	3.0
Stress of constant care	2.9	3.1
Child's aggressive behavior	2.6	2.4
Child's physical/medical condition	2.3	2.7
Lack of supportive family situation	2.0	2.1
Need for employment outside the home	1.9	2.6
Needs of other children	1.6	2.3
Money	1.6	1.8

Note. Scale: 1 = *not at all*, 5 = *a great deal*.

Table 3 shows the rank order of mean scores indicating the extent to which different factors might have contributed to the placement decision for those who said they would eventually place their child.

Discussion

The results of this study indicate that mothers of children with severe developmental disabilities who received a cash subsidy of $225 per month for up to 10 months reported decreased family stress, particularly related to financial stress, and enhanced life satisfaction. This was true regardless of marital status, employment status or education, child's age, diagnosis or level of functioning, family income, or county of residence.

That stress around financial issues was reduced bears a clear conceptual link to receipt of the subsidy. One would expect financial stress to decrease as money is introduced. Our finding regarding increased life satisfaction is a little more difficult to explain given the available data. It may be that additional money allows families to do and purchase things that contribute to general life satisfaction, or mothers may realize some psychological benefit to being recognized by the state for their contributions, which is expressed as enhanced satisfaction with life. In any case, this finding deserves further research in order to explain how cash subsidies influence overall life satisfaction.

One of the primary goals of cash subsidy programs is cost-savings due to reduction in out-of-home placement. Our findings indicate that indeed mothers were less likely to anticipate out-of-home placement of their child after receiving the subsidy for approximately 10 months. In general, lower income and black mothers were less likely to plan placement. However, those mothers who did change their minds about future placement did not differ significantly along a number of socioeconomic variables from those who planned placement. Questions remain regarding the factors that influence parental decisions to place. The subsidy appears to have had an effect on this decision. The reduction in stress and increase in life satisfaction that mothers experienced may have contributed to their feeling that they could continue to care for their children at home. The sample of families stating that they planned placement was too small to fully explore the interrelations among out-of-home placement and various social, cultural, and economic factors.

In summary, the Michigan's Family Support Subsidy Program has had a positive impact on participating families. As similar programs are instituted or piloted in other states, they should be evaluated to determine how they assist families. Longitudinal research is required to test the efficacy of subsidies over time as a policy option for supporting families of children with developmental disabilities.

References

Agosta, J. M., & Bradley, V. J. (Eds.) (1985). *Family care for persons with developmental disabilities: A growing commitment.* Boston: Human Services Research Institute.

Herman, S. E. (1984). *Baseline study on family support services in the state of Michigan.* Lansing: Department of Mental Health.

Stein, R. E., & Riessman, C. K. (1980). The development of an Impact-on Family Scale: Preliminary findings. *Medical Care, 18,* 465–472.

Zimmerman, S. L. (1984). The mental retardation family subsidy program: Its effects on families with a mentally handicapped child. *Family Relations, 33,* 105–118.

This article is based on research supported by grants from the Michigan Developmental Disabilities Council, the University of Michigan Rackham Faculty Grant Program, and Wayne State University. The views expressed herein are solely those of the authors and do not represent the opinions or policies of any agency of the State of Michigan. We give special thanks to the families who cooperated with us in this study. The first author conducted this research while Associate Director of the Bush Program in Child Development and Social Policy at the University of Michigan.

Authors

Judith C. Meyers, Ph.D., 4020 John Lynde Rd., Des Moines, IA 50312. **Maureen O. Marcenko, Ph.D.,** Assistant Professor, School of Social Work, and Associate Director, Developmental Disabilities Institute, Wayne State University, 285 Justice Bldg., Detroit, MI 48202. Requests for reprints should be sent to the second author.

Aging and Developmental Disabilities: Demographic and Policy Issues Affecting American Families

David Braddock, Ph.D.
1999

The aging of our society, coupled with the increasing longevity of persons with developmental disabilities, is the primary focus of this commentary. These two key forces are working in a powerful synergy that is stretching state service-delivery systems well beyond their capacities to meet current and projected demands for residential, vocational, and family support services for individuals with developmental disabilities. Large and growing waiting lists are very common in the states today. This commentary is based on testimony presented at the United States Senate Special Committee on Aging's Forum on Aging and Developmental Disabilities (Braddock, in press).

Structure of Residential Care in the United States

Formal, supervised out-of-home residential services were being provided to 394,284 persons in the states in 1996, according to a national study completed this past year at the University of Illinois at Chicago (Braddock, Hemp, Parish, & Westrich, 1998). Fifty-one percent of the individuals (about 200,000 persons) lived in 1 to 6 person settings, such as small group homes, supervised apartments, foster care, and supported living placements (see Figure 1). The vast majority of these settings were operated by private, nonprofit service providers. An additional 55,227 persons resided in facilities for 7 to 15 persons, 100,729 individuals were living in large public or private institutions for 16 or more persons, and 38,438 persons lived in nursing homes.

The structure of the residential care system has changed markedly over the past 20 years, as state-operated residential institutions reduced their census by two thirds, from 150,000 to under 60,000 persons. Concurrently, the number of persons residing in 1- to 6-person settings expanded 10-fold—from about 20,000 individuals in 1977 to the present figure of just under 200,000 persons. Overall system capacity, however, grew by only

Figure 1 Out-of-home MR/DD residential placements by settings in the United States: 1996. *Source*: Department of Disability and Human Development, University of Illinois at Chicago, 1998.

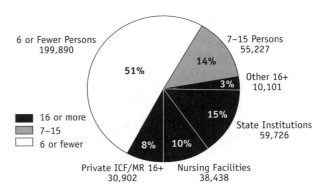

Residential Services Total: 394,284

36% over the 20-year period, an average growth rate of just 2% per year. Given that the general population of the United States increased by 22% during the past 20 years, the entire system of residential care grew at a very modest pace. This is remarkable in light of the fact that public funding for residential and community services expanded from $3.5 billion in 1977 to $22.8 billion in 1996, a growth rate of 167% after adjusting for inflation.

The Medicaid program was the principal catalyst of system expansion, both in terms of persons served and resources allocated (Braddock & Hemp, 1996). In 1996, 71% of all public resources in the nation's mental retardation/developmental disabilities (MR/DD) service system was associated with the federal–state Medicaid program through the Intermediate Care Facility for the Mentally Retarded (ICF/MR) authority or the Home and Community Based Services (HCBS) Waiver program. The ICF/MR program has been instrumental in the financing of large public and private institutions; the HCBS Waiver program supports a wide array of community services and supports for people with developmental disabilities and their families. The dominant national trend today is clearly toward implementing more family and community supports in the states while closing and consolidating state-operated institutions (Braddock & Hemp, 1997).

Aging Caregivers and the Growing Demand for Services

The aging of our society directly influences demand for developmental disabilities services. This occurs because the majority of people with developmental disabilities in the United States currently reside with family caregivers. As these caregivers age beyond their caregiving capacity, formal supervised living arrangements must be established to support their relatives who have disabilities. It is logical to assume that the size of the cohorts of people with developmental disabilities living with aging family caregivers in each state would correspond closely to the size of waiting lists for residential services in those states.

The aging of our society is a product of several forces, primary among them the size of the baby boom generation (persons born during 1946 to 1964), declining fertility rates, and increased longevity. Baby boomers will begin to reach age 65 in about 11 years—in 2010. The number of persons in our society age 65+ years is projected by the U.S. Bureau of the Census to be 35 million persons in the year 2000; the number will double by the year 2030 to 70 million (see Figure 2) due to the aging of the baby boom cohort (U.S. Bureau of the Census, 1996). Currently, 12.8% of the U.S. general population is age 65+ years. Census Bureau demographers anticipate that this percentage will grow steadily for the next 3 decades, finally leveling off at 22% of the U.S. population in 2030. Problems loom even larger in countries such as Japan and Germany, where the 65+ cohort is projected to approximate one third of their general populations by the year 2040 (U.S. Bureau of the Census, 1997).

Understanding the impact of aging on the increased demand for developmental disabilities services in the states requires an appreciation of the prevalence of developmental disabilities in our society. Fujiura (1998) recommended using a prevalence rate of 1.2% based on the Survey of Income and Program Participation (U.S. Bureau of the Census, 1992), for which data were collected from 91,000 U.S. households. The 1.2% rate includes persons with mental retardation, cerebral palsy,

Figure 2 Growing numbers of Americans age 65+ years: 1980–2030. *Source*: U.S. Bureau of the Census (1996).

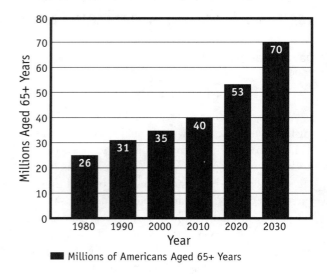

■ Millions of Americans Aged 65+ Years

Figure 3 Distribution of individuals with a developmental disability by living arrangement, 1996. *Source:* Adapted from Braddock et al. (1998) and Fujiura (1998).

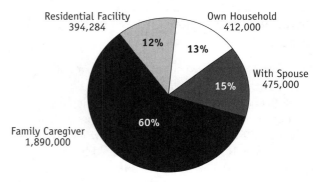

Total Estimated Population with a Developmental Disability: 3.17 Million

autism, epilepsy, and other childhood disabilities originating prior to 22 years of age. Fujiura's analysis indicated that in 1991, 60% of persons with developmental disabilities in the United States resided with family caregivers as opposed to living on their own or within the formal out-of-home supervised residential care system in the states.

I updated Fujiura's 1991 data based on the more current Braddock et al. (1998) study of the formal out-of-home residential system, and on U.S. population growth through 1996. The results are presented in Figure 3,

Aging and Developmental Disabilities: Demographic and Policy Issues Affecting American Families   David Braddock

Figure 4 Distribution of individuals with a developmental disability living with family caregivers, 1996. *Source:* Adapted from Braddock et al. (1998) and Fujiura (1998).

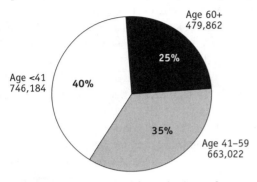

Total Estimated Population of Persons with a Developmental Disability Living with Family Caregivers: 1.89 Million

Table 1 Individuals With Developmental Disabilities Living in Households With Caregivers Age 60+ Years, 1996

State	Individuals/ households[a]	State	Individuals/ households[a]
Alabama	8,362	Missouri	10,378
Alaska	402	Montana	1,580
Arizona	8,898	Nebraska	3,048
Arkansas	4,694	Nevada	2,787
California	49,374	New Hampshire	1,985
Colorado	5,611	New Jersey	15,789
Connecticut	6,378	New Mexico	2,630
Delaware	1,345	New York	32,391
District of		North Carolina	13,483
Columbia	1,017	North Dakota	1,110
Florida	40,145	Ohio	21,109
Georgia	10,949	Oklahoma	6,235
Hawaii	2,209	Oregon	6,150
Idaho	1,764	Pennsylvania	27,115
Illinois	20,602	Rhode Island	2,219
Indiana	10,208	South Carolina	6,432
Iowa	5,631	South Dakota	1,291
Kansas	5,019	Tennessee	9,766
Kentucky	7,325	Texas	29,129
Louisiana	6,808	Utah	2,547
Maine	2,270	Vermont	1,011
Maryland	8,526	Virginia	11,115
Massachusetts	11,745	Washington	8,747
Michigan	17,453	West Virginia	3,780
Minnesota	7,283	Wisconsin	8,572
Mississippi	4,777	Wyoming	691
United States	479,862		

Source: Braddock (in press).

[a] Estimated.

which indicates that 1.89 million of the 3.17 million persons with developmental disabilities in the U.S. population in 1996 were receiving residential care from family caregivers. This "informal" system of residential care served about *five times* the numbers served by the formal residential care system (394,284 persons).

Fujiura's data, based on the 1991 Survey of Income and Program Participation, indicated that 25% of individuals with developmental disabilities across the United States lived with family caregivers age 60+ years, and an additional 35% were "in the households of middle-age caretakers, for whom transition issues were near term considerations" (p. 232). In Figure 4, I reconfigured Figure 3 to draw specific attention to the size of the aging family caregiver cohort (479,862 persons in 1996).

How large is the aging caregiver cohort in each of the states? State-by-state estimates can be generated by taking into account differences both in terms of states' utilization of out-of-home placements and in terms of differences in the size of states' cohorts over age 60+ years. For example, 10% of persons with developmental disabilities in Michigan live in out-of-home settings, whereas the figure is 27% in North Dakota (Braddock et al., 1998). Also, the percentage of older individuals in the general population in the "oldest" state, Florida (18.5%), is three times the percentage of older individuals in the youngest state, Alaska (5.2%) (U.S. Department of Census, 1997). State-by-state estimates of individuals with developmental disabilities living with older (60+ years) caregivers appear in Table 1.

Increased Longevity of Persons With Developmental Disabilities

A second factor impinging on the growing demand for MR/DD services is related to increases in the lifespan of individuals with developmental disabilities. The mean age at death for persons with mental retardation was 66.2 years in 1993—up from 18.5 years in the 1930s and 59.1 years in the 1970s. The mean age at death for the general population is 70.4 years (Janicki, 1996). Janicki, a noted authority on aging and mental retardation who is affiliated with the University of Illinois at Chicago's Rehabilitation Research and Training Center on Aging with Mental Retardation, has observed that with continued improvement in their health status, individuals with mental retardation—particularly those without severe impairments—can be expected to have a life-span equal to that of the general population. Longevity has increased dramatically for persons with significant developmental problems such as Down syndrome. Average age at death in the 1920s was 9 years for this group; it rose to 30.5 years in the 1960s and 55.8 years in 1993 (Janicki, Dalton, Henderson, & Davidson, in press).

As the lifespan of persons with developmental disabilities increases, they require long-term care for *longer* periods of time. This directly impacts on the finite capacities of service delivery systems in the states. The increased life expectancy of persons with developmental disabilities between 1970 and the present accounts for a significant percentage, perhaps as much as 20% or more, of the long-term care resources now being consumed by such persons in the formal out-of-home long term care service system.

The likelihood of older persons with developmental disabilities living into their own retirement and outliving their family caregivers has increased substantially in recent years. This has, in turn, stimulated a growing need for more services and supports. The need to provide these services is frequently unanticipated by federal, state, and local agencies, often resulting in a crisis situation for families in the most extreme cases of need. It is unfortunately not an exaggeration to note that many family caregivers must die before the relative with disabilities they are caring for receives appropriate residential and community services from the state system.

Waiting Lists in the States

The size of the state cohorts of individuals with developmental disabilities living with aging family caregivers (Table 1) correlates strongly with the size of waiting lists reported by the states, $r = .649$, $p < .01$. According to data collected by the University of Minnesota in 1997, an estimated nationwide total of 83,101 persons with developmental disabilities are on formal state waiting lists for residential services (Prouty & Lakin, 1998). This figure is nearly equivalent to the total service system expansion during the previous 20 years (104,000 persons). A second recent survey conducted by the Arc/United States (Davis, 1997) confirms the magnitude of waiting lists in the states today. Thus, demographic trends clearly suggest that waiting lists will accelerate markedly in the states as baby boomers age, unless a concerned state–federal effort is mounted to address this issue.

Some states keep detailed waiting lists on service needs for persons with developmental disabilities. Some do not keep "official" lists, although state officials informally acknowledge that significant demand for needed services exists. In their 1997 survey of waiting lists in the states, Prouty and Lakin (1998) noted a 38% increase in persons requesting residential services compared to a survey conducted 5 years earlier in 1992 by Hayden and DePaepe (1994). Eleven states did not furnish waiting list data in the 1997 survey (California, Iowa, Kansas, Maine, Maryland, Michigan, Mississippi, Ohio, Texas, Virginia, and West Virginia), and 5 states indicated that the waiting list was zero (District of Columbia, Hawaii, Illinois, North Dakota, and Rhode Island). One of the states indicating zero persons awaiting services was Illinois, which is remarkable because the state has long lagged behind most other states in the development of family-scale residential alternatives. We need more accurate waiting list data from states such as Illinois. States should not cover up this problem. They should conduct rigorous needs assessments for services and develop plans to serve the burgeoning number of families awaiting services in the states.

The close connection between aging caregivers and growing waiting lists in the states can be illustrated in the vivid example of Maryland. Maryland's Developmental Disabilities Administration provided residential waiting list data to the *Baltimore Sun* (March 23, 1997). The *Sun* reported that 4,682 persons were waiting for services in 1997. Thirty-nine percent of these individuals were

Figure 5 Caregiver age for adults with developmental disabilities on residential waiting lists in Maryland: 1997. *Source: Baltimore Sun*, March 23, 1997 (compiled from waiting lists of the Maryland Developmental Disabilities Administration).

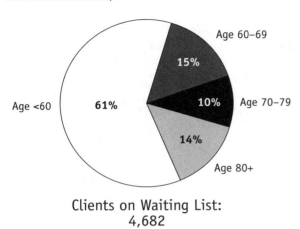

Clients on Waiting List:
4,682

living with caregivers age 60+ years (see Figure 5). Twenty-four percent of the 4,682 persons waiting for services had caregivers age 70+ years, and 14% were age 80+ years. It is not likely that Maryland represents an aberration among the states. Because of the state's fairly large general population, its percentage of aging caregivers on the waiting list (39%) may well approximate the pattern in most states. There is no doubt that aging family caregivers are extremely oversubscribed on state waiting lists and that the Maryland data are indicative of a serious national problem requiring this Committee's concerted attention.

State Initiatives to Address Waiting Lists

Several states have begun initiatives to address the problem of waiting lists. New Jersey, for example, appropriated $30 million in FY 1999 to reduce its waiting list for community residential services. Between 1986 and 1996, the New Jersey waiting list increased from 767 to 4,600 persons. The "urgent" category in 1996 consisted of 2,286 persons. The New Jersey Department of Human Services, Division of Developmental Disabilities, projects the need for a 10-year waiting list education initiative with appropriations of $30 million per year through the year 2008. New Hampshire has enacted a special appropriation to address the waiting list and is requiring an annual status report to the governor regard-

ing progress in addressing the waiting list. Connecticut, Texas, Massachusetts, and Oregon have also commenced waiting list initiatives. Lakin (1998) noted that waiting list initiatives in the states generally involve re-allocating resources in the following ways:

- The closure/consolidation of institutions
- The conversion of ICFs/MR to HCBS programs
- Capping reimbursement for existing program
- Augmenting state funding with Medicaid funding
- Expanding family support and subsidies to prevent or delay the need for placement
- Promoting flexibility in residential and day programs for persons leaving high cost programs.

Policy Considerations and Recommendations

Aging of the nation's population, marked improvement in the life-span of persons with developmental disabilities, and our country's traditional reliance on families to provide most developmental disabilities long-term care are currently having profound impacts on the states, and these impacts will increase dramatically in the years ahead. We can anticipate increased pressures on family caregivers, especially in states with a large percentage of older citizens, and in those many states that have yet to develop an extensive array of community services and supports. A major problem is the fact that only 3% of the total funding base of $22.8 billion in the developmental disabilities field is currently targeted toward family support services. A similar minuscule percentage of total funding (4%) is allocated for consolidated activity in supported living, personal assistance, and support employment. The remaining 93% of the field's funding base finances residential and vocational facilities, including large public and private institutions, sheltered workshops, and other primarily facility-based services.

The federal government should encourage greater flexibility in resource allocation through use of the HCBS Waiver and other Medicaid Waivers. In-home support programs and cash subsidies frequently prevent more costly placements in institutions, nursing homes, and other residential settings where costs often exceed $100,000 per year. States and community providers need greater flexibility to access HCBS Waiver funds for families and consumers on waiting lists. The Medicaid state plan amendment process is cumbersome in many respects. The federal government should provide additional incentives to states to reallocate Medicaid ICF/MR funding to community and family support objectives that address waiting list and aging caregiver issues. Personal assistance legislation (MICASA, the Medicaid Community Attendant Services Act, H.R. 2020) should be supported. Improved coordination between Older Americans Act services and the MR/DD service system should be stressed.

The states should also be encouraged to adopt waiting list reduction initiatives and to conduct independent special studies of the number of persons awaiting various developmental services in the states. The state developmental disabilities planning councils and university affiliated programs should assist in carrying out such studies. A special initiative for family support appropriations is currently pending in the Developmental Disabilities Act appropriation bill before Congress. This special appropriation should be supported. A portion of these DD Act funds might be targeted for developing models in the states for serving aging caregivers and for carrying out carefully designed waiting list studies to inform the state planning process required under the Developmental Disabilities Act.

References

Braddock, D. (in press). Aging and developmental disabilities: Demographics and policy issues affecting American families. *Can we rest in peace? The anxiety of elderly parents caring for baby boomers with disabilities* (A forum of the U.S. Senate Special Committee on Aging, September 18, 1998). Washington, DC: U.S. Government Printing Office.

Braddock, D., & Hemp, R. (1997). Toward family and community: Mental retardation services in Massachusetts, New England, and the United States. *Mental Retardation, 35*, 241–256.

Braddock, D., & Hemp, R. (1996). The impact of proposed Medicaid spending reductions on persons with developmental disabilities in the United States. *Journal of Disability Policy Studies, 7*(1), 1–32.

Braddock, D., Hemp, R., Parish, S., & Westrich, J. (1998). *The state of the states in developmental disabilities* (5th ed.). Washington, DC: American Association on Mental Retardation.

Davis, S. (1997, November). *A status report to the nation on people with mental retardation waiting for community services.* Arlington, TX: Arc/United States.

Fujiura, G. T. (1998). The demography of family households. *American Journal on Mental Retardation, 103*, 225–235.

Hayden, M. F., & DePaepe, P. (1994). Waiting for community services: The impact on persons with mental retardation and other developmental disabilities. In M. F. Hayden & B. H. Abery (Eds.), *Challenges for a service system in transition: Ensuring quality community experiences for persons with developmental disabilities* (pp. 173–206). Baltimore: Brookes.

Janicki, M. P. (1996, Fall). Longevity increasing among older adults with an intellectual disability. *Aging, Health, and Society, 2*, 2.

Janicki, M. P., Dalton, A. J., Henderson, C. M., & Davidson, P. W. (in press). Mortality and morbidity among older adults with intellectual disability: Health services considerations. *Disability and Rehabilitation.*

Lakin, K. C. (1998). On the outside looking in: Attending to waiting lists in systems of services for people with developmental disabilities. *Mental Retardation, 36*, 157–162.

Prouty, R., & Lakin, K. C. (Eds.). (1998, May). *Residential services for persons with developmental disabilities: Status and trends through 1997.* Minneapolis: University of Minnesota, Research and Training Center on Community Living, Institute on Community Integration.

U.S. Bureau of the Census. (1992). *Survey of income and program participation 1991 panel: Technical documentation (June, 1992 revision).* Washington, DC: U.S. Department of Commerce.

U.S. Bureau of the Census. (1996, April). *Current population reports. Special studies (P23-190).* Washington, DC: U.S. Government Printing Office.

U.S. Bureau of the Census. (1997). *International data base.* Washington, DC: Bureau of the Census, International Program Center, Information Resources Branch.

U.S. Department of Commerce. (1997). *Statistical abstract of the United States, 1996.* Washington, DC: U.S. Government Printing Office.

Author

David Braddock, Ph.D., Professor of Human Development and Head, Department of Disability and Human Development, University of Illinois at Chicago, 1640 W. Roosevelt Rd., Chicago, IL 60608.

On the Importance of Helping Families: Policy Implications From a National Study

Arnold Birenbaum, Ph.D. and Herbert J. Cohen, M.D.
1993

Abstract

This study is a companion to our 4-year study (Birenbaum, Guyot, & Cohen, 1990) on financing health care for individuals with autism or severe mental retardation. We reported on nonmedical expenditures and opportunity costs pertaining to maintaining a child or young adult with serious developmental disabilities in the home or in residential care and discussed policy implications for assisting their families. We proposed that (a) personal care and family support should be included in health care requirements, (b) family-centered care should be promoted, (c) appropriate programs and care should be provided for young adults no longer in school, (d) financing and organizing of family supports and subsidies should be administratively simple, (e) Medicaid should be expanded to increase use of home- and community-based services, and (f) financial support should be provided to families.

In this paper we have linked new findings from a national study on care for people with developmental disabilities and policy proposals for assisting families. We recently reported the results of a 4-year study on financing health care for individuals with autism or severe mental retardation (Birenbaum, Guyot, & Cohen, 1990).

The 1985–1986 data collected from 308 subjects under age 25 with autism and from 326 children and young adults with severe or profound mental retardation produced some interesting findings and contrasts concerning cost of medical and health care, financing, and utilization of these services. The highlights are:

- None of the children had expenditures in excess of $50,000 and very few reached the upper $20,000s.
- The average annual health care expenditure for children with autism was about $1,000 and for young adults with autism, about $1,700 compared to the $414 average cost for all American children. They received an average of four physician visits annually, slightly above the average for children in the general population. Hospitalization accounted for one third of the health care expenditures among children with autism, but for two thirds among young adults with the disorder.

- For children and young adults with severe mental retardation, the average expenditure on health care was about $4,000 because two thirds of them had physical impairments. They averaged about 12 physician visits annually, whereas those over 18 averaged 8 visits. Children were hospitalized about eight times the national rate for all children and young adults, about twice the national rate for their age peers.

- For both groups, people with autism or mental retardation, there was little use of preventive or habilitative services, and, consequently, these services were but a tiny fraction of health care expenditures. For the individuals whose primary physicians judged that they would benefit from physical or speech therapy, less than one quarter were receiving these services.

- Inequities abound in the financing of health care. Almost 20% of the parents of children with severe or profound mental retardation and 10% of the parents of autistic children had experienced refusals or limitations in the health insurance they could purchase for their child. In both disability groups, about 15% of those with private insurance had policies that specifically excluded coverage for some of the child's health care.

- Because the individuals with autism in this study were from families with higher incomes than were those with mental retardation, they were twice as likely to be covered by private insurance. Seven percent of the individuals with autism and 4% of those with severe or profound mental retardation had no insurance coverage. As a consequence, the percentage of the uninsured who did not visit a physician in the 12-month study period was three times higher than that for insured individuals.

- Only 60% of all children in this study had routine dental examinations within the 12-month study period, a worse record than the average American child.

- Income differences between the two groups of families were dramatically revealed when out-of-pocket expenses were compared. For children with autism, the average out-of-pocket expense for health and personal care was almost $1,000, about 3% of family income, but a very few families, about 2%, had expenses greater than 15% of their income. Families with a child who had severe or profound mental retardation typically spend almost $2,000 out-of-pocket, an average of 7% of their income, but as many as 10% spent over 15% of their total income. Medical debts over $2,000 burdened 1% of the families with children who had autism and 5% of the families with children who had severe or profound mental retardation.

We also answered the following questions because they had implications for understanding whether family support would be cost effective: How much do parents spend on babysitting, home modification, and other services and adaptations when a child with severe developmental disabilities lives at home? How do these total amounts compare with the cost of providing 24-hour a day care for either children with severe mental retardation or autism who live in residential placements? Are total amounts different or are they the same when the costs accrued for individuals with severe mental retardation are compared to those for children with autism? What do parents give up (opportunity-costs) when they provide in-home care?

Braddock (1987) collected data on the cost of residential placements for individuals with developmental disabilities in all the states. These data are useful and provide a perspective on costs of out-of-home care. Yet there is no analysis in his work on the savings to the taxpayer when families provide at-home care nor of the impact of family allowances to encourage families to maintain their children with developmental disabilities in their own homes. To address these issues, we have presented in this paper comparative findings on costs for these families of individuals with severe developmental disabilities and concluded with a detailed discussion of the policy implications of our findings.

Space limitations do not permit us to go into the elaborate methodology we employed to assure represen-tativeness in sampling in this national data-gathering effort. Although this was not a probability sample, we avoided the pitfalls found in using convenience samples drawn from patients at specialized out-patient health care facilities. To find families eligible for the study, we cast a wider net, using the census of children in need of special education in 11 school districts. The methodology employed is reported in Birenbaum, Guyot, and Cohen (1990).

Central to the policy recommendations found in this paper were the data collected on nonmedical expenditures pertaining to maintaining the child or young adult with serious developmental disabilities in the home or in residential care. Although biased toward families from urban and suburban households, we examined the expenditures for health care and other services for individuals living in residential placement as well as those living at home in nine highly populated states. This unique sample enabled us to make some comparisons on expenditures for those people with developmental disabilities living in a variety of residential placements with those living with their families.

The term *residential placement* is comprehensive, meaning all formally established living arrangements: foster care, group homes, community residences, Intermediate Care Facilities for the Mentally Retarded (ICF/MR), and nursing homes. In our study, the great majority of the children, adolescents, and young adults in residential placement lived in foster care and other family-like settings. Therefore, no pejorative connotations or images of large institutions should be attached to the term *residential placement*.

Characteristics of Individuals in Residential Placement

The ultimate step for an overburdened family is to place their child with severe disabilities in residential care. We found that of the 308 individuals with autism, 24 individuals (8%) were in residential placement and of the 326 who had severe or profound mental retardation, 72 individuals (22%) were in such placement. Half of these children with mental retardation were in large institutions, about one fourth were in group homes, and about one fourth were in foster homes. Approximately two thirds of all of the offspring in residential care were from homes with only a single parent. Whether or not only one parent was in the homes of these children at the time of placement could not be ascertained from our cross-sectional data. If single parent families predominated at the time of placement, residential care is clearly serving particularly needy families. Among sites, the huge variation in the proportion of individuals in placement appears to depend largely upon the availability of alternative services.

A striking fact is that individuals in residential placement differed less from those at home in their functional abilities than in their socioeconomic backgrounds. One expected difference was that the mean age of all the children, adolescents, and young adults at home was about 12 years, but for those in placement, it was 17 years. Parents varied greatly in how many years after the child's birth they made the placement decision, but few placed their children when they were infants. If parents had made their placement decisions primarily upon the severity of the child's condition, the data would show that the functional ability of children at home would consistently exceed that of children in placement. This was not the case.

Because children with more obvious impairments are diagnosed earlier, one would expect the children in placement to have an earlier age of diagnosis. However, for the children with severe mental retardation, the average age for the requested initial diagnoses was one year, and the reported average age for the children with autism was 4. In eight functional abilities from walking to speaking intelligibly, the children in residential placement were no more impaired than were the children living at home. In fact, we were surprised to find that the children with severe or profound mental retardation in our sample who lived at home had more difficulty climbing stairs than did those in residential placement.

However, we did find that a deficit in a key social skill distinguished children in placement from those at home. Children in placement sought out the company of other people far less frequently than did children at home. A plausible explanation is that over the years the child's inability to express affection or enjoyment of contact discourages the parents in their persisting efforts to care for their child at home. The causal relation may go in the other direction as well. In placement, fewer demands are placed on the young people to socialize, and the simple enjoyment of socializing decreases through decreased experience. Only a longitudinal study design could answer definitively whether failure to seek company occurs as often prior to placement as afterwards.

Household Composition

In examining household composition, we found that the families were remarkably similar in these respects: marital status of mother, number of siblings who live at home, and presence of additional siblings with the same disabling condition.

Socially advantaged families tended to seek out or more easily obtain residential placement for their children. The mean income of families of children with severe mental retardation who placed their children was about $8,000 higher than that of families who kept their children at home, but the $14,000 average difference among families with children who had autism was not statistically significant because the variation in income was high in both groups. Residence outside a central city was a particularly strong predictor of placement.

A caveat regarding these findings is that the study sites varied so greatly in the proportion of children in residential programs that site variation alone might greatly influence the findings. Actually, data from a single site, the Wayne County special education district, which serves both Detroit and its suburbs, supports this possible explanation. The 121 individuals with autism and the 50 with severe or profound mental retardation were all served by the same intermediate school district that provided programs up to the individual's 26th birthday. An analysis for all the sites showed the same results: Children in placement were older but did not have more severe disabilities, and their families came overwhelmingly from the suburbs.

Expenses to Modify and Repair the Home

The average out-of-pocket expenses to modify physical surroundings totaled about $100 for children with autism and about $250 for children with severe mental retardation. About 10% of the families had expenses for home and car modification that exceeded $2,000 per year. Unfortunately, a few families with children who had autism had unusual expenses that did not entirely solve the problems in keeping their children home. One family of three children in a suburban Wayne County location had to make considerable home modifications because their 6-year-old son continually tried to run away. They redesigned the interior of the house and placed alarms on the windows and bolts on all the doors. In another family, a daughter with autism slipped into the kitchen almost daily to dump food and cleaning supplies on the kitchen floor. She also frequently turned on the faucets, flooding the bathroom. Her mother estimated that the family had paid $400 to repair the bathroom floor but that a water-damaged rug and a ruined bed accounted for $1,050 in replacement costs that the family was postponing. All together, about 10% of the families spent more than $350 to replace damaged furnishings.

The major expenses of families with children who had severe or profound mental retardation were for purchasing a van that could carry a wheelchair and for one time interior modifications to permit wheelchair access.

Child Care Needs

Children, adolescents, and young adults with serious developmental disabilities required care far in excess of their healthy peers. Yet one fourth of the children living at home did not have two parents to care for them. The single parent households were usually headed by mothers, but a few fathers were coping alone, as were a few grandmothers. For all children living in metropolitan areas, the proportion was about the same, 23% in single parent homes. However, the two groups of families diverged when the members with developmental disabilities were young adults. Adults with autism were more likely to live in a two-parent family; adults with severe mental retardation were less likely to do so.

Parents reported whether their 10- to 24-year-old children could take care of themselves at home alone. According to the respondents, only one third of those with autism could take care of themselves, even for a few minutes. Less than one fifth of the offspring with severe or profound mental retardation could take care of themselves. Only one fourth of these 10- to 24-year-olds received regular care from someone outside the household, about half from a relative. Among those who had help in child care, the lowest quartile used less than 6 hours a week and the highest quartile used more than 40 hours a week.

The experiences of a farm family in Iowa with three children illustrate the difficulties in obtaining even occasional babysitting. Sylvia was an 11-year-old girl with severe mental retardation who was unable to feed or dress herself. Her brothers, ages 4 and 5, were not old enough to care for her. The mother had tried to find an adult to babysit, but only teenagers were available. When Sylvia was younger her grandparents cared for her occasionally,

but now that she had grown and they had become infirm, they could no longer lift her from her wheelchair. Her parents wanted to take a one-night trip to a livestock show, but they could find no one to stay with their children. A respite center known to the mother did accept clients for 3 or 4 day stays, but she felt it would be hard for her daughter to be away from home that long when all they wanted was a single night's care.

Families in our sample bore the financial burden of child care. Whether a child went to the home of a paid sitter or a sitter came to the home, in no instance did a health insurance policy pay for even part of the child care costs. Medicaid paid some child care costs for children at home for only about 1% of the 634 children with developmental disabilities in this study.

Special camps are the best known summer programs for children with developmental disabilities because they are sponsored by active voluntary associations such as the United Cerebral Palsy Association and the Association for Retarded Citizens. At our study sites, about 10 to 15% of the children went to camp. School summer programs, however, served about half of the children and young adults. Overnight respite care was received by only about one tenth of the children for a few nights a year.

The usual inconveniences of moving the family residence are amplified by the need to find new providers of services for the child with disabilities. The average individual in both of the disability groups that we studied moved about twice in 10 years, a rate that is somewhat lower than the national average. The extreme variation runs from the stable one third who have lived at the same address since birth to the very mobile 5% who have moved more than eight times in 10 years.

Expenditure Comparison With Individuals in Residential Placements

America's expenditures on child care are not supportive of families. In the interviews, all of the expenses incurred by families and charitable organizations to maintain these children and young adults with severe disabilities in their homes averaged about $550 annually for those with autism and about $950 annually for individuals with mental retardation. For children with mental retardation and physical impairment, the family had substantial expenses beyond the cost of programs and other caregivers. During the 12 months of the study, a few families had substantial expenses related to construction of ramps and other home modifications or to purchasing a van to accommodate the wheelchair when they would have preferred a sedan.

The private expenditures to keep a child home seem insignificant when contrasted with the reported Medicaid and Supplemental Security Income (SSI) payments to care for a child in residential placement: $16,000 for the typical individual with autism and $27,000 for an individual with severe mental retardation.

Indirect Costs of the Child's Disability to the Family

The inability of all the young adults with severe mental retardation and most of the adults with autism to engage in paid employment resulted in a substantial indirect cost that was calculated as lost lifetime earnings. The pattern for mothers of children with severe mental retardation was consistent across the age range through age 24. About one fourth of the mothers worked full-time, about 20% part-time, and over half were not employed. Many interrupted their employment when their children were born and had yet to return. Current data from the Bureau of Labor Statistics on paid employment show that mothers with young children work full-time at a rate at least 12 percentage points above the rate of mothers of children with severe mental retardation. Nationally, among all mothers whose youngest child is between ages 6 and 13, 48% are in full-time paid employment and another 18% are in part-time employment. This places them more than 20 percentage points above the mothers of children with severe mental retardation.

Opportunity losses were dramatically illustrated when we compared employment among mothers whose child or young adult with severe mental retardation was in placement to those whose child or young adult was at home. Almost 80% of the mothers of individuals in residential care were employed, whereas only 50% of those mothers who were the primary caretakers held a job. When the child was living away, almost three fourths of the mothers who worked were working full-time.

It is interesting that for mothers with children who had developmental disabilities and were living in residential care, the proportion working full-time rose to about 40%, not far below the national average. The indirect costs in income of the children's chronic disabilities due to the mothers' foregoing work were substantial.

Discussion, Policy Implications, and Recommendations

There are six important family policy implications that are derived from this report on national data comparing families with a member who had a developmental disability and lived with them and families with counterparts in residential placement. In the course of this discussion, we have mentioned legislative proposals that can advance the goals of establishing more normal ways to live. First, because of their disability, the health care requirements of these children, adolescents, and adults should be viewed broadly so as to include personal care and family support. In the routine circumstances of a 5-year-old boy free of chronic illness and disability, an annual medical check-up may be the only health care service he needs, and this type of care is entirely distinct from his parents' need for a Saturday night babysitter. However, the medically involved child, for example, a 15-year-old boy with spina bifida, may have benefitted from corrective surgery, physical therapy, the installation of a home elevator, and a sitter who can perform clean, intermittent catheterization. We believe that it is appropriate to regard all of these services as health-care related because, in the absence of a health condition, none of them would be necessary for a 15-year-old. Case management should coordinate the whole gamut of necessary care.

Second, financing should promote family-centered care. To state the case in bold terms, the family should be regarded as the unit for receiving services. The tendency of Americans in the late 20th century to look at individuals without seeing them as members of families results in a distorted view. Specifically, it is unrealistic to believe that excellent services have been provided to children with severe mental retardation and physical disabilities when they receive appropriate schooling but their parents and siblings obtain no assistance in bearing the physical, mental, emotional, and social burdens of care. When parents are empowered, they should be able to call upon services to assist them in keeping their son or daughter who has disabilities in their home beyond childhood. The natural desire of parents to nurture their children during their growing years should be especially encouraged for children whose progress is measured in centimeters. Whenever families decide that they can no longer bear the burden of care, the transition to a residential placement should be facilitated. The

Association for the Care of Children's Health has put forward a comprehensive overview of family-centered care that is itemized in checklists for all participants (Shelton, Jeppson, & Johnson, 1987).

Third, young adults with serious, chronic conditions continue to need appropriate programs and personal care after they have completed school. It follows that although there is an agency in each state that is accountable for this service, it often provides only lip service to these needs. Some forward-looking special education directors have attempted to piece together programs for their graduates who have severe disabilities, but the heavily burdened education system cannot be expected to fill this policy vacuum. The need is for systematic commitment of resources at state and federal levels. In its absence, parents are left not knowing how their sons and daughters with disabilities will be cared for in the decades ahead when they will no longer be able to care for them.

Fourth, financing and organizing of family supports and subsidies should be administratively simple. Long-term care needs should be included in comprehensive thinking about children with severe developmental disabilities. Just as fresh thinking about long-term care for elderly citizens includes new ways to expand home care, so should thinking about children with chronic conditions include many varieties of child care and family services. The majority of older children with autism and with severe mental retardation cannot be left at home alone, even for 15 minutes. This burden of constant attention requires occasional alleviation, but the only alleviation that is financially supported is to place the child in a residence. From the parents' perspective, residential placement is cost effective because they pay nothing after the first month. Medicaid eligibility rules deem that the family income belongs to the child during the first month, but thereafter, only the child's own income and assets, typically nil, share in the payment. The paradox of this situation is that home care is cost effective from a societal perspective but costly to the family because they must either find the free caregivers among relatives or pay the whole bill. If a single source were to pay for both long-term residential care and for its substitutes, then the payer would have monetary incentive to provide a range of child care, home care, day programs, and respite services as alternatives to residential care.

This recommendation fits the national trend toward reducing the numbers of children and young adults en-

tering institutions. From the 1977 total of about 91,000 children and youth under the age of 21 in public and private institutions for individuals with mental retardation, the number fell to about 60,000 in 1982 and to about 48,500 in 1987 (Lakin et al., 1989). This massive shift has been accompanied only by a relatively small corresponding increase in family support services.

Fifth, Medicaid can be expanded to increase the use of home- and community-based services. Medicaid waivers have been a flexible but complicated method for states to obtain permission from the Health Care Financing Administration (HCFA) to use federal funds for services provided outside of institutions. For people covered by a waiver, the state has two freedoms: one, to provide specific services not included in the mandatory or optional state services and, two, to decline to provide those services to others served by Medicaid. In recent years HCFA has preferred not to issue new waivers, but to encourage states to use their options flexibly.

The fundamental deficiency of family support services is addressed by the Medicaid Quality Services to the Mentally Retarded Amendments of 1988, sponsored by Representative Henry Waxman (H.R. 5233). A succinct analysis prepared by the Congressional Budget Office estimates participation, services, and federal costs (Congressional Budget Office, 1988). The Waxman bill gives states the option of providing community habilitation services to individuals with mental retardation or related conditions. We believe that these services would be especially helpful for young adults who are no longer served by the special education system. Among the services covered are prevocational, adaptive living, educational, and supported employment. The individuals eligible for these services are those qualified for SSI, approximately 100,000 people, according to a Congressional Budget Office estimate, which also projects new enrollments at 42,000 by 1993. Some of the major benefits of this bill to individuals who have severe mental retardation or autism can be estimated from our data. Although all of the individuals with developmental disabilities in our study were categorically eligible for SSI, many were ineligible due to the amount of family income and assets. Only 40% of those living at home across the age span from birth to 24 received SSI benefits. A larger proportion of young adults at home, about 85%, received SSI benefits. The unserved young adults could receive SSI benefits under current regulations, whereas the unserved 72% of the families of children may need assistance that could come from changes in regulations or from alternative sources. The recent Supreme Court ruling (February 1990) should speed up recognition of the Social Security Administration's responsibility to provide support to people with severe developmental disabilities during childhood.

Sixth, financial support for families is a necessity. Support for unpaid caregivers comes in three forms: tax credits or deductions (e.g., the federal government child and dependent care tax credit); direct payments to family members, as in the Michigan program of family support; and direct services to the unpaid provider, ranging from training to respite.

Tax breaks are always unobtrusive and often inequitable, but easy to administer. The long-standing federal tax deduction for a blind person leads to the question, why not for the deaf? Because the federal dependent care income tax credit applies to all children below age 15 and to spouses with disabilities, the obvious gaps are older offspring with disabilities and the frail elderly relative, but Congress has resisted expanding the scope. The amount of tax that the federal government loses in the child care tax credit, which largely goes to middle and upper income families, is more than the amount spent on all Headstart and other day care programs for disadvantaged children. This inequity promotes a two-tier system of child care.

Family financial support programs have the advantage of giving families flexibility to meet their needs as they define them. An impressive example is the Michigan family support program for children under age 18. Families of children who have severe mental retardation, mental retardation and physical impairments, or who have autism are eligible for a subsidy of $225 per month as long as the family income is under $60,000. Since starting the program in 1984, Michigan now supports over 3,000 families. The initial hope that a substantial number of families would bring their children home from residential placement proved to be false. Only 60 children have returned. The basic reason to mount such programs is that they help to relieve the burden on families.

In sum, the current focus on achieving independence for people with disabilities neglects the members of their household. The people who share a household with a person who has serious disabilities carry a burden beyond those of most people. If policy makers address the immediate family as the unit that needs services due to a member's disability, then respite services and other family supports would be common rather than the rarity we found them to be. Empowerment of people with disabilities cannot ignore those who provide day-to-day care.

References

Braddock, D. (1987). *Federal policy toward mental retardation and developmental disabilities*. Baltimore: Brookes.

Birenbaum, A., Guyot, D., & Cohen, H. J. (1990). *Health care financing for severe developmental disabilities* (Monograph 14). Washington, DC: American Association on Mental Retardation.

Congressional Budget Office. (1988). *Estimated costs and provisions of H.R. 3454 and H.R. 5233* (Staff Working Paper). Washington, DC: Congress of the United States.

Lakin, K. C., Jaskulski, T. M., Hill, B. K., Bruininks, R. H., Menke, J. M., White, C. C., & Wright, E. A. (1989). *Medicaid services for persons with mental retardation and related conditions* (Project Report 27). Minneapolis: University of Minnesota, Institute on Community Integration.

Shelton, T. L., Jeppson, E. S., & Johnson, B. H. (1987). *Family-centered care for children with special health care needs*. Washington, DC: Association for the Care of Children's Health.

Authors

Arnold Birenbaum, Ph.D., Professor, Department of Sociology, St. John's University, Grand Central and Utopia Parkways, Jamaica, NY 11439. **Herbert J. Cohen, M.D.,** Professor of Pediatrics, Rose F. Kennedy Center, Albert Einstein College of Medicine, 1410 Pelham Parkway S., Bronx, NY 10461.

PART FIVE

Looking Ahead

Looking back over AAMR's 125 year history, we can readily see that families have come a long way. From initial invisibility or vilification, families ended the 20th century as primary players in mental retardation services. The long journey was marked first by an acknowledgement that family care is a good model, if only to inform institutional practice. Mid-century, researchers cast a sympathetic, although somewhat patronizing, eye toward family emotional responses to handicap, and clinicians responded by viewing parents and siblings in the role of patients. At the same time, however, activist parents began an advocacy movement that attested both to service needs and to parental capabilities. More recently, researchers, responsive to a more inclusive philosophy and armed with newer methodologies, have taken an increasingly sophisticated look at family adjustment, and have begun to view the totality of family responses to disability (positive as well as negative) across the whole lifespan. Laws and service models have encouraged parents and professionals to work together, and "family support" is beginning to change the way we think about service delivery. There are new challenges too. Adults with mental retardation are more likely than before to outlive their own parents. Moreover, these adults are increasingly marrying and having families of their own.

Looking ahead we cannot see as well. We have been encouraged to include this final section forecasting how families of children with mental retardation will fare in the years to come and what directions family research might take. The uncertainties around the 2000 election underscored our reservation about prognostication. It's easy to be wrong. Even if we are well-informed, we can never anticipate how readily events can take a different direction. Indeed, parents cannot even predict their own family's outcome with any degree of certainty; half of those who pledge "until death do us part" with such conviction at the altar will divorce within a decade.

So we look ahead gingerly, focusing first on three broad social trends that seem inexorable regardless of the political winds and that will likely have a dramatic influence on family well-being. Families, we believe, will be increasingly affected by the internet, scientific advances, particularly psychopharmacology, and residential services. We conclude with some thoughts about family research in the decade or so to come.

The Internet

Computers, already in half of American homes, are rapidly becoming as ubiquitous as telephones. Information (and misinformation) about disabilities is now just clicks away. We see three ways that the Internet is increasingly affecting families. First, parents are becoming much more sophisticated consumers, and parent-professional relationships are becoming redefined, at least in the power differentials that come with knowledge. With hundreds of known causes of mental retardation, it is unlikely that a given professional will know as much about a particular rare syndrome as the parent who has searched out information from websites. Thus, the professional's role becomes altered from providing information to assisting parents in sorting through the information they bring and supporting their efforts to problem solve about alternatives.

Secondly, parents are finding emotional and functional support through the Internet, as they hear from and talk to other parents with similar experiences. A parent of a child newly diagnosed with Down Syndrome, for example, can readily access supportive testimonials from similar parents; letters from individuals with Down Syndrome; postings about special needs; information, references and links to local, national, and international organizations; and, of course, chats. Thirdly, many parents will feel more supported as they keep in touch with family members, long distance friends, and service providers better through e-mail than they have been able to do by telephone or in person.

At present, however, the Internet does not benefit families equally. A recent survey found that internet usage increases with education (e.g., 33.1% of individuals with just high school degrees but 63.9% of those with college degrees) and that internet access varied with race and ethnicity, with rates three times as high for Whites and Asian/Pacific Islanders as for African Americans and Hispanics (Kaye, 2000). Moreover, although persons with disabilities are also part of the computer revolution, their Internet access and usage is lower than for those without disability in every education and race/ethnicity group (Kaye, 2000). Looking ahead, then, the Internet will clearly empower and support families in coping with mental retardation and developmental disabilities. Yet because of unequal access, we can expect considerable diversity in what knowledge and concerns families bring to professionals and what families need and expect to receive from them.

Psychopharmacology

Recent advances in psychopharmacology have been staggering, and the increase in the specificity and effectiveness of behavior control drugs seems exponential (Reiss & Amen, 1998; Rush & Frances, 2000; Thompson & Symons, 1999). The major impact of psychotropic drugs in mainstream psychiatry is highly relevant to treatment programs for persons with mental retardation. Persons with mental retardation are at heightened risk for behavior problems and psychiatric disorder, a phenomenon termed "dual diagnosis." (Dykens, 2000; Pfeiffer & Baker, 1994). Over the past decade there has been greatly increased attention to dual diagnosis, making it more likely that emotional and behavioral problems will be properly identified and targeted for intervention. While psychological programs that focus on behavior problem reduction are essential, psychotropic medications will be a prominent part of future treatment plans.

There are well-deserved reservations about prescribing psychotropic medication for persons with mental retardation, owing largely to a history of excessively using antipsychotic medications for behavior control despite their sedating and other adverse effects (Kalachnik, 1999). Yet regardless of reservations, these practices continue. A recent survey of 120 group homes found that 27% of clients were prescribed a psychotropic medication and, of these clients, 78% received an antipsychotic medication (Amen, Sarphare, & Burrow, 1995). To be sure, many of these are newer atypical antipsychotics (e.g., risperidone) that are preferred over traditional ones because they are safer and less likely to cause further cognitive impairment; they may be more effective for individuals with severe or profound mental retardation (Kern, 1999; Rush & Frances, 2000). However, increasing awareness of underlying psychiatric conditions, such as unipolar or bipolar disorder, or obsessive-compulsive disorder, will suggest other, more appropriate, medications (Kalachnik, 1999). One example is the new selective serotonin reuptake inhibitor antidepressants (SSRIs) (e.g., Prozac, Zoloft, Paxil, Lovox, Celexa); these are promising for clients with profound and severe mental retardation, with evidence of effectiveness with wide-ranging behaviors, including agitation, aggression, impulsiveness, compulsiveness, anxiousness, panic, self-injury, and sleep problems (Kern, 1999).

Family researchers have shown that parents of children with mental retardation experience heightened stress and burden of care across the life cycle, with particularly high points at times of developmental transition (Wikler, 1986, this volume). Yet parental stress may not be related as much to cognitive disability as to contending with disruptive problem behaviors (Baker, Blacher, & McIntyre, 2000). The increasing effectiveness of psychotropic medication in reducing behavior problems and mental health symptoms in persons with mental retardation predictably will facilitate adjustment in community settings, reduce the cost of care, and change family life for the better.

Residential Services

There will always be a need for residential programs, although their nature is rapidly changing. The residential trends of recent decades — decreased institutional census, closure of large institutions, increased community based alternatives for adults, and supports for families to keep children at home — show every sign of continuing. Braddock et al. (1998) reported that 113 state residential facilities, in 36 states, have closed, or plan to close by the year 2000. The number of persons with mental retardation in large state residential facilities peaked in 1967 at 228,500. The census has decreased in every subsequent year, to 51,056 in 1999 (Prouty and Lakin, 2000). Looked at another way, the number of residents per 100,000 population was 116 in 1967 and down to 19 in 1999. Plans are under way in most states to find community alternatives for the remaining residents. Long-term-care community settings have increased dramatically, from 336 in 1960 to 70,635 in 1996 (Prouty & Lakin, 1997). Also, community-based living arrangements have become smaller, so that by 1999 33% of persons receiving residential services lived in homes for three or fewer individuals (Lakin, Prouty, Polister, & Anderson, 2000).

As residential census has dropped, however, the average annual cost per resident has soared, to $107,500 (Prouty and Lakin, 2000). Although there has been much debate as to whether community programs are less expensive, a study by Stancliffe and Lakin (1998) is notable. These authors controlled for differences between residents remaining in institutions and those in community settings and found, among other things, that the adjusted expenditure for persons in the community was 66% of that of their counterparts who remained in institutions.

What is the implication of these residential trends for families? First, given the high financial as well as emotional costs of residential treatment, whether institutional or community-based, families are likely to receive increasing support to keep a child with mental retardation at home. As states seek to avoid the high costs of residential care, propelled yet higher by a tight labor market (Braddock, 1998), we can anticipate that state-funded family support services will expand in scope and become available to more families. Second, families with adults, while being encouraged to "launch" them into more independent living, will have increasing access to small community-based homes nearby. The result will be greater continuing involvement of parents, siblings, and relatives in the life of the family member living out of the natural home. Studies have consistently found that family involvement is greater in community residences than institutions (Stancliffe & Lakin, 1998), and when the placement is closer to the family home (Baker & Blacher, 1993; Baker, Blacher, & Pfeiffer, 1996). Thus, looking ahead, we see marked benefits to families with a mentally retarded member from the availability of information and support via the internet, from behavior management through medication, and from more available residential options. Developments in these areas are supported through international social trends, business investment (e.g. pharmaceutical industry), and governmental cost-saving goals. Support for family researchers has a more tenuous basis.

Family Research

Looking ahead at family research in mental retardation, we are encouraged by recent directions taken by family researchers. We are less encouraged about funding trends, and worry that decreasing support for the social and behavioral sciences, and for intervention in particular, will unduly influence what we study and how we study it. That said, however, we anticipate productive family research directions, influenced by evolving philosophy, social policy, and family needs. We expect:

Increased attention to the whole family life cycle. The emphasis of the last decade or so on changing family needs and resources across the life cycle (Carter & McGoldrick, 1989; Turnbull & Turnbull, 1990) will be an important underpinning for future study. We anticipate, in particular, increased attention to families of young adults, as these individuals age out of mandated schooling (Blacher, 2001), and continuing analysis of families with older adults (Seltzer & Heller, 1997). We also anticipate that "family" will be more inclusive and less limited to the study of mothers.

Increased attention to culture. Family researchers will increasingly study critical issues within cultural groups other than Anglo-American (Magana, 2000). The widely held belief among family researchers that "culture matters" is beginning to be reflected in studies of mental retardation in minority families (Blacher, Shapiro, Lopez, Diaz, & Fusco, 1997; Chen & Tang, 1997; Magana, 1999 (this volume); Rogers-Dulan, 1998). This trend toward a more diverse and truly representative picture of families and disability will be further driven by our nation's changing demographics, federal funding guidelines mandating minority representation, and a greater number of minority researchers.

Increased attention to mental health problems in mental retardation. Family researchers, looking beyond the mainly epidemiological studies to date, have much to contribute to a better understanding of the etiology of mental health problems as well as psycho-social interventions. As school, vocational, social, and residential programs for people with mental retardation become more normalized, an individual with maladaptive behaviors especially stands out. Professionals are now more sensitized to the phenomenon of "dual diagnosis," and, as noted, new promise from psychotropic drugs is bringing this mainstream psychiatry concern into the mental retardation literature. There is a pressing need to understand more about why persons with mental retardation are at such heightened risk for behavioral difficulties, and to devise ways to intervene earlier (Crnic, Baker, Blacher, & Edelbrock, 1998).

Increased attention to family support programs. We have noted that family support programs are increasing, and yet with a paucity of sound evaluation research. Proponents argue that the benefits are to be seen in greater consumer satisfaction, more quality caregiving, increased family quality of life, and decreased need for out-of-home placement. Good evaluation research is already overdue. To date most evaluation has involved cost analysis. We anticipate, however, that as more significant funds (especially Medicaid waivers) are allocated to programs such as cash subsidies and respite care, family researchers will weigh in.

Increased study of specific syndromes. In recent decades the mental retardation field has been dominated by emphasis on broad constructs that cut across levels and types of disability (e.g., normalization, mainstreaming, inclusion, deinstitutionalization, choice, quality of life, permanency planning, family support). Yet many notable advances in knowledge have come from research on specific syndromes, focused on etiology or behavioral manifestations (Dykens, Hodapp, & Finucane, 2000). In the immediate future the near-complete mapping of the human genome will have far-reaching impacts and be a stimulus to further study of specific syndromes (Moser, 1995). Although not family research *per se*, the increased study of syndrome-specific behavior, as well as related areas, such as prenatal diagnosis and gene therapy, intimately involve family decision making and well-being.

Research approaches will continue to evolve with these and other content concerns, with new methodologies, with the focus of research funding, and with developments in thinking about mental retardation and social policy. We note three research directions that we would encourage and that seem likely extensions of the best recent family study:

Increased longitudinal research. Families are not static, and family issues of interest are not usually well-addressed by single-assessment research designs. Although longitudinal studies are costly, and they have their own associated problems (e.g., attrition, changing measures), longitudinal studies have been extraordinarily productive in the family research arena. Even over short critical periods (e.g. the transition into, or out of, school) longitudinal designs give a more valid picture of development and an opportunity to go beyond simple explanatory models to investigate moderators and mediators of outcome. We anticipate more emphasis on longitudinal research and also on multi-site/multi-investigator studies (e.g., Seltzer & Krauss, this volume).

Increased emphasis on the positive. Family researchers' past emphasis on negative impact of disability has been criticized as being too unidimensional, missing the complexity of families' experience. In recent years, researchers have begun to examine positive outcomes (Helff & Glidden, 1998), measured variously as perceived positive impact, resilience, empowerment, positive adaptation (Singer & Powers, 1993), cognitive coping (Turnbull et al., 1993), accommodation (Gallimore et al., 1996), and transformations (Scorgie & Sobsey, 2000). In program evaluation, there is a renewed emphasis on consumer satisfaction and on "family generalization," the broader impact of interventions on family functioning (Baker et al., 1991, this volume). We expect that family researchers will further broaden their dependent measures in an effort to more fully capture the family experience.

Improved cross-influence of research and practice. "Research to Practice" is a popular phrase, a favorite convention theme. Yet much research appears to be conducted with little attention to, or awareness of, implications for practice. At the same time, practices in the mental retardation field often seem to be proceed without empirical evidence, marching to different drumbeats, like values and advocacy. Although basic research, unbound by practical considerations, will always be essential, we note that there is an increasing emphasis on fiscal accountability; it is likely that this will encourage more researchers to aim at practical questions and to clearly present the implications of their findings for practice.

At the same time, we would encourage more research from practice. AAMR's early papers, like those in this volume by Doll, Vaux, Murray, Mikelson, and Boggs, highlight how persons intimately involved in services have a unique view of the issues and questions that deserve more careful study. Although federal support will continue to be the cornerstone of research in mental retardation, we would hope that state governments, private agencies, and foundations take more interest in funding research within their service programs. Moreover, we would hope for more researchers on the staff of such programs as well as greater collaboration between service providers, family members, self-advocates, and researchers.

All in all, families who have a member with mental retardation have many reasons to be hopeful about the immediate future. It is inspiring to see how far we have come during the last half of the 20th century.

References

Aman, M. G., Sarphare, G., & Burrow, W. H. (1995). Psychotropic drugs in group homes: Prevalance and relation to demographic/psychiatric variables. *American Journal on Mental Retardation, 99,* 500–599.

Baker, B. L., & Blacher, J. (1993). Out-of-home placement for children with mental retardation: Dimensions of family involvement. *American Journal on Mental Retardation, 98,* 368–377.

Baker, B. L., Blacher, J., & McIntyre, L.L. (2000). *Families and dual diagnosis: understanding the impact across the lifespan.* In Ann R. Poindexter (Ed.), NADD 17th Annual Conference Proceedings: Bridging the Gap (pp. 187–192). NADD: Kingston, NY.

Baker, B. L., Blacher, J., & Pfeiffer, S. I. (1996). Family involvement in residential treatment. *American Journal on Mental Retardation, 101,* 1–15.

Baker, B. L., Landen, S. J., & Kashima, K. L. (1991). Effects of parent training on families of children with mental retardation: Increased burden or generalized benefit? *American Journal on Mental Retardation, 96,* 127–136.

Blacher, J. (2001). The transition to adulthood: Mental retardation, families, and culture. *American Journal on Mental Retardation, 106,* 173–188.

Blacher, J., Shapiro, J., Lopez, S., Diaz, L., & Fusco, J. (1997). Depression in Latina mothers of children with mental retardation: A neglected concern. *American Journal on Mental Retardation, 101,* 483–496.

Braddock, D. (1998). Mental retardation and developmental disabilities: Historical and contemporary perspectives. In D. Braddock, R. Hemp, R., S. Parish, & J. Westrich, J. *The state of the states in developmental disabilities,* 5th ed. Washington, D. C.: American Association on Mental Retardation.

Carter, B., & McGoldrick, M. (Eds.) (1989). *The changing family life cycle. A framework for family therapy.* Boston: Allyn & Bacon.

Chen, T. Y., & Tang, C. S. (1997). Stress appraisal and social support of Chinese mothers of adult children with mental retardation. *American Journal on Mental Retardation, 101,* 473–482.

Crnic, K., Baker, B. L., Blacher, J., & Edelbrock, C. (1998). *Children with mental retardation: Family processes and dual diagnosis.* NICH Grant 3479-1459.

Dykens, E. M. (2000). Annotation: Psychopathology in children with intellectual disability. *Journal of Child Psychology and Psychiatry, 41,* 407–418.

Dykens, E.M., Hodapp, R. M., & Finucane, B. M. (2000). *Genetics and mental retardation syndromes: a new look at behavior and interventions.* Baltimore: Paul Brookes.

Gallimore, R. G., Coots, J. J., Weisner, T. , Garnier, H., & Guthrie, D. (1996). Family responses to children with early developmental delays II: Accommodation intensity and activity in early and middle childhood. *American Journal on Mental Retardation, 101,* 215–232.

Helff, C. M., & Glidden, L. M. (1998). More positive or less negative? Trends in research on adjustment of families rearing children with developmental disabilities. *Mental Retardation, 36,* 457–464.

Kalachnik, J. E. (1999). Monitoring psychotropic medication. In N. A. Wieseler & R. H. Hanson (Eds.). *Challenging behavior of persons with mental health disorders and severe developmental disabilities,* pp. 151–203. Washington, D.C.: American Association on Mental Retardation.

Kaye, H. S. (2000). Computer and internet use among people with disabilities. *Disability Statistics Report (13).* Washington D.C.; U.S. Department of Education, National Institute on Disability and Rehabilitation Research.

Kern, C. A. (1999). Psychopharmacotherapy for people with profound and severe mental retardation and mental disorders. In N. A. Wieseler & R. H,. Hanson (Eds.). *Challenging behavior of persons with mental health disorders and severe developmental disabilities* (pp. 103–123). Washington, D.C.: American Association on Mental Retardation.

Lakin, K. C., Prouty, R., Polister, B., & Anderson, L. (2000). Over three quarters of all residential service recipients in community settings as of June 1999. *Mental Retardation, 38,* 378–379.

Magana, S. M. (1999). Puerto Rican families caring for an adult with mental retardation: Role of familism. *American Journal on Mental Retardation, 104,* 466–482.

Magana, S. M. (2000). Mental retardation research methods in Latino communities. *Mental Retardation, 38,* 303–315.

Moser, H. W. (1995). A role for gene therapy in mental retardation. *Mental Retardation and Developmental Disabilities Research Reviews, 1,* 4–6.

Pfeiffer, S. I., & Baker, B. L. (1994). Residential treatment for children with dual diagnosis of mental retardation and mental disorder. In J. Blacher (Ed.). *When there's no place like home: Options for children living apart from their natural families,* pp. 273–298. Baltimore: Paul H. Brookes.

Prouty, R., & Lakin, K. C. (Eds.). (1997). *Residential services for persons with developmental disabilities: Status and trends through 1996.* Minneapolis: University of Minnesota, Research and Training Center on Community Living, Institute on Community Integration.

Prouty, R., and Lakin, K. C. (2000). *Residential services for persons with developmental disabilities: Status and trends through 1999.* Minneapolis, MN: University of Minnesota, Research and Training Center on Community Living.

Reiss, S. & Amen, M. G. (1998). *Psychotropic medications and developmental disabilities: The international consensus handbook.* Washington, D.C.: American Association on Mental Retardation.

Rogers-Dulan, J. (1998). Religious connectedness among urban African American families who have a child with disabilities. *Mental Retardation, 36,* 91–103.

Rush, A. J., & Frances, A. (2000). Expert consensus guideline series: Treatment of psychiatric and behavioral problems in mental retardation. *American Journal on Mental Retardation, 195,* 159–228.

Scorgie, K., & Sobsey, D. (2000). Transformational outcomes associated with parenting children who have disabilities. *Mental Retardation, 38,* 195–206.

Seltzer, M. M., & Heller, T. (1997). Families and caregiving across the life course: Research advances on the influence of context. *Family Relations, 46,* 321–323.

Singer, G. H. S., & Powers, L. E. (Eds.) (1993). *Families, disability, and empowerment: Active coping skills and strategies for family interventions.* Baltimore: Paul H. Brookes.

Stancliffe, R. J., & Lakin, K. C. (1998). Analysis of expenditures and outcomes of residential alternatives for persons with developmental disabilities. *American Journal on Mental Retardation, 102,* 552–568.

Thompson, T., & Symons, F. J. (1999). Neurobehavioral mechanisms of drug action. In N. A. Wieseler & R. H. Hanson (Eds.). *Challenging behavior of persons with mental health disorders and severe developmental disabilities* (pp. 125–150). Washington, D.C.: American Association on Mental Retardation.

Turnbull, A. P., Patterson, J. M., Behr, S. K., Murphy, D. L., Marquis, J. G., & Blue-Banning, M. J. (Eds.) (1993). *Cognitive coping, families, and disability.* Baltimore: Paul H. Brookes.

Turnbull, A. P., & Turnbull, H. R. (1990). *Families, professionals, and exceptionality: A special partnership* (2nd ed.). Baltimore: Brookes.

Wikler, L. M. (1986). Periodic stresses of families of older mentally retarded children: An exploratory study. *American Journal on Mental Retardation, 90,* 703–706.

Articles Reviewed

Adams, J. L., Campbell, F. A., & Ramey, C. T. (1984). Infants' home environments: A study of screening efficiency. *American Journal of Mental Deficiency, 89*(2), 133–139.

Affleck, G., Allen, D., McGrade, B. J., & McQueeney, M. (1982). Home environments of developmentally disabled infants as a function of parent and infant characteristics. *American Journal of Mental Deficiency, 86*(5), 445–452.

Affleck, G., Tennen, H., & Rowe, J. (1988). Adaptation features of mothers' risk and prevention appraisals after the birth of high-risk infants. *American Journal on Mental Retardation, 92*(4), 360–368.

Allen, D. A., & Affleck, G. (1985). Are we stereotyping parents? A postscript to Blacher. *Mental Retardation, 23*(4), 200–202.

Allen, D. A., Affleck, G., McQueeney, M., & McGrade, B. J. (1982). Validation of the parent behavior progression in an early intervention program. *Mental Retardation, 20*(4), 159–163.

Allen, D. A., & Hudd, S. S. (1987). Are we professionalizing parents? Weighing the benefits and pitfalls. *Mental Retardation, 25*(3), 133–139.

Anderson, K. A., & Garner, A. M. (1973). Mothers of retarded children. *Mental Retardation, 11*, 36–39.

Anderson, V. H., Schlottmann, R. S., & Weiner, B. J. (1975). Predictors of parent involvement with institutionalized retarded children. *American Journal of Mental Deficiency, 79*(6), 705–710.

Andrew, G., Kime, W. L., Stehman, V. A., & Jaslow, R. I. (1965). Parental contacts along the route to institutional commitment of retarded children. *American Journal of Mental Deficiency, 70*, 399–407.

Andron, L., & Sturm, M. L. (1973). Is "I do" in the repertoire of the retarded? A study of the functioning of married couples. *Mental Retardation, 11*, 31–34.

Appell, M. J., Williams, C. M., & Fishell, K. N. (1964). Changes in attitudes of parents of retarded children effected through group counseling. *American Journal of Mental Deficiency, 68*(6), 807–812.

Bailey, D. B. Jr., Skinner, D., Correa, V., Arcia, E., Reyes-Blanes, M. E., Rodriguez, P., Vazquez-Montilla, E., & Skinner, M. (1999). Needs and supports reported by Latino families of young children with developmental disabilities. *American Journal on Mental Retardation, 104*, 437–452.

Bailey, D. B., Blasco, P. M., & Simeonsson, R. J. (1992). Needs expressed by mothers and fathers of young children with disabilities. *American Journal on Mental Retardation, 97*(1), 1–10.

Baker, B. L., Landen, S. J., & Kashima, K. J. (1991). Effects of parent training on families of children with mental retardation: Increased burden or generalized benefit? *American Journal on Mental Retardation, 96*, 127–136.

Baker, B. L., Blacher, J., & Pfeiffer, S. I. (1996). Family involvement in residential treatment. *American Journal on Mental Retardation, 101*(1), 1–14.

Baker, B. L., & Blacher, J. B. (1993). Out-of-home placement for children with mental retardation: Dimensions of family involvement. *American Journal on Mental Retardation, 98*(3), 368–377.

Baker, B. L., Heifetz, L. J., & Murphy, D. M. (1980). Behavioral training for parents of mentally retarded children: One-year follow-up. *American Journal of Mental Deficiency, 85*(1), 31–38.

Bakken, J., Miltenberger, R. G., & Schauss, S. (1993). Teaching parents with mental retardation: Knowledge versus skills. *American Journal on Mental Retardation, 97*(4), 405–417.

Baran, S. J. (1979). Television programs about retarded children and parental attitudes toward their own retarded children. *Mental Retardation, 17*, 193–194.

Barber, T. M. (1956). Better parent education means more effective public relations. *American Journal of Mental Deficiency, 60*, 627–632.

Barnett, W. S., & Boyce, G. C. (1995). Effects of children with Down syndrome on parents' activities. *American Journal on Mental Retardation, 100*(2), 115–127.

Articles Reviewed

Bass, M. S. (1963). Marriage, parenthood, and prevention of pregnancy. *American Journal of Mental Deficiency, 68,* 320–335.

Beckman, P. J. (1991). Comparison of mothers' and fathers' perceptions of the effect of young children with and without disabilities. *American Journal on Mental Retardation, 95*(5), 585–595.

Beckman, P. J. (1983). Influence of selected child characteristics on stress in families of handicapped infants. *American Journal of Mental Deficiency, 88*(2), 150–156.

Beckman, P. J. (1984). Perceptions of young children with handicaps: A comparison of mothers and program staff. *Mental Retardation, 22*(4), 176–181.

Beckman, P. L. J., & Strong, B. (1993). Influence of social partner on interactions of toddlers with disabilities: Comparison of interactions with mothers and familiar playmates. *American Journal on Mental Retardation, 98*(3), 378–389.

Begab, M. J. (1956). Factors in counseling parents of retarded children. *American Journal of Mental Deficiency, 60,* 515–524.

Begab, M. J. (1960). Review of Farber, Bernard et al. "Family crisis and the retarded child" (1960). *American Journal of Mental Deficiency, 65,* 384–385.

Begab, M. J. (1958). A social work approach to the mentally retarded and their families. *American Journal of Mental Deficiency, 63,* 524–529.

Begun, A. L. (1989). Sibling relationships involving developmentally disabled people. *American Journal on Mental Retardation, 93*(5), 566–574.

Belan, E. (1956). Parents meet the state school. *American Journal of Mental Deficiency, 61,* 34–37.

Birenbaum, A., & Cohen, H. J. (1993). On the importance of helping families: Policy implications from a national study. *Mental Retardation, 31,* 67–74.

Birenbaum, A. (1992). Courtesy stigma revisited. *Mental Retardation, 30*(5), 265–268.

Birenbaum, A., & Cohen, H. J. (1993). Mini-symposium: Helping families. *Mental Retardation, 31*(2), 67–74.

Blacher, J. (1984). Sequential stages of parental adjustment to the birth of a child with handicaps: Fact or artifact? *Mental Retardation, 22*(2), 55–68.

Blacher, J., & Baker, B. L. (1992). Toward meaningful family involvement in out-of-home placement settings. *Mental Retardation, 30*(1), 35–43.

Blacher, J., & Meyers, C. E. (1983). A review of attachment formation and disorder in handicapped children. *American Journal of Mental Deficiency, 87,* 359–371.

Blacher, J., Baker, B. L., Feinfield, K. A. (1999). Leaving or launching? Continuing family involvement with children and adolescents in placement. *American Journal on Mental Retardation, 104,* 452–465.

Blacher, J., Nihira, K., & Meyers, C. E. (1987). Characteristics of home environment of families with mentally retarded children: Comparison across levels of retardation. *American Journal of Mental Deficiency, 91*(4), 313–320.

Blacher, J., Shapiro, J., Lopez, S., Diaz, L., & Fusco, J. (1997). Depression in Latina mothers of children with mental retardation: A neglected concern. *American Journal on Mental Retardation, 101*(5), 483–496.

Blacher, J. B., Hanneman, R. A., & Rousey, A. B. (1992). Out-of-home placement of children with severe handicaps: A comparison of approaches. *American Journal on Mental Retardation, 96*(6), 607–616.

Black, M. M., Molaison, V. A., & Smull, M. W. (1990). Families caring for a young adult with mental retardation: Service needs and urgency of community living requests. *American Journal on Mental Retardation, 95*(1), 32–39.

Blair, C., Ramey, C. T., & Hardin, J. M. (1995). Early intervention for low birthweight, premature infants; Participation and intellectual development. *American Journal on Mental Retardation, 99*(5), 542–554.

Blue-Banning, M. J., Turnbull, A. P., & Pereira, L. (2000). Group action planning as a support strategy for Hispanic families: Parent and professional perspectives. *Mental Retardation, 38,* 262–275.

Boggs, E. (1952). Relations of parent groups and professional persons in community situations. *American Journal of Mental Deficiency, 57,* 109–115.

Booth, T., & Booth, W. (2000). Against the odds: Growing up with parents who have learning disabilities. *Mental Retardation, 38,* 1–14.

Bostock, N. L. (1956). How can parents and professionals coordinate for the betterment of all retarded children? *American Journal of Mental Deficiency, 60,* 428–432.

Bostock, N. L. (1958). The parent outlook. *American Journal of Mental Deficiency, 63,* 511–516.

Botuck, S., & Winsberg, B. G. (1991). Effects of respite on mothers of school age and adult children with severe disabilities. *Mental Retardation, 29*(1), 43–47.

Boyd, D. (1951). The three stages in the growth of a parent of a mentally retarded child. *American Journal of Mental Deficiency, 55*, 608–611.

Braddock, D. (1999). Aging and developmental disabilities: Demographic and policy issues affecting American families. *Mental Retardation, 37*, 155–161.

Braddock, D. (1986). Federal assistance for mental retardation and developmental disabilities I: A review through 1961. *Mental Retardation, 24*(3), 175–182.

Braddock, D., & Hemp, R. (1997). Toward family and community mental retardation services in Massachusetts, New England, and the United States. *Mental Retardation, 35*(4), 241–256.

Braddock, D., Hemp, R., & Parish, S. (1997). Emergence of individual and family support in state service-delivery systems. *Mental Retardation, 35*(5), 497–498.

Bradley, R. H., & Caldwell, B. H. (1979). Home observation for measurement of the environment: A revision of the preschool scale. *American Journal of Mental Deficiency, 84*(3), 235–244.

Bradley, R. H., & Caldwell, B. M. (1977). Home observation for measurement of the environment: A validation study of screening efficiency. *American Journal of Mental Deficiency, 81*(5), 417–420.

Bradley, R. H., Rock, S. L., Caldwell, B. M., & Brisby, J. A. (1989). Uses of the HOME inventory for families with handicapped children. *American Journal on Mental Retardation, 94*(3), 313–330.

Bricker, W. A. (1970). Identifying and modifying behavioral deficits. *American Journal of Mental Deficiency, 75*, 16–21.

Brinker, R. P., Seifer, R., & Sameroff, A. J. (1994). Relations among maternal stress, cognitive development, and early intervention in middle- and low-SES infants with developmental disabilities. *American Journal on Mental Retardation, 98*(4), 463–480.

Brody, G. H., Stoneman, Z., Davis, C. H., & Crapps, J. M. (1991). Observations of the role relations and behavior between older children with mental retardation and their younger siblings. *American Journal on Mental Retardation, 95*(5), 527–236.

Bromley, B., & Blacher, J. (1989). Factors delaying out-of-home placement of children with severe handicaps. *American Journal on Mental Retardation, 94*(3), 284–291.

Bruder, M. B. (1987). Parent-to-parent teaching. *American Journal of Mental Deficiency, 91*(4), 435–438.

Bruns, D. A. (2000). Leaving home at an early age: Parents' decisions about out-of-home placement for young children with complex medical needs. *Mental Retardation, 38*, 50–60.

Buck, C., Valentine, G. H., & Hamilton, K. (1969). A study of microsymptoms in the parents and sibs of patients with Down's Syndrome. *American Journal of Mental Deficiency, 73*, 683–692.

Buckhalt, J. A., Rutherford, R. B., & Goldberg, K. E. (1978). Verbal and nonverbal interaction of mothers with their Down's syndrome and nonretarded infants. *American Journal of Mental Deficiency, 82*(4), 337–343.

Budd, K. S., & Greenspan, S. (1985). Parameters of successful and unsuccessful interventions with parents who are mentally retarded. *Mental Retardation, 23*(6), 269–273.

Buium, N., Rynders, J., & Turnure, J. (1974). Early maternal linguistic environment of normal and Down's Syndrome language-learning children. *American Journal of Mental Deficiency, 79*(1), 52–58.

Burgess, C. B. (1953). Parent use of the enrollment process in a residential school. *American Journal of Mental Deficiency, 58*, 170–174.

Cahill, B. M., & Glidden, L. M. (1996). Influence of child diagnosis on family and parental functioning: Down syndrome versus other disabilities. *American Journal on Mental Retardation, 101*(2), 149–160.

Caldwell, B. M., & Guze, S. B. (1960). A study of the adjustment of parents and siblings of institutionalized and non-institutionalized retarded children. *American Journal of Mental Deficiency, 64*, 845–861.

Caldwell, B. M., Manley, E. J., & Nissan, Y. (1961). Reactions of community agencies and parents to services provided in a clinic for retarded children. *American Journal of Mental Deficiency, 65*, 582–589.

Caldwell, B. M., Manley, E. J., & Seelye, B. J. (1961). Factors associated with parental reaction to a clinic for retarded children. *American Journal of Mental Deficiency, 65*, 590–594.

Castellani, P. J., Downey, N. A., Tausig, M. B., & Bird, W. A. (1986). Availability and accessibility of family support services. *Mental Retardation, 24*(2), 71–79.

Chen, T. Y., & Tang, C. S. (1997). Stress appraisal and social support of Chinese mothers of adult children with mental retardation. *American Journal on Mental Retardation, 101*(5), 473–482.

Cheng, P., & Tang, C. S. (1995). Coping and psychological distress of Chinese parents of children with Down Syndrome. *Mental Retardation, 33*(1), 10–20.

Cherry, K. E., Matson, J. L., & Paclawskyj, T. R. (1997). Psychopathology in older adults with severe and profound mental retardation. *American Journal on Mental Retardation, 101*(5), 445–458.

Cheseldine, S., & McConkey, R. (1979). Parental speech to young Down's syndrome children: An intervention study. *American Journal of Mental Deficiency, 83*(6), 612–620.

Clare, L., Garnier, H., & Gallimore, R. (1998). Parents' developmental expectations and child characteristics: Longitudinal study of children with developmental delays and their families. *American Journal on Mental Retardation, 103*(2), 117–129.

Clark, D. B., Baker, B. L., & Heifetz, L. J. (1982). Behavioral training for parents of mentally retarded children: Prediction of outcome. *American Journal of Mental Deficiency, 87*(1), 14–19.

Clayton, J. M., Glidden, L. M., & Kiphart, M. J. (1994). The questionnaires on resources and stress: What do they measure? *American Journal on Mental Retardation, 99*(3), 313–316.

Cleveland, D. W., & Miller, N. (1977). Attitudes and life commitments of older siblings of mentally retarded adults: An exploratory study. *Mental Retardation, 15*(3), 38–41.

Cole, D. A. (1986). Out-of-home child placement and family adaptation: A theoretical framework. *American Journal of Mental Deficiency, 91*(3), 226–236.

Coleman, J. C. (1953). Group therapy with parents of mentally deficient children. *American Journal of Mental Deficiency, 57*, 700–704.

Condell, J. F. (1966). Parental attitudes toward mental retardation. *American Journal of Mental Deficiency, 71*, 85–92.

Cook, J. J. (1963). Dimensional analysis of child-rearing attitudes of parents of handicapped children. *American Journal of Mental Deficiency, 68*, 354–361.

Crnic, K. A., Friedrich, W. N., & Greenberg, M. T. (1983). Adaptation of families with mentally retarded children: A model of stress, coping, and family ecology. *American Journal of Mental Deficiency, 88*(2), 125–138.

Crutcher, H. B. (1948). Family care of mental defectives. *American Journal of Mental Deficiency, 53*, 345–352.

Cunconan-Lahr, R., & Brotherson, M. J. (1996). Advocacy in disability policy: Parents and consumers as advocates. *Mental Retardation, 34*(6), 352–358.

Cuskelly, M., & Gunn, P. (1993). Maternal reports of behavior of siblings of children with Down syndrome. *American Journal on Mental Retardation, 97*(5), 521–529.

Diamond, K. E., & LeFurgy, W. G. (1992). Relations between mothers' expectations and the performance of their infants who have developmental handicaps. *American Journal on Mental Retardation, 97*(1), 11–20.

Dingman, H. F., Eyman, R. K., & Windle, C. D. (1963). An investigation of some child-rearing attitudes of mothers with retarded children. *American Journal of Mental Deficiency, 67*, 899–908.

Dodd, B., McCormack, P., & Woodyatt, G. (1994). Evaluation of an intervention program: Relation between children's phonology and parents' communicative behavior. *American Journal on Mental Retardation, 98*(5), 632–645.

Doll, E. A. (1937). The institution as a foster parent. *Journal of Psycho-Asthenics, 42*, 143–148.

Donovan, A. M. (1988). Family stress and ways of coping with adolescents who have handicaps: Maternal perceptions. *American Journal on Mental Retardation, 92*(6), 502–509.

Drewry, H. H., & Staff. (1953). Information for parents of mentally retarded children in New York City. *American Journal of Mental Deficiency, 57*, 495–497.

Dunst, C. J., Trivette, C. M., & Cross, A. H. (1986). Mediating influences of social support: Personal, family, and child outcomes. *American Journal of Mental Deficiency, 90*(4), 403–417.

Dupras, A., & Tremblay, R. (1976). Path analysis of parents' conservatism toward sex education of their mentally retarded children. *American Journal of Mental Deficiency, 81*(2), 162–166.

Dybwad, R. F. (1963). The widening role of parent organizations around the world. *Mental Retardation, 1,* 352–358.

Dyson, L., Edgar, E., & Crnic, K. (1989). Psychological predictors of adjustment by siblings of developmentally disabled children. *American Journal on Mental Retardation, 94*(3), 292–302.

Dyson, L. L. (1991). Families of young children with handicaps: Parental stress and family functioning. *American Journal on Mental Retardation, 95*(6), 623–629.

Dyson, L. L. (1993). Response to the presence of a child with disabilities: Parental stress and family functioning over time. *American Journal on Mental Retardation, 98*(2), 207–218.

Dyson, L. L. (1997). Fathers and mothers of school-age children with developmental disabilities: Parental stress, family functioning, and social support. *American Journal on Mental Retardation, 102*(3), 267–279.

Eden-Piercy, G. V. S., Blacher, J., & Eyman, R. K. (1986). Exploring parents' reactions to their young child with severe handicaps. *Mental Retardation, 24*(5), 285–291.

Edlund, C. V. (1971). Changing classroom behavior of retarded children: Using reinforcers in the home environment and parents and teachers as trainers. *Mental Retardation, 9*(3), 33–36.

Edmundson, K. (1985). The "discovery" of siblings. *Mental Retardation, 23,* 49–51.

Eheart, B. K., & Ciccone, J. (1982). Special needs of low-income mothers of developmentally delayed children. *American Journal of Mental Deficiency, 87*(1), 26–33.

Eheart, B. K. (1982). Mother-child interactions with nonretarded and mentally retarded preschoolers. *American Journal of Mental Deficiency, 87*(1), 20–25.

Engberg, E. J. (1952). Keeping in step. *American Journal of Mental Deficiency, 56,* 771–774.

Engelhardt, J. L., Brubaker, T. H., & Lutzer, V. D. (1988). Older caregivers of adults with mental retardation: Service utilization. *Mental Retardation, 26*(4), 191–195.

Erickson, M. T. (1969). MMPI profiles of parents of young retarded children. *American Journal of Mental Deficiency, 73,* 728–732.

Erickson, M., & Upshur, C. C. (1989). Caretaking burden and social support: Comparison of mothers of infants with and without disabilities. *American Journal on Mental Retardation, 94*(3), 250–258.

Essex, E. L., Seltzer, M. M., & Krauss, M. W. (1999). Differences in coping effectiveness and well-being among aging mothers and fathers of adults with mental retardation. *American Journal on Mental Retardation, 104,* 545–563.

Fantuzzo, J. W., Wray, L., Hall, R., Goins, C., & Azar, S. (1986). Parent and social-skills training for mentally retarded mothers identified as child maltreaters. *American Journal of Mental Deficiency, 91*(2), 135–140.

Farrell, M. J. (1957). What the institution expects of parents. *American Journal of Mental Deficiency, 61,* 675–678.

Feldman, M. A., & Walton-Allen, N. (1997). Effects of maternal mental retardation and poverty on intellectual, academic, and behavioral status of school-age children. *American Journal on Mental Retardation, 101*(4), 352–364.

Feldman, M. A., Case, L., Towns, F., & Betel, J. (1985). Parent education project I: Development and nurturance of children of mentally retarded parents. *American Journal of Mental Deficiency, 90*(3), 253–258.

Ferrara, D. M. (1979). Attitudes of parents of mentally retarded children toward normalization activities. *American Journal of Mental Deficiency, 84*(2), 145–151.

Fliederbaum, S. (1951). Effect of parent group participation in state schools. *American Journal of Mental Deficiency, 56,* 180–184.

Floyd, F. J., & Phillippe, K. A. (1993). Parental interactions with children with and without mental retardation: Behavior management, coerciveness, and positive exchange. *American Journal on Mental Retardation, 97*(6), 673–684.

Floyd, F. J., Costigan, C. L., & Phillippe, K. A. (1997). Developmental change and consistency in parental interactions with school-age children who have mental retardation. *American Journal on Mental Retardation, 101*(6), 579–594.

Flynt, S. W., & Wood, T. A. (1989). Stress and coping of mothers of children with moderate mental retardation. *American Journal on Mental Retardation, 94*(3), 278–283.

Flynt, S. W., Wood, T. A., & Scott, R. L. (1992). Social support of mothers of children with mental retardation. *Mental Retardation, 30*(4), 233–236.

Font, M. M. (1951). Parental reactions to psychologic measurement. *American Journal of Mental Deficiency, 56*, 48–51.

Fowle, C. M. (1968). The effect of the severely mentally retarded child on his family. *American Journal of Mental Deficiency, 73*, 468–473.

Frankel, R. (1979). Parents as evaluators of their retarded youngsters. *Mental Retardation, 17*, 40–42.

Fredericks, H. D., & et al. (1971). Parents educate their trainable children. *Mental Retardation, 9*(3), 24–26.

Freedman, R. I., Griffiths, D., Krauss, M. W., & Seltzer, M. M. (1999). Patterns of respite use by aging mothers of adults with mental retardation. *Mental Retardation, 37*(2), 93–103.

Freedman, R. I., Krauss, M. W., & Seltzer, M. M. (1997). Aging parents' residential plans for adult children with mental retardation. *Mental Retardation, 35*(2), 114–123.

Freeman, S. W., & Thompson, C. L. (1973). Parent-child training for the MR. *Mental Retardation, 11*(4), 8–10.

French, A. C., Levbarg, M., & Michal-Smith, H. (1953). Parent counseling as a means of improving the performance of a mentally retarded boy: A case study presentation. *American Journal of Mental Deficiency, 58*, 13–20.

Frey, K. S., Greenberg, M. T., & Fewell, R. R. (1989). Stress and coping among parents of handicapped children: A multidimensional approach. *American Journal on Mental Retardation, 94*(3), 240–249.

Friedman, D. L., Kastner, T., Plummer, A. T., Ruiz, M. Q., & Henning, D. (1992). Adverse behavioral effects in individuals with mental retardation and mood disorders treated with cabamazepine. *American Journal on Mental Retardation, 96*(5), 541–546.

Friedrich, W. N., & Friedrich W. L. (1981). Psychosocial assets of parents of handicapped and nonhandicapped children. *American Journal of Mental Deficiency, 85*(5), 551–553.

Friedrich, W. N., Greenberg, M. T., & Crnic, K. (1983). A short-form of the Questionnaire on Resources and Stress. *American Journal of Mental Deficiency, 88*, 41–48.

Friedrich, W. N., Wilturner, L. T., & Cohen, D. S. (1985). Coping resources and parenting mentally retarded children. *American Journal of Mental Deficiency, 90*(2), 130–139.

Fujiura, G. T. (1998). Demography of family households. *American Journal on Mental Retardation, 103*(3), 225–235.

Fujiura, G. T., Roccoforte, J. A., & Braddock, D. (1994). Costs of family care for adults with mental retardation and related developmental disabilities. *American Journal on Mental Retardation, 99*(3), 250–261.

Gallimore, R., Weisner, T. S., Kaufman, S. Z., & Bernheimer, L. P. (1989). The social construction of ecocultural niches: Family accommodation of developmentally delayed children. *American Journal on Mental Retardation, 94*, 216–230.

Gallimore, R. G., Weisner, T. S., Bernheimer, L. P., Guthrie, D., & Nihira, K. (1993). Family responses to young children with developmental delays: Accommodation activity in ecological and cultural context. *American Journal on Mental Retardation, 98*, 185–206.

Gallimore, R., Coots, J., Weisner, T., Garnier, H., & Guthrie, D. (1996). Family responses to children with early developmental delays II: Accommodation intensity and activity in early and middle childhood. *American Journal on Mental Retardation, 101*(3), 215–232.

George, J. D. (1988). Therapeutic intervention for grandparents and extended family of children with developmental delays. *Mental Retardation, 26*(6), 369–375.

Giannini, M. J., & Goodman, L. (1963). Counseling families during the crisis reaction to mongolism. *American Journal of Mental Deficiency, 67*, 740–747.

Giliberty, F. R., & Porter, E. L. H. (1954). Beginnings of a home training program. *American Journal of Mental Deficiency, 59*, 149–151.

Glidden, L. M., & Johnson, V. E. (1999). Twelve years later: Adjustment in families who adopted children with developmental disabilities. *Mental Retardation, 37*, 16–24.

Articles Reviewed

Glidden, L. M. (1993). What we do not know about families with children who have developmental disabilities: Questionnaire on resources and stress as a case study. *American Journal on Mental Retardation, 97*(5), 481–495.

Glidden, L. M., & Floyd, F. J. (1997). Disaggregating parental depression and family stress in assessing families of children with developmental disabilities: A multisample analysis. *American Journal on Mental Retardation, 102*(3), 250–266.

Glidden, L. M., & Pursley, J. T. (1989). Longitudinal comparisons of families who have adopted children with mental retardation. *American Journal on Mental Retardation, 94*(3), 272–277.

Glidden, L. M., Valliere, V. N., & Herbert, S. L. (1988). Adopted children with mental retardation: Positive family impact. *Mental Retardation, 26*(3), 119–125.

Goldberg, S., Marcovitch, S., MacGregor, D., & Lojkasek, M. (1986). Family responses to developmentally delayed preschoolers: Etiology and the father's role. *American Journal of Mental Deficiency, 90*(6), 610–617.

Goodman, L., & Rothman, R. (1961). The development of a group counseling program in a clinic for retarded children. *American Journal of Mental Deficiency, 65,* 789–795.

Goodman, L., Budner, S., & Lesh, B. (1971). The parents' role in sex education for the retarded. *Mental Retardation, 9,* 43–45.

Gordon, E. W., & Ullman, M. (1956). Reactions of parents to problems of mental retardation in children. *American Journal of Mental Deficiency, 61,* 158–163.

Gowen, J. W., Johnson-Martin, N., Goldman, B. D., & Appelbaum, M. (1989). Feelings of depression and parenting competence of mothers of handicapped and nonhandicapped infants: A longitudinal study. *American Journal on Mental Retardation, 94*(3), 259–271.

Graliker, B. V., Fishler, K., & Koch, R. (1962). Teenage reaction to a mentally retarded sibling. *American Journal of Mental Deficiency, 66,* 838–843.

Grant, G., & McGrath, M. (1990). Need for respite-care services for caregivers of persons with mental retardation. *American Journal on Mental Retardation, 94*(6), 638–648.

Grebler, A. M. (1952). Parental attitudes toward mentally retarded children. *American Journal of Mental Deficiency, 56,* 475–483.

Grimes, S. K., & Vitello, S. J. (1990). Follow-up study of family attitudes toward deinstitutionalization: Three to seven years later. *Mental Retardation, 28*(4), 219–225.

Gumz, E. J., & Gubrium, J. F. (1972). Comparative parental perceptions of a mentally retarded child. *American Journal of Mental Deficiency, 77*(2), 175–180.

Gutmann, A. J., & Rondal, J. A. (1979). Verbal operants in mother's speech to nonretarded and Down's syndrome children matched for linguistic level. *American Journal of Mental Deficiency, 83*(5), 446–452.

Hannah, M. E., & Midlarsky, E. (1999). Competence and adjustment of siblings of children with mental retardation. *American Journal on Mental Retardation, 104*(1), 22–37.

Hanneman, R., & Blacher, J. (1998). Predicting placement in families who have children with severe handicaps: A longitudinal analysis. *American Journal on Mental Retardation, 102*(4), 392–408.

Hanson, M. J., Vail, M. E., & Irvin, L. K. (1979). Parent and parent advisory observation measures as indicators of early intervention programs effects. *Mental Retardation, 17,* 43–44.

Hanzlik, J. R., & Stevenson, M. B. (1986). Interaction of mothers with their infants who are mentally retarded, retarded with cerebral palsy, or nonretarded. *American Journal of Mental Deficiency, 90*(5), 513–520.

Harris, V. S., & McHale, S. M. (1989). Family life problems, daily caregiving activities, and the psychological well-being of mothers of mentally retarded children. *American Journal on Mental Retardation, 94*(3), 231–239.

Haworth, A. M., Hill, A. E., & Glidden, L. M. (1996). Measuring religiousness of parents of children with developmental disabilities. *Mental Retardation, 34*(5), 271–279.

Hayden, M. F., & Heller, T. (1997). Support, problem-solving/coping ability, and personal burden of younger and older caregivers of adults with mental retardation. *Mental Retardation, 35*(5), 364–372.

Haywood, H. C. (1976). The ethics of doing research . . . and of not doing it. *American Journal of Mental Deficiency, 81*(4), 311–317.

Heifetz, L. J. (1977). Behavioral training for parents of retarded children: Alternative formats based on instructional manuals. *American Journal of Mental Deficiency, 82,* 194–203.

Heifetz, L. J., & Franklin, D. C. (1982). Nature and sources of the clergy's involvement with mentally retarded persons and their families. *American Journal of Mental Deficiency, 87* (1), 56–63.

Heilman, A. E. (1950). Parental adjustment to the dull handicapped child. *American Journal of Mental Deficiency, 54,* 556–562.

Helff, C. M., & Glidden, L. M. (1998). More positive or less negative? Trends in research on adjustment of families rearing children with developmental disabilities. *Mental Retardation, 36*(6), 457–464.

Heller, T., Miller, A. B., & Factor, A. (1997). Adults with mental retardation as supports to their parents: Effects on parental caregiving appraisal. *Mental Retardation, 35,* 338–346.

Heller, T., & Factor, A. (1988). Permanency planning among Black and White family caregivers of older adults with mental retardation. *Mental Retardation, 26*(4), 203–208.

Heller, T., & Factor, A. (1991). Permanency planning for adults with mental retardation living with family caregivers. *American Journal on Mental Retardation, 96*(2), 163–176.

Heller, T., & Factor, A. (1993). Aging family caregivers: Support resources and changes in burden and placement desire. *American Journal on Mental Retardation, 98*(3), 417–426.

Heller, T., Markwardt, R., Rowitz, L., & Farber, B. (1994). Adaptation of Hispanic families to a member with mental retardation. *American Journal on Mental Retardation, 99*(3), 289–300.

Heller, T., Miller, A. B., Hsieh, K., & Sterns, H. (2000). Later-life planning: promoting knowledge of options and choice-making. *Mental Retardation, 38,* 395–406.

Helm, D. T., Miranda, S., & Chedd, N. A. (1998). Prenatal diagnosis of Down syndrome: Mothers' reflections on support needed from diagnosis to birth. *Mental Retardation, 36*(1), 55–61.

Herman, S. E. (1994). Cash subsidy program: Family satisfaction and need. *Mental Retardation, 32*(6), 416–421.

Herman, S. E. (1991). Use and impact of a cash subsidy program. *Mental Retardation, 29*(5), 253–258.

Herman, S. E., & Hazel, K. L. (1991). Evaluation of family support services: Changes in availability and accessibility. *Mental Retardation, 29*(6), 351–357.

Herman, S. E., & Marcenko, M. O. (1997). Perceptions of services and resources as mediators of depression among parents of children with developmental disabilities. *Mental Retardation, 35*(6), 458–467.

Herman, S. E., & Thompson, L. (1995). Families' perceptions of their resources for caring for children with developmental disabilities. *Mental Retardation, 33*(2), 73–83.

Hersh, A., Carlson, R. W., & Lossino, D. A. (1977). Normalized interaction with families of the mentally retarded—to introduce attitude and behavior change in students in a professional discipline. *Mental Retardation, 15,* 32–33.

Hill, B., & Bruininks, R. H. (1984). Maladaptive behavior of mentally retarded individuals in residential facilities. *American Journal of Mental Deficiency, 88*(4), 380–387.

Hodapp, R. M., & Zigler, E. (1993). Comparison of families of children with mental retardation and families of children without mental retardation. *Mental Retardation, 31*(2), 75–77.

Holroyd, J., & McArthur, D. (1976). Mental retardation and stress on the parents: A contrast between Down's syndrome and childhood autism. *American Journal of Mental Deficiency, 80* (4), 431–436.

Horsefield, E. (1942). Suggestions for training the mentally retarded by parents in the home. *American Journal of Mental Deficiency, 46,* 533–537.

Howarth, A. M., Hill, A. E., & Glidden, L. M. (1996). Measuring religiousness of parents of children with developmental disabilities. *Mental Retardation, 34*(5), 271–279.

Hoyle, J. S. (1951). Home conditions and employment of mental defectives. *American Journal of Mental Deficiency, 55,* 619–621.

Intagliata, J., & Doyle, N. (1984). Enhancing social support for parents of developmentally disabled children: Training in interpersonal problem solving skills. *Mental Retardation, 22*(1), 4–11.

Joyce, K., Singer, M., & Isralowitz, R. (1983). Impact of respite care on parents' perceptions of quality of life. *Mental Retardation, 21*(4), 153–156.

Kanner, L. (1953). Parents' feelings about retarded children. *American Journal of Mental Deficiency, 57,* 375–383.

Kashima, K. J., Baker, B. L., & Landen, S. J. (1988). Media-based versus professionally led training for parents of mentally retarded children. *American Journal on Mental Retardation, 93*(2), 209–217.

Kaufman, A. V., James P., & Campbell, V. A. (1991). Permanency planning by older parents who care for adult children with mental retardation. *Mental Retardation, 29*(5), 293–300.

Kazdin, A. E. (1973). Issues in behavior modification with mentally retarded persons. *American Journal of Mental Deficiency, 78*, 134–140.

Kelman, H. R. (1957). Some problems in casework with parents of mentally retarded children. *American Journal of Mental Deficiency, 61*, 595–598.

Kenneth, K. F. (1977). The Family Behavior Profile: An initial report. *Mental Retardation, 15*(4), 36–40.

Kenney, E. (1967). Mother-retarded child relationships. *American Journal of Mental Deficiency, 71*, 631–636.

Kenowitz, L. A., & Edgar, E. (1977). Intra-community action networks: The ICAN System. *Mental Retardation, 15*(3), 13–16.

Keogh, B. K., Garnier, H. E., Bernheimer, L. P., & Gallimore, R. (2000). Models of child-family interactions for children with developmental delays: child-driven or transactional? *American Journal on Mental Retardation, 105*, 32–46.

Kirkham, M. A. (1993). Two-year follow-up of skills training with mothers of children with disabilities. *American Journal on Mental Retardation, 97*(5), 509–520.

Klaber, M. M. (1968). Parental visits to institutionalized children. *Mental Retardation, 6*, 39–41.

Kogan, K. L., & Tyler, N. (1973). Mother-child interaction in young physically handicapped children. *American Journal of Mental Deficiency, 77*(5), 492–497.

Koller, H., Richardson, S. A., & Katz, M. (1992). Families of children with mental retardation: Comprehensive view from an epidemiologic perspective. *American Journal on Mental Retardation, 97*(3), 315–332.

Kornblatt, E. S., & Heinrich, J. (1985). Needs and coping abilities in families of children with developmental disabilities. *Mental Retardation, 23*(1), 13–19.

Krauss, M. W. (1993). On the medicalization of family caregiving. *Mental Retardation, 31*, 78–80.

Krauss, M. W. (1993). Child-related and parenting stress: Similarities and differences between mothers and fathers of children with disabilities. *American Journal on Mental Retardation, 97*(4), 393–404.

Krauss, M. W., Seltzer, M. M., & Goodman, S. J. (1992). Social support networks of adults with mental retardation who live at home. *American Journal on Mental Retardation, 96*(4), 432–441.

Krauss, M. W., Seltzer, M. M., Gordon, R., & Friedman, D. H. (1996). Binding ties: The roles of adult siblings of persons with mental retardation. *Mental Retardation, 34*(2), 83–93.

Lakin, C., Prouty, B., Anderson, L., & Sandlin, J. (1997). Nearly 40% of state institutions have been closed. *Mental Retardation, 35*(1), 65

Leberfeld, D. T., & Nertz, N. (1955). A home training program in language and speech for mentally retarded children. *American Journal of Mental Deficiency, 59*, 413–416.

Lehmann, J. P., & Roberto, K. A. (1996). Comparison of factors influencing mothers' perceptions about the futures of their adolescent children with and without disabilities. *Mental Retardation, 34*(1), 27–38.

Levy-Shiff, R. (1986). Mother-father-child interactions in families with a mentally retarded young child. *American Journal of Mental Deficiency, 91*(2), 141–149.

Lillie, T. (1993). A harder thing than triumph: Roles of fathers of children with disabilities. *Mental Retardation, 31*(6), 438–443.

Llewellyn, G. (1995). Relationships and social support: Views of parents with mental retardation/intellectual disability. *Mental Retardation, 33*(6), 349–363.

Lubetsky, M. J., Mueller, L., Madden, K., Walker, R., & Len, D. (1995). Family-centered/interdisciplinary team approach to working with families of children who have mental retardation. *Mental Retardation, 33*(4), 251–256.

Lutzer, V. D., & Brubaker, T. H. (1988). Differential respite needs of aging parents of individuals with mental retardation. *Mental Retardation, 26*(1), 13–15.

Lynch, E. C., & Staloch, N. H. (1988). Parental perceptions of physicians' communication in the informing process. *Mental Retardation, 26*(2), 77–81.

Magaña, S. M. (1999). Puerto Rican families caring for an adult with mental retardation: Role of familism. *American Journal on Mental Retardation, 104*(5), 406–482.

Articles Reviewed

Mahoney, G., & O'Sullivan, P. (1990). Early intervention practices with families of children with handicaps. *Mental Retardation, 28*(3), 169–176.

Mahoney, G., Finger, I., & Powell, A. (1985). Relationship of maternal behavior style to the development of organically impaired mentally retarded infants. *American Journal of Mental Deficiency, 90*(3), 296–302.

Mahoney, S. C. (1958). Observations concerning counseling with parents of mentally retarded children. *American Journal of Mental Deficiency, 63*, 81–86.

Marchant, J., & Wehman, P. (1979). Teaching table games to severely retarded children. *Mental Retardation, 17*(3), 150–152.

Marshall, N. R., Hegrenes, J. R., & Goldstein, S. (1973). Verbal interactions: Mothers and their retarded children vs. mothers and their nonretarded children. *American Journal of Mental Deficiency, 77*(4), 415–419.

Mary, N. L. (1990). Reactions of black, Hispanic, and white mothers to having a child with handicaps. *Mental Retardation, 28*(1), 1–5.

Mash, E. J., & Terdal, L. (1973). Modification of mother-child interactions: Playing with children. *Mental Retardation, 11*(5), 44–49.

Mason, L. F. (1953). Developing and maintaining good parental relationships. *American Journal of Mental Deficiency, 57*, 394–396.

McCallion, P., & Tobin, S. S. (1995). Social workers' perceptions of older parents caring at home for sons and daughters with developmental disabilities. *Mental Retardation, 33*(3), 153–162.

McDonald, A. C., Carson, K. L., Palmer, D. J., & Slay, T. (1982). Physicians' diagnostic information to parents of handicapped neonates. *Mental Retardation, 20*(1), 12–14.

Menolascino, F. J. (1965). Psychiatric aspects of mongolism. *American Journal of Mental Deficiency, 69*, 653–660.

Menolascino, F. J. (1965). Psychoses of childhood: Experiences of a mental retardation pilot project. *American Journal of Mental Deficiency, 70*, 83–92.

Mercer, J. R. (1966). Patterns of family crisis related to reacceptance of the retardate. *American Journal of Mental Deficiency, 71*, 19–32.

Meyerowitz, J. H. (1967). Parental awareness of retardation. *American Journal of Mental Deficiency, 71*, 637–643.

Meyers, J. C., & Marcenko, M. O. (1989). Impact of a cash subsidy program for families of children with severe developmental disabilities. *Mental Retardation, 27*(6), 383–387.

Michaels, J., & Schucman, H. (1962). Observations on the psychodynamics of parents of retarded children. *American Journal of Mental Deficiency, 66*, 568–573.

Mickelson, P. (1947). The feebleminded parent: A study of 90 family cases; an attempt to isolate those factors associated with their successful or unsuccessful parenthood. *American Journal of Mental Deficiency, 51*, 644–653.

Mickelson, P. (1949). Can mentally deficient parents be helped to give their children better care? *American Journal of Mental Deficiency, 53*, 516–534.

Mink, I. T., Nihira, K., & Meyers, C. E. (1983). Taxonomy of family life styles: I. Homes with TMR children. *American Journal of Mental Deficiency, 87*(5), 484–497.

Mink, I. T., Meyers, C. E., & Nihira, K. (1984). Taxonomy of family life styles: II. Homes with slow-learning children. *American Journal of Mental Deficiency, 89*(2), 111–123.

Mink, I. T., & Nihira, K. (1987). Direction of effects: Family life styles and behavior of TMR children. *American Journal of Mental Deficiency, 92*(1), 57–64.

Mink, I. T., Blacher, J., & Nihira, K. (1988). Taxonomy of family life styles: III. Replication with families with severely mentally retarded children. *American Journal on Mental Retardation, 93*(3), 250–264.

Mink, I. T., Nihira, K., & Blacher, J. (1991). Scientific paradigms and validation: A response to Widaman. *American Journal on Mental Retardation, 96*(2), 221–224.

Mink, I. T. (1993). In the best interests of the family: Some comments on Birenbaum and Cohen's recommendations. *Mental Retardation, 31*(2), 80–82.

Minnes, P. M. (1988). Family resources and stress associated with having a mentally retarded child. *American Journal on Mental Retardation, 93*(2), 184–192.

Morris, E. (1955). Casework training needs for counseling parents of the retarded. *American Journal of Mental Deficiency, 59*, 510–516.

Murray, M. A. (1959). Needs of parents of mentally retarded children. *American Journal of Mental Deficiency, 63*, 1078–1088.

Articles Reviewed

Myers, B. A. (1991). Treatment of sexual offenses by persons with developmental disabilities. *American Journal on Mental Retardation, 95*(5), 563–569.

Nihira, K., Meyers, C. E., & Mink, I. T. (1983). Reciprocal relationship between home environment and development of TMR adolescents. *American Journal of Mental Deficiency, 88*(2), 139–149.

Nihira, K., Mink, I. T., & Meyers, C. E. (1981). Relationship between home environment and school adjustment of TMR children. *American Journal of Mental Deficiency, 86*(1), 8–15.

Nihira, K., Tomiyasu, Y., & Oshio, C. (1987). Homes of TMR children: Comparison between American and Japanese families. *American Journal of Mental Deficiency, 91*(5), 486–495.

Nihira, K., Weisner, T. S., & Bernheimer, L. P. (1994). Ecocultural assessment in families of children with developmental delays: Construct and concurrent validities. *American Journal on Mental Retardation, 98*(5), 551–566.

Nixon, C. D., & Singer, G. H. S. (1993). Group cognitive-behavioral treatment for excessive parental self-blame and guilt. *American Journal on Mental Retardation, 97*(6), 665–672.

Nugent, M. A. (1940). A home training and teaching program for mentally defective children to be taught by parents in the home. *American Journal of Mental Deficiency, 45*, 104–109.

Orr, R. R., Cameron, S. J., & Day, D. M. (1991). Coping with stress in families with children who have mental retardation: An evaluation of the Double ABCX model. *American Journal on Mental Retardation, 95*(4), 444–450.

Orr, R. R., Cameron, S. J., Dobson, L. A., & Day, D. M. (1993). Age-related changes in stress experienced by families with a child who has developmental delays. *Mental Retardation, 31*(3), 171–176.

Orsmond, G. I., & Seltzer, M. M. (2000). Brothers and sisters of adults with mental retardation: Gendered nature of the sibling relationship. *American Journal on Mental Retardation, 105*, 486–508.

Peck, J. R., & Stephens, W. B. (1960). A study of the relationship between the attitudes and behavior of parents and that of their mentally defective child. *American Journal of Mental Deficiency, 64*, 839–844.

Peck, J. R., & Stephens, W. B. (1965). Marriage of young adult male retardates. *American Journal of Mental Deficiency, 69*, 818–827.

Pendler, B. (1988). A parent's response to "Are we professionalizing parents?" *Mental Retardation, 26*, 49–51.

Piper, M. C., & Ramsay, M. K. (1980). Effects of early home environment on the mental development of Down syndrome infants. *American Journal of Mental Deficiency, 85*(1), 39–44.

Poling, A., & LeSage, M. (1995). Evaluating psychotropic drugs in people with mental retardation: Where are the social validity data? *American Journal on Mental Retardation, 100*(2), 193–200.

Popp, C. E., Ingram, V., & Jordan, P. H. (1954). Helping parents understand their mentally handicapped child. *American Journal of Mental Deficiency, 58*, 530–534.

Poulson, C. L. (1988). Operant conditioning of vocalization rate of infants with Down syndrome. *American Journal on Mental Retardation, 93*(1), 57–63.

Pruchno, R. A., & Patrick, J. H. (1999). Effects of formal and familial residential plans for adults with mental retardation on their aging mothers. *American Journal on Mental Retardation, 104*(1), 38–52.

Pueschel, S., & Murphy, A. (1976). Assessment of counseling practices at the birth of a child with Down's syndrome. *American Journal of Mental Deficiency, 81*(4), 325–330.

Ramey, C. T., Mills, P., Campbell, F. A., & O'Brien, C. (1975). Infants' home environments: A comparison of high-risk families and families from the general population. *American Journal of Mental Deficiency, 80*(1), 40–42.

Ramey, C. T., & Smith, B. J. (1976). Assessing the intellectual consequences of early intervention with high-risk infants. *American Journal of Mental Deficiency, 81*(4), 318–324.

Ramey, S. L., Krauss, M. W., & Simeonsson, R. J. (1989). Research on families: Current assessment and future opportunities. *American Journal on Mental Retardation, 94*(3), ii–vi.

Ramsey, G. V. (1967). Review of group methods with parents of the mentally retarded. *American Journal of Mental Deficiency, 71*, 857–863.

Rankin, J. E. (1957). A group therapy experiment with mothers of mentally deficient children. *American Journal of Mental Deficiency, 62*, 49–55.

Rao, S. S. (2000). Perspectives of an African American mother on parent-professional relationships in special education. *Mental Retardation, 38*, 475–488.

Articles Reviewed

Ray, J. S. (1974). The Family Training Center: An experiment in normalization. *Mental Retardation, 12* (1), 12–13.

Redner, R. (1980). Others' perceptions of mothers of handicapped children. *American Journal of Mental Deficiency, 85*(2), 176–183.

Reese, M. R., & Serna, L. (1986). Planning for generalization and maintenance in parent training: Parents need I. E. P. s too. *Mental Retardation, 24*(2), 87–92.

Reilly, W. N. (1942). Let the parent live again. *American Journal of Mental Deficiency, 46,* 409–413.

Ricci, C. S. (1970). Analysis of child-rearing attitudes of mothers of retarded, emotionally disturbed, and normal children. *American Journal of Mental Deficiency, 74*(6), 756–761.

Richards, M. (1953). The retarded child in a state school and the problems he presents from a parent's viewpoint. *American Journal of Mental Deficiency, 58,* 56–59.

Rimmerman, A. (1989). Provision of respite care for children with developmental disabilities: Changes in maternal coping and stress over time. *Mental Retardation, 27*(2), 99–103.

Roach, M. A., Orsmond, G. I., & Barratt, M. S. (1999). Mothers and fathers of children with Down syndrome: Parental stress and involvement in childcare. *American Journal on Mental Retardation, 104,* 422–436.

Robbins, F. R., & Dunlap, G. (1992). Effects of task difficulty on parent teaching skills and behavior problems of young children with autism. *American Journal on Mental Retardation, 96*(6), 631–643.

Robbins, M. M. D. (1957). What parents expect the institution to do for their children. *American Journal of Mental Deficiency, 61,* 672–674.

Rogers-Dulan, J. (1998). Religious connectedness among urban African American families who have a child with disabilities. *Mental Retardation, 36*(2), 91–103.

Rogers-Dulan, J., & Blacher, J. (1995). African American families, religion, and disability: A conceptual framework. *Mental Retardation, 33*(4), 226–238.

Ronai, C. R. (1997). On loving and hating my mentally retarded mother. *Mental Retardation, 35*(6), 417–432.

Roos, P. (1963). Psychological counseling with parents of retarded children. *Mental Retardation, 1,* 345–350.

Rosen, L. (1955). Selected aspects in the development of the mother's understanding of her mentally retarded child. *American Journal of Mental Deficiency, 59,* 522–528.

Rousey, A., Best, S., & Blacher, J. (1992). Mothers' and fathers' perceptions of stress and coping with children who have severe disabilities. *American Journal on Mental Retardation, 97*(1), 99–109.

Rousey, A. B., Blacher, J. B., & Hanneman, R. A. (1990). Predictors of out-of-home placement of children with severe handicaps: A cross-sectional analysis. *American Journal on Mental Retardation, 94*(5), 522–531.

Routh, D. K. (1970). MMPI responses of parents as a function of mental retardation of the child. *American Journal of Mental Deficiency, 89,* 610–616.

Rowitz, L. (1992). A family affair. *Mental Retardation, 30,* iii–iv.

Rowitz, L. (1985). Social support: The issue of the 1980s. *Mental Retardation, 23*(4), 165–167.

Ruzicka, W. J. (1958). A proposed role for the school psychologist: Counseling parents of mentally retarded children. *American Journal of Mental Deficiency, 62,* 897–904.

Ryckman, D. B., & Henderson, R. A. (1965). The meaning of a retarded child for his parents: A focus for counselors. *Mental Retardation, 3*(4), 4–7.

Saetermoe, C. L., Widaman, K. F., & Borthwick-Duffy, S. (1991). Validation of the Parenting Style Survey for parents of children with mental retardation. *Mental Retardation, 29*(3), 149–157.

Salisbury, C. L. (1985). Internal consistency of the short-term of the Questionnaire on Resources and Stress. *American Journal of Mental Deficiency, 89*(6), 610–616.

Salisbury, C. L. (1986). Adaptation of the Questionnaire on Resources and Stress-Short Form. *American Journal of Mental Deficiency, 90*(4), 456–459.

Salisbury, C. L. (1989). Construct validity of the adapted Questionnaire on Resources and Stress short form. *American Journal on Mental Retardation, 94*(1), 74–79.

Salisbury, C. L. (1990). Characteristics of users and nonusers of respite care. *Mental Retardation, 28*(5), 291–297.

Salzberg, C. L., & Villani, T. V. (1983). Speech training by parents of Down syndrome toddlers: Generalization across settings and instructional contexts. *American Journal of Mental Deficiency, 87*(4), 403–413.

Sampson, A. H. (1947). Developing and maintaining good relations with parents of mentally deficient children. *American Journal of Mental Deficiency*, 52(2), 187–194.

Sandler, A. G., Warren, S. H., & Raver, S. A. (1995). Grandparents as a source of support for parents of children with disabilities: A brief report. *Mental Retardation*, 33(4), 248–250.

Sarason, S. B. (1952). Individual psychotherapy with mentally defective individuals. *American Journal of Mental Deficiency*, 56, 803–805.

Scheerenberger. (1970). Generic services for the mentally retarded and their families. *Mental Retardation*, 8, 10–16.

Scher, B. (1955). Help to parents: An integral part of service to the retarded child. *American Journal of Mental Deficiency*, 60, 169–175.

Schilling, R. F., Schinke, S. P., Blythe, B. J., & Barth, R. P. (1982). Child maltreatment and mentally retarded parents: Is there a relationship? *Mental Retardation*, 20, 201–209.

Schonell, F. J., & Rorke, M. (1960). A second survey of the effects of a subnormal child on the family unit. *American Journal of Mental Deficiency*, 64, 862–868.

Schonell, F. J., & Watts, B. H. (1956). A first survey of the effects of a subnormal child on the family unit. *American Journal of Mental Deficiency*, 61, 210–219.

Schumacher, H. C. (1945). Contribution of the child guidance clinic to the problem of mental deficiency. *American Journal of Mental Deficiency*, 50, 277–283.

Scorgie, K., & Sobsey, D. (2000). Transformational outcomes associated with parenting children who have disabilities. *Mental Retardaiton*, 38, 195–206.

Scott, B. S., Atkinson, L., Minton, H. L., & Bowman, T. (1997). Psychological distress of parents of infants with Down syndrome. *American Journal on Mental Retardation*, 102(2), 161–171.

Scott, R. L., Sexton, D., Thompson, B., & Wood, T. A. (1989). Measurement characteristics of a short form of the questionnaire on resources and stress. *American Journal on Mental Retardation*, 94(3), 331–339.

Seitz, S., & Hoekenga, R. (1974). Modeling as a training tool for retarded children and their parents. *Mental Retardation*, 12(2), 28–31.

Seitz, S., & Terdal, L. (1972). A modeling approach to changing parent-child interactions. *Mental Retardation*, 10(3), 39–43.

Seltzer, M. M., & Kraus, M. W. (1989). Aging parents with adult mentally retarded children: Family risk factors and sources of support. *American Journal on Mental Retardation*, 94, 303–312.

Seltzer, M. M. (1985). Informal supports for aging mentally retarded persons. *American Journal of Mental Deficiency*, 90(3), 259–265.

Seltzer, M. M., Krauss, M. W., & Tsunematsu, N. (1993). Adults with Down syndrome and their aging mothers: Diagnostic group differences. *American Journal on Mental Retardation*, 97(5), 496–508.

Shapiro, J., & Simonsen, D. (1994). Educational/support group for Latino families of children with Down syndrome. *Mental Retardation*, 32(6), 403–415.

Sheimo, S. L. (1951). Problems in helping parents of mentally defective and handicapped children. *American Journal of Mental Deficiency*, 56, 42–47.

Singer, G. H. S., Irvin, L. K., & Hawkins, N. (1988). Stress management training for parents of children with severe handicaps. *Mental Retardation*, 26(5), 269–277.

Skeels, H. M., & Dye, H. B. (1939). A study of the effects of differential stimulation on mentally retarded children. *Journal of Psycho-Asthenics*, 44, 114–136.

Slater, M. A. (1986). Modification of mother-child interaction processes in families with children at risk for mental retardation. *American Journal of Mental Deficiency*, 91, 257–267.

Smith, E. M. (1952). Emotional factors as revealed in the intake process with parents of defective children. *American Journal of Mental Deficiency*, 56, 806–812.

Smith, G. C. (1997). Aging families of adults with mental retardation: Patterns and correlates of service use, need, and knowledge. *American Journal on Mental Retardation*, 102(1), 13–26.

Smith, G. C., Majeski, R. A., & McClenny, B. (1996). Psychoeducational support groups for aging parents: Development and preliminary outcomes. *Mental Retardation*, 34(3), 172–181.

Smith, G. C., Tobin, S. S., & Fullmer, E. M. (1995). Elderly mothers caring at home for offspring with mental retardation: A model of permanency planning. *American Journal on Mental Retardation*, 99(5), 487–499.

Spreen, O., & Anderson, C. W. G. (1966). Sibling relationship and mental deficiency diagnosis as reflected in Wechsler test patterns. *American Journal of Mental Deficiency*, 71, 406–410.

Stark, J. (1992). Presidential address 1992: A professional and personal perspective on families. *Mental Retardation, 30*(2), 247–254.

Stayton, S. E., Sitkowski, C. A., Stayton, D. J., & Weiss, S. D. (1968). The influence of home experience upon the retardate's social behavior in the institution. *American Journal of Mental Deficiency, 72,* 866–870.

Stern, E. M. (1951). Problems of organizing parents' groups. *American Journal of Mental Deficiency, 56,* 11–17.

Stoddard, H. M. (1959). The relation of parental attitudes and achievements of severely mentally retarded children. *American Journal of Mental Deficiency, 63,* 575–598.

Stone, M. M. (1948). Parental attitudes toward retardation. *American Journal of Mental Deficiency, 53,* 363–372.

Stone, N. D. (1959). Clinical team treatment of a mentally retarded child and his parents: Casework with the mother. *American Journal of Mental Deficiency, 63,* 707–712.

Stone, N. D. (1967). Family factors in willingness to place the mongoloid child. *American Journal of Mental Deficiency, 72,* 16–20.

Stoneman, Z. (1989). Comparison groups in research on families with mentally retarded members: A methodological and conceptual review. *American Journal on Mental Retardation, 94*(3), 195–215.

Stoneman, Z., & Crapps, J. M. (1990). Mentally retarded individuals in family care homes: Relationships with the family-of-origin. *American Journal on Mental Retardation, 94*(4), 420–430.

Stoneman, Z., Brody, G. H., & Abbott, D. (1983). In-home observations of young Down syndrome children with their mothers and fathers. *American Journal of Mental Deficiency, 87*(6), 591–600.

Stoneman, Z., Brody, G. H., Davis, C. H., & Crapps, J. M. (1987). Mentally retarded children and their older same-sex siblings: Naturalistic in-home observations. *American Journal on Mental Retardation, 92*(3), 290–298.

Stoneman, Z., Brody, G. H., Davis, C. H., & Crapps, J. M. (1988). Childcare responsibilities, peer relations, and sibling conflict: Older siblings of mentally retarded children. *American Journal on Mental Retardation, 93*(2), 174–183.

Stoneman, Z., Brody, G. H., Davis, C. H., Crapps, J. M., & and others. (1991). Ascribed role relations between children with mental retardation and their younger siblings. *American Journal on Mental Retardation, 95*(5), 537–550.

Strazzulla, M. (1954). A language guide for the parents of retarded children. *American Journal of Mental Deficiency, 59,* 48–58.

Suelzle, M., & Keenan, V. (1981). Changes in family support networks over the life cycle of mentally retarded persons. *American Journal of Mental Deficiency, 86*(3), 267–274.

Tannock, R. (1988). Mothers' directiveness in their interactions with their children with and without Down syndrome. *American Journal on Mental Retardation, 93,* 154–165.

Tannock, R., Girolametto, L., & Siegel, L. S. (1992). Language intervention with children who have developmental delays: Effects of an interactive approach. *American Journal on Mental Retardation, 97*(2), 145–160.

Terdal, L., & Buell, J. (1969). Parent education in managing retarded children with behavior deficits and inappropriate behaviors. *Mental Retardation, 7,* 10–13.

Thorin, E., Yovanoff, P., & Irvin, L. (1996). Dilemmas faced by families during their young adults' transitions to adulthood: A brief report. *Mental Retardation, 34*(2), 117–120.

Thorne, F. C., & Andrews, J. S. (1946). Unworthy parental attitudes toward mental defectives. *American Journal of Mental Deficiency, 50*(3), 411–418.

Thurston, J. R. (1959). A procedure for evaluating parental attitudes toward the handicapped. *American Journal of Mental Deficiency, 64,* 148–155.

Thurston, J. R. (1960). Attitudes and emotional reactions of parents of institutionalized cerebral palsied, retarded patients. *American Journal of Mental Deficiency, 65,* 227–235.

Townsend, P. W., & Flanagan, J. J. (1976). Experimental preadmission program to encourage home care for severely and profoundly retarded children. *American Journal of Mental Deficiency, 80*(5), 562–569.

Turnbull, A. P., & Turnbull, H. R. (1982). Parent involvement in the education of handicapped children: A critique. *Mental Retardation, 20*(3), 115–122.

Articles Reviewed

Turnbull, A. P., & Turnbull, H. R. (1988). Toward great expectations for vocational opportunities: Family-professional partnerships. *Mental Retardation, 26*(6), 337–342.

Tymchuk, A. J. (1975). Training parent therapists. *Mental Retardation, 13,* 19–22.

Tymchuk, A. J., Andron, L., & Rahbar, B. (1988). Effective decision-making/problem-solving training with mothers who have mental retardation. *American Journal on Mental Retardation, 92*(6), 510–516.

Upshur, C. C. (1982). An evaluation of home-based respite care. *Mental Retardation, 20*(2), 58–62.

Upshur, C. C. (1982). Respite care for mentally retarded and other disabled populations: Program models and family needs. *Mental Retardation, 20*(1), 2–6.

Vaux, C. L. (1935). Family care of mental defectives. *Journal of Psycho-Asthenics, 40,* 168–189.

Waisbren, S. E. (1980). Parents' reactions after the birth of a developmentally disabled child. *American Journal of Mental Deficiency, 84,* 345–351.

Walden, T. A., Knieps, L. J., & Baxter, A. (1991). Contingent provision of social referential information by parents of children with and without developmental delays. *American Journal on Mental Retardation, 96*(2), 177–187.

Walker, G. H. (1949). Some considerations of parental reactions to institutionalization of defective children. *American Journal of Mental Deficiency, 54,* 108–114.

Wardell, W. (1952). The mentally retarded in family and community. *American Journal of Mental Deficiency, 57,* 229–242.

Wardell, W. (1947). Case work with parents of mentally deficient children. *American Journal of Mental Deficiency, 52*(1), 91–97.

Warfield, M. E., & Hauser-Cram, P. (1996). Child care needs, arrangements, and satisfaction of mothers of children with developmental disabilities. *Mental Retardation, 34*(5), 294–302.

Watson, L. S., & Bassinger, J. F. (1974). Parent training technology: Potential service delivery system. *Mental Retardation, 12*(5), 3–10.

Watts, E. M. (1969). Family Therapy: Its use in mental retardation. *Mental Retardation, 7*(5), 41–44.

Weingold, J. T. (1952). Parents' groups and the problem of mental retardation. *American Journal of Mental Deficiency, 56,* 484–492.

Weller, L., Costeff, C., Cohen, B., & Rahman, D. (1974). Social variables in the perception and acceptance of retardation. *American Journal of Mental Deficiency, 79*(3), 274–278

Whitcraft, C. J., & Jones, J. P. (1974). A survey of attitudes about sterilization of retardates. *Mental Retardation, 12*(1), 30–33.

White, B. L. (1959). Clinical team treatment of a mentally retarded child and his parents: Group counseling and play observation. *American Journal of Mental Deficiency, 63,* 713–718.

Whitman, B. Y., Graves, B., & Accardo, P. (1987). Mentally retarded parents in the community: Identification method and needs assessment survey. *American Journal of mental deficiency, 91*(6), 636–638.

Whitney, E. A. (1951). Mental Retardation—1950. *American Journal of Mental Deficiency, 56,* 253–263.

Whitney, E. A. (1952). Mental Retardation—1951. *American Journal of Mental Deficiency, 56,* 737–746.

Widaman, K. F. (1991). Properly characterizing clusters of families who have children with mental retardation: A comment on Mink, Blacher, and Nihira. *American Journal on Mental Retardation, 96*(2), 217–220.

Wikler, L. M. (1986). Periodic stresses of families of older mentally retarded children: An exploratory study. *American Journal of Mental Deficiency, 90*(6), 703–706.

Wildman, P. R. (1965). A parent education program for parents of mentally retarded children. *Mental Retardation, 3,* 17–19.

Willoughby, J. C., & Glidden, L. M. (1995). Fathers helping out: Shared child care and marital satisfaction of parents of children with disabilities. *American Journal on Mental Retardation, 99*(4), 399–406.

Wilson, J., Blacher, J., & Baker, B. L. (1989). Siblings of children with severe handicaps. *Mental Retardation, 27*(3), 167–173.

Wolf, L., & Zarafas, D. E. (1982). Parents' attitudes toward sterilization of their mentally retarded children. *American Journal of Mental Deficiency, 87*(2), 122–129.

Worchell, T. L., & Worchel, P. (1961). The parental concept of the mentally retarded child. *American Journal of Mental Deficiency, 65,* 782–788.

Wortis, H., Jedrysek, E., & Wortis, J. (1967). Unreported defect in the siblings of retarded children. *American Journal of Mental Deficiency, 72,* 388–392.

Articles Reviewed

Yates, M. L., & Lederer, R. (1961). Small, short-term group meetings with parents of children with mongolism. *American Journal of Mental Deficiency, 65,* 467–472.

Yoshida, R. K., & Gottlieb, J. (1977). A model of parental participation in the pupil planning process. *Mental Retardation, 15,* 17–20.

Zetlin, A. G. (1986). Mentally retarded adults and their siblings. *American Journal of Mental Deficiency, 91*(3), 217–225.

Zetlin, A. G., & Turner, J. L. (1985). Transition from adolescence to adulthood: Perspectives of mentally retarded individuals and their families. *American Journal of Mental Deficiency, 89*(6), 570–579.

Zirpoli, T. J., Wieck, C., Hancox, D., & Skarnulis, E. R. (1994). Partners in policymaking: the first five years. *Mental Retardation, 32,* 422–425.

Zuk, G. H. (1959). The religious factor and the role of guilt in the parental acceptance of the retarded child. *American Journal of Mental Deficiency, 64,* 139–147.